INDEX TO
HATHAWAY'S REGISTER

The Lost Tribes of
North Carolina, Part 1

HATHAWAY'S REGISTER

Available in Reprint

NORTH CAROLINA HISTORICAL AND GENEALOGICAL REGISTER

Volume 1, No. 1 through Volume III, No. 3

(All published.)

Compiled and Published by

JAMES ROBERT BENT HATHAWAY

ELEVEN NUMBERS. 1760 PAGES. WRAPPERS.
REPRINTED: BALTIMORE, 1964-1970.

The set: $37.50

An invaluable record of the early families and history of the old Albemarle region of North Carolina, this monumental work contains over 50,000 names of early settlers and information about them. Contents include land grants, court records, conveyances, births, deaths, marriages, wills, petitions, licenses, oaths, and queries and answers on family history for the present counties of Beaufort, Bertie, Camden, Chowan, Currituck, Dare, Gates, Halifax, Hyde, Martin, Northampton, Pasquotank, Perquimans, Tyrrell, and Washington, and the Virginia counties of Surry and Isle of Wight.

Reprint of the original edition of 1900-1903.

"The genealogical spirit is truly rising in our southern states.... Our publications relative to Carolina genealogy are sparse, and this is a welcome addition."—N. Y. GENEALOGICAL AND BIO-GRAPHICAL RECORD, Vol. XXXI, No. 4. October, 1900.

RAY'S
INDEX AND DIGEST

TO
HATHAWAY'S

North Carolina Historical and
Genealogical Register

With

GENEALOGICAL NOTES AND
ANNOTATIONS

Compiled and Edited by
WORTH S. RAY

GENEALOGICAL PUBLISHING CO., INC.
BALTIMORE   1971

Originally Published As
The Lost Tribes of North Carolina, Part I
Austin, Texas, 1945

Reprinted
Southern Book Company
Baltimore, 1956

Reprinted with an added Half-title
Genealogical Publishing Company
Baltimore, 1971

Library of Congress Catalog Card Number 67-121942
International Standard Book Number 0-8063-0479-0

Made in the United States of America

PREFACE

The North Carolina Historical and Genealogical Register was published by James Robert Bent Hathaway at Edenton, North Carolina, beginning in January, 1900 and continuing until July, 1903. It was issued quarterly, each number containing approximately 150 pages, crowded with valuable North Carolina historical and genealogical data, largely abstracted by the editor and publisher, from the public records. In the first volume there were 640 pages, in the second 640 and in the three numbers of the third volume there were 480 pages, making altogether 1760 pages of material Mr. Hathaway collected in the brief life of this remarkable publication. Not less than 50,000 names appear in the publication from the beginning until the end. Not all of these names, by any means, may be found in this imperfect index, but by reason of the foresight of the founder, who arranged a great part of his material in alphabetical order, (particularly the lists of revolutionary soldiers, and the marriage bonds) a literal transcription of every name is found unnecessary for a workable guide to the contents. Mr. Hathaway's is a monumental work and a rich heritage to the researcher interested in the early families of the Old North State, and the only thing lacking has been an index, which doubtless the pioneer publisher would have himself supplied had his life been spared.

It is this omission which the writer has undertaken with an unpracticed hand to supply. The unorthodox manner in which the index is constructed, the interpolation of citations occasionally from Grimes and other accepted sources, designed to point out additional authority on the subject; the insertion of "side bar remarks" and genealogical notes throughout the work (in the nature of footnotes) may not prove likeable, or popular, but should not detract from the value of the factual records quoted. But here they are. Take them or leave them.

The index is not perfect, nor are the notes. It and they are full of mistakes. So is Grimes, so is Wheeler, Martin, Williamson and nearly all other books that have ever been written about North Carolina. In this instance, many, if not all such mistakes were noticed by the writer when it was too late to correct them and others have been discovered since the volume came off the press. If you see them, just pass them over and let them go. Nothing can now be done about it. This is a wartime job, produced in spite of aggravating wartime regulations, which seem necessary. It may not be much of a job, but it has been largely a labor of love and is the best available, since it seems to be the only one ever attempted. If you don't readily find the name wanted, keep searching among the "connected" names and other material referred to and it will probably turn up.

The numbers 1-442, mean Volume 1, page 442; 2-164 mean Volume 2, page 164, and 3-222 mean Volume 3, page 222, and so on, all the way through. This is very simple. The work, crude though it may be, should make your file of Hathaway's H. & G. Register of much greater value.

WORTH S. RAY.

INDEX TO THE INDEX

(Genealogical Notes Only)

INDEX

AND DIGEST TO HATHAWAY'S NORTH CAROLINA HISTORICAL
AND GENEALOGICAL REGISTER.

BY WORTH S. RAY

ANCRUM, JOHN 2-243.

ANDERSON, ANN, land grant (1762) 1-21.

ANDERSON, ELIZABETH 1-166, 1-26.

ANDERSON FAMILY (After 1800) 3-324.

ANDERSON, CAROLUS, with BOOK FAMILY 1-165.

ANDERSON, GEORGE, 1-165.

ANDERSON, JAMES, wife ELIZABETH (1700) 2-617,
2-619; wife DEBORAH (1706) 3-377.

ANDERSON, JOHN married NICHOLSON 1-64; col -
lector of rents (1701) 2-78; will, (1744)
1-164; wife JEAN (1699) 3-370.

ANDERSON, JOSEPH, Attorney General, CHOWAN,
(1741) 1-448; land on Indian Town Creek,
(1734) 3-453; witness deed (1729) 2-547;
Clerk of Court (1731) 1-456; member of
Court (1743) 1-447; see also 1-110, 2-609
and 3-164.

ANDERSON, ROBERT (1719) 1-629; witness with
ISAAC HILL (1717) 1-629.

ANDREWS, ABNER, of BERTIE COUNTY (1762)2-324

ANDREWS FAMILY, connected with HILL FAMILY,
2-305.

ANDREWS, JOHN, of ROWAN COUNTY, will, 1-26.

ANDREWS, SAMUEL, Exr. of THOMAS (1746)2-627.

ANDREWS, STEPHEN, master of Brig INDUSTRY in
1773. 1-436.

ANDREWS, THOMAS, will (1737) 1-26; another
THOMAS ANDREWS, will (1746) 2-627.

ANDREWS, WILLIAM, Exr. of THOMAS (1746)2-627.

APPLEWHITE, HOLLAND, mentioned in will of
HENRY WEST (1752) 1-80. (She a woman).

ARBUTHNOT, JOHN 1-134.

ARCHBELL FAMILY, connected with JESSE BRYAN
family 2-562, 2-563.

ARCHDALE, JOHN, GOVERNOR. In BLOUNT genealogy
1-35; died 1705, 2-302, 3-266; letter to
GOVERNOR HARVEY 1698, 3-35 to 3-39; son in
law (stepson?) EMANUEL LOWE 3-72; connected
with EDWARD MOSELEY 3-257; Lord Proprietor
(landgrave?) 2-302.

ARCHDALE, ANN, mentions DANIEL AKEHURST in a
statement, 3-243.

ARCHER, BENJAMIN (and JOHN LONG) 3-139.

ARCHER, STEPHEN, bought lands (1732) 2-450,
2-451.

ARDENE, JOHN (1702) buys land from WILLIAM
DUKENFIELD, on SALMON CREEK, 2-455; kin
of DUKENFIELD 1-26, 2-456, 3-262.

ALFORD, JOHN SR. died (1690) 3-363.

ALFORD, TABITHA mentioned in will of CHAS.
JONES (1695) 1-54.

ARLING, JOHN, and wife MARY (1731) 2-450.

ARKILL, WILLIAM, of PERQUIMANS, wife HANNAH
3-324; land grant (1740) 1-18; bought
land from WILLIAM BRANCH (1729) 2-448; inspector at EDENTON (1748) 1-452; ABRAHAM
ENDLESS (ENLOE?) Exr. of his estate(1754)
1-457.

ARMISTEAD, STARKEY (1793) son of WILLIAM AR-
MISTEAD 2-324.

ARMISTEAD FAMILY, wills (1793) 2-324, 2-498.

ARMOUR, JOHN, will (1728) 1-516; married widow BAILEY, later widow of SIMON BRYAN 1-328;
related to BRYAN family 1-28; mother was
MARY STANTON (1720) 1-76.

ARMOUR, ROBERT 1-516.

ARMOUR, WILLIAM, of PASQUOTANK, will (1719)
1-27; on jury in ALBEMARLE (1702) 1-610.

ARMSTRONG, ANDREW, Lieut. in Rev. 1-421.

ARMSTRONG, JAMES, will (1685) mentions RICH-
ARD GRAY 1-164; Lieut. Col. N. C. Cont.
Line 1-419.

ARMSTRONG, JOHN, Captain and later COLONEL
in N. C. Cont. Line 1-417; one died CURRI-
TUCK (1753) wife was AFIAH 1-167.

ARMSTRONG SOLOMON, married MARGARET DONALD-
SON (1765) 3-413.

ARMSTRONG, THOMAS, Lieut. N. C. Continental
Line, 1-420; another died in BOSTON, MASS.
(1735) will in N.C. names children. 2-303.

ARMSTRONG, WILLIAM, Lieut. and later CAPTAIN
(or were there two?) in N. C. Continental Line 1-415, 1-416.

ARNOLD, BENEDICT, Master of Brig HARRIOT at
Edenton (1774) 2-465, 1-416.

ARNOLD, EDWARD (Spelled ARNELL) land grant
(1761) 1-21.

ARNOLD, JOHN, wife MARY (1701) 3-373; will,
(1735) 1-26.

ARNOLD, LAWRENCE, will (1690) 1-26, wife
SARAH (1745) 3-379; wife (1702) was JANE
RICHARDS 3-374.

ARNOLD, WILLIAM 3-164, 3-163.

ARRENTON, EZEKIEL, will (1808) 3-324.

ARRENTON, ISAAC, will (1816) 3-324.

ARRENTON, RACHEL, married THOMAS HEA (1785)
3-418.

ARRENTON, WILLIAM, will (1806 and 1810) 3-324.

ARTHUR, JOHN, land grant (1717) 1-9; connection with MOORE family 1-165; sold land
to ADAM COCKBURN (1724) 2-449.

ASBELL FAMILY, wills 2-498.

ASBELL, RICHARD, will (1695) 1-26.

ASBELL, MARTIN wife HANNAH (1717) 3-379.

ASBELL, SOLOMON, of BERTIE COUNTY (1769)
3-447.

ASHE, JOHN BAPTIST, will (1731) 1-26; appears in court (1733) 1-453; complained against GOV. BURRINGTON (1732) 1-453; one of the name Lieut. Colonel in N. C. Cont. Line 1-421; in 1777 2-339; one mentioned with SAMUEL ASHE 3-13.

ASHE, SAMUEL, 3-13.

ASHBURN FAMILY WILLS 2-497.

ASHBURN, BENJAMIN, will (1808) 2-497.

ASHBURN, ELISHA will (1801) 2-497.

ASKEW, AARON, will (1770) BERTIE 2-323.

ASKEW, DAVID, will (1811) BERTIE 2-497.

ASKEW FAMILY WILLS, Bertie 2-497.

ASHLEY FAMILY WILLS 1-516.

ASHLEY, EDMUND, affidavit 3-252.

ASHLEY, JOHN, Bertie, orphan (1770) 3-448; estate 3-446.

ASHLEY THOMAS (1746) 2-629, 2-324; lived on SALMON CREEK (1719) 1-444; Exr. of SAMUEL RATLIFF (1723) 1-70.

ASHLEY, THOMAS, JR. married HICKS 1-50.

ASHLEY, WILLIAM, will (1762) 3-163.

ASHWORTH, RICHARD, inserted with ROGER MONTAGUE (1697?) 2-300; on jury in ALBEMARLE (1702) 1-610.

ASSEMBLY OF CAROLINAS. THOMAS CARY, GOVERNOR (1708) 2-225; officers of (1713)3-228; against Sabbath breaking 3-263; dissolution of (1717) 3-228, 3-229; exporting of debtors, 2-281, 2-282.

ATKINS, DANIEL, land grant (1716) 1-14.

ATKINS, DAVID, sold land (1730) 2-452; witnessed RICKS deed (1716) 1-616

ATKINSON, IRVIN, married MARY ROBERTS (1831) and moved to GEORGIA 1-562.

ATTAWAY, THOMAS, married DOROTHY BAILEY 3-202 in North Carolina 1689 3-431.

AVELIN, PETER, will (1710) 1-26

AVENT, THOMAS, deed to ROBERT GREEN (1716) 1-295; deed to RICHARD MOORE, 1-295.

AVERITT FAMILY WILLS, Bertie 2-323

AVERITT, HENRY, will (1771) Bertie 2-323.

AVERITT, THOMAS, witness deed to JOHN MARKS (1717) 1-617; grandson of THOMAS MARKS (1702) 2-612.

AVERITT, NATHANIEL, constable CHOWAN (1731) 1-449; son in law of THOMAS HARRISON (1716)-1-295.

AVERY FAMILY GENEALOGY 1-636.

AVERY, ELIZABETH, dau of JOHN (1719) married WILLIAM SMITH 1-75; another same name, married ELISHA PARKER (1790) 3-419; ROBERT AVERY had dau. ELIZABETH 3-379.

AVERY, FREDERICK, will (1800) 3-164.

AVERY, JOHN, son of ROBERT and wife RUTH (1753) 3-379.

AVERY ROBERT and wife RUTH 3-379.

AVERY, SARAH, dau. ROBERT and RUTH 3-379.

AVERY, PENINAH (COPELAND) 2-261

AVERY, THOMAS, of CHOWAN 1722) 2-149.

AUSTELL, WILLIAM (his family) 1-635.

AUSTIN, CORNELIUS, affidavit (1777) witnessed by WILLIAM BENNETT 2-571, 2-572.

AUSTIN, DANIEL, same as preceding.

AUSTIN, ROBERT, wife SARAH (1696) 3-407.

AUSTIN, SARAH, wife of ROBERT (1696) 3-402

AXTELL, THOMAS (Account of family) 1-633.

AXTELL, WILLIAM, of New York, was a grandson of THOMAS JONES, of BERTIE COUNTY (1730) 1-445.

AYCOCK, WILLIAM, patent to lands in NORTHAMPTON CO. N. C. (1746) 1-447.

DANIEL AKEHURST. From page 40 of "Virginia Carys": "Among the old records of Albemarle County, North Carolina, at Edenton, are several affidavits filed July 18, 1713, concerning a slave named Stephen, who had been sold some years before by Ann Akehurst to Miles Cary, Jr. The witnesses are "Miles Cary, the elder, age "42", whose signature is the unmistakable autograph of our first Clerk of Warwick, age "43", and Elizabeth Cary "age 34", who says that she went to dwell in the house of Daniel Akehurst in 1695. This Akehurst was a Quaker. He lived in Warick (County, Virginia), but had been the Proprietor Archdale's Deputy in North Carolina Council, subsequently secretary for the Proprietors, and died in 1699. The York County (Virginia) records show that in 1701, "Mr. Miles Cary, Jr." was attending to business for "Ann Akehurst, executrix of Daniel Akehurst, deceased."

The will of DANIEL AKEHURST, Deputy in the Council, discloses that he probably left no male descendants. In his will he mentions only his wife Ann and daughter Filia Christy Akehurst, and directs that his estate be delivered to Thomas Symonds for his daughter's use, his wife Ann and Symonds be named his executers. The will was probated in Warwick County, Virginia, and was witnessed by Mary Cary and Miles Cary. 1-133.

PETER ADAMS, of Chowan County, in his will of 1745 (1-167), speaks therein of his brother John, of Wrentham, New England. If the family of ADAMS, to which two Presidents belong ever had representation in the South, the names of the Chowan Adamses, suggest they perhaps may have belonged. Peter was a common name in the Presidents' family.

BACON, PETER, Capt. 10th Reg. N. C. Continental Line (Col. Abraham Shepard) 1-425.

BADHAM, WILLIAM, merchant of PASQUOTANK (1720) 1-444; Justice Chowan Precinct (1731) 1-449 land grant (1727) 1-12; bought land from CHRISTOPHER GALE (1733) 2-610; widow MARTHA was MRS. DUNSTON 3-134; will (1736) 1-29.

BADHAM, WILLIAM, JR. 14 years old (1750) JOHN HALSEY, his uncle 1-451; received land grant (1782) 1-21; 2-257.

BAGLEY FAMILY WILLS - PERQUIMANS - After 1800 3-325.

BAGLEY, JOSEPH, of PERQUIMANS, owner of sloop FRANKLIN (1775) 1-436.

BAGLEY, THOMAS, wife SUSANNAH (1712) 3-379; 3-334, 3-164, 2-328; will (1727) 1-31.

BAGLEY, WILLIAM, mentioned with JOHN COSARD, 3-330.

BAGSTER, NATHANIEL, had daughter MARY 3-210.

BAINES FAMILY WILLS 1-530, 2-257 and 2-504.

BAINES and BRANCH FAMILY connected 3-325.

BAINES, GEORGE SR. grant on Yeppim River (1783) 1-21 (near Perquimans line; also on Queen Anne's Creek 1-22.

BAINES, GEORGE JR. land grants 1-24; joined WILLIAM HOSKINS (1783) 1-22.

BAINES, ISAAC, land grant (1793) near Perquiman's line 1-24.

BAILEY, BARZILLAC, master of schooner DOVE (1749) 1-433.

BAILEY, BENJAMIN, Lieut. 7th Reg. N. C. Cont. Line 1-422.
BAILEY, DAVID, Pasquotank, BRIAN kin 2-326.
BAILEY FAMILY GENEALOGY, note bottom of page 1-278, 1-279.

BAILEY FAMILY WILLS 1-179.

BAILEY, GABRIEL, Exr. NATHANIEL GORDON (1815) 3-335.

BAILEY, JOHN, widow MARY deed (1716) witnessed by THOMAS DANIEL and JOHN ADDERLY 1-297 deeded land by RICHARD WASHINGTON 1-299; deed HENRY CLARK 1-290; THOMAS LEE mar'ed his widow 1-297; will (1716) 1-33.

BAILEY PATRICK, marriages in his family 1-305 son of Patrick 3-219; old one died(1691) 3-363; children born 3-218; married widow of SAMUEL RATCLIFF 1-305.

BAILEY, RICHARD, wife DEBORAH and son HENRY (1689) 3-371.

BAILEY, THOMAS, indicted for preaching (1725) 2-132, 2-133. Was son of RICHARD BAILEY and wife REBECCA (1702) 3-374.

BAKER, BLAKE, son of HENRY BAKER of CHOWAN (1737) 1-29; brother of ZADOCK BAKER and others 2-469; related to EDMUND CHANCEY 1-36; called brother in will of WILLIAM KINCHEN JR. (1758) 1-56; was Clerk of Superior Court (1787) 1-449, 2-305.

BAKER FAMILY WILLS 2-40, 2-41, 2-51, 2-328, 2-502, 2-503.

BAKER, HENRY, merchant of ISLE OF WIGHT CO. VA. (1703) 2-468; his children 2-469; WILLIAM DANIEL witnessed his deed (1736) 3-130; proposed to start mill (1748) 1-452; petitioned for ferry in BERTIE (1725) 3-451; deed to WILLIAM SKINNER of Nansemond County, Va. (1738) 3-128; his will in Chowan (1737) 1-29; Justice for Chowan (1731) 1-449; left will (1730) Bath Baker his heir 3-132; witnessed deed by WILLIAM SPARKMAN (1729) 2-451; deed to ROBERT THOMAS (1736) 3-130.

BAKER, JAMES (of Nansemond Co. Va.) deed to JOHN PORTER, JR. (1728) 2-443; same 2-454; Had son William 2-633.

BAKER, JOHN, chose his mother RUTH BAKER as his guardian at 14 2-469; will in BERTIE (1756) 1-27.

BAKER, MOSES, will (1734) 1-31.

BAKER, RICHARD, bought land from FRANCIS HARRELL, of Nansemond Co. Va. (1731)2-450.

BAKER, RUTH, was daughter of EDMUND CHANCEY of PASQUOTANK bottom of page 1-29; sold land to HENRY BAKER (JR.) land left her in will of HENRY BAKER, deed (1739) 3-132.

BAKER, SAMUEL, orphan of HENRY BAKER, ZACH. CHANCEY, guardian (1745) 1-452.

BAKER, SARAH, Zachariah Chancey, guardian in (1745) 3-470.

BAKER, SARAH, dau. of CAPT. HENRY BAKER, chose THOMAS LUTEN, as guardian (1742) 1-447.

BAKER, WILLIAM, will (1745) 2-625; wife Elizabeth (1718) 1-622.

BAKER, ZADOCK, son of HENRY and brother of BLAKE BAKER 2-469.

BALES, EDEN will (1762) 2-327.

BALES, JOHN, witnessed deed (1719) 1-622.

BALES, THOMAS 2-284.

BALL, THOMAS, witnessed deed by JOHN HAWKINS (1715) 1-287; sold land to THOMAS COOK (1717) 1-630; will CHOWAN CO. (1722) 1-32.

BALLARD, ABRAHAM 1-181.

BALLARD, JETHRO, will 2-40.

BALLARD JOHN, owned lands by JOHN JORDAN & JOHN WHITE, JR. (1712) 1-629; wife MARY (1725) 2-449; servant (1717) 1-618.

BALLARD, JOSEPH, lived on BEAVER DAM SWAMP (1733) 2-453; one left will (1729) 1-31.

BALLARD, RALPH 1-11; land grant (1722) 1-19.

BALLARD, THOMAS, Bertie, surety JOHN DAWSON Estate (1770) 3-446, 3-448.

BALLENTINE, GEORGE, will (1723) 1-180; one GEORGE BALLENTINE m. ROE 1-374.

BALLENTINE, JOHN (Suffolk, Va.) 2-103.

BANKS, JOHN, sold land to JOHN URMSTONE, minister (1716) on ALBEMARLE SOUND, with ROBERT MOORE a witness 3-455.

BAPTIST CONGREGATION, first one organized in North Carolina, account of 1-283.

BAPTIST, DR. BENJAMIN, died (17630 with EDWARD HATCH, Executor 2-470.

BAPTIST, MARY CLARK, wife of DR. BENJAMIN BAPTIST (1753) 2-470.

BARBER, CHARLES, land grant next to THOMAS JONES (1712) 1-7; wife ELIZABETH 1-296; in BERTIE, on Cashy River and SALMON CREEK by HENRY WHEELER and WILLIAM JONES (1716) and on TURKEY CREEK 1-296.

BARBER, ISAAC, Executor of HINCHA GILLIAM in will (1802) 3-333; witness for JESSE COPELAND 3-198.

BARBER, ISRAEL, will (1819) 3-327.

BARBER, JACOB, son in law of JOHN BUCK 1-30.

BARBER FAMILY WILLS 3-326, 3-327.

BARBER, JOEL will (1808) wife MOURNING, with names of children 3-327; witness for JACOB WYATT (1787) 3-198.

BARBER, JOHN, will PASQUOTANK (1692) 1-30; in CURRITUCK, the same (1762) ANN and SAMUEL BERNARD witnesses 2-297; will in CHOWAN in (1762) wife MASSINAH, mentions brother SAM BERNARD 1-133.

BARBER, JOSEPH will 3-166.

BARBER, MARGARET was MARGARET GREGORY 1-44.

BARBER, SAMUEL, will (1835) mentions cousin REBECCA WALLACE 3-327.

BARBER, WILLIAM, wife was DORCAS (1755) 3-379.

BARCLIFT, ANN, was ANN PARISH, of BERTIE 1-66.

BARCLIFT, ANN MARWOOD, took name from wife of GEORGE DURANT, see note bottom 3-167; the Barclifts were related to the KNOWLES family 3-326.

BARCLIFT FAMILY WILLS, of PERQUIMANS COUNTY - 3-165.

BARCLIFT, NOAH will 3-166.

BARCLIFT, WILLIAM, married ANN DURANT (1696) daughter of GEORGE DURANT and wife ANN - 3-148; will (1733) 1-31.

BARKER FAMILY GENEALOGY 2-477 to 2-479.

BARKER, THOMAS, married PHEREBY PUGH, the widow of FRANCIS PUGH 2-477, 2-479; was an attorney for SARAH HOWARD, daughter of JAMES HOWARD (1744) 2-623; was in BERTIE on road petition (1744) 2-625; born in RHODE ISLAND and came to BERTIE (1735) see account 1-515; made contract with SALISBURY 1-445; PHEREBY BARKER was born a MISS SAVAGE 2-470; was treasurer of the PROVINCE (1755-1756) 1-442.

BARKSDALE, WILLIAM, of HALIFAX COUNTY 2-60.

BARLOW, ROBERT, will in HYDE COUNTY 1-178.

BARLOW, ROGER, Executer of THOMAS FORSTER (1749) 3-305.

BARLOW, THOMAS, was Master of the Sloop TRYALL (1749) 1-435.

BARDIN, JOHN, bought land joining WILLIAM BRIDGER (1718) 1-634.

BABBCOCK, THOMAS, will (1721), had daughter MARGARET GREGORY 1-32.

BABBCOCK, WILLIAM, will (1730) 1-31; see also 3-251.

BAREFIELD, RICHARD, will (1754) 1-27.

BAREFIELD, WILLIAM, Quaker, 3-259; proved his rights (1712) mentions THOMAS MATTHEWS and JOHN ROBINSON 2-299.

BAREFIELD, THOMAS, will in BERTIE in (1768) 3-329.

BARNABAS, COOK, Master of the Sloop GREYHOUND (1749) 1-434.

BARNCASTLE, BEVERLY, will (1844) and account of his relatives 2-504.

BARNSFORD, ANNE, will (1721) 1-32.

BARNES, ANN, married THOMAS WHITE (1755) a list of children 3-400.

BARNES, BENJAMIN, witness for PHILLIP LEWIS in GATES COUNTY 2-59.

BARNES, ELIZABETH, of PERQUIMANS 3-165, also 2-549.

BARNES FAMILY WILLS 2-41, 2-42.

BARNES, HENRY, will (1812) 2-503; see 1-103.

BARNES, JACOB, son of JEREMIAH (1739) 3-379.

BARNES, JEREMIAH, married MARY LUTEN or LATEN (1705) 3-410, 3-376; also see wife SARAH (1724) 3-379.

BARNES, JOHN, wife ANNE (1725) 3-379; he guardian of LEWIS COBB, son of JOHN COBB (1769) in BERTIE 3-447; wills of same JOHN BARNES in BERTIE (1773-83) 2-324.

BARNES, MARY, bought land from MATTHEW ODOM next to HENRY KING (1730) 2-610.

BARNES, NANCY, was daughter of JOHN MARTIN (will 1816) 2-533.

BARNES, NATHANIEL witnesses bill of JOHN CULPEPPER (1678) 1-614.

BARNES, RICHARD, deed of gift to MARY CARTER (1723) 2-449; list of children given 2-257; land grant (1725) 1-19; deed to EDWARD HARE (1731) 2-451.

BARNES, SAMUEL 3-257.

BARNES, THOMAS deed to JOHN ELLIS 1-333-4.

BARNES, WILLIAM bought land from EDWARD HOWARD (1719) 1-630.

BABOS, MOSES, will (1733) 1-31.

BARTIE, WILLIAM, will in PERQUIMANS (1799)
wife DIANA BOUTWELL & Children 3-167; sister ELIZABETH or EMILY MUNS (1832) 3-323.

BARTLETT, JOHN, and wife ANN (1724) 3-380.

BARTLETT, SAMUEL, master of schooner BETTY
(1749) 1-434.

BARTLETT, WILLIAM, wife ANN, and children in
(1700) 3-372, 3-374.

BARRADELL, JOSEPH, surveyor BERTIE (1744 - 5)
2-625.

BARRETT, JOHN, will (1803) daughter TEMPER -
ANCE, etc. 2-501.

BARRINGTON, BENJAMIN, and children, proved
rights (1700) 1-305.

BARROIE, JOSEPH; witness with FRANCIS PETITT
(1732) 2-452.

BARRON, ALEXANDER, witness with WILLIAM LAT-
TIMORE (1721) 2-618.

BARRON, ANDREW, deed (1715) to HENRY JARVI -
GAN, of Nansemond Co. Va. 1-615; owned
lands next to OWEN McDANIEL (1720) 2-618;
granted land (1714) on POPLAR RUN 1-9; also same (1720) 1-12, 1-615.

BARRON, EDMUND, Tithable in CURRITUCK very
eraly date, with DAVID BLAKE, SAMUEL
BARNES, the VINCES, JOHN SCARBOROUGH and
others 3-257.

BARRON, JAMES, witnessed deed (1738) with
ANDREW and DAVID MEADE 3-132.

BARRON, THOMAS, mentioned with JAMES BARRON
1-234.

BARRON, WILLIAM, mentioned 3-34, 3-35.

BARROW, ANN (Daughter of JOHN and SARAH BAR-
ROW) married JOHN BENTLEY (1694) 3-406.

BARROW, MAJOR DAVID (1777) 2-438.

BARROW, ELIZABETH, died (1697) 3-364.

BARROW FAMILY Births of children 3-206, 3-207
3-211.

BARROW FAMILY WILLS, PERQUIMANS (All after
1800) 3-326.

BARROW, JAMES, of CHOWAN, will (1719) 1-33;
witness deed of EDWARD MOSELEY (1714)
1-293; was son of JOHN and SARAH BARROW
3-215, 3-408

BARROW, JOHN, wife SARAH (1696) 3-408, 3-
216; will (1718) 1-33; acting Justice in
(1697) 3-408; see 3-379, 1-489.

BARROW, JOSEPH, wife JEAN (1724) 3-379; wife
SARAH (1730) 3-379.

BARROW, RICHARD (son of Elizabeth Lillington, 1741) 1-57.

BARROW, THEOPHILUS, will (1825) ISAAC WHITE
a witness 3-326.

BARROW, WILLIAM, petition to Council 3-76;
charged with plot (1701) in ALBEMARLE
1-610; will (1715) 1-33; wife ELIZABETH
COOK (1697) 3-370, 3-408; will 1-172;
names of sons 1-172; see also 3-163 and
3-260.

BARRY, JOHN 1-529.

BARRY, THOMAS, Bertie County (1795) 2-329.

BARRY, WILLIAM, will (1721) daughter MARY
BARRY married JOHN MEADS 1-31.

BASNETT, WILLIAM, mentioned in oldest document on records of North Carolina (1669)
3-87.

BASSETT, WILLIAM witnessed deed (1731) 2-610.

BASS, EDWARD, from Norfolk County, Va. bought
land from ABRAHAM HILL (also of Nansemond)
in (1720). His wife was ELIZABETH 2-616;
he and his wife LOVE deed land to JOSEPH
REDDIN on HORSE PEN SWAMP, joining ABRAHAM
HILL (1726) 2-446; 2-615.

BASS FAMILY WILLS 1-533, 2-326.

BASS, JACOB, will (1810) 2-502.

BASS, JOHN, married LOVE HARRIS in 1696, of
NANSEMOND COUNTY, Va. (both of them)
3-407; bought land from ABRAHAM HILL in
(1720) deed witnessed by WILLIAM HINTON
2-616; had grandson, AARON JOHNSTON mentioned in his will (1732) 1-31.

BASS, LEMUEL, made deed (1737) 3-130.

BASTABLE, WILLIAM, was son in law of RICH-
ARD TURNER (1719) 1-79.

BATCHELDER, RICHARD 1-293.

BATE, HUMPHREY, of BERTIE, son of MARY
MHOON (1832) 2-532.

BATE, JAMES (prob. BATES) and THOMAS HEN-
MAN witness PETTIVER deed (1720) 2-607.

BATE, HENRY (Dr.) BERTIE (1739) 2-466.

BATES, JAMES, of YORK COUNTY, VA. deposition of JOHN SMITH (1695) 2-151; witness
to deed of JOHN CAKE (1720) 2-608 (1717)
1-17; witnessed deed with CHRISTOPHER
DUDLEY (1715) 1-287; land grant (1717) 1-17.

BATH, North Carolina, an historical account
3-20 to 3-27.(1715) 2-276 to 2-281.

BATH COUNTY, items from records relating to
1-441, 1-442

BATHEY, JOHN, to son TRISTRAM 3-128.

BATEMAN FAMILY. Births of children 3-210

BATEMAN FAMILY WILLS 1-521, 3-164.

BATEMAN, HANNAH died (1692) 3-220.

BATEMAN, JONATHAN, wife MARGARET, had son
JONATHAN born (1676) 3-210, 3-363.

BATEMAN, JONATHAN had wife ELIZABETH (1705)
3-376; she was ELIZABETH ARNOLD in(1693)
married by JONATHAN WHEDBEE 3-205.

BENBERRY, WILLIAM, constable in ALBEMARLE PRE-
CINCT (1707) 3-147; evidently had son WIL-
LIAM, estate divided (1762) 1-446; the 1st
one died leaving will (1709) 1-34; another
left will in CHOWAN (1755) 1-27; his wife
was BRIDGETT 1-455; his children 1-455.

BENNETT, EDWARD, will (1637) ALBEMARLE 1-178;
Births of his children 3-208.

BENNETT, JAMES, deals with the CHOWAN INDIANS
(1734) 3-125.

BENNETT, JANE married WILLIAM HARBORT 3-203.

BENNETT, JOHN, will in CURRITUCK (1710) mentions cousin WILLIAM JONES of England 1-34;
bought land from CHARLES MORGAN (1716) and
JOSHUA PORTER and RICHARD BENNETT were the
witnesses 1-618 (this probably JOHN JR.)

BENNETT, JOHN, SR. deed to THOMAS STACEY(1715)
2-619; one sold servant to BENJ. TULLE in
CURRITUCK (1699) 1-609; he and wife ROSE
deed to FRANCIS BEASLEY 1-625.

BENNETT, JOHN B., brother of WILLIAM BENNETT
2-258; connected with JOHN BEASLEY 3-327.

BENNETT, JOSEPH, had son JOHN mentioned in
will of JOHN HODGSON (1712) 1-52; see also
1-13 for his land grant (1719).

BENNETT, LYDIA, her will (1807) mentions connections. Will in CHOWAN 1-531.

BENNETT, NEHEMIAH 1-185.

BENNETT, RICHARD with JOSHUA PORTER witness a
JOHN BENNETT deed (1716) 1-618.

BENNETT, SARAH, probably daughter of JACOB
SHARP named (1746) 2-627.

BENNETT, SOLOMON, mentioned with NATHANIEL
BENNETT 1-182.

BENNETT, WILLIAM land grant on county line &
the river side 1-17; one grant (1794) 1-22;
mentioned in connection with MICHAEL Mc-
KEEL 3-342; witness to affidavit made by
DANIEL AUSTIN (1777) 2-573; his estate in
(1805), of course a later one 2-259.

BENTON FAMILY. Wills. 2-43.

BENTON, EPAPRODITUS, owned land next to ED-
WARD ARNOLD 1-21; and next to MOSES HALL
(1758) 1-20; these BENTONS lived on EAST
SIDE of CHOWAN RIVER 3-444; see also 2-293.

BENTON, FRANCIS, appointed to divide, JOSEPH
WITHERINGTON to assist, the FAIRLESS estate (1746) 2-627.

BENTON, JAMES witness to deed by WILLIAM PAR-
KER (1719) 3-126; bought land from JOHN
BENTON (1736) on West side of BENNETT'S
CREEK 3-125.

BENTON, JESSE, orphan of MARY BENTON of BER-
TIE (1770) 3-448.

BENTON, JOHN, road overseer (1748) at EDEN-
TON 1-452; bought land from LITTLETON
SPIVEY (1735?) 2-610.

BENTON, MARY, her orphans named (1770)
including ROBERT and JESSE 3-448.

BENTLEY FAMILY. Wills 1-179, 2-500.

BENTLEY FAMILY. Births of children 3-209.

BENTLEY, JOHN, deed to CONSTANCE LUTEN
with power of attorney (1710) to one
THOMAS CLARK 1-296; his will (1695)
an elder one, of course, mentions bro-
in-law WILLIAM BARROW and JENKINS WIL-
LIAMS 1-30; his wife was ANN BARROW
married (1694); there as early as
(1689) 3-430; deed to ALEXANDER SMITH
(1711) 1-292.

BENTLEY, MARTHA, will in BERTIE 2-329.

BENTLEY, PETER, died before (1771) leaving orphans in BERTIE 3-450.

BENTLEY, WILLIAM, witness with SIMON DAN-
IEL and HENRY GOODMAN (1732) 2-609; &
bought lands from SAMUEL MERRITT of
GATES COUNTY (1718) 1-628.

BENN, CHRISTOPHER. His wife was ELIZABETH,
daughter of THOMAS JORDAN, from NANSE-
MOND COUNTY, VA. (1760) 1-446.

BERKLEY, SIR WILLIAM, an account of him
and his family connections extended
note at bottom of page 1-306.

BERKELEY - LATER PERQUIMANS - PRECINCT
Births, deaths and marriages therein
from the original records at HERTFORD
N. C. 3-199 to 3-220; deaths in BERK-
ELEY PRECINCT 3-401- to 3-406.

BERTIE PRECINCT. Act providing for its
erection (1722) 2-412, 2-413; list of
tithables in before 1700 3-34, 3-35;
Act providing for courthouse 2-413,
2-414; proceedings relating to courthouse in (1741) 2-199, 2-202; Ray family of BERTIE COUNTY 2-541; see 3-308.

BERTIE COUNTY, miscellaneous records obtained from 3-443 to 3-451; marriage
bonds on file (1788 to 1809) 2-364 to
2-379; (1762-1787) 2-314 to 2-320;
(1820 to 1834) 2-589 to 2-593; other
miscellaneous court records (1720 to
1750) 2-520 to 2-634; an account of its
history and formation 3-308; BLACKMAN'S
LANDING in Bertie 3-92, 3-93.

BERTIE COUNTY WILLS. (See under ABSTRACTS)

BRENARD, ANN, witnessed will of JOHN BAR-
BER (1762) 2-297

BERNARD, SAMUEL 2-297.

BERRY, CHARLES 1-518.

BERRY, JOHN, died without will 1-33.

BERRY, EDWARD, wife MARY (1703) 3-375; sold
land to JOHN BENNETT, CHOWAN 1-625.

BERRYMAN, RICHARD, land grant (1719) on
BENNETT'S CREEK 1-9; wife MARTHA (1718)
1-624; see also 2-451.

BEST, JOHN, a witness (1731) 2-451.

BETTERLY, THOMAS, of PERQUIMANS had power of Attorney from CHARLES FOSTER (1719) 1-627; bought land from THOMAS PARRIS (1718)1-628.

BEVERLY, JOHN, bought land from WILLIAM EARLY (1704) 3-465.

BIGGS, JOHN. His mother was SUSANNAH GREEN in (1732) in BATH. 1-45.

BIGGS, TIMOTHY made bond not to transport persons out of the Colony 3-138; a creditor of the owners of the ship LOYAL 2-300; his wife was MARY 3-220; see also 3-45.

BILLET, JOHN, will (1710) 1-32.

BILLUPS, LANGLEY and AGATHA BRINKLEY 3-328.

BIRAM, JOHN 2-329.

BIRCH, WILLIAM and wife GRACE (1739) 3-134.

BIRD, EDMUND, of BERTIE (1767) 3-442

BIRD, EDWARD, son of JOHN BIRD and wife RE-BECCA (1701) 3-373.

BIRD FAMILY. Mentioned in will of JOHN D. GALE (1825) 2-515.

BIRD, JAMES power of attorney from MARY FLEM-ING (1717) 1-299.

BIRD, JOHN, married REBECCA PETERSON (1697) 3-408, 3-370; had daughter MARY BIRD who was niece of GEORGE BELL (1745) 2-626; her father may have been JR. as first JOHN made will (1744) in BERTIE 2-625; in(1702) he assigned his rights to FRANCIS GARGAN-US 1-614; one of which was JOHN BIRD, JR. 3-139; see also 3-147.

BIRD, MARY had son WILLIS BIRD under tuition of JAMES JENKINS (1770) 3-448.

BIRD, THOMAS and RICHARD BROWN were witnesses together (1719) 2-608; he was constable in place of RICHARD WILLIFORD, in BERTIE (1744) 2-605.

BIRD, WILLIAM, from NANSEMOND COUNTY, VA. He made deed there (1735) to JOHN WALTON, JR. 3-129; bought land from JAMES HOMES (Helmes) in BERTIE (1728) 2-444.

BIRTHS, DEATHS and MARRIAGES in BERKELEY PRE-CINCT 3-199 to 3-220, 3-363 to 3-410, 3-368 to 3-401.

BISHOP, JOHN and wife HANNAH (1739) 3-380.

BISHOP, MOSES. His family 2-545.

BISSELL FAMILY. Wills. 1-532.

BLACHOW, JOHN witnessed deed (1719) 1-627.

BLACK, JAMES and JOSEPH BLACK sold land on ROANOKE (1732) 2-451

BLACK, JOHN and wife SARAH (1709) division of their estate 2-258.

BLACK, SAMUEL (1788) division of his estate is shown 2-258.

BLADES, ABRAHAM, will 3-45.

BLACKALL, DR. ABRAHAM member Court for CHOWAN (1743) 1-447; deed to MARTHA DUN-STON, widow of JOHN 1-446; had something to do with EDENTON original town site or site of courthouse (1744) 1-453; His estate divided (1769) 1-456; His family 3-466.

BLACKALL, SARAH, of EDENTON, will (1754) had daughter SARAH BOWDEN. 1-28.

BLACKBURN, ANN administratrix of the estate of OLIVER BLACKBURN, she of BEAUFORT and he of BATH 2-303.

BLACKBURN, JOHN, bought land from BENJAMIN FREEMAN (1719) 1-629.

BLACKBURN, OLIVER appears on records (1726) 2-302.

BLACKWELL, MICAJAH, will (1765) 2-327.

BLAIR FAMILY. Wills 1-520.

BLAIR, GEORGE, genealogical account of the family, women connected with the EDENTON TEA PARTY. See note at bottom of page. 2-458.

BLAIR, WILLIAM, succeeded BLAKE BAKER as CLERK of the COURT (1787) 2-305; connected with GOV. JAMES IREDELL 3-327.

BLAKE DAVID, brought suit against WILLIAM STEWARD 3-431; connected with THOMAS WHITE 3-247; member of the jury CHOWAN (1704) 1-444; wife was MARY 3-213; contract with THOMAS WHITE 3-247; connection with ROBERT BEASLEY (1689) 3-433.

BLAKE, JOHN WYATT born (1749) 2-471.

BLAKE, THOMAS died 3-366.

BLAND, RICHARD, of YORK COUNTY, VA. 2-151; Justice of YORK 2-151.

BLEWETT, ABRAHAM (BLEWETT) and JOHN NAIRN witness deed (1718) CHOWAN 1-627; wife was JEANETT 1-625; sold land to LAWRENCE MARTIN (1718) next to ROBERT LANIER and EDWARD HOWARD 1-625.

BLEY, WILLIAM (BLY) bought land from WIL-LIAM WARD (1740) 3-136; will presented (1748) 2-632; proved rights of JOHN and JAMES BLY (1744) 2-624.

BLISH, JOHN, guardian of ELLENER GIBSON (1716) 1-46.

BLITCHENDEN, THOMAS wife MARY and names of children (1715) 3-380.

BLANCHARD, AARON, Justice for CHOWAN (1731) 1-449; wife was ZILPHA and children 1-451.

BLANCHARD, ABRAHAM, wife MARY 1-452.

BLANCHARD, BENJAMIN (1702) 1-293, 3-242; land grant (1701) on BEAVER DAM SWAMP 1-6.

BLANCHARD, EDWARD, land grant (1803) next to JACOB CULLEN, ELISHA HUNTER and MARY SMITH 1-25.

BLANCHARD, EPHRAIM, wife ISABELLA, made deed to THOMAS FLETCHER (1716) 1-397; land grant (1722) on MEHERRIN NECK, in GATES COUNTY 1-11.

BLANCHARD FAMILY. Wills 1-525.

BLANCHARD, MICAJAH, land grant (1790) on WAR-WICK SWAMP 1-23.

BLANCHARD, ROBERT, had sister SARAH who was his administrator 1-450.

BLOUNT, ANN, married JAMES HARVEY (1774)3-386

BLOUNT, BENJAMIN, wife ELIZABETH deeds land on HAWKINS BRANCH (1719) 2-457; was son-in-law of NATHANIEL EVERETT (AVERITT) in (1718) 1-519; was brother of JACOB BLOUNT and son of THOMAS BLOUNT (1718) 1-519; left will TYRRELL COUNTY (1739) 1-29; see also 1-291.

BLOUNT, CHARLES WORTH. His wife was MARY CLAYTON 3-166; was sheriff of CHOWAN CO. (1755-1756) 1-456; history of 1-460; his will (1807) 3-325; see also 2-355.

BLOUNT, CHRISTIAN, was daughter of THOMAS BLOUNT, mentioned by JEREMIAH PERRY (1694) 1-57.

BLOUNT, EDMUND (1804) 2-258; note relating to bottom of page 1-322.

BLOUNT, ELIZABETH. Will (1732) 1-34.

BLOUNT FAMILY. Notes relating to 1-34, 1-35.

BLOUNT FAMILY. Division of estates 2-257.

BLOUNT FAMILY GENEALOGY. 1-522 to 1-524; & 1-460 to 1-462 inclusive.

BLOUNT FAMILY GRAVEYARD with the LITTLEJOHN FAMILY on CHESHIRE'S HILL 1-39.

BLOUNT FAMILY. Wills 1-522, 1-523.

BLOUNT, FREDERICK, of PASQUOTANK. His widow married TEMPLEMAN (1784) 2-304.

BLOUNT, JACOB, married BARBARA GRAY 1-523; Justice of CHOWAN PRECINCT (1731) 1-449; had brother JOHN BLOUNT (1722) 1-456; had daughter ANN married JAMES HARVEY (1774) 3-386; he was a nephew of THOMAS READING (1734) 1-70; is said to have married also a daughter of JAMES LONG and his wife ELIZABETH 2-468. (He is known to have been twice married).

BLOUNT, JAMES was son in law of SAMUEL SLADE (1746) 1-72; there was a JAMES BLOUNT Sr. and a JAMES BLOUNT JR. 1-292; and the sen-ior in (1669) lived in ISLE OF WIGHT COUN-TY bottom note 1-34; will of the elder (1685) mentions family connections 1-34; His son was evidently called "Sr" on later records, as in land grant (1716) 1-16; an-other land grant (1697) on Mattacomack Creek 1-5; James Sr. sold land to James Jr (1711) 3-441; one married first KATHERINE TYLER and second MARY TYLER (1712) 3-302; one left will (1716) 1-33; another will with HARMON HILL, Executor (1751) 1-28; another will (1725) 1-34, 1-35; one JAMES mentioned in will of LOVICK WORLEY with WILLIAM GRAY (1754) 1-80, 1-294, 1-3.

BLOUNT, JOHN was son of JAMES BLOUNT called his "late father" (1718) 1-526; mentions "my sister Anne" 1-526; with wife ELIZABETH (1718) sold land to ED-WARD WINGATE on Queen Anne's Creek for-merly property of JOHN BLOUNT deceased (1718) 1-526; John and JACOB were the nephews of THOMAS READING 1-70; had a land grant (1696), reissued from (1684) 1-6; lived at MULBERRY HILL, his fami-ly (the son of James) 1-35; sold land (1716) 1-520; was a Justice in CHOWAN PRECINCT (1731) 1-449; married SARAH VAIL (connections mentioned) 1-132; had land grant near MULBERRY HILL (1721) 1-10; was son of JAMES BLOUNT and wife ANN of ISLE OF WIGHT COUNTY came to CHOWAN in (1669) 2-325; land joined that of his father (1714) 1-9; 1-445.

BLOUNT, JOHN, the son of THOMAS BLOUNT (1729) moved to NEW ENGLAND, and deed-ed N. C. lands to WILLIAM DOWNING 2-446; land joined MATTHEW BROWN (1717) 1-16; married MARY DAVIS, of Henrico Co. Va. (1695) 3-407; another JOHN married ELIZ-ABETH DAVIS, daughter of JOHN and wife MARY, related to BURTONS (1687) full account of family 2-325.

BLOUNT, JOSEPH, was sheriff of CHOWAN CO. (1757) and brother of CHARLES WORTH BLOUNT 1-456; was connected with DURANT and LITTLEJOHN families 1-522.

BLOUNT, MARTHA, married THOMAS WEST as her first husband, and had daughter by name MARTHA who married EDWARD BRYAN and her grand-daughter ELIZABETH BRYAN married THOMAS WHITMELL 1-445.

BLOUNT, MARTHA ANN, married JOSHUA SKIN-NER (1730) 3-396.

BLOUNT, MARY had lawsuit with JOHN WOR-LEY, in ALBEMARLE (1707) 1-510; an-other MARY, widow of FREDERICK BLOUNT married a TEMPLEMAN (1784) 2-304.

BLOUNT, READING, was a Captain and later a major in N. C. Cont. line 1-420.

BLOUNT, RICHARD HINES, an account of his family connections 1-639, 1-640.

BLOUNT, THOMAS answers complaint of WIL-LIAM DUKENFIELD 3-65, 3-56; married MARY SCOTT 3-318; tried to beak up the match between his son JAMES BLOUNT and the widow HOOPER (1701) in ALBEMARLE 1-510; was the oldest son of THOMAS BLOUNT and MARY SCOTT, the widow of JOSEPH SCOTT of PERQUIMANS, who married later THOMAS LEE (1716) 1-297; Assembly met at the elder CAPT. THOMAS BLOUNT'S home in PERQUIMANS (1696) 1-612, 1-255, 3-55, who may have been bother of the JAMES BLOUNT who died (1685) 3-318; one had daughter ZILPHA BLOUNT who married JOHN EDWARDS 1-59; son went to NEW EN-GLAND (1729) 2-446; the one who mar-ried the widow MARY SCOTT was called "Jr" 3-202, 1-397; left will in TYRRELL COUNTY (1701) 1-30

BOBBITT, JOHN witnessed deed of RICHARD LONG (1718) 1-528, was sued (1732)2-298; was brother in law of JOHN GREEN (1718) 1-534 and witnessed deed (1713) 2-518.

BODDIE, JOHN married ELIZABETH JEFFRIES (the
widow POTTLE) 1-53.

BODDIE, NATHAN, an account of his family
1-639.

BODLEY, JOSHUA, agent of Lord Granville, see
note 1-522; will 1-521.

BODIEST, JACOB, died (1714) 1-34.

BOGHART, DANIEL 2-329.

BOGUE, CHARITY (1790) witnessed will of one
JOSEPH GUYER 3-172.

BOGUE, HANNAH, daughter of WILLIAM 3-218.

BOGUE, JOSEPH 3-325.

BOG (BOGG, BOGUE) THOMAS. Master schooner
SNOW LILLY (1754) 1-435.

BOGUE, ROBERT. Was a cousin of WILLIAM MOORE
of PERQUIMANS (1725) 1-82.

BOGUE, WILLIAM. His wife was ELLENER (1717)
3-380, 3-217 and in (1701) 3-373; had
grandson WILLIAM HILL mentioned in his
will (1721) 1-32.

BOND, ELIZABETH, was the daughter of BENJA-
MIN REYNAUD (1712) 1-71.

BOND FAMILY. Notes relating to. 3-121; wills
in PERQUIMANS 3-164, also 2-42, 2-43, &
1-527, 1-528; in BERTIE 2-327 and 2-499.

BOND FAMILY. Genealogy of JAMES BOND who
married MARY HOSKINS, and the BOND FAMI-
LY 3-117, 3-118.

BOND, GEORGE, married MARY RHODES in BERTIE
(1806) 2-377.

BOND, HANCE, deceased (1748) wife was SARAH
1-452.

BOND, HENRY, an orphan, and WILLIAM WALTON
to be his guardian (1737) 1-448.

BOND, JOHN, left will in (1738) 1-29.

BOND, LEWIS, was the son of RICHARD BOND &
his wife SARAH 1-450; he died in CHOWAN
in(1754) 1-453; left will there 1-28.

BOND, RICHARD, was of Nansemond County, Va.
1-132; was the father of HENRY BOND, one
of seven children 2-469; his widow SAR-
AH BOND, married JAMES COSTEN of MENHER-
RIN NECK 2-469.

BOND, ROBERT, will (about 1736) had daughters named GOODALL 1-29.

BOND, SAMUEL. His wife was ELIZABETH (1706)
3-376; left will in PERQUIMANS (1721)
1-32.

BOND, THOMAS, left will in BERTIE 2-327.

BOND, WILLIAM, will 1-291; other BOND FAMI-
LY WILLS 1-181.

BONDFIELD, CHARLES. Was Clerk of the SUPERI-
OR COURT of the EDENTON DISTRICT (1779)
1-448.

BONNER, BRYAN T. 3-178.

BONNER, EDWARD, of CURRITUCK, left will
in (1711) 1-24

BONNER FAMILY. GENEALOGY of the BONNERS
of BEAUFORT COUNTY 3-115 to 3-120,
3-171, 3-405, 3-406. Wills of BONNER
FAMILY 1-519; connection of BONNERS
with the BLOUNTS, WILLIAMS and FORE-
MAN FAMILIES 2-171 to 3-178; related
to CRAWFORDS and BRYANS and the JESSE
BRYAN FAMILY 3-561, 3-562.

BONNER, HENRY. Grant of WILLIAM YATES land
1-11; grant on MATTACOMACK CREEK (1718)
1-13; deed to JAMES BLOUNT (1716) 1-295;
deed to JOSEPH JESSUP of Perquimans in
(1715) 1-293; other land grants 1-11 &
1-12; was brother in law of JAMES WELCH
(1711) 1-84; father in law of PATCHETT
(1710); he married SARAH, daughter of
HENDERSON LUTEN 2-470; in(1714) was the
attorney of WILLIAM JONES 1-292; he had
daughters MARY and DEBORAH BONNER (1739)
2-469; he deeded land to WILLIAM BONNER
(1716) 1-295; there was a HENRY BONNER,
JR (1734) 2-453, 2-454; he and THOMAS
BONNER both left wills in CHOWAN COUNTY
his (1738) 1-27; he sold land to GEORGE
MARTIN (1732) 2-452; he was member of
the General Court in(1727) with BARNABY
McKINNIE, JOHN ALSTON and others 3-290;
both he and son HENRY BONNER JR. witness
BLANCHARD deeds (1736) 3-129; other land
grants received 1-15, 1-17 and 1-18.

BONNER, JOHN BRYAN 2-178.

BONNER, NORFLEET 1-159.

BONNER, THOMAS. Witness with BENJAMIN SANDER-
SON to deed by JOHN DAVIS (1720) 2-613;
left will (1755) 1-519; and another THOS.
received land grant (1782) near EDENTON
1-21.

BONNER, WILLIAM. Received land grant (1719)
1-17; he married a daughter of HENDERSON
LUTEN and niece of WILLIAM LUTEN 2-469;
witnessed indenture contract between ALEX-
ANDER RAY and WILLIAM CHARLTON JR. (1718)
1-629; his land joined the town of EDEN-
TON 1-17; came into court (1749) 1-452;
left will in BERTIE (1775) 2-329; see also
1-299.

BOON FAMILY. List of wills, etc. 2-616, 2-617.

BOONE FAMILY. List of revolutionary soldiers
who bore the name 2-186.

BOON, JACOB, deed from WILLIAM BOON and wife
ELIZABETH (1721) 2-616.

BOON, JAMES, and wife ELIZABETH deed to WIL-
LIAM BOON (1721) 2-617; sold land to JOHN
HOMES (1717), with EDWARD HOWARD a witness 1-627; owned land next to PETER EVANS
(1718) 1-620; neighbor to WILLIAM MAULE
(1719) 2-454; records his mark with EDWARD
GILLIAM (1744) 2-625; sold land to STEPHEN
HOWARD (1721) 2-617; to one SESSIONS also
1-105; see 1-627.

BOON, JOHN mentioned in will of DANIEL PHIL-
LIPS (1726) 1-68.

BOON, JOSEPH, and NICHOLAS BOON, members of COL. ROBERT PATTERSON'S Co. from MEHERRIN river (1729) 1-443; will 1-183

BOON, MARY. Mentioned (1746) by ROBERT FOS- TER, as his grand-daughter in his will. 1-43.

BOON, NICHOLAS, received deed (1721) from WILLIAM BOON and wife ELIZABETH 2-616; left will (1728) 1-183.

BOON, THOMAS. Wife was MARTHA BROWN 2-457; deed by him to WILLIAM BOON lands on So. side MEHERRIN river (1721), with ROBERT HICKS a witness 2-617.

BOON, WILLIAM. He, too, was member of ROBT. PATTERSON'S Co. from MEHERRIN river (1721) 1-443; part of his patent to land sold by MARTHA BROWN, widow of WILLIAM BROWN 2-457; His wife was ELIZABETH and they sold land to THOMAS BOON, JR. 2-616; see 2-457.

BOON, WILLIS, revolutionary soldier, appli- cation for pension as such 1-126.

BOOTH, GEORGE, of PRINCESS ANNE County sued JOSEPH WICKER, of CURRITUCK (1712) 2-466.

BOOTH, JAMES. His will 2-44.

BOOTH, RICHARD, sold land to WILLIAM EARLY on West shore of CHOWAN river (1712)2-512.

BORITZ FAMILY, of CHOWAN County, an account relating to bottom of page 1-523.

BORITZ, WILLIAM. Land grant (1787) 1-23.

BOSWELL, FAMILY WILLS 3-327, 3-328.

BOSWELL, GEORGE, of PERQUIMANS (1741) his will 1-27.

BOSWELL, JOSHUA. Will 3-164.

BOSWELL, THOMAS, wife SANE (Jane?) (1702) with children named 3-373; she was called ANNE (1713) 3-380; one THOMAS in Bertie (1808) 2-503.

BOSWELL, WILLIAM (1734) will 1-30.

BOUCHER, HELEN 2-163

BOUCHER, JOHN, witness to deed by JOHN BLOU- NT to EDWARD WINGATE (1718) 1-626.

BOUCHER, THOMAS 3-68; merchant in BOSTON in (1733) with GEORGE MONK 2-303.

BOULTON, JONATHAN, land grant on Rockyhoek Creek (1793) 1-24.

BOUND, RICHARD, of Perquimans, left will in (1720) 1-32.

BOUNDARY LINES between TYRRELL and BEAUFORT (1741) 2-255, 2-256; letter to GOV. SAM- UEL JOHNSTON relating to 3-104, 3-105.

BOUTWELL, DIANA married WILLIAM BARTIE 3-167

BOVELY, JOHN, will (1707) left property to JOHN BELL 1-71.

BOWEN, NATHAN 2-502.

BOWLER FAMILY 3-117.

BOYD, REV. ADAM, Chaplain the Revolution in N. C. An account of him 2-480; was Judge Advocate 1st Regt. N. C. Conti- nental Line, under Col. James Moore. 1-415.

BOYD FAMILY. Wils of 1-520.

BOYD, JOHN, of BERTIE County sold land to JOSEPH ANDERSON where SAMUEL BUNCH re- sided (1738) once owned by THOMAS POL- LOCK (1738) 3-129; also bought land from ROBERT HALTON (1736) 3-125; left will in CHOWAN (1737) 1-29; there was one in Pasquotank (1741) 1-27; Rev. John Boyd mentioned 1-134.

BOYD, MARTHA 2-328

BOYD, THOMAS land grant (1714) 1-15; mar- ried in PASQUOTANK the widow of JOHN WEST deceased 3-349, 1-509; they were married (1702) 1-609; he witnessed deed (1717) of GERARD LYNCH 1-300; he was step-father of JOHN and BENJAMIN West 3-249.

BOYD, WILLIAM obtained grant of land (1780) next to JULIUS BUNCH 1-21; in (1784) on ROCKYHOCK Creek or Neck 1-22; see 2-257.

BOYD, WINNIFRED, will (1720) 1-33.

BOYCE, ANN was the wife of WILLIAM BOYCE the Executor of JOHN BARBER (1692) 1-30.

BOYCE, CHRISTOPHER, bought land from JONATHAN KITTRELL (1739) 3-133.

BOYCE, EPAPRODITUS, his father was EPAPRODIT- US BOYCE also 3-134; he sold land to JOHN BOYCE (1709) and they appear to have been brothers and sons of the first EPAPRODIT- US BOYCE 3-134; mentioned 1-108.

BOYCE, HARDY. His wife was NANCY, both left wills after 1800 2-503.

BOYCE FAMILY. Wills 2-503, 1-525, 1-526, in Perquimans County 3-327.

BOYCE, JEMIMAH, will (1829) mentions JEMIMA and DAVID WHITE 3-327.

BOYCE, JOHN, will 1-175; in (1816) 3-327.

BOYCE, MARY married (1795) JOSEPH COPELAND in CHOWAN 1-252.

BOYCE, MOSES owned lands on BENNETT'S Creek next to RICHARD PARKER (1736) and SAMUEL and JOHN HINES 3-126; much later one left will (1811) 3-327.

BOYCE, WILLIAM, of Maryland (1703) in PRINCE GEORGE'S County 1-30; will in BERTIE 2-329; will (1688) 1-30.

BOYKIN, EDWARD. Will 1-183.

BOZMAN, CHLOE 1-532.

BOZMAN FAMILY. Some genealogy in connection with HARRISONS 3-472.

BOZMAN, JAMES married a SORSBY 2-635.
BOZMAN, JOHN, BERTIE (1810) 2-503.

BOZMAN, JOSEPH, married CHLOE HARRISON, perhaps daughter of WILLIAM HARRISON (1791) 3-472

BOZMAN, RALPH. He was an uncle of ISAAC WILSON, who died (1724) 1-83; patented lands next to THOMAS BRAY (1717) 2-452; died & left will (1745) 1-185.

BOZMAN, SAMUEL, sold land to SAMUEL PURSAIN (PURSELL?) in (1718) 1-527; see BOZMAN FAMILY genealogy 3-472.

BRADDY, JOHN, of MARRATTOKE, deed to WILLIAM JOHNSON (1723) 2-608.

BRADY, JAMES bought land (1739) from JOHN BRADY, which came to them through their father 3-136.

BRADY, JOHN sold land to JAMES (1739) with JACOB ODOM as a witness 3-136.

BRADLEY, JOHN, left will 1-178; his widow was RACHEAL (1745) 2-526.

BRADLEY, RICHARD, will 1-178.

BRADSHAW, EDWARD. Was a Quaker. 3-259.

BRADWELL, DAVID. His estate was administered by his widow HESTER (1771) Bertie. 3-450.

BRAINER, MICHAEL 3-166.

BRAINER, SARAH. Her will 3-327.

BRANCH, FRANCIS, land grant on MATTACOMACK Creek 1-9; was a Justice for CHOWAN PRECINCT (1731) 1-449; his wife was ANNE, in CHOWAN, who was mentioned in will of JOHN WHEATLEY 3-442; he witnessed deed with JOHN YELVERTON to RICHARD WILSON in (1718) 1-524; deeded land to MARY GARDNER, called "friend" (1739) 3-132; will (1739) 1-29; see also 1-98.

BRANCH, GEORGE, proved rights in CHOWAN (1735) mentions MARGARET THOMAS 2-465.

BRANCH, ISSACHAR, married the daughter of WILLIAM STEWART (1739) 2-469; sold lands to EDMUND GALE on Queen Anne's Creek in (1735) 3-128; one ISSACHAR BRANCH died in (1801) mentions GEORGE RAINES, SR. and others 3-325.

BRANCH, JOB, left will (1802) 3-325.

BRANCH, WILLIAM, bought land on MATTACOMACK Creek (1704) from JOHN DAVIS 2-455; the Court for CHOWAN PRECINCT was held at his home(1711) 3-441; land grant (1717) on BONNER'S COVE Creek 1-16; left will(1721) 1-32; deeded land to COL. EDWARD MOSELEY (1717) witnessed by Col. THOMAS SWANN & ELIZABETH SWANN 1-518; Edward Titman was bound to him 3-442 (this in 1711.).

BRANCH, WILLIAM (JR.). He executed deed in (1729) to WILLIAM ARKILL, witnessed by JOHN LOVICK 2-448; he died before (1747) and his widow married ROBERT KINGHAM 2-470; he had orphans FRANCIS and ELIZABETH BRANCH 2-470; He had son in law who was HUMPHREY ROBINSON 1-89.

BRASSEUR, JOHN makes affidavit in (1689) with EDWARD STREATER 3-432.

BRASWELL, RICHARD was connected with JAS BRYAN in BERTIE (1731) 1-34.

BRASWELL, ROBERT left will (1736) 1-180.

BRASWELL, VALENTINE. He and his wife JEAN in (1721) relinquished dower to BARNABY McKINNIE to land sold JOHN POPE 1-470.

BRASWELL, WILLIAM. His wife was MARY in deed of (1711) 1-288; deed to JOHN DICKINSON in (1717) 1-300, 1-299; had deed from JAMES BRYAN (1715) 1-287; he and MARGARET (maybe his wife) witnessed deed of JOHN SMITH to PHILLIP BROWN (1718) 1-629; he and wife MARY deeded lands to HENRY WHEELER on MORATTOCK river (1718) 1-299.

BRATTON, JOHN 3-166.

BRATTON, NATHANIEL 3-325.

BRAVEBOY, JOHN deed to JOHN WAIT (1732) 2-452.

BRAY, HENRY. His will (1745) 1-28

BRAY, THOMAS, patented land on Rockyhoek Creek (1716) 1-15; next to JOHN WATSON (1717) 1-9; sold land to ROBERT EVANS (1716) WILLIAM SHARP a witness 1-300; married before(1715) MARTHA POLLOCK, daughter of THOMAS POLLOCK and received deed as marriage portion (1716) 1-615, 1-616; bought land from JOHN EARLY and wife MARY (1718) 1-627; was from New Kent County, Virginia 2-288; sold land to FRANCIS BRANCH (1719) 2-512; bought land from Lawrence McGue (1717) 1-616; obtained patents to lands (1717) 1-17; PAUL BUNCH bought land from him 2-511; see 2-453.

BRAY, WILLIAM, copy of petition for his relief (1696-7) 3-251; his will as "Sr." (1725) 1-31; see also 1-33.

BRENT, JAMES will in CURRITUCK (1753) 1-27

BRENT, JOHN (1726) witnessed will of JOHN PAGE 1-67.

BRENT, THOMAS will CURRITUCK (1712) 1-34; same (1727) 1-34.

BRETT, DANIEL, minister 3-409.

BREVARD, JOHN, Lieutenant in 9th Regt. N. C. Continental Line 1-424.

BREVARD, JOSEPH, Ensign in 10th Regt. N. C. Continental Line (Col. Abraham Shepard) 1-426

BREWER, GEORGE, will (1739) 1-177.

BRICE, FRANCIS 2-325, 2-342.

BRICE, PETER, Ensign 9th Regt. N. C. Continental Line 1-424.

BRICE, WILLIAM, mentioned in will of ALICE WHITEHEAD 1-81, 3-81, 3-270; refers to an Indian named THOMAS BLOUNT 3-81, 3-82; will (1712) 1-32.

BRISKELL, JOHN, ordinary license (1747) 2-829.

BROWN, PRISCILLA, and sister SARAH daughters of THOMAS BROWN were related to THOS. BAR- FIELD 1-61

BROWN, PETER (1716) administrator of the esta- te of DANIEL BROWN 1-33.

BROWN, RICHARD, and WILLIAM CRAWFORD witnessed deed of WILLIAM HOOKER (1718) 1-524; died leaving will (1734) 1-30.

BROWN, SAMUEL witnessed deed (1718) from JOHN COUNCIL (Of Va.) to THOMAS BRITT 1-528.

BROWNE, THOMAS deed (1717), with BENJ. FOREMAN ISAAC HILL and RICHARD WASHINGTON 1-300; witnessed will of GEORGE WILLIAMS (1735) (This prob. Thomas Jr.) 2-296; THOMAS SR. died leaving will (1718) 1-33.

BROWN, THOMAS, JR. land grant (1720) 1-19; will (1748) at WILMINGTON 1-27; witnessed will of GEORGE WILLIAMS (1735) 2-296.

BROWN, WALTER of BERTIE, will (1735) mentions cousin JESSE DRAKE 1-30; also 1-169, the latter testator spelling it BROWNE.

BROWN, WILLIAM and wife MARTHA (1714) deed to GEORGE and JOHN SMITH 2-456; deeded land in CHOWAN to WILLIAM JONES (1718) 1-524; died leaving will (1719) 1-33.

BROWN, WILLIAM, son of BEAL BROWN mentioned in will of BENJAMIN RICKS 1-71.

BROWNELL, WILLIAM deed (1715) to CAPT. THOMAS LEE, witnessed by EDWARD MOSELEY 1-291.

BROWNING, JOHN SR. sold lands to ROBERT MOSS about (1720) 2-514; had son in law WILLIAM MORRIS (1720) 2-513; died leaving will in (1733) 1-31.

BROWNRIGG FAMILY. Genealogy of, in connection with EDENTON TEA PARTY families 3-300 to 3-304.

BROWNRIGG, GEORGE was twice married 2-537.

BROWNRIGG, RICHARD 1-530, 2-257; married SARAH CAMPBELL see note 1-48.

BROMLEY, GEORGE deed (1716) from JOHN JONES & THOMAS LUTEN mentioned 1-391; received land grant (1719) on Rockyhock 1-13; deeds land to THOMAS COOK (1728) 2-608; one of the name went to BOSTON (1717) 1-521.

BRINN, JAMES, division of his estate 2-259.

BRYAN, ALLEN, married (1784) SARAH ARPS 3-418.

BRYAN ANNE, daughter of LEWIS BRYAN, was born 1697, see note 2-602; she married JOHN GRAY 2-502,-2-507, and her sister ELIZABETH was wife of THOMAS WHITMELL 1-47; both were sis- ters of SIMON and EDWARD BRYAN 2-326.

BRYAN, ANNE, of CRAVEN COUNTY, widow, will in (1760) names children, and grandson JOHN DAWSON 1-175.

BRYAN, CATHERINE, executor estate of WILLIAM BRYAN (1744) 2-522; this was at WINDSOR in BERTIE COUNTY 2-520.

BRYAN, ELIZABETH, PERQUIMANS (1797) will 3-167.

BRYAN, ELIZABETH, daughter of LEWIS BRYAN married THOMAS WHITMELL 1-47.

BRYAN, ESTHER, was daughter of WILLIAM BRYAN and ESTHER SMITH, and married her first cousin JONATHAN SMITH; she had two brothers (sons of WILLIAM BRYAN) BLAKE BRYAN and ARTHUR BRYAN, the last named for his uncle ARTHUR SMITH IV of SMITHFIELD, VA. 1-471.

BRYAN, EDWARD (and JOHN BRYAN) were re- lated to LAWRENCE McGEE 1-61; EDWARD sold land to JOHN (1714) land patented to THOMAS MANN, joining the widow BAR- NES 2-136; bought land from THOS. MANN and wife BRIDGETT (1713) 1-103; account of his family 2-325; his mother was ELIZABETH HUNTER, from SURRY COUNTY VA. 2-325; he married MARTHA WEST daughter of THOMAS WEST and MARTHA BLOUNT 1-445; he and NEEDHAM BRYAN were present as Justices (1748) 2-531 for BERTIE 2-528; witnessed will of ISAAC HILL (1710) in BERTIE 1-52; the one in BERTIE and HERTFORD left will (1746) 1-27; another died BERTIE leaving will (1762)2-325; this last one master of sloop SUSANNA (1755) 1-435, and the same(1749) 1-435; Master of "TRYALL" (1761) 1-435. (This note seems to deal with two EDWARDS).

BRYAN FAMILY NOTES. The WILLIAM BRYAN record 1-577 to 1-584; notes on JOSEPH BRYAN 1-476, 1-477; English ancestry 2-536; 1-470, 1-471; wills of BRYAN FAM- ILY in BERTIE 2-325, 2-326.

BRYAN, HARDY died leaving will in CRAVEN COUNTY 1-175; a later HARDY BRYAN was COMMISSARY in the 7th Regt. N. C. Cont. Line during revolution 1-422; said to have been the son of WILLIAM BRYAN and ELIZABETH SMITH 1-578, and grandson of NEEDHAM BRYAN 1-577, and married WINNI- FRED McCULLERS 1-578; will CRAVEN 1-175

BRYAN, JAMES. One left will in BERTIE in (1731), Richard Braswell mentioned 1-34; another on North side MEHERRIN in 1733-4 1-31.

BRYAN, JENNET, daughter of EDWARD BRYAN in Bertie 2-536.

BRYAN, DAVID, son of SIMON 2-326.

BRYAN, JESSE, son of WILLIAM BRYAN of CRA- VEN COUNTY, a full account of his con- nections and descendants 2-557; his mother was ANN 2-459; was in BERTIE in (1775) 2-326.

BRYAN, JOHN bought land from JOHN NAIRNE (1720) ROBERT HICKS witness 2-513; sold land to WILLIAM CRAWFORD 2-284; and to JOHN EVERIT (1734) 2-454; was an exec- utor of RALPH EAVES (1741) 2-468; with NEEDHAM BRYAN (1745) was Justice in BERTIE 2-525; same at CASHY BRIDGE in (1749) 2-532; his wife was ALICE (1717) (probably from NANSEMOND CO. VA) 1-520; called a son of EDWARD BRYAN in deed of 1722 2-284; another JOHN had dealings with the Indians (1781) 3-453.

BRYAN, JOSEPH. An account of his family 1-521.

BRYAN, JOSEPH married daughter of DAVID BAILEY of PASQUOTANK. Their family 1-631, 1-632.

BRYAN, LEWIS, married ELIZABETH HUNTER, from SURRY COUNTY, VA. to BERTIE in (1713; daughter ANNE BRYAN married JOHN GRAY 2-325 and 2-602 and to 3-607; they were parents of EDWARD BRYAN who married MARTHA WEST 2-325; their daughter ELIZABETH married to THOMAS WHITMELL 1-17; LEWIS BRYAN witness to will of JOHN SOAKE (1732) 1-74; son SIMON BRYAN married ANNE (WEST) JACOCKS (see JACOCKS).

BRYAN, MARTHA, will in BERTIE (1808) 2-500.

BRYAN, MATTHEW, lived on East Side ROCKYHOCK, where he was granted lands (1714) 1-13; lived next to HENRY LILES and MAJ. LUTEN 1-3; and in (1713) was neighbor of WILLIAM WOODLEY 1-620; and of THOMAS WILLIAMS 1-9; His wife was KATHERINE and they sold land to HENRY LILES (1715) with JOHN HARDY a witness to the deed 1-620.

BRYAN, NEEDHAM and THOMAS HART were CHURCH wardens in BERTIE PRECINCT (1729) 2-305; he was a member of BERTIE COURT (1741) 2-199; he and EDWARD BRYAN, THOMAS WHITMELL and ROBERT HUNTER appointed Commissioners of the Peace for BERTIE (1746) 2-528; he and JOHN BRYAN and THOMAS WHITMELL (1745) were Justices of BERTIE 2-525; his name mentioned in suit of WILLIAM MAULE v. WILLIAM MARSHALL as overseer of lands occupied (1724) by WILLIAM BLOUNT 2-297; died leaving will in BERTIE (1767) 2-326.

BRYAN, RICHARD, was in CURRITUCK PRECINCT in (1695) 1-612; owned lands before(1700) in ALBEMARLE PRECINCT, and 494 acres in PAS - QUOTANK (1704) 1-304. (Ancestor of WIL - LIAM J. BRYAN - see this compiler's note.)

BRYAN, SIMON, brother of EDWARD and Son of LEWIS BRYAN married widow ANNE JACOCKS (1749) 2-332, 1-323; account of his family 1-28 & 1-164; his wife ANNE JACOCKS was born WEST 1-28.

BRYAN, THOMAS 2-350; his will in CRAVEN COUNTY (1760) 1-175.

BRYAN, WILLIAM, Church warden CRAVEN COUNTY 2-304; of (1730) 1-447 as witness in Court; will in CRAVEN COUNTY (1746) 2-557; same proved in BERTIE (1744); there was a younger WILLIAM BRYAN in BERTIE (1769) 3-447; another (the younger?) made deed of gift to KESIAH BRYAN in Bertie (1771) 3-450; the genealogical record of the first WILLIAM BRYAN 1-557 to 1-584.

BRYAN, WINIFRED,married first GEORGE DURANT REED who died (1809) leaving will 2-542; she was daughter of EDWARD BRYAN and wife MARTHA WEST, see note bottom 2-542.

BRYANT, JAMES, wife SARAH, made deed to WIL - LIAM BRASWELL (1715) 2-287.

BRYANT, EDWARD, of CHOWAN (1711) 3-441

BRYANT, JOHN, will in EDGECOMBE COUNTY (1734) mentions friend JOHN POPE 1-30.

BRYANT, WILLIAM and JAMES BRYANT, SR. witness to deed by JOHN COUNCIL (of Va.) to JOHN BRITT (1718) 1-528.

BRYANT, WILLIAM, witnessed deed of HENRY WHEELER to RICHARD WASHINGTON (1715) 1-295; and he and RALPH MASON witness to deed (1714) mentions JOHN DEW 1-329. (These BRYANS and BRYANS, the compiler believes were the same family.)

BRYTO, WILLIAM, left will (1703) 1-30.

BUCK, JOHN, will (1710) mentions sons in law (probably step-sons) JACOB and SAMUEL BARBER 1-30.

BUCK, RICHARD 1-87.

BUCKNER, ROBERT, 2-147.

BUDGATE, DANIEL, 3-164.

BUFKIN, MARY, deed (1729) to THOMAS HOLLIDAY 2-448.

BUFKIN, RALPH, wife MARY (1725) 3-380.

BULLOCK, DANIEL, Lieut. 9th Regt. N. C. Continental Line in revolution 1-424.

BULLOCK FAMILY. Wills 3-166, 1-531.

BULLOCK FAMILY. Genealogical account of the Bullocks of GEORGIA 1-467 to 1-469.

BUNCH, CULLEN,land grant (1792) on ROCKYHOCK Creek 1-24.

BUNCH, EDMUND, married MARTHA JORDAN in (1829) 1-560.

BUNCH FAMILY. Wills 1-520; in Bertie 2-327; 2-499, 2-500; account of 3-170.

BUNCH, ISAAC, witnessed will of JOS. EVANS (1827) 3-332.

BUNCH, ISHMAEL, two land grants on COWHALL and BEAR SWAMP 1-23.

BUNCH, JESSE, land grant (1751) next to THOMAS HUBBARD 1-20.

BUNCH, JOSHUA 3-166.

BUNCH, JULIUS, land grant (1761) next to SAMUEL PATCHETT 1-21.

BUNCH, PAUL, sold lands (1734) formerly belonged to THOMAS BRAY 3-611; recorded his mark (1744) in BERTIE 2-523; bought land from SAMUEL WOODWARD (1735) 3-128; one PAUL BUNCH died in Chowan (1726) & left will 1-31.

BUNCH, SARAH, witness to will of SEVERN SCOTT (1799) 3-191.

BUNCH, SHADRACK, land grant (1782) next to JULIUS BUNCH 1-22.

BUNTEN, THOMAS, died (1744) WILLIAM TAYLOR, Executor of estate 2-620.

BUNCOMBE, EDWARD, Colonel in N. C. Continental Line 1-420.

BUNCOMBE FAMILY. Genealogical account, showing connections of EDWARD BUNCOMBE son of JOSEPH. Bottom note 1-526.

BUNCOMBE, Col. EDWARD, will and note 1-526.

BUNCOMBE, JOSEPH. His wife was ANN DURANT and their daughter MARY BUNCOMBE married SAM-UEL SUTTON before (1753) 1-452, 2-469; sold land to GEORGE BURRINGTON (1733), J. PRATT, a witness 3-609.

BUNDY, CALEB, his wife was JANE MANERS 3-204; He left will in PASQUOTANK (1721) 1-32.

BUNDY, BENJAMIN will (1728) 1-31.

BUNDY, WILLIAM, mention of CALEB (1700) 3-38.

BUNDY, JOSIAH. He and DANIEL LAMB witnessed will of THOMAS SAUNDERS (1827) 3-350.

BUNDY, MARY, married NICHOLAS SIMMONS 3-204.

BUNDY, SAMUEL, son of WILLIAM BUNDY and wife ELIZABETH 3-208.

BUNDY, SARAH, daughter of WILLIAM BUNDY and wife MARY 3-213

BUNDY, WILLIAM, married daughter of JOSEPH SCOTT (1683) 3-201 (She was the widow of JOHN PEARRE); he left will in PASQUOTANK (1700) 1-443.

BUNTIN, JOHN, a headright for EDWARD KEIS -- LAND about (1697) 2-299.

BURKES, THOMAS, master of sloop LOYAL (1749) 1-433.

BURN FAMILY. Note in Bertie 2-503; wills in BERTIE 3-324.

BURNS, JAMES, will (1733) in BERTIE 1-30.

BURN, MICHAEL, granted ORDINARY license at the JAMES STEWART place in BERTIE (1744) 2-524; his wife JUDITH administratrix of his es-tate (1746) 2-529.

BURNS, THOMAS owned land next to ANN ANDERSON 1-21.

BURKETT, JOHN, bought land (1720) from JOHN PETTIVER 3-454; made deed to JOHN WILLIAMS of CHOWAN (1711) 3-442; made deed to his brother THOMAS (1715) witnessed by JAMES BATES and CHRISTOPHER DUDLEY in CHOWAN - 1-287.

BURKETT, LEMUEL, wife SARAH and children men-tioned in inventory (1808) 2-258.

BURKETT, THOMAS married widow of WILLIAM HOUGH-TON (1753) 2-469; (This must have been the younger one, because) as was dead by (1734) and his widow MARY made deed with JOHN CAKE 2-453.

BURGESS, ELIZABETH, will in GATES COUNTY (1819) grandsons named BOYCE 2-43.

BURGESS, STEPHEN, left will (1729) 1-31; anoth-er STEPHEN left will (1735) 1-30.

BURGESS, STEPHEN, of (1777) mixed up in mat-ters relating to plots against the Govern-ment; made affidavit that he met with oth-ers at home of THOMAS HARRISON 2-576.

BURGWIN, JOHN, will (1766) 1-45.

BURNBY, JOHN, of PASQUOTANK, will (1705) 1-34.

BURNHAM, CALEB, 3-166.

BURRINGTON, GEORGE deed (1725) to EDMUND PORTER and WILLIAM STEWART 2-444; 3-237;

BURRINGTON, GOVERNOR. Restoration of the Governorship (1725) signed by JOHN RICH-ARD 3-197; example of his tyranny (1732) 2-129; charged (1732) with misbranding mares 1-453.

BURROWS, HUMPHREY. His wife was SARAH 3-217.

BURTON, HUTCHINS, married TABITHA MINGE 2-154

BURTON, JOB, deceased (1744) spelled BERTON THOMAS BARKER, administrator 2-635.

BURTON FAMILY. Genealogical account of the family 1-467.

BURTON, JOHN. Died in Henrico County, Va. in (1687) grandfather of ELIZABETH DAVIS, the wife of JOHN BLOUNT 2-325.

BURTONSHALL, JACOB, will (1816) 2-503

BURTONSHALL, RICHARD 3-268; one of the head-right of HENRY MANDEVILLE 2-300; his wife was PRISCILLA 3-300.

BURTONSHALL, SUSAN, married GEORGE FLETCHER (1701) 3-409.

BURRUSS, JOHN will (1715) 1-33

BURRUSS, SOLOMON 1-532.

BURWELL, COL. LEWIS and THOMAS GODWIN, Ex-ecutors of COL. JOHN LEAR 3-254.

BUSH, DAVID. His children (1765) 2-257.

BUSH, JOHN, will (1768) names nephew, JOHN O'Neal; owned lands in CHOWAN (1716) 1-615; witnessed deed (1717) 1-300.

BUSH, MARY, daughter of WILLIAM BUSH 1-299

BUSH, WILLIAM, will (1715) land next -- FRANCIS MACLENDEN 1-615; (1717?) sold land to ANDREW STEVENSON 1-300; to WIL-LIAM CRAWFORD 2-284; witnessed deed to THOMAS MACLENDEN 1-300; sold land to JOHN DAVIS (1715) 1-615; owned lands next to LAWRENCE MARTIN 2-607; sold land to ROBERT EVANS (1721) 2-617; bought land from GEORGE WINNS (1718) 1-620; witnessed deed to JOHN BIRD (1721) 2-618.

BUSH, WILLIAM SR. and wife MARTHA, sold land to WILLIAM HOOKER, on WICACON CREEK 1-95.

BUSH, WILLIAM (JR.) Adjutant of 8th Regiment N. C. Cont. Line, with COL. JAMES ARM-STRONG 1-423.

BUSTIN, THOMAS, brother in law of JOHN PAT-NALL (1711) 1-69.

BUTLER, CHRISTOPHER, son of CHRISTOPHER BUT-LER sold land where his father had lived (1718) 1-624; land grant (1749) on ALBE-MARLE SOUND 1-20.

BUTLER, DAVID 2-293.

BUTLER, JACOB, will in CHOWAN (1745) names son GHRISTOPER and brother DAVID 1-184; appear in court at KENTON (1744) 1-453; married widow of THOMAS HAUGHTON (1759) (one did) 1-454; was "friend" of WILLIAM ROPER (1729)

BUTLER FAMILY. Wills 1-184, 1-185, 2-502, 1-531

BUTLER, KESTER, orphan in BERTIE (1767) 3-443.

BUTLER, JETHRO 2-502.

BUTLER, JOHN, of TYRRELL COUNTY, will (1773) 1-185; was alias ABEL JOHNSON (1721) 3-618.

BUTLER, CAPT. SAMUEL, about to fight duel and was arrested (1800) 2-286.

BUTLER, TOBIAS, will BERTIE 2-328.

BUTLER, WILLIAM, wife DOSIAH (1696) 3-369.

BUTTERTON FAMILY. Wills 2-326.

BIRD, JOHN, and wife REBECCA, admr. JACOB PETERSON JR. (1704) 1-612; witnessed deed to WILLIAM BOND (1699) 2-611; will, JOHN HARDY Exr. 1-172.

BYRUM, BRIAND (1772) 1-528, 1-529.

BYRUM, GIDEON (1776) 2-257.

BYRUM, JOHN (1730) with JOSEPH & EDWARD JORDAN 2-449; THOS. BYRUM 1-183.

BAKER FAMILY. HENRY BAKER, "merchant of Isle of Wight County, 1703, mentioned on 2-568 was the father of the HENRY BAKER mentioned in most of the other items appearing under the name. The son died at BUCKLANDS in CHOWAN COUNTY in 1739, and left, among other children a third HENRY BAKER, who inherited Bucklands, which fell in HERTFORD when that county was organized. There was still another HENRY BAKER, not of this family, who died in SURRY COUNTY, VA. in 1700.

The first HENRY BAKER, believed to have been a son of LAWRENCE BAKER, was a wealthy and influential merchant on Lawne's Creek Plantation in Isle of Wight County, Virginia, and a close neighbor of the HARDYS, (Of Hardy's Mill), BLOUNTS and BRYANS, who came to North Carolina from the same locality. He was closely connected with MAJ. NICHOLAS HILL, whose widow Silvester (Bennett) Hill, a niece of GOV. RICHARD BENNETT, in her will in 1707 (W. & M. (1) 7 p.254) mentions "My loving friend Mary, wife of HENRY BAKER, "and "My God-Daughter, MARY, daughter of HENRY and MARY Baker." HENRY BAKER (of Isle of Wight Co. Va.) died there in 1712, leaving children HENRY, JAMES, LAWRENCE, WILLIAM, SARAH, MARY, CATHERINE and ELIZABETH (Ibid). He served on the County Court of Isle of Wight County in 1685, 1698 and 1702; was Burgess in 1692, 1693, and was Lieutenant Colonel of Isle of Wight Militia, being 67 years old at the time of his death. He gave his oldest son, HENRY BAKER, 2,500 acres of land at BUCKLANDS, in North Carolina. This latter Henry Baker, before moving to Chowan County, N. C., served as Sheriff of Nansemond County in Virginia, was Captain of Militia, and as Burgess from Nansemond County in 1723-26. He was twice married, first to Angelica Bray, daughter of Col. David Bray, son of Col. James Bray, of JAMES CITY COUNTY, Va., member of the Council in 1690, second, to RUTH CHANCEY, daughter of EDMUND CHANCEY, of Pasquotank County; his children by both marriages being HENRY, JOHN, BLAKE, DAVID, ZADOCK, SARAH, RUTH and MARY. Mary married TSCHARNES DE GRAFFENREID, the grandson of the old BARON who founded NEW BERN. HENRY BAKER, of the third generation, also an older son married CATHERINE BOOTH and died in 1770, leaving HENRY, (IV) BRAY and LAWRENCE, the last born at Bucklands in 1745, a member of the Provincial Congress of N. C. This HENRY IV BAKER married as his second wife ANNA MARIA BURGESS, who died in 1808, and they were the parents of DR. JOHN BURGESS BAKER (b. 1802) who resided at GATESVILLE, where he died in 1837, the father of GEN. LAWRENCE S. BAKER (b. 1830), who married ELIZABETH EARL HENDERSON.

BLOUNT FAMILY. The BLOUNTS, like the BAKERS and many others who settled in the old ALBEMARLE PRECINCT, were from ISLE OF WIGHT COUNTY, VIRGINIA. According to family tradition there were "three brothers", who were the emigrants. Traditions are often erroneous, but diligent research, in this instance, confirms the stereotyped phrase. There is a mere scintilla of evidence that they were the sons of a THOMAS BLOUNT, who also settled on Lawne's Creek Plantation, but confirmative records have not been found by this compiler. The theory sounds reasonable and logical. The three brothers were (1) JAMES (2) THOMAS and (3) RICHARD BLOUNT. James and Thomas Blount were the ancestors who came to North Carolina, while Richard Blount appears to have remained in Virginia.

Mr. Hathaway on page 34 of Volume 1, tells us that there is evidence that JAMES BLOUNT was living with his family in ISLE OF WIGHT COUNTY, Virginia in 1660; John Bennett Boddie in his "Seventeenth Century Isle of Wight", on page 567, says that "JAMES BLOUNT sold JOHN ROSS seven head of cattle in Isle of Wight County May 13, 1673" quoting from the record. The will of JAMES BLOUNT was proven in CHOWAN PRECINCT, N. C. July 17, 1686 (1-34) and he left children, JAMES, JOHN, THOMAS, ANN and ELIZABETH. Ann married a SLOCUM and Elizabeth married a HAWKINS. In some enlightening notes Mr. Hathaway has taken some pains to review the descendants of this JAMES BLOUNT. There is little that any writer could possibly add to this.

As for THOMAS BLOUNT, the light is not quite so clear. From the notes it appears that he was called "Jr.", who married MARY, the widow of JOSEPH SCOTT, apparently in Virginia somewhere. Thus he must have been a nephew of JAMES and a son of James' brother THOMAS BLOUNT. Was he the THOMAS BLOUNT who lived on Kendrick's Creek in Tyrrell County and died there in 1701, leaving wife MARY and "all my children"? He is seemingly the father of the Blount who was brother-in-law of CHURCHILL READING, of Bath County, who in his will in 1734, mentions his nephews JOHN and JACOB BLOUNT, and of BENJAMIN BLOUNT, who "was brother of JACOB BLOUNT and son of THOMAS BLOUNT", son in law of NATHANIEL EVERETT (or AVERITT), but who also may have married a READING. These facts and the fact that he (BENJAMIN) left will in TYRRELL COUNTY in 1739, proved in 1740, indicates strongly that he was one of the sons of THOMAS BLOUNT who married MARY SCOTT and died in Tyrrell in 1701. Since this BENJAMIN had a son JACOB, was he not the JACOB who married BARBARA GRAY "of the THOMAS BLOUNT line" mentioned by Mr. Hathaway? (1-523.)

In discussing the JAMES BLOUNT line Mr. Hathaway on (1-522) makes it clear that the JACOB BLOUNT who married BARBARA GRAY, was not of that line, but of the "THOMAS BLOUNT line", so that, if we eliminate the RICHARD BLOUNT family, of Virginia, unless THOMAS BLOUNT of TYRRELL was JACOB'S ancestor, then Jacob must have been a "waif", which we know he was NOT. This JACOB BLOUNT was the father of two sons, both of whom were Governors of Tennessee, and otherwise greatly esteemed and remembered in the "Annals" of that commonwealth. In one of the histories of that State, widely quoted as an authority, it is stated:

"In 1669, THOMAS BLOUNT, great grandfather of WILLIAM BLOUNT, with two brothers, emigrated to Virginia, where one of the brothers settled and became the head of a long line of descendants. The other two brothers moved to North Carolina and settled in the vicinity of AIREMARLE. JACOB BLOUNT, father of WILLIAM BLOUNT, was born in BERTIE COUNTY, N. C., in 1726, and was married to BARBARA GRAY, a lady of Scotch ancestry in 1744, by whom he had eight children. On the death of his wife he married a daughter of EDWARD SALTER, by which union there were five children. JACOB BLOUNT was a member of the North Carolina Assembly in 1775-76. His death occurred at his country seat in Pitt County in 1789. WILLIAM BLOUNT, eldest son of JACOB BLOUNT, was born in BERTIE COUNTY, N. C., March 26, 1749. He was married February 12, 1778 to MARY, a daughter of COL. CALEB GRAINGER. He and his father (JACOB) participated in the battle of the Alamance, May 16, 1771, and all the brothers were leading spirits in the revolutionary war. His half-brother, Willie, was Judge of the Supreme Court of Tennessee, and Governor of the State from 1809 to 1815. From 1780 to 1790 William Blount was a member of the General Assembly of North Carolina, and in 1783-84 and 1786-87 of the Continental Congress. Governor William Blount was appointed Territorial Governor of Tennessee by General George Washington in 1790," etc.

Without ever having seen a list of the children of Jacob Blount, or an account of his immediate parentage, it occurs to the compiler that he was the JACOB, son of BENJAMIN BLOUNT, of Tyrrell County who died in 1740, and that among other sons he had WILLIAM, (b. 1749) JOHN GRAY (b. 1752), READING (b. 1757), THOMAS (b. 1759), and by his second marriage, WILLIE (b. 1768). Also there was evidently a JACOB, date of birth not found, who went to Tennessee, after his brothers, and resided there for a time, at Knoxville, since his name appears there on the county records.

RICHARD BLOUNT, the third one of the original brothers, (said to have been the emigrants to Virginia) remained in Virginia, where his name occurs on the records a number of times. His wife was MARY (last name unknown), who after the death of RICHARD BLOUNT became the wife of THOMAS FLOOD, then married JOHN WASHINGTON, of Surry County, and after he died, married, it is said, the fourth time, a CHARLES FORD. By Richard Blount and wife MARY there was only one son, THOMAS BLOUNT whose will was proven in Surry County, Virginia, March 7, 1709. This THOMAS BLOUNT married (1) ELIZABETH BRIGGS, and (2nd) PRISCILLA BROWNE, the widow of RIVER JORDAN, of the COL. GEORGE JORDAN family. It is probable that THOMAS BLOUNT had no children by PRISCILLA (Browne) JORDAN, his second wife, who after his death married WILLIAM THOMAS, of SURRY COUNTY, a grandson of MAJ. NICHOLAS HILL heretofore mentioned. THOMAS BLOUNT and his first wife ELIZABETH BRIGGS had these children: THOMAS, RICHARD, WILLIAM, HENRY, BENJAMIN, ELIZABETH m. HOWELL EDMUNDS, MARY m. JOHN FLOOD and another daughter (name unknown) who married JOEL BARKER. It would be tiresome to extend this line further, here, suffice to say, that many of them lived in SURRY and BRUNSWICK COUNTY, the son-in-law HOWELL EDMUNDS (who married ELIZABETH BLOUNT) being the Sheriff of that county in 1727-28, and the ancestor of THOMAS EDMUNDS who married a daughter of the distinguished lawyer THOMAS ELDRIDGE, of Brunswick.

BRYAN FAMILY. The BRYANS also came from ISLE OF WIGHT COUNTY, VIRGINIA, and they were all of the same parent stock. In Mr. Hathaway's accounts (independent of the actual records) he deals with different branches of the family, such as the William Bryan record 1-577 to 1-584, the EDWARD BRYAN family 2-325, the JESSE BRYAN family 2-557, etc. No one need take what this compiler says seriously, if they disagree, but, an intense study of the Bryan family has convinced me that what is said here is true.

HODGES COUNCIL, who made his will in Isle of Wight County, Virginia, in 1699, was the grandfather of nearly all of the Bryans of this record. His daughter CHRISTIAN HODGES married EDWARD BRYAN in Isle of Wight County, probably by 1655. The wife of HODGES COUNCIL was LUCY HARDY, a member of the HARDY FAMILY who owned the old HARDY MILL on Lawne's Creek Plantation in Isle of Wight County, acquired by GEORGE HARDY in 1646-7, away back in the "dark ages" of Virginia History. This EDWARD BRYAN was the grandfather of EDWARD, NEEDHAM, JESSE, SIMON, JOHN, WILLIAM and most of the BRYANS of this remarkable record. RICHARD BRYAN, who while his name occurs once or twice on the records, "beat it" to the upper reaches of the Rappahannock Country and settled in KING GEORGE COUNTY, and became the ancestor of WILLIAM JENNINGS BRYAN, through the marriage of one of his descendants with a LILLARD. He was one of the sons, I think, of EDWARD BRYAN and his wife CHRISTIAN HODGES. This compiler has the complete record, stored away in his files. So, thus it happens, that the BRYANS are all descendants of the old HARDY MILL neighborhood, marked only on the older maps of the lower side of the JAMES RIVER in Virginia. The account of the English ancestry of the BRYANS shown on or at 2-536, may be a clue to the English ancestry and the origin of the family, but throws no light on details and is therefore of little value. The name was spelled BRIAN in England, and it was from this family that the redoubtable sea-faring old warrior, BRIAN HARRISON, related to the Harrisons into which the Bryans afterwards so often married, obtained his name.

BURTON FAMILY. HUTCHINS BURTON married TABITHA MINGE (2-154). In York County, Va. ROBERT HARRISON married ELIZABETH COMINS, and they had a son ROBERT, and a daughter AMADEA, married JAMES MINGE, whose son ROBERT MINGE married MARY HUNT, a widow and had TABITHA MINGE who married HUTCHINS BURTON. At HENDERSON, N. C. on the South side of Main Street, there is a long lane leading to a house back in the trees built in 1750 by HUTCHINS BURTON. Burton hanged himself from the attick stairwell in this old house. It is called "haunted". The house is two stories high with a central door flanked by pilasters. Hutchins Burton was the grandfather of Governor HUTCHINS BURTON, of North Carolina and the father of the celebrated COL. ROBERT BURTON.

CABARRUS, AUGUSTINE, petitioned for liberation of a negro woman (1735) 2-304; was brother of STEPHEN CABARRUS and Executor of his will 1-538; they had brother BARTHOLOMEW CABARRUS in France 1-539.

CABARRUS, STEPHEN, ran for Congress in CHOWAN in(1783) 2-296; county named for him 1-539; owned lands next to GEORGE BAINES Jr. in (1794) 1-24; left will at Pembroke, CHOWAN COUNTY (1807) 1-539.

CAHOON, WILLIAM, land grant (1786) joins land of BENJAMIN COFFIELD 1-23.

CAIL, RICHARD 3-169.

CAIN, HARDY, of EDGECOMBE, left will (1754) & his wife was RACHEL 1-188.

CAIN, JOHN, died in EDGECOMBE, leaving will & family (1757) 1-188.

CAIN, WILLIAM, SR., left will (1732), wife ELIZABETH, son HARDY and others 1-37, 1-38.

CAKE, JOHN, 2-330, 3-331; bought land from John Hall (1720) with JAMES BATES a witness; 2-608; his wife was MARY, and they deeded land to THOMAS WALLIS (1734) 2-456.

CAKE, ROBERT, guardian of HALLENBACK orphans (1771) BERTIE 3-450.

CAMRILL, ALEXANDER (Campbell?) deed to land from THOMAS BRAY (1720) 2-454; left will in (1726) naming wife ANN 1-36.

CAMPBELL, ALEXANDER, was in BERTIE COUNTY in (1726) 2-467.

CAMPBELL, ARCHIBALD, with RICHARD GRILLS and JOHN CHERRYHOLMS witnesses to deed by EDWD. MOSELEY (1718) 1-626.

CAMPBELL, CHARLES, bought land from THOMAS SPIVEY in (1720) 3-614.

CAMPBELL, CORNELIUS, Master of ship ANNE (1749) 1-433, 3-330; one was grandson of DAVID RYAN (1762) 1-69.

CAMPBELL HUGH, 3-72; petition of 3-259; 1-186.

CAMPBELL, JOHN (1702) 3-242. (See Below).

CAMPBELL, JAMES, to sell property of one ANDREW OLIVER, deceased (1747) 2-630; Master sloop RANGER (1749) 1-435; Justice in BERTIE(1770) 3-448; 2-330; will 1-186.

CAMPBELL, CAPT. JOHN. His landing (1749) 2-633; land grant (1743) 1-19; witnessed deed of THOMAS SPIVEY to CHARLES CAMPBELL (1720) 2-614; land grant 1-18; married first, MARY HILL, second MARTHA 1-48; Justice in CHOWAN (1767) 3-443; to look after schooling of WILLIAM and JAMES STEWART (1747) 1-453; left will in BERTIE (1781) 2-330; 1-186.

CAMBRIDGE, FRANCIS, will in MARYLAND (1710)1-42

CAMBRIGHT, FRANCIS (perhaps same as above)will in MARYLAND (1710) 1-40.

CAMPEN, JAMES, Ensign in Revolution N. C. Cont. Line 1-417; Lieutenant 2-634; query relating to his family 2-634.

CANE, NATHANIEL 3-169.

CANNINGS, JOSEPH, will (1729) 1-38.

CANNON, EDWARD, will (1729) at BATH 1-194; daughter SARAH married WOODWARD 1-195.

CANNON, JACOB, witnessed will of ELIZABETH KNOWLES (1824) 3-339; witnessed will of THOMAS WILSON (1785) 3-197; one left will (1831) 3-330.

CANNON, JOHN, land granted next to JOHN TAYLOR (1681) 1-4.

CANNON, JOSEPH 3-196.

CANNON, ROBERT, died at the home of a DURANT in BERKELEY (1690), from NEW ENGLAND 3-363.

CANADY, MARY, daughter of PATRICK 3-214.

CANADY, PATRICK, son of PATRICK 3-216.

CANADY, PATRICK, and wife ELIZABETH (1686) 3-214.

CANADY, RICHARD, witnessed deed to JEFF LYLES (1715) CHOWAN 1-290; witnessed deed of JACOB BLOUNT (1718) 1-619; left will (1744) 1-191.

CANADY, SAMUEL, a member of Patterson's Co. from CHOWAN (1720) deed from WILLIAM BOON and wife ELIZABETH (1721) 2-616; will (1727) 1-197.

CANADY, THOMAS, witnessed deed (1718) from JACOB BLOUNT and wife ELIZABETH 1-619.

CAPE FEAR RIVER. Ferry ordered erected over in (1727) 3-290.

CAPPS, MATTHEW, witnessed deed of WILLIAM BRASWELL to HENRY WHEELER (1715) 1-299; sold land to JAMES ANDREWS (1716), with EDWARD HOWARD a witness 1-295.

CAPEHART, GEORGE and wife MARY deeded land to PETER CHRISTIAN SHROCK (1746) 2-629; deed from NEHEMIAH WARRING, BERTIE in (1744) 2-621.

CAPEHART FAMILY. Wills 2-506.

CAPEHART, MICHAEL (1778) will 2-331.

CARY REBELLION between 1706 and 1710; see note bottom of 3-226; depositions various persons relating to 3-224, 3-226.

CARY, ELIZABETH (of Warwick County, Va.) stayed at DANIEL AKEHURST home (1695) 2-151.

CARY, JAMES was 64 years old in(1702) born in (1638) 1-609. Lived in ALBEMARLE PRECINCT.

CARY, MILES, register, 3-40; the Elder 2-151

CARY, MILES, JR. 2-151.

CARY, PENELOPE, married JAMES SWAIN (1806) in BERTIE COUNTY 2-378.

CARY, THOMAS, Governor, succeeded ROBERT DANIELL 3-262; met at JOHN HECKLEFIELD home (1708) 1-454, 3-224; ordered arrested 3-267; of Warwick County, Va. 2-151; deed to EDWARD MOSELEY (1714)1-294.

CARY, COL. THOMAS, Governor. Letter from to the Proprietors (1708) 3-85, 3-86; bought land from NATHANIEL CHEVIN (1715) 2-455; letter to JOHN PORTER 3-85, 3-86; Governor (1704-5) 2-220; signers of Proclamation issued (1704-5) 3-220; nearest kin to JOHN LIGO who died (1717) 1-60.

CARD, WILLIAM, with JOHN CHESHIRE witness to deed (1718) 1-625; witness with WILLIAM BRYAN and JAMES BRYAN to deed by JOHN COUNCIL (Of Va.) (1718) 1-628.

CARLETON, ARDEN, deed to THOMAS BRAY in (1715) witnessed by SAMUEL WOODWARD 1-296.

CARLINTON, CATH, land grant (1718) 1-17.

CARLLATON, ARTHUR and wife CATHERINE, had son JOHN born (1697) 3-317.

CARROLL, BUTLER, revolutionary soldier 2-578.

CARMAN, WILLIAM, married ELIZABETH NOYS(1694) 3-406.

CARPENTER, MARY, married THOMAS WAFF, she the daughter of STEPHEN CARPENTER (1805) 1-538.

CARPENTER, STEPHEN, will (1805) EDENTON 1-538.

CARTER, ALEXANDER, owned lands next to JOHN PIFKIN (1730) 2-451; his wife was ANN and their daughter MARY received deed of gift from RICHARD BARNES (1723) 2-449; she may have married BARNES, since ALEXANDER CARTER (1733) bought lands from MARY BARNES, which had been granted to RICHARD 2-610.

CARTER, ARCHELAUS, witnessed will of THOMAS CASPER (1827) 3-509.

CARTER FAMILY. Wills 3-46, 3-506, 3-507.

CARTER, EDWARD, sued (1720) by WILLIAM BADHAM merchant of PASQUOTANK 1-444.

CARTER, HENRY (Of Bath) left will (1735) 1-36

CARTER, ISAAC, BERTIE COUNTY, had ISAAC, WYLIE HUGH and JAMES CARTER 2-155, 3-156.

CARTER, JAMES. His wife was PRUDENCE. Deed to JOHN HOLCOMBE (1717), EDWARD HOWARD witness 1-626.

CARTER, JOHN, will(1801) mentions son JESSE and WILLIAM CARTER 3-328.

CARTER, ROBERT, records his mark or brand in BERTIE COUNTY (1744) 2-624; see 2-331.

CARTERET PRECINCT. Account of its formation and history 3-309.

CARTWRIGHT, PETER. Robert STUART his apprentice in PASQUOTANK (1763) 1-446.

CARTWRIGHT, THOMAS. His petition to the GOVERNOR and COUNCIL, relating to CAPT. JOHN HUNT (1695) 3-250.

CARTWRIGHT, WILLIAM, will (1732) mentions godson JOSEPH STOAKLEY and brother THOMAS CARTWRIGHT 1-38; another WILLIAM CARTWRIGHT, will (1734) mentions sons THOMAS and CALEB and others 1-37

CARTWRIGHT FAMILY. Wills. GRACE (1728) THOMAS (1705-6) JOHN (1714) ROBERT (1746)1-193

CASE, JONATHAN, revolutionary soldier 2-579

CASE, ROGER, and wife ELIZABETH sold land to JOHN KELLEY (1720) 3-618.

CASEY, JOHN. Master of the sloop DOVE(1749) 1-435.

CASTELLAW, JAMES, on petition with NEEDHAM BRYAN, THOS. WHITMELL and others (1741) 3-199; was Justice of BERTIE in (1745) 2-636; died about 1749, left will and SARAH SANDERLIN and THOMAS WHITMELL are his executors 2-633.

CASTELLO (Castellaw?) PHILLIP, received deed from OWEN McDANIEL (1720) 3-618.

CASTELLAW, THOMAS, applied for administration on the estate of his father JAMES CASTELLAW (1749) 2-633.

CASTELLAW, WILLIAM, of BERTIE, will (1749) names mother SARAH and brothers and sisters, his mother and THOMAS WHITMELL his executors, witnesses SARAH SANDERLIN and HARDY SAMMARK 1-196; he recorded his brand (probably the Sr.) (1746) 2-628.

CASTLETON, GEORGE. Bill of sale to MARY SCOTT (1685) 3-429; he married the widow HANNAH PERISHO (By Mr. Thomas Gordon) in the year (1679-80) 3-200; this one was son of GEORGE CASTLETON and wife MARY, of Newcastle, in England 3-200.

CASWELL, FRANCIS (Of ALLIGATOR) will (1712) mentions brother MATTHEW 1-57.

CASWELL, MATTHEW, witnessed deed to JOHN PASSELL, in Chowan (1717) 1-619; left will in TYRRELL County (1745) 1-36.

CASWELL, RICHARD, Governor of N. C., letter to RUTLEDGE, of S. C. (1777) 2-379; see 2-235; letter to JOHN ASHE 2-237.

CASWELL, SAMUEL, will (1817) 2-509.

CATCHMAID, GEORGE. John Hunt testifies as to his last will in VIRGINIA 3-64, 3-65; he executes deed to GEORGE DURANT 3-424, 3-425; charges made against his estate 3-82.

CATCHMAID FAMILY. History in will of JOHN BERKELEY in England 1-33

CATHCART, FANNIE 3-355.

CATHCART, JAMES, sued AARON ADAMS in (1737) 3-467.

CATHCART, WILLIAM, 2-199; married PENELOPE, daughter of WILLIAM MAULE by (1745) 2-626.

CATHERINE CREEK was on line between GATES and CHOWAN COUNTY, as now. 1-5.

CEAR, HENRY, deed to ANDREW BARRON to land surveyed for EDWARD COBB on South side MEHERRIN (1709) 1-615.

CAULDRON, JOHN, Executor of ALEXANDER SIMPSON (1737) 1-73.

CALDWELL, ROBERT, will (1750) mentions wife SARAH, and brother JOSHUA CALDWELL of SOMERSET Co. Md, SAMUEL BEALE wit. 1-195.

GAIL, JOHN. Josiah Freeman made guardian of his orphans in BERTIE (1771) 3-450.

GALE FAMILY. Wills 3-329.

GALE, NATHANIEL, will (1821) 3-329.

CALF, ROBERT, receipt to GERRARD LYNCH for goods sold HENRY KING (deceased) 1715. 1-615. (Gerard Lynch married widow of Henry King); witness with JOHN SMITH, CHOWAN (1717) 1-617; received deed from TREBLE KEEFE (1718) 1-625.

CALLOWAY, CALEB, Speaker of the Assembly in N. C. prior to (1706) 2-130; his wife was Elizabeth Lawrence and they were married by JEREMIAH TAYLOR about (1669)3-199; He was witness to oldest deed on record in N. C. (1661) 3-423; JOHN WATTS, of ACCOMAS COUNTY, Va. died at his home (1696), 3-402; he died in (1706) 3-402; the older CALEB CALLOWAY died (1687) 3-364; he had a daughter Eliza 3-216; son John 3-211; the will of Caleb died (1706) 1-190.

CALLOWAY, ELIZA, daughter of CALEB 3-216.

CALLOWAY FAMILY. Births of children 3-207; wills of family 3-168.

CALLOWAY, JOHN, son of CALEB, birth 3-211.

CALLOWAY, JOHN, married JOHANNA (1750) 3-381.

CALLOWAY, JOSHUA, wife ELIZABETH (1716) 3-380; will of 1-190.

CALLOWAY, MARY, date of birth 3-211; the daughter of CALEB died (1698) 3-402.

CALLOWAY, THOMAS married ISABEL GARRETT (1728) 3-410.

CALLOWAY, WILLIAM, died (1692) 3-220.

CALLOWAY, ZEBULON, son of JOHN (1752) 3-381.

CALLAHAN, CORNELIUS, overseer of the road in (1732) 1-450; see also 2-615.

CALLAHAN, DENNIS, deeded lands to MULFORD LANGSTON adjoining THOMAS HARRIS (1729)2-446.

CALVERT, JOSEPH, 2-614; bought land from THOMAS WHITMELL (1720) 2-614.

CHADWICK, EBENEZER, sued by Enoch Ward (1726) 2-290.

CHADWICK, EPHRAIM, sued (1726) 2-290.

CHADWICK, SAMUEL. The Chadwick brothers, SAMUEL, EPHRAIM and EBENEZER, of CARTERET COUNTY were whale fishermen, who came in (1726) to the N. C. waters from New England 2-398.

CHAMBERLAYNE, EDMUND (1721), witnessed deed in (1721) from JOHN PETTIVER (Of York County Va.) to HENRY NORMAN, to tract of land adjoining JOHN DAVENPORT 2-135.

CHAMBERLAIN FAMILY. Members mentioned in will of HANNAH ABERCROMBIE, of Pasquotank(1754) 1-167.

CHAMBERS, GEORGE, in Court in CHOWAN COUNTY (1706) with DAVID BLAKE 1-444.

CHAMBLE, JOHN, recorded his mark (1744) 2-523.

CHAMPION, EDWARD, brother of ORLANDO CHAMPION, sons of EDWARD CHAMPION (1722) 2-143; will of Sr. (1718) 1-188.

CHAMPION, HENRY, land grant (1794) near the town of EDENTON 1-24.

CHAMPION, JOSEPH, land grant (1730) Queen Anne's Creek 1-12; sold land to THOMAS LUTEN, JR. (1730) witnessed by JOHN BALLARD 2-450.

CHAMPION, JOHN, land grant (1737) 1-19; will in CHOWAN (1749) 1-188.

CHAMPION, ORLANDO deeds (1721) 2-514; deed to THOMAS and MARY WEST (1716) 1-295; came from ISLE OF WIGHT COUNTY, about (1715) 1-188, note; witnessed deed from EDWARD MOSELEY (1718) 1-625; received land grant (1736) near the late THOMAS MATTHEWS 1-12; bought land from WILLIAM JONES next to the widow BOND (1728) 2-447; land grant (1720) 1-10; bought the EDMUND GALE place on Queen Anne's Creek (1734-5) 1-109; died early in (1745) leaving will, JOSEPH BLOUNT and JOS. ANDERSON, executors 1-188.

CHANCEY, EDMUND, will in PASQUOTANK (1753) was father in law of HENRY BAKER 1-36; wife was SARAH (1705) 3-376; was listed among the Governor's Deputies 3-253.

CHANCEY, WALLY, was brother in law of JOHN SNEAD (1743) 1-72.

CHANCEY, WILLIAM, JR. will (1736) mentions JOHN BOYD 1-36.

CHANCEY, ZACHARIAH, was guardian to SARAH BAKER (1745) 2-470; his home burned in (1745) 2-468; and his wife was REBECCA (1737) 3-381.

CHAPMAN, "GRANDFATHER" of JOHN PIERCE will (1726) 1-68.

CHAPMAN, CHARLES, will (1770) 1-190.

CHAPMAN, JOHN, will 1-190.

CHAPMAN, MARY, 3-168, 1-190.

CHAPMAN, WILLIAM and ALEXANDER CHAPMAN (1689) 3-431.

CHAPPELL, HENRY, will (1826) DANIEL WHITE an Executor 3-329.

CHAPPELL FAMILY. Wills 1-535, 3-168, 3-328, 3-329.

CHAPPELL, JONATHAN. His father was ROBERT CHAPPELL, MARY RUTTER mentioned (1734) 2-453.

CHAPPELL, RICHARD, will (1734) 1-37.

CHAPPELL, ROBERT, witnessed deed with ELIZA and THOMAS ROUNDTREE (1737) 3-132; may have been father of JONATHAN CHAPPELL 2-453.

CHAPPELL, SAMUEL, will (1825) had daughter PENINAH and KESIAH, son ISAAC 3-329.

CHOWAN PRECINCT. Abstracts from the records of the court (1711) 3-441, 3-442; history of its beginning and establishment 3-307, 3-308, 3-309; THOMAS HENMAN Clerk of in (1720) 3-287.

CHOWNE, JOSEPH, transported three times; his headrights proven about (1704) 3-244.

CHRISTIAN, MATTHEW, witness deed by THOMAS WIGGINS (1728) 3-451.

CHRISTMAS, JONATHAN, with JOHN BAYLEY was witness to deed of RICHARD WASHINGTON and his wife HANNAH (1719-1720) 3-508; Christmas was sued by WASHINGTON (1724) 3-297.

CHURCH. Money disbursed on account of up to (1760) 3-108 to 3-110.

CHURCH, ALLEN. He married WINNIFRED (1709) & JESSE HODGES was security 3-379.

CHURCH FAMILY. Wills 3-504.

CHURCH, JOSEPH. Will (1723) his wife was JULIAN, had son RICHARD 1-39, 1-132.

CHURCH, JOHN, power of attorney to CHRISTOPHER DUDLEY (1709) 1-98.

CHURCH, RICHARD, son of JOSEPH 1-39 (1723); He and wife JANE made deed to EDWARD HOW - ARD (1715) with PETER PARKER a witness 1-293.

CHURCH, THOMAS, was Master of schooner LEOPARD (1749) 1-434.

CLARK & WEIR owned lots in old town of EDENTON which escheated 1-23.

CLARK, CHRISTOPHER, Master of the sloop WIL - LIAM (1774) which cleared for the BARBA - DOES 1-436; left will in BERTIE (1800) at 3-506.

CLARK, COLIN, Master of the schooner MARTIN (1775) 1-436; he married JENET GRAY Mc - KENZIE, account of their family 3-503 & 3-604.

CLARK FAMILY. Genealogy of 3-603, 3-604, and 3-173, 2-174; connection with NORFLEETS 1-466.

CLARK, GAVIN HOGG, of NASH COUNTY N. C. his wife was REBECCA HILLIARD 3-506.

CLARK, GEORGE, will in BERTIE County in(1722) 1-39; of LONDON, owned the ship LOYAL and was creditor of TIMOTHY BIGGS (1689)3-300.

CLARK, JOHN, will in PERQUIMANS (1717) men - tions heirs named TRUMBULL 1-39; certificate for JAMES WEALCH 3-281.

CLARK, MARTHA, deed from JOHN HAWKINS (1716) 3-519.

CLARK, SAMUEL with JOHN CLARK bought land of THOMAS CLARK (1718) 1-523; Samuel married (a later one) SALLIE ANN HODGES 3-173.

CLARK, THOMAS, left will CHOWAN COUNTY (1705) 3-62 (1714) deed 1-293; see also 1-88; ROBERT FOSTER died at his home (1696)3-402 and he received land grant(1701) 1-5.

CLARK, THOMAS, was a Colonel in the N. C. Continental Line 1-415.

CLARK, WILLIAM proved the headright of HENRY CREAK 3-300.

CLARKSON, SAMUEL RUSSELL left will in WIND-SOR, N. C. (1809) 3-508, which names his friends and relatives; witnessed will of ALEXANDER URQUHART (1804) 2-551.

CLAPHAM, JOSEPH, will in BERTIE (1733) sons SAMUEL and JOSIAS 1-38, 1-196.

CLARY, JOHN. Will (1825). Son JOHN and THOM-AS LONG, Executors; son JOHN died (1828) married daughter of WILLIAM RELFE, and FRANCIS TOMS, Executor. A113-330.

CLANTON, W. Witness to deed by EPAPRODITUS BENTON (1730) 3-448.

CLAPPER, MRS. REBECCA, married ABRAHAM WAR - REN (1701) 3-409.

CLAYTON, ASHER, will (1801) PARTHENIA LEIGH a witness 3-328.

CLAYTON, ELIZABETH will (1737) 1-36.

CLAYTON, HENRY, a Justice 3-329; will (1725) 1-39; he married ELIZABETH, the widow of JAMES COLE by (1718) 1-528; received land grant (1716) on YOPPIM river 1-14; lived in EDGECOMBE (1735) 3-465.

CLAYTON FAMILY. Wills 3-167.

CLAYTON, JOHN, 3-166; deputy surveyor of BLADEN COUNTY (1736) 3-303.

CLAYTON, MARY, administratrix estate of NICH-OLAS FAIRLESS (1745) 3-626.

CLAYTON, ZEBULON, of PERQUIMANS. His widow was ELIZABETH (1737) 3-470; she appointed guardian of GEORGE PARRIS and MILES GALE (1737) 1-448.

CLEARE, ANN, daughter of TIMOTHY 3-215.

CLEARE, HANNAH, will (1726) mentions daughter HESTER WINSLOW 1-39.

CLEARE, MARY wife of TIMOTHY CLEARE died in (1694) 3-402; he married afterwards ELIZ-ABETH 3-213. (Should be HANNAH).

CLEARE, PETER (1765) 1-535.

CLEARE, SARAH, daughter of TIMOTHY and wife MARY 3-219.

CLEARE, TIMOTHY, 1-454; he and CORNELIUS JONES present petition to House (1713) 1-454; he was called "friend" in will of DANIEL JONES (1713); he married MARY BUNDY (1685) 3-201; connected with estate of DAVID BLAKE (1690) 3-434; mentioned in will of JAMES LOADMAN (1694) 1-58; proves the rights of his wife (1690) 3-439; will proven in PERQUIMANS (1724) wife HANNAH 1-189.

CLELAND, JOHN, married SUSANNAH ROBINSON the daughter of HUMPHREY ROBINSON by (1752) 1-59.

CLEMENTS, GEORGE, will (1794) 3-331.

CLEMENTS, WILLIAM, and DELIGHT NIXON witness will of JOHN PETTYJOHN (1832) CHOWAN COUNTY 2-19.

CLEMMIT, JOHN, Bertie, will (1734) mentions BELL FAMILY 1-37.

CLIFT, JONATHAN, witness to deed (1734) 2-453

CLIFTON, THOMAS, gives care of NATHANIEL OVERTON, 6 years old (1746) 2-627.

CLOUD, EZEKIEL, died (1851) note relating to his family 2-159.

COBB, CHARLES, married POLLY MORGAN, daughter of JOHN MORGAN who died (1826) 2-531.

COBB, EDWARD, sold lands on MEHERRIN CREEK to ANDREW BARRON before (1715) 1-615.

COBB FAMILY. Wills 2-330.

COBB, HENRY, will in BERTIE (1763) 2-330.

COBB, JAMES, Master schooner UNION in (1749) 1-434.

COBB, JESSE, called "grandson" in will of BETHIAH KINGTON (1807) 2-525.

COBB, JOHN, witness to will of WILLIAM STEEL with BENJ. HARDY (1716) 2-547; he married into the WHITFIELD FAMILY 1-569; was the father of LEWIS COBB, tuition to JOHN BARNES 3-447; was orphan son of NATHANIEL COBB (1769), James Pritchard, guardian 3-447; sent letter to House of Burgesses 3-75; one JOHN COBB left will in BERTIE (1809) 2-506.

COBB, MARY, the headright of RICHARD BURTONSHALL 9 no date) 3-276.

COBB, NATHANIEL, was the father of JOHN COBB an orphan 16 years old (1769) 3-447.

COBB, THOMAS, witnessed will of A. W. MEBANE (1846) 2-532.

COCKBURN, ADAM, land grant (1723) land grant on MARY BRANCH joining COL. EDWARD MOSELEY, DANIEL HARRISON and others 1-11; another grant (1720) South side MEHERRIN 1-19; lived with PARRIS family 3-231; had daughter SUSANNAH in Scotland (1754)1-446 was assistant to CHRISTOPHER GALE in(1724) 1-446; his wife was DOROTHY perhaps 3-235.

COCKBURN, DOROTHY was wife of ADAM FARLOW 3-235, 3-236.

COCKBURN, SUSANNAH, daughter of ADAM COCKBURN and wife DOROTHY 1-446.

COCKRAN, THOMAS, 2-332.

COCKRELL, EDWARD, deed (1717) to JOHN MARKS, witnesses ROBERT HICKS and THOMAS AVERITT 1-617; he bought land from MARTIN CHARLES and wife MOURNING (of ISLE OF WIGHT COUNTY, VA.) (1716) sold the land about same time to DANIEL HARRISON Rockihock Creek 2-619.

COCKS, ROBERT, will (1767) 3-167.

COFFIELD, BENJAMIN, owned land next to WILLIAM CAHOON 1-23; land grant (1790) on GREEN HALL 1-23; had brothers FREDERICK and ISAAC (one did) and they were sons of WILLIAM COFFIELD, who left will (1811) 2-507; Benjamin left will (not found).

COFFIELD FAMILY. Genealogy at bottom of (1-538); wills 2-507

COFFIELD, JOHN, married ELIZABETH HOSKINS 1-538.

COFFIN, ABNER, Master of the sloop SUNFLOWER (1749) 1-435.

COFFIN, CHRISTOPHER, Master of sloop FORTUNE (1749) 1-434.

COGWELL, HENRY, will (1719) 1-39.

COINS, BENJAMIN, of PERQUIMANS, will (1734) mentions JAMES McBRIDE 1-37.

COLBY, SPENCER, Master schooner MARLBOROUGH (1749) 1-435.

COLE, CAPT. JAMES, House Messenger at ASSEMBLY (1708) 1-454; court held at his home in ALBEMARLE (1702) 1-609; files road petition (1702) 1-609; his will in PERQUIMANS about (1712) 1-40; his wife ELIZABETH after his death married HENRY CLAYTON - 1-628; he came from NANSEMOND COUNTY, Va. (1698) 3-408.

COLE, JAMES, JR. married MARY PETERSON the widow of JACOB PETERSON (1698) 3-408.

COLE, JOHN, born in NANSEMOND COUNTY, VA. married ELIZABETH TETTERTON (1698)3-408.

COLE, WILLIAM, was Justice of WARWICK Co. Va. affidavit (1713) 2-151.

COLEFOX, JONATHAN (Colfax?) Master of schooner MARIAM (1749) 1-435.

COLEMAN, ROBERT, of BATH (1721) was related to the ISLER FAMILY 1-39.

COLEMAN, WILLIAM, will - 1-187.

COLLISON, JOHN, will in BERTIE (1736) 1-26.

COLESTON, BARBARA, with WILLIAM KIRBY witnessed will of WILLIAM COPPAGE in (1811) 3-330.

COLSON, DANIEL, grandson of RICHARD TURNERVILLE (Turbeville?) 1-78.

COLSON, MARY, will (1732) mother of wife of JAMES LUNDY 1-37.

COLSON, WILLIAM, witnessed the will of JOHN TURNER (1770), 3-191, died (1736) 1-194.

COLSON, MIRIAM, witnessed will of DEMPSEY TURNER (1782) 3-191.

COLSON, NELLIE, witnessed JOSHUA TURNER'S will (1794) 3-191

COLSON, JOSEPH , deed from THOS. WHITMELL 2-614.

COLLY, DANIEL, deceased. THOMAS WALTON adminis-trator, Chowan (1751) 1-451.

COLLY, SMITH and wife MARY (1732) 3-381.

COLLINS, EDWARD, administrator of estate THOM-AS COLLINS (1744) 3-625.

COLLINS FAMILY. Wills 2-505, 3-167.

COLLINS, JAMES, mentioned in will of FRANCIS NEVILL (1725) 1-64; he married daughter of JOHN RELF, and left will (1723) 1-58.

COLLINS, JOHN, made affidavit (1777) 2-575; he married LYDIA GRAY (1767) 3-108; bought land from JOHN ODOM (1727) Chowan 2-443; he sold land to JOHN EUER (1735) 3-127; JAMES REA was one of his creditors 3-467; and he left will in BERTIE (1752) 1-36.

COLLINGS, JOSEPH, of BERTIE, received deed from JOHN HILL and wife ANN (1769) 3-447.

COLLINS, JOSIAH, land grant (1785) 1-38; was a Judge 2-205.

COLLINS, LUKE, connected with the WATSON fami-ly 2-554; left will (1802) in BERTIE COUN-TY 3-505.

COLLINS, MARY, married ROBERT ROE (1769) 3-414.

COLLINS, RICHARD, will (1701) mentions ROGER MONTAGUE 1-37.

COLLINS, THOMAS, appointed guardian of RICHARD and SUSANNAH TOMLINSON, orphans of RICHARD TOMLINSON, in the place of CHARLES BENCH -(1771) 3-449; his estate EDWARD COLLINS ad-ministrator (1744) 2-625; he was an orphan of JAMES COLLINS 14 years old (1732) 1-449; was guardian of orphans of MICHAEL HILL in BERTIE (1771) 3-460.

COLLINS, WILLIAM, of PASQUOTANK 3-283; he and MARY CLARK were administrators of EDWARD SMITH (1694) PASQUOTANK 1-443; his widow married JONATHAN JACOCKS lived in PASQUO-TANK, where JACOCKS was a merchant. JACOCKS married second MARY BLOUNT (b. 1696)daugh-ter of JOHN BLOUNT and ELIZABETH DAVIS -3-283, 3-284; one WILLIAM in right of his wife ELLENER, administrator of JAMES FROST deceased (1744) 2-625; another sued MARY LAMB, widow of JOSHUA LAMB (1694) 1-612.

COLLINS FAMILY. An account of the connection of the family with the HILL FAMILY 2-637, in BERTIE; item showing business relations with ODOM FAMILY in CHOWAN (1717) 1-618.

COLLINGS, WILLIAM, witnessed deed from WILLIAM BRASWELL to JOHN DICKINSON(1717) 1-300.

COLONIAL DAMES OF NORTH CAROLINA. An account of the formation of 1-458 to 1-460; also 2-381 and 3-382.

COLYER, MARY married THOMAS HOLMES (1695) 3-408

COMBES, JESSE, married MARY BROGDEN (1799) in BERTIE 2-373.

COMBES, MARTHA, married JONATHAN ADAMS (1783) 3-111.

COMBES, ROBERT, married MILLIE PERISHO (1781) 3-111.

COMBES, THOMAS, and MARY COMBES witnessed deed by DAVID JONES (1715) 1-624.

COMBES, WINNIFRED 1-195.

COMMANDER, JOSEPH MATTHEW was an heir of JOHN HARVEY 3-253; petition of WILLIAM BRAY, states he was provost Marshall 3-251.

COMINFORT, RICHARD, of CURRITUCK 3-264.

COMPTON, HENRY, will (1735) 1-37.

CONE, ANDREW, son of R. COMINFORT (R?) 1-40.

CONNOLLY, DANIEL, witness with JOHN KLIRTH (1720) 2-618.

CONNOR, DEMPSEY, will in PASQUOTANK (1752) 1-36; married NANCY BLOUNT 1-35; one left will (1774).

CONNOR, H. G. of WILSON, N. C. an address by in 1902 at meeting of COLONIAL DAMES of N. C. 3-3 to 3-19.

CONNOR, JOHN, will in PASQUOTANK (1753)1-38; witness with DANIEL RICHARDSON (1717) 1-615; witness to deed of WILLIAM DUKEN-FIELD (1717) 1-299.

CONNOR, LEWIS, of NORFOLK, VA. to JOHN O'SHEAL (1729) JOSEPH and CALEB ELLIOTT witnesses 3-448.

CONSTANT, JAMES married widow of RICHARD BOND (1732) 1-450.

CONWAY, MARY, will (1753) 1-137.

COOK, MRS. ELIZABETH married WILLIAM BARTON (1696) 3-408.

COOK FAMILY. Wills 3-309.

COOK, JOHN, married ELIZABETH ELMER (1696) 3-382; deed to THOMAS BALE (1719)1609;

COOK, SAMUEL, and JOHN COOK, recorded their marks and brands (1745) 3-326.

COOK, THOMAS, will (1734) ED. GALE, Exexr. 1-37; Alexander Lillington and William Sherrill were his nearest kin 1-38; he died (1677) 3-365.

COOPER, ANTHONY ASHLEY, an account 3-486.

COOPER, ELIZABETH, wife of first ALEXANDER LILLINGTON, children 1-477.

COOPER FAMILY. Genealogical notes showing connection with BYRUM family 3-502.

COOPER, FRANCES, of PRINCESS ANNE COUNTY, Va. married JOHN F. MOSELEY, who mar-ried second AGNES SPENCER, of Charlotte County, Va. 3-471.

COOPER, JONATHAN, will (1825) 3-509.

COOPER, SOLOMON, revolutionary soldier 1-425.

COOPER, THOMAS, owned land adjoining THOMAS HARRISON (1714) 1-105; see also 3-341.

COOPER, WILLIAM, orphan, tuition by SOLOMON PENDER (1771), BERTIE 3-450.

COTTON, JOSIAH, married ELIZABETH SKINNER in 1777 3-382; died (1781) 3-382; one was a Captain in 7th Regt. North C. Continental Line 1-422.

COTTON, MARTHA, daughter of JOHN COTTON married JOHN SPEIR and died by (1726) 2-298; another MARTHA COTTON was daughter of Col FREDERICK JONES and SARAH SWANN, who married JOHN COTTON, of CHOWAN, later BERTIE and HERTFORD 1-479.

COTTON, SAMUEL, will 1-191.

COTTON FAMILY Wills 1-191.

COULSON, WILLIAM, will (1712) 1-40.

COUNCIL, ARTHUR, Captain in 6th Regt. N. Carolina Continental Line 1-421.

COUNCIL, HARDY, bought land from WILLIAM WHITEHEAD (1721) 2-619.

COUNCIL, HENRY, witness to deed by WILLIAM WHITEHEAD to MABEL KING (1721) 2-619.

COUNCIL, JOHN, of NANSEMOND COUNTY, Va. His attorney ROBERT HICKS (1718) 1-625; sold land to JOHN BRITT North side MEHERRIN river in (1718), also to THOMAS BRITT, witnessed by WILLIAM BRYANT (BRYAN) JR. and JAMES BRYAN SR. 1-628; also sold land to ALEX SHIVERS same time and place 1-628.

COUNCIL, ROBERT, Lieutenant in 1st Regt. N. C. Continental Line 1-416.

COURTS AND COURT HOUSES, an ACT for settling them 3-428, 3-429, 3-430; and prison bound (1747) 2-191, 2-192; rules of practice in (1709) 2-206, 3-207; at Edenton, Act relating to erection of, signed by CALEB CALLOWAY 2-130; old records at Edenton 1-144 to 1-156; courthouse at Queen Anne's Town later Edenton 2-100.

COWAN, DAVID, lieutenant in 10th Regt. N. C. Continental Line 1-425.

COWAN, ESTHER, an account of her family and connection with the HARRISONS 3-472.

COWAN, GARRETT will (1721) 1-39.

COWAN, WILLIAM, orphan in (1768) in BERTIE - 3-444.

COWAND FAMILY. Connected with MITCHELL (1796) 3-348; family wills 2-509; Ezekiel Cowand and Jonathan Cowand witness will of BENJ. STONE (1812) 2-546.

COWARD, JOHN. His estate looked after by JOS. WIMBERLY (1744) 2-523.

COWARD, WILLIAM, bought land from RICHARD WILSON (1721) witnessed by THOMAS MATTHEWS, which formerly belonged to JOHN YELVERTON 2-618; owned land next to JOHN KAIRNE and CORNELIUS HARNETT (1721) 1-619; sold land to THOMAS GARRETT (1724) Orlando CHAMPION a witness 2-290; with JOHN JORDAN JR. witnessed deed of SAMUEL WOODWARD 2-393.

COWLISLE, THOMAS, was proven as a headright of WILLIAM HUTCHINSON 3-282.

COWPER, CALEB 3-330.

COWPER FAMILY. Wills 2-46.

COX FAMILY. Wills 1-194, 3-329, 2-506.

COX, CHARLES. Will 1-194.

COX, EDWARD, WILL 1-194.

COX, JOHN, of ONSLOW COUNTY, will (1743) 1-36.

COX, JUDITH, witness to deed by GERARD LYNCH (1716) Chowan County 1-619.

COX, MARY, will (1827) BENJ. TOMS Exr. 3-329.

COX, THOMAS, will CURRITUCK (1743) 1-36.

CRADDOCK, CHARLES, mentioned in will of JOHN HOPKINS (1721) 1-51; lived on West side of SCUPERNONG 3-268.

CRADDOCK, RICHARD, 1-193.

CRAFT, JOHN, will (1760) 2-330.

CRAIG, RICHARD, will (1695) mentions "friend" PATRICK BAILEY 1-37; see also 3-281.

CRAIKE, THOMAS 2-343.

CRAIN, JOSEPH witnessed deed to TECMAS HAWKINS (1728) 2-447.

CRANDON, JAMES, Master of the SWALLOW (1749) 1-433.

CRANK, THOMAS and WILLIAM SHARPE witnesses to deed by SAMUEL WOODWARD (1718)1-628; he lived on CHOWAN river neighbor to LUKE WHITE (1718) 1-625.

CRAVEN PRECINCT. An account and history of its formation, etc. 3-309.

CRAVEN, JAMES, Clerk of Chowan County(1742) 2-190; left will (1755) 1-36; permitted to erect mill (1747) known as BENNETT'S 1-452; one was licensed as a lawyer in BERTIE 2-630; land grant at mouth of ROCKYHOCK (1744) 1-19; he and ABRAHAM BLACKALL mentioned as to EDENTON town lots(1744) 1-453; in (1750) appointed to train WILLIAM BADHAM (aged 14) to be a merchant in CHOWAN 1-451.

CRAWFORD FAMILY. Genealogical account showing connection with BRYAN family 2-358, 2-359.

CRAWFORD, MICHAEL on vestry of St. James Parish, at WILMINGTON (1740) 2-304.

CRAWFORD, WILLIAM. He and JOHN EARLY owned adjoining lands (1719) 1-627; sold land to WILLIAM BUSH 2-284; he and JOHN ELLIS witness to deed to THOMAS JOHNSON (1718) 1-621; at Indian Town 3-442; witness deed of RICHARD BROWN Chowan (1718)1-624; made deed to JOHN BRYAN (son of EDWARD) (1722) Chowan 2-284; sold land on BENNETT CREEK to WILLIAM HEWS (1737) 3-127; witness deed of JOHN EARLY to DENNIS McCLENDEN (1717) 1-300. Wills 1-36, 1-190.

CRAWLEY, DANIEL bought land (1720) 2-618.

CRAWLEY, DAVID, bought land from HENRY JONES (1720) 2-618.

CREA, THOMAS, married the widow of JAMES HOWARD before (1744) 2-623.

CREATH, HENRY. Among his headrights were WILLIAM CLARK and RICHARD STANLEY 2-300.

CREECH, HENRY, will (1709) 1-40.

CREECY FAMILY. Wills 1-553, 3-330, 3-168; note on genealogy of 1-533, 1-37; 1-534.

CREECY, JOHN, wife MARY (1743) 3-382; his will (1764) 3-168.

CREECY, JOSEPH, Sheriff of PERQUIMANS in (1757) 1-448; land grant (1780) next to JAMES MING (MINGE) 1-21; married SARAH STANDING (1738) widow of EDWARD STANDING 2-469; one married PENELOPE SKINNER (1780) 3-382; taught WILLIAM, son of TIMOTHY TRUELOVE 1-457; land grant on YOPPIM RIVER (1784) 1-22.

CREECY, JOSHUA S., genealogy of 1-534.

CREECY, LEMUEL, genealogy of 1-533; married MRS. PENELOPE CREECY (1784) 3-382; land grant in (1795) on line of PERQUIMANS 1-24, 1-25; he and NATHANIEL ALLEN arrested, about to fight a duel (1800) 2-296.

CREECY, LEVI, Perquimans, founder of the family will (1734) 1-37.

CREECY, MILES SKINNER, son of JOHN SKINNER and wife PENELOPE 3-382.

CREECY, SARAH, married JOSHUA SKINNER, their children named 3-396.

CREECY, THOMAS, of BATH, will (1730) mentions a grandson JAMES REYNOLDS 1-37

CREECY, WILLIAM, will (1812) mentions his brother NATHAN CREECY; ALFRED MOORE an executor 3-330.

CRETCHINGTON, SAMUEL, 3-278; wife MARY (1703) 3-375.

CREWS, JOHN, and wife ELIZABETH 3-366.

CREWS, THOMAS and ELIZABETH CLAYTON witnessed deed (1728) from JOHN JORDAN to SAMUEL WOODWARD, Chowan 2-445.

CRICKETT, JOHN, wife ANNE died in BERTIE (1767) 3-444; he was Justice in Bertie 3-443.

CRICKETT, JOSEPH and wife MARY witnessed deed to LUKE WHITE (1737) 3-127.

CRICKETT, THOMAS Master of the sloop WILLING MAID (1775) 1-436.

CRIMINAL PROCEDURE, Act of Assembly relating to (1715) 2-363.

CRISP FAMILY. Genealogy of 1-38, 1-39, 1-490.

CRISP, FRANCIS, deed of sale proved in BERTIE (1748) 2-631.

CRISP, NICHOLAS. Sketch of 1-38, 1-39 (1734) 2-610; he and ISAAC HILL were executors of JOHN PLOWMAN 1-68; his will (1726) mentions relationship to DURANT FAMILY 1-38;

he was brother-in-law of CHARLES WILKINS (1733) 1-82; his son JOHN CRISP married ELIZABETH SCOLLEY 1-490.

CROKER, RICHARD, Master of brig ELIZABETH in (1749) 1-434.

CROOKE, CLEMENT, merchant at ST. KITT'S (1761) meaning St. Christopher's, had minor sons STEPHEN and EDWARD CLEMETTS (1791) 2-304.

CROMER, MARTIN, bought land from NORTON MOORE and wife MARY (1719) 1-629; made deed to WILLIAM MACKEY (1733) 2-609; he was from Ireland and died (1733), will 1-37.

CROMBIE, JOHN a witness to a HARDY deed (1717) 1-619; and witnessed a BALL deed 1-620; bought land from WILLIAM STOCKEY 1-623; witnessed deed of KATHERINE MOIBY (1717) 1-299; deeded lands to JACOB HARDY (1721) William Hardy and JOHN WALKER witnesses 2-614.

CRONEY, DENNIS, will (1735) 1-36

CROPLEY, JOHN, and wife ANN (1675) 3-407; will (1685) 1-194; had daughter MARY who married JAMES BEASLEY (1675) 3-407.

CROPLEY, MARY, daughter of JOHN and ANN 3-407.

CROPLEY, VINES, part of his tract sold by WILLIAM HARRISON to his son WILLIAM HARRISON (1728) 2-445; was Constable of CHOWAN PRECINCT (1717) 1-153; deed of gift to THOMAS BEASLEY (1736) 3-129; land grant next to GEORGE FORDYCE (1694) on ALBEMARLE SOUND 1-4; land next to WILLIAM PRIVETT 1-8; he and wife SARAH sold land to WILLIAM STEWART (1717) 1-300; and in (1694) to WILLIAM HARRISON 1-286; had grant also next to ANNE SIMONS 1-4; died about (1720) report of estate returned by ROBERT BEASLEY 1-39.

CROPLEY, WILLIAM, deed of gift to THOMAS BEASLEY, has family genealogy 1-115 (1739; deed to CORNELIUS LEARY lands on REEDY BRANCH (1738) 3-132.

CROSBY, JOHN, witness to deed (1717) 1-299; member of Patterson's Company from CHOWAN (1720) 1-443; see 2-295.

CROSS FAMILY. Wills 2-45, 2-46.

CROSS, JOSEPH, died (1728) 1-38.

CROSSLAND, ELIZABETH, daughter of RICHARD SHERRILL (1693) 1-37.

CROXON, ARTHUR, wife BARBARA (1721) 3-381; left will (1765) 3-167.

CRUIKSHANK, JOHN, document relating to his family (1630) 3-616.

CRUIKSHANK, PATRICK, mentioned by PATRICK GERMACK (1708) 1-45.

CULLEN, CAPT. THOMAS sued THOMAS HURST 1-613.

CULLIPHER, NATHANIEL 2-509.

CULPEPPER, HENRY, of MARTIN COUNTY makes an affidavit (1777) 2-571.

CULPEPPER, JOHN, married SARAH MAYO in (1688) 3-203; he and wife SARAH (1691) 3-248.

CULPEPPER, JOHN, related in business to COR-
NELIUS JONES 3-248; will mentioned (1695)
PATRICK HENLEY and wife SARAH, executrix
of, in PASQUOTANK 3-259 (looks like SARAH
married PATRICK HENLEY after JOHN CULPEP-
PER died -WSR) suit against DANIEL SNOCKE
by ANTHONY DAWSON (1690) 3-435; deceased
(1702) Matthew Pritchard. Executor in Albemarle 1-610; he is mentioned (1678)1-614

CULY, JOHN 3-210.

CULLINFORT, KENDRICK will (1712) mentions AN-
DREW CONE 1-40.

CUMMINGS, CHARITY 3-168.

CUMMINGS, JOHN and ALEXANDER BRODIE married
into the family of DR. ABRAHAM BLACKALL
by (1759) 1-456.

CUMMINGS, WILLIAM, an attorney (1796) Note on
his family history 1-537.

CUNIFFE, JOHN 2-331.

CUNNINGHAM, ELIZABETH (1809) widow of JAMES
CUNNINGHAM 3-261.

CUNNINGHAM, JAMES, married ELIZABETH ELLIS in
CHOWAN COUNTY (1795) 1-252.

CUNNINGHAM, JOHN, will in CHOWAN (1778) about
to sail on a voyage, if does not return
balance to his son JOHN CUNNINGHAM 1-537.

CUNNINGHAM, JOHN, will in CHOWAN (1799) mentions wife PEGGY, daughter LYDIA and ELIZ-
ABETH NORFLEET and B. NORFLEET 1-537.

CUNNINGHAM, MAURICE, tithable East side HAR-
VEY'S CREEK, on list with VINCENT WHITE
and ISAAC BOWDEN 3-253.

CUNNINGHAM, THOMAS, JR. mentioned in will of
ALEXANDER DUNCAN of WILMINGTON (1767) and
JAMES MOORE and MAURICE MOORE are also
among those mentioned 1-201.

CUNNINGHAM, WILLIAM mentioned among the
rights of THOMAS DEARHAM (1701) 1-305.

CUNNINGHAM, WILLIAM (two of them) were revolutionary soldiers 2-583.

CURRITUCK COUNTY. List of inhabitants on an
old document including JOHN HAWKINS, DAVID
JONES, MARY COBB, RICHARD ROSE and many
others 3-275, 3-276.

CURRITUCK COUNTY. List of early tithables
taken, no date given, contains the name of
JACOB PETERSON who dates back of (1700)
3-257.

CURRITUCK COURT HOUSE. Contract for building by ROBERT PEYTON [1723) 2-134.

CURRITUCK COUNTY. Order to elect Burgesses
in 3-275.

CURRITUCK PRECINCT. Petition for a CLERK of;
JOSEPH WICKER elected 3-221

CURETON, JOHN 2-331.

CURL, UPHAM, wife of ROSCOE CURL of NORFOLK
COUNTY, Va. (1771) 3-449.

CURL, WILLIAM ROSCOE, wife UPHAM (1771) 3-449.

CURLEE, JAMES deed to JOHN EARLY (1713) 1-101;
witness to deed (1717) 1-619; bought land
from GEORGE SMITH on WICACON CREEK (1714)
2456; was a grandson of ELINER EARLY in
(1733) 1-42.

CURLEE, WILLIAM, witnessed the execution of
a Power of Attorney by HENRY SUTTON and his
wife (1715) 2-288.

CURRY, JAMES, will (1849) mentions PEGGY MIZELL
wife of AARON MIZELL 2-509.

CURRY FAMILY. Wills 2-509.

CUTLETT, THOMAS will (1706) 1-37.

GOV. THOMAS CARY and the CARY REBELLION. THOMAS CARY (according to WHEELER'S) was
appointed deputy governor by Sir Nathaniel Johnston. The Lords Proprietors disapproved of the
choice and directed their Deputies to select one of their own number as Governor of North Carolina .
The Deputies selected WILLIAM GLOVER. Cary, who was selected as deputy governor, had been collector of rents of the Lords Proprietors, and had neglected to settle his accounts. For awhile he
seemed to yield to the sway of Glover, but, aided by his friends, he seized the records of the
Province, and proclaimed himself governor.
        The Colony was now a scene of anarchy; the laws were suspended and justice fled. The res-
pectable portion of the colony adhered to Glover, while Cary possessed the force. A General Assembly was called, which met at Captain Hecklefield's, on Little River, to decide this vexed question. Members appeared under writs of election issued by President Glover; while another set appeared under writs of election issued by President Cary. Glover and Cary sat in separate rooms
with their respective councils. Great confusion prevailed, and the partisans of Glover, irritated
by the persecutions from Cary and his adherents, sought refuge in Virginia. Thus was the Colony of
North Carolina, for a time, again under a domination contrary to the proprietary government. At
this period EDWARD HYDE arrived with the commission of Lieutenant Governor; but Cary refused to
yield. With an armed brig and a smaller vessel he made an attempt upon EDENTON, but was repulsed
and retired to BATH. The proprietors called upon Governor Spottswood, of Virginia, who by July 1
1711, had succeeded in quieting the rebellion. HYDE was appointed governor the next year and issued a proclamation in 1712, granting a pardon to all the insurgents, except THOMAS CARY, JOHN POR-
TER and three others.
        According to a dependable authority, COL. THOMAS CARY, the "rebel" of 1711, was a son of
Walter Cary, of Cheping Wycomb, county Bucks, England, and was a step-son of JOHN ARCHDALE, the
beloved Quaker, called, I believe, one of the most popular of the proprietary governors of North
Carolina, who had poured oil on the "troubled water" brought about by the CULPEPPER REBELLION.

CARTER FAMILY. These CARTERS were from VIRGINIA, as evidenced by a deed mentioned on 2-156; that they were connected with the old "King" Carter family is likely. Genealogists have hunted in vain for actual proof that the Col. John Carter, of the Watanga settlement in Tennessee was related to the LANDON CARTER family of Virginia, which seems reasonable, since his eldest son was named Landon, evidently for some forbear. On the Tennessee records the names John, Isaac, Hugh, Jesse and Wylie Carter have repeatedly appeared for over 150 years, and this record shows 2-155, 2156 identical names were bourne by the Bertie Carters. It appears that the Carter genealogists have been looking in the wrong place for the ancestors of this family.

CHARLTON FAMILY. Originally this was an "Eastern Shore" family in Accomac County, Virginia, from whence came many of the early emigrants to the old ALBEMARLE PRECINCT in North Carolina.

CHEW FAMILY. The Chew family came originally to YORK COUNTY, Virginia. From there members of the family migrated, some to North Carolina, some to the falls of the Rappahannock at Fredericksburg, Va., some to the vicinity of Winchester, some to Maryland. The Maryland Chews intermarried with some of the first families of that commonwealth.

JONATHAN CHRISTMAS was also from YORK COUNTY, VIRGINIA, a descendant, possibly even a grandson of old DOCTORIS WILLIAM CHRISTMAS, of YORKTOWN, whose will was proven in 1654, witnessed by PETER STARKEY, ancestor of the Starkeys who went down into North Carolina. It seems reasonable that Peter Starkey was son-in-law of Doctoris Christmas, of Yorktown, and that the distinguished Starkeys of North Carolina may have acted as the magnet that brought hither this JONATHAN CHRISTMAS. WILLIAM CHRISTMAS was a noted landscape architect and city planner in the old North State, perhaps a hundred years ahead of the times, who laid out the cities of WARRENTON and the State Capitol, RALEIGH. ROBERT CHRISTMAS, of this same clan, migrated to the State of GEORGIA, following the American Revolution, where he was one of the members of the Court in Greene County, before whom the trial of ELIJAH CLARKE was held, who was charged with some irregularities, which the court saw fit to waive in favor of the gallant old revolutionary patriot.

COBB FAMILY. The Cobb family of this record originated in YORK COUNTY, VIRGINIA, also, and in Isle of Wight County. William Blount, the distinguished member of the Philadelphia Congress, and later Territorial Governor of Tennessee, son of JACOB BLOUNT, presided over the first court ever held West of the Blue Ridge at the home of WILLIAM COBB, on the banks of the Watanga river. It can be no mere co-incidence that the site of this old COBB home is within a stone's throw of the old home and the family cemetery where COL. JOHN CARTER, mentioned above, with his son LANDON is buried, in Carter County, Tennessee.

COLE FAMILY. There is a reference on 2-151 to WILLIAM COLE, Justice of WARWICK COUNTY, Virginia. He was not only a Justice of Warwick, where MILES CARY, a cousin of COL. THOMAS CARY, was Clerk, but was also Secretary of the Colony of Virginia. The James Cary of our NORTH CAROLINA RECORD appears to have been contemporaneous with this distinguished William Cole - perhaps a brother. The suggestive items in Mr. Hathaways records that lead one to conclude that they are of the same family, is frequent references to the LEIGHS, who married into the family of the old Justice of Warwick. This COLE family is the one from which came DOLLY PAYNE, daughter of JOHN PAYNE and MARY COLE, who became the famous DOLLY (PAYNE) MADISON, one of our "first ladys" and wife of JAMES MADISON. Dolly's grandparents lived in Hanover County at what was called then "Coles Hill". Their North Carolina cousins were some distance away, and the genealogists, on that account have long overlooked them.

COOPER FAMILY. Old man JUSTINIAN COOPER, according to his will, apparently left no direct male descendants when he died in Isle of Wight County, but the Coopers of this North Carolina record bear the earmarks of his family, in their associates and intermarriages. The wife of Justinian Cooper was a HARRISON, and there have been innumerable connections since that time between the Harrison and Cooper families.

COTTON FAMILY. This is another ISLE OF WIGHT COUNTY family. In his "Seventeenth Century Isle of Wight" John Bennett Boddie says: John Cotton married Martha, daughter of WILLIAM GODWIN. He owned two hundred acres in Isle of Wight in 1704, but afterwards moved to Nansemond and then to NORTH CAROLINA. He may have been a brother or relative of THOMAS COTTON, who made his will in Surry (Va.) in 1718, and leaves "wife Mary my plantation and land and after her death to my cousin Thomas Cotton, son of Walter Cotten and Elizabeth his wife. His will was witnessed by John Barker, Sr., John Johnson and Grace Bailey. One of John Cotten's sons married Sarah, widow of William Bridgers of Northampton (County, N. C.), and William Bridgers mentions his father John Dew and his brother William Bryant (BRYAN?) in his will. This John Dew was probably the son of Capt. Thomas Dew, of Nansemond, Speaker of the House of Burgesses.

JOHN CULPEPPER and the "CULPEPPER REBELLION". John Culpepper, prior to the events here recorded, had been surveyor-general of South Carolina (Wheeler), and one MILLER, preceding Governor Eastchurch into North Carolina, holding the tripple office of governor, secretary and collector. The people were aroused by this man's extortion and tyranny, and led on by the redoubtable JOHN CULPEPPER they seized the president and six members of the council and slapped them in jail; then they called a Legislature, appointed courts of justice, and exercised all the rights and powers of government for two years. When Eastchurch arrived his authority was derided. He died before the Governor of Virginia could send him aid. JOHN CULPEPPER was tried of his "offenses" in England, and acquitted, then Harvey took over and John Jenkins was appointed to succeed him. One of Culpepper's associates was Receiver General and another was no less a person than GEORGE DURANT a Judge of the Court.

DAIL, HENRY, of PERQUIMANS County, will (1828) wife SARAH. WILLIAM SUTTON wit. 3-331.

DALRYMPLE, JOHN, of WILMINGTON, will (1742) wife was MARTHA, a son of SIR JOHN DALRYM- PLE, of England. ROGER MOORE Exr. 1-201.

DAWSON, COL. JOHN, married CHARITY ALSTON, will executed (1749), she his second wife. Ac- count of his family and children 2-308,1-199

DALTON, LETITIA, daughter of SAMUEL DALTON and NANCY REDD; they were married (1757) Ac- count of the family 2-479, 2-480.

DANIEL, AARON, married ELIZABETH WHITFIELD the daughter of MATTHEW WHITFIELD, whose bro- ther WILLIAM WHITFIELD married RACHEL, the daughter of NEEDHAM BRYAN. 1-567, 1-568.

DANIEL, CORNELIUS, killed a panther with a gun in (1718) 3-282.

DANIEL, ELIZABETH, will in TYRRELL (1752) wid- ow of THOMAS DANIEL, mother of ROBERT LAN- IER DANIEL and AARON DANIEL 1-199.

DANIEL, EZEKIEL, son of JOHN DANIEL, of NORTH- AMPTON County who left will (1754) 1-199.

DANIEL FAMILY. Wills 1-199.

DANIEL, HENRY MAY. Account of family 2-460.

DANIEL, JAMES, revolutionary soldier 3-585; a Lieutenant 9th Regt. N. C. Continental Line 1-424.

DANIEL, JAMES, proved his rights (1697) NICE LYNCH, JOHN CRUMWELL and others 1-141.

DANIEL, JENNINGS, witness (1720) with JAMES WAINWRIGHT to deed by WILLIAM HAVETT and wife to JOHN WILLIAMS 2-613.

DANIEL, JOHN, wife SARAH, of NORTHAMPTON COUN- TY (1754) will 1-199.

DANIEL, JOHN BLOUNT, descended from partici - pants in EDENTON TEA PARTY; account of his family 2-460.

DANIEL, JONATHAN, wife MARY (1700) deeded land next to THOMAS HOSKINS 2-611.

DANIEL, OWEN was an assigned headright of NATH- ANIEL CHEVIN, Chowan Court (1703) 3-138; left will in Chowan dated (1700) 1-40; MARY FOX entered land on SALMON CREEK back of MR. PARROTT, which she bought of him, but Daniel died before perfecting title. Date not given 3-143.

DANIEL, HON. ROBERT, landgrave, lieutenant general, vice admiral and deputy govern- or (1704) 1-301; petition addressed to 3-258; issued Major's commission (1702) 2-202; present at General Assembly with Thomas Cary, Governor (1708) 1-454; peti- tion by ISAAC WILSON to 3-141; issues an order remitting quit rents signed by THOS. SNOWDEN, Clerk 3-264, 3-265; petition to by inhabitants of Matchapungo 2-193; asks leave to be excused from council (1708) 1-454; met with council at home of JOHN HECKLEFIELD (1703) 1-611; dates when GOV- ERNOR 3-259; patents issued by 3-76,2-193.

DANIEL, SARAH, was daughter of DANIEL HEN - DRICKS, had brother ABRAHAM HENDRICKS in (1768) see HENDRICKS will, ELISHA WHIT - FIELD an executor 2-340.

DANIEL, ROBERT, grandson of ROBERT ROGERS in (1736) 1-69.

DANIEL, SIMON, was son in law of ROBERT ROG- ERS and his wife ELIZABETH, and father of a ROBERT DANIEL 1-69; with HENRY GOODMAN he witnessed deed of JOHN PIPKIN in NAN - SEMOND County, Va. (1732) 2-609.

DANIEL, SUSANNAH, was sister in law of JOHN JONES of CHOWAN who left will (1711) 1-56.

DANIEL, THOMAS, with THOMAS WEST witnessed deed of LEONARD LOFTON to Col. Thomas Pollock (1715) 1-285; left will in TYR - RELL COUNTY (1749) father of ROBERT LAN- IER DANIEL 1-199; witnessed a Power of At- torney by JOHN HOLBROOK to JOHN HARDY in (1715) 2-288; witnessed deed of ARTHUR KAVANAUGH (1714) 1-286; sold land to ED - WARD MOSELEY (1716) 1-299; witnessed deed of THOMAS LEE who married the widow of JOHN BAILEY (1716) 1-297; see 3-95, 3-96.

DANIEL, URIAH, married AMEY HARROD in Chowan County (1795) 1-252.

DANIEL, WILLIAM, land grant (1721) Northwest side BENNETT'S creek 1-10; sold 200 acres there to WILL PEEL (1727) 3-127; 1-112; left will (1740) 1-198; helped to lay out road on Bennett's Creek (1737) 1-448; he and CHARITY ALSTON witnessed deed together (1739) 3-133; was sued by WILLIAM WHIT- FIELD in EDENTON (1726) 1-457; was on com- mittee with WILLIAM SPEIGHT 1-448; wit - nessed deed (1739) from JOHN SINGLETON and wife to THOMAS PILAND in Bertie 3-134.

DANIEL, WILLIAM, married ELIZABETH UPTON in PERQUIMANS County (1799) 3-422; in (1804) was witness to THOMAS UPTON'S will 3-355.

DANIEL, WILLIAM, was a Captain in the 6th Regt. of the N. C. Continental Line in the Revolution 1-421.

DANN, JOHN and wife MARY (1680) 2-300.

DARBY, LEWIS, an orphan, tuition by ANDREW OLIVER in BERTIE (1771) 3-450.

DARDEN, JACOB, mentioned as the son of ANN LEIGH in her will (1733) 1-58.

DARDEN, WEST, mentioned in the will of his fa- ther, JOSEPH DARDEN (1743) 1-40.

DARDEN, JOSEPH, will in BERTIE (1733) his wife was ALICE, children WEST, JOSEPH and HENRY and daughters AMERICA and REBECCA 1-40.

DARE, VIRGINIA. The Indian legend of this girl and a poem about her 2-639.

DARGAN, JEREMIAH, of BERTIE, will (1786) 2-332; executor of will of BENJAMIN MOORE in (1780) 2-347.

DARLING, RICHARD, lived on lands sold by ROG- ER SNELL to JOHN YELVERTON (1702) 2-456; left will (1702) 1-41.

DARLING, THOMAS, deed to CAPT. THOMAS LEE in (1716), William Mitchell and JOHN EDWARDS witnesses 1-297.

DAUGHTERS OF AMERICAN REVOLUTION. North CAROLINA SOCIETY of 1-596, 1-597.

DAUGHTRY FAMILY. Wills 2-47.

DAUGHTRY, THOMAS, will (1757) 1-202.

DAUGHTRY, MANDUE, son in law of THOMAS MAND will (1736) 1-61.

DAUGHERTY, GEORGE, Lieutenant in 6th N. C. Continental Line in Revolution 1-421.

DAUGHERTY, PETER, claimed as a headright by GEORGE LASITER, of Nansemond Co. Va. (1702) together with THOMAS DAVIS and JOSEPH ASHLEY 3-141, 3-142.

DAVENPORT, AGNES, daughter of RICHARD DAVENPORT, born (1691) 3-217.

DAVENPORT, EPHRAIM, of CHOWAN, will (1852) 1-541.

DAVENPORT, ISAAC, son of RICHARD DAVENPORT and wife JOANNA b. (1685) 3-213; another ISAAC DAVENPORT married in RICHMOND VIRGINIA Helen Blair Tredwell, of the LEWIS BRYAN FAMILY 2-557, 2-558.

DAVENPORT, JOHN and his wife ANNE (1705)3-376; made deed to THOMAS GAYLORD (1719) 2-457; of Scupernong River (1716) 1-294, 3-382 & 3-268.

DAVENPORT, RICHARD, was born in 1642, and was 66 years old (1708) 3-148; his wife was JOHANA, and they had son RICHARD born year (1674) 3-213; as owner of lands in (1665) he writes about THOMAS HARRIS and NATHANIEL NICHOLSON 3-106.

DAVENPORT, SUSAN, daughter of RICHARD and ELIZ. JOHANNA born (1688) 3-215.

DAVIES, JONATHAN, makes bond (1777) 2-209; and has wheat reaping party 2-214.

DAVIES, RICHARD and wife SARAH (1718) with names of children 3-382.

DAVIS, ARTHUR, bought land from WILLIAM BROWN (1718), with JOHN DEW a witness 1-625; he and wife make deed (1720) to BARNABAS McKINNIE, witnessed by WILLIAM LATTIMORE and JOHN ALSTON 1-470.

DAVIS, EDWARD, bought land (1717) from FRANCIS BROWN 1-300.

DAVIS FAMILY. Wills 1-197, 1-198; was connected with the WHITE FAMILY in Isle of Wight County 3-146.

DAVIS, GEORGE, will (1797) had son MILES DAVIS, HENRY COBB a witness 2-333.

DAVIS, HANNAH, married SAMUEL CHARLES (1722) 3-381.

DAVIS, HENRY, will (1738) 1-40.

DAVIS, HUGH, will (1724) mentions heirs named HARMON 1-41.

DAVIS, ISAAC will in CURRITUCK in (1742) mentions son CORNELIUS DAVIS 1-40.

DAVIS, JAMES will (no date) 1-41.

DAVIS, JOHN, wife MARY deed in BATH (1720) to THOMAS HOSKINS, land next to EDWARD STANDING 2-613; deed in (1704) to WILLIAM BRANCH 2-455; of Pasquotank (1753) mentions son in law WILLIAM GORDON 1-40; the one in BATH lived on SLOCUM Creek near William Branch and HENRY BONNER 1-294.

DAVIS, MARGARET, was mother of JOHN SLOCUMB who died (1712) 1-77.

DAVIS MARY, died in (1739) 3-405; Mary Davis of HENRICO COUNTY (Va.) married JOHN BLOUNT (1695) 3-407.

DAVIS, OTHNIEL, Mariner, was commander of the sloop NEVILLE (1719) 2-301, 2-302.

DAVIS, PETER, on Manwarring River, will in (1719) 1-41.

DAVIS, RICHARD, will (1737), had a daughter married MOSES HALL 1-40.

DAVIS, SAMUEL. He and his wife ANN, of Pasquotank, came from ISLE OF WIGHT COUNTY, Virginia 2-146; he married a daughter of THOMAS MERRIDAY who died in (1740) 1-60; she was a servant in ISLE OF WIGHT COUNTY of Captain JAMES BLOUNT, and in (1660) they came to NORTH CAROLINA; SAMUEL DAVIS was their oldest son 1-612.

DAVIS, SARAH, will (1817), Peninah White was a witness 3-330.

DAVIS, SOLOMON, will (1737) mentions grandson DANIEL KAIN 1-40.

DAVIS, THOMAS, married ANN PENDLETON, daughter of HENRY PENDLETON of PASQUOTANK 1-65.

DAVIS, WILLIAM, will (1719) 1-41.

DAVIDSON, ELIZABETH, will (1822) 2-511.

DAVISON, JOHN, deed to lands on MEHERRIN river to RICHARD BARNES, of NANSEMOND COUNTY, Virginia (1711) JOHN ODOM a witness 2-285; he recorded his mark in Bertie (1746) 2-628; will (1768), wife EDY, and HUMPHREY HARDY a witness 2-332; one with wife MARY sold land to JOHN KING (of Va) in (1718) 1-627.

DAVIDSON, WILLIAM, a Colonel in the N. Carolina Continental Line 1-420.

DAWKINS, GEORGE, will at EDENTON (1764) Fred Blount and THOMAS BLOUNT witnesses 1-540.

DAWS, WILLIAM will (1746), had sons WILLIAM and NICHOLAS, witness EDWARD CAMPEN 1-201; one proved nine rights in Chowan (1711) 3-442.

DAWSON, ANTHONY, sued FRANCIS FOSTER for an adz (1689) and obtained jury verdict in PERQUIMANS 3-431; witness to the marriage of RICHARD ATKINSON of Va. 3-406; witness to Bill of Sale to MARY SCOTT (1689) 3-429.

DAWSON, HENRY, Capt. in Rev. N. C. 1-422.

DAWSON, HENRY, together with JOSHUA KENT and ELIZABETH TWINE, witnessed power of attorney by JOHN ARCHDALE to EMANUEL LOWE in (1703) 3-72; witness with BLAKE BAKER to will of WILLIAM KINCHEN, JR. in EDGECOMBE County (1758) 1-56.

DAWSON, FRANCIS, deceased (1714) ELIZA DAWSON Administratrix 1-41.

DAWSON, JOHN, brother-in-law of BARNABY THOMAS who left will (1735) of which his brother PHILLIP THOMAS was Executor (1735) 1-77; he was witness to deed by HENRY HEDGPETH (Of Nansemond Co. Va.) in (1732) 2-609; had a ferry in BERTIE COUNTY (1768) 3-446; made assignment deed with EDWARD WILLIAMS (1707) 1-92; witnessed deed by ISAAC WILLIAMS and wife MARY of Bertie in (1732) 2-610; bought 100 acres from FRANCIS PUGH (1728) 2-608; his last will in EDGE-COMBE (1749) wife MARY and children 1-199; another JOHN DAWSON of Bertie left estate (1770) with PENELOPE DAWSON administrator and probably his widow 3-448; he and JOHN JORDAN, JR. witnessed will of JOHN JORDAN of CHOWAN County (1717) 1-300.

DAWSON, GEORGE, brother of RICHARD DAWSON who died (1796) 2-333.

DAWSON, RICHARD, will (1796) in BERTIE COUNTY mentions relatives including GEORGE OUTLAW and DAVID TAYLOE, also nephews 2-333.

DAWSON, WILLIAM, mentioned in will (1796) in BERTIE County 2-333.

DEACON, JOHN, Master of sloop PEGGY (1749) 1-435.

DEANE, GEORGE, SR., of Chowan County; will in (1700) 1-40.

DEAR, DANIEL, with JOHN SMITH witness to deed to ROBERT CALF (1718) 1-625.

DEAR, GEORGE, land grant (1694) 1-4; he and JAMES WARD witness to deed (1718) in CHOWAN County 1-623; owned lands on ROCKYHOOK CREEK in (1680) 1-614.

DEBNAM, CHARLES 3-279.

DEBTORS' Act of Assembly relating to 3-54 and 3-55; Act to prevent their transportation out of the Government 3-78.

DEEDS and CONVEYANCES in CHOWAN 1700 to about 1730 2-135 to 2-146; copies obtained at EDENTON Courthouse 2-465 to 2-471; from BERTIE County up to 1712; Tyrrell County up to 1729; Washington County to same date and GATES COUNTY up to 1778 1-284 to 1-300; original deeds in courthouse at Edenton 2-443 to 2-457; in CHOWAN 1-615 to 1-630; see also 1-85 to 1-116, and 1-120 to 1-131 for the town of EDENTON; and 3-125 to 3-136; & the oldest one recorded in North Carolina at HERTFORD (1661) 3-423

DEPT, JOHN (Spelled DEIPT, here) will in (1725) 1-41.

DEPT, PENELOPE, will (1735) 1-41.

DELAMAR, FRANCIS (sometimes De La Mar) BEAUFORT will in (1739) 1-40; see also 2-148 & 3-259.

DELAMAR, ISAAC, Executor of JOSEPH STOAKLEY (1729) 1-75.

DELAMAR, STEPHEN, will (1732), mentions his nephew JOSEPH STOAKLEY 1-41.

DELANO, DANIEL, Executor of will of SOLOMON HENDRICKS (1833) who had son DELANO HENDRICKS and whose wife was MARY 3-338.

DELANO, BENJAMIN, master of the sloop SUSANNAH (1749) 1-434

DELANO, ICHABOD, will (1774) JOSEPH WHITE an Executor of will 3-169

DELANEY, HENRY sued NATHANIEL EDWARDS for damages to a horse he had borrowed to run a race with one owned by WILLIE JONES in (1769) 3-302.

DELOW, HENRY, was Clerk of the CHOWAN COURT (1746) 1-452.

DEMPSEY, PATIENCE, will (1764), WILLIAM ASHLEY and JOHN ANDREWS witnesses 2-332.

DEMPSEY, ISAAC, son of PATIENCE (1764) 2-332.

DEMPSEY, JAMES, son of PATIENCE (1764) 2-332.

DEMPSEY, JOSEPH, son of PATIENCE (1764) 2-332.

DEMPSEY, THOROUGHGOOD (1764) 2-332.

DENBY, JOHN (Of Nansemond Co. Va.) bought land from WILLIAM HORN and wife MARGARET with ELIAS STALLINGS a witness in (1730) 2-448.

DENMAN, CHARLES and wife SARAH with names of Children (1728) 3-382.

DENMAN, RICHARD and wife ANN 3-219.

DENSON, DARBY, lived between GASHY river & SALMON creek in BERTIE (1719) 1-444.

DENT, CHARLES, of CHOWAN was dead (1750) & left son CHARLES DENT about 1-451.

DEREHAM, ELIZABETH, will (1716) her father in law (step father?) was JAMES LEIGH 1-41.

DEREHAM, RICHARD. His deposition relating to the CARY REBELLION 3-224 to 3-225.

DEREHAM, THOMAS, of BATH 3-287.

DE ROSSETT FAMILY. Genealogical sketch of this family by MRS. MEARS 2-483 to 2-494.

DE ROSSETT, MOSES JOHN, will at WILMINGTON 1-199.

DECROW, SARAH 3-169.

DE GRAFFENREID, BARON STEPHEN 3-272.

DESHONE, PETER, witness to deed by JOHN GRAY (1719) 2-454.

DEVAN FAMILY. Wills of 2-510.

DEVAN, SARAH, will (1803) mentions husband JEREMIAH DEVAN, and ELIZABETH BRYAN the daughter of WILLIAM BRYAN; Jeremiah's will same page 2-510.

DEVEREAUX, GEORGE P. 3-511.

DEW, FRANCIS, bought land (1717) from JAMES WILKINSON, with JOHN MAINER and JAS WOOD witnesses 1-618.

DEW, JOHN, with SAMUEL RICKS, witnessed deed of THOMAS KIRBY, JR. to his mother(1718) 1-630; was witness to deed by WILLIAM BOON and wife ELIZABETH (1721) 2-616; also he bought land from WILLIAM HOOKER in (1716) 2-287.

DEW, JOHN, JR. was witness to deed by WILLIAM BOON (1721) 2-616.

DEW, LEWIS, to JOHN HARDY, with power of at - torney (1715) 2-288.

DEWMAN, CHARLES and James WILLIAMSON witness a deed to HENRY CLAYTON (1718) 1-628.

DICKSON, CHRISTIAN, witness to deed by WILLIAM LOW (1720) 2-617.(May be DICKINSON).

DICKSON, MRS. ELIZABETH (Dickinson) mentioned in will of THOMAS POLLOCK (1732) 1-67; & ELIZABETH DICKINSON married ANTHONY HATCH ---list of children 3-386.

DICKINSON, EDWARD, signs petition about (1704) with others 3-244.

DICKINSON, HENRY (1806) his estate settled men- tions ANDREW KNOX 2-261.

DICKINSON, JOHN, bought land from JOHN BROWN on North side MEHERRIN river (1719) 1-623; witnessed deed from FRANCIS BROWN to ED - WARD DAVIS (1700) 1-300; bought land from WILLIAM BRASWELL (1700) 1-300; left will (1742) 1-200.

DICKINSON, JOSEPH, was married by (1803) to POLLY GREGORY, daughter of JAMES GREGORY 1-446.

DICKINSON, MARY will in (1753) 1-200.

DICKERSON, NATHANIEL, revolutionary soldier 2-585.

DICKINSON, PENELOPE, sister of HENRY 2-261.

DICKINSON, REBECCA, will (1750) 1-200.

DICKINSON, DR. SAMUEL, BERTIE 3-28, 2-506.

DICKINSON, WILLIAM, died (1687) was a servant to ALEXANDER ~~ INGTON (1687) 3-364.

DIGBY, JAMES, JR. 3-170.

DILLARD, GEORGE, will (1780) 2-332

DIX, JOHN, and wife ALICE, son WILSON DIX born (1702) 3-374.

DIXON, HENRY, Lieutenant Colonel in the N. C. Continental Line 1-418.

DIXON, ROBERT (1720) was son in law of WILLIAM LOWE (of Prince George County, Va. 1-59.

DIXON, THOMAS and WILLIAM BRYAN have lawsuit EDGECOMBE COUNTY (1755) 1-447; with JOHN EARLY appointed to clear creek (1744) in BERTIE COUNTY 3-620.

DIXON, WINN1 Leutenant in 10th Regt. N. C. Continental Line under Col. ABRAHAM SHEPARD 1-425.

DOBBS, GOV. ARTHUR, commission to CHARLES ELLIOTT to be attorney general (1759) signed by RICHARD SPEIGHT, Secretary. 1-457; will of one ARTHUR DOBBS (1749) 1-40.

DOBY, WILLIAM, witness to will of ROBERT MOORE, with NICHOLAS JONES, first proba- ted in SUSSEX COUNTY, VA. (1808) 3-341.

DOCTON, JACOB, will (1764) daughter ELIZA- BETH married a PERRY 3-169.

DOE, CHARITY, died (1747) 3-405.

DOE, RALPH, married CHARITY SHERWOOD (1734) list of children 3-383.

DOGGETT, SAMUEL, Master of sloop ABIGAIL - (1749) 1-453.

DOIELE, THOMAS (DOYLEY) witnessed deed of ROBERT PATTERSON (1711) in HERTFORD Co. 2-287.

DONALDSON, ANDREW, will (1762) left land in LANCASTER COUNTY, VA. 3-169; another and later ANDREW DONALDSON with ANN HINES & ROBERT ROE, witnessed will of WILLIAM HINES (1784) 3-174; still another died (1768) and was related to the HARVEYS & WHITES and PERRYS 3-406.

DONALDSON FAMILY. Wills of 3-169; relation to SKINNER and HARVEY FAMILY 2-508, 3-169, 3-406.

DONALDSON, MARGARET, married SOLOMON ARM - STRONG (1765) 3-413.

DONALDSON, SPENCER, son of ANDREW, left land in LANCASTER COUNTY, Va. (1762) 3-169; left his own will, wife PENINAH in (1824) and mentions SAMUEL SUTTON 3-330, 3-331.

DONBET, JAMES, witnessed deed by WILLIAM HORN (1729) 2-448.

DONE, HENRY, will (1785), mentions JOHN HIGH and was related to the BRINKLEY FAMILY 3-169.

DONOVAN, DANIEL, witnessed deed by WILLIAM FALLAUGH (1716) 1-297.

DORMAN, RICHARD, married ANN NICHOLSON in (1690) list of their children 3-438.

DORTCH, WILLIAM, patented lands EDGECOMBE COUNTY (1746) 1-447.

DOUGALL, ARTHUR, with HENRY LYSLE, witnessed deed of WILLIAM WALSTON (1719) 1-629.

DOUGHTIE, EDWARD, owned lands next to ABRA- HAM ODOM (1735) 3-129.

DOUGLAS, DAVID, in NORTHAMPTON, will (1753) daughter MARTHA married a CARROLL, wit - nesses CHRISTMAS RAY, John Douglass 1-198, 1-199.

DOUGLAS, JAMES, will in BERTIE (1752) had son KESIAH DOUGLAS 1-199.

DOUGLAS, ROBERT and wife ANN sold land to AR-
THUR CARLTON (1716) with JAMES WILLIAMSON
as witness 1-295.

DOWDY, EDWARD, of NANSEMOND COUNTY, VA., sold
land to ABRAHAM ODOM (1732) 2-452.

DOWERS, WILLIAM, and wife HANNAH (1717) 3-383;
he and JOHN NEW witness to deed by ROBERT
HAWKINS (1721) 2-618; sued by EDWARD OUT-
LAW in BERTIE (1725) 2-470.

DOWNING, WILLIAM, Justice of the General Court East of CAPE FEAR about (1689-1725)
2-298; he was brother in law of WILLIAM
SHARPE (1717) in CHOWAN 1-618; bought land
from JACOB BLOUNT and wife ELIZABETH in
(1718), Richard CANADY a witness 1-619; he
was a merchant in (1715) and sold out to
WILLIAM SHARP (ship's carpenter) 1-288;
gave power of attorney to WILLIAM SHARP in
(1716) witnessed by JOHN ODOM and ALICE
MUNDAY 1-293; he and EDWARD MOSELEY were
Executors of THOMAS LEE (1726) 2-467; one
left will (1739) named friend STEPHEN LEE
1-40; whose deed he had witnessed (1730)
2-449; took deed from WILLIAM SHARP(1722)
2-143; witnessed deed by EDWARD HOWCOTT
in CHOWAN (1717) 1-616; his widow married
THOMAS LEE (of Lee's Mill, in Washington
County) who prior to that had married the
widow of THOMAS BLOUNT 2-133.

DRAPER, CHALKLEY, one of executors of will of
JOHN COX (1807) 3-329.

DRAPER, JOSEPH, will (1795), sons NATHAN and
JOSIAH 3-330; another son of SILAS DRAPER
3-170.

DRAPER, SILAS, will (1791) his children named
had one called CHALKLEY DRAPER 3-170.

DRAPER, SAMUEL will (1828) WILLIAM and BENJA-
MIN GREGORY, Executors 3-330.

DRAPER, NATHANIEL, of FLEA POINT, house as a
place of worship (no date) 2-198.

DRAPER, PETER, will (1764) sons JOSEPH and
SILAS and others, CORNELIUS MOORE was a
witness 3-169.

DRAUGHAN, WALTER, will (1758), daughters THOM-
ASINE and BRIDGET, other children named,
JOHN CAKE, a witness 2-332.

DREW, PATIENCE, wife of JOHN DREW deposition
and deed to ABRAHAM MOOR of Nansemond Co.
Va. (1771) 3-449.

DRIGGERS, WINSLOW, with EDWARD WILLIAMS wit -
ness to deed of JAMES WILLIAMS and wife
ELIZABETH to LUKE WHITE (1734) 3-127.

DRINKWATER, JOHN, Clerk of BEAUFORT and HYDE
Precincts (1713) 3-277; will in BATH in
(1718) 1-199.

DRUMMOND, GOV. WILLIAM, executed by BERKELEY
in (1679) son JOHN and daughter SARAH who
married SAMUEL SWANN, who later married
a LILLINGTON and had SARAH who married
Col. FREDERICK JONES. History 1-306.

DRUMMOND, SARAH, widow of the GOVERNOR, died
and left will (1679) 1-40.

DRURY, JOHN patent to lands in (1695) 3-130;
owned lands next to JOSEPH BALLARD and
WILLIAM BROWN (1733) 2-453; witness to
deed of JAMES HEDGEPETH (1737) 3-131.

DUDLEY, AMBROSE, revolutionary soldier who
served with 10th N. C. Regt. Continental
Line, Col. ABRAHAM SHEPARD 3-97.

DUDLEY, CHRISTOPHER, power of attorney from
JOHN CHURCH (1709) 1-98; he and JOHN
GORDON witness to deed by HENRY HILL of
Nansemond County, Va. (1716) 2-447; also
witnessed deed to WILLIAM DUKENFIELD in
(1716) 1-294; and he and wife ANN made deed
to WILLIAM KELLY, of Nansemond County, Va.
(1717) 1-620; and one to JAMES BATES in
CHOWAN (1715) 1-287; three of them in a
row 3-314; he left will (1744) with JOHN
STARKEY a witness 1-200.

DUDLEY FAMILY. Wills: Thomas 1755; Christopher 1744, John 1748, Thomas 1753, Edward
1744-5 1-200

DUDLEY, GOV. JOSEPH, mentioned 3-104.

DUDLEY, MARY was daughter of WILLIAM LEWIS in
(1731) 1-59.

DUDLEY, STEPHEN, witnessed deed of THOMAS GAR-
RETT (1715) 3-289.

DUDLEY, THOMAS will (1753) mentions son CHRIS-
TOPHER 1-200.

DUERS FAMILY. Wills 2-510, 2-511.

DUGALL, JOHN deed to PETER GRAY (1718) Henry
and PATIENCE SPELLER witnesses. 1-622.

DUKE, JAMES will (1807) 2-47.

DUKE, JOHN, and JOHN DRURY, witnesses to deed
by ANN MOOR, of Nansemond Co. Va. (1734)
2-453; his wife was ALICE (1705) 3-376.

DUKENFIELD, NATHANIEL 2-351; Sir NATHANIEL
DUKENFIELD, George Ryan's Grist Mill in
BERTIE (1771) 3-449; suerty for CHARLES
JACOCKS (1770) Bertie 3-448.

DUKINFIELD, RICHARD. Letter written him in
(1708) by JOHN ARDENE 2-455.

DUKENFIELD, WILLIAM, suit brought against him
by FREDERICK JONES and others, assigns of
ROBERT HARRISON, of YORK COUNTY, Virginia
after 1697 for debt of that date to HARRI-
SON 3-69, 3-70; letter from to JOHN ARCH-
DALE relating to INDIANS no date 3-64; in
CHOWAN (1711) 3-441; sold lands on SALMON
CREEK to JOHN ARDENE (1702) 2-455; was
deputy escheator (1707) 1-7; deed to JON-
ATHAN JACOCKS (1717) 1-299; was kinsman
of JOHN ARDENE (1712) 1-26; chart of his
family in England in will (1721) 1-41; obtained grant on ROCKYHOCK 1-6; married the
widow of FRANCIS HARTLEY (1694) 3-407; a
bond to HENRY KING (1713) 2-288; lawsuit
settled (1713) 1-291; made deed to THOMAS
WEST next to HENRY KING (1715) 1-292; sold
land to JOHN LOVICK 1-618; appeared in
suit with HANNIBAL HOSKINS (1690) 1-613;
witness with JOHN HAWKINS (1694) 3-247

DUNBAR, WILLIAM (1746) son in law SAM SLADE 1-72.

DUNCAN, ABRAHAM, will, BEAUFORT (1751) wife MARY and children of brothers 1-201.

DUNCAN, ALEXANDER, of WILMINGTON (1768) mentions brother ROBERT, JOHN RUTHERFORD, JAMES MOORE and THOMAS CUNNINGHAM, JR. "who has lived with me", MARY GRAINGER, wife of CALEB, MAURICE MOORE and wife & others 1-201.

DUNNING, JOHN and ABRAHAM SMITH witness deed by JOHN JORDAN JR. (1730) 2-449.

DUNNING, SAMUEL (1802) 2-510.

DUNNING, WILLIAM 2-522.

DUNSTON, BARNABY HELY, deed to JENKINS HANS - FORD (1749) 2-632; see 1-447.

DUNSTON, JOHN, and wife FRANCES (1696) 3-369; he and wife MARTHA receive deed from ABRA- HAM BLACKALL (1748) 1-446; one JOHN was Master of the Brig JOHNSTON (1775) 2-466. Will (1726) 1-41.

DUNSTON, EDMUND 2-510.

DUNSTON, MRS. MARTHA, accounts with WILLIAM BADHAM, merchant (1736) 1-448; she mar - ried (1738) JEREMIAH MITCHENER 1-448.

DUNSTON, MARY and sister ELEANOR, were the hrs of WILLIAM BADHAM (1737) 1-448.

DURANT, ANN, wife of GEORGE DURANT, the elder, died Jan. 23 (1694) 3-402; her will (1695) 1-41; her daughter ANN born (1681) 3-211; one ANN DURANT married JOSEPH BUNCOMBE & had daughter MARY married SAMUEL SUTTON by (1750) 1-453; ANN DURANT married WILLIAM BARCLIFT (1698) 3-408.

DURANT, CHRISTOPHER 2-218.

DURANT FAMILY. Births of children 3-205; wills 1-203, 1-204, 1-205.

DURANT, GEORGE (the 1st) was 49 years of age in 1680, 1-139; was born(1632) 1-203; an account of his family, with items from the family Bible 1-203, 1-204, 1-205, 1-268; copy of his will abstracted (1688) 1-203; attorney general of N. C. (1676) 3-40; gave power of attorney to wife ANN (1675) 2-470; Court held at his home (1685) EDWARD MAYO among those present 1-613; married to ANN MARWOOD (1658) in Northumberland County, Virginia 1-203; bought lands from the In - dians in DURANT'S NECK, in Perquimans Co. 1-203; his son GEORGE died(1671) 1-204; & GEORGE DURANT son of Thomas & Elizabeth - was born (1696) 1-204; will of his wife ANN (1695) 1-41; George Durant son of JOHN DURANT & Sarah Jooke, account 1-205.

DURANT, JOHN, who married SARAH JOOKE was grandson of first GEORGE DURANT and ANN MARWOOD 1-205; daughter ELIZABETH was born (1691) 3-218; another JOHN DURANT died (1699) 3-402; one was on list of tithables in Durant's Neck before(1700) 3-143; and MRS. DURANT was on the same list.

DURANT, MARY, was great grand-daughter of the first GEORGE DURANT, and she married CHRISTIAN REED, and JOSEPH REED married ELIZABETH DURANT 3-184, 3-185.

DURANT'S NECK. List of tithables in that section before (1700) 3-143, 3-144.

DURANT, THOMAS, wife ELIZABETH (1696-8) and their children; he was the son of GEORGE DURANT and wife ANN, and married ELIZA GASKILL, note 1-218; witnessed with THOM- AS SWANN articles of agreement between THOMAS WHITE and DAVID BLAKE (1695)3-247

DURANT, PARTHENIA, daughter of GEORGE DURANT and wife ANN MARWOOD, married JOSEPH SUT- TON (1695) 3-407.

DURANT, MRS. SARAH, married WILLIAM STEPHENS 3-410; another SARAH married RICHARD WHEDBEE (1709) see list of children 3-399;

DURANT, SARAH, married ELIAS ROWDEN in (1690) they were married by ALEXANDER LILLINGTON 3-204; this SARAH is mentioned in the will of her mother (1695) 1-41

DURANT, THOMAS, appointed by GOV. HARVEY to take charge of collections about (1696) 3-90; a much later THOMAS was Master of the sloop LYON in (1763) 2-296.

DURANT, WILLIAM (spelled in this instance DURANCE, but evidently intended for DURANT) made affidavit (1777) 2-209; SAMUEL DU- RANCE will in TYRRELL COUNTY (1756) uses the same spelling 1-204

DURANT - WILLIAMS FAMILIES. Note relating to the connection between these two families 1-501.

DWYER FAMILY. Wills 2-332.

DWIGHT, MATTHEW, will (1737) mentions his wife ELIZABETH 1-40.

DYALL, THOMAS. His wife was MARY, and they gave power of attorney to HENRY KING, in which acknowledgment is made of a sale to LEONARD LANGSTON of 100 acres of land in (1715) The witnesses to the instrument were WILLIAM WHITFIELD, JOHN CORE and JOHN DAWSON 1-289.

GOV. ROBERT DANIEL. The popular conception of Governor Daniel's genealogical history is that he was born in England, whereas the weight of the suggestive, if not positive evidence is that he was born in York or Warwick counties, in Virginia. No one has been able to determine with certainty the exact year in which MILES CARY, the emigrant, arrived in Virginia, but it was prior to 1644-5 at least. He was from Bristol, England, and brought over with him his "known kinsman" ROGER DANIEL and his son ROGER DANIEL JR. The latter was the father of GOV. ROBERT DANIEL, who with two brothers, JOHN and WILBERT fled to the BARBADOES to escape the wrath of BERKELEY after the rebellion stirred up by NATHANIEL BACON. Wilbert Daniel remained in the Island only a few months after which he returned to Virginia. Prior to his going there on November 13, 1678, he had been one of the subscribing witnesses to the will of HENRY ISHAM, at Vorina, in Henrico County, whose wife was the widow Katherine Royal, and whose son HENRY ROYAL in 1693 witnessed with DARBY DANIEL (uncle of Governor Robert) the will of his step son HENRY COPELAND, in Elizabeth CityCounty. John Daniel, the other brother, remained in the Barbadoes for some time and the St. James Parish Records there show the birth of two sons John (in 1678) and THOMAS (1679). ROBERT DANIEL had married DOROTHY CHAMBERLAINE, sister of EDWARD PYE CHAMBERLAINE, by whom he had one son, ROBERT; and JOHN DANIEL, his brother, married ANN ___. Thomas Daniel, born in 1679 married ELIZABETH LANIER, daughter of THOMAS LANIER (who was also living for a time in the Island) and both Thomas Daniel and Thomas Lanier died in TYRRELL COUNTY, N. C. about 1750, as disclosed by these Hathaway records. Robert Daniel's first wife died before he sailed on the "MARY" for the Carolinas in April 1679, bringing with him to Charleston his housekeeper and servant MARY COOPER and his son, ROBERT, a child-in-arms at that time.

Arriving in the Province of the Carolinas, Robert Daniel married a second wife, SARAH LOGAN, by whom he had several children, including SARAH (b. 1703), married Algernon Wilson; MARMADUKE DANIEL, MARTHA (b. 1704); JOHN DANIEL, born (1707) and ANN DANIEL, born (1710), according to the Annals of the Parish of St. Thomas and St. Dennis, of Charleston, S. C. SARAH DANIEL died July 31, 1721.

DOROTHY CHAMBERLAINE, the first wife of ROBERT DANIEL, had a sister who appears to have been the wife of JOHN LEAR, Clerk of Nansemond County, Virginia, hence Robert Daniel and the old Clerk were brothers-in-law. Dorothy also had a nephew MARMADUKE CHAMBERLAINE, for whom Governor Daniel named his second son. ROBERT DANIEL, the Governor's oldest son, married and had a number of children and many descendants, while MARMADUKE DANIEL's descendants intermarried into the famous BUFFINGTON FAMILY, of South Carolina (originally from Spottsylvania County, Virginia) which in turn hadrepresentatives who intermarried with prominent Cherokee Indian families and scattered throughout Georgia, Alabama and later to the Indian Territory and Oklahoma.

ROBERT DANIEL in a distant way was a kinsman of THOMAS CARY, who was born in England, the son of Walter Cary, whose widow, after Walter's death, became the wife of that lovable character and Governor of North Carolina, following the Culpepper troubles, JOHN ARCHDALE, Thomas Cary being the step-son of JOHN ARCHDALE and a distant cousin of ROBERT DANIEL. Robert Daniel was a landgrave, a Lieutenant General and Deputy Governor of the Province of North Carolina from 1704 to 1708. Unostentaciously he was in sympathy with the Quakers, dissenters and others who had been barred from holding office and exercising other privileges as citizens and during his incumbency the first church in North Carolina was established and the first seeds of the wholesomepolicy of the separation of Church and State were sown. Strange to say, THOMAS CARY, stepson of the popular JOHN ARCHDALE, who was chosen against the wishes of the Proprietors to succeed Daniel, soon became a thorn in the flesh of the whole colony, was deposed by the deputies and refused to surrender the office to WILLIAM GLOVER who had been elected Governor in his place. Then it was that the "double parliaments" met at the home of old JOHN HECLEFIELD on LITTLE RIVER, Glover presiding in one room and Thomas Cary in another. The gallant ROBERT DANIEL sent his regrets and asked to be excused (1-454) from attendance at the session.

DARDEN FAMILY. This is an old ISLE OF WIGHT COUNTY family. In an excellent genealogical work containing a chart of this family the compiler finds this statement, which is typical of many such compilations: "STEPHEN DARDEN settled in Nansemond County, Va. in 1640, and his son Capt. JOHN DARDEN, revolutionary soldier, married MISS DANDRIDGE, sister of MARTHA WASHINGTON". From 1640 to the beginning of the revolution was 135 years, which is a long time for the son of a settler of 1640 to live and still be a revolutionary soldier. Captain JOHN, according to the same account had two sons, JOHN (also a revolutionary soldier) born in 1734, and JACOB the next birth in the family. STEPHEN DARDEN may have been the first American ancestor of the family, but certainly there were several generations between 1640 and the birth of any member of the clan who could possibly have served in the revolution. One JACOB DARDEN made his will in Isle of Wight County in 1719. His wife was ANNE. He and Anne sold one-half of his patent to land in Isle of Wight to HENRY POPE in 1698. Jacob was alive and active in 1684, when he sold 100 acres to William Murphey in Isle of Wight County. (Boddie's 17thCentury pp 635, 596.). After the death of Jacob Darden his wife Anne married a LEIGH and her will was proven in BEAUFORT, North Carolina, which shows JACOB had changed his residence from Virginia, or his widow did after his death. The will was proven in (1733) 1-58, and gives us the names of their children: SAMUEL, JACOB, JOSEPH, JAMES; daughter ANN married ABRAHAM ADAMS, and JANE DARDEN married a WATKINS; the son JACOB DARDEN married (according to John Bennett Boddie p. 217), a daughter of GEORGE WILLIAMSON and the grand-daughter of that well known character COL. JOSEPH BRIDGER. It is not only possible, but probable, reverting now to the published chart referred to above, that Jacob Darden, a son of Jacob and Miss Williamson, were the parents of the JACOB DARDEN who married MARY HILLIARD and had (1) ZIEPHIA DARDEN who married JOSHUA ROUNDTREE (2) CYNTHIA DARDEN who married NEEDHAM BRYAN (which one, I don't know)and JACOB DARDEN who never married. The JACOB who married MARY HILLIARD had a brother WILLIAM, one of whose daughters married MANNING ROUNDTREE (an old N. C. family, of course), and a brother GEORGE married MARTEA BURCH and moved to GEORGIA after the revolution and they were the ancestors of the famous Texan STEPHEN HEARD DARDEN, well known in the annals of that commonwealth.

GEORGE DURANT. At the risk of having this work condemned, utterly, this compiler has long been convinced that one of the greatest genealogical tragedies of which he knows is the statement, long since perpetuated in print, that the wife of GEORGE DURANT was ANN MARWOOD. Neither in Dr. Swem's monumental index, or the equally prolific and voluminous records of the Provincial periods of North Carolina does the name MARWOOD appear. This name, obviously a scrivener's poor effort at writing the name "NORWOOD" in the old English style, has literally spoiled a great family history. A further statement, in the space available here, is not possible.

EAMES, GEORGE and wife SUSANNAH, son JOHN born (1694) 3-367.

EARL, ANN, daughter of Rev. Daniel Earl (1785) 1-542. Her will on same page mentions many of her connections.

EARL, REV. DANIEL, will in CHOWAN COUNTY (1785) names children and son in law CHARLES JOHNSON, wife CHARITY EARL 1-542; succeeded CLEMENT HALL as Rector of St. Paul's Parish EDENTON in(1758) 3-411.

EARLE, JOHN, member of Grand Jury with DAVID BAYLEY and others, which indicted GEORGE BURRINGTON for trespass (about 1723-1724) 3-237.

EARLY, ELINER, will (1732) mentions her grandson JAMES CURLEE 1-42.

EARLY FAMILY. Wills 2-333.

EARLY, JOHN and wife MARY (1713) sell land to GEORGE SMITH 1-100; bought land from JAMES CURLEE (1713) JOHN HARDY a witness 1-101; sold land to WILLIAM DAVIS on west side of WICACON Creek (1713) with JOHN BRYAN a witness 1-100; he and WILLIAM CRAWFORD owned adjoining lands (1719) 1-627; he and wife MARY deed lands to PETER PARKER (1700) at 3-131; he and wife MARY sell land to WILLIAM WILSON (1716) next to JOHN BUSH and WILLIAM CRAWFORD 1-615; he and William Rasberry and THOMAS DIXON appointed to clear a creek (1744) 2-620; JACOB LEWIS was his neighbor (1714) 2-456; made deed to JOHN HALE (1711) 3-441; he and MARY sold land to DENNIS MACLENDEN (1717) witnessed by WILLIAM CRAWFORD and FRANCIS MACLENDEN 1-300; made deed to JOHN ROSEBERRY (or Rasberry) in (1711) CHOWAN 3-441; he was a brother of REBECCA SHEETES (1732); MARY, wife of JOHN EARLY, gave Power of Attorney to MICHAEL HILL (1711) 3-441.

EARLY, JOHN SR. will in BERTIE (1740) wife ANN and son JOHN executors. List of his children 1-208.

EARLY, WILLIAM, sold land to JOHN BEVERLY in (1704) 1-119; sold land to PETER EVANS adjoining COL. POLLOCK (1706) John Jordan a witness 1-95; witnessed deed to COL. POLLOCK (1703) and to WILLIAM STEMMOS 2-611; his wife was ELIENER and they had son in law HENRY SUTTON (1704) to whom they gave land bought of RICHARD BOOTH (1701) 2-612.

EASON, ABNER, had son JACOB EASON (1764) and was son in law of JACOB DOCTON 3-170,2-333.

EASON, GEORGE, will (1774) had JESSE, MOSES, ABNER and GEORGE EASON sons 3-170.

EASON FAMILY. Wills (BERTIE) 2-511 and 3-170.

EASON, WILLIAM, of PERQUIMANS COUNTY died in (1718-1719), one WILLIAM married ANNE LAVINIA ROOTES 2-537.

EASTER FAMILY. Wills in HYDE COUNTY. MARY in (1751), ABRAHAM (1751), JOHN (1751) and also a JOHN (1732) 1-207, also 1-42.

EASTER, SOLOMON, mentioned in the will of WILLIAM JOY (1725) 1-55.

EATON, JAMES will in CHOWAN (1729) 1-42.

EATON, PINKETHMAN, Major in the N. C. Continental Line 1-418.

EATON, WILLIAM, of GRANVILLE COUNTY, N. Carolina, patented lands there in(1746) 1-447; was Sheriff of Granville County (1753) and left will (1759) 1-41.

EAVES, RALPH, left will (1741) executors were JOHN STARKEY and JOHN BRYAN 2-468.

EBORN, HENRY, will (1732) 1-42.

EDEN, CHARLES, order relating to powder(1719) 3-281; issues proclamation dissolving the Assembly (1717) 3-228, 3-229; came as Royal Governor (1713) and lived in BATH 3-24; married into GOLLAND family 2-622; files complaint against WILLIAM MAULE 3-151, 3-152; left will (1721) in which he mentions DANIEL RICHARDSON, JAMES HENDERSON and JOHN LOVICK, the latter his executor 1-42, 1-43.

EDEN, PENELOPE, daughter of Governor EDEN, married (1) JOHN LOVICK (2) _____ (3) GEORGE PHENEY and (4) Governor GABRIEL JOHNSTON 1-86.

EDENTON - TOWN OF - Built on lands of JACOB and THOMAS PETERSON 3-143; first called ANNE'S TOWN 3-284; list of tithables there in (1702) 3-84, 3-85, 1-142; Act of Assembly relating to lands where town is located 2-237, 2-274; the old CANNON INN at EDENTON 1-593 to 1-595; list of citizens of the town (1777) taking oath 2-205,2-206; deeds and conveyances of lots in the town 1-120 to 1-131; bond relating to building of the courthouse signed by JOSEPH HEWES and others 2-225, 2-226; early miscellaneous records obtained at 2-146 to 2-153, & 2-465 to 2-471; same, 3-125 to 3-136.

EDENTON TEA PARTY. An account of the historic event of 1774, attended by 56 ladies of the town 2-120 to 2-124; the descendants of WINNIFRED HOSKINS, the BROWNRIGGS and LEARYS 3-300 to 3-304; 3-116 to 3-124; 2-163 to 2-170; the LOWREYS and BLAIRS 2-602 to 2-607; 2-458 to 2-464.

EDGERTON, PATRICK married MARY FISHER (1705) 3-410.

EDGERTON, WILLIAM, of CHOWAN (1711) 3-442; received land grant on YOPPIM river (1723) 1-11.

EDLIN, JOHN, assigns his interest in certain lands (1678-9) to JAMES PERISHO —mentions JOHN GREEN and others 3-434; his wife was SARAH and his son JOHN was born (1677) 3-209.

EDMUNDS, SAMUEL, of CHOWAN, will (1720) mentions daughter married HENRY MIDDLETON and other children 1-43 and 1-209; his wife was MARY and they sold land to JOHN EDWARDS on TURKEY SWAMP (1716), and JOHN EDWARDS was his executor 1-296; he lived between Cashy River and Salmon Creek in BERTIE in (1719) 1-444.

EDWARDS FAMILY. Wills of ISAAC, EDWARD, HENRY and CATHERINE EDWARDS 1-207.

EDWARDS, HUMPHREY, will in BATH (1711) 1-43

EDWARDS, JOHN married ZILPHA BLOUNT, daughter of THOMAS BLOUNT and wife MARY 1-59; they were witnesses to deed by PETER HERD (HEARD) (1720) 2-614; he was executor of the will of SAMUEL EDMUNDS (1720) 1-43; and witness to deed by WILLIAM JONES (1715) 2-289; and from JOHN WILLIAMS (1716) 1-296; he bought land from SAMUEL EDMUNDS (1716) 1-296; witnessed deed from JAMES HOOPER (1716) 1-296; sold lands to SOLOMON JORDAN by (1718)1-625.

EDWARDS, JOHN, whose wife was DORCAS had son in law JAMES ROBERTS who married their daughter CORNELIA EDWARDS (1718), MATTHEW ED - WARDS a witness 1-621; together JOHN and DORCAS made deed to EDWARD MOORE (1716)2-285 and bought land from CHARLES BARBER (1716) on TURKEY CREEK 1-296; deeded lands in (1718) next to THOMAS JONES and THOMAS HOLBROOK 1-621; they sold lands to SOLOMON JORDAN in (1714) 1-103.

EDWARDS, JOHN, (probably the one who married ZILPHA BLOUNT) together with SAMUEL EDMUNDS lived between CASHY RIVER and SALMON CREEK in (1719), in BERTIE 1-444; and JOHN ED- WARDS was killed in BERTIE in (1750) 2-470.

EDWARDS, MARY, with RICHARD FRYER witnessed a deed to WILLIAM JONES (1719) 1-627.

EDWARDS, MATTHEW and WILLIAM JONES were witness to a deed by MARTIN GARDNER to JOHN WIL - LIAMS (1718) 1-623; witness another time in (1718) 1-621.

EDWARDS, NATHANIEL, borrowed a horse from HENRY DELANEY to run in a race with a horse be- longing to WILLIE JONES (1769) 2-302; he & THOMAS HART and DRURY GEE sign bond (1768) in a suit with HENRY DELANEY 3-468; his wife was JANE EATON, daughter of WILLIAM EATON of GRANVILLE COUNTY in (1759) 1-49.

EDWARDS, TITUS, was an executor of the will of THOMAS BARFIELD (1768) 2-329; his wife was RACHEL and he left will in BERTIE in(1785) 3-333.

EDWARDS, WILLIAM, will (1785) names wife TABI- THA, his sons, and brother TITUS EDWARDS 2-333.

EDWARDS, ZILPHA, daughter of THOMAS BLOUNT, was witness to deed by PETER HERD(1720) 2-614.

EGAN, JOHN, letter written by him to COL. JAMES BLOUNT (1779) 2-195, in CHOWAN COUNTY;2-205

EGAN, JAMES died in BLADEN COUNTY leaving will (1737), mentions "wife and daughter" makes WILLIAM CARY his Executor 1-206.

EGAN, ROBERT, and JOHN EGAN, among the citizens of EDENTON who took the oath of allegiance in June (1778) 2-205; he was living in NEW YORK CITY (Robert Egan) at the time of his death (1796) but his will was proven in EDENTON, his wife was ELIZABETH and mention is made of SARAH COTTEN and ALLEN RAMSEY in said will 1-542.

EGGERTON, PATRICK was granted lands on YOPPIM RIVER in (1719) next to JOHN PORTER 1-17; witnessed a deed by DAVID JONES in (1720) 2-614; had sons HENRY and WILLIAM EGGERTON in (1733) 1-450; his wife was MARY in(1705) 3-376.

EGGERTON, WILLIAM made deed to WILLIAM BEN- BERRY of lands heired from his father (about 1733) 3-128; sold land to THOM- AS MING (MINGE?) in (1731) 2-451.

EGLINTINE, HENRY. His wife was ELIZABETH & their daughter SARAH was born (1681) 3-211.

EGLINTINE, SARAH, daughter of HENRY 3-211.

EICHORN, CONRAD, land grant (1714) next to LEWIS WILLIAMS 1-14.

ELDRIDGE, WILLIAM, will (1751) in NORTHAMP- TON COUNTY, mentions MATTHEW and CHARITY MOORE, his brother SAMUEL EDRIDGE and others, with WILLIAM RICHARDSON and RE - BECCA DAWSON, witnesses 1-206.

ELLIOTT, ABRAHAM, will (1812), mentions wife JULIANA, with CHARLES MOORE and JAMES MOORE witnesses 3-331.

ELLIOTT, ANDREW, witness (1735) to will of THOMAS ARMSTRONG, of BOSTON, Mass., proved in North Carolina 2-303.

ELLIOTT, CALEB and JOSEPH ELLIOTT witness a deed of LEWIS CONNOR in NORFOLK COUNTY, Va. registered in N. C. (1729) 2-448; Caleb & Richard Wilson and MEDIA WHITE witness to deed in (1729) 2-451; his wife's name was MARY in (1743) 3-383; one CALEB ELLIOTT left will (1775) witnessed by three members of the BUNCH FAMILY 3-170; children 3-383.

ELLIOTT, CHARLES, appointed attorney general by Governor DOBBS (1759) 1-457, 2-305.

ELLIOTT, EPHRAIM and wife SARAH, had KEZIAH ELLIOTT born (1752) 3-383; he left will in (1799) perhaps a later one 3-331

ELLIOTT, EXUM, witness with MYLES ELLIOTT to will of MARY SMITH (1817) 3-351.

ELLIOTT FAMILY. Wills 3-331 to 3-332.

ELLIOTT, GEORGE, will in PASQUOTANK (1727) mentions god-daughter MARY WALLACE 1-42.

ELLIOTT, JOSHUA and wife ANNE (1740) 3-383.

ELLIOTT, MICAJAH, brother of JOSEPH ELLIOTT who left will (1831) 3-332.

ELLIOTT, MILES, brother of STEPHEN and WILLIS ELLIOTT (1825) 3-332.

ELLIOTT, STEPHEN, will names brothers (1825) makes JOSIAH TOWNSEND, Executor 3-332.

ELLIOTT, THOMAS, will (1729) in PERQUIMANS mentions son MOSES 1-42; sold lands to AARON ELLIOTT (1726) and bought land from ROBERT WILSON the same year 2-293.

ELLIOTT, TOWNSEND, was the son of EPHRAIM EL- LIOTT who left will (1799) and brother of STEPHEN, CALEB, MILES and JOSIAH ELLIOTT 3-331.

ELLIS, AARON, of BERTIE COUNTY, his admx was CATHERINE ELLIS (about 1769) 3-446.

ELLIS, ELIZABETH, married DAVID HARRIS (1695) by JOSEPH SUTTON 3-407; another ELIZABETH ELLIS married JAMES CUNNINGHAM in CHOWAN County (1795) 1-252.

ELLIS, GEORGE, will in PASQUOTANK (1721) mentions wife HANNAH and brother THOMAS PALIN 1-42.

ELLIS, MOSES, will in CHOWAN (1771) daughters CELIA and ANN 3-449.

ELLIS, SYLVIA, of BERTIE, an orphan, with EZE-KIEL WIMBERLY, her guardian (1771) 3-450.

ELKER, ELIZABETH, daughter of RICHARD ELKER & wife ANN, born (1678) 3-209.

ELKER, MARGARET, was drowned 3-365.

ELKER, RICHARD, his wife was ANN 3-209 (1678)

EMANSON, HENRY, was a witness (1720) 2-618.

ENGLE, PETER, will (1722) mentions God son WIL-LIAM MOORE 1-42.

ENLOW, ABRAHAM, grandson of GUILFORD SILVERTH-ORN (1737) writes a note 1-73; with the name spelled "ENDLESS" in (1754) he and his wife ELIZABETH petition with reference to the estate of WILLIAM ARKILL, deceased – 1-457.

ERWIN FAMILY. Genealogy of the ERWIN-JONES family, descendants of ANNIE ISABELLA IREDELL and CADWALLADER JONES 3-165.

ESCHEATED LANDS. How lands were escheated in North Carolina 3-87.

ESTATES OF DECEASED PERSONS. Act of the North Carolina Assembly relating to 3-58, 3-59.

ESTATES. Division of estates of deceased persons and families in CHOWAN COUNTY, from about (1740 to 1800), giving list of heirs generally named. The names of the owners of these estates are arranged in alphabetical order. 2-256 to 2-273.

ETHERIDGE, HENRY will (1742) names wife LUCY – 1-42.

ETHERIDGE, LUKE, will (1742) wife CHRISTIAN, see 1-42.

ETHERIDGE, MARMADUKE, will (1734) leaves legacies to children of SARAH BELL, including CALEB BELL and others 1-42.

ETHERIDGE, WILLIAM, will (1837) mentions wife MARTHA and his five oldest children by his first marriage. Then see note 2-512.

EURE FAMILY. Some of the names are mentioned in will of MARY LEE in GATES COUNTY (1836) 2-59

EURE, JAMES, bought land from JOHN COLLINS in (1735) 3-127.

EUBANK, GEORGE, of BERTIE COUNTY, will (1732) mentions three members of the WHITMELL family 1-42; he brought suit against JOHN GREEN and JOHN BOBBITT (1732) 2-298.

EVANS, ANN, daughter of RICHARD EVANS, died in (1700) 3-402.

EVANS, BENJAMIN, was son in law of THOMAS PAR-KER of CHOWAN (1716) 1-617; sold land to FRANCIS THOMAS (1730) with JOHN PARKER a witness 3-449.

EVANS FAMILY. Wills of 1-205, 1-206, 1-541.

EVANS, JAMES of PERQUIMANS, deeded lands to THOMAS LUTEN next to HENRY BONNER and WIL-LIAM JONES (1720) Thomas MONTAGUE and BEAL BROWN, witnesses 2-513.

EVANS, JOHN, deed to BENJAMIN EVANS (1718) JOHN JORDAN a witness 1-622; also deed to JOHN WHITE, son of GEORGE next to JOHN JORDAN (1717) John and JANE JORDAN witnesses 1-626; received land grant (1718) joining JOHN JORDAN and SAMUEL PADGETT 1-12.

EVANS, JONATHAN, wife was MARY (1717) 3-383.

EVANS, JOSEPH, son of WILLIAM EVANS records his brand-mark (1746) 2-628; leaves will (1827) NATHAN and EXUM WHITE his executors. 3-332.

EVANS, MARY was daughter of THOMAS LUTEN 2-293.

EVANS, MICHAEL, will (1795) 2-333.

EVANS, PETER, deeded lands to WILLIAM EVANS in CHOWAN (1715) 1-285; was surviving executor of JACOB SHARP, whose relict married RICHARD FIGURES by (1749) 2-633; had son ROBERT EVANS (1715) 1-285; owned land next to JAMES BOON on GUM BRANCH (1718) 1-620; appointed to help distribute estate of WILLIAM BAKER (1745) 2-626.

EVANS, RICHARD, suit against ROBERT BRIGHT-WELL (1689) 3-431; also against THOMAS LILLY same year 3-430; died leaving will in PERQUIMANS (1692) with ALEXANDER LIL-LINGTON, Executor 1-42.

EVANS, ROBERT, bought land from THOMAS BRAY (1716) 1-300; he and wife ANN sold land to JOHN WOOD (1719) 2-608; Ann adminis-tered his estate (1746) 2-626-8; sold lands to PETER PARKER (1729) 2-615; RICH-ARD HAYS and WILLIAM SHARP witnessed his deed (1716) to THOMAS BRAY 1-616.

EVANS, SARAH, was daughter of WILLIAM WILLS of ONSLOW (1742) 1-80.

EVANS, SUSANNAH 3-57.

EVANS, THOMAS, power of attorney to THOMAS SNOWDEN (1703) 3-73; will in CHOWAN in (1731) 1-42.

EVERARD, SIR RICHARD, Governor 3-230; Burring-ton's attack on 3-229; Everard riot in EDENTON (1728) 1-439, 1-440.

EVERARD, RICHARD, JR. 3-230.

EVERENDEN, THOMAS, JR. bought land from JOHN SIMONS (1729) 2-446.

EVERITT, NATHANIEL, wife MARY. He left will (1720) witnessed by BENJ. BLOUNT 2-454; deed to THOMAS LEE and others 1-297; was father in law of BENJ. BLOUNT (1718)1-619.

EVERITT, THOMAS, wife DOROTHY (1700) 2-456.

EVERTON, JERMIAH dau SARAH FOREHAND 1-41.

EVINS, ELIZABETH 3-406; THOMAS EVINS 3-216.

EXUM, JEREMIAH (1707) 1-94; RICHARD EXUM 1-90.

REV. DANIEL EARL. This man was an English Clergyman, who came to Virginia sometime prior to 1758, when he succeeded REV. CLEMENT HALL as the Rector of ST. PAUL'S PARISH in the town of EDENTON, which position he held until the time of his death in 1785 (1-542). His wife was ELIZABETH GREGORY, a member of an old and respected NANSEMOND COUNTY, Virginia, family, the daughter of JAMES GREGORY, who was a son of MAJ. JOHN GREGORY (16 Va. Mag. 203). REV. EARL and his wife ELIZABETH GREGORY had two children, both daughters. They were ANN EARL who died leaving a will in CHOWAN COUNTY in 1796 (1-542) and ELIZABETH EARL who married CHARLES JOHNSON. Charles Johnson and Elizabeth Earl were the parents of ELIZABETH EARL JOHNSON who became the wife of DR. ALEXANDER HENDERSON, a son of PLEASANT HENDERSON and SARAH MARTIN. Their daughter ELIZABETH EARL HENDERSON married GEN. LAWRENCE S. BAKER, a descendant of HENRY BAKER, the old ISLE OF WIGHT COUNTY, Va. merchant, heretofore mentioned in these notes. Rev. DANIEL EARL, in the spelling of his name, omitted the final "e" sometimes attached to the name EARLE in the Virginia and South Carolina records, and so far as is known was not related to the EARLES of Westmoreland County, Va. and Spartanburg County, S. C. He evidently left no male descendants to carry on the name of EARL.

WILLIAM EATON. This William Eaton was born on SKEMONI CREEK near the York River in York County, Virginia. He was the son of SARAH PINKETHMAN (daughter of William Pinkethman, a lawyer and tobacco merchant) and WILLIAM EATON. He had an older brother PINKETHMAN EATON, who was mentioned in the will of their grandfather WILLIAM PINKETHMAN, who died in 1713. His older brother PINKETHMAN EATON had a son PINKETHMAN EATON, who was born according to the Bruton Parish Register, in 1748. This was MAJ. PINKETHMAN EATON, of the North Carolina Continental Line, who was WILLIAM EATON'S nephew. WILLIAM EATON, of this record, was one of the founders and a member of the first court of GRANVILLE COUNTY, N. C. SARAH PINKETHMAN, mother of WILLIAM EATON, had a sister, REBECCA PINKETHMAN, who married ROBERT COBBS as his first wife; after her death ROBERT COBBS married ELIZABETH ALLEN (daughter of DANIEL ALLEN) and this last couple were the parents of SARAH COBBS who married ROBERT JONES, JR. and they were the parents of GEN. ALLEN JONES and WILLIE JONES famous in North Carolina revolutionary history. MARTHA COBBS, another daughter of ROBERT COBBS and ELIZABETH ALLEN, married SAMUEL WELDON, of HENRICO COUNTY (Dale Parish) and they were the parents of DANIEL WELDON who married MARTHA EATON, one of the daughters of WILLIAM EATON, of GRANVILLE COUNTY. After the death of his wife SARAH COBBS, Robert Jones, Jr., father of Gen. Allen and Willie Jones and their sister CHARLOTTE JONES, married MARY EATON, another daughter of WILLIAM EATON, of Granville. By this last marriage ROBERT JONES JR. (who was attorney general of North Carolina) had one daughter ELIZABETH JONES (half-sister of ALLEN and WILLIE JONES) who married August 10, 1781, BENJAMIN WILLIAMS, Governor of North Carolina from 1799 to 1802, who resided in MOORE COUNTY.

In the Department of ARCHIVES and HISTORY, at Raleigh, N. C. some years ago this compiler found an old record book (the first, apparently), a mere fragment of which gave a brief account of the organization of the original Granville county. The first entry, in a faded state, gives an account under date of September 3, 1746, contains an abstract of the Act of the Assembly providing for the erection of the upper part of Edgecomb County into a new county by the name of GRANVILLE. It provided that the courthouse should be erected at ROCKY CREEK, "as near as may be to the BOILING SPING". WILLIAM PERSON and WEST HARRIS were appointed commissioners to confer with the court of EDGECOMB County, and PERSON was appointed Sheriff of the new county. Court to meet at the home of EDWARD JONES, and so it met there on December 2, 1746. Present at the first meeting were the following persons: WILLIAM ETON (Eaton), JOHN MARTIN, JAMES PAYNE, EDWARD JONES, JOHN WALKER and GIDEON MACON. At a second meeting, those present were: JAMES PAYNE, JOHN WADE, JOHN MARTIN, WEST HARRIS and JONATHAN WHITE. At that time the territory embraced in GRANVILLE included (in addition to other territory) all of the present counties of GRANVILLE, VANCE, WARREN and FRANKLIN counties.

EDWARD JONES, at whose home the first meetings of the court were held in Granville county, came from Virginia, and at that time lived, as near as can be ascertained in the North - western part of what is now Franklin County near Shocco Springs - then referred to as the BOILING SPINGS. His wife was ABIGAIL SUGRE, the daughter of a French Huguenot family who had settled with that colony at Manikintown, in Virginia. From the will of Edward Jones, proven in Granville County in 1750, we learn that his children were SUGAR, JAMES, EDWARD, DANIEL, SARAH, OBEDIENCE, RABON and PRISCILLA. Priscilla Jones married GIDEON MACON, who was one of the members of the first Granville county court, as shown above. He was the brother of MARTHA MACON, of New Kent County, who married ORLANDO JONES, son of Rev. Rowland Jones, of Bruton Parish in York County, Va. These were Martha Washington's near relatives. GIDEON MACON'S daughter, ANN HUNT MACON became the wife of CAPT. JOHN ALSTON of the family so often mentioned in these records. CAPT. SUGAR JONES, son of EDWARD JONES, played an important role in the early Indian Wars in North Carolina. His wife was SARAH FRANKLIN, who after his death married NATHANIEL HENDERSON, son of JUDGE RICHARD HENDERSON and brother of PLEASANT HENDERSON, who married SARAH MARTIN, daughter of Col. James Martin, of Snow Creek, N. C.

COL. NATHANIEL EDWARDS, who in 1769 borrowed a horse from HENRY DELANEY to match against one owned by COL. WILLIE JONES, of Halifax (2-302) and which operation finally resulted in a lawsuit with resort to the courts (2-468), was a son in law of WILLIAM EATON, the old SHERIFF of Granville County, N. C., and member of its first court, having married JANE EATON, his daughter (1-41). Col. Edwards lived in BRUNSWICK COUNTY, Virginia, which, of course, was not far away. He had the following children, as disclosed by his will written in 1771: SARAH (m. AMBROSE DANIEL) Isaac, William, Anne (m. RIDLEY), REBECCA (wife of ALLEN JONES, of "Mount Gallant" in Northampton County, N. C., and brother of Col. WILLIE JONES, who owned the horse he wanted to beat) and Elizabeth Edwards, who is said to have married HENRY WILLIS. Allen Jones' daughter, REBECCA EDWARDS JONES married (1) LUNSFORD LONG, son of Col. Nicholas Long, and (2) CADWALLADER JONES, of the PETER JONES family.

FAGAN, RICHARD. Division of his estate in TYR-
RELL COUNTY in (1777) names heirs 1-449.

FAIR, OBEDIAH, was headright of JOSEPH PEIRY in
(1701) 2-300.

FAIRCLOTH, EDWARD, called "son" in the will of
PHILLIP TORKSEY (1727) 1-78.

FAIRCLOTH, WILLIAM, Lieutenant in 10th Regt. N.
C. Continental Line 1-425.

FAIRLESS, NICHOLAS, Estate; MARY CLAYTON administratrix (1745) 2-526.

FAISON, FRANCIS DIANA, was daughter of HENRY
FAISON and SALLIE THOMPSON. Sallie Thompson
was daughter of WILLIAM THOMPSON of SAMPSON
County, N. C. 2-158.

FAISON FAMILY. Genealogy of the family, which
was from SOUTHAMPTON COUNTY, VA., and its
connection with the THOMPSON and HILL FAM-
ILY, the latter of BRUNSWICK COUNTY, VA.
Also connected with the DUDLEYS 2-158,3-312
3-313.

FALCONER, JAMES, sold land to JOHN SHOLER before
(1717) 1-617.

FALCONER, JOHN, signs table showing prices of
merchandise (1699) 2-203; witnessed deed of
JOHN SWAIN to JOHN PORTER (1718) 1-624; was
witness with GEORGE GUILFORD (1721) 2-618;
received land grant (1720) on YOPPIM RIVER
1-9; bought land from WILLIAM MOODY (1710)
1-296; sold 52 acres on DRUMMOND'S POINT to
JOHN SHOWLER (1715?) 1-294; witness to deed
from THOMAS SPIERS to EDWARD COCKRILL(1728)
2-443; he and SARAH FALCONER witnessed deed
(1733) 2-611.

FALCONER, THOMAS, deed to land (1733) witnessed
by SARAH and JOHN FALCONER 2-611.

FALK, RICHARD (Probably FOLK) will (1712) his
wife ELIZABETH 1-44.

FALLOW, WILLIAM, deed to WILLIAM BONNER in(1716)
to land bought of DINA (DIANA) LEE 1-399;
land grant (1714) on ROCKYHOCK CREEK 1-8;
bought land from DAVID LEE (1716), DANIEL
DONOVAN a witness 1-8.

FANNY, JOHN, an orphan, MATTHEW HUBBARD to care
for him (1711). His father was JOHN 3-444.

FARR, RICHARD, held note against JOHN JOHNSTON
in (1746) 2-301; died leaving will in(1757)
1-213.

FARROW, FRANCIS, will (1722) 1-4.

FARLEE, JAMES, will in CHOWAN, (1727) EDWARD
MOSELEY, Executor 1-43.

FARLEY, ELISHA, son in law of HENRY MIDDLETON
(1738) 1-61.

FARLOW. DOROTHY, MRS. Her grand-daughter was
wife of ADAM COCKBURN (1725) 3-336; had two
grandchildren named HALSEY 3-134.

FARLOW, JAMES, land grants (1711) on Beaver Dam
1-7; (1712) on Rockyhock 1-7; (1732) on BEAV-
ER DAM SWAMP 1-11; deed (1716) from ROBERT
HICKS 1-291; (1718) from JONATHAN KITTRELL &
wife ANN 1-630; grant (1717) 1-16.

FARLOW, JOHN witness with MARY TOMS (1699)
2-432.

FARLOW, WILLIAM. His wife was MARY, sold land
to CHARLES RICKETTS(1713) next to JOHN
HARRIS and JOHN MARKS 1-99; land grant in
(1721) joined DAVID AMBROSE and WILLIAM
WOODLEY 1-1C.

FARMER, JOSEPH 2-335.

FARMER, THOMAS (1760) 1-543.

FEARE FAMILY "Mother Fearre" in will of WIL-
LIAM LEWFORD (1732) 1-57.

FAVIEL, RICHARD, will (1738) 1-44.

FELTON FAMILY. Wills in GATES COUNTY 2-48; wills
in CHOWAN COUNTY 1-543; wills in PERQUIMANS
3-333.

FELTON, RICHARD, of CHOWAN COUNTY, will (1776)
1-543.

FELTON, WILLIAM, in CHOWAN COUNTY (1817) 1-543.

FELTS, HUMPHREY, will (1726) in PERQUIMANS,
WILLIAM LONG, Executor 1-43.

FENDALL, ELIZABETH, widow of JOHN FENDALL sold
land to HENDERSON WALKER (1698) 2-456.

FENDALL, JOHN, married ELIZABETH LILLINGTON in
(1694), daughter of ALEXANDER LILLINGTON &
wife ELIZABETH 3-406, 1-43.

FENDALL, JOSIAS died in (1692) 3-220; his wife
was MARY 3-406.

FENDALL, ROBERT, owned land that had belonged
to THOMAS GILLIAM on Albemarle Sound (1708)
1-291, died leaving will (1711) 1-43.

FENIX, JOHN 3-285.

FERRELL, NICHOLAS, witness to deed by JOHN
WHITE (1717) in CHOWAN 1-624; sold land bt
from WILLIAM JACKSON and wife ELIZABETH to
JOHN WHITE, JR. (1719) 1-628.

FERGUSON, ADAM. Genealogy of his immediate family in CRAVEN COUNTY 2-297.

FERGUSON, SARAH, daughter of ADAM FERGUSON married JAMES TOOLE, of PRINCESS ANNE COUNTY,
Virginia, list of children(1761) 2-297.

FEWOX, JAMES, proved his headrights (1702) including JANE WHEELER and others 2-299; left
will (1711), SAMUEL HARDY son of WILLIAM is
mentioned 1-43.

FEWOX, ROBERT, of SCUPERNONG, sold land to WIL-
LIAM HARDY (1714) witnessed by MARY LAWSON
1-285; deed to JOHN HASSELL (1717) with MAT-
THEW CASWELL a witness 1-619; deed to AN-
THONY ALEXANDER (1719) witnessed by JOSEPH &
LEMUEL ALEXANDER 2-615.

FIELDS, JOHN 2-334.

FIELDS, MILLS R. 2-48.

FIGURES, BARTHOLOMEW 1-211.

FIGURES, RICHARD, married ELIZABETH, the widow
of JACOB SHARP by (1749) 2-633.

FRILEY, WILLIAM, to THOMAS EVANS and MATTHEW ADAMS, assignment of Patent in CHOWAN in(1720) 2-615; deed to JAMES JONES (1724) lands surveyed for RICHARD ROSE 2-291.

FILBERT, NICHOLAS, an early settler near EDENTON for whom FILBERT CREEK named 3-147.

FILGO, ANTHONY, will (1777) his wife was ANN & son in law JAMES LAUGHLIN 2-334.

FINCH, JEREMIAH was dead in (1725) 2-298.

FINCH, ROWLAND PORTER, Church warden in BEAUFORT (1739) 2-303.

FINCH, THOMAS, his headrights proved by WILLIAM OUTLAW (1744) 2-624; directed to furnish tuition to an orphan MARY STAPLES (1745) 2-626

FIRST CHURCH IN NORTH CAROLINA. Its location and history 1-256 to 1-267.

FISHER, JAMES land grant on YOPPIM RIVER 1-5; he married MARY SMITH widow of FRANCIS SMITH in (1701) 3-409; they had son JAMES born (1702) 3-373; in (1688) his wife was ANN 3-215; also in (1692) 3-219; JAMES FISHER and MARY RICHARDS married in NEWPORT PARISH, Isle of Wight County, Va. (1701) 3-409.

FISHER, MARY married PATRICK EDGERTON (1705) 3-410.

FISKE, REV. SAMUEL, deceased in (1772). MARY FISK, Administratrix, sues JOSEPH JONES and other Church wardens 2-304.

FITZPATRICK, BRYAN sold THOMAS HOLLOWAY on SOUTH SIDE OF ROANOKE Sound (1707) JOHN PETTIVER a witness 1-931; he and CORNELIUS FITZPATRICK were tithables (1702) in BERTIE 3-85; lived at ALLIGATOR (1709) where he died that year and left will in which he named a son CORNELIUS 1-44.

FITZPATRICK, CORNELIUS, will (1715) related to the WHEDBEE family 1-44; tithable (1702) in BERTIE 3-85; one was a son of BRYAN FITZPATRICK 1-44.

FITZPATRICK, ISAAC, mentioned in will of JOHN LUDFORD (1735) 1-57; one ISAAC married MARY BATEMAN (1796) 3-442.

FLATTY CREEK was located in PASQUOTANK COUNTY not far from NEW BEGUN Creek 3-266.

FLEETWOOD, ASHLEY, witnessed the will of JOHN WHITEMAN (1831) 3-362.

FLEETWOOD FAMILY. Wills 2-334, 2-513.

FLEETWOOD, GEORGE, called son of ASHLEY FLEETWOOD, married PARTHENIA MEWBORN by (1824) 3-343.

FLEETWOOD, HARDY, married SARAH REDDITT by (1804) 2-543

FLEETWOOD, WILLIAM, will (1792) had sons WILLIAM, JOHN, HENRY and ASHLEY and daughters 2-335; paid tuition of NATHAN ASHLEY (1770) in BERTIE 3-448; named guardian of MARY PARROTT (1749) 2-633; Executor of JACOB BARCOT (PARROTT?) (1738) 1-66.

FLEMING, JAMES. His widow MARY sold land in (1717) 1-299; and to JAMES BIRD the same year 1-399; he witnessed deed to EDWARD HOWCOTT (1716) 1-293;another(?) JAMES FLEMING and wife MARY deed to JAMES MAGIOHON (1720) 2-454; JAMES FLEMING deed to NICEODAS CRISP and JOHN JORDAN (1720)2-457; the first JAMES witnessed deed (1716) to WALTER DRAUGHAN by THOMAS GARRETT SR. 1-298; JAMES FLEMING and wife MARGARET to JOHN CHAMPION (1720) 2-608.

FLEMING, MARY, married STEPHEN WILEY (1761) 3-412.

FLETCHER, ELIZABETH, married SAMUEL PASSONS in (1695) 3-407; she was born in (1675) 3-206

FLETCHER FAMILY. Wills 3-333; births 3-206.
                                              3-383
FLETCHER, GEORGE, married SUSAN BURTONSHALL (1701) 3-409.

FLETCHER, MARGARET, daughter of RALPH (1784) 3-171.

FLETCHER, RALPH, of PERQUIMANS was born in (1632) 2-298; his wife was ELIZABETH 3-214, 3-215, 3-409; he was a member of the court of PERQUIMANS (1688) 3-429.

FLETCHER, RALPH, JR. married JANE MORGAN in (1698) 3-408; they had son RALPH born in (1703) 3-374; son JOSHUA born (1718)3-383

FLETCHER, SARAH, daughter of RALPH and ELIZABETH born (1681) 3-311.

FLETCHER, THOMAS bought land from EPHRAIM BLANCHARD in (1711) 1-297; he died and left will (1734) 1-43.

FLOOD, NICHOLAS, mentioned in will of WILLIAM SAVAGE (1780) also DR. SAMUEL DICKINSON of NORTH CAROLINA 2-28.

FLOOD, DR. WILLIAM and his sons NICHOLAS and WILLIAM mentioned in will of WILLIAM SAVAGE of CHOWAN COUNTY (1780) 2-28.

FLOYD, JOHN, will (1809). His wife was JEMIMA and he mentions TITUS MOORE 2-513.

FLOYD, RANDALL, will (1818) names children and wife RACHEL 2-513.

FLOYD, THOMAS. Joseph Hughes administered on his estate in BERTIE (1767) 3-443.

FOARD, ALEXANDER, qualified as Register for BERTIE COUNTY (1767) 3-443.

FOARD, ELIAS, was an orphan of JOHN FOARD & tuition turned over to SAMUEL MILBURN (1771) 3-450.

FODDY, THOMAS, married ELIZABETH HARMON in (1698) 3-408.

FOLGER, BARZILLA, Master of sloop HEPSEBETH (1749) 1-434.

FOLK, SARAH, will (1734) was SARAH MHOON 2-513

FOLK, WILLIAM (spelled FOULK) of NANSEMOND County, Va. deed (1716) THOMAS JORNIGAN & RICHARD TAYLOR witnesses 1-298.

FONVILLE, JOHN, of CRAVEN COUNTY, will (1741) names sons JOHN, PETER, DAVID and ISAAC, Wm. WHITFORD, Exr. 1-133.

FOOTE FAMILY. Related to the BONNERS OF BEAU- FORT and their genealogy included together 2-115 to 2-120.

FORBES, JAMES, his headright and that of ALICE his wife assigned to ISAAC GUILFORD (1701) 2-300.

FORDICE FAMILY. Children of GEORGE FORDICE and wife MARY 3-146.

FORDYCE, GEORGE, land grant (1694) next to NICH- OLAS SIMONS 1-4; proved his rights (1700) 1-612, 3-146; GEORGE JR. sold land to THOM- AS HORTON, which his father GEORGE had sold to NICHOLAS SIMONS (1715) Rebecca Pierce and MARY SIMONS mentioned 1-293; GEORGE of CHOW- AN, his nearest kin (1713) was WILLIAM HOU- GHTON 1-44; sold land to NICHOLAS SIMMONS (1698) in Chowan 1-626.

FOREHAND, ANN, married ELIJAH OVERTON in (1785) 3-418.

FOREHAND, BENJAMIN married MARTHA HALSEY (1783) 3-417.

FOREHAND, DANIEL married JEMIMA EVERIDGE (1791) 3-422; son of DANIEL left will (1784) whose wife was SARAH, JOSEPH WHITE and ELIZABETH ROUNDTREE witnesses 3-171. (Mentions EZEKI- EL HOLLOWELL).

FOREHAND, JOHN witness to marriage of THOMAS FOREHAND, SR. (1844) 2-93.

FOREHAND, SARAH, daughter of ELIAS STAILINGS of (1778) will 3-187; another SARAH FOREHAND a daughter of JEREMIAH EVERTON (1736) 1-42.

FOREHAND, THOMAS, SR. married CATHERINE HOLLO - WELL (1844) JOHN FOREHAND a witness, CHOWAN 2-93.

FOREHAND, WILLIAM T. married ELIZABETH TWINE in CHOWAN (1862) 2-415.

FOREMAN, BENJAMIN, SR. deed to MATTHEW SOLEAR - (SHOWLAR?) next to ROBERT SHARER (1717) JOHN DIER (DEW?) a witness; also deed to JOHN BLACKBURN next to ROBERT SHARER (1717) with JOHN DEW a witness 1-300.

FOREMAN, WILLIAM, witnessed will of WILLIAM DAN- IEL (1740) 1-198.

FORSTER, DIANA (FOSTER?) married THOMAS WHITE by (1694) in ALBEMARLE 1-611.

FORSTER, EDWARD, father in law of SETH SOUTHEL 3-31.

FORSTER, FRANCIS, met with ASSEMBLY (1708) with THOMAS CARY 1-454.

FORSTER, ROBERT, appointed CLERK OF CHOWAN in (1731) 1-449; he and JOHN JONES witness to deed (1728) from HENRY TO CHARLES KING in CHOWAN COUNTY 2-443; appointed Clerk of BER- TIE in (1744) 2-620; licensed to practice as attorney (1733) 1-450.

FORT, BENJAMIN, deed to BOON (1721) 2-616.

FORT, GEORGE, will in (1719) with ELIAS FORT his executor 1-44.

FORT, JOHN, will (1745) mentions his son AR- THUR FORT 1-43.

FOSCUE, JOHN, of HYDE will (1751) wife named ABIGAIL and children 1-211.

FOSCUE, SIMON, of HYDE, will (1751), eldest son RICHARD 1-211; man of this name among the inhabitants of MATCHAPUNGO when ROBERT DAN- IEL was Governor 2-193.

FOSTER, CHARLES, made deed to RICHARD LEWIS and THOMAS BETTERLY in form of Power of Attorney (1719) 1-627; he and EDWARD FOS- TER witness to deed (1716) 1-619; made power of attorney to JOHN LOVICK (1718) 1-627.

FOSTER, DIANA, the widow of WILLIAM FOSTER mar- ried THOMAS WHITE 3-245; this the same as DIANA FORSTER 1-611.

FOSTER, EDWARD witnessed deed with CHARLES FOSTER made by LAWRENCE McGUE (McGEE?) (1716) 1-619; this probably the same as FORSTER 3-31.

FOSTER, FRANCIS, associated with WILLIAM GLOV- ER and others (1708) 3-261; a later one left will (1819) 3-333; first one signed proclamation with WILLIAM GLOVER 3-261; his wife was FRANCES in (1715) names his children 3-383; brought suit against ANTHONY DAWSON (1689) 3-431; the one of ACCOMAC COUNTY, Va., son of WILLIAM FOSTER and wife Margaret, married MRS. HANNAH GOSBY (1694) 3-407; signed order of adjournment of the Assembly (1713) 3-228; the later one was called brother by ELIZABETH GOODMAN in her will (1836) 3-335.

FOSTER, GEORGE, was 60 years old in (1690) 1-139.

FOSTER, HANNAH will (1727) George GORDON her executor 1-43

FOSTER, JAMES, will (1725) wife was HANNAH 1-43.

FOSTER, COL. JOHN, consigned goods to Madam ANNA SOUTHEL 3-254; one married ANN WIL - LIAMS in Perquimans (1689) 3-203; he re- ceived land grant (1694) 1-4; children of JOHN and wife ELIZABETH born 3-371.

FOSTER, MARY, will of (1806), BENJAMIN PENDLE- TON and SALLIE PENDLETON witnesses 3-332.

FOSTER, NANCY, of EDENTON, will (1783) men - tions her mother ANN WILLIAMS 1-544.

FOSTER, MAJ. RICHARD (1670) 3-470.

FOSTER, ROBERT, died (1696) at home of THOMAS CLARK 3-402; Robert of BERTIE died leav- ing will (1746) mentioned daughter ANN COT- TON and grand-daughter MARY BOON 1-43.

FOSTER, WILLIAM, of ACCOMAC County, Va. mar- ried MARGARET (1694) 3-407; but another WILLIAM FOSTER married DIANA HARRIS (1675) who is the DIANA HARRIS of this record 3-200; still a later WILLIAM had wife ANNE (1741) 3-383.

FOURKE, JOHN, will in (1729) 1-43.

FOURRE, PETER and JOHN FOURRE on the list of tythables East of Harvey's Creek to the W. side of FLATTY CREEK with ANTHONY MARKHAM and MAURICE CUNNINGHAM (no date) 3-253.

FOX, GEORGE, famous QUAKER, visits North Carolina (1672) 3-307.

FOX, JAMES, was father in law of JOSEPH HASSELL who married his daughter ANNE FOX. James FOX died 1754 2-296.

FOXWORTH, MOSES received land grant (1717) next to JOHN and THOMAS PARKER 1-17; he and wife MARTHA made deed to JAMES MAGLOHAN in (1721) 2-619; he received deed from ROBERT HICKS in (1716) 1-293.

FOY, DANIEL, was executor of FRANCIS FOY (1760) 2-297; died leaving will in CHOWAN in(1762) 1-543.

FOY, FRANCIS, appeared in CHOWAN-County (1756) 2-469; he died about (1760) 2-297.

FRALEY, WILLIAM, sued WILLIAM HANCOCK in(1702) in ALBEMARLE COUNTY 1-609.

FRANCIS, ELIZABETH, will (1844) 2-514.

FRAZIER, JERMIAH, will in CHOWAN (1798) had son RICHARD and others 1-543.

FRAZIER, THOMAS, will in CHOWAN (1773) wife MARGARET, daughter BARSHEBA. JOHN DARDEN a Witness 1-543.

FREEMAN, BENJAMIN sold land to JOHN BLACKBURN before (1719) 1-629.

FREEMAN FAMILY. Wills 2-512, 2-513, 2-333, 2-334 2-47; see will of JOSEPH SPEIGHT in GATES COUNTY (1792) 2-74.

FREEMAN, JAMES was orphan of WILLIAM FREEMAN & was looked after by SOLOMON FREEMAN of BERTIE (1771) 3-450.

FREEMAN, JOHN, bought land from GEORGE WHITE in (1729) 2-452; he and wife TABITHA, made deed to THOMAS FREEMAN (1737) with RICHARD TATUM and THOMAS ROUNDTREE 3-129; made deed to RICHARD WILSON (1719) 1-629; he made will in (1729) 1-43; another JOHN made will in(1776) 1-543;

FREEMAN, JOHN JR., made deed to JAMES SUMNER in (1740) of land given him by JOHN FREEMAN, SR. 3-135; bought lands from the Indians (1733) with ROBERT HICKS a witness 2-609; received land grant (1749) on BENNETT'S CREEK 1-20;he and HUMPHREY HARDY sureties on ALEX NOARD'S bond as Register of BERTIE COUNTY(1767)3-444.

FREEMAN, JOSIAH, guardians of the orphans of JOHN CAIL, of BERTIE (1771) 3-450.

FREEMAN, MOSES, looked after the tuition of JOHN, orphan of JOHN FANNY, ten years old 3-444.

FREEMAN, RICHARD, will in CHOWAN (1761) sons AMOS and DEMPSEY FREEMAN 1-543.

FREEMAN, SOLOMON, looked after tuition of the orphan WILLIAM FREEMAN (1771) 3-450.

FREEMAN, THOMAS, bought land from JOHN FREEMAN (1737) 3-129.

FREEMAN, WILLIAM, of CHOWAN, will (1736) son AARON and other children 1-211; bought land from THOMAS GARNETT SR. (1716) 1-625; witnessed deed by JOHN ARLENE and wife MARY (1731) 2-450; one WILLIAM will (1824) had daughter MARY COPELAND 2-512.

FRENCH, RICHARD, will (1712) related to JOHN OLD 1-44.

FRIAR, SION, will (1795) mentions brother WILLIS COOPER 2-335.

FRILEY, WILLIAM, deed to THOMAS EVANS and MATT ADAMS (1720) 2-615.

FROMAN, JOHN, with JOHN HARRIS, witnessed deed by THOMAS BRAY (1718) 1-622, 1-623.

FROST, WILLIAM, deed to MARTIN CROMINS (1721) witnessed by ALEX BARRON and WILLIAM LATIMORE 2-618; left will (1717) 1-44; deed to JAMES FROST (1717) 1-298.

FROTHINGTON, SAMUEL wife MARY (1706) 3-377.

FRUGEEFF, JAMES, married MARTHA POOL (1694) in HENRICO COUNTY 3-409.

FRY, CATHERINE, will 2-334; wife of WILLIAM FRY of BERTIE (1770) 3-448.

FRY, THOMAS, family related to DR. PATRICK MAULE note 1-210; left will(1724) 1-478.

FRYER, RICHARD, witnessed deed by WILLIAM JONES (1719) 1-627; WILLIAM FRYER 3-132.

FRYLEY, WILLIAM and wife GRACE deed to BENJAMIN BLOUNT (1716) 1-291.

FULLINGTON, JOHN, to WILLIAM BURCH of KING & QUEEN COUNTY Va. (1733) 3-131.

FULLINGTON, ROBERT and RICHARD FULLINGTON were granted lands sold by HENRY JONES in year (1728) 2-447.

FOSCUE FAMILY. This name does not appear prolifically on these records, but it belongs to one of the really old families of North Carolina. FREDERICK FOSCUE, in 1806, LEWIS FOSCUE in 1818, NATHAN FOSCUE in 1832, 1833 and 1834 served in the Legislature of the old North State from down in JONES COUNTY, according to JOHN HILL WHEELER'S records. Hon. Frederick F. Foscue, of this family, removed to COOSA COUNTY, Alabama, and in 1849 was elected to the House of Representatives; he then married and removed to MARENGO COUNTY, where in 1853 he was again elected to represent the people. Very soon thereafter he moved to Texas and settled and was almost immediately chosen as a Representative from his district to the Texas House, where he voted for the ordinance of Sececession, offered his services to the South and fought gallantly to his death. Here was an honored descendant of old SIMON FOSCUE of Hyde, who lived in the turbulent times of ROBERT DANIEL and THOMAS CARY. His descendants are to this day, upright citizens of the Great Commonwealth he selected as his home.

GAFFIS, ARTHUR, will (1729) mentions friend JAS. WINWRIGHT 1-45.

GAINES, REBECCA, daughter of MORDECAI WHITE who left will (1776) in BERTIE; she and JESSE HARDY were his executors 3-362.

GALE, CHRISTOPHER, with JAMES BLOUNT and others appointed JUSTICE of GENERAL COURT in (1712) 3-267; received land grant near EDENTON now ROPE WALK (1728) 1-12; was Chief Justice in (1724) 1-445; met with General Court at home of RICHARD SANDERSON (1715) at home of CAPT. JOHN HECKLEFIELD (1712) 2-148; his first wife was SARAH LAKER, the widow of GOV. THOMAS HARVEY 1-45, see also 3-220; gave power of Attorney to FREDERICK JONES and JOHN DRINK - WATER (1716) 1-297; in his will (1734) mentions his wife's former husband JOHN ISMAY 1-45; he lived and died on his plantation near the town of EDENTON 1-45.

GALE, EDMUND, was brother of CHRISTOPHER GALE - 1-45; was Justice of the General Court East of Cape Fear 2-298; WILLIAM LEWIS was guardian of his orphans (1741) 1-457; commissions issued to him and THOMAS POLLOCK in (1725) signed by J. LOVICK 2-131, 2-132; land grant on MATACOMACK CREEK (1728) 1-12; bought home in EDENTON from ORLANDO CHAMPION (1734) 1-109 his wife was MARY and he left will (1738) & named sons EDMUND and ROGER 1-45; see 2-639.

GALE, JOHN, was Master of the sloop POLLY (1774) which cleared for JAMAICA 1-436.

GALE, MILES, was son of CHRISTOPHER GALE (1734) 1-45; deed by him (1729) JOSEPH ANDERSON & JAMES POTTER, witnesses 3-447; he had son MILES GALES (1747) 2-467; ELIZABETH CLAYTON was the latter's guardian (1737) 1-448; she was his aunt 1-45.

GALE, PENELOPE, was daughter of CHRISTOPHER GALE 1-45 (She married LITTLE, and had daughter PENELOPE).

GALE, SARAH, with PATRICK MAULE witnessed deed by JONATHAN WHITE at EDENTON (1723) 2-443.

GALLEY, JOHN, will in EDENTON (1729) 1-45.

GALLOWAY, THOMAS, related in some way to ROBERT ROGERS whose will (1736) mentions 1-69.

GAMMON, HENRY, servant of SIR RICHARD EVERARD (1725) makes oath relating to Ex Governor BURRINGTON'S conduct 3-230.

GANLETT, PETER, an INDIAN was dead (1702) THOMAS POLLOCK administrator 1-45.

GANNIN, CHARLES deeded lands to WILLIAM SCOTT in (1736) witnessed by WILLIAM WHITFIELD and ISAAC WILLIAMS 3-130.

GARFOOT, GREGORY will (1702) mentions uncle WILLIAM PARGITER 1-45.

GARGANUS, ELIAS ALEXANDER, proved his rights in (1702) in ALBEMARLE PRECINCT 1-611.

GARGANUS, FRANCIS was a headright of NICHOLAS TYLER about (1697) 2-299; had JOHN BIRD'S headright assigned to him (1702) 1-614.

GARDNER, JAMES, will in BERTIE (1790) 2-335.

GARDNER, JOHN and RICHARD WESSON witnessed deed by ABRAHAM SANDERS (1734) 2-610.

GARDNER, MARTIN, died leaving will in BERTIE (1760) 1-44; he and his wife ANN deeded lands to JOHN WILLIAMS in (1718) 1-622; another one left will (1784) in BERTIE, had son BRYAN GARDNER 2-335.

GARDNER, WILLIAM, and his wife MARTHA sold land to LUKE WHITE they had bought of JAMES WILLIAMS and his wife ELIZABETH (1737) 3-127; he and JOHN GARDNER were witnesses to a deed (1734) 2-611.

GARRETT, DANIEL and his wife SARAH sold land on CONABY CREEK to JOHN BALL (1713) 1-102; called brother of ANN CHESSON (1727) 1-38; another one's lands in BERTIE divided in (1807) among children named 1-449. (DAVID)

GARRETT, EVERARD married ELIZABETH FREEMAN in (1808) in BERTIE 2-378.

GARRETT FAMILY, wills 1-546.

GARRETT, ELLENER, married MOSES BAKER 1-449.

GARRETT, HUMPHREY, deceased (1752) WILLIAM WILSON, administrator 1-451.

GARRETT, ISABEL, married THOMAS CALLOWAY in (1728) 3-410.

GARRETT, JOHN, executor of will of JANE HAMBLETON (1733) 1-49; administrator of JOHN HAMBLETON and wife JANE (1734) 1-450.

GARRETT, MARY, will (1796) names several grand children. Solomon HENDRICKS witness 3-172; another MARY'S will in BERTIE (1820) 2-515.

GARRETT, SARAH was grand-daughter of WILLIAM RHODES (1753) 1-69.

GARRETT, THOMAS land grant on line between GATES and CHOWAN (Catherine's Creek) (1697) 1-5; he and wife THOMASINE made deed to JOHN GOODWIN (1722) 3-144; witnessed RICHARD BERRYMAN deed (1732) 2-451; sold land to THOMAS HOBBS (1718) witnessed by JAMES GOODWIN 1-625; made deed to RICHARD BERRYMAN (1717) 1-299; another land grant on Catherine's Creek (1701) 1-8; left will in (1733) 1-45; after his death his son THOMAS was called "SR". (?).

GARRETT, THOMAS, JR. (1718) land grant on the WARWICK SWAMP 1-8; he may have been the one whose wife was THOMASINE 1-625; THOMAS GARRETT Sr. and wife BETHEA deed witnessed by THOMAS ROUNDTREE (1716) 1-298; made deed to WILLIAM FREEMAN (1716) 1-625; THOMAS SR and wife BETHEA to THOMAS JR. (1719) 1-628; he and wife BETHEA to THOMAS GODDIN (1715) witnessed by STEPHEN DUDLEY 2-288; one was Justice for CHOWAN PRECINCT (1731) 1-449; THOMAS JR. mentioned about (1715) 3-237; THOMAS SR. and wife BETHEA deed witnessed by CHRISTOPHER DUDLEY and JOHN GODDIN 2-287.

GARRETT, WILLIAM, bought land (1723) from ZACH NIXON 2-608.

GARRISH, EDWARD, left will in PERQUIMANS COUNTY (1827), names wife CATHERINE, and mentions JONATHAN WHITE, son of JOSIAH WHITE witnessed by DAVID and ROBERT WHITE 3-335.

GARRISH, JAMES, will (1834) 3-335.

GARLAND, THOMAS sued SAMUEL SPRUILL (1721)1-444

GARLAND, H. M. S. Bill of Expenses in saving stores from 3-154.

GARNETT, RALPH, of PASQUOTANK owned lands in (1704) 1-303.

GASCOIGNE, WILLIAM, petition relating to a road to HOSKIN'S MILL and BLOUNT'S BRIDGE about (1694) 3-245; served on jury in ALBEMARLE (1702) 1-610.

GASKILL, JANE, widow to ROBERT WINDLEY made a deed (1707) to JOSEPH JORDAN 1-291.

GASKINS FAMILY. Wills in BERTIE 2-514, 2-515.

GASKINS, WILLIAM, sued HENRY PALIN in ALBEMARLE PRECINCT (1697) 1-611. (This name probably GASCOIGNE. WSR).

GATES COUNTY and HERTFORD. Petition of HENRY BAKER to establish a ferry between (1725) 3-451.

GATLIN, EDWARD, will in CRAVEN COUNTY in(1725) 1-45.

GATLIN FAMILY. Wills 2-50, 2-51.

GATLIN, JOHN, mentioned in will of HENRY GEORGE (1711) 1-46.

GATLIN, WILLIAM, was a witness with CHARLES MORRIS in (1734) 2-453.

GAVIN, CHARLES of CHOWAN, and wife MARY 1-617; bought land from RICHARD HOWCOTT and wife ELLENER (1718) 1-627; witnessed deed from THOMAS ROGERS and wife (1716) 1-294.

GAYLORD, THOMAS, bought land from JOHN DAVENPORT (1719) 2-457.

GEE, CHARLES, deceased father in (1716) of JAMES GEE, of SURRY CO. VA. 1-296.

GEE, JAMES (of SURRY COUNTY, VA.) deeded to WILLIAM BRIDGES, of ISLE OF WIGHT COUNTY, VA. (1716) a patent he had heired from his father CHARLES GEE 1-296.

GENERAL COURT. Members of appointed by CHRISTOPHER GALE, Chief Justice 3-284.

GEORGE, HENRY, his sister's eldest son was JOHN GATLIN (1711) and her youngest son was WILLIAM MITCHELL, JR. 1-46.

GERKIN, ZACARIAH, was son in law of NATHANIEL EVERITT (or AVERITT) in (1718) 1-619; he witnessed deed to THOMAS LEE (1716)1-297

GERMACK, PATRICK, was related to the CRUIKSHANK FAMILY, his will (1708) 1-45.

GIBBS, HENRY, died (1744) widow SUSANNAH 2-620; his estate divided by LUKE MIZELL, COL. ROBERT WEST and ROGER SNELL (1744) 2-622; his widow had married JOHN SAVAGE by (1746) 2-627.

GIBBS, CAPT. JOHN, was Governor (1689) by seizure of the office 2-197; petition for his removal (he lived in CURRITUCK) signed by WILLIAM ALLEN, BEN LAKER and others 3-56

GIBLE, MARY was wife of ED HARWOOD and ARTHUR MABSON 2-303.

GIBLIN, SARAH will (1805) mentions "NORFLEET HARRIS' three children" 2-514.

GIBSON, ELINER died intestate (1713) & JOHN BLISH was guardian of her children 1-46.

GIBSON FAMILY. Wills 1-545.

GIBSON, GIDEON, bought land (1721) from WILLIAM MAULE and wife PENELOPE next to WILLIAM JONES 2-617.

GIBSON, JAMES, will (1765) mentions kinsman WILLIAM BARCLIFT 3-171.

GIBSON, SAMUEL, will (1802) had five children not named, wife ABIGAIL 3-333.

GIDDON, BENJAMIN, and wife JOHANNA in (1695) 3-368.

GILBERT, JOSEPH in (1720) owned lands next to EDWARD STANDING and JOHN DAVIS 2-613; was probably the same land he owned in (1728) on Queen Anne's Creek 2-446; land granted him in (1712) was next to THOMAS HOSKINS 1-6; one of the name had land grant early as (1680) 1-3; patented lands (1729) that had been sold by WILLIAM ARKILL to WILLIAM BRANCH (1737) 3-129; a later JOSEPH left will (1806), wife PATSY and JOSHUA WHITE executors 3-334.

GILBERT, FRANCIS, will (1725) 1-46.

GILBERT, THOMAS was granted land (1711) on ROCKYHOCK NECK 1-7; and (1715) on CHINKAPIN SWAMP 1-15; lands on CHOWAN RIVER joined EDWARD MOSELEY 1-13; his wife was MARY and they sold to SAMUEL WOODWARD (1713) 1-99, 1-100.

GILLCREST, JOHN, one of petitioners to KING in (1680) from ALBEMARLE PRECINCT 3-51.

GILES, JOHN, and wife PHILANTA (of Isle of WIGHT COUNTY, Va.) sold land (1701) to LEWIS WILLIAMS, which had been granted to THOMAS WOODWARD (father of his wife PHILARITE —Boddie p. 130 - who was daughter of THOMAS WOODWARD)1-92.

GILES, MATTHEW, will (1713) mentions RICHARD DAVENPORT and JAMES MINGE 1-46.

GILL, SARAH, will (1839) mentions children & son JAMES GILL executor 2-515.

GILLIAM, ELIZABETH, married JOHN H. PUGH in (1803) Bertie 2-376.

GILLIAM FAMILY. Wills 2-515.

GILLIAM, HENRY, witness with THOMAS D. MARTIN to will of DANIEL GORDON (1813) in MANCHESTER, Va. 3-335; he left will in (1835) 2-51.

GILLIAM, HINCHA, will (1798) mentions wife ANN, William Creecy and ISAAC BARBER 3-333.

GILLIAM, JOHN R. witness to will (1845) of MARGARET TAYLOE 2-549; see 2-498.

GILLIAM, MOSES, witness to the will of FRANCIS SOWELL (1795) who mentions his wife TAMER and children 2-357; his own will 2-515.

GILLIAM, SAMUEL (Spelled GUILLAMS) bought land from JONATHAN KITTRELL (1719) "mentioned in my patent", JOHN WILLIAMSON and ROBERT HICK witnesses 1-630; witnessed deed of JAMES RIDDICK to ANDREW HAMBLETON (1726) land by ABRAHAM ODOM 2-293.

GILLIAM, THOMAS, married SARAH WOOLARD and she married second EDWARD SMITHWICK by (1703) 1-612; was mentioned in will of WILLIAM STEVENS (1695) 1-74; mentioned in petition of EDWARD and JOHN SMITHWICK 3-79; he and wife SARAH file petition in regard to land in CHOWAN, adjoining spot where first church was erected 3-80, 1-87, 1-613; he was on jury in ALBEMARLE (1702) 1-610; he patents 560 acres on EDENTON BAY (1697) 1-5.

GILLIAM, WILLIAM, will (1827) mentions cousin BENJAMIN FOLK and WILLIAM J. GILLIAM 2-515.

GILLIAM, ZACHARIAH (in LONDON, ENGLAND) will (1678) 1-45.

GLAISTER, JOSEPH, with GABRIEL NEWBY, executor of will of MARY HAIG (1718) 1-51; was brother of MARY TOMS (1713) 1-79; died leaving will (1718) mentions cousin THOMAS PALIN 1-46.

GLAISTER, MARY, of PASQUOTANK, will (1740) mentions various connections of the GLAISTER FAMILY, including SARAH HUNNICUT (which proves that this was the Virginia GLAISTER FAMILY from which sprang GLAISTER HUNNICUT WSR) 1-217.

GLASGOW, ELIZABETH wife of ROBERT 3-366.

GLEANINGS IN ENGLAND relating to N. C. FAMILIES 3-463 to 3-467.

GLISTEN, DANIEL, will (1790) ARTHUR JARNIGAN a witness 2-335.

GLISTEN, JAMES, will (1781) had brother DANIEL GLISTEN and others 2-335.

GLISTEN FAMILY. Wills 2-335.

GLISTON, JOHN (spelled GLISSON) will (1734) 1-46.

GLOVER, CATHERINE, widow of GOV. WILLIAM GLOVER, married TOBIAS KNIGHT 1-56, 1-637.

GLOVER, CHARLES WORTH, appears in the INDIAN war (1711-1712) 1-637; he was imprisoned by EMANUEL CLEAVES in BATH COUNTY about this same time 3-269; born (1688)1-637.

GLOVER FAMILY. History of and connection with DAVIS and BLOUNT family 1-637; GLOVER FAMILY wills in Bertie 2-515. (NOT GLOVER).

GLOVER, JOSEPH was witness to power of attorney by JOHN WEBSTER and others of HAMPTON VIRGINIA (1714) 1-296.

GLOVER, THOMAS, born (1685) apparent brother of CHARLES WORTH GLOVER born (1688) and of JOSEPH GLOVER born (1691) possibly the sons of GOVERNOR WILLIAM GLOVER, whose first marriage may have been with MARY DAVIS, a sister of ELIZABETH DAVIS who married JOHN BLOUNT, the parents of CHARLES WORTH BLOUNT 1-637, 1-460.

GLOVER, WILLIAM, President. Bill against him and THOMAS CARY, JOHN PORTER and FRANCIS FOSTER (1708) 3-261; he was a Justice in (1704) 3-440; witnessed appointment by WILLIAM LEE (1697) 3-248; his widow CATHERINE married TOBIAS KNIGHT 1-56; letter to him from THOMAS ABINGTON (1697) 3-53; accepts complaint from COL. JOHN HUNT 3-68; President of the Assembly and Lord Deputies in (1707) 1-457; brought suit against THOMAS HAUGHTON in ALBEMARLE (1702) 1-609; was a Clerk of the GENERAL COURT (1695) 3-301 & 3-35; he was deceased by (1712-13) 1-277, 1-215.

GOBSON, JAMES, his wife was MARY (1738)3-383.

GODBY, CARY, his wife was MARY, and as his widow (1720) deeded lands to THOMAS POLLOCK 2-613; he, himself sold lands to POLLOCK on SALMON CREEK (1717) witnessed by THOMAS WEST 1-617.

GODFREY, ELIZABETH was born (1652) 1-443; the births in family shown 3-219 and 3-209.

GODFREY, FRANCES, was daughter of WILLIAM & wife JANE (1689) 3-216.

GODFREY, HUGH, and RICHARD LEIGH were executors of will of JOSEPH GODFREY (1831) 3-335.

GODFREY, JOSEPH, will (1831) had sons HUGH & ZADOCK GODFREY 3-335.

GODFREY, THOMAS. His wife was ELLENER (1726) father of JOSEPH 3-384; he left will in (1774) 3-171

GODFREY, TULLEY, called son in will of MARY FOSTER (1806) 3-332.

GODLY, JOHN will (1731) 1-46.

GODDIN, JOHN, witnessed deed by THOMAS GARRETT SR. in (1715) with CHRISTOPHER DUDLEY 2-287

GODDIN, WILLIAM, appointed Justice of Peace in BERTIE with others (1749) 2-632.

GODWIN, COL. THOMAS and MAJ. LEWIS BURWELL Executors of JOHN LEAR, sue THOMAS POLLOCK 3-254.

GOLDSMITH, DANIEL was tobacco inspector at EDENTON (1759) 2-299.

GOLFE, EDWARD was headright of JOHN DANN in (1680) 3-300.

GOLLAND, MARY, of WILMINGTON, will (1766) mentions JOHN BUROWIN 1-45.

GONSOLVO, ELIZABETH, had daughter ELIZABETH PARKER (1685) 3-435.

GONSOLVO, LAWRENCE married (1693) daughter of JOHN JOHNSON 1-54.

GOODALL, GILBERT (spelled GOODALE here)will (1712) mentions GEORGE DURANT SR. 1-46.

GOODALL, JOHN, married daughter of ROBERT BOND 1-29.

GOODALL, JOSEPH, was witness to a deed executed by ANTHONY ALEXANDER (1716) to JOSHUA WALES 1-621.

GOODBEE, CARY (Undoubtedly the same as CARY GODBY heretofore mentioned) deeded lands to JAMES WILKINSON (1716) joining Col. THOMAS POLLOCK 1-520.

GOODING, ANN, will in GATES COUNTY (1805) JOHN VANN a witness and BEASLEY grandchildren mentioned 2-50.

GOODLAT, ALEXANDER, will (1710) 1-46.

GOODMAN, ELIZABETH will (1837) mentions brother FRANCIS FOSTER and children 3-335.

GOODMAN FAMILY. Wills of WILLIAM (1780) HENRY (1778) JOEL (1795) HENRY (1817) MARY (1823) also (1847) WILLIAM (1839) and BARNES GOODMAN (1862). 2-48, 2-49.

GOODWIN, CALEB, will (1819) 3-334.

GOODWIN FAMILY. Wills 1-546, 3-333, 3-334.

GOODWIN, JACOB will (1803) wife PEACHA and son CALEB 3-333, 3-334.

GOODWIN, JOHN he and wife MARY sold lands next to CHRISTOPHER DUDLEY (1715) 2-288.

GOODWIN, MOSES, with JOHN GOODWIN and EDWARD WHITE (1734?) witness deed of EPAPRODITUS BRINKLEY, of PERQUIMANS 2-610.

GORDON, ELIZABETH, was wife of MARMADUKE NORFLEET who died (1750) in NORTHAMPTON COUNTY N. C. 2-306; another ELIZABETH married EDWARD GREEN in CHOWAN COUNTY(1827) 1-359.

GORDON, BENJAMIN with JOHN GORDON, witnessed a deed from WILLIAM DOE to THOMAS BRAY (1716) in CHOWAN COUNTY 1-616.

GORDON, DANIEL, died leaving will (1812) MANCHESTER, VA. (Across the river from RICHMOND) 3-335

GORDON FAMILY. Wills 1-218, 2-49, 2-50, 3-335.

GORDON, GEORGE, wife FRANCES (1698) 3-377; was executor of HANNAH FOSTER (1727) 1-43; another of (1766) list of his children 3-263

GORDON, JACOB witnessed will of ABRAHAM NORFLEET, SR. in CHOWAN (1784) 2-13; probably grandson of JOHN GORDON of PERQUIMANS (1754) 1-44; will in GATES COUNTY (1817) 2-50.

GORDON, JOHN (printed JON) witnessed deed of ARTHUR KAVANAGH (1715) 2-289; he bought land from JOHN ROBINSON (1715) 2-290; was a neighbor of LAWRENCE McGUE in CHOWAN in (1716) 1-616; he and CHRISTOPHER DUDLEY witness to deed (1716) from JOHN WATSON to HENRY HILL 2-447, 1-292.

GORDON, JOHN N. witness to will (1824) of ELIZABETH HAYES 3-337.

GORDON, MARY mentioned in will (1792) of JOHN ROBINS as daughter 3-186; one was the widow of ROBERT GORDON (1736) 2-303.

GORDON, NATHANIEL, will in PERQUIMANS (1755) 1-44;another NATHANIEL will (1815) wife was MARY ANN, and GABRIEL BAILEY was one of the executors 3-335.

GORDON, PATRICK, attended Court in CHOWAN (no date) 1-446.

GORDON, ROBERT, married SARAH RAY (1769) 3-106; one ROBERT died (1736) and his widow MARY was executrix 2-303.

GORDON, SARAH, married STEPHEN NORFLEET; she the daughter of JOHN GORDON and MISS BAKER 2-635.

GORDON, WILLIAM, was son in law of JOHN DAVIS (1753) 1-40.

GRANT FAMILY. Wills 1-219.

GRADY, HENRY with URIAH JONES witnessed deed by STEPHEN LEE (1730) 2-449.

GRADY, WILLIAM deed (1718) to JAMES RUTLAND next to THOMAS JOHNSON 1-621.

GRAHAM, EBENEZER, will GATES COUNTY in(1795) had son JOHN BAKER GRAHAM and was brother in law of HENRY BAKER of Scotland Neck 2-51.

GRAINGER, EDWARD, sued RICHARD HARROLD year (1694) 2-465.

GRAINGER, JOSHUA, will in WILMINGTON (1741) names sons JOSHUA and CALEB GRAINGER 1-45.

GRAINGER, MARY, of NEW HANOVER, was sister of SARAH WALTERS 1-30.

GRANBERRY, JOSEPH, lived at the FOLLY in GATES COUNTY (1754) 1-453.

GRANBERRY, NANCY, will in GATES COUNTY (1836) had son GEORGE GORDON 2-51; she was daughter of ELIZABETH RUTLAND will (1831) 2-545.

GRANBERRY, SAMUEL, of BERTIE, will (1774)2-336.

GRANBERRY, PENELOPE, was the daughter of MOSES MOORE, will (1817), and had sister TABITHA MOORE, NELLY CULPEPPER and POLLY RUTLAND 2-531.

GRANBERRY, WILLIAM, and wife MARY of BERTIE (1771) 3-449.

GRANDIN, DANIEL, Clerk of the General Court in (1749) 2-305.

GRANVILLE, LORD, sent FRANCIS CORBIN from LONDON to lay off his lands (1744) 1-445; EDWARD MOSELEY appointed DEPUTY to represent his heirs 3-257.

GRAVES, RICHARD, will (1730) 1-219, 1-220.

GRAY, ALLEN, of ONSLOW, will (1765) 1-44.

GRAY, ANN, will (1731) with WILLIAM WALLACE Executor note 1-46; ANN of BERTIE (1770) THOMAS CLARK, administrator 3-448.

GRAY, MRS. CLARKY, nee GORDON, account of the family 3-121.

GRAY FAMILY. Wills of in BERTIE 2-514.

GRAY, GEORGE, of EDENTON will (1785) 1-546.

GRAY, JANET married REV. J. McKENZIE 2-603.

GRAY, JOHN, with WILLIAM BRAY, witnessed deed by JOHN BRYAN (1734) 2-454; joined JOHN BLOUNT in signing bond for THOMAS WHITMELL as Sheriff of BERTIE (1745) 2-628; sold land to JOHN CHERRYDIME adjoining JAMES BOON and WILLIAM MAULE (1719) 2-454; ANNE GRAY, wife of JOHN GRAY, probably daughter of LEWIS BRYAN and ELIZABETH HUNTER, and was born (1697) 1-577; in (1720) he witnessed deed of NATHAN HOLLY and wife JEAN to BARNABY McKINNIE 1-469; was Deputy Collector under JOHN BLOUNT of CHOWAN about (1722) 1-445; foreman of Grand Jury for BERTIE COUNTY (1746) 2-628; one JOHN GRAY Captain in 3rd Regiment N. C. Continental Line 1-413; an early JOHN GRAY had wife TABITHA (1701) 3-409; one married ANNE BRYAN (as above) 2-602; the latter were the ancestors of HENRY CLAY 1-473; JOHN GRAY and wife TABITHA 3-214; witnessed deed to lands next to PETER EVANS and JAMES BOON (1718) died leaving will in BERTIE in(1750) children JOHN, WILLIAM, ANN, BARBARA, JANET McKENZIE, LUCRETIA, AMELIA and LOUISA 1-45.

GRAY, PETER, sold land to JOHN EDWARDS in(1718) 1-622; sold tract of land adjoining JAMES BOON (1719) to JOHN ODOM, JR. 2-608; with MARY GRAY and ROBERT ANDERSON (1719) witnessed deed of ROBERT MOORE 1-629; in(1692) witnessed deed of ROBERT WHITE to HENDERSON WALKER 1-297; in (1711) was exempted from maintaining bridge over BLACK WALNUT RUN 3-441; witnessed deed by DAVID BLAKE, PERQUIMANS, to ROBERT BEASLEY in (1687) 3-433.

GRAY, PRISCILLA, was the daughter of THOMAS GREGORY, of Pasquotank (1740) 1-45.

GRAY, STEPHEN (Spelled STEVENS) will (1796) was son of WILLIAM GRAY, mentions JOSEPH BLOUNT and was "brother" of WILLIAM LEE 2-336.

GRAY, THOMAS, married SARAH BEASLEY (1701)3-409

GRAY, WILLIAM, will (1799) mentions daughter ANN BLOUNT and others 2-514; he and WILLIAM MAULE witness deed to THOMAS WHITMELL (1720) 2-614; sold lands to JAMES TURNER (1721) and also to JOHN BRYAN 2-140; he & JAMES BLOUNT mentioned in will of LOVICK WORLEY (1754) 1-80.

GRAVES, JAMES (spelled GREAVES) Master sloop RUTH (1755) 1-435.

GREEN, BARNEFOLD, of near OCCOCOK INLETT, submits petition (no date, but very early) 3-87; is mentioned as headright of NICHOLAS TYLER (1697) 2-299; died leaving will in BATH (1711) mentions daughter in law ANN SMITHWICK 1-46.

GREEN, HENRY, of CRAVEN, called the son of HENRY PARKER (1734) 1-56.

GREEN, JOHN, was brother in law of JOHN BOBBITT (1718) 1-623, 1-524; bought land of RALPH MASON (1714) 1-529; and from MATTHEW STURDIVANT (1716) 1-295; witnessed deed with HENRY BAKER (1729) 2-451; deed to THOS CHARLES (1721) 2-518; wife was ANNA 2-517; witnessed deed with THOMAS SMITH to WILLIAM LOVE 1-623; and with JAMES HINTON in (1732) 2-454; will BLADEN (1749) 1-218.

GREEN, MOSES, proves will of WILLIAM WESTON (1748) 2-631.

GREEN, RICHARD, bought land from JOHN ALSTON (1733) 2-610; left will naming his children (1742) 1-218.

GREEN, ROBERT, bought land from THOMAS AVENT and wife ELIZABETH, on MORATTUCK RIVER at MOUNT ROYAL (1716) 1-295.

GREEN, JACOB, of BATH will (1752) no children of his own, mentions brothers, etc. 1-218.

GREEN, THOMAS, was brother of JACOB GREEN & had son RICHARD GREEN (1752) 1-218.

GREEN, SAMUEL, together with WILLIAM STEWARD bought land from JOHN EDLIN adjoining JAMES PERISHO (1678) 3-434.

GREEN, SUSANNAH, of BATH, will (1735) names her own BIGGS CHILDREN and others 1-45.

GREEN, THOMAS (the brother of JACOB above) list of children (1758) 2-263; another THOMAS left will (1760) names other children and daughter in law HANNAH GREEN & son in law BENJAMIN HOOKER, and wife ELIZABETH 2-335, 2-336.

GREEN, WALTER, married DEBORAH CHASTON (This is probably CHASTAIN) 3-202.

GREEN, WILLIAM, bought land from HENRY JONES (1713-1716) being part of JONES patent & at MOUNT ROYAL, where ROBERT GREEN bought land from THOMAS AVENT, who witnessed the instant deed 1-294.

GREENWOOD, FREDERICK, of EDENTON, left will (1852) wife MARGARET and WILLIAM H. HARRISON, CLERK, nephew CHARLES F. GREENWOOD, and brother MARTIN GREENWOOD of NORFOLK, VA. 1-547.

GREENWOOD, MARTIN, Norfolk, Virginia, was a brother of FREDERICK GREENWOOD, of EDENTON 1-547.

GREGORY, ABSILIA, daughter of BENJAMIN GREGORY (1827) and her aunt was DEBORAH WARD married ROUNDTREE 3-362.

GREGORY, BENJAMIN, married daughter of ABSILIA WARD, see will (1827) 3-362.

GREGORY FAMILY. Wills 1-545, 2-49; 3-335.

GREGORY, HOSEA, father of JOHN 3-335

GREGORY, DEMPSEY married MARY XELFE 2-297.

GREGORY, ISAAC will (1822) names children & wife and RICHARD LEIGH Executors 3-335.

GREGORY, JAMES, estate divided (1803) GATES COUNTY, mentions son in law JOSEPH DICKINSON and children 1-446.

GREGORY, JOHN, nephew of JOHN LEWERTON, of BERTIE (1740) 1-57.

GREGORY, LEMUEL, will in BERTIE (1845) mentions son DAVID and daughters, MARY, SEELY & MARGARET, also sons JOB, JAMES W. and wife MARGARET 2-516.

GREGORY, MARGARET (1721) daughter of THOMAS BABECOCK 1-32; of PASQUOTANK left will in (1753) daughters MARY HUMPHRIES and MARGARET BARBER 1-44; also 2-297.

GREGORY, LUKE. His wife was SARAH WILKINS in (1733) daughter of CHARLES WILKINS, CHOWAN 1-82; he is mentioned in will of JOB PRATT (1736) 1-66; he had daughter who married HENDERSON STANDING (1754) 2-469; he was deceased by (1745) and widow SARAH administered on his estate 1-455

GREGORY, PENNY married LAMB RAY (1831) 2-592.

GREGORY, PETER and wife LETITIA were PASQUO-TANK headrights (1701) 3-300.

GREGORY, RICHARD, of PASQUOTANK, left will in (1719) wife MARGARET (will 1753) 1-47; the son RICHARD GREGORY will in CURRITUCK (1758) mentions brother in law ISAAC BRIGHT 1-44.

GREGORY, THOMAS, will in PASQUOTANK (1740) mentions daughter PRISCILLA GRAY 1-45; another THOMAS left will (1712) had son LUKE 1-46; one THOMAS witnessed LANGLEY BILLUPS will (1829) 3-328.

GREGORY, SAMUEL, will in CHOWAN (1744) mentions sons SAMUEL, LUKE and THOMAS 1-216.

GREGORY, WILLIAM, of PASQUOTANK, will (1751) 1-216; another (1748) 1-44; another WILLIAM GREGORY married SARAH MOORE (1785) 3-418; the first WILLIAM had wife JUDITH left will (1753) 1-216.

GREGORY, WILLIS, son of WILLIAM (1751) wife was ELIZABETH 1-216.

GREY, JOHN married ELIZABETH RUTTER (1703) 3-410. (Probably GRAY).

GREY, RICHARD, of PERQUIMANS (1729) wife was ANN 1-46. (Probably GRAY).

GRIFFIN, EDWARD, will (1790) wife PENELOPE 2-336.

GRIFFIN, ELIZABETH, will (1824) HUMPHREY HARDY Executor 2-515.

GRIFFIN FAMILY. Wills 1-547, 3-334; 3-171.

GRIFFIN, JAMES, bought lands (1717) from THOMAS SPIVEY 1-300.

GRIFFIN, HUMPHREY 3-125.

GRIFFIN, JOHN deeded lands to WILLIAM PARKER (1736) on West side BENNETT'S CREEK 3-125.

GRIFFIN, MARTIN, will (1718) 1-46.

GRIFFIN, MICAJAH, witnessed will of ELISHA PENDER (1830) 2-536.

GRIFFIN, WILLIAM, wife MARY will (1735) 1-45.

GRIFFITH, JOHN will (1727) wife JEMIMAH 1-46.

GRILLS, RICHARD, witness to EDWARD MOSELEY deed (1718) 1-626; with ALEXANDER MARSHALL he executed Power of Attorney (1715) to JOHN HARDY 2-288; left will in BERTIE 1-46.

GRIMES, HUGH, was appointed Constable in BERTIE COUNTY (1744) 2-621.

GRIMES, SAMUEL will in BERTIE COUNTY (1783) names his wife PHEREBY and all his children; WILLIAM PUGH an executor, and the witnesses were WILLIAM and JESSE BRYAN and NOAH HINTON 2-336. (See note at bottom of same page cited).

GROSVENOR, SARAH, daughter of SARAH FALCONER (1744) 2-469.

GROSVENOR, WILLIAM, witnessed deed (1719) of WILLIAM to HENRY HAUGHTON 1-629; he died leaving will (1721) 1-46.

GROVER, JAMES SWINHOW one left will (1807) wife ELIZABETH, another left will (1817) wife ABSILA 2-515.

GUEST, JOHN, was member of jury in ALBEMARLE PRECINCT (1702) 1-610.

GUILFORD, GEORGE (Spelled GUILLIFORD) was witness to a deed by JOHN YELVERTON in (1731) 2-618.

GUILFORD, ISAAC and JOHN PETTINGER appear together on the record 2-299.

GUIRKEN, ZACHARIAH, was mentioned in the will of JOHN WALKER (1709) 1-83.

GULLIER, WILLIAM, was a godson of TIMOTHY McCARTY who died (1718) 1-63.

GUMMS, ABRAHAM, together with ABRAHAM JAMES was executor of the will of MATTHEW GUMMS in (1754) 1-455.

GUMS, JOHN (may have been GUMMS) appeared in Court at CHOWAN in (1749) 1-451.

GUMS, MATTHEW, of PERQUIMANS, was the son in law of RICHARD SKINNER, as mentioned in deed (1722) 2-145; in (1739) he and his wife ELIZABETH sold land to CHARLES McDOWELL next to lands of JAMES THIGPEN - 3-132.

GUMS, SARAH, was a sister of ELISHA GUMS, a grandson of RICHARD SKINNER, the emigrant to North Carolina 2-465.

GUNFALIS, LAWRENCE. His wife was SARAH and son JAMES was born (1684) 3-212; LAWRENCE died (1687) 3-564.

GUSTON, HENRY in (1739) deeded 350 acres of land which JOHN HINTON had bought of WILLIAM WRIGHT, the witnesses to the deed being WILLIAM DANIEL and CHARITY ALSTON 3-133.

GUSTIN, HENRY, lived in EDGECOMBE in (1739) and sold MICHAEL BRINKLEY lands in that County 3-132; in (1727) he was engaged in business at CASIA and ROANOKE, with JAMES MILLIKEN and JAMES CASTELLAW as partners 2-304.

GUYER, JOHN, left will (1804) in which he said JOHN PERISHO was the son of "his wife" 3-334.

GWINN, JOHN, left will (1843) daughters MARTHA JONES and MILLY BARR 2-51.

JOSEPH GLAISTER who died in 1718 leaving will (1-46) was a Quaker Minister and a former associate and contemporary of the JORDANS of Isle of Wight County, Virginia. The records of the Virginia Yearly Meeting Book (1702-1844) has the entry for July 18, 1709: "Benjamin Jordan and JOSEPH GLAISTER are appointed to draw up the state of this meeting in order for LONDON. They are also appointed Country Correspondents", also on the 23rd day and 7th month, 1711, the minutes say "Benjamin Jordan, Clerk, with JOSEPH GLAISTER, is continued as Correspondent" This was at "Chuckatuck". At "Levy Neck", July 19, 1708 an entry says "Benjamin Jordan and JOSEPH GLAISTER are appointed to draw up the state of this meeting," etc. It is thus interesting to note these items showing conclusively that this JOSEPH was the same one who lived in the general neighborhood of Capt. Chritopher Lawne's Plantation, from whence came the Blounts, Whites, Harrisons and so many others on this record. JOSEPH had a sister, MARY TOMS (1-79) and his daughter SARAH became the wife of WYKE HUNNICUTT and thus the ancestress of a numerous family of that name found in nearly all of the "deep South" States.

GODDIN FAMILY. On these records the name is sometimes spelled GODDING, and on the Virginia records sometimes GODIN, but on the old Family Bible in Virginia (1 Tyler 172) it is spelled GODDIN. In the Fairfax Harrison account it is spelled GODDING, but DAVID GODDIN'S name on the old New Kent St. Peter's Parish Register is spelled "GODDIN" long before 1700, although the exact date is not given there. From the "Harrisons of Skimeno" which deals muchly with the Jordans as well as the Harrisons - the same Jordans mentioned in the preceding note - the author on page 7 gives an interesting incident, based on a lawsuit that arose between one JAMES HARRISON (son of the emigrant RICHARD) and old ISAAC GODDIN. ISAAC GODDIN was a Justice or Commissioner of the Peace in YORK COUNTY, VIRGINIA in 1678, when he had the "run in" with the obstreperous JAMES HARRISON, but it was not until 1686, some eight years later, that the participants in this neighborly litigation almost came to blows. Thereafter James was hailed before MATTHEW HOWARD (Lord Effingham) to give an account of his unseemly conduct, leaving that august presence loaded with a fine of 500 pounds of hard earned tobacco. At the hearing conducted with all due solemnity, it was brought out by the testimony of one SUSANNA BETTS and a certain JOHN BERRY that the following events had occurred:

"That about the last of January, the past year (1685-6), deponents were at the house of ISAAC GODDIN, and there JAMES HARRISON came in the presence to borrow a rundlett of the said Goddin, and the said Goddin told him that he had never a one but a two gallon rundlett, and if that would serve him he should have it". Harrison's answer was "Dam the rundlett, it is not fit for my use" and otherwise used certain threatening and abusive language to the said GODDIN which is set forth in its somewhat lurid detail. Whereupon the said GODDIN told him: "James, my hands are tied to keep the peace". Then the said JAMES HARRISON replied, exclaiming "God dam the peace"; and further "ye deponents sayeth not".

If the student of psychology will now turn to Vol. II of these remarkable records and read the numerous affidavits and depositions set forth on pages 208 to 217, and in other parts dealing with the "loyalists and tories" of early revolutionary days, in which, coupled with such activities we find the name of WILLIAM BRIMMAGE, THOMAS and JAMES HARRISON, DANIEL LEGGETT and numerous other members of the HARRISON family he will be struck with the similarity of the conduct of this JAMES HARRISON who sued ISAAC GODDIN and the Harrisons involved in these troublous events. It may not mean anything, but it is certainly singular and highly interesting.

WILLIAM GLOVER. This man who served as Deputy Governor in the hectic days when the troublesome THOMAS CARY attempted to rule or ruin, and thus precipitated the infamous "CARY REBELLION" came from the North side of the James River in Henrico County, Virginia, to Albemarle Precinct about 1691. With shelves of various source books and records from both North Carolina and Virginia, however, the compiler has been unable to discover the maiden name of his wife CATHERINE, who after his death married TOBIAS KNIGHT, and seems only to have bourne her GLOVER husband one or two daughters. The idea has been advanced that his first wife may have been Mary Davis, and that THOMAS, JOSEPH and CHARLES WORTH GLOVER were sons of his by this first marriage (1-637, 1-460). This idea is suggestive and has some force, but proof is lacking. Deputy Governor WILLIAM GLOVER was a Justice in Henrico County in 1688, as the following item from page 279 of the Bound Volume of Records for Henrico for 1677-1692, shows:

"John Womack, accused by FRANCIS CARTER, to MR. WILLIAM GLOVER, one of ye Justices for this county * * being by said GLOVER bound over to this court, the said complaint referred to a jury," etc. That he left there for parts unknown is revealed by the following item from page 404 of the Bound Record for 1683-1701:

"Captain WILLIAM RANDOLPH, deputy commander on the North Side JAMES RIVER (Henrico County, Virginia) representing to the court that by departure of MR. WILLIAM GLOVER, there is a place in his troops become void which cannot be supplied at present" etc. William Glover was a close friend of the Randolphs and is one of the witnesses to a transfer of patented lands in 1687 by Henry Randolph Jr. to his sister MARGERY BRIGGS. And it is singularly interesting to note that WILLIAM GLOVER, GENT, of Henrico County, who had so much touble in the Province of North Carolina with a certain THOMAS CARY, should have been intimate with and a neighbor to JOHN PLEASANTS, of Virginia, who married DOROTHY, the daughter of another and different THOMAS CARY (but of the same family line), as witness the following item from the Henrico Records:

"JOHN PLEASANTS, of Henrico County, Gent, to JOHN ELLIS, same county, planter, conveys a tract of land included in patent to MR. WILLIAM GLOVER, of same COUNTY, GENT, bearing date 28th of April 1691, and by him (Glover) sold to JOHN ELLIS, and by him sold to JOHN PLEASANTS, said land being on the North side of James River, Henrico County, bounded N. E. by lands of JOHN DAVIS and ROBERT BURTON. Nov. 1, 1701." Yes, William Glover's first wife might have been a DAVIS.

GRIMES FAMILY. The will of SAMUEL GRIMES in 1783 (2-336) suggests that the Grimes family and the BRYANS were related. Sampson Grimes of Duplin County, married BATHSHEBA WINDER and their son JESSE GRIMES was born in 1788. He married twice and had a large family of children, and one of his sons died with DAVID CROCKETT in the Alamo in Texas in 1836. GRIMES COUNTY, TEXAS, is named for JESSE GRIMES, son of Sampson Grimes and Bathsheba Grimes of Duplin County, N. C.

HACKLEY, HENRY, deed of gift to THOMAS HARRIS land on SALMON CREEK (1728) with JOHN OT-WAY and ABRAHAM ODOM witnesses 3-129.

HADDOCK, JANE, married SAMUEL HEATH (1697)3-408

HAGAN, JOHN, will (1793), had brothers ALEXAN-DER and JAMES HAGAN sister MARGARET in Md. DAVID STONE and EDWARD BRYAN Exrs. 2-518.

HAIG, MARY, will in PASQUOTANK (1718) GABRIEL NEWBY and JOSEPH GLAISTER Exrs. 1-51.

HAIG, WILLIAM, will in PASQUOTANK (1718) names wife MARY 1-51; another WILLIAM will (1735) 1-52.

HAILES, JAMES and EDWARD WILLIAMS witness deed from WILLIAM JONES to CHARLES JORDAN (1731) 2-452.

HALE, JOHN, deed from JOHN EARLY (1711) 3-441.

HALFORD, DIANA and MARY NASH witnessed will of THOMAS HOGG (1696) 2-465.

HALL, ANN, will in PERQUIMANS (1741) mentions daughter SARAH JENNETT 1-47.

HALL, REV. CLEMENT, will (1749) with FRANCIS HALL and WILLIAM JACKSON administrators - 1-456; succeeded as Rector of ST. PAUL'S PARISH in Edenton by REV. DANIEL EARL 3-411.

HALL, EDWARD and wife RACHEL had children born (1754-1755) 3-384.

HALL, ENOCH, was Chief Justice of N. C. (1749) 2-305; was appointed by GOV. GABRIEL JOHN-STON (1747) 1-446.

HALL FAMILY. Wills 3-173; births 3-207, 3-384.

HALL, HEZEKIAH, will (1733) daughter SARAH and wife ANN, DAVID SHEPARD Exr. 1-49.

HALL, JOHN, will (1690) wife CATHERINE 1-48; & another JOHN HALL with wife BLESSING deeds land to JOHN CAKE (1720) with JAMES BATES a witness 2-608.

HALL, ISAAC, will (1826) ALFRED MOORE witness - 3-337.

HALL, MOSES, owned lands (1735) adjoining JOHN NORFLEET, the HUBBARDS and PARKERS 3-126; also his lands joined EPAPRODITUS BENTON in (1758) and other BENTONS 1-20; he and JOHN COLLINS and MOSES ODOM witnesses to deed by HENRY ROBINSON of BERTIE (1734) 3-125; was from NANSEMOND COUNTY, Virginia (1734) and sold land to JOHN HUBBARD 3-128; listed as son in law of RICHARD DAVIS (1737) 1-40.

HALL, NATHANIEL, will (1734) 1-49.

HALL, RACHEL, will (1810) had daughter SARAH WAFF, grandchildren named MOORE, and JOHN and JOSHUA SKINNER were executors 3-337.

HALL, ROGER, received land grant in CHOWAN in (1681) 1-3; and owned lands next to JOSEPH GILBERT and others (1720) 2-613.

HALL, WILLIAM, married ANN MATTHEWS (1703)3-410 lived in PERQUIMANS and sold land to HENRY CLAYTON deceased JAMES COLE (1719) 1-628.

HALL, WILLIAM and wife MARY (1725) 3-384; he received land grant (1711) 1-16; his wife was ANNE in (1705) 3-376.

HALLUM, JEREMIAH, will (1784) wife JUDITH, witnessed by ABRAHAM PERRY and WILLIAM WHITE 2-341.

HALLUM, JOHN, and wife PRUDENCE, children born (1685) 3-213; John was sued by JOHN HAR-RIS (1689) 3-430.

HALLUM, SAMUEL, son of JOHN 3-216.

HALLUM, THOMAS, son of JOHN and PRUDENCE 3-218

HALSEY, DANIEL and wife MARY sold to THOMAS WEST certain WILLIAM DUKENFIELD lands in (1716) with CHRISTOPHER DUDLEY a witness 1-294; he married the daughter of ROBERT HICKS in CHOWAN 1-49; he and wife MARY sold lands to JOSEPH HUDSON in (1715)1-285; was granted lands on ROCKYHOCK CREEK in (1711) 1-7; witnessed deed from RICHARD LEWIS to HENRY LISLE (1715) 1-294; owned land next to ANDREW SALSBURY (1715) 1-290; died leaving will (1719) 1-294.

HALSEY FAMILY. Wills 1-547, 3-335.

HALSEY, JAMES, land grant (1717) 1-16.

HALSEY, JOHN (1744) names of his children are given 1-455; he was the uncle of WILLIAM BADHAM when he was 14 years old (1750) 1-451; was Sheriff of CHOWAN (1749) 1-451, 1-452.

HALSEY, MALACHI, received land grant (1790) on ROCKYHOCK NECK 1-23.

HALSEY, MARTHA, married BENJAMIN FOREHAND in (1783) 3-417; she was daughter of DANIEL HALSEY and married three times, her sec-ond husband being WILLIAM BADHAM 3-450.

HALSEY, MARY, was also a daughter of DANIEL HALSEY in (1730) 3-449; but another MARY was daughter of ROBERT HICKS (John Hal-sey's wife) 3-467; the latter's estate divided and all heirs named 1-449.

HALSEY, MILES 1-548; received land grant in (1722) joining JAMES FARLOW 1-11.

HALSEY, THOMAS, will (1774) wife was CATHER-INE, and ANDREW KNOX was Executor 3-174.

HALSTEAD, HENRY with HENRY LAWLY was granted lands in (1716) 1-16.

HAMILTON, ANDREW, bought land from JOHN COL-LINS and wife MARTHA (1725) 2-293.

HAMBLETON, EMILY, will (1849) 2-522.

HAMBLETON FAMILY. Wills 1-222.

HAMBLETON, JAMES, sold land to THOMAS PILAND (1729) 2-446.

HAMBLETON, JANE, will (1733) names JOHN GAR-RETT, Executor 1-49; see also 1-222.

HAMBLETON, JOHN, will (1706) daughter in law MARY HOPGOOD 1-50; his wife was JANE 1-450; from NANSEMOND CO. (Va) 2-444.

HAMLIN, MARTHA, was a sister of ROBERT MOORE who died (1807) and daughter of HANNAH MOORE who died (1802) 3-341.

HANCOCK FAMILY. Births of children (about 1680) 3-207, 3-208, 3-211, 3-215.

HANCOCK, STEPHEN, was son of ROGER HANCOCK, of DORSETSHIRE, England, and married MARGARET DRAKE in 1673; 3-200; he died (1691) 3-363; they had son STEPHEN born (1680) 3-211; and daughter MARY born (1637) 3-215.

HANCOCK, THOMAS. His wife was MARY and she died (1702) on Castleton's Creek 3-402.

HANCOCK, WILLIAM and WILLIAM BARROW employed by WILLIAM BLOUNT in a plot or scheme in(1701) 1-610; he was sued by WILLIAM FRYLEY of AL-BEMARLE PRECINCT (1702) 1-609.

HANKINS, THOMAS, division of his estate CHOWAN COUNTY (1837) mention of HATHAWAY 2-264.

HANSFORD, JENKINS, acknowledgment of deed to him by BARNABY H. DUNSTON (1749) 2-632.

HANSFORD, THOMAS, was a Justice with NEEDHAM & EDWARD BRYAN at CASHY BRIDGE (1749) 2-632; was overseer of the road (1744) from his ferry in BERTIE 3-625.

HANSON, JOHN, died in (1732) his wife was MARY administratrix his estate 1-450.

HANDRICK, RICHARD, will in PERQUIMANS in (1712) Francis Corpew and JOHN PAYNE are mentioned 1-52.

HANDWICK, THOMAS, charged with tuition for SARAH SHEHAN in BERTIE (1770) 3-448.

HANDWORKER, DANIEL. Will (1729) 1-49.

HANKEY, JOHN married JUDITH ATTAWAY (1688) 3-203

HANWORTH, WILLIAM, married JANE BENNETT (1688) 3-203; he died (1692) 3-230.

HARD, JOHN, JR. proved his rights in ALBEMARLE (1702) 1-609.

HARDING, JOHN, of CHOWAN and CASHEY RIVER (1711) 3-441.

HARDING, JOSIAH, will (1752) in NORTHAMPTON Co. 1-226; he was called brother in will of THOMAS SPARROW (1717) 1-77.

HARDING, RICHARD, of PERQUIMANS will (1741)1-226 his wife MARY left will (1743) and mentioned SKINNER connections 1-226.

HARDISON, HARDY, kept an Ordinary in BERTIE in (1769) 3-447.

HARDISON, JASPER, lived in TYRRELL PRECINCT in 3-317; he left will (1733) and mentioned a daughter JUDITH SUTTON 1-49.

HARDISON, THOMAS, was administrator of the es - tate of WILLIAM GARRETT (1735) 1-45.

HARDEN, THOMAS, will (1809) 2-529.

HARDIN, WILLIAM, will in CURRITUCK (1748) wife JANE had son in law THOMAS DUDLEY 1-226.

HARDY, EDITH, was the wife of WILLIAM HARDY who had brother JOHN HARDY (1717) 1-619.

HARDY, EDWARD, charged with tuition of JOAB MITCHEL orphan of JAMES MITCHELL (1771) 3-450.

HARDY, MADAM ELIZABETH, married EDWARD SALTER (1731) 3-410.

HARDY FAMILY. Wills: 1-553, 2-520, 2-519 and 2-503. Connection of the family with the HILL, WHITMELL families 1-47.

HARDY, HUMPHREY appointed guardian of AGNES KNOTT orphan of NATHANIEL KNOTT (1769) 3-447; he and JOHN FREEMAN signed bond of ALEXANDER FOARD as Register of BERTIE in (1767) 3-443, 3-444; executor of will of SAMUEL PERRY (1773) 2-350; will of (1804) 2-519; wife was RACHEL and left will(1807) naming connections, FREEMAN, and others 2-519.

HARDY, HUMPHREY, will in BERTIE (1810) wife MARTHA, mentions "JOSEPH HARDY'S wife ELIZ-ABETH, daughter of ABRAHAM SHEPPERD" (Did Abraham Shepperd marry his daughter?) also mentions BENJAMIN HILL of Hertford 2-519, 2-520.

HARDY, HUMPHREY H. executor of will of MARTHA YOUNG (1849) mentions WILLIAM and JAMES PEELE among others 2-556.

HARDY, JOHN, will in BERTIE (1719) wife REBECCA and brothers WILLIAM, THOMAS and JACOB HAR-DY 1-49 (mentions also ROBERT WEST and THOMAS POLLOCK and children) his daughter ELIZABETH HARDY married NATHANIEL HILL 1-47; he and REBECCA made deed of gift about (1717) to his brother WILLIAM HARDY 1-618; they lived on SALMON CREEK next to THOMAS WEST 1-300; in (1713) ABEL TURNER gave JOHN HARDY power of attorney to collect debts due his father HENRY TURNER, with ISAAC HILL a witness 1-99; he and WILLIAM CHARLTON witnessed deed (1717) 1-623; he was apprenticed (1695) to WILLIAM STEVENS 1-74; his daughter ELIZABETH married NATH-ANIEL HILL in (1792) 1-52; he was executor of the estate of WILLIAM LEWERTON, Chowan (1710) 1-60; he and his brothers WILLIAM and JACOB lived between SALMON CREEK and CASHY river in BERTIE (1719) 1-444; he witnessed deed of MARY LAWSON to COL. THOM-AS POLLOCK (1714) 2-136; ALEXANDER MARSHALL power of attorney to sell him lands 1-288; in (1714) he proves an account 1-145; he witnessed deed (1713) by CHARLES BANNER & wife ELIZABETH to JOHN PLOWMAN 1-103.

HARDY, JACOB, witnessed deed by JOHN HAWKINS to his brother THOMAS HAWKINS (1713) with JOHN BYRD 1-103; bought lands from JOHN CROMBIE on CASHOKE CREEK SWAMP (1721) & deed witnessed by WILLIAM HARDY and JOHN WALKER 2-614; Jacob sold this land (1722) to JAMES CASTELLAW 2-294, 2-295.

HARDY, JOSEPH, was foreman of the grand jury in BERTIE County (1747) 3-630.

HARDY, LAMB, left will in BERTIE COUNTY in (1797) in which he names wife WINIFRED sons THOMAS and WILLIAM PARROTT HARDY & brothers WILLIAM P. and BENJAMIN 2-339.

HARDY, MATTHEW, in (1743) was chosen by PENEL-
OPE LITTLE, daughter of WILLIAM LITTLE as
her guardian 1-447; in (1738) witnessed a
deed by EDWARD HOWCOTT to JAMES POTTER 3-131

HARDY, REBECCA, wife of JOHN HARDY 1-172; wit-
nessed deed from EDWARD HOWCOTT to BEAL
BROWN (1719) 2-607, and 2-457; wife of JOHN
HARDY (1717) in CHOWAN 1-618.

HARDY, RICHARD, of WILMINGTON, will (1758) mentions wife SARAH, witness was JAMES GREG-
ORY 1-228.

HARDY, ROBERT, copy of letter (1776) apppinted
Commissioner at Port of EDENTON for pur-
chasing military supplies 3-440; received
land grant (1755) near FRANCIS PUGH'S Ferry 1-20; was master of schooner SION in
(1749) 1-434, as was JOHN HARDY of the
sloop HANNAH (1775) 1-436 and of the BETSY
1-436.

HARDY, SAMUEL, son of WILLIAM (1711) mentioned
in will of JAMES FEWOX 1-43.

HARDY, WILLIAM made deed (1715) to WILLIAM
SPRUILL, with WILLIAM WILKINSON as a witness 1-285; his wife was EDITH FEWOX the
sister of ROBERT FEWOX 2-139; she was the
daughter of JAMES FEWOX 1-43; he was the
brother of JOHN HARDY of CHOWAN 1-618; and
of JACOB HARDY whose deed he witnessed in
(1721) 2-514, see bottom page 1-43; in
(1717) he witnessed deed of WILLIAM ROSE
1-613; in (1717) he sold land to JOHN HAS-
SELL on SCUPERNONG, with JOSHUA ALEXANDER
a witness 1-619; a later WILLIAM HARDY
died leaving will (1784) in BERTIE, mentioning brothers EDWARD and JESSE and son
LAMB HARDY as executors, and ABRAHAM LEE
and STEPHEN LEE witnesses 2-339.

HARE, EDWARD, deeded land to MOSES HARE next to
THOMAS SPEIGHT (1733) 2-611; he and MOSES
witnesses with THOMAS HALE to will of JU-
DITH HARE (1732) 2-608; he and CHARLES MOR-
RIS and WILLIAM GATLING were neighbors in
(1733) 2-453

HARE FAMILY. Lived in GATES COUNTY. Wills 2-52,
2-53, 2-608.

HARE, ISAIAH, was appointed guardian (1767) of
HESTER BUTLER in BERTIE 3-443.

HARE, JOHN, married SARAH SHADDOCK (1698) 3-408;
married JANE DOVATED (?) (1697) 3-408; had
son RICHARD HARE born (1699) 3-370; he was
dead (1735) and had son JOSEPH HARE 3-127.

HARE, JOSEPH, son of JOHN HARE (1735) 3-127.

HARE, JUDITH, left will (1732) or made deed to
WILLIAM SPEIGHT, Moses HARE a witness 2-608.

HARE, MOSES with MOSES ODOM (1731) witnessed a
deed by RICHARD BARNES to EDWARD HARE 2-451;
he received deed to land from JOHN ODOM
about (1623) which is now illegible 2-607.

HARE, SAMUEL. His wife was JANE (1699) 3-371.

HARE, SARAH with ROBERT HICKS in (1718) witness
to deed by THOMAS CLARK 1-623.

HARE, THOMAS will in BERTIE in (1785) daughter
PENELOPE and wife PENELOPE and several other children mentioned 2-341.

HARLE, SARAH, will in BERTIE (1779) had two
daughters married LANE and daughter married AMOS DAVISON 2-341.

HARLOW, AMAZIAH master of the schooner EN-
DEAVOR (1749) 1-433.

HARLOW, ELIZABETH married ROBERT INKOSON in
(1672) 3-200

HARLOW FAMILY. Births of children 3-209.

HARLOW, JAMES, his rights mentioned 3-153.

HARLOW, JOHN, deed (1727) to EDMUND GALE adjoining lands bought of WILLIAM CHARLTON
2-444; owned land next to JOHN WARBURTON
(1759) 1-21; division of his estate and
heirs (1750) 3-264; his sons WILLIAM &
JOHN HARLOE mentioned (1717) 3-149; sold
land to EDMUND GALE 2-607; JOHN son of
THOMAS and ALICE HARLOE 3-218; one JOHN
died (1693) 3-220; JOHN HARLOW of CHOWAN
left will (1762) 1-132.

HARLOE, THOMAS, and ELIZABETH CHASTONE were
married (1672) 3-200.

HARMON, CALEB. His wife was MARY (1760) list
of their children 3-384.

HARMON, DANIEL, son of RICHARD HARMON and his
wife MARGARET 3-384.

HARMON, ELIZABETH married THOMAS FODDEY(1698)
3-408.

HARMON FAMILY. Births of children 3-207, 3-219.

HARMON, JAMES, will in CHOWAN (1787) mentions
wife MARY TURNBULL and children 1-554.

HARMON, JOHN, wife SUSANNAH (1750) births of
their children given 3-384.

HARMON, NICHOLAS, will in BERTIE (1802) witnesses were JAMES and CHRISTIAN TAYLOR
2-518.

HARMON, ROBERT, will (1717). JOHN WYATT was
his executor 1-51; in (1698) Robert HAR-
MON'S wife was ELIZABETH 3-408, and their
children are listed 3-384, see 3-212.

HARMON, SARAH, married ANTHONY WHERRY, JR. in
(1699) 3-408; and the date of SARAH HAR-
MON'S birth is shown at 3-211.

HARMON, THOMAS, will in PASQUOTANK (1720) 1-51.

HARMON, WILLIAM JR. in (1727) he made deed
of lands to JOHN HARRISON in BERTIE, adjoining VINES CROPLEY and WILLIAM HARRI-
SON, bought of said HARRISON'S father, &
witnesses were THOMAS PIERCE, FRANCIS PET-
TIT and VINES HARRISON 2-444.

HARNETT, CORNELIUS, the elder, mentioned 3-7;
given permission to maintain a ferry over
CAPE FEAR river (1727) 3-290.

HARNEY, SELBY, granted lands in (1786) in the
town of EDENTON 1-25.

HARRAMOND, HENRY, master of the sloop NANCY
in (1774) 1-436.

HARRELL, ABRAHAM, in BERTIE, settlement of his
estate (1768) and family history 3-445.

HARRELL, MENKING, of BERTIE (1767) His estate ordered divided 3-443.

HARRELL, FRANCIS, of NANSEMOND COUNTY, VIRGINIA, sold lands (1731) to RICHARD BAKER adjoining RICHARD PARKER. The witnesses were JAMES PARKER, JOHN ARLINE and THOMAS ROUNDTREE 2-450; in (1734) he sold land to THOMAS BAKER, with RICHARD TAYLOR and RICHARD TAYLOR, JR. as witnesses 3-125.

HARRELL, HARDY. Genealogical information about his family. Said to be related to the WASHINGTON family. Some moved to South Carolina, etc. 2-157.

HARRELL FAMILY. Wills: 2-54, 2-55, 2-56, 2-157 2-225, 2-226, 2-336, 2-337, 2-338, 3-337 - 2-516, 2-517.

HARRELL, ISOM, witnessed the will of JAMES PURVIS (1785) 2-351.

HARRELL, JACOB, in (1828) witnessed the will of REV. MARTIN ROSS, with JOHN E. WOOD; his son MARTIN ROSS JR. having married ELIZA TOWNSEND 3-348.

HARRELL, JESSE, witnessed the will of JOHN F. SPIVEY in BERTIE (1763) 2-355.

HARRELL, JOEL, with ARTHUR and ISOM HARRELL a witness to the will of JAMES PURVIS (1785) 2-351.

HARRELL, JOHN, qualified as a Justice of BERTIE in (1746) 2-628; in (1744) returned the division of the estate of FRANCIS PUGH 2-623; died in (1749) and JOHN HARRELL JR. was the administrator 2-633; in (1767) JOHN HARRELL was orphan of JOSEPH, with MAJ. THOMAS PUGH his guardian 3-443, see also 3-337.

HARRELL, JOSEPH, was deceased in (1767), and his widow ANN married JAMES WILLIAMS, they had one son JOHN HARRELL 3-444, 3-443.

HARRELL, JOSIAH was a Justice in BERTIE (1767) 3-444; and in (1768) 3-445.

HARRELL, RICHARD, sold lands (1735) to CHRISTOPHER BOYCE, adjoining lands of JONATHAN KITTRELL, the witnesses being THOMAS JOHNSON, NICHOLAS FAIRLESS and TITUS BOYCE 3-128; he died leaving will in (1762) with NICHOLAS STALLINGS, JAMES and JOHN SCOTT, witnesses 3-172. (Had sons DEMPSEY, JAMES and JOHN HARRELL).

HARRELL, SAMUEL, son of JOHN HARRELL of VIRGINIA in (1739) sold lands to PETER PARKER and DANIEL PARKER and ROBERT PARKER were witnesses 3-134.

HARRELL, THOMAS, will (1831) left son CHARLES HARRELL and daughters who married ELLIOTT and PERRY 3-337.

HARRINGTON, GEORGE, will in CHOWAN (1718) wife was JUDITH HAUGHTON 1-51.

HARRINGTON, HUMPHREY, will (1713) mentions his brother JOHN HARRINGTON 1-52.

HARRIS, AMOS, will in BERTIE (1796), witnessed by ALLEN KNOTT and ELIZABETH HARRIS 2-521; mentions RACHEL WALSTON.

HARRIS, DANIEL, patented lands in GRANVILLE COUNTY on South side of FISHING CREEK in (1746) 1-447.

HARRIS, DAVID, married ELIZABETH ELLIS in (1695) 3-407; births of their children 3-370, 3-372, 3-374.

HARRIS, DIANA, was married (1675) to WILLIAM FOSTER by REV. MR. TAYLOR 3-200. (After his death she married again, see other notes). She was the widow of THOMAS HARRIS and after FOSTER'S death married 3rd THOMAS WHITE 3-274.

HARRIS FAMILY. Wills 1-553, 1-554.

HARRIS, JOHN, probably son of THOMAS HARRIS and wife DIANA, married about (1687-8) ELIZABETH WALLER 3-203; in (1689) he sued JOHN HALLUM 3-430; he witnessed deed with GEORGE TURMODGER (1711) 1-626; one JOHN had wife SUSANNAH 3-216; one died (1711) and his wife was MILDRED 1-52; court was held at the home of JOHN HARRIS in (1689) with HENRY WHITE, ALEX LILLINGTON and CALEB GALLOWAY among those present 2-298.

HARRIS, MARTHA, married WILLIAM VOSE (1669) maybe sister of THOMAS HARRIS 3-200.

HARRIS, THOMAS, wife DIANA, an account of his family and death (1665), son JOHN and grand-daughter SARAH married NATHANIEL NICHOLSON 3-274; another THOMAS HARRIS was standard keeper (1771) in BERTIE 3-451; Thomas who married DIANA left will (1665) 2-148; he sued CHRISTOPHER HOLLY (1683) 3-283; and another THOMAS HARRIS died in (1679) in BERKELEY 3-365.

HARRIS, WILLIAM, land grant joined one JOHN SPARKMAN in (1742) 1-18; he and wife ANN sold land to ARGYLE SIMONS, which joined lands of JONATHAN HARRISON 1-85.

HARRISON, ANN, of BERTIE, was administrator of the estate of CHRISTOPHER HARRISON (1769) 3-446.

HARRISON, BARBARA, was mentioned as the widow of JOSHUA HARRISON (no date) 2-469.

HARRISON, BENJAMIN, makes affidavit relating to what occurred at the home of his father THOMAS HARRISON (1777) DANIEL LEGGETT and WILLIAM BRIMAGE loyalist activities 2-208, 2-209; BENJAMIN HARRISON (possibly a different one) and PHILLIP LIGHTFOOT were executors of FRANCIS LIGHTFOOT of Virginia (1731) 2-298.

HARRISON, CHLOE, married JOSEPH BOZEMAN in (1791), and she was the daughter of WILLIAM HARRISON who was born (1733) and died in (1805) 3-472.

HARRISON, CHRISTOPHER in (1768) was guardian of JOHN ROUSE, orphan of DAVID ROUSE in BERTIE 3-445; also appointed guardian for JOHN OXLEY, orphan of JOHN OXLEY in (1767) 3-443; died (1769) 3-446.

HARRISON, DANIEL, owned lands (1723) joining ADAM COCKBURN and others 1-11; bought land in (1716) from EDWARD COCKRELL (2-519) and left will in CHOWAN (1726) 1-50.

HARRISON, ELIZABETH, mother of JOSEPH HARRISON who deeded lands on ROCKYHOCK CREEK (1729) to DANIEL HARRISON 2-447; she was a cousin of JAMES HODGES (1722) 1-51.

HARRISON FAMILY. An account taken from an old Bible in the BOZEMAN family relating to the genealogy of the HARRISONS 3-472.

HARRISON, GEORGE, surety on bond of REUBEN HARRISON in BERTIE COUNTY (1790) who married ANN MITCHELL 2-365; a later GEORGE with a brother REUBEN was son of WINNIFRED HARRISON who died in BERTIE (1844) 2-522.

HARRISON, HANNAH, wife of WILLIAM HARRISON (who was born 1733) died in 1804 3-472; see 1-52.

HARRISON, EDMUND, witnessed the will (1685) of JOHN CROPLEY, father of VINES CROPLEY 1-194.

HARRISON, EDWARD in (1738) was brother of VINES HARRISON, who died that year 1-48.

HARRISON, JAMES, makes affidavit relating to occurrences on a path to home of THOMAS HARRISON's (1777) among the loyalists 2-210, and 2-211.

HARRISON, JAMES JR. gives evidence against DANIEL LEGGETT and others as to their loyalist activities (1777) he being the son of JAMES HARRISON 2-214.

HARRISON, JOHN, deceased, leaves will (1710) in which he mentions brother THOMAS HARRISON & sister HANNAH HARRISON 1-52; another one left will (1693) mentions sons WILLIAM, JOHN and daughter ELIZABETH 1-48; in (1717) JOHN witnessed deed by VINES CROPLEY to WILLIAM STEWART 1-300; John of BERTIE in (1727) bgt land from WILLIAM HARMON JR. which joined lands of VINES CROPLEY and WILLIAM HARRISON and which HARMON had bought from their (the HARRISONS') father; and this deed was witnessed by THOMAS PIERCE, FRANCIS PETTIT and VINES HARRISON 2-444; a JOHN HARRISON (1777) had son THOMAS HARRISON mentioned in affidavit of JAMES HARRISON 2-210; a certain JOHN HARRISON married (name not given) in January (1783) with JOSHUA SLADE as surety on the marriage bond 3-111.

HARRISON, JONATHAN owned land (1701?) on the No. side of ALBEMARLE RIVER, adjoining lands bought by ARGYLE SIMONS from WILL HARRIS and his wife ANN 1-65.

HARRISON, JOSEPH in (1729) sold lands to DANIEL HARRISON on Rockyhock Creek left to JOSEPH HARRISON by his father, except one-half to his wife ELIZABETH for life, deed witnessed by ROBERT HICKS and JOHN HALSEY 2-447; was seemingly the son of DANIEL HARRISON died leaving will in CHOWAN (1726) with wife ELIZABETH, EDWARD PADGET, Exr. 1-50; GEORGE PHENEY, who married the widow of JOHN LOVICK - (Penelope Eden, daughter of Gov. Charles Eden) mentions in his will (1737) "my nephew JOSEPH HARRISON" 1-66; ROBERT HARRISON in his will (1713-14) mentions son JOSEPH 1-232.

HARRISON, JOSHUA. His widow's name was BARBARA (no date) 2-469; Vines HARRISON had in (1738) brothers JOSHUA, WILLIAM and EDMUND 1-48.

HARRISON, JOSIAH, supplied DANIEL LEGGETT with vituals (1777) see affidavit 3-397.

HARRISON, MARTHA, married MARTIN WHITE of BERTIE in (1808) 2-379.

HARRISON, MARY, married EZEKIEL WHITE in BERTIE (1780) 3-318; another MARY married WILLIAM HOLLAND in North Carolina about 1740 3-318.

HARRISON PLANTATION was patented in (1714) by MARTIN CHARLES 3-135.

HARRISON, REBECCA, daughter of ROBERT HARRISON and wife ELIZABETH died (1706) 3-404.

HARRISON, REUBEN, with EZEKIEL WHITE (who married MARY HARRISON) witnessed will of TIMOTHY MIZELL (1792) 2-348; he married ANN MITCHELL in BERTIE COUNTY in (1790) with GEORGE HARRISON security on the bond 2-365; a later REUBEN was the son of WINNIFRED HARRISON mentioned in her will (1744) 2-522.

HARRISON, ROBERT and wife ELIZABETH, daughter was REBECCA (1706) in PERQUIMANS Precinct 3-404; ROBERT HARRISON of YORK COUNTY, Va. assigns account against WILLIAM DUKENFIELD to FREDERICK JONES about (1697) and suit was brought 3-69, 3-70; see also 1-610; still another ROBERT HARRISON died leaving will in (1713) names sons ROBERT and JOSEPH, daughters SARAH and ELIZABETH 1-232.

HARRISON, SARAH, and MARGARET were granddaughters mentioned in will of MARY SWANN (1771) 3-188, 3-189; an earlier SARAH in (1713) was daughter of ROBERT HARRISON 1-232.

HARRISON, SUSANNAH, was the wife of THOMAS HARRISON who sold land to JOHN WORLEY in (1715) and SUSANNAH gave power of attorney same date to ZACHARIAH JUNKIN (probably JUNKIN) to acknowledge her deed 1-288.

HARRISON, THOMAS, mentioned in deposition of PETER MAYFIELD regarding facts in the CULPEPPER REBELLION, Harrison having stored certain tobacco in his home 3-43; THOMAS HARRISON (1679) was aged 34 years according to his own statement 3-42; he is mentioned also in affidavit of MARY WALKER a hundred years later (1777) 2-575; this last THOMAS had a son named BENJAMIN 2-208; see also 2-212, 2-216, 2-576; one Thomas married ELIZABETH HARDISON (1784) 3-112; an earlier THOMAS was son in law of NATHANIEL AVERIT in (1716) 1-295; his age (1680) 1-139; a THOMAS HARRISON (1680) lists himself, his wife ELIZABETH, son THOMAS and ELIZABETH HARRISON JR. 2-301; one owned lands in (1714) on CHOWAN SOUND next to THOMAS COOPER and wife ELIZABETH 1-105; the one in TYRRELL (1777) said he wished he had never been born 2-215; a much later THOMAS A. HARRISON married LOUISA M. COLLINS (1842) 3-92.

HARRISON, VINES, was a witness with FRANCIS PETTIT (1728) to deed by WILLIAM HARRISON to his son WILLIAM of lands that were a part of the VINES CROPLEY tract next to JOHN NORCOMB and WILLIAM WHITE North side ALBEMARLE SOUND 2-445.

HARRISON, VINES, owned lands in (1727) next to JOHN HARRISON and WILLIAM HARRISON bought from WILLIAM HARMON, JR. 2-444; he obtained his name from VINES CROPLEY note 1-48; he was a witness in (1733) to a deed by THOMAS EVERENDEN to FRANCIS PETTIT 1-109; He died in CHOWAN between February and 24th of March (1738) leaving will naming brothers JOSHUA, WILLIAM and EDMUND and sister SARAH FELTS (probably wife of Humphrey Felts) 1-48.

HARRISON, WILLIAM, father of VINES HARRISON, sold lands to his son WILLIAM on the North side of ALBEMARLE and part of the Vines CROPLEY lands (1726) adjoining JOHN NORCOM and WILLIAM WHITE, the witnesses being VINES HARRISON and WILLIAM PETTIT 2-445; either the father or the son in (1717) witnessed deed by VINES CROPLEY to WILLIAM STEWART 1-300; WILLIAM SR. bought the land he sold his sons by deed from VINES CROPLEY on ALBEMARLE SOUND dated (1714) which had been patented to CROPLEY (1694) and wife SARAH 1-286; in (1727) the senior HARRISON sold a part of these lands to CORNELIUS LEARY, witnessed by WILLIAM SMITH and THOMAS HARRELL 2-445.

HARRISON, WILLIAM, was brother of VINES HARRISON mentioned in his will 1-48.

HARRISON, WILLIAM, was born DEC.17, 1733 and died April 25, 1805 (place of birth not given (from old Bible, and his wife was HANNAH (last name not given) genealogical notes pertaining to his family 3-472.

HARRISON, WINIFRED, died in BERTIE COUNTY (1844) named sons GEORGE and REUBEN, and JONATHAN WHITE, Executors. 3-522.

HARRISON, WILLIAM, was Lieutenant in the 7th Regiment, North Carolina Continental Line 1-422.

HAHROD, AMY, married URIAH DANIEL in CHOWAN in (1795) 1-252.

HARWOOD, EDWARD, of PASQUOTANK, married MARY GIBLE and he died by (1737) 2-303.

HARWOOD, MARY, administered on the estate of EDWARD HARWOOD about (1737) 2-303.

HART, THOMAS, and NEEDHAM BRYAN were Church wardens of SOCIETY PARISH (1729) in BERTIE COUNTY 2-305; he died leaving will in NORTHAMPTON COUNTY (1748) wife MARY and son HENRY executors 1-222.

HART, JOHN, of BERTIE, died in (1746) wife was MARY children BENJAMIN, JESSE, JOHN and DAVID and SARAH and LUCY HART 1-222.

HART, MARY (widow of JOHN) died in NORTHAMPTON COUNTY (1751) her witnesses being JAMES WRIGHT, JOHN GORDON, JESSE HART and GEORGE BRACE 1-222.

HARTLEY, FRANCIS, Court for ALBEMARLE PRECINCT was held at his home (1688) 2-298; he died in PERQUIMANS leaving will (1692) wife SUSANNA and THOMAS HARVEY being his executors and ANN and THOMAS DURANT witnesses 1-227; his widow SUSANNA in (1696) married WILLIAM DUKENFIELD 3-407 and 1-610.

HARVEY, ANN died (1768) 3-406.

HARVEY, BENJAMIN, SR. division of his lands among the sons of his son WILLIAM about (1787) 1-449.

HARVEY, BENJAMIN, son of MILES HARVEY and his wife ELIZABETH, born (1754) 3-385; his wife was JULIANA (one Benj) in (1758) 3-385.

HARVEY, D. AFRICA, mentioned in will of DAVID PERKINS (1733) 1-67.

HARVEY, DOROTHY, will in PASQUOTANK (about 1720) mentions brother THOMAS TOOKE of ISLE OF WIGHT COUNTY, VA. and his seven children, all named 1-51.

HARVEY, EDWARD, died (1771) 3-406.

HARVEY, ELIZABETH, died (1760) and another in (1773) the last a daughter of JOHN HARVEY and wife SARAH 3-406.

HARVEY FAMILY. Wills (GATES CO.) 2-56; also see 3-174; was related to the WILLIAMS family 3-195; genealogical account of the PERQUIMANS HARVEYS of HARVEY'S NECK who came from WARWICKSHIRE, England 3-476 to 3-480; births of children 3-385; 3-446.

HARVEY'S CREEK TITHABLES taken by FRANCIS DELAMARE no date, but very early) and including CAPT. JOHN HUNT, JOHN GRIFFIN STEPHEN MUNDAY, MAURICE CUNNINGHAM and ROBERT and VINCENT WHITE and CHARLES JONES 3-253.

HARVEY, JAMES, married ANN BLOUNT, daughter of JACOB BLOUNT, sister of JOHN GRAY and GOV. WILLIAM BLOUNT of TENNESSEE 1-534; he died (1777) and is buried at COLONEL BLOUNT'S home "Blount Hall" in PITT County, N. C. 3-406, 1-635.

HARVEY, JOHN, came to N. C. with GOV. JOHN JENKINS 1-534. He settled at HARVEY'S neck and may have been son of GOV. THOMAS HARVEY 1-534; one JOHN of HYDE died leaving will (1758) mentions daughter MARY MARTIN and other children 1-47; another JOHN and wife MARY had children in (1746) 3-385; still another one and wife SARAH and children (1773) 3-395.

HARVEY, JOHN MARKS, was the son of JOHN HARVEY of HYDE who died (1758) 1-47.

HARVEY, JOSHUA died (1775) 3-406.

HARVEY, MARY, daughter of COL. THOMAS HARVEY, married COL. ROBERT WEST, son of ROBERT WEST and MARTHA CULLEN 3-367.

HARVEY, MILDRED, married ABNER NEALE, and had sons CHRISTOPHER and ABNER NEALE 3-480.

HARVEY, MILES- His wife was ELIZABETH(1752) children named 3-385; he was son in law of EDWARD SALTER (1734) 1-74; he died (1776) 3-406.

HARVEY, RICHARD, will (1732-33) had sons JOHN, RICHARD, PETER, LEMUEL, JONAS and JAMES HARVEY, daughter BRIDGETT and his wife was MARY 1-49.

HARVEY, RICHARD, was executor of the will of
JOHN KENT (1719) 1-56; and he left will in
WILMINGTON (1758) in which he names his
wife SARAH 1-47.

HARVEY, SARAH, was the daughter of BENJAMIN LA-
KER who left will (1701) 1-58.

HARVEY, COL. THOMAS, and wife ELIZABETH dates
of birth of their children 3-384, 3-385;
genealogy of his family 1-225; he was DEP-
UTY GOVERNOR (1694) 3-406; in (1695) with
DANIEL AKEHURST 3-259; also see 3-35 to
3-39; and 3-476, 3-477, 3-259; left a will
making JOSEPH COMMANDER, SAMUEL COMMANDER
and JOHN WHITEHEAD his heirs, but will has
never been found 3-263; he and his wife
SARAH LAKER had daughter MARY who married
COL. ROBERT WEST 3-829; he wrote letter to
Governor of Virginia (1696) 3-52, 3-53; a
THOMAS HARVEY married MARGARET FLETCHER in
(1701) 3-409; he and wife MARGARET mention-
ed (1705) 3-376; granted land (1722) which
joined SAMUEL WOODWARD 1-11; as executors
of JOHN HARVEY sued JAMES and JOHN TOOKE
the executors of THOMAS COMMANDER (1695)
1-141; THOMAS (son of Governor) married
ELIZABETH, daughter of COL. JAMES COLE of
Perquimans; the Governor's 1-52; widow SAR-
AH LAKER married CHRISTOPHER GALE 1-52;
JOHN, son of THOMAS HARVEY and wife SARAH
was born (1689) 3-216; will of THOMAS HAR-
VEY, proved (1729) gives names of wife
ELIZABETH and their children 1-52; another
THOMAS had wife MARY (1767) 3-386; JOHN,
son of the Governor and Sarah, died (1691)
3-363; a THOMAS HARVEY (son of BENJAMIN)
married daughter of ALBRIDGTON JONES of
SOUTHAMPTON, Virginia (1773) 3-386.

HASELTON, Captain of the sloop FLYING FISH in
(1748) 1-446.

HASK, ANTHONY. Wife was TABITHA 3-368.

HASKETT, ANTHONY, son of ANTHONY HASKETT JR.
was born (1706) 3-377.

HASKETT FAMILY. Wills 2-56, 3-173 and 3-334 &
3-337.

HASKETT, JOSEPH, was the son of ANTHONY 3-386.

HASSELL, ABRAHAM, bought land on SCUPPERNONG in
(1734) from EDWARD HASSELL, with JOHN PAGET
and JOHN HASSELL witnesses 2-452.

HASSELL, EDWARD, and wife ELIZABETH of SCUPER-
NONG sold lands to ABRAHAM HASSELL (1734)
2-452.

HASSELL, JAMES. His appointment as Chief Justice signed by MATTHEW ROWAN as Governor in
(1753) 2-296.

HASSELL, JOHN bought land from ROBERT FEWOX in
(1717) 1-619; sold land to JOHN LAWSON of
SCUPPERNONG (1717) 1-619; also sold lands to
SARAH WILKINSON the wife of COL. WILLIAM
WILKINSON (1719) 1-628.

HASSELL, JOSEPH, married ANN FOX, daughter of
JAMES FOX, who died in (1754), and SUSANNA
FOX, great grand-daughter of JAMES, married
WILLIAM ALEXANDER 2-296.

HATCH, ANTHONY. He was powder receiver at LIT-
TLE RIVER on the CHOWAN West Shore in (1719)
by letter from CHARLES EDEN 3-281.

HATCH, ANTHONY, was son to MRS. ELIZABETH
HUNT (wife of CAPT. JOHN HUNT?) on
LITTLE RIVER (1696) 1-32; he was receiv-
er of powder money at PASQUOTANK 1-444;
he died leaving will in PERQUIMANS in
(1726) mentions brother in law GEORGE
DURANT 1-50; his widow ELIZABETH will
(1726) married TULLY WILLIAMS 1-50;
his daughter ELIZABETH married WILLIAM
REED, see notes by MR. HATHAWAY 1-464,
1-50; he is mentioned in will of ARTHUR
WORKMAN (1696) 1-32; with GEORGE DURANT
in (1713) he bought land from JOHN PET-
TIVER, of PERQUIMANS 1-102; one ANTHONY
HATCH married (1735) ELIZABETH DICKIN-
SON (his son) 3-386; he was a Justice
of the General Court in (1714); he died
leaving will (1744) in which he mentions
wife ELIZABETH and brother JERMON and
makes EDMUND HATCH executor 1-232.

HATCH, BENJAMIN (one of them) married SALLY
WHITFIELD, daughter of NEEDHAM WHITFIELD
1-569.

HATCH, DURANT (General) was born (1763) and
died (1763) married ELIZABETH NORMENT &
may have been son of EDMUND HATCH of
EDENTON 3-316.

HATCH, EDMUND, maybe son of ANTHONY HATCH JR.
will (1744) with MARY CLARK BAPTIST was
an executor of DR. BENJAMIN BAPTIST in
(1753) of CRISP CREEK near EDENTON 2-470;
he was Clerk of the County Court of
CHOWAN in (1744) 1-454.

HATCH, LEMUEL, of PERQUIMANS left will (1776)
naming children; he was a descendant of
ANTHONY HATCH 1-47.

HATCH, SAMUEL was Master of the sloop DEFI-
ANCE in (1774) 1-436.

HATHAWAY, BURTON W. died leaving will (1855)
1-567.

HATHAWAY, JAMES, a genealogical account of
his family 2-637; one JAMES HATHAWAY was
born (1713-14) 2-637.

HATHAWAY, NATHANIEL, was Master of the brig
ABIGAIL bound for the BARBADOES (1774)
2-302.

HATFIELD, GEORGE, died leaving will (1775)
in which he gives the names of all his
brothers WILLIAM, RICHARD, JOHN, DAVID,
BENJAMIN and sister MARTHA, with FOS-
TER TOMS, administrator 3-174.

HATFIELD, RICHARD will proved (1809) mentions
his son AMAZIAH BIGGS HATFIELD and "all
my children", and wife MARY, with NATHAN
LONG and DEMPSEY HARRELL witnesses 3-337.

HAUGHTON, ALEXANDER, was schoolmate of CORNE-
LIUS NORCOM who died in (1755) 1-455.

HAUGHTON, CHARLES, of CHOWAN, left will in
(1754) mentions son JEREMIAH 1-47; one
CHARLES received land grant (1782) next
to JONATHAN HAUGHTON 1-22; another the
same year next to JACOB SIMMONS 1-22; he
had daughter ELIZA HAUGHTON married THOM-
AS SATTERFIELD by (1759) 1-456; and an
earlier CHARLES HAUGHTON obtained a grant
(1748) upon the lines of CHARLES WILKINS
and COL. MOSELEY, land which formerly
belonged to PEARCE 1-20.

HAUGHTON FAMILY. Wills 1-554, 1-555, 1-556.

HAUGHTON, GEORGE land grant in (1716) joining EDMUND PORTER 1-14.

HAUGHTON, JEREMIAH, son of CHARLES HAUGHTON of CHOWAN, who left will (1754) 1-47.

HAUGHTON, JONATHAN, received grant of land in (1784) on the South side of Yoppim river 1-22.

HAUGHTON, MALACHI, left will in EDENTON (1847) wife was ELIZA B. 1-556; he was an attorney of some prominence and some of his descendants WHITFIELD live in COLUMBUS, MISSISSIPPI note 1-556.

HAUGHTON, MARGARET chose RICHARD HAUGHTON her guardian (1745) 1-456.

HAUGHTON, MARY, was daughter of ELIZABETH, who married (1) THOMAS HAUGHTON (2) JOHN PENRICE (3) JACOB BUTLER; the daughter MARY HAUGHTON became wife of THOMAS MINGE in (1738) 2-298, 2-470.

HAUGHTON, THOMAS, married ELIZABETH and had MARY who married THOMAS MINGE 2-298; his widow married JACOB BUTLER (1759) 1-456; he was sued by WILLIAM GLOVER in ALBEMARLE PRECINCT in (1702) 1-509; RICHARD HAUGHTON was guardina of his children(1744) 1-455.

HAUGHTON, RICHARD, guardian of THOMAS HAUGHTON orphans (1744) 1-455.

HAUGHTON, WILLIAM, land grant (1716) joining the land of LEWIS WILLIAMS 1-14; he deeded land to THOMAS HAUGHTON on YOPPIM river in(1725) 2-447; in (1749) his children were RACHEL, JAMES and ESTHER HAUGHTON 1-451; after his death his widow (1753) married THOMAS BURKETT 2-469.

HAVET, WILLIAM, witnessed deed from JOHN HASSELL to SARAH WILKINSON (1719) 1-628; he and wife MARY deeded lands to JOHN WILLIAMS in(1720) with JENNINGS DANIEL a witness 2-613; he obtained land grant (1719) next to the lands of HENRY CLAYTON 1-18; he bought land from JOHN VOLWAY in (1720) 2-612; he sold land in (1718) to MARY WOOD, daughter of MRS. MARY CLARK, widow of THOMAS CLARK (whom he may have married?) 1-623.

HAWKINS, BENJAMIN was a witness with JOHN BOYD and SIMON ALDERSON to the will of EDWARD TRAVIS of BEAUFORT (1739) 1-495.

HAWKINS, EDWARD, will (1777) wife ELENER, witnessed by ROBERT TITUS and PETER HAYS 2-340.

HAWKINS FAMILY. Births of children 3-209; genealogy of the family 1-638 and 2-605.

HAWKINS, FRANCIS, died (1676) 3-365.

HAWKINS, JAMES SR. sold land bought from JAMES HOOPER to his brother THOMAS HAWKINS (1725) with WILLIAM DOWNING and JAMES BLOUNT the witnesses 2-447; he was brother of the THOMAS HAWKINS who left will (1732) 1-50.

HAWKINS, THOMAS (JR.) was son of the THOMAS who left will (1732) and a nephew of JAMES HAWKINS, SR. 1-50.

HAWKINS, JOHN, ESQ. was a Lord DEPUTY and met with the Assembly at JOHN HECKELFIELD'S house in (1707) with GOVERNOR WILLIAM GLOVER 1-457; he sold land to WILLIAM KETOR in BERTIE (1715) 1-293; owned land next to WILLIAM REEVES in (1719) 1-528; deeded lands on KEZIAH RIVER to RICHARD ROSE (1716) 1-298; his wife was MARY and they sold land to HENDERSON WALKER in (1703) 3-511; his name appears on an order for the election of Burgesses in CURRITUCK early (no date) 3-275; he and JOHN WEST and JOHN HUNT were present at a court held at home of RICHARD POPE (1694) of which EDWARD MAYO was Clerk. 3-465; in(1706-7) signs proclamation with WILLIAM GLOVER vouding all offices as then held 3-261; his mother was MRS. MICHAEL LYNCH and his grandmother was MRS. ALICE WADE, when he was a minor (no date) 3-140; in (1694) he signed the bill of ANNA SOUTHELL, with WILLIAM DUKENFIELD 3-247; in (1716) he made deed to JOHN PLOWMAN with JOHN BOYD a witness 2-519; in (1701) his wife was MARGARET 3-372; he and EDWARD MAYO were at the house of WILLIAM REED (1697) and he was also present at court 3-465; in (1715) he made deed to JOHN IUERTON, witnessed by THOMAS BALL 1-207; he was the executor of the will of ALICE WADE (1701) 1-32; there are two JOHN HAWKINS' wills, relating to different persons of the name, one probated APRIL 10, (1717) and the other APRIL 20 (1717) 1-51; SARAH, the widow of one of these, died (1719) leaving will 1-228; and a later JOHN HAWKINS leaves will (1744) 1-228; the last will was in PASQUOTANK and SARAH'S will was in PERQUIMANS 1-228, 1-229.

HAWKINS, THOMAS, SR. will (1793) in BERTIE names children and daughter ELIZABETH HARDY 3-341; his son THOMAS (perhaps) died in (1704) 3-402; and another THOMAS HAWKINS was a THOMAS CARY DEPUTY (1708) 1-454; and may have been the one who lived at HAWKINS' NECK (1728) 3-446; Thomas Hawkins married ALICE DAVIS 3-81; he signed the Deer Skin BOND of (1689) 3-81; a THOMAS was the son of JOHN and MARY HAWKINS (1704) 3-375; in (1716) Thomas Hawkins sold land to JOHN FALCONER on ALBEMARLE SOUND 1-294; one THOMAS HAWKINS died and left will in (1730) mentions brother JAMES 1-50.

HAWKINS, ROBERT, of BATH made deed of gift to MARGARET HAINBROOK (1721) of land in CRAVEN COUNTY 2-618.

HAWKS, MARIAN (widow) of CHARLESTON, S. C. gave power of attorney to WILLIAM WILLIAMS (1729) witnessed by JOHN ISMAY 2-446.

HAWTHORNE, JOHN, of SURRY COUNTY, VA. sold lands to FRANCIS McCORRY (1718) 1-623.

HAYS, HARDY, will (1784) wife was SARAH and gives names of his children 2-339.

HAYS FAMILY. Wills 2-516, 2-339.

HAYS, JOHN, witness to deed (1717) with THOMAS WEST 1-617.

HAYS, PETER 2-340.

HAYS, RICHARD, will (1786), wife EDY and BENJ. MIRES, Executors 2-339.

HAYMAN, HENRY will proved (1727) but written in (1697) which must have been at or near time of his death, names son WILLIAM, daughter ANN and child in esse, and brother THOMAS HAYMAN 1-50, 1-51.

HAYWOOD, JOHN of EDGECOMBE, sons WILLIAM, EGBERT and JOHN (no date) 1-47.

HAZARD, JAMES in (1731) was the orphan of ROGER HAZARD 1-449.

HAZARD, ROGER, had orphan JAMES (1731) 1-449; & was a witness to deed to TIMOTHY TRUELOVE in (1718) with ROBERT HICKS 3-518.

HEALE, JOHN, of CHOWAN, appointed Constable in (1711) 3-442.

HEED, PETER (HEARD?) sold lands (1720) to HENRY MIDDLETON adjoining JEFFREY LILES and HENRY CLARKE, witnessed by ZILPHA and JOHN EDWARDS 2-514.

HEATH, SAMUEL, married JANE HADDOCK in (1697) 3-408.

HEARE, SAMUEL, in (1702) his wife was JANE 3-373.

HECKLEFIELD, JOHN, copy of document appointing him Captain of militia on N. E. side of the PERQUIMANS river 3-256; no date on this paper, but in another note the date is given as in (1702) 1-609; the Lord Deputies met at his house on Little River in (1704) and at various other times 1-610, 1-454, 3-260, 2-88; he was Provost Marshall (1718) 3-281; he died leaving will (1721) mentions son JOHN HECKLEFIELD, with EDMUND GALE and GEO. DURANT as executors 1-51. (Grimes p 160 says there was filed with this will another executed 1718, and that Gov. Charles Eden, Edmund Gale and George Durant were also legatees, and that he mentions sister in law MARY COX).

HECKSTALL, WILLIAM, will (1848) 2-522.

HEDGEPETH, HENRY of NANSEMOND CO. VA. sold land to EDWARD HARE (1732), witnessed by JOHN DAWSON, THOMAS SPEIGHT and MOSES HARE 2-609.

HEDGEPETH, JAMES, of NANSEMOND CO. Va., made a deed (1737) witnessed by CHARLES KING and JOHN DRURY 3-131.

HEDGEPETH, JOHN, of NANSEMOND CO. VA. sold land to THOMAS SPEIGHT (1717) with CUTHBERT HEDGEPETH a witness 3-129.

HEIDELBERG, CHRISTIAN, was a witness (1721) with ORLANDO CHAMPION 2-518.

HENBY FAMILY.   Will 3-336, 3-173.

HENBY, SYLVANUS, will (1767) mentions son JOHN and JOSEPH OUTLAW 3-173.

HENBY, THOMAS, one of the witnesses to the will of SYLVANUS HENBY (1767) 3-173.

HENDERSON, ALEXANDER, was Master of the sloop PEGGY in (1749) 1-435.

HENDERSON, CAPT. DAVID bought land (1706) 1-92.

HENDERSON, DAVID lived in (1719) between CASHY RIVER and SALMON CREEK in BERTIE 1-444; he had a sister GENNON HENDERSON and a nephew GEORGE HENDERSON in (1735) 1-49; he died leaving will (1735) in which they were named 1-231; and GEORGE HENDERSON died in (1736) 1-231; see also 3-244.

HENDERSON, GEORGE, died leaving will (1736) in which he mentioned ANDREW MOORE, ANDREW SCOTT and HUGH SCOTT; JOHN RAY was one of his executors 1-231; in another abstract of this will ROBERT IRVING and GEORGE POWELL are mentioned 1-48.

HENDRIXEN, ISAAC, will (1840) 2-522.

HENDRICKS, DANIEL, will (1768) in BERTIE Co. mentions wife ELIZABETH, daughter SARAH DANIEL and ELISHA WHITFIELD 2-340; another and earlier DANIEL had his estate divided among his children by LUKE MIZELL, WILLIAM LATTIMORE and JOSEPH JORDAN 2-522.

HENDRICKS, JOB, will (1788), mentions grandsons, including SOLOMON and JOB, also JOSEPH, DEMPSY and PENINAH, with RALPH FLETCHER and JOSEPH PERISHO executors 3-172.

HENDRICKS, SOLOMON will (1833) mentions sons DANIEL, DELANO, DAVID, JOSIAH and others with DAVID WHITE and JOSIAH NICHOLSON executors; his wife was MARY and he also had a son ABEL HENDRICKS 3-338; in one note SOLOMON HENDRICKS, son of THOMAS and ELIZABETH HENDRICKS was born (1759)3-386.

HENDRY, ROBERT, was an inspector in BERTIE (1771) 3-450.

HENLEY, JOHN, died leaving will (1729) names wife ISABELLA and children 1-50.

HENLEY, PATRICK, petition addressed to PHILLIP LUDWELL (1689-1694) 3-91, 3-93; was sued by THOMAS WHITE (1694) 3-146; he was dead in ALBEMARLE PRECINCT in (1702) and MATTHEW PRITCHARD was his executor 1-610.

HENLEY, SARAH married MATTHEW PRITCHARD 3-260.

HENLEY, PA. (PATRICK?) affidavit found on the records at EDENTON (1696) 1-599, 1-600.

HENRY, ROBERT SR. will (1806) wife ELIZABETH sons ROBERT and JAMES and WILLIAM and daughter NANCY who married a FREEMAN. He mentions LEWIS OUTLAW and son JAMES HENRY 2-519.

HEPWORTH, JOSHUA, his mark recorded (1689) 3-431.

HERRING, ABRAHAM, recorded his mark in BERTIE in (1745) 2-626.

HERRINGTON, CLINCH, was son in law of JOHN MASON, SR. (1737) 1-60.

HERRINGTON, HEZEKIAH, of New England, left a will in BERTIE (1754) wife HANNAH 1-222.

HERMAN, ROBERT, left will (1714) named his wife REBECCA 1-52.

HERRITAGE, WILLIAM will CRAVEN (1769) 1-228.

HERON, JOHN, land grant in (1720) on South side of BEAR SWAMP 1-9.

HERRON, JOSEPH, was Sheriff of CHOWAN (1747 and (1749) 1-451.

HEWES, GEORGE, bought land on RIVER POCOSIN in (1732) from RICHARD BROTHERS 3-127.

HEWES, JOSEPH, the "Signer" from NORTH CAROLINA genealogy of his family 1-474, 1-475; he was a merchant at EDENTON 1-550; he was the uncle of NATHANIEL ALLEN 1-517; he left a will in (1773) and died in PHILADELPHIA while a member of the Continental Congress 1-474 and 2-170; will (1778) 1-550.

HEWES, WILLIAM, bought land from WILLIAM CRAW - FORD on BENNETT'S CREEK (1737), and there was a GEORGE HEWES and WILLIAM HUGHES JR. 3-127.

HICKS, AFRICA, wife of ROBERT HICKS left will in (1711) mentions sons PATRICK and GREGORY McGREGORY 1-52; (Grimes p. 163 says she mentions her sister ANN PALIN (widow) and others not shown in the Hathaway abstract).

HICKS, DAVID, will (1732) mentions son in law THOMAS ASHLEY 1-50.

HICKS, GRACE, was the daughter of THOMAS LUTEN of CHOWAN 1-444.

HICKS, ROBERT, obtained three land grants (1715) 1-14; he married ESTHER LUTEN, daughter of THOMAS LUTEN, was Register of CHOWAN PRE - CINCT and owned the land on which a part of the town of EDENTON is built 1-49; he was of SANDY POINT and left will (1734) 1-49; he sold land to MOSES FOXWORTH in (1716) with JAMES LONG a witness 1-293; made deed to JOHN or JONATHAN WHITE SR. (1723) 2-443 and he and ESTHER were witnesses together in (1717) 1-618; he witnessed deed from WILLIAM to JAMES HINTON in Chowan in (1718) 1-624; he had only two children living in (1748), THOMAS HICKS and MARY HALSEY 3-305; in (1717) he bought land from FRANCIS MAC- LENDEN, witnessed by WILLIAM WILLIAMSON 1-516; he witnessed a deed to JOHN BRYAN in (1720) 2-513; was attorney for JOHN COUNCIL of NANSEMOND COUNTY, VA. in (1718) 1-625; obtained land grant with WILLIAM BADHAM in (1727) 1-12; and a grant for himself in (1713) on Rockyhock Creek 1-3; he witness to deed of JOHN WHITEMARSH (1715) 1-299; & sold land to JAMES FARLOW (1716) 1-291.

HICKS, SAMUEL, and RICHARD McCLURE witnessed a deed of JOB RIDDICK to JOHN SIMPSON in (1739) 3-134.

HICKS, THOMAS, will (1722) mentions CHRISTOPHER SUTTON, son of JOSEPH SUTTON, and others apparently in ENGLAND 1-50.

HIGGINS, WINNIFRED, of HALIFAX COUNTY, N. C. mar- ried a HOSKINS 1-549; (She was WINNIFRED HOSKINS of the Edenton Tea Party, perhaps).

HIGGS FAMILY. Wills 2-338, 2-520.

HIGGS, JUDITH, left will (1796) in BERTIE COUN- TY. Jacob HIGGS a witness 2-338.

HIGGS, ABRAHAM, will (1782), wife SARAH and sons JOHN and ABRAHAM HIGGS. Wife, NOAH HINTON and GEORGE WILLIAMS, Executors 2-338.

HILL, ABRAHAM, of NANSEMOND COUNTY, Virginia, deeded land to WILLIAM HINTON (1720) witnessed by EDWARD BASS and THOMAS ROUNDTREE 2-515; the ABRAHAM HILL whose wife was JUDITH is said to be the son of HENRY HILL, genealogical account of his family, his descendants, and the records and abstracts relating to his family at some length and detail 1-472 to 1-477; owned lands (1728) that joined SARAH BOND and WILLIAM JONES 2-444; ABRAHAM of WAKE COUNTY, N. C. was son of ABRAHAM of CHOWAN COUNTY (account of his family) 2-159; Abraham married CATHERINE WALTON (1756) in Chowan 1-293; his importation by HENRY HILL proved (1710) 2-305; ABRA- HAM and wife JUDITH sold land to JACOB SPIVEY (1732) 2-456; the one from NANSE- MOND COUNTY, VA. bought land from WILLIAM JONES of PERQUIMANS (1727) 2-445; he and ISAAC HUNTER witnessed deed of FRANCIS PUGH to DANIEL PARKER (1734) 3-131; was granted land (1759) at head of LOSING SWAMP 1-20; one ABRAHAM lived in (1726) on what was known as HORSE PEN SWAMP 2-445.

HILL, BENJAMIN, was the administrator of the estate of GEORGE GOULD (1749) 2-633; sat with JOHN HARRELL and JAMES CASTELLAW as Justice at CASHEY BRIDGE (1747) 2-630; he was born in (1697) according to note at bottom of page and married a MISS LATHAM 1-48; one of his daughters married JOHN CAMPBELL, son of JAMES, and another was the wife of ALEXANDER McCULLOUGH; he left will in BERTIE COUNTY in (1758) in which he mentions daughters MARY, SARAH, PRIS- CILLA and son HENRY 1-48; genealogy of his family on the same page; in (1733) he was the executor of JOHN JERNIGAN 1-54; qualified as Justice of BERTIE COUNTY in (1746) 2-628; he and ALEXANDER COTTEN proved will of JOHN RODOLPH (1744) in BER- TIE COUNTY 2-620; he and THOMAS JONES & RICHARD WILLIAMS witnessed deed by PENEL- OPE LITTLE (1737) 3-130; account of the relationship between the HILL and COLLINS family 2-637.

HILL, HENRY, son of BENJAMIN, nothing known of him 1-48. But see 1-292, 3-125, 2-447, 2-305.

HILL, EDWARD. His commission as JUDGE of AD- MIRALTY issued in (1697) signed by MILES CARY, as Register 3-39, 3-40.

HILL, ELIZABETH, daughter of ABRAHAM HILL may have married EDWARD BASS by (1720) 2-616.

HILL FAMILY. Account of its connection with the FAISON FAMILY, and the genealogy of descendants of a certain WILLIAM HILL 3-310 to 3-314; Maryland connections of the Hill family 2-157; wills of the fam- ily in Gates County 3-51; other Hill fam- ily wills 1-552, 1-553; the Hill family of DUPLIN COUNTY 2-157, 2-158.

HILL, GEORGE, of BATH, left will in (1722) & mentioned his son HARMON HILL 1-50.

HILL, GREEN, of BUTE COUNTY. Query in Q & A department as to his ancestry 2-157.

HILL, HARDY, of BERTIE COUNTY, left will in (1777), names his wife JANET, and daugh- ter ELIZABETH; his wife, and THOMAS and LUKE COLLINS named as Executors of the will; THOMAS LAWRENCE and ASA LAWRENCE were the witnesses 2-340.

HILL, HANNAH, daughter of JACOB HILL and wife ELIZABETH was born (1723) 3-386; in (1689) HANNAH HILL was grandmother of JAMES PERISHED 3-430; she obtained an order for the management of JAMES PERISED'S cattle until the said James should chose his guardian (1790) 3-437, 3-438.

HILL, HENRY, bought lands from JOHN FREEMAN in (1733) on BENNETT'S CREEK 2-609; of NANSEMOND CO. VA. bought land from JOHN WATSON (1713 -15) 2-447; he deeded lands on BENNETT'S CREEK to the INDIANS (1733) 2-609; proved his rights for importation of HENRY, MARY and ABRAHAM HILL, and JOHN, WILLIAM and ELIZA HINTON (1710) 2-305.

HILL, ISAAC, in (1721) was the executor of JOHN PLOWMAN 1-68; in (1724) was a member of the General Court with WILLIAM DOWNING and THOMAS POLLOCK at EDENTON 2-468; he was either the grandfather or great grandfather of Hon. WHITMELL HILL: 1-52; he witnessed deed (1717) from ROBERT WEST to SOLOMON JORDAN 1-621; he and THOMAS POLLOCK owned adjoining lands in (1720) 2-614; he witnessed deed by SOLOMON JORDAN in (1718) 1-625; some genealogy of his descendants - including the REEDS, JACOCKS and REAS 2-536; one ISAAC HILL married MARGARET JENNINGS in Middlesex County, Va. 1-637; in (1717) one ISAAC witnessed deed from THOMAS BROWNE to to RICHARD WASHINGTON 1-300; he left will in BERTIE COUNTY (1710) in which he names his children and makes ROBERT WEST his executor, the witnesses being EDWARD BRYAN, WILLIAM MAULE and JOHN HALE 1-52.

HILL, JACOB, his wife was ELIZABETH, births of their children (1721) 3-386.

HILL, JOHN. One JOHN is said to have married a NANCY CURRIER 3-315; JOHN HILL of BATH left will (1721) to which HARMON HILL was a witness 1-49; another JOHN HILL of BATH left will (1731) 1-221 (These two seem to be the same, though they are of different dates); JOHN HILL (a later one) and HUMPHREY BATE were sureties for THOMAS WHITMELL (1749) 2-632; he and wife ANN a deed to JOSEPH COLLINS of BERTIE in (1769) 3-447; a JOHN HILL of NORTHAMPTON left a will in (1747) had sons NATHANIEL, DANIEL, LEWIS and PETER HILL 1-221;JOHN & HARDY —2-340

HILL, HARMON, of BEAUFORT, will (1755) wife was SARAH, and children married into the HANCOCKS, RICE and SLADE families 1-221.

HILL, MARY, in (1771) was an orphan of MICHAEL HILL, and THOMAS COLLINS her guardian 3-450

HILL, MICAJAH, married RUTH PERRY (1763) 3-413.

HILL, MICHAEL, his orphans, of BERTIE, in (1771) THOMAS COLLINS was their guardian 3-450; division of his estate (1770) 3-448; he was the son of NATHANIEL HILL and ELIZABETH HARDY (daughter of JOHN and REBECCA HARDY) and NATHANIEL HILL was the son of ISAAC HILL 2-536; proves P. of Atty (1711)3-441

HILL, MOSES and JACOB PERRY (1719) witnessed deed of JAMES PERRY and wife PATIENCE to JOHN PERRY 2-137; in (1720) he bought land from THOMAS SPIVEY and wife MARY 2-608; in (1762) he left will in BERTIE COUNTY and youngest daughter JUDITH HILL and son in law DANIEL FREEMAN 2-339.

HILL, NATHANIEL, and JOHN DEW, were among the Justices present at a court held for BERTIE PRECINCT (1724) 2-466; he was the youngest son of ISAAC HILL 1-52; and married ELIZABETH HARDY, daughter of JOHN HARDY and his wife ELIZABETH 1-52 note at bottom of page; was the executor of SAMUEL RATLIFF in (1723) 1-70.

HILL, PRISCILLA, was the daughter of BENJAMIN HILL 1-48.

HILL, RICHARD, of BATH, in CRAVEN PRECINCT, left will (1723) in which he mentioned brother FRANCIS and son in law EVAN JONES 1-50 ; he and THOMAS ROUNDTREE witnessed deed by THOMAS SPIVEY (1720) 2-612.

HILL, ROBERT, was in EDGECOMB COUNTY before (1736) 2-467; may have been the son of ROBERT TYRRELL HILL who left will(1736) wife ANN and son ROBERT, daughter SARAH with CULLEN POLLOCK and ROBERT WEST his executors 1-221; alive (1740) 2-468.

HILL, SAMUEL, of WARWICK COUNTY, VA. left will (1693) 1-52.

HILL, SION. An account which says that he married DRUSILLA LANE, had son RICHARD HILL and first cousin HENRY HILL; and the RICHARD HILL had son DR. DUNCAN HILL who was born (1799) 2-310.

HILL, THOMAS, of EDGECOMBE COUNTY (1740) is mentioned with ROBERT HILL of same 2-468; a THOMAS B. HILL married REBECCA NORFLEET, daughter of REUBEN, and had a son WHITMELL HILL married LAVINIA BARNES and WINNIFRED HILL married WILLIAM NORWOOD - 2-606.

HILL, HON. WHITMELL married his first cousin WINNIFRED BLOUNT, daughter of ELIZABETH WHITMELL and THOMAS BLOUNT 2-297, 2-506.

HILL, COLONEL (WILLIAM?); his account for the building of a warehouse (1744) is allowed 2-621. H. G. Connor says he came from BOSTON 3-7.

HILL, WILLIAM, in (1724) witness to contract between FRANCIS and THOMAS ROUNDTREE to build a mill on CATHERINE CREEK 2-289; in (1721) a William Hill was grandson of WILLIAM BOGE (BOUGE) 1-32; bought land in (1734) from JAMES BENNETT and the CHOWAN INDIANS on INDIAN TOWN SWAMP, with THOMAS JONES and ROBERT FORSTER witnesses 3-125; one was son (1721) of JACOB HILL and wife ELIZABETH 3-386; witnessed in will of BASIL SANDERSON in ANTIQUA (1721) 1-76; he married MARY SPIVEY, daughter of THOMAS SPIVEY by (1729) 1-75; he bought land from BASIL SANDERSON (1721) 2-139; married MARY SPIVEY daughter of THOMAS SPIVEY and wife MARY before (1720) 2-612.

HILL, WILLIAM, of BRUNSWICK COUNTY, list of his children (from will) and his descendants and a genealogy of this particular branch of the HILL FAMILY, and its connections with the HENRY FAISON family and the CHRISTOPHER DUDLEY family 3-310, and 3-311, 3-312 and 3-313.

HILL, WILLIAM, of CHOWAN, will (1751) and the one in NORTHAMPTON will (1748) 1-221.

HILLARY, SAMUEL, will in BATH (1712-13) SAMUEL WOODWARD Executor, with ALEXANDER OLIVER & HENRY TURNER, witnesses 1-221.

HILLIARD, CHARITY, wife of ROBERT HILLIARD who left will (1751) 1-230.

HILLIARD, ANN, was daughter of WILLIAM HILLIARD of NORTHAMPTON COUNTY (1754) and her mother was also ANN 1-230.

HILLIARD, ELIAS, was son of WILLIAM HILLIARD in (1756) 1-230.

HILLIARD, JACOB, son of JEREMIAH HILLIARD and had brothers ROBERT and JEREMIAH (1751) 1-230.

HILLIARD, JAMES, son of WILLIAM HILLIARD and wife ANN (1756) 1-230.

HILLIARD, JEREMIAH, appears (1751) to have had children JACOB, ROBERT, JEREMIAH, LAWRENCE, MARY and SAMPSON HILLIARD 1-230.

HILLIARD, JOHN, died in NORTHAMPTON in (1748) names wife MARY and sons ROBERT and JOHN & daughter SARAH 1-29-30.

HILLIARD, LAWRENCE, was son JEREMIAH HILLIARD (1751) 1-230.

HILLIARD, MARY, wife of JOHN HILLIARD of NORTH-AMPTON COUNTY (1748) 1-229, 1-230, 2-606.

HILLIARD, ROBERT, will in EDGECOMBE (1751) wife was CHARITY 1-230.

HILLIARD, WILLIAM, of NORTHAMPTON, left will in (1756) in which he names all his children & his wife ANN, the witnesses being HENRY HART, JOSEPH BRIDGERS and CHARLES COTTON 1-230.

HILLIARD, REBECCA, married GAVIN HOGG CLARK, (son of WILLIAM McKENZIE CLARK and MARTHA BODDIE WILLIAMS) 2-603, 2-606. (See for HILLIARD GENEALOGY).

HILLINGWORF, PETER, a witness with JOHN ISMAY in (1729) 2-446.

HINES, JOHN and wife HANNAH (1755) 3-386.

HINES, MOSES, left will in GATES COUNTY in (1803) wife was RUTH, with JESSE B. BENTON and KE-DAR PARKER witnesses 2-56.

HINES, PETER, son of JOHN HINES and wife HANNAH born (1755) 3-386.

HINES, RICHARD, of NANSEMOND COUNTY, VA. sold land to JOHN PIPKIN, granted to CHARLES SCOTT (also of Nansemond Co.) (1735) JOHN HINES, GEORGE WILDS (WILDE) and WILLIAM BULLOCK, witnesses 3-126; he also sold to MOSES BOYCE in (1736) 3-126.

HINES, SAMUEL with JOHN HINES was witness to a deed (1736) by RICHARD HINES 3-126.

HINES, WILLIAM, will (1785) mentions brothers MOSES, CHRISTOPHER, PETER and JOSHUA HINES; his wife was ANN (she may have been nee ANN DONALDSON, who first married a COLLINS) and his wife's sons JEREMIAH and JOHN COL-LINS; his wife and ANDREW DONALDSON were his executors 3-174.

HYMER, HENRY, will (1772) 1-228.

HINTON FAMILY. Genealogical account of the HINTON FAMILY, descendants of COL. JOHN HINTON, of CHOWAN, showing connections with the KIMBROUGHS, SMITHS, BRYANS and other families, also the LANES and HILLS, 1-463, 1-464, 1-465 and 1-466; Wills of the family 1-553, 2-53, 2-54, and 2-238.

HINTON, AMOS, son of JAMES HINTON, whose estate was divided (1761) 2-263.

HINTON, AARON, son of JAMES HINTON, whose estate was divided (1761) 2-263.

HINTON, DEMPSEY, brother of AMOS and AARON HINTON (1761) 2-263.

HINTON, ELIZABETH, widow of WILLIAM HINTON, whose estate was divided (1737) 1-263.

HINTON, JACOB, estate divided (1778) list of his children 2-264.

HINTON, JAMES, bought land from WILLIAM HIN-TON in (1718), ROBERT HICKS a witness 1-624; division of his estate and names of his children (1761) 2-263.

HINTON, JOHN, deceased (1737) his widow ELIZ-ABETH, Executor 2-469; a later one died and estate divided (1763) wife was SARAH 2-263; JOHN HINTON, of CHOWAN. left will (1730) sons HARDY, JOHN, WILLIAM and MAL-ACHI, wife MARY and daughters ANN ALSTON, MARY, JUDAH, RACHEL, ROSE, SARAH, CHARI-TY. 1-50; JOHN HINTON son of JAMES (1751) 2-263; one JOHN bought lands (1734) from JAMES BENNETT and the CHOWAN INDIANS 3-125; the JOHN who died (1730) lived in that part of CHOWAN now GATES COUNTY see NOTE 1-50; JOHN HINTON, son of JAMES HIN-TON in (1745) bought land from THOMAS WALTON JR. on CATHERINE CREEK 1-118; the widow of JOHN HINTON married THOMAS HOLLI-DAY in (1732) 1-450.

HINTON, MALACHI, was one of the sons of COLON-EL JOHN HINTON, of CHOWAN who died in (1730) 1-50.

HINTON, MICAJAH, was the son of WILLIAM HINTON and his wife ELIZABETH, whose estate was divided (1737) 2-263, 2-469.

HINTON, NANCY, married LEWIS BRYAN, who was a daughter of MAJ. JOHN HINTON, of WAKE COUNTY, N. C. 1-577.

HINTON, NOAH, was the son of WILLIAM HINTON & wife ELIZABETH (d. 1737) 2-263; he died about 1803, and gives names of brothers & other relatives, including the THOMPSONS 2-518.

HINTON, REUBEN, son of WILLIAM and brother of NOAH 2-263.

HINTON, RACHEL, was daughter of JOHN HINTON & wife SARAH (1763) 2-263.

HINTON, WILLIAM, died (1736) names of all his children 1-447; estate divided in (1737) names given again, the same; wife was ELIZABETH 2-263; he witnessed a deed by JOHN LEWIS in (1733) 2-609; he bought land in (1720) from ABRAHAM HILL, Nansemond County, Virginia 2-615; deed (1718) made to JAMES HINTON 1-624.

HINTON, ZADOCK, son of JACOB (1778) 2-264.

HOBBS, ABRAHAM and wife MARY (1696) 3-369.

HOBBS FAMILY. Wills 1-553.

HOBBS, SAMUEL, witnessed the will of JOHN OLIVER in (1816) 2-535

HOBBS, THOMAS in (1753) left six minor children in care of MARY HOBBS 2-470; he bought land from WILLIAM ROUNDTREE of PERQUIMANS (1734) 2-453; a THOMAS HOBBS estate divided (1778) between children named 2-264; the first one (1745) sold land to his son JOHN HOBBS on South side of CATHERINE CREEK, part of a grant to THOMAS ROUNDTREE in (1720) 1-118.

HOBDAY, ROBERT, charged with the tuition (1770) in BERTIE of MALACHI SIMMONS 3-448.

HOBSON, FRANCIS, will (1766) names neices and nephews CANNADY 2-340, 3-445.

HOBBY, JACOB, of EDGECOMBE COUNTY, will (1758) wife JEMIMAH and son MATTHEW 1-231.

HOBBY, LAWRENCE, a witness with HENRY WHEELER of a deed by JOHN BAILEY (1717) 1-299; made deed to THOMAS DRAKE in CHOWAN (1717) which was witnessed by RICHARD WASHINGTON 1-515; was a member of PATTERSON'S COMPANY in CHOWAN in (1720) 1-443.

HOCKS, WILLIAM JR. in (1733) owned lands next to MOSES HARE and JOHN DAVIDSON 2-511.

HOCKINS, JOHN (HAWKINS) married MARY BATEMAN (1701) 3-409.

HODGES FAMILY. A genealogical account of some descendants 2-173.

HODGES, JAMES will (1722) mentions wife SARAH CATHERINE and cousin ELIZABETH HARRISON 1-51

HODGES, JOHN, will in BERTIE in (1827) mentions son WHITMELL, daughter ELIZABETH RHEA and younger children WILLIAM, SARAH, JESSE and MARY 2-522.

HODGSON, CHARLES, witnesses indenture contract of JOHN BALLARD (1717) 1-518.

HODGSON, JOHN was a member of the CHOWAN court in (1743) 1-447; he exhibited inventory of THEOPHILUS PUGH (late of Virginia) in (1745) 1-452; an earlier one's widow married ROGER SNELL (1679) 1-73; he died in (1747) and his widow PENELOPE was administrator 1-457; he was son in law of SAMUEL PAGET and wife ELIZABETH (1737) 3-135; the earlier one left will in CHOWAN (1712) witnessed by JOSEPH BENNETT 1-52; the later one received land grant in (1738) which joined GEORGE CAPEHART 1-12; a list of his orphans in (1751) 1-451.

HODGSON, SAMUEL was one of the orphans of JOHN HODGSON (1752) 1-451.

HOGUN, JAMES, was a Colonel and Brigadier General in the North Carolina Continental Line in revolution 1-422; JAMES HOGAN, evidently earlier, was the father in law of MARMADUKE NORFLEET who died in (1762) 1-63.

HOGG, ANN, daughter of JAMES HOGG and wife ANN - was born (1681) 3-211; she died (1693) 3-220.

HOGG, GAVIN, with GEORGE OUTLAW and JOSEPH BRYAN was an executor of ANTHONY COPELAND in (1817) in BERTIE 2-509; he was also an executor of MOSES GILLIAM in (1822) 2-515.

HOGG, JAMES, was the son of JOHN HOGG of Yorkshire in ENGLAND and he married ANN KENT the daughter of THOMAS KENT and his wife Ann 3-200; they had a son JAMES 3-212; a daughter ANN 3-220; a daughter HANNAH 3-367; JAMES HOGG proved his rights about (1706) 1-305; James and Ann also had son JONATHAN HOGG 3-212.

HOGG, JANET, married COLIN McKENZIE HAWKINS & had many descendants 1-538, 1-539

HOGG, RICHARD, of BLADEN, died about (1769) mentions a sister in England, and their father was WILLIAM HOGG. ROBERT and JOHN HOGG his executors, and THOMAS BAILEY was a witness 1-221.

HOGG, SARAH was the daughter of JAMES HOGG & his wife ANN KENT 3-215.

HOGG, THOMAS left will (1696) in which he mentioned JOHN DACOST, and DIANA HALFORD & MARY NASH were witnesses 2-465; another THOMAS HOGG of CRAVEN sued JOHN MURPHY in (1737) 2-303.

HOGG, THOMAS, was a Lieutenant in the First Regiment North Carolina Contiental Line 1-416.

HOGGARD'S MILL was on CASHY RIVER in BERTIE in (1769) 3-447.

HOGGARD, WILLIAM left will in BERTIE COUNTY in (1823) in which he mentions sons ELISHA and JAMES and son JOHN and several others, DAVID and SOLOMON RICE were witnesses 2-521.

HOLDEN, ROBERT, mentioned in affidavits relating to CULPEPPER REBELLION 3-43.

HOLDEN, THOMAS, recorded his mark in BERTIE COUNTY in (1771) 3-449.

HOLDER, ELISHA, SR. left will (undated) in it he mentions sons AARON, SHADRICK and others 2-519; ELISHA HOLDER JR left will in BERTIE (1826) and had SOLOMON, JOHN & wife WINNY 2-519.

HOLDER, THOMAS, left will in BERTIE in (1774) mentions wife SUSANNAH, and sons JOHN, THOMAS and ELISHA HOLDER 2-340.

HOLLY, CHRISTOPHER, was sued by THOMAS HARRIS in 1683 in ALBEMARLE COUNTY 3-283.

HOLLY, BENJAMIN was the son of JAMES HOLLY who died (1795) see will 2-339.

HOLLY FAMILY. Wills 2-521, 2-522 and 2-239.

HOLLY, JAMES, will (1795) gives names of his children, JOSHUA FREEMAN witness 2-339.

HOLLY, NATHANIEL, will (1782) mentions wife SARAH and names children, JOHN FREEMAN & TIMOTHY WALTON, Executors; LEWIS OUTLAW one of the witnesses 2-339.

HOLLY, MOORE, son of JAMES HOLLY, was brother of ANN HOLLY, who married AMOS BRITTAN & of ELIZABETH HOLLY who married LEWIS OUTLAW 2-339, 2-501; daughter m. LANDRAM 2-522

HOLLY, PENELOPE, sister of MOORE HOLLEY, ANN BRITTAN and ELIZABETH OUTLAW, left will in (1853) 2-522.

HOLMES, JOHN, of NANSEMOND COUNTY, VIRGINIA, bought land from WILLIAM FOULK (FOLK) of same place 1-298. (1716)

HOLMES, EDWARD, of NANSEMOND COUNTY, VIRGINIA, bought land from WILLIAM FOULK (FOLK) of same place (1716) witnessed by JOHN JERNIGAN (JARNEGAN), RICHAR TAYLOR and JOHN RALES 1-298.

HOLMES, REV. JOHN, sued JOHN POPE and JOHN BROWN, Church Wardens of the N. W. PARISH of BERTIE (1739) 2-303.

HOLMES, THOMAS, married MARY COLYER in (1695) 3-408. JAMES HOMES to WILLIAM BIRD 2-444.

HOLLAND, FREDERICK, was son of HENRY HOLLAND in (1768) 3-444. DANIEL HOLLAND, CRAVEN 1-230

HOLLAND, HENRY, appears to have had sons HENRY and JOSEPH (1768) 3-444; bought land (1728) bought land from WILLIAM SPEIGHT of NANSEMOND COUNTY, Virginia 2-444; and sold same to THOMAS VAUGHAN also of NANSEMOND COUNTY, VIRGINIA 2-444.

HOLLAND "son in law" of ELIZABETH MARSTON (1732) in BATH 1-62.

HOLLAND, JOSEPH, son of HENRY HOLLAND, left will (1790) had daughter SARAH THOMAS 2-341.

HOLLOWAY, ELIZABETH, married JONATHAN BATEMAN, JR. (1697) 3-408.

HOLLOWAY, THOMAS, in (1697) his wife was ELIZABETH 3-408; in (1719) his wife was MARY & they had several children born 3-386, 3-387

HOLLOWAY, WILLIAM, the son of HANNAH HOLLOWAY, who left will (1807) 3-336.

HOLLOWELL, EDMUND, in his will (1729) names his brothers JOHN and THOMAS 1-49.

HOLLOWELL, EZEKIEL, was in (1784) executor will of DANIEL FOREHAND, with JOSEPH WHITE and ELIZABETH ROUNDTREE witnesses 3-171

HOLLOWELL FAMILY. Wills 1-556, 2-520, 3-172, 3-173, 3-336.

HOLLOWELL, LUKE, will (1735) names sons WILLIAM, JOEL, JOHN and REUBEN and wife ELIZABETH 1-48.

HOLLOWELL, REUBEN, son of LUKE, of PERQUIMANS, left will (1753), mentions brothers LOUY, JOHN and ABNER, witnessed by NICHOLAS STALLINGS 1-227.

HOLLOWELL, THOMAS, witnessed will of PETER DRAPER (1764) 3-169.

HOLLOWELL, WILLIAM, left will in (1766) named wife ELIZABETH and "all my children" with JESSE HOLLOWELL the executor 2-339.

HOLLIDAY, JOHN, left will in BERTIE (1818) with WILLIAM MOORE, JR. and JEREMIAH LEGGETT, Executors 2-521.

HOLLIDAY, THOMAS, was granted lands (1730) 1-12; married the widow of JOHN HINTON in (1732) 1-450; his widow married WALTER LONG about (1750) 2-305; query as to his descendants from about (1730)3-316.

HOLLIDAY, SAMUEL, apparently brother of the THOMAS HOLLIDAY, whose descendants are requested 3-316.

HOLBROOK, JOHN, gave Power of ATTORNEY (1715) to JOHN HARDY, witnessed by THOMAS WEST & THOMAS DANIEL 1-288; he and wife DOROTHY sold land in BEAUFORT PRECINCT about (1720) to PATRICK MAULE 2-612; he left will in BERTIE (1740) mentions son JOHN and his wife DOROTHY 1-48; in (1744) JAMES McDOWELL, his administrator presented his account 2-623.

HOLBROOK, THOMAS, owned lands next to THOMAS JONES and JOHN EDWARDS in (1718) 1-621.

HOLDBROUGH, JOSEPH, left will in BATH in (1711) in which he mentions his brother JOHN HOLDBROUGH 1-52.

HOLLENBECK, JASPER, left orphans and in (1771) ROBERT CAKE was their guardian in BERTIE 3-450.

HOLT, THOMAS, of CHOWAN, left will in (1776) wife MARY and son in law EDWARD COFFIELD with JESSE BROWN a witness 1-551.

HOMES, JAMES (HOLMES) of BERTIE deeded lands to WILLIAM BIRD of NANSEMOND COUNTY, VA. (1728) 2-444. (The HOLMES family shown previously was from NANSEMOND COUNTY, so we are sure they were the same).

HOMES, JOHN, had been on the tax list CHOWAN since (1703) 1-443; indenture of a JOHN HOMES resigned by EDWARD GILMAN to JOHN WYNNS (1745) 2-628.

HOMES, THOMAS, was the father in law of DAVID LAWLER, whose wife was ELIZABETH 1-58.

HOOD, THOMAS, had something to do with the estate of THOMAS REASONS (1769) 3-446.

HOOKS, JOHN, left will (1732)and named all of his sons and daughters 1-49.

HOOKS, THOMAS, and wife ANNA sold lands to JOHN SMITH of BERTIE (1771) 3-449; lived on the road from BLACKMAN'S to OLIVER'S FERRY in BERTIE 3-448.

HOOKER, BENJAMIN died leaving will in BERTIE in (1774) mentions wife ANN, names sons HARDY, JOHN and other children 2-340; he and SIMON HOOKER recorded their marks in BERTIE in (1745) 2-626.

HOOKER, ELISHA, was son of BENJAMIN HOOKER of (1774) 2-340.

HOOKER, HARDY, was the eldest son of BENJAMIN HOOKER (1774) 2-340.

HOOKER, HULDA, married a POWERS by (1774)2-340.

HOOKER, SIMON, registered his mark in BERTIE in (1745) 2-626.

HOOKER, WILLIAM, will in CHOWAN (1717) eldest son, WILLIAM JR., and son in law SAMUEL SIZEMORE, William Crawford and FRANCIS BROWN witnesses 1-230, also 1-51; he sold lands to JOHN DEW in (1716) patented to TREBLE KEEFE, with THOMAS KIRBY a witness (this in HERT-FORD COUNTY) 1-287.

HOOKER, WILLIAM, of BERTIE, left will (1737) & named sons JOHN, WILLIAM, JAMES, STEPHEN & NATHAN, wife was not named, the WYNNS and BAKERS were witnesses 1-230.

HOOPER, JAMES granted lands on LONG BRANCH in (1715) 1-15; sold land to JOHN WORLEY (1720) with THOMAS TAYLOR a witness 2-615; & JOHN HOOPER of "SOUTH SHORE" sold land to JAMES HAWKINS (1716) with JOHN EDWARDS a witness 1-297.

HOOPER, WILLIAM, the "SIGNER". Claimed by H. G. Connor to be from BOSTON 3-7; (this compiler doesn't believe that); letter from to GOVERNOR CASWELL 3-240; his home built by DR A. J. DeROSSETT 2-489.

HOOPER, WIDOW, about to marry JAMES BLOUNT, the son of WILLIAM (1701) 1-610.

HOPKINS, ARNOLD in (1711), with PETER GRAY and others exempted from the highways for maintaining the bridge over BLACK WALNUT RUN 3-441.

HOPKINS, JOHN, granted land on YOPPIM river in (1696) 1-5; left will (1721) mentions CHARLES CRADDOCK 1-51; left will in CHOWAN (1753) 1-47; his wife was SARAH in (1696) 3-369.

HOPKINS, SAMUEL, was son of JOHN HOPKINS and his wife SARAH, and was born (1696) 3-369.

HOPWOOD, MARY, was the step daughter of JOHN HAMBLETON (1706) 1-50.

HORN, HENRY, was a witness to a deed by STEPHEN LEE in (1729) 2-447.

HORN, JOHN, with WILLIAM HOLMES and RICHARD TAYLOR witnessed deed from WILLIAM FOULK (FOLK) to JOHN JERNIGAN (JARNIGAN) of NANSEMOND CO. VA. 1-298; his wife was SARAH and they had a son JOHN HORN (1746) about 6 years old committed to the tuition of JOHN WYNNS 2-627.

HORN, MICHAEL, witnessed deed by WILLIAM HORN to ELIAS STALLINGS (1729) 2-448.

HORN, MOSES and THOMAS HORN, witnessed the will of WILLIAM RUFFIN (1781) 2-352; in (1744) he proved his rights in MOSES, JOEL and MARY HORN 2-625.

HORN, RICHARD, was a member of PATTERSON'S COMPANY, from MEHERRIN river in CHOWAN (1729) 1-443.

HORN, WILLIAM, Rights claimed on account of the importation of WILLIAM HORN and ELIZABETH ADAMS by THOMAS LOVETT, who sold such rights to MAJ. ALEXANDER LILLINGTON about (1702) 3-139; his wife was MARGARET (1723) and he & JOHN DRURY were witnesses 2-448; in (1729) MOSES HORN sold lands to ELIAS STALLINGS & MICHAEL HORN was witness 2-448.

HORNADAY, ISAIAH, said to have married SU-SANNA CARR in NORTH CAROLINA, no date given 1-636; Susannah Carr was daughter of WILLIAM A. CARR and she was born in (1774) perhaps married in RANDOLPH CO. N. C. 2-157; they had a son EZEKIEL HORNADAY and CHRISTIAN, CHRISTOPHER, LEWIS and JOHN HORNADAY were brothers of ISAIAH and all entered lands in CHATHAM COUNTY, N. C. (no dates); said to have come from IRELAND 2-157.

HORNBEE, WILLIAM, will (1808) had two daughters married ARRENTONS and one a BATEMAN; related to the STANDINS 3.336, 3-337

HORNER, ELLENER, left will (1719) mentions daughter ANN SAFFORD 1-51.

HORNETT, CORNELIUS (Should be HARNETT) with THOMAS STOBBS (or STUBBS) witnessed a deed by JOHN BROWNING to his son in law WILLIAM MORRIS 2-613.

HORNIBLOW, JOHN, signs a bond for the famous (or infamous) BENEDICT ARNOLD; he was the owner of the old "KING'S ARMS" an Inn in the town of EDENTON. The date of the bond is (1774). 3-299.

HORST, SAMUEL. His wife was JANE (1705) 3-375.

HORTH, THOMAS, will (1735) his daughter married a MING or MINGE - MARTHA 1-48.

HORTON, ELIZABETH, an orphan chose THOMAS PIERCE as her guardian about (1742) 1-447

HORTON, THOMAS, granted land at the mouth of the YOPPIM RIVER (1704) 1-6; another grant (1719) 1-18; the last to WILLIAM.

HORTON, WILLIAM, witnessed deed (1732) with CORNELIUS LEARY to THOMAS PIERCE 2-452; he sold land to CHARLES HORTON in (1722) on YOPPIM POCOSON witnessed by JOHN BLOUNT 2-284.

HOSEA, JOSEPH, left will (1785) sons SAMUEL and JOSEPH, witnessed by WILLIAM HOSEA & MARY STANTON 3-175.

HOSKINS, HANNIBAL, with wife MARGARET appear in (1690) in a lawsuit with WILLIAM DUKINFIELD 1-613; his wife was MARGARET FUREE and they were married by FRANCIS HARTLEY, ESQ. in (1690) 3-204.

HOSKINS, EDMUND, married ELIZABETH BLOUNT in (1802) 3-300; list of descendants of this couple who moved to Texas, married into the BROWNRIGGS, GILLS and others 1-300, 1-304.

HOSKINS FAMILY, Genealogy of the descendants of WINNIFRED HOSKINS of the EDENTON TEA PARTY 3-116 to 3-118; wills of the family 1-549, 1-550, 2-57.

HOSKINS, MARGARET, will in GATES COUNTY in (1838) had daughter married CHARLES CUNNINGHAM 2-57.

HOSKINS, MARTHA, was the widow of JAMES TROTTER and the sister of WILLIAM HOSKINS about (1756) 2-305.

HOSKINS, MARY, married JAMES BOND (1787) she daughter of RICHARD HOSKINS 3-116.

HOSKINS, RICHARD, of CHOWAN, was the son of WIL-
LIAM HOSKINS and wife SARAH WHEDBEE (and
WILLIAM HOSKINS was the son of THOMAS HOS -
KINS and ELIZABETH BOWLING), and RICHARD
married WINNIFRED WIGGINS (daughter of JOHN
WIGGINS and CATHERINE BAKER) and his wife
WINNIFRED HOSKINS was the Secretary of the
EDENTON TEA PARTY 3-122; he received a grant
of land at GREEN HALL (1782) 1-21; and an-
other about the same location (1794) 1-34;
for genealogy of their descendants see 3-300
to 3-304; 3-116 to 3-124.

HOSKINS, SAMUEL, received land grant (1792) on
MATTACOMACK SWAMP 1-24; he married NANCY
ROBERTS, and died (1802) 3-117; had children
ELIZABETH who married JOHN HOGAN of HALIFAX
COUNTY, and WILLIAM and MARY HOSKINS 3-118.

HOSKINS, THOMAS SKINNER, married HARRIET WILLI-
AMS WILSON, of CAMDEN COUNTY, N. C. and had
son BLAKE BAKER HOSKINS C. S. A. 3-121. The
HOSKINS family lived, many of them, in the
immediate vicinity of EDENTON 3-124.

HOSKINS, THOMAS, the founder of the HOSKINS FAM-
ILY, appeared in N. C. by (1670); genealogy
of his descendants 3-310, 2-311, 2-312; one
THOMAS married the widow of MOSES HUNTER in
(1769) 3-446; one received land grant next
to NICHOLAS CRISP (1712) 1-8; and another in
(1719) 1-17; he was to erect a mill on the
road from EDENTON to the Virginia line in
(1748) 2-459; one left a will (1733) with
JOHN BENBURY as Executor; see NOTE 1-49.

HOSKINS, WILLIAM was dead by (1692) and there is
a list of his goods at time of death 3-258;
a later one received a land grant (1749) on
WALLOWING ROOT SWAMP 1-20; he was said to
be the son of THOMAS HOSKINS and his wife
ELIZABETH BOWLING (or BOLLING) of KENT, in
ENGLAND 3-116.

HOUCK, RICHARD, was the grandson of THOMAS MAT-
THEWS of CHOWAN and his wife PRISCILLA will
(1732) 1-62.

HOUGHTON, DAVID was deceased (1754) and left
widow MARY and three sons 2-264.

HOUGHTON, ELIZABETH, was the daughter of THOM-
AS HOUGHTON and was born (1697) 3-369.

HOUGHTON, GEORGE, was the son of THOMAS born
in (1688) 3-218.

HOUGHTON, JONATHAN , land grant (1784) 1-22.

HOUGHTON, MATTHEW, was the son of THOMAS, born
(1707) 3-377.

HOUGHTON, THOMAS and his wife MARY 3-377; 3-217

HOUGHTON, RICHARD. His mother was dead (1743)
and he was administrator 1-447.

HOUGHTON, THOMAS left will in ONSLOW (1733)
1-48; he and wife SARAH 3-367, 3-217.

HOUGHTON, WILLIAM, land grant on YOPPIM RIVER
(1720) 1-9; he made deed to JOHN PORTER in
(1715) witnessed by THOMAS CARY, JOHN LIL-
LINGTON and JOHN and JOSHUA PORTER 1-294.

HOUSE FAMILY headrights to JAMES FENOX 2-299 in
the year (1702).

HOUSE FAMILY. Wills in BERTIE 2-339; 1-233,
2-340.

HOUSE, BAYLIS, son of GEORGE HOUSE in (1771)
1-233.

HOUSE, GEORGE, will in BERTIE in (1771) gives
list of children and grandchildren, and
the executor was his son in law JAMES
MOORE 1-233; another GEORGE left will in
BERTIE (1796) 2-340.

HOUSE, JAMES, sold land to JOHN WHITE JR., on
North part of CHOWAN RIVER, with ANTHONY
HOLLIDAY and LUKE WHITE witnesses (1714)
1-104; JAMES HOUSE of ISLE OF WIGHT COUN-
TY, VA. bought land from JOHN WHITE SR. &
wife SARAH (1697) part of a patent to LEWIS
WILLIAMS 3-131.

HOUSE, THOMAS, will (1803) mentions brother
WILLIAM HOUSE and sister SALLY MOORE, and
brother WILLIAM HOUSE and TITUS MOORE were
his executors 2-518; he lived in BERTIE
PRECINCT in (1728) (one did) 2-470; and
left will there in (1734) in which he mentions his son BAYLIS HOUSE 1-49.

HOUSE OF BURGESSES. An address to the GOVERNOR
and Council about (1703) 2-223; communica-
tion from to the House of Deputies 3-50.

HOW, WILLIAM, of BOSTON, deed to SAMUEL SMITH
of NANSEMOND COUNTY, VA. (1736) with WIL-
LIAM SMITH and ROBERT REDDICK witnesses
3-126.

HOWARD, BENJAMIN, with JAMES BAKER, witnessed
the will of ELIJAH HOWARD in BERTIE (1820)
2-521; married SARAH MIDDLETON (1775) 3-109

HOWARD, CHARLES, of CRAVEN COUNTY (1754) names
son CHARLES and son in law JACOB SHARKBOX;
FRANCIS FONTAINE and ANN SPINKS were witnesses 1-234.

HOWARD, EDWARD, bought land from RICHARD CHURCH
and wife JANE (1715) with JOHN JORDAN and
JOHN WILLIAMS witnesses 1-293; he was witness to deed to JOHN BRYAN (1717) 1-520; he
and ROBERT HICKS were witnesses to a deed
from JAMES BOON to STEPHEN HOWARD in (1721)
2-517; he also witnessed deed (1715) CHOWAN
from PETER EVANS to WILLIAM EVANS 1-285; he
and ROBERT LANIER witnessed deed of ABRAHAM
BLEWETT and wife JANET (1718) 1-525; and one
from MATTHEW CAPPS (1716) 1-295; in (1719)
he sold land to WILLIAM BARNES that had been
granted to RICHARD WILLIAMS 1-530; with
TREBLE KEEFE he witnessed deed by JAMES CAR-
TER and wife (1717) 1-526

HOWARD, ELIJAH, left will in BERTIE (1820)2-521

HOWARD, JAMES, had daughter SARAH and his widow married (by 1744) THOMAS CREA 2-523;
he left will (1729) in BERTIE, wife SARAH,
sons SOLOMON and others, and brother ELI-
JAH 1-234.

HOWARD, JOHN, was Master of the sloop DEFIANCE
in (1775) 3-466; one was Master of sloop
THREE FRIENDS (1749) 1-433.

HOWARD, KATHERINE, witnessed the will of JAMES
BYRUM in BERTIE in (1806) which mentions
daughters ELIZABETH and MARTHA COOPER 2-502.

HOWARD, KITRAIN, was a witness to the will of JOHN SMITHWICK (1761) with JOHN HOWARD who mentions grandson JOHN SUTTON 2-354.

HOWARD, MOSES, married SUSAN PERRY (1790) 3-419

HOWARD, STEPHEN, bought land from JAMES BOON (1721) on South side of CHOWAN RIVER 2-617.

HOWARD, WILLIAM, was a servant of THOMAS SPEIGHT in (1702) 3-85; he made affidavit in the loyalist and Tory troubles (1777) that he was at the house of JONATHAN DAVIS and was placed under bond with BENJAMIN HOWARD as his surety 3-367.

HOWCOTT, EDWARD, received a land grant (1716) on ROCKYHOCK CREEK 1-16; he sold land to EDWARD MOSELEY (1715) with ROBERT HICKS & ELIZABETH SWANN witnesses 1-291; made deed to JAMES POTTER, of CHOWAN (no date)1-294.

HOWCOTT FAMILY. Wills 1-551; 1-49.

HOWCOTT, JOHN, bought land from JOHN WATSON in (1717) with ROBERT HICKS and WILLIAM BROWN as witnesses 1-617; he sold land to SAMUEL WOODWARD (1713) 2-608; and in (1716) to WILLIAM DOE, with JOHN NAIRNE a witness 1-292; died leaving will in CHOWAN in(1733) mentions daughter ELIZABETH BRANCH 1-49.

HOWE, ALEXANDER, will in BERTIE (1780) had son THOMAS HOW; executors were COL. JOHN HARDY of PITT County, luke COLLINS and HUMPHREY HARDY 2-341. JOSEPH HOWES 2-468.

HOWE, MARY, will (1814) 2-520.

HOWE, ROBERT, was Colonel and Brig. General in N. C. Continental Line; also a MAJOR GENERAL 1-416.

HOWELL, ROBERT, and his wife SARAH proved his rights (1746) 2-627.

HOWELL, MILES, of GATES COUNTY will (1839) 3-57.

HUBBARD, JOHN, sold land to WILLIAM PARKER in (1735) next to MOSES HALL, which he had inherited from his father, with WILLIAM PARKER and JAMES HUBBARD witnesses; the land of JOHN NORFLEET also joined 1-111.

HUBBARD, THOMAS dead (1771) heirs were MARY McGUIRE and CHARITY HUBBARD 2-265; he left will in CHOWAN (1770) naming daughter CHARITY, son in law EPHRAIM McGUIRE, daughter MARY and ABRAHAM NORFLEET, son of ABRAHAM NORFLEET, with SARAH NORFLEET (another daughter?) as witness 1-551; he was granted lands (1751) next to JESSE BUNCH 1-20; sold land to GEORGE ALLEN (1732) with DAVID AMBROSE a witness 2-510.

HUBBARD, MATTHEW in (1767) was ordered to take JOHN FANNEY under his care until next court 3-444.

HUBBLE, JOHN, married ELIZABETH HAWKINS before (1719) 1-51.

HUCKINS FAMILY. Wills 1-222.

HUCKINS, DANIEL, will in BATH (1733) his wife was ANN; mentions "all my children"; RICHARD SCOTT a witness 1-222.

HUDGINS, HUMPHREY, will in GATES COUNTY in (1822) 3-57.

HUDGINS FAMILY. Wills 2-57.

HUDSON, ABEDNIGO, of NEW BERN, administration on his estate (1787) ANNE HILL a widow, formerly HUDSON, relict 3-466.

HUDSON FAMILY. Notes relating to the family taken from the old HARRISON FAMILY BIBLE, including MARY the wife of HENRY HUDSON (about 1686) 3-475.

HUDSON, JOHN, will (1772) mentions brother URIAH HUDSON and others 3-172.

HUDSON, JOSEPH, bought land from DANIEL HALSEY in (1702) 1-385; he and THOMAS SPIRES witnessed deed of THOMAS YEATES to THOMAS LUTEN (1721) 2-615.

HUDSON, URIAH, was brother of JOHN HUDSON & mentioned in his will 3-172 (possibly the nephew instead) he died leaving will (1830) mentions connections with the WINSLOW and PERRY FAMILIES, with JOHN WHITE a witness 3-338.

HUGHES, GEORGE, will (1764) wife SARAH and a son in law JOHN MIZELL 2-340; he proved the rights of himself, his wife SARAH & MARY, ANN, ELIZABETH, ELISHA, JEMIMAH, WILLIAM, GEORGE and THOMAS HUGHES (1745) 2-626.

HUGHES FAMILY. Wills 2-517, 2-518.

HUGHES, JOSEPH, was administrator of the estate of THOMAS FLOYD (1767) in BERTIE 3-443.

HUGHES, WILLIAM, his wife ELIZABETH 3-212; he had a son WILLIAM 3-215.

HUGHEY, JOSEPH, married JANE ERWIN (1737) 3-470.

HUGHTON, THOMAS and wife SARAH had son CHARLES HUGHTON born (1702) 3-374.

HUMPHREY, RICHARD, will in CHOWAN (1796) had a son JONATHAN and daughters SARAH and MARY SMALL, and MARGARET HUMPHREY 1-550; a later RICHARD (1800) (maybe the same) had DAVID, THOMAS and MARGARET 2-265.

HUMPHREYS, WILLIAM left will (1798) had sons WILLIAM, JOHN and THOMAS and daughters PARTHENIA, SUSANNA & LYDIA 3-175; a later WILLIAM (perhaps the same) will (1833) had son in law GEORGE S. BARCLIFT 3-338.

HUNNICUTT, SARAH, was SARAH GLAISTER, the daughter of JOSEPH GLAISTER, Quaker 1-217. (She was the wife of WYKE HUNNICUTT -WSR).

HUNT, JOHN met with the Court at the home of GEORGE DURANT in (1685) 1-512 testified in regard to troubles in the CARY REBELLION 3-225, 3-226; was ordered to survey land (1695) 3-250; statement as to JOHN CATCHMAID'S will while GLOVER was Clerk 3-64, 3-65; died at his home on LITTLE RIVER in PERQUIMANS PRECINCT in (1712) mentioning no children of his own; only grandchildren named EVANS. THOS. COMMANDER witness 1-228.

HUNT, MEMUCAN, of GRANVILLE COUNTY, N. C. was appointed by the Legislature of (1782) the Commissioner of Confiscated Property for the Hillsboro District 2-160.

HUNT, THOMAS, of PASQUOTANK (may have been the brother of COL. JOHN) left will proved in (1696) in which he mentions "younger brother ANDREW HUNT, of Co. BUCKS, ENGLAND" & also appoint him my executor; also mentions "Sons JOHN HAWKINS and THOMAS HAWKINS"; EDWARD SMITH, WILLIAM COLLINGS and John CAFEY (CASEY?) witnesses 1-228.

HUNTER, ARTEMESIA, married GEORGE BOZEMAN(1817) and had son JOSEPH JAMES BOZEMAN; George died in WINDSOR (1820) 3-472. (He was the son of JOSEPH BOZEMAN and CHLOE HARRISON; ESTHER COWAND and CHLOE BOZEMAN were daughters of WILLIAM HARRISON and wife HANNAH)

HUNTER, CADER, died leaving will (1790) names children HUMPHREY and HARDY HUNTER 2-341.

HUNTER, CATHERINE in (1769) in BERTIE was ward of THOMAS WIGGINS 3-447.

HUNTER, EPHRAIM, with RICHARD TAYLOR was witness to deed of JOSEPH HARE (Of Nansemond Co. Virginia) to ROBERT THOMAS, of lands inherited from his father JOHN HARE (1735) 3-127; he and JOHN WESTON in (1746) were appointed to office 3-527.

HUNTER FAMILY. Wills 1-221 (includes ANN, WILLIAM and JOHN) 2-51, 2-52, 2-519, 2-341.

HUNTER, HARDY, left will (1794) his wife was RACHEL, anf sons HUMPHREY, CADER, WILLIAM, TIMOTHY and JOSHUA HUNTER, and one daughter married a PERRY (SARAH) 2-341.

HUNTER, HENRY, was foreman of the Grand Jury in BERTIE (1749) 2-533; and a Deputy Sheriff in (1746) 2-627; his wife was SARAH WHITMELL and they had THOMAS, SARAH, FANNY and ANN HUNTER 3-449.

HUNTER, HUMPHREY, will (1805) brother of CADER HUNTER, JOSEPH BLOUNT a witness 2-519.

HUNTER, ISAAC, son of NICHOLAS HUNTER, and the grandson of WILLIAM HUNTER (late of Va.) who patented lands on MEHERRIN'S SWAMP issuing out of BENNETT'S CREEK 3-133; ISAAC left will in CHOWAN COUNTY (1752) and mentions daughter who married JONATHAN PARKER 1-47.

HUNTER, JAMES, was the son of WILLIAM HUNTER in (1770) and his mother was SARAH HUNTER, & he had brothers and sisters named 2-265.

HUNTER, JOB, was the guardian of orphans of one MOSES NEWBORN, Bertie (1769) 3-447.

HUNTER, JOHN, left will in CHOWAN (1771) wife ALA and children; THOMAS and SARAH WALTON and ELISHA HUNTER witnesses 1-548.

HUNTER, MOSES, his estate (1768) mentions PATTY HOSKINS widow of said HUNTER, but HENRY HUNTER is taking over 3-446

HUNTER, NICHOLAS, of BEAUFORT (1749) wife was REBECCA 1-48.

HUNTER, NICHOLAS and wife REBECCA give POWER OF ATTORNEY to THOMAS ROUNDTREE to sell certain lands (1728) 2-446; these lands had been patented by WILLIAM HUNTER in (1701) and were sold by ROUNDTREE under this power in (1729) 2-445.

HUNTER, ROBERT, Treasurer to receive monies for lots sold at BLACKMAN'S LANDING in (1752) 3-92, 3-93; he left will BERTIE in (1753), wife was ELIZABETH WHITMELL and daughter SUSANNAH BENTON 1-47.

HUNTER, SARAH, widow of WILLIAM HUNTER (1749) 1-451.

HUNTER, THOMAS and wife REBECCA were Executors of THOMAS SWANN (1739) 2-302.

HUNTER, WILLIAM, of NANSEMOND COUNTY, VIRGINIA, was the father of NICHOLAS HUNTER, whose attorney (1729) was THOMAS ROUNDTREE 2-445; he left will (1732) 1-50; Sarah was his widow in CHOWAN 1-451; he received another land grant (1722) next to JOHN PORTER and others 1-11.

HUNTLEY, CHARLES entered lands above those of GEORGE DEARE on ROCKYHOCK CREEK in (1680) 1-614

HURST, JOHN, left will in (1769) and mentioned wife JUDITH, son WILLIAM and a daughter MARY GREET 2-340.

HURST, THOMAS, was sued by CAPT. THOMAS CULLEN in (1685) 1-613.

HUSBANDS, RICHARD, left will (1732) mentioned wife JANE and sons RICHARD and JOHN 1-50.

HUTCHISON, WILLIAM, proves his rights (no date) including MOSES WHITAKER, FRANCIS ELLIS & WILLIAM HUTCHINSON (four trips) 3-282; date given as (1702) 1-009.

HYDE, EDWARD, Governor, with NATHANIEL CHEVIN, WILLIAM REED and THOMAS PETERSON members of the COUNCIL (1712) 2-152, 3-267.

HYDE PRECINCT. List of FREEHOLDERS living there in (1715) including BONNERS, BRIGHTS, BARROWS and many others 3-425.

HYMAN FAMILY, mentioned in will of CLARISSA LEGGETT (1842) 2-526; also in the will of WILLIAM SPARKMAN (1785) 2-356.

HYMAN, HUGH, was appointed to look after tuition of RACHEL REDDITT, daughter of WILLIAM & SUSANNAH REDDITT (1747) 2-630.

HYMAN, JOEL, mentioned in will of JOHN PENDER (1805) who calls him brother-in-law and had sister MARY HYMAN 3-535; left will in (1817), with WILLIAM PENDER a witness 2-521.

HYMAN, MARY, was wife of JOEL HYMAN (1817)2-521; mentioned as daughter with ANN DEW in the will of ALEXANDER RAY in BERTIE (1769) 2-353

HYMAN, SAMUEL, will (1847) WM. SOUTH men. 2-521.

HYSMITH, DANIEL (1744) proved his rights 2-624.

HYTER, THOMAS, an INDIAN CHIEFTAN 2-609.

HARRISON FAMILY. The numerous HARRISONS of this record are all seemingly the descendants of FOUR PERSONS of the name who came into ALBEMARLE PRECINCT shortly after BACON'S REBELLION out of VIRGINIA. They lived contiguously, were of the same generation and could have been, and probably were, brothers. At the time of their coming and always afterwards and until this good day they were related to the HILLS, SPEIGHTS, BENNETTS, SIMMONS, HARMONS, JORDANS, BRYANS, CROPLEYS, VINES and JONES FAMILIES. Their names were JOHN, ROBERT, THOMAS and EDWARD HARRISON. We know that THOMAS was born about 1645 and presumably the others were relatively and consecutively about the same period, and they were therefore contemporaneous with the second BENJAMIN HARRISON, son of the Clerk of the Virginia Council in 1633, about whose origin practically nothing is known. In CHARLES CITY County at this particular period there was a certain WILLIAM HARRISON, whose sons they may have been, if an obvious speculation may be indulged.

JOHN HARRISON died in CHOWAN in 1693. Children, WILLIAM, JOHN and ELIZABETH are named in his will (1-48).

ROBERT HARRISON died in ALBEMARLE in 1713 (1-232). His wife was ELIZABETH and his children ROBERT, JOSEPH, REBECCA (d. 1706 3-404), SARAH and ELIZABETH.

THOMAS HARRISON was born about 1645 (3-42, 1-139) and his first wife was ELIZABETH (3-301), though he appears to have married a second time to a widow JOANNA about 1680. His children were JOHN, THOMAS, HANNAH (1-52) and ELIZABETH (3-301).

EDWARD HARRISON is the most interesting of the four brothers (?), since he has managed to elude the sleuthing genealogists for nearly 300 years. He did NOT migrate to NEW ENGLAND, as so many of them have insisted, but after signing a petition of the followers of NATHANIEL BACON in Blissland Parish (of New Kent County, Va.) in 1677, he slipped quietly away with his family into ALBEMARLE COUNTY, N. C. where he joined his brother in law JOHN CROPLEY and other relatives, and lived happily ever afterwards. He had married a daughter of MR. LUKE CROPLEY, of London, a wealthy merchant, who after the death of his wife's mother, again married MARY BENNETT, the widow of the still wealthier THOMAS BLAND, a sister of SYLVESTER HILL, wife of MAJ. NICHOLAS HILL, of York County, Virginia, and daughter of EDWARD BENNETT an uncle of GOVERNOR RICHARD BENNETT. EDWARD HARRISON and his wife had three sons (1) WILLIAM (2) JONATHAN and (3) DANIEL HARRISON, some of whose descendants were as follows:

(1) WILLIAM HARRISON married SARAH VINES, daughter of JOHN VINES. His wife was a sister of ANNE VINES who married JOHN CROPLEY, and of THOMAS VINES who married MARY HILL (These last the grand - parents of ANN VINES who married ISAAC COLLIER, who had son MYHILL COLLIER who married a BENJAMIN HARRISON (see later). JOHN CROPLEY who married ANN VINES had a son VINES CROPLEY (1-39) and WILLIAM HARRISON had a son VINES HARRISON (1-48). In order to convey some idea of the dates applicable it is appropriate to say that MARY CROPLEY a sister of VINES CROPLEY married JAMES BEASLEY (son of ROBERT BEASLEY and wife SARAH) in 1675, and when VINES CROPLEY died about 1720, ROBERT BEASLEY (son of JAMES?) was the administrator of his estate. The children of WILLIAM HARRISON and his wife SARAH VINES were JOHN (3-444), JOSHUA, WILLIAM and EDMUND HARRISON, and a daughter SARAH who married HUMPHREY FELTS (1-48). Likewise VINES HARRISON.

(2) JONATHAN HARRISON in 1701 owned lands on the North side of ALBEMARLE RIVER and among his close neighbors was ARGYLE or ARGALL SIMMONS and WILLIAM HARRIS and his wife ANNE (1-4, 1-95). JONATHAN HARRISON was the father of at least two sons, DANIEL HARRISON and JOSEPH HARRISON, who married ELIZABETH SIMMONS. DANIEL HARRISON, son of Jonathan, bought lands from his cousin JOSEPH HARRISON, the son of (3) DANIEL HARRISON in 1729 (2-447). The SIMMONS family, to which ARGALL SIMMONS belonged, lived in ST. ANDREW'S PARISH in Brunswick County, Virginia, and perhaps acted as the magnet that drew JOSEPH, son of JONATHAN back to that part of the country before his death. The records of that period indicate that a number of these HARRISONS went along at the same time. At any rate in the year 1763, JOSEPH HARRISON died in BRUNSWICK COUNTY (Va.) leaving a will in which he named six children: WILLIAM, DANIEL, BENJAMIN, SIMMONS, PATTY and NANCY HARRISON who married HENRY MANGUM JR. (Later a prominent N. C. family). WILLIAM HARRISON (son of JOSEPH, son of JONATHAN, son of WILLIAM) is said (by the family genealogists) to have married ELIZABETH SIMMONS,(an evident error, since that was his mother's name) though the old family Bible shows her name was HANNAH, and gives him a daughter CHLOE and a daughter ESTHER(3-472). According to the family genealogical account he and his wife ELIZABETH (sic) had JOSEPH, BENJAMIN, ANN, ELIZABETH (m. JOHN HILL BRYAN), SUSANNAH (m. WILLIAM BRYAN), MARY (m. SPEIGHT), REBECCA (m. WILLIAM ISLER), PENELOPE HARRISON and SIMMONS HARRISON. The last, SIMMONS HARRISON, was born in JONES COUNTY, N. C. in 1777 and died in SUMPTER COUNTY, Ala., in 1855. He married HOLLAND SPEIGHT (b. 1781 in JONES COUNTY N. C.) and they had children: NANCY SPEIGHT HARRISON (m. JACOB GILES), MARY R. HARRISON (m. NATHAN BRYAN BUSH), ELIZABETH (m. JOSEPH PIERCE), REBECCA (m. JAMES BRYAN SHINE), HOLLAND (m. WHITE), MATILDA (m. WILLIAM HARRISON GREEN, a cousin), BENJAMIN HARRISON, SIMMONS (b. 1817), LARISSA (m. KIRKLAND) and SUSAN CHARLOTTE HARRISON (m. ELIJAH BRASIER BLALOCK). This last couple were the parents of MRS. R. W. FINLEY, of AUSTIN, TEXAS.

(3) DANIEL HARRISON, died leaving a will in CHOWAN, proved January 14, 1726-7, in which he mentions his son JOSEPH and wife and executrix ELIZABETH, "friend" HILL SAVAGE and co-executor EDWARD PADGETT. William Williams, John Falconer and Martha Hammond were the witnesses. (1-50 - GRIMES p. 153).

NOTE: WILLIAM HARRISON married SARAH VINES. Their son was JONATHAN HARRISON, who had son JOSEPH HARRISON married ELIZABETH SIMMONS; and they in turn had BENJAMIN HARRISON, who the books say, had a daughter JUDITH HARRISON. THOMAS VINES (brother of SARAH) married MARY HILL, whose g-dau. ANNE VINES who married ISAAC COLLIER; and they in turn had MYHILL COLLIER who married JUDITH HARRISON. Thus the two lines run back together once more; a trait of these families.

HARDY FAMILY. This family has already been partially mentioned in these notes under the head of "BRYAN FAMILY" (page 20). An exhaustive genealogical account of the HARDYS will be found on pages 216 to 280 of Landon C. Bell's "OLD FREE STATE" Volume II; which account, however omits the N. C. branch of the family entirely. The origin, however, is pretty well stated and the connections with numerous other families are clearly shown.

HILL FAMILY. The HILL FAMILY in all of its ramifications could not possibly be handled in a foot note, such as this purports to be, but the compiler will here make just a few brief observations, one of which is that the genealogy of the family which appears at 3-310 to 3-314, dealing with the family of a certain WILLIAM HILL is wholly inadequate to paint a picture of the Hills as a whole. This WILLIAM HILL whose family is connected with the FAISON, DUDLEY and other families is only one of a large group of persons of the name who were contemporaneous with him. He is mentioned as being "of Brunswick County, Virginia" because the latter days of his life was spent there, and only a small part of it in North Carolina, whence his descendants moved, and because he left a will in Brunswick County. The best account of his family will be found set out, beginning on page 86 of the Virginia Magazine of History & Biography Volume No. 48. A study of that article convinces the reader that the WILLIAM HILL in question came to Lunenburg County, Virginia, from New Kent County, and that he was a brother in law of the famous Clement Reade who married MARY HILL, evidently a daughter of ISAAC HILL (said to have married MARGARET JENNINGS in Middlesex County, Virginia in 1708.). An interesting item, however, in the Hathaway account, was the marriage of FRANCES DIANA FAISON to WILLIAM E. HILL the fourth son of WILLIAM LANIER HILL, who was a grand-daughter of HENRY FAISON, member of an old family from YORK COUNTY, VIRGINIA, to NORTHAMPTON COUNTY, N. C. What was not known to the writer of the Hathaway Account, was the fact that the DUPLIN COUNTY FAISON family - a part of it, at least - transferred their citizenship from North Carolina to Texas. Among the early settlers in FAYETTE COUNTY, TEXAS, was HENRY FAISON, from North Carolina. In an old cemetery at LaGrange, Texas, which this writer has visited, he found a prominent tombstone or marker, reading as follows: "HENRY FAISON. Born in SAMPSON COUNTY, N. C., APRIL 6, 1824; Died at LA GRANGE, TEXAS on October 17, 1853." There are appended to this account at the bottom of 3-313, requests for certain information, among these being one asking for the "Ancestry of Christopher Dudley prior to 1828." The trouble about this is that one does not know WHAT CHRISTOPHER DUDLEY the writer had in mind. There were several of them. The one that was related to the writer collaterally was the father of the famous and distinguished HON. GUILFORD DUDLEY. Guilford Dudley's father CHRISTOPHER DUDLEY married ELIZABETH DANIEL, the youngest daughter of JOHN DANIEL, who died in GRANVILLE COUNTY, N. C. in 1763, a certified copy of whose will I have. The will of this CHRISTOPHER DUDLEY was copied by this writer personally from the records at HALIFAX, N. C. in 1939, it bearing the date 1777, and in it he names the following children: RANSOM DUDLEY, CHRISTOPHER DUDLEY, SARAH DUDLEY, LINTON DUDLEY, ANN DUDLEY (wife of HENRY MACHIN) GUILFORD DUDLEY, ELIZABETH DUDLEY and AGATHA DUDLEY. GUILFORD DUDLEY, HENRY MACHIN and O. DAVIS were the executors named. There is neither time not space to go into it here, but the records show that GUILFORD DUDLEY, the son of this particular CHRISTOPHER DUDLEY was born in CAROLINE COUNTY, VIRGINIA, a tip which the genealogists are welcome to. GUILFORD DUDLEY died near NASHVILLE, TENNESSEE.

MEMUCAN HUNT. The name of his home on the outskirts of WILLIAMSTON in Granville County (now Vance) North Carolina was "BURNSIDE". By his familiars, such men as JUDGE JOHN WILLIAMS, RICHARD BULLOCK and ROBERT BURTON he was called "MUKE" HUNT. When independence came to the Colonies MEMUCAN HUNT was the first State Treasurer of North Carolina and was a member of the Provincial Congress. Doubtless MEMUCAN HUNT had a number of children, but this writer has been unable to supply their names, and only knows of two, DR. THOMAS HUNT and his brother WILLIAM HUNT. The old home "BURNSIDE" still stands in the old WILLIAMSTON settlement in Vance County, a few miles from the town of HENDERSON. Dr. THOMAS G. HUNT, the son, inherited the place about 1820, after the death of MEMUCAN HUNT. It was sold to REDDICK HAMILTON before 1740, when DR. HUNT left North Carolina and came to TEXAS and settled in WASHINGTON COUNTY, at a place called "GAY HILL " not far from the present BRENHAM, where he died and is buried, a fact that few people, and perhaps not many descendants of the family know.

DR. THOMAS HUNT (son of MEMUCAN) married (1) BETTY DUKE, daughter of GREEN DUKE and his wife ELIZABETH WADE, who was a planter of some distinction, it is said, in VIRGINIA. They were the parents of eight children: MARY HUNT, SALLY HUNT, JAMES HUNT, ELIZABETH HUNT, THOMAS HUNT, ALBERT HUNT, WILLIAM HUNT and JOHN HUNT. The son "JAMES HUNT" was DR. JAMES ANDERSON HUNT, who was born in GRANVILLE COUNTY, N. C. Dec. 22, 1808, and died at CALDWELL, TEXAS, January 19, 1892. His parents were married in the year 1800. Dr. James Anderson Hunt was a "BINGHAM" pupil, and obtained his medical education at TRANSYLVANIA UNIVERSITY, Lexington, Kentucky.

DR. JAMES ANDERSON HUNT (son of DR. THOMAS HUNT, son of MEMUCAN) married ANNA ADAIR BRIDGES, HARRODSBURG, KENTUCKY, March 19, 1838. She was the daughter of JUDGE JOHN L. BRIDGES, of Kentucky, and his wife NANCY ADAIR, daughter of GOVERNOR JOHN ADAIR, of Kentucky. Dr. Hunt and ANNA ADAIR BRIDGES were married at "WHITE HALL" near Harrodsburg, Kentucky. They had the following children: WILLIAM, ELIZA, CATHERINE, ANNA, MARIAN, ISABELLA, HENRY, GALLIE, JOHN, BEN, ROWAN HUNT.

BEN BRIDGES HUNT (son of DR. JAMES ANDERSON HUNT) was born at HARRODSBURG, KY. Feb. 19, 1857, and died at CALDWELL, TEXAS, in 1904. He married LAURA BELL PARKS and had the following children: JAMES DUDLEY, MABEL, WAILIE, BEN BRIDGES, HORACE HAMILTON, EDITH, GLADYS, WARREN WOOD, LAURA BELLE and AILA HUNT.

BEN BRIDGES HUNT II, an attorney and writer of considerable note, and a commentator on current events who is widely quoted, resides in AUSTIN, TEXAS, his home for many years past.

WILLIAM HUNT (another son of MEMUCAN HUNT) had one son MEMUCAN HUNT, born in GRANVILLE COUNTY, N. C., who emigrated to Texas, where he became Secretary of the Navy of the REPUBLIC OF TEXAS in Sam Houston's Cabinet. Memucan Hunt (son of William) married a HOWARD, and settled in Galveston. In addition to serving in the Cabinet of the Republic, Mr. Hunt was also, in the pompous language of diplomacy, "Minister Plenopotentiary and Envoy Extraordinary, from the Republic of Texas to the United States of America," and was a Commissioner on the part of Texas to run the boundary line between Texas and the United States. Mr. Hunt, in 1845, was a candidate for the Constitutional Convention held for the purpose of writing a new Constitution for the State of Texas, but was defeated for the post by one BACHE, who was a grandson of BENJAMIN FRANKLIN. After his death this Texas MEMUCAN HUNT'S widow married at least twice. This particular branch of the Hunt family intermarried with the KITTRELL family, the descendants of which are numerous today in Texas.

ILANDS, RICHARD, will (1735) wife ELIZABETH and son ROBERT and daughter JANE and ELIZABETH RAWLINGS 1-53.

INDIANS AND INDIAN TRIBES. Articles of agreement with the BAY RIVER Indians 1-598, 1-599; Commission to audit accounts since the year of the INDIAN MASSACRE (1711) 3-279 to 3-281; petition of the CHOWAN INDIANS relating to their reservation 3-76; petition of BENJAMIN BLANCHARD and others relating to the CHOWAN INDIANS 3-242, 3-243; war declared against the CORE and NYNEE TRIBES (1703) 3-204; Indian commission met at home of WILLIAM BLOUNT (1781) to effect a settlement of dispute between the Indians and the executors of WILLIAM KING 3-453; Act passed relating to the Indians (1715) 3-275, 3-276; Act relating to the TUSCARORA INDIANS 3-426, 3-427, 3-428; Articles of peace with the TUSCARORAS on record at EDENTON 3-218, 3-219; order to lay out reservation for the YAWPIM 3-73; article relating to lands of WILLIAM BABBCOCK and the Indians in PASQUOTANK 3-251; items of interest relating to the INDIAN WAR of (1711-1712) 1-437, 1-438.

INDICTMENT. Copy of Bill of Indictment returned under the Government of the LORDS PROPRIE-TORS 3-153.

INKIRSON, ROBERT, and wife ANNE (1701-2) 3-373.

IREDELL FAMILY. Genealogical account showing the descent of GOV. JAMES IREDELL, and his connection with the McCULLOCH FAMILY, the O'FINIS and McCARTNEYS, and an account of his marriage to HANNAH, daughter of SAMUEL JOHNSTON 2-3, 2-163, and this precedes an account of the JOHNSON FAMILY 2-163, 2-170.

IREDELL, MRS. HANNAH, of the EDENTON TEA PARTY and her family genealogy 2-163; died leaving will (1823) 2-6.

IREDELL, HON. JAMES, GOVERNOR and ASSOCIATE JUSTICE of the SUPREME COURT, appointed by GEORGE WaSHINGTON, and his last will and testament (1790) 2-3; was licensed to practice law in BERTIE (1770) 2-446; his son JAMES mentioned in will of WILLIAM W. JOHNSTON in (1819) 2-253.

IRBY, HENRY, left will (1733) names sons WILLIAM and HENRY and daughter ANN 1-53.

ISHAM, JAMES, of DUPLIN, will (1753) wife JANE and sons JAMES and CHARLES ISHAM 1-323.

ISLER, CHRISTIAN, will CRAVEN COUNTY (1747) children JOHN, WILLIAM, ELIZABETH and SUSANNAH; wife ELIZABETH 1-53.

ISLER, ELIZABETH, wife of CHRISTIAN ISLER and daughter of ROBERT COLEMAN of BATH (1721) 1-31, 1-53.

ISLER, FREDERICK, brother of CHRISTIAN and JOHN ISLER of CRAVEN (1747) 1-53

ISMAY, JOHN, in (1728) witnessed deed by JAMES BAKER (Of NANSEMOND COUNTY, VA.) to JOHN PORTER 2-444; he died leaving will (1729) and his widow CATHERINE married CHRISTOPHER GALE 1-53.

INGRAM, ABRAHAM, of ONSLOW, left will there in (1744) naming sons DAVID ISAAC and ABRAHAM INGRAM 1-323.

IRVING, ROBERT, died leaving a will in CURRITUCK in (1735) and one of the witnesses was HUMPHREY VINES 1-323.

IVES, JOHN, will in CRAVEN in (1750) names sons JOB and JONAS and other children 1-323.

IVES, THOMAS will (1751) CURRITUCK, wife MARY JOHN WOODHOUSE and JAS. PARKER wits. 1-330.

ISHAM FAMILY. The abstract of the will of JAMES ISHAM as shown (1-323) is not quite as complete as that of the same will shown in GRIMES (p. 180) which is as follows:

ISHAM JAMES (DUPLIN COUNTY) Sons: JAMES, CHARLES. Daughter: MARGARET. Wife and Executrix: JANE. Executors: EVAN ELLIS and EDWARD HARRISON, JUNIOR. (Brothers in law). Witnesses: WILLIAM HOUSTON, WILLIAM McKEE, JOHN DUNN. Clerk of the Court: JOHN DICKSON.

That gives us a little more light. It may be that the wife of JAMES ISHAM was JANE HARRISON, a sister of EDWARD HARRISON; or the wife of EDWARD HARRISON was a sister of JAMES ISHAM; or that both JAMES ISHAM and EVAN ELLIS married HARRISONS, or else EVAN ELLIS had sisters who married EDWARD HARRISON and JAMES ISHAM. Anyway you imagine it, here was a brother in law relationship between JAMES ISHAM and EDWARD HARRISON.
The presence of a family by the name of ISHAM in DUPLIN COUNTY, N. C. in the middle of the eighteenth century, gives the genealogist a peg on which to hang a lot of unclaimed garments. Some of them have looked far and long, in vain, seeking to find how and where some of the HARRISONS acquired ISHAM as a given name, when the particular HARRISONS in which they were interested were seemingly no relation to the HARRISONS who married into the RANDOLPHS and ISHAMS of Virginia; and here we find a North Carolina family of HARRISONS, mixed up in marriage with an ISHAM FAMILY there. The name EDWARD suggests, of course, descent from the NEW KENT (Blissland Parish) EDWARD who married into the CROPLEY FAMILY, settled on ALBEMARLE SOUND and became the ancestor of a large group of the name, as shown on this record. (See p. 73 of this study).
JOHN HARRISON, somewhere in Virginia, married SARAH DANIEL, a daughter of JOHN DANIEL, born in YORK COUNTY, and among the children of JOHN HARRISON and SARAH DANIEL was a son ISHAM, as shown by JOHN'S will in 1762. ISHAM HARRISON was a brother of JAMES HARRISON, who married ELIZABETH HAMPTON, and also had a son ISHAM, whose various descendants spread through SOUTH CAROLINA, ALABAMA, MISSISSIPPI and on into TEXAS, where they are still numerous. WILLIAM HARRISON left will in NORTHAMPTON COUNTY, N. C. in 1786, and among children named in his will was a son ISHAM.

JACKSON, AARON, son of WILLIAM and MARY JACKSON, was born (1723) 3-387; left will (1772) and names children, MOSES, SAMUEL, CHARLES, WILLIAM, PARTENIA and PRISCILLA 3-176.

JACKSON, DANIEL, will in CHOWAN (1743), sons DANIEL, SAMUEL, DAVID and JOAB and wife ANN 1-328.

JACKSON, ELIZABETH, daughter of WILLIAM, was b. (1711) 3-387.

JACKSON, ELLENER, witnessed deed (1728) from WILLIAM JONES to SARAH BOND 2-444.

JACKSON FAMILY. Wills 1-328, 1-329, 2-6, 3-176.

JACKSON, ISAAC, of BATH, will (1716) had daughter RACHEL ADAMS and friend JOHN JORDAN 1-58

JACKSON, JOHN sold land to NICHOLAS FERRELL near BALLARD'S BRIDGE (1716) witnessed by PETER PARKER and JOHN HOLBROOK 1-292; had land grant (1711) on INDIAN TOWN CREEK and MOSSY SWAMP 1-7; was a grandson of EDWARD SIMMONS (1735) 1-73; he and WILLIAM CRAWFORD witness to deed by LUKE WHITE (1718) in CHOWAN 1-625.

JACKSON, MARY, was daughter of WILLIAM FROST who died (1717) 1-44.

JACKSON, MOSES, was son of WILLIAM JACKSON and wife MARY, and born (1720) 3-387.

JACKSON, PARTHENIA, was the daughter of WILLIAM and MARGARET JACKSON born (1719) 3-387.

JACKSON, PRISCILLA, daughter of WILLIAM and MARY JACKSON was born (1729) 3-387.

JACKSON, RICHARD in (1720) witnessed deed of NATHANIEL HOLLY and wife JEAN to BARNABY McKINNIE 1-470; ISAAC RICKS witness to same deed 1-470; bought land from BARTHOLOMEW CHAVERS (1722), with BARNABY McKINNIE as witness 2-143.

JACKSON, RUTH, daughter of WILLIAM JACKSON and wife MARY, born (1729) 3-387.

JACKSON, THOMAS, surveyor of BERTIE COUNTY was succeeded by ALEXANDER COTTEN (1744) 2-625; was appointed deputy sheriff 2-625; presented his bill for repairs on courthouse (1747) 2-630; paid for painting the courthouse in BERTIE (1746) 2-628; was an inspector BERTIE in (1743) 2-623; left will (1746) wife was HESTER, with GRIFFIN FAMILY mentioned in his will 1-328.

JACKSON, WILLIAM. His wife was MARY 3-387; she a daughter of WILLIAM FROST 1-44; one in (1707) had wife named SARAH 3-377; an earlier WILLIAM died leaving will in PASQUOTANK (1695) who had son DANIEL 1-54; another left will in (1735) with sons MOSES and AARON 1-54; one & wife ELIZABETH witnessed deed to JOHN WHITE (1735) 1-628; WILLIAM JACKSON SR. lived in PASQUOTANK (1704) 1-303; one received land grant on BEAR SWAMP (1790) 1-25; and one died (1808) with wife ELIZABETH and daughter name RACHEL JACKSON 2-265. See also 1-444.

JACKSON, ZACHARY, was the son of WILLIAM JACKSON (1704) 1-444.

JACOCKS, ANN, daughter of ROBERT WEST married (2) SIMON BRYAN, daughter of LEWIS BRYAN 2-629.

JACOCKS, CHARLES WORTH married ANNE WEST, a daughter of ROBERT WEST and wife MARY, a daughter of GOV. THOMAS HARVEY and SARAH LAKER; ANNE JACOCKS married (2) SIMON BRYAN, son of LEWIS BRYAN and his wife ELIZABETH HUNTER; who administrator of estate of CHARLES WORTH JACOCKS (1747) 2-629.

JACOCKS, JONATHAN. The first JONATHAN was of age in (1707) 1-613; he was son of THOMAS JACOCKS and wife ANN, who lived on LITTLE RIVER as early as (1689) 3-283; he married first ELIZABETH COLLINS, widow of WILLIAM COLLINS of PASQUOTANK and he was a merchant 3-284; he married second MARY BLOUNT (b. 1696) daughter of JOHN BLOUNT and wife ELIZABETH DAVIS, and moved to BERTIE, where both died (1735) naming the children THOMAS, CHARLES WORTH, JOSEPH & ELIZABETH 3-284 (Also JONATHAN II).

JACOCKS, JONATHAN II, died leaving will in BERTIE (1787), wife ELIZABETH and WHITMELL and HENRY HILL, executors; had among others a son JONATHAN III, who died leaving will (1811) in BERTIE 2-343, 2-525.

JACOCKS FAMILY. Genealogical notes on the family, showing connections with BLOUNTS, JOHN DAVIS of HENRICO, BRYANS, HILLS and various others 1-330.

JACOCKS, THOMAS. Genealogy of his family 1-330; he died (1692) 3-220; his wife was REBECCA SCOILEY of BOSTON 2-296; in (1760) one THOMAS was Master of ship SWALLOW between EDENTON and BOSTON 2-296.

JAMES, BETTIE, her children placed under the tuition of CHARLES SOWELL, of BERTIE in (1770) 3-448.

JAMES, EDWARD, left will (1720) mentions his cousin JOHN MURPHY and son in law DOZIER PITTS 1-55.

JAMES, FRANCIS, deceased. SARAH JAMES administrator (1754) in CHOWAN 1-455.

JAMES, FREDERICK, son of ANN JAMES placed under tuition of JOHN NORWOOD (1768) 3-445.

JAMES, JOHN, bought land from WILLIAM JORDAN in (1729) 3-451.

JAMES, WILLIAM, of PASQUOTANK, left will in (1733) in PASQUOTANK, in which he named his daughter FRANCES McKEEL and others 1-54.

JANNET, ABRAHAM (JARRETT?) and his wife MARY (1729) 3-387.

JARMAN, THOMAS, will in ONSLOW COUNTY (1749) proved (1760) children were THOMAS, JOHN, MOSES, LAWRENCE, WILLIAM, MARY and NANCY; CALEB MANER, witness 1-330.

JARNEGAN FAMILY (JERNIGAN, JONEGAN, ETC.) Wills 1-296, 2-343, 2-524, 2-522, 2-523.

JARNIGAN, GODWIN, will in BERTIE (1820) mentions children and daughter MARTHA BUTLAW with JOHN MIZELL a witness 3-523.

JARNIGAN, HENRY, son of HENRY of NANSEMOND County Va. bought lands (1715) 1-615.

JARNIGAN, HENRY, left will in BERTIE in (1733)
mentioned sons HENRY, THOMAS, GEORGE and
JAMES and wife TEMPERANCE; BENJAMIN HILL WAS
and EXECUTOR 1-54; he bought land from WIL-
LIAM FOULK (FOIK) of NANSEMOND COUNTY, VA.
(1716), witnessed by THOMAS and JOHN JARNI-
GAN and RICHARD TAYLOR (All of Nansemond
County, Virginia) 1-298.

JARNIGAN, JOHN, (Of Nansemond County, Va.) received deed from WILLIAM FOULK (FOIK) of the
same place (1716) 1-298; in (1744) in BERTIE
he proved his rights, including ELIZABETH,
JOHN and JAMES JARNIGAN and DEMPSEY BRASWELL
2-625; in (1746) the will of JOHN JARNIGAN
was proven, óf which his wife ELIZABETH was
executrix 2-628.

JARNIGAN, JOSEPH, was one of the Justices in BER-
TIE in (1771) 3-450.

JARNIGAN, NEEDHAM, was Sheriff of BERTIE COUNTY
in (1795) 1-456.

JARNIGAN, SAMUEL, left will in BERTIE (1825) in
which he mentions children including son
ALLEN and daughter PHEREBEE and wife RACHEL
2-523.

JARNIGAN, THOMAS, from NANSEMOND COUNTY, Va. witnessed deed from WILLIAM FOULK (FOIK) (1716)
1-298; one was son of HENRY JARNIGAN 1-54;
he sold land to JOHN WEBB in (1737) 3-129; &
also to ANN ODOM in (1737) 3-129; and he and
WILLIAM CHARLTON and ROBERT HICKS are men -
tioned in land transfer (1717) 1-620; he sold
land to AARON ODOM (1737) which he had peten-
ted in (1726) 1-115; and in a deed to JOHN
WEBB, JR. the same year same was witnessed
by ANN ODOM. LUKE RAWLS mentioned 1-115.

JARRELL, THOMAS, bought land from JOHN LOVICK in
(1721) 2-613.

JARRETT, JOHN, of CARTERET COUNTY, died leaving
will in (1745) in which he mentions his wife
CATHERINE 1-329. (See GRIMES p. 183 for a
complete list of the children, and others
mentioned in this will).

JASPER, RICHARD, will (1722) mentions children &
son in law JOHN HEATH 1-55.

JASPER, SAMUEL, left will in HYDE (1752) in which
he names his children 1-330.

JEFFRIES, CAPTAIN married MRS. JOANNA TAYLOR in
(1705) 3-410.

JEFFRIES, CHRISTOPHER, left will (1735) mentions
ELIZABETH POTTLE, daughter of JOSEPH POTTLE
1-53.

JEFFRIES, ELIZABETH, will (1742) mentions son
JOHN HILLIARD, son ROBERT HILLIARD, son WIL-
LIAM HILLIARD, grandson JACOB HOLLAND, son
of JEREMIAH HOLLAND, son in law JOHN BODDIE
and others 1-53.

JEFFRIES, RICHARD, and wife ELLENER, deeded land
in (1731) to RICHARD FULLINGTON 2-609; he &
EDWARD CHAMPION and WILLIAM SELEY in (1729)
witnessed deed by MARGARET PADGETT 2-447; he
and CATHERINE DONOVAN were witnesses to deed
(1730) to RICHARD FULLINGTON from JOHN PAGET
on SAWPIT BRANCH 2-448.

JEFFRIES, ROBERT, and ROBERT FULLINGTON wit-
nessed deed to DAVID ATKINS (1730)2-452;
he and GABRIEL COSAND witnessed deed by
JOHN STONE (1730) 3-450; he sold land to
BARTHOLOMEW SCOTT in (1728) with JOHN
OXLEY a witness 2-443; in (1725) he and
DAVID AMBROSE witnessed deed of JOHN BAL-
LARD 2-449; his wife was ELLENER, and they
sold land on ROCKYHOCK CREEK to RICHARD
FULLERTON (FULLINGTON?) in (1731) with
HENRY BONNER and JAMES HUNTER as witness-
es 1-105.

JENKINS, CHARITY. She had been CHARITY COPE-
LAND as she left will in CHOWAN (1791) in
which she mentions sister SARAH COPELAND,
with BENJAMIN GREGORY a witness 2-5.

JENKINS, CHARLES, died leaving will HERTFORD
COUNTY (1773) names children and kin named
MURFREE, also WINBORNES 1-329.

JENKINS, EPHRAIM, one of the sons of JOHN JEN-
KINS will (1780); also the EPHRAIM (broth-
er of JOHN?) mentions brothers IRVIN and
ZADOCK JENKINS 2-342.

JENKINS FAMILY. Wills 2-342, 2-523, 2-524.

JENKINS, HENRY. He and TIMOTHY CLEARE recorded their brand or mark, CLEARE apparently
doing this for JENKINS (APRIL 1690)3-434;
3-438

JENKINS, JAMES, tuition of WILLIS BIRD four-
year old son of MARY BIRD, turned over to
him in BERTIE (1770) 3-448.

JENKINS, JOHANNA, was married to ROBERT BEAS-
LEY by ALEXANDER LILLINGTON (1689) 3-203;
she and ROBERT BEASLEY recorded their
marks at a court held (1689) at the house
of MRS. MARY SCOTT (who married a BLOUNT)
3-429. (DAVID SHERWOOD was among those who
registered at the same time and place).

JENKINS, JOHN proved headrights (10) in (1744)
including his wife ANNE and children JAMES,
ELIZABETH, CASIA, MARY, JOHN, ANNA, CADER
& LEWIS 2-622; he bought land from RICHARD
BERRYMAN (1732) witnessed by THOMAS GARRETT
and THOMASINE GARRETT 2-451; he died leaving will in BERTIE in (1779) in which his
wife was called MARY, with many children
named including ISAAC, ZADOCK and EPHRAIM,
2-342; he made deed to THOMAS HOBBS of
land originally granted to THOMAS GARRETT
on the north side of WARWICK SWAMP, MOSES
HILL a witness 1-114; JOHN JENKINS, who had
been GOVERNOR of the Colony died DEC. 17,
(1681) 3-220; he it was (the GOVERNOR)
who witnessed the relinquishment of the
land on Durant's Neck to GEORGE DURANT in
the year(1662) 3-424, 3-425.

JENKINS, LEWIS, was the son of EDWARD JENKINS &
was ten years old in (1707) 3-378; and
JOHN JENKINS (1744) had a son LEWIS 2-622.

JENKINS, THOMAS, was Master of the sloop NEWCAS-
TLE in (1749) 1-434.

JENKINS, WILLIAM, was the bro.in law of JOHN
BENTLEY (1695) 1-30.

JENKINS, WINBORN left will in GATES COUNTY in
(1813), mentions wife and sons ISAAC, JOHN,
WILLIS and JETHRO JENKINS 2-57.

JENNETT, ABRAHAM will (1742) in PERQUIMANS. Had son ABRAHAM and others, wife MARY, and RICHARD SKINNER and WILLIAM LONG executors 1-328.

JENNETT, JOHN, of TYRRELL will (1738) his wife was DOROTHY; children named 1-328.

JENNETT, JOHN, SR. of TYRRELL will (1748) among others had son ABRAHAM 1-328.

JENNINGS, ANN, widow of JOHN JENNINGS, of PAS - QUOTANK will (1719) mentions son EDWARD POPE 1-55.

JENNINGS, JOHN, of PASQUOTANK, will (1734) names wife ELIZABETH, witnessed by ANN BRYAN 1-54; another JOHN of PASQUOTANK, will (1751)names wife LUCY and children 1-328.

JENNINGS, DOROTHY, was the grandmother of the children of RICHARD ROADS (RHODES) and his wife ELIZABETH, and petitions to have them placed in her care (about 1698-1700) 3-145.

JENNINGS, THOMAS, of NEW HANOVER, will (1744) his wife was ELIENER and had son THOMAS 1-327, 1-328.

JENNINGS, WILLIAM, of PASQUOTANK, will in (1686) daughter ANN LATHAM and son in law RALPH GARNET and daughter MARY 1-327; WILLIAM of CURRITUCK will (1713) proved (1739) wife MARY, witnessed by JOHN and MARGARET NORTON 1-328.

JENUEE, JOHN, and KENNEDY O'BRIEN were witnesses to a deed (1729) 2-448.

JESSUP, DANIEL, mentioned in the will of JOHN WINN in (1739) 1-81.

JESSUP, JOSEPH, was father in law of EDWARD MINGE (1734) 1-62; he left will in PERQUIMANS in (1735) and mentions daughter MARY MOYE and STEPHEN THOMAS 1-54.

JESSUP, MORGAN, was son in law of JOHN MARTIN & so was THOMAS JESSUP (about 1735) 1-62.

JESSUP, THOMAS was executor of the will of EDWARD MAYO (1724) 1-63; and son in law of JOHN MARTIN 1-62; one left will (1818) 3-338.

JESSUP, RACHEL, will (1824) 3-338.

JESSUP, TIMOTHY O. will (1805) mentions sister PENINAH JESSUP married a WILLARD, Executors were CALEB ELLIOTT and RESTORE LAMB 3-338.

JEWELL, BENJAMIN, mentioned in the will (1743) of JOHN SLADE 1-72.

JEWELL, JOSEPH, will (1736) mentions wife FRANCES and sons JOHN, BENJAMIN, SAMUEL and JAMES JEWELL 1-54.

JOHNSON, ABEL, lived in (1719) between CASHR RIVER and SALMON CREEK in BERTIE 1-445; he was called "alias JOHN BUTLER" and his wife was RACHEL, and they sold land to THOMAS MITCHEL in (1721) with SOLOMON JORDAN witness 2-618; he bought land from THOMAS BALL (1718) next to COL. ROBERT WEST 1-620; and he sold land to JOHN HARDY of BERTIE in (1718) in BERTIE 1-621.

JOHNSON, CHARLES E. Genealogical account of the JOHNSON FAMILY and BLOUNT connections 2-168.

JOHNSON FAMILY. Account of its connection with the Skinners and BLOUNTS 2-168; wills of the family 2-4, 2-5.

JOHNSON, ISAAC, came from ROANOKE, N. C. with the KILGORE COLONY and fought in the revolution 3-314.

JOHNSON, ISRAEL, imported into the Colony of N. C. about(1697) by WILLIAM HANCOCK 2-299, 2-300.

JOHNSON, JAMES. His wife was RACHEL 3-215.

JOHNSON, JOHN and wife MARY (1726) 3-387; one was the son of THOMAS JOHNSON 3-217; JOHN JOHNSON will (1693) mentions wife SARAH & son in law LAWRENCE GONSOLVO 1-54; the orphan of one JOHN turned over to PETER PAYNE by EDENTON Court (1748) 1-452; another JOHN of NORTHAMPTON COUNTY died (1745) and in will mentions daughter MARY BRIDGES 1-53. 2-343

JOHNSON, JOSHUA, was the son of JOHN JOHNSON & he was turned over to PETER PAYNE, and was 18 years old in (1748) 1-452.

JOHNSON, LEWIS of BATH COUNTY, will (1711) 1-56.

JOHNSON, MARY, received land grant in (1720) next to THOMAS JOHNSON 1-19.

JOHNSON, SIR NATHANIEL. Letter from him to the Deputy Governor of North Carolina, dated about 1705, relating to the death of JOHN ARCHDALE 3-266.

JOHNSON, RACHEL, died at the home of SAMUEL SWANN in (1697) 3-401.

JOHNSON, RICHARD received deed to land from JAMES LONG in (1702-3) 2-456.

JOHNSON, MRS. SARAH, married WILLIAM LONG in (1697) 3-408.

JOHNSON, SUSANNAH, died leaving will in (1718) in which she mentions her god son EDWARD FREDERICK RAZOR and daughter FRANCES RAZOR 1-55.

JOHNSON, THOMAS received grant of land (1714) 1-14.

JOHNSTON, AARON, was the grandson of JOHN BASS in (1732) 1-31.

JOHNSTON, CHRISTOPHER died about 1780 and in the administration of his estate in the hands of THOMAS ENDLESS, WILLIAM and ANN JOHNSON appear as the heirs 3-265.

JOHNSTON FAMILY. Wills 2-523 and 1-327; 3-289.

JOHNSTON, GABRIEL (GOVERNOR) Letter from JOHN RUTHERFORD relating to his will, addressed to SAMUEL JOHNSTON in (1755) 3-289, 3-290; will in BERTIE COUNTY (1753) 1-53, in which he mentions his wife FRANCES and other relatives; letter written by him to ELEAZER ALLEN at CAPE FEAR in (1735) 2-303; probably arrived in North Carolina in SEPTEMBER (1734) 2-304; in (1747) he commissioned ENOCH HALL as CHIEF JUSTICE of N. C. 1-446.

JOHNSTON, GABRIEL, and his wife PENELOPE sold lands to JOHN CAMPBELL in (1741) 1-54.

JOHNSTON, ISABELLA, was the sister of MRS. HAN-NAH IREDELL and had the same ancestry, but no descendants, as she never married 2-169.

JOHNSTON, JOHN left will in BERTIE (1790) he was the brother of SAMUEL JOHNSTON, and had brothers in law SAMUEL and WILLIAM WILLIAMS who were his executors; THOMAS and JEREMIAH LEGGETT were the witnesses 2-343, 2-523.

JOHNSTON, GOV. SAMUEL. Letter to from NEW YORK and Mass., (1785) and from JAMES MADISON to in (1789) 3-104, 3-105, 3-106; he was the son of SAMUEL JOHNSTON, public treasurer in (1738-1739) 3-288; received land grant in (1742) of an Island in CHOWAN RIVER next to JOSEPH PARKER 1-18; died leaving will in ONS-LOW (1756) with CARY GODBIE and WILLIAM WIL-LIAMS witnesses 1-53; a SAMUEL JOHNSTON was appointed JUDGE in (1774) 1-448; genealogical notes relating to his family 2-163 to 2-170; elder SAMUEL from NANSEMOND VA. 2-394.

JOHNSTON, SAMUEL W. will 2-523

JOHNSTON, THOMPSON N. (Of HILLSBORO, N. C.) will (1826) related to JAMES WEBB 2-523.

JOOKE, SARAH, married (1684) JOHN DURANT, son of GEORGE DURANT and ANN his wife; John died in 1699, and she married 2nd WILLIAM STEPHENS died 1702 with THOMAS GILLIAM his executor 1-268.

JOSEY, WILLIS, with MOSES HORN, witnessed will of WILLIAM RUFFIN (1781) 2-352.

JOY, WILLIAM, of PASQUOTANK left will in (1725) wife MARGERY; SOLOMON EASTER mentioned 1-55.

JOYNER, THOMAS, of HALIFAX COUNTY, N. C. married ALICE BLOUNT, and he may have been the son of MATTHEW JOYNER 2-154.

JONES, ABRAHAM and ISAAC PIPKIN were vestrymen of St. Barnabas Church (1771) 3-304.

JONES, ALBRIDGETON, had daughter AGATHA who married THOMAS HARVEY 3-386.

JONES, ALLEN, son of ANNA ISABELLA IREDELL and CADWALLADER JONES born (1846) 2-166. (no items found of ALLEN JONES of Halifax).

JONES, ARTHUR, had brother DANIEL JONES who left will (1713) in PERQUIMANS 1-56.

JONES, CADWALLADER, married ANNIE ISABELLA IRE-DELL, daughter of JAMES IREDELL II; the genealogy of his family 2-163 to 2-170.

JONES, CHARLES and wife SARAH sell land to JOHN EARLY in (1719) 1-627; will of CHARLES JONES (an earlier one) mentions (1695) SARAH and TABITHA ALFORD 1-54; about 1690 he ran an attachment against estate of RICHARD BENTLEY SAWYER 3-433, 3-434.

JONES, CORNELIUS, with TIMOTHY CLEARE, ROBERT DANIEL and others were members of the LOWER HOUSE which met at the home of CAPT. JOHN HECKLEFIELD on Little River in (1708) 1-454; he and TIMOTHY CLEARE present petition from the HOUSE (1708) 1-454; in (1734) a CORNE-LIUS JONES was the son in law of THOMAS TAY-LOR; 1-78; he proved some rights 2-300; one married HANNAH VOSSE (1687) 3-203; married SARAH (MAYO) CULPEPPER 3-248.

JONES, CORNELIUS, had a lawsuit with GEORGE GRIFFIN in PASQUOTANK COURT and beat the case, and had to enjoin GRIFFIN to stop him from further prosecution of the case 3-145; CORNELIUS died in (1714)and left will leaving son CORNELIUS, daughters ELIZABETH and ANN and wife ELIZA-BETH 1-55.

JONES, DANIEL of PERQUIMANS left will (1713) mentions wife SARAH, brother ARTHUR JONES and friend TIMOTHY CLEARE 1-56.

JONES, DAVID, was brother of THOMAS JONES & sold land to THOMAS YEATS in (1717) 1-298; also to CONSTANCE LUTEN in (1715) witnessed by THOMAS and MARY COMBES 1-624; he and THOMAS JONES brothers in (1728) in CHOWAN 2-443; had a land grant on TINDALL SWAMP (1715) 1-15; sold land to ROBERT FULLERTON (1720) with PATRICK EGGERTON a witness 2-514.

JONES, EDWARD, left will (1720) names daughters PRISCILLA and ABIGAIL and cousin PRISCILLA, brother JAMES JONES and bro. in law WINN ROOS 1-55.

JONES, ELIZABETH, the wife of PETER JONES d. in (1700) 3-402; the widow of THOMAS JONES died (1750) 1-445.

JONES, EPAPRODITUS, sold land to ELISHA BAL-LARD in (1738) and the witnesses to the deed were, MARY, ANDREW, DAVID MEADE & JAMES BARON 3-132; in about(1737) in GATES COUNTY he bought land from JOHN ODOM, with WILLIAM and LEONARD LANSTON as witnesses 1-115; one of the name died in HERTFORD COUNTY leaving will in (1768) and his wife was REBECCA 2-3.

JONES, EVAN, was the son in law of RICHARD HILL (1723) as shown by his will 1-50; he was a cousin of LUCY RICKS 1-71; and in (1740) a grandson of ROBERT PALMER 1-65; THOMAS POLLOCK was the attorney of EVAN JONES, and the children of THOMAS HOLLOWAY were related to JONES in some way (1790) 3-281; he died in CRAVEN CO. in (1753) leaving son LOVICK JONES and a daughter SARAH; the witnesses were JAMES JONES, JOHN TANNYHILL and CHARLES JONES and THOMAS LOVICK and ROGER JONES were his executors 3-323.

JONES, FRANCIS, died (1713) without leaving a will, and ARTHUR JONES appears to have been the nearest of kin 1-56. (A leter FRANCIS JONES died in EDGECOMBE (1755) with many children -see GRIMES p. 191)

JONES, COL. FREDERICK, Chief Justice, married a daughter of SAMUEL SWANN and the grand-daughter of ALEXANDER LILLINGTON 3-145; in (1732) he was the administrator of his brother WILLIAM HARDING JONES 1-450; the name of his wife was SARAH SWANN, and his daughter MARTHA JONES married JOHN COT-TEN, of CHOWAN 1-479; he was the attor-ney for JOHN CRUIKSHANK (1718) 2-616; in (1697) he was one of the assignees of an account against WILLIAM DUKENFIELD from ROBERT HARRISON of YORK COUNTY, Virginia 1-610, 3-69; had power of attorney from CHRISTOPHER GALE with others in (1716) 1-297, 1-298; was CHIEF JUSTICE of N. C. in (1720) see WOODS DEED 2-608.

JONES, COL. FREDERICK. His wife's sister a MISS SWANN married JOHN BAPTISTA ASHE 3-149; his will proved in CHOWAN (1723) mentions his daughters JANE, MARTHA and REBECCA, and his sons WILLIAM HARDING, THOMAS and FREDERICK JONES, and his brother THOMAS JONES of VIRGINIA 1-55; his son FREDERICK married MARY, probably the daughter of EDWARD MOSELEY see deed (1730) 2-448; another FREDERICK, who was perhaps his grandson left will (1758) in CRAVEN and mentions his mother MRS. MARY MOORE, which will was witnessed by ELIZABETH SPEIGHT 1-325; and a much later FREDERICK JONES left will in GATES COUNTY in (1838) in which all of the old names have disappeared 2-57; the earliest account of FREDERICK JONES makes him a resident of JAMES CITY COUNTY in (1702-3) 3-139.

JONES FAMILY. Wills: 1-323, 1-324, 1-326, 1-327, 2-4, 3-175, 3-338.

JONES, GEORGE, had son ELISHA JONES aged 10 yrs placed under the tuition of HENRY EVERIT (1744) 2-623.

JONES, GRIFFIN, was administrator of the estate of WILLIAM ROOSE (1722) 1-71; EDWARD JONES (1720) had brother in law WINN ROOSE 1-55.

JONES, HENRY sold land to WILLIAM GREEN (1713) with THOMAS AVENT and JOHN NAIRNE witnesses 1-294; his wife was ELIZABETH and together they sold land in (1728) to JOHN BALLARD 2-447; he made deed to DAVID CRAWLEY (1718) 1-623.

JONES, DR. ISAAC N., of WASHINGTON, ARK., married ELIZABETH LITTLEJOHN, aunt of ROBERT McALPIN LITTLEJOHN 1-272; one ISAAC JONES much earlier died in (1734) with wife MARY and sons ISAAC, JOHN and NEHEMIAH 1-54.

JONES, JAMES, was a brother of EDWARD JONES in (1720) 1-55; and a much later one of same name received a grant of land in (1793) 1-24.

JONES, JANE, of CURRITUCK, was the daughter of WILLIAM STAFFORD (1750) 1-446.

JONES, JESSE, left will in (1806). His wife & BELSOM KITTRELL were executors 2-525.

JONES, JOHN JR. (presupposes a "Sr") helped prove the will of JOHN PATCHETT (PAGETT) in CHOWAN (1711), with DAVID JONES and a WILLIAM TANNER 3-441; one (perhaps the SR) received a land grant in CHOWAN (1693) 1-4; and another one in (1720) 1-19; one's wife was MARY and they sold land to MARTIN GARDNER in (1718) 1-622; and to GEORGE BROMLEY in (1716), with THOMAS LOTEN a witness 1-291; granted land on TIMBER BRANCH(1714) 1-3; another in (1720) 1-10; same lapsed to THOMAS WILLIAMS next to SAMUEL PAYNE 1-14; the first JOHN JONES (apparently) of CASHOKE in CHOWAN left will (1711) and mentions wife ELIZABETH and sister in law SUSANNAH DANIEL 1-56; JOHN and JUDITH JONES sold land to RICHARD BOND (1739) 3-132; will of JOHN JONES (probably the JR) in (1727) with SAMUEL PAGETT executor, names children 1-55; another left will (1735) mentions daughters MARY BONNER and ANN COTTEN and a grandson ABRAHAM JONES 1-54; witnessed deed with FREDERICK and WM. HARDING JONES (1732) 2-451.

JONES, JOHN, Master of the sloop RANGER in (1749) 1-435; also Master of the sloop INDUSTRY the same year 1-434.

JONES, JONATHAN, married MARGARET VOSS in the year (1688) by ALEXANDER LILLINGTON 3-203; CORNELIUS JONES married HANNAH VOSS the same year 3-203; he received a land grant about 1694 on MATTACOMACK CRK 1-4; he was the son of JONATHAN JONES & wife MARGERY 3-368; one JONATHAN left will in PASQUOTANK in (1740) and had son CORNELIUS, etc. 1-53.

JONES, JOSEPH, was surveyor of the roads in BERTIE in the place of JOHN BROWN in (1744) 2-625; a much later JOSEPH had a son in law named DANIEL SAINT, whose wife was MARGARET, died (1793) 3-191.

JONES, JOSIAH, received a grant of land on ROCKYHOCK CREEK or NECK in (1790) 1-23.

JONES, MARMADUKE, settled in WILMINGTON about 1750, with his wife and two daughters; his wife had been a MRS. IVY, and one of the daughters, ANN MOORE, married JAMES MOORE, son of MAURICE MOORE, while her older sister MARY married DR. MOSES JOHN de ROSSETT 2-491, 2-492.

JONES, MARTHA and her son THOMAS PICKETT sold land to JOHN SANDERS on CYPRESS SWAMP in (1738) 3-132.

JONES, MARY (who had been a MRS. BEASLEY) in (1699) married JOHN MORGAN 3-409; another MARY married PETER ALBERTSON in (1701) 3-409.

JONES, PETER, died August 4 (1679) 3-365; a later PETER JONES had wife ELIZABETH and had a son PETER JONES born in (1700) 3-371; a PETER JONES was executor of the will of THOMAS CLARK in (1719) 1-39; and patented land on TOPPIM CREEK the same year 1-13; he was brother in law of JOHN PIERCE, the father of COPELAND PIERCE (1726) 1-58; a PETER JONES, SR. died leaving will in PERQUIMANS in (1752) leaving sons JOHN, WILLIAM and PETER and daughters MARY, HANNAH, SARAH SUTTON, MARGARET HENBY, grandsons THOMAS SHERWOOD, and daughter REBECCA DENMAN 1-323; an earlier PETER died in (1731) and still a different one died leaving will (1753) with an altogether different set of children 1-324; John Pierce (above) was brother in law of the PETER JONES who married MARY PIERCE, daughter of THOMAS PIERCE 1-69; the PETER JONES and wife ELIZABETH above mentioned had daughter REBECCA born (1694) 3-367.

JONES, PHILLIP, of SURRY COUNTY, VA. deeded land to JOHN LEONARD of the same place in (1718) next to lands of WILLIAM REEVES 1-523.

JONES, PRISCILLA. One was a cousin of EDWARD JONES, who also had a daughter of the same name 1-55; and still another was the daughter of FRANCIS TOMS in (1729) 1-623.

JONES, RICHARD, proved certain headrights in (1680) including WILLIAM JONES and a JOHN SAWYER 2-300 (CHARLES JONES in 1690 ran an attachment against the estate of a RICHARD BENTLEY SAWYER, in an effort to collect a claim or debt) 3-434; he m. JANE HARRIS 1-91.

JONES, ROBERT, married MARY EATON, daughter of
WILLIAM EATON, of GRANVILLE COUNTY, and he
is mentioned in EATON'S will (1759) 1-41;
leased land from the TUSCARORA INDIANS as
ROBERT JONES JR. about 1767 3-443, 3-444.

JONES, ROBERT JR. leased lands from the TUSCARO-
RA INDIANS about (1767) 3-443, 3-444.

JONES, ROGER, and ROLAND PORTER FINCH were wardens of the CHURCH in BEAUFORT in (1739)
3-303; he was one of the executors of the
will of EVAN JONES in (1753) with THOMAS
LOVICK 3-323.

JONES, SAMUEL, left will in CHOWAN (1726) and had
sons THOMAS, SAMUEL, WILLIAM, HEZEKIAH and
ZACHARIAH and daughter JANE 1-55.

JONES, THOMAS, granted land on TINDALL SWAMP in
(1711) 1-7; grant in (1715) 1-15; grant in
(1726) of land next to JOHN PAINE 1-19; land
next to widow LEWERTON (1712) 1-7; his widow ELIZABETH was grandmother of WILLIAM AX-
TELL of New York (1730) 1-445; his widow
ELIZABETH executor of his will (1712-13) in
which he names brother WILLIAM JONES, sons
THOMAS and JOHN and son in law LUKE HARMON
1-55; a THOMAS was attorney for WILLIAM WHIT-
FIELD (1732) 3-302; owned a Shallop (1701)
statement about by JOHN COLES of Nansemond
County, Va. 3-246; he and VINCENT WHITE are
executors of the will of ROBERT WHITE in AL-
BEMARLE PRECINCT in (1698) 1-504; a THOMAS
was the orphan of JOHN JONES (1767) placed
under the tuition of JAMES HOLLEY 3-444; he
sought a division of the estate of JAMES
GILMAN in (1767) 3-443; the son THOMAS, apparently, married the widow of EDMUND POR-
TER in (1730) about 1-445; a THOMAS was the
attorney for HENRY BAKER in (1725) 3-452;
and he and BENJAMIN HILL were witnesses to a
deed in (1737) 3-130; his wife was SARAH in
(1730) 3-387; THOMAS JONES was mentioned in
the will of ROBERT WHITE in ALBEMARLE PRE-
CINCT in (1698) who was the father of VIN-
CENT WHITE 1-504; THOMAS JONES left a will
in CHOWAN in (1763) wife ELIZABETH and sons
THOMAS and WILLIAM and daughters; and another THOMAS left will the same in (1797) and
mentioned daughters MARY BRIN and ELIZABETH
BEASLEY and grand-daughters named SWEENEY
2-4; still another THOMAS JONES elft will
at ENDENTON, who must have been of a different set from ENGLAND as the children of REV.
DANIEL EARL were his nephews and nieces 2-3;
in (1737) THOMAS JONES and JOSEPH ANDERSON
were to be guardians of ELLEN and MARY DUN-
STON 1-448.

JONES, WILLIE, of HALIFAX COUNTY, N. C. married
ELIZABETH MONTFORT and had two sons, WILLIE
and ROBERT and daughters PATSY and SALLIE;
PATSY married JOHN W. EPPES and SALLIE mar-
ried (1) GOV. HUTCHINS BURTON and (2) COL.
ANDREW JOYNER (no issue) 1-278.

JONES, WILLIAM, and wife FRANCES, in (1713) sold
lands to ORLANDO CHAMPION in GREEN HALL or
BEECH NECK 1-101; of BATH, sold lands (about
(1720) to EDWARD MOSELEY, witnessed by MAU-
RICE MOORE, JEREMIAH VAIL and LYONEL READING
2-613; WILLIAM JONES and wife PRISCILLA had
son WILLIAM born (1732) 3-387; a WILLIAM
JONES married REBECCA WILEY in (1790) 3-419;
and one had a land grant (1717) next to land
of MARY JONES and THOMAS WEST 1-17.

JONES, WILLIAM, of PERQUIMANS, sold land to
SARAH BOND in (1728) which joined lands
of ABRAHAM HILL, ROBERT HICKS and ELLENER
JACKSON as witnesses 2-444; he made deed
to CHARLES JORDAN (1728) witnessed by JOB
MEADER and wife 2-444; he was exempted
from certain road duties in (1730) and was
born in (1670) 1-449; he sold land to W.
LEWIS, son of RICHARD LEWIS in (1717)
1-618; with his wife MARY sold lands to one
MARTIN GARDNER (1719) 1-627; also in (1739)
he sold lands to EDWARD ARNOLD which was
part of a patent issued to HENRY BAKER, by
BAKER sold to EDWARD RICKETTS, who sold it
to JOHN ODOM, from whom WILLIAM JONES had
bought it, which land joined JOHN WINBORN,
JOHN THOMAS and JAMES ELLIS; ISAAC HUNTER
a witness 3-133; he and ISAAC WILLIAM are
appointed overseers of a road in (1747)
1-450; the road mentioned ran by way of the
home of one WILLIAM VINCENT, starting near
a plantation where ROBERT ROGERS formerly
lived, and on to an old plantation where
SIMON DANIEL formerly lived, from there to
the place of MOSES ODOM JR., by THOMAS
BARNES and on to CHOWAN RIVER; this order
passed in (1747) 1-450; WILLIAM JONES and
wife REBECCA sold land to DAVID ATKINS in
(1716) 1-294; he left will in PASQUOTANK in
(1733) and named daughter REBECCA 1-54; but
the one in CHOWAN died about 1723 leaving
will naming his sons, daughters and other
connections, with THOMAS LUTEN executor
1-54; WILLIAM HARDING JONES will (1732) on
same page 1-54; WILLIAM JONES, of HALIFAX
COUNTY died (1759) mentions sons SIMON,
WILLIAM, HENRY and BRITTON and daughters
SARAH, WINNIFRED, ANNE and SYLVIA and his
wife SARAH 1-53; the WILLIAM JONES of BER-
TIE left will (1736) wife ANNE and son EPH-
RAIM JONES 1-53; one WILLIAM had land grant
adjoining RICHARD SKINNER (1729) 1-12; received power of attorney (1714) from CAPT.
HENRY BONNER 1-292.

JONES, COL. WILLIAM HARDING, was the brother of
COL. FREDERICK JONES, and died (1732) leaving will, with ANNE JONES widow 1-450.

JONES, ZACHARIAH, was brother of ELIZABETH HEAS-
LEY and the son of THOMAS JONES who died
in CHOWAN with will (1797) 2-4.

JORDAN, ARTHUR. There were two by this name who
died in NORTHAMPTON COUNTY, one who died
in (1752) and the other in (1755) leaving
wills; both had sons named ARTHUR and the
first had a daughter FORTUNE, clearly sug-
gesting descent from the JORDANS to which
the Attorney General of Virginia belonged
1-328.

JORDAN, CHARLES, patented lands in CHOWAN in
(1719) next to SAMUEL PADGETT, THOMAS HICKS
JOHN JORDAN and JAMES FARLOW 1-13; he sold
a part of this land in (1726) to ROBERT
WILSON, with JOHN and JOSEPH JORDAN as the
witnesses 2-292; in (1760) a CHARLES JORDAN
was granted permission to erect a mill
1-456.

JORDAN FAMILY. Wills in BERTIE COUNTY are listed at 2-342, 2-524, and 3-5.

JORDAN, JEAN, with JOHN JORDAN and HAGAR WATHEY
witnessed a deed in (1730) from JOHN WHITE
to THOMAS HOLLIDAY on LONG BRANCH 2-449.

JORDAN, JOHN. One of the name left will(1720) and named daughters MARGARET and MARY JORDAN 1-55; one sold land to JOHN PARKER of CHOWAN (1718) JOHN EVANS a witness 1-622; JOHN EVANS married JEAN JORDAN, who made a deed (1717) witnessed by JOHN and JEAN JORDAN 1-626; the same witnessed deed from PETER PARKER to WILLIAM COPELAND in (1716) 2-619; JOHN witnessed deed (1715) from RICHARD CHURCH and wife JANE to EDWARD HOWARD 1-293; he (JOHN) sold land to FRANCIS THOMAS in (1730) with ABRAHAM SMITH & JOHN DUNNING witnesses 2-449; he was treasurer of HYDE PRECINCT (1719) 1-444; he obtained grant (1712) next to RICHARD SOWELL and one COTTEN ROBINSON 1-15, 1-16; he owned land adjoining WILLIAM COPELAND 1-15; JOHN JORDAN sold JOHN JORDAN JR. his son lands in (1718) witnessed by JOHN J. EVANS 1-622; one owned lands (1717) next to MOSES FOXWORTH 1-12; & next to THOMAS PADGETT in (1719) which he sold to PHILLIP MAGUIRE, with JOHN PARKER as witness 1-628; in (1727) JOHN JORDAN sold land to JOHN JORDAN SR., with CHARLES JORDAN and ROBERT HICKS witnesses 2-443; JOHN JR. sold land to SAMUEL WOODWAR (1728) 2-445.

JORDAN, JOSEPH, of BERTIE, married RUTH SPEIGHT, daughter of THOMAS SPEIGHT and wife MARY a sister of RACHEL who married THOMAS JORDAN 1-446; he was a witness to a deed by ROBERT WINDLEY in (1707) 1-291; FRANCIS THOMAS married MARY JORDAN, sister of THOMAS and JOSEPH, to whom JOSEPH deeded land in (1730) 2-449; JOSEPH JORDAN, LUKE MIZELL and WILLIAM LATTIMORE appointed in (1744) to divide the estate of DANIEL HENDRICKS 2-622.

JORDAN, JOSEPH, and his wife FILIA CHRISTIAN, subpoened as witnesses in EMANUEL JORDAN v. ANN HENLEY (1713) 2-150; JOSEPH JORDAN estate in (1801) had widow MOURNING and sons JACOB, JOSEPH and WILLIAM JORDAN 2-266; one JOSEPH married SUSANNA LLOYD in (1770) in BERTIE 3-448; and he was a JUSTICE in BERTIE (1771) 3-449; JOSEPH, the son of THOMAS JORDAN died leaving will in (1817) witnessed by BENJAMIN COSAND and SUSANNA JORDAN 3-339

JORDAN, MATTHEW, died leaving will (1763) and mentions his NEWBY relatives 3-175.

JORDAN, NATHAN, had a land grant on MILL SWAMP in (1807) 1-25.

JORDAN, RACHEL, wife of THOMAS JORDAN, was the daughter of THOMAS SPEIGHT (1760) 1-446.

JORDAN, SOLOMON, and wife KATHERINE sold lands to JOSEPH SKITTLETHORPE in (1718) 2-137; in (1716) sold land to WILLIAM NUTSHELL in WASHINGTON COUNTY, N. C. 1-297; and (1719) lived between CASHY RIVER and SALMON CREEK 1-445; sold land (1718) to ROBERT WEST, with ISAAC HILL a witness 1-625; left will (1722) ROBERT WEST and wife Executors 1-55.

JORDAN, THOMAS father in law of CHRIST. BENN 1-446

JORDAN, WILLIAM (1732) TYRRELL 1-54.

JURKIN, ZACK. (JUNKIN?) witnessed deed (1716) from NATHANIEL AVEITT to his son in law THOS. HARRISON 1-295.

JACKSON FAMILY. JOHN JACKSON (1-7, 1-292), RICHARD JACKSON (1-470, 2-143) and WILLIAM JACKSON (1-54) were seemingly the ancestors of the numerous JACKSONS of this record. We are convinced that they were closely related to, if not direct descendants of RICHARD JACKSON, who patented lands on LAWNE'S CREEK in Isle of Wight County, Virginia, in 1641. This land adjoined land owned by GEORGE HARDY, JUSTINIAN COOPER (and his wife ANNE HARRISON) and one THOMAS and ALICE BENNETT. RICHARD JACKSON'S wife was a daughter of the last named couple. She was a sister of WILLIAM BENNETT (1-17, 1-22) and GRACE BENNETT, the wife of the first GREEN HILL, was her niece. Another sister of the wife of RICHARD JACKSON married JOHN HARDY and was the ancestress of the HARDY FAMILY of N. C., or at least some of them, while her daughter married EDWARD BRYAN and became the grandmother of the older BRYANS of this record. ALICE BENNETT, the mother in law of RICHARD JACKSON, had first married a PIERCE, related in some way to CAPT. WILLIAM PIERCE, who came to Virginia with SIR THOMAS GATES in the year 1709, and was a member of the Virginia Council in 1631, and who also owned lands on MULBERRY ISLAND (in Warwick County)and LAWNE'S CREEK, in ISLE OF WIGHT. (See BODDIE'S SEVENTEENTH CENTURY ISLE OF WIGHT COUNTY, pp 289 to 294).

JARNIGAN FAMILY. One of the interesting families of this record is the JARNIGAN family, which is so often mis-spelled. Descendants I have known pronounced the name "JERNIGAN" as if spelled with an "e", but invariably spelled it with the "a". At least two descendants of this family were distinguised members of the bar in the State of Tennessee and Kentucky, Spencer and Chesley Jarnigan. From what I can gather some of the members of the family from the old ALBEMARLE stock went west and settled in JEFFERSON COUNTY, TENNESSEE, and later at KNOXVILLE, where the BLOUNTS had also sent representatives. SPENCER JARNIGAN was born there and studied law under the famous HUGH LAWSON WHITE, afterwards United States Senator and a Justice of the SUPREME COURT OF TENNESSEE. An old history of the Bench and Bar of Tennessee speaks of Spencer Jarnigan as a "plain, unimaginative man with a clear head and sound judgment".

JORDAN FAMILY. The JOHN JORDAN (1-444, 1-622 and 1-12) could possibly have been the son of RICHARD JORDAN, who with his wife ALICE, deeded lands to their son JOHN in ISLE OF WIGHT COUNTY, Virginia in 1678, as shown by Virginia Magazine of History & Biography, and whose parentage is not revealed, but who obviously belonged in some way to the family of Col. GEORGE JORDAN, one time ATTORNEY GENERAL of Virginia (1670). These JORDANS, therefore are NOT the JORDANS who were such ardent QUAKERS, who lived mostly in NANSEMOND COUNTY and were descended from SAMUEL JORDAN of "Jordan's Journey, up the JAMES. The scarcity of material relating to these particular JORDANS in Virginia has been very noticable, but such scarcity is now accounted for by the fact that they migrated to NORTH Carolina, as revealed by Mr. Hathaway's collection. The frequent occurrence of the names ARTHUR and RIVER among them is of itself a most convincing identification.

COL. FREDERICK JONES. Was son in law of HON. SAMUEL SWANN (1-477, instead of 3-145 as mis-stated in the text of the index hereto) and in 1820 was CHIEF JUSTICE of North Carolina (3-608). His forbears settled in YORK COUNTY, Virginia, though the ancestor patented lands in WARWICK, or on the WARWICK RIVER in 1628, as evidenced by the following note (p 644 Boddie's 1th Century Isle of Wight): "RICE JONES, Planter of Warwick River. 50 acres, 2 Dec. 1628. Lying on Estly side of WARWICKSQUIECKE RV. Nly on land of MARTHA KEY, Sly on land of PHETTIPACE CLAUSE. Due as his first dividend. Doe unto FRANCIS WEST for transportation of said JONES from Canada in the JOHN AND FRANCIS in 1623 and by these presents made over to said JONES.". In all other records we have found of the family of RICE JONES thereafter, until some of his descendants moved to JAMES CITY COUNTY, they are referred to as of "YORK COUNTY". RICE JONES had several children, one of whom, RACHEL, married (1) CAPT. RICHARD CROSHAW, brother of MR. JOSEPH CROSHAW, (2) one MARTIN PALMER, whose wife immediately preceding had also been a widow, the relict of CAPT. WILLIAM COBBS, of York County. June 25, 1677, MARTIN PALMER, then the husband of RACHEL (Jones) CROSHAW, was appointed the administrator of BENJA-MIN CROSHAW, son of CAPT. RICHARD CROSHAW, and the guardian of his children; he had also, in 1675, been the administrator of the estate of CAPT. WILLIAM COBBS. Martin Palmer in 1678 in YORK COUNTY happened also to be a member of the jury in a suit brought by JOHN COTTON against JOHN HARRIS and a PHILLIP COCKE. RICE JONES, a son of the first RICE JONES and a brother of RACHEL JONES, married in Middlesex County, Va. in 1678, JANE, a sister of PHILLIP COCKE, and the daughter of NICHOLAS COCKE. One GEORGE LYDDALL was assigned a patent to 1750 acres of land in YORK COUNTY by MR. JOSEPH CROSHAW, a brother of the son in law of RICE JONES, and then in 1702, RICHARD LITTLEPAGE, with ANN LYDDALL as a witness sold land in KING WILLIAM COUNTY, VA. to FREDERICK JONES and THOMAS JONES of JAMES CITY COUNTY. This was COL. FREDERICK JONES who died 21 years later in CHOWAN COUNTY, N. C. leaving to his brother THOMAS JONES, GENT., certain lands called the "HORN QUARTER" in KING WILLIAM COUNTY, Virginia. These two were grandsons of the original RICE JONES, of YORK COUNTY, long since deceased.

Now, what makes this story of COL. FREDERICK JONES still more interesting is that, long afterwards JOHN COTTON, a grandson or great grandson of the JOHN COTTON who sued JOHN HARRIS and PHILLIP COCKE in York County, Virginia, in 1678 (with MARTIN PALMER, son in law of the first RICE JONES, on the jury) married MARTHA JONES, daughter of COL. FREDERICK JONES, and died in 1728(1-479) leaving children JOHN, WILLIAM, SAMUEL, THOMAS, ARTHUR, JAMES, JOSEPH and ALEXANDER COTTON, his wife MARTHA, daughters PRISCILLA and SUSANNAH, son in law JOHN THOMAS, son in law JOHN SPEARS, daughter MARY HOLLAND and daughter MARTHA BENTON, widow of FRANCIS BENTON; and also the fact that CAPT. WIL-LIAM COBBS, whose relict for a brief time, apparently, had been the previous wife of MARTIN PALMER, had among other sons a ROBERT COBBS. This ROBERT COBBS married (1) REBECCA PINKETHMAN, daughter of WILLIAM PINKETHMAN, by whom he had, among other children, perhaps, two daughters: ELIZABETH COBBS, who married JAMES SHIELDS, and REBECCA COBBS (who was still unmarried about 1715); then ROBERT COBBS married (2) ELIZABETH ALLEN (daughter of DANIEL ALLEN) and had two more daughters, one of whom, MARTHA COBBS, married DUDLEY RICHARDSON, and the other, SARAH COBBS, married ROBERT JONES, JR., (3-443, 3-444) of this record. ROBERT JONES, JR. was the father of COL. ALLEN JONES, of "MOUNT GALLIANT", NORTHAMPTON COUNTY, N. C., and GEN. WILLIE JONES of "THE GROVE" in HALIFAX COUNTY. This ROBERT JONES JR., who appears to have lived to a ripe old age, was seemingly contemporaneous with the sons of COL. FREDERICK JONES, and he is said to have been the son of another ROBERT JONES, of SURRY COUNTY, who was doubtless a grandson of the original RICE JONES, the ancestor of the tribe. After the death of ROBERT COBBS, grand-father of WILLIE and ALLEN JONES, his widow ELIZABETH ALLEN married SAMUEL WELDON, of HENRICO COUNTY, VIRGINIA, and became the father of DANIEL WELDON and a number of other sons, for whom the town of WELDON in HALIFAX COUNTY was named. ROBERT JONES, JR., after the death of his wife SARAH COBBS, married MARY EATON, daughter of COL. WILLIAM EATON, of GRANVILLE COUNTY, by whom he had one daughter ELIZABETH JONES, who married AUG. 10, 1781, HON. BENJAMIN WIL-LIAMS, GOVERNOR of N. C. about 1700, who, was therefore a half-brother in law of WILLIE and ALLEN JONES. Both Willie and Allen Jones played important roles in the revolutionary history of NORTH CARO-LINA, and SARAH JONES, daughter of ALLEN married GEN. WILLIAM R. DAVIE, the light of whose fame as a statesman during the days following the revolution, is still reflected in the history of the OLD NORTH STATE which he adopted and lived in and served until old age forced him back into his beloved South Carolina home. JONESBORO, TENNESSEE, was named for WILLIE JONES. The shadows of these men were long and sheds luster on the sheen of a great commonwealth, as well as the name of JONES.

MATTHEW JONES. One of the most numerous of the JONES FAMILIES in Northeastern North Car-olina, was the descendants of MATTHEW JONES, of MULBERRY ISLAND, in Warwick County, Virginia. Prop-erly speaking they really descend from ANTHONY JONES, who was born about 1604 in England. He was a burgess from Isle of Wight County in 1643 (Boddie p. 96). ANTHONY was the father of ABRAHAM JONES, who had son MATTHEW. This is the family to which TIGNAL, ALBRIGTON or BRITTAN and the RIDLEY JONES set belonged. The ramifications of the genealogy of this set is somewhat clarified by the numerous accounts that have been published, particularly the one in Vol. 9, Tyler's Magazine beginning at pp 136-7, etc. FRANCIS JONES, of this family, died in EDGECOMBE COUNTY in 1755, leaving a will in which he mentions his wife MARY (RIDLEY) and children JUDITH, NATHANIEL, TIGNAL, JOHN JAMES, MAT-THEW, ALBRIDGTON, RIDLEY, MARY, BETTIE DAY JONES, LYDIA and JEREMIAH. It is not only possible, but probable that this set was related in some way to the ALLEN and WILLIE JONES set, and the NATHANIEL JONES of CARY, in Wake County. TIGNAL JONES who married PENELOPE CAIN has many descendants who went to Texas, and a TIGNAL JONES has been Clerk of BASTROP COUNTY TEXAS for more than thirty years at this writing (1945.)

EDWARD JONES, of WARREN COUNTY, and his family, have already been mentioned under the note relating to WILLIAM EATON, in which it is stated that the first county court ever held for GRANVILLE COUNTY was at his home. The fact that his daughter PRISCILLA married GIDEON MACON, and was a de-scendant of the MACONS of NEW KENT who married into the REV. ROWLAND JONES family suggests that ED-WARD may have been of the ROWLAND JONES strain, and thus indirectly related to MARTHA (DANDRIDGE-JONES) WASHINGTON. The CHAMPION FAMILY of this record were related to that set, and the much men-tioned ORLANDO CHAMPION heired his name from ORLANDO JONES, son of Rev. Rowland JONES, Rector of old BRUTON PARISH in VIRGINIA. (CORRECTION: JOHN COTTON (above) m. MARTHA GODWIN instead of JONES.)

KAIN, DANIEL, mentioned as grandson in will of SOLOMON DAVIS (1739) 1-40.

KANNADY, MARY died (1692) 3-220.

KASWELL, SARAH, in (1713) lived in PASQUOTANK PRECINCT (now a part of TYRRELL COUNTY) in ALBEMARLE COUNTY 3-265.

KAVANAUGH, ARTHUR (of SURRY COUNTY, VIRGINIA) sold land to THOMAS WHITMELL (of same County and State) in (1714) witnessed by JOHN KEETER and LAWRENCE MAGUE in N. C. 1-286; & the same year he sold land on a branch of INDIAN TOWN CREEK, which KAVANAUGH obtained by patent in (1707); witnessed by ROBERT HICKS and JON. GORDON - to THOMAS HICKS 1-289

KEETER, JOHN, witnessed deed by ARTHUR KAVANAUGH to THOMAS WHITMELL (1714) 1-286.

KEETER, MARTHA, and her son, bought land from JOHN HAWKINS (1716) 2-619.

KEETER, LEMUEL, in will (1849) gives list of descendants of the KEETER FAMILY 2-525, 2-526.

KEATON, JOHN, deed to JOHN KEATON, JR. in (1733) 2-509; sold land to RICHARD BOND on MAIDEN HAIR NECK (1736) 3-127; left will in (1734) in PERQUIMANS and mentions daughter ELIZABETH WIGGINS 1-56; JOHN KEATON SR. sold land to JOHN KEATON, JR. (or with him) and wife HANNAH, patented by JOHN KEATON, deceased & JOHN KEATON JR. (50 acres) to LUKE MIZELL, said land being on or in MAIDEN HAIR NECK; MATTHEW YOUNG and ROBERT LASSITER were the witnesses 2-450.

KEATON, JOSEPH, will (1824) mentions various relatives and grandchildren, including children of his son in law NEHEMIAH WHITE; shows relation with the WINSLOW family also; JAMES LEIGH and WILLIAM KNOWLES witnesses 3-339.

KEATON, ZACHARIAH, married in (1704) the widow of ZACHARIAH JACKSON and had daughter named LUCY 1-444.

KEARNEY, EDMUND, was an assignee of TIMOTHY BLOODWORTH (Of Nansemond County, Va.) in the year (1719) v. EPAPRODITUS BENTON and THOMAS JARNIGAN (In Nansemond County Va. Court) 2-149.

KEARNEY, MICHAEL, gave his brother EDWARD KEARNEY (Of Virginia) a power of attorney in (1719) 2-455; MICHAEL KEARNEY was in the PROVINCE of N. C. 2-149.

KEARNEY, ROGER, married MARY ST. LEGER in (1735) 2-465.

KEEFE, TREDLE, and wife ELLENER sold lands to a ROBERT CALF in (1718), with JOHN SMITH and DANIEL DEAR witnesses 1-625; he also sold a tract in (1738) on BENNETT'S CREEK to JOHN ALSTON 1-284; he had power of attorney from WILLIAM SHARP in (1716) 1-293; he died and left will in BERTIE in (1723) mentions wife ELLENER, sons TREDLE and JOHN, JAMES BATE & MARGARET and ELIZABETH KEEFE 1-56; in (1725) his widow ELLENER married RICHARD OLDNER in BERTIE 2-470.

KEISLAND, EDWARD, named JOHN BUNTIN as a headright about (1697) 2-299.

KEITH, ELIZABETH, servant to SAMUEL WILSON, died in (1685) 3-366.

KELLY, JOHN (late of ROANOKE in CURRITUCK) left will (1764) witnessed by EDWARD and WILLIAM MANN 2-6; JOHN of PASQUOTANK died in (1759) and the witnesses were JOHN & SARAH McBRIDE 1-331.

KELLY, MATTHEW, of PASQUOTANK died in (1699) and his will was witnessed by HENRY WHITE and JOSEPH DAVIS 1-333.

KELLY, SARAH, left will in PASQUOTANK in (1699) with THOMAS BOYD a witness 1-331.

KELLY, SMITH, left will in (1731) and named a son NICHOLAS KELLY 1-56.

KELLY, WILLIAM, bought land from CHRISTOPHER DUDLEY in (1717); KELLY was from NANSEMOND COUNTY, Virginia 1-620; in (1723) the wife of WILLIAM KELLY was HANNAH and they sold land to EDWARD WESSON on the North side of WARWICK SWAMP that year 2-295; A WILLIAM left will in CHOWAN in (1815) witnessed by JOSIAH and CALEB ELLIOTT 2-6.

KEMP, GEORGE, left will in (1723) and named his wife MARY 1-56.

KERBY, THOMAS (often spelled KIRBY - but they were the same) and wife ESTHER sold land in (1718) to JOHN PROCTOR on WASHINGTON'S BRANCH adjoining RICHARD WASHINGTON 1-622; he bought land from HENRY WHEELER (1716) 1-299; in (1716) he appointed his son THOMAS KIRBY JR. to acknowledge a deed 1-295; in (1712) he sold land to HENRY WHEELER on TURKEY CREEK, with RICHARD WASHINGTON and RICHARD HORNE as witnesses 1-295; then in (1716) he sold lands to RICHARD HORNE 1-295; in (1718) he sold lands that had been part of a grant to HENRY WHEELER to one MATTHEW RUSHING 1-629; he and his wife ESTHER in (1718) sold lands to RICHARD WASHINGTON 1-627; he died in (1719) leaving a will in which he named oldest son THOMAS, second son CHARLES, youngest son EDWARD & daughters MABEL and ESTHER and wife ESTHER 1-56; in about (1720) THOMAS KERBY, JR. deeded lands left him by his father on TURKEY CREEK to his mother ESTHER KERBY; SAMUEL RICKS and JOHN DEW being the witnesses 1-630.

KENDALL, OBEDIAH, died (1692) 3-364

KENNEDY, ANN, died at EDENTON in (1777); she was ANN HAUGHTON, and mentions her brothers & their children, and PENELOPE, daughter of SAMUEL JOHNSTON and cousins TAYLOR 2-7.

KENNEDY, ELIZABETH in (1768) was orphan of ELIZABETH KENNEDY and 8 years old 3-445; and ELIZABETH was the name of the wife of PATRICK KENNEDY 3-367.

KENNEDY, JAMES, son of PATRICK and his wife ELIZABETH was born in (1694) 3-367.

KENNEDY, PATRICK, and wife ELIZABETH sold plantation on BANKS CREEK in (1689) to TIMOTHY CLEARE, with PETER GRAY and JAMES LOADMAN witnesses 3-435.

KENT, ANN, married JAMES HOGG, son of JOHN HOGG of YORKSHIRE, ENGLAND in (1679) 3-300.

KENT, ELIZABETH, daughter of THOMAS KENT and his
wife ANN, married WILLIAM CHARLES, son of
WILLIAM CHARLES and his wife ABIGAIL (1683)
3-202; she was born (1667) and had sister
MARY KENT born (1673) 3-205.

KENT, JOHN, son of SAMUEL KENT and wife JANE was
born (1704) 3-375; an older JOHN KENT died
leaving will (1719), with RICHARD HARVEY as
executor 1-56.

KENT, JOSEPH, died in (1789) leaving wife RACHEL
with ALEX SLAUGHTER a witness 2-344.

KENT, JOSHUA in (1703) witnessed a power of attorney given by JOHN ARCHDALE to EMANUEL
LOWE 3-72.

KENT, SAMUEL, father of JOHN KENT born in (1704)
3-375.

KENT, THOMAS, died in (1673) 3-365; probably the
father in law of WILLIAM CHARLES 3-202.

KENT, WILLIAM, was Master of the schooner SUKEY
in (1775) 1-436.

KENYON, DUKE, brother of THOMAS, WILLIAM, SARAH,
JOSEPH and BENJAMIN KENYON, died leaving
will (1738); DUKE BOGUE an executor of his
will 3-176.

KENYON, ROGER, died (1777) leaving will and giving names of his children 3-176; he is mentioned in a lawsuit in (1732) 2-305.

KENYON, JOAB, left will (1797) and the name of
his wife was MARWOOD 3-176.

KENNON, WILLIAM (no K in name) married LEWIS
in Virginia; list of children given, and
what became of them 2-155.

KENNON, MARY, daughter of WILLIAM KENNON and MISS
LEWIS, married THOMAS HARRISON, and ELIZA-
BETH WOODSON KENNON (daughter of JOHN KEN-
NON and ELIZABETH WOODSON) born in GRAN-
VILLE COUNTY, N. C. (1783) married DAVID L.
WHITE 2-155.

KINYON, ANN MARWOOD, died leaving will (1805) EL-
BURY TURNER, executor 3-339.

KINYON, LEVI, died leaving will (1833) 3-339.

KILLINGSWORTH, FRANCIS, of JOHNSTON COUNTY, will
(1751) wife Rebecca 1-331.

KILLINGSWORTH, RICHARD sold lands to MICHAEL DOR-
man which he had aptented (1699) sale in
(1722) 2-295; he died leaving will EDGECOMB
in (1733), wife MARY 1-331.

KING, CHARLES and THOMAS PILAND were witnesses to
a deed by RICHARD BARNES in (1723) 2-449; &
he and ELIZABETH KING were witnesses to deed
of THOMAS KNOX in (1737) with ISAAC WILLIAMS
3-130; two CHARLES KINGS left wills in BER-
TIE (1818 & 1819) the first naming grandsons
and the second children, with wife ELIZABETH
2-525.

KING, DAVID, in (1769) was allowed to keep FERRY
from WINDSOR to VIRGIN'S POINT 3-447.

KING FAMILY. Wills of the family in BERTIE at
2-525; also see 2-6, 2-57, 2-58.

KING, HENRY left orphan named WILLIAM KING, &
WILLIAM VIRGIN was appointed his guardian (1768) 3-445; he received a grant of
land (1728) on CYPRESS SWAMP 1-18; also
a grant in (1741) 1-18; the one who was
perhaps the ancestor left will in CHOWAN
(1714) naming sons MICHAEL, HENRY, CHARLES,
and daughters ELIZABETH, CATHERINE, ANN
and MARY, to whom he left land in NANSE-
MOND COUNTY, Virginia 1-56; in (1715) receipt from ROBERT CALF to GERARD LYNCH for
merchandise taken up by HENRY KING deceased (LYNCH had married the widow of
HENRY KING) 1-615; HENRY KING (JR)owned
land next to MARY BARNES and MATTHEW ODOM
in (1730) 2-610; and he had made a deed
to CHARLES KING in (1728) witnessed by
JOHN JONES and ROBERT FORSTER 2-443.

KING, JOHN, patented lands on BENNETT'S CREEK
SWAMP and on MIDDLE SWAMP (now in GATES
COUNTY) in (1697) 1-5; he was a physician
2-113, 3-348; and was from NANSEMOND
COUNTY, Virginia (1719) 2-512; he deeded
part of the land on BENNETT'S CREEK in
(1731) to JOHN BENTON, with HENRY BONNER,
JOHN WILLIAMS and CONSTANCE LUTEN as the
witnesses 2-452; he and DANIEL PUGH were
witnesses to deed by BENJAMIN SMALL in
(1731) 2-550; JOHN KING and JONATHAN GOD-
WIN were JUSTICES OF NANSEMOND COUNTY, in
Virginia (1771) 3-449; JOHN King, son of
JOHN KING deeded lands to JOHN BENTON in
BERTIE COUNTY in (1739) 3-134.

KING, KATHERINE, widow of HENRY KING, married
GERARD LYNCH before (1717) 1-300.

KING, KADER, died leaving will in (1815) mentions wife POLLY and sons WILLIAM and
NOAH KING; AARON SPIVEY and JOHN ALLEN
were the witnesses 2-525.

KING, MABEL, was the daughter of NATHAN KIRBY
in (1721) 2-619.

KING, MICHAEL, died leaving will in BERTIE in
(1741) wife ISABEL; children MICHAEL, HEN-
RY, JOHN, PENELOPE, CATHERINE, ISABEL &
MARY 1-56; he was son of HENRY KING who
died (1714) 1-56; he lived in (1719) between CASHY RIVER and SALMON CREEK in
BERTIE COUNTY 1-445; in (1717) he was the
minor son of HENRY 1-300.

KING, NOAH, was the son of KADER KING 2-525.

KING, SOLOMON, in (1747) he set up a billiard
table in the town of EDENTON 2-470.

KING, THOMAS, with JOHN GRAY, lived on CY-
PRESS SWAMP and witnessed deed of GRAY to
FRANCIS SANDERS (1739) 3-132; in (1682)
a THOMAS KING signed the bond of TIMOTHY
BIGGS and JONATHAN WITTER not to transport certain persons out of the Colony
3-138.

KING, THOMAS BARNES, in (1815) was the grandson of JAMES PARKER, whose daughter SARAH
was his mother 2-538.

KING, WILLIAM, his executors in (1781) had a
dispute with the Indians about certain
lands 3-453; one WILLIAM was the son of
HENRY KING of BERTIE (1768) 3-445; the
estate divided in (1804) children 1-448.

KINGHAM, ROBERT, married the widow of WILLIAM BRANCH in (1747) 2-470; this one or an older Robert KINGMAN (thought to be the same) made an affidavit during the CARY REBELLION (about 1706-10) 3-226.

KINGERLE, GEORGE, had wife ELIZABETH in (1698) 3-370.

KINCHEN, WILLIAM SR. obtained a land grant (1745) in CRAVEN COUNTY 1-445.

KINCHEN, WILLIAM, JR. of EDGECOMBE, left a will in (1758) and mentions brothers BLAKE BAKER and HENRY DAWSON 1-56

KINGSBURY, JOHN, was Captain of ARTILLERY in the N. C. Continental Line 1-426.

KINSE, KATHERINE, married WILLIAM TURNER (1693) 3-406.

KINSEY, JOHN. His wife was CATHERINE 3-218; died (1692) 3-220.

KINGTON, BATHIA, will (1815) had a grandson JESSE COBB 3-525.

KIRK, THOMAS, bought land from JAMES TURNER in (1716), deed witnessed by DAVID ATKINS and ISAAC HILL 2-285; then he sold land to ROBERT CALF in (1717) with JOHN NAIRNE as a witness 1-618.

KITTRELL, ANN, and THOMAS WHITMELL JR. witnessed will of HEZEKIAH THOMPSON in (1771) 2-358.

KITTRELL, BELSON, married NANNY WEST (1803)2-376 he was the executor of the will of RICHARD NORTH in (1805) 2-534; and witnessed marriage of JOHN KITTRELL to POLLY WEST (1797) in BERTIE COUNTY 2-371.

KITTRELL, DEMPSEY, died in (1797) leaving a will with wife MARTHA; AARON and JONATHAN SPIVEY were executors; witnesses MARTHA BATE and JEREMIAH LEGGETT 2-344.

KITTRELL, GEORGE, one of the executors of will of PHILIP WARD in (1777) 2-361; left will in GATES COUNTY in (1832) naming wife MILLY and his children 2-58.

KITTRELL, ISAAC married ELIZABETH REED in (1805) in BERTIE COUNTY 2-377.

KITTRELL, JOHN, bought land from WILLIAM WOOD in (1739) with RICHARD TAYLOE a witness to the deed 3-133; an earlier JOHN left will in (1793) father of DEMPSEY 2-344; JOHN KITTRELL (JR) married MARY LASSITER in (1794) 2-368; married POLLY WEST in BERTIE (1797) BELSON KITTRELL a witness 2-371.

KITTRELL, JONATHAN and wife ANN sold lands on BENNETT'S CREEK in (1718) to JAMES FARLOW, with ROBERT HICKS and SAMUEL GILLIAM as witnesses 1-630; in (1739) when of BERTIE he sold lands to JOHN ARLINE (Of NANSEMOND COUNTY, VA.) which he had bought from JOHN KING, deceased being land for son JOHN KITTRELL; the witnesses were JOHN KITTRELL, SARAH KITTRELL & JAMES HOMES 3-132, 3-133; in (1723) he sold land to RICHARD PARKER (Of Nasemond Co. Va.) GEORGE & JAMES SPIVEY witnesses 2-283; and to RICHARD BAKER -CALEB SPIVEY 3-133; will left (1747) 2-631.

KITTRELL, JONATHAN JR. and JOHN COLLINS and others appointed as road overseers (1744) 2-621; one JONATHAN owned lands next to CHRISTOPHER BOYCE (1735) 3-128; he and wife ANN sold land (1719) to SAMUEL GILLIAM, with JOHN WILLIAMSON and ROBERT HICKS as witnesses 1-630.

KITTRELL, SARAH, married DANIEL BOGHART, who died in (1796) naming his wife's brothers and sisters in his will 2-329.

KITTRELL, WILLIAM, was brother in law of DANIEL BOGHART in (1796) 2-329.

KORNEGAY, GEORGE, died in CRAVEN COUNTY (1773) leaving will naming wife SUSANNA and all his children 1-331.

KNIGHT, ANN, mentioned in the will of THOMAS PENDLETON in will (1732) 1-67.

KNIGHT, DEMPSEY, was executor of the will of AMBROSE WIGGINS of GATES County (1805) who mentioned brother PUGH WIGGINS and others 2-80.

KNIGHT, MRS. FOSTER, married EDWARD FOISON in (1701) 3-410.

KNIGHT FAMILY. Wills 2-58.

KNIGHT, JOHN, witnessed a deed by THOMAS MILNER to JANE KNIGHT (both of NANSEMOND CO. VA.) in (1737), which land was part of a patent to COL. THOMAS MILNER in (1708) 3-130.

KNIGHT, LEWIS ALEXANDER, died leaving will in PASQUOTANK in (1731) in which his sons are named 1-56.

KNIGHT, ROBERT, received a grant of land in (1749) which joined lands of JACOB ODOM 1-20.

KNIGHT, SIMON, proved his rights (1694) 3-244; also 1-609.

KNIGHT, TOBIAS in (1717) signed proclamation dissolving the Assembly 3-229; he was the CHIEF JUSTICE in (1718) 3-282; he married CATHERINE, the widow of WILLIAM GLOVER by (1712) 3-276, 3-277; he had been SECRETARY to CHARLES EDEN 3-24; he died leaving will in (1719) 1-56.

KNIGHT, WILLIAM died in BERTIE COUNTY in (1751) leaving will naming wife MARTHEW (MARTHA?) and children JOHN, WILLIAM and NEHEMIAH & "all my children" 1-331.

KNOTT, JOHN, married PRISCILLA LAWRENCE in BERTIE in (1806) 2-377.

KNOTT, JOSEPH, died in BERTIE (1780) leaving a will, wife SARAH, HENRY SPELLER and GEORGE OUTLAW 2-343.

KNOTT, NATHANIEL, of BERTIE, died and his orphans were wards of HUMPHREY HARDY (1769) 3-447.

KNOTT FAMILY. Wills in BERTIE 2-344.

KNOWLES, ELIZABETH died leaving will in (1824) leaving CHARLES, ASBERRY and WILLIAM, sons, with JACOB CANNON a witness 3-339.

KNOWLES, ABNER, was the son in law of ELIZABETH BARCLIFT will (1808)   3-326.

KNOX, AMBROSE had the sloop Two Brothers assigned to him in (1777) 2-217.

KNOX, ANDREW. Children born to them about(1750) wife was CHRISTIAN 3-387; he and wife CHRISTIAN witnessed will of THOMAS HALSEY (1774) 3-174; he died leaving will (1776) mentions wife CHRISTIAN and children, and names SAMUEL JOHNSTON and REV. HENRY PATILIO guardians of his children 3-176; ANDREW KNOX was the MASTER of the sloop FRANKLIN, Joseph BAGLEY owner (1775) 1-436; DR. ANDREW KNOX was related to the COFFIELD family and the WARRENS 1-538; the Doctor patented lands(1805) 1-24; one ANDREW was an heir of S. P. KNOX in (1833) 2-266.

KNOX, JOHN, died in CHOWAN, leaving will in (1730) mentions wife MARGARET, daughter MARY, son THOMAS, with JOHN PORTER and wife Executors 1-331.

KNOX, JOHN, who married JANE GRACY (according to this account) and came from Scotland to America in 1740, settled in ROWAN County, N. C., and his son JAMES was Grandfather of JAMES KNOX POLK the President. 3-315.

KNOX, THOMAS. He and his wife MARGARET sold land to JOHN DRURY (1737) part of lands patented to CHARLES WILKES in (1695) 3-130; bought lands (1734) MOSES HALL & MOSES ODOM wits 3-125; deed to WILLIAM JONES (1737) with CHARLES and ELIZABETH KING, witnesses 3-130.

THOMAS KIRBY of this record belonged to an old YORK COUNTY, VIRGINIA, family, and his emigrant ancestor, another THOMAS KERBY, married a daughter of DOCTORIS WILLIAM CHRISTMAS, while the son of the first THOMAS married MARY RAY, daughter of THOMAS RAY and his wife MARY CHRISTMAS, of the same parentage. The last will of this writer's oldest known ancestor, THOMAS RAY, now an undecipherable rag on the records of YORK COUNTY, Virginia, probated, as near as can be made out, on the 24th of June 1653, gives the names of the following signers, as witnesses thereto: HENRY FREEMAN, THOMAS RAY, THOMAS KERBY and PETER STARKEY. The will of DOCTORIS WILLIAM CHRISTMAS was proved in December, of the following year (1654) and the witnesses to his will were HENRY FREEMAN, THOMAS KERBY and PETER STARKEY. On the old CHARLES PARISH REGISTER there are fragments of records of members of these families, but obviously NOT ALL OF THEM. But enough is gleaned to enable the student to piece in the missing items needed to connect these NORTH CAROLINA Starkeys, Kerbys, Rays and Freemans, as limbs from these old stems. All of these witnesses were apparently sons in laws of DOCTORIS WILLIAM CHRISTMAS. PETER STARKEY married BRIDGET CHRISTMAS, HENRY FREEMAN married ____ CHRISTMAS and THOMAS RAY married MARY CHRISTMAS. No slightest clue reveals the name of the daughter who married THOMAS KERBY, but that one did there is little doubt. No clairvoyancing is needed to deduce that the THOMAS KERBY who in 1712 lived on TURKEY CREEK and sold land to HENRY WHEELER, joined by his wife ESTHER, with RICHARD WASHINGTON as a witness (1-295); and sold land to RICHARD WASHINGTON in 1718 (1-627); and the JONATHAN CHRISTMAS who witnessed a deed by RICHARD WASHINGTON in (1720) (2-608) and was sued by WASHINGTON in 1724 (2-297); and the historically known presence in this same section of North Carolina of PETER STARKEY, EDWARD STARKEY, JOHN STARKEY and others of prominence, were direct descendants of the signatories of the THOMAS RAY WILL on NEW POCOSON, in YORK COUNTY, Virginia, in 1653.

As for the FREEMANS, the same may be said of them - some of them took the same course and came to North Carolina. The RAYS and FREEMANS were related to the KINGS, as witness the will of KING FREEMAN in Bertie in 1793, the father in law of BLAKE BAKER (2-334), and the writer's father, who was WILLIAM KING RAY, of Tennessee and Texas. These ancient families had ways of perpetuating family history by the use of certain names which branded their off-spring. One ALEXANDER SKIPWORTH married a daughter of THOMAS RAY (the emigrant) and this accounts for the SKIPWORTH RAYS in Virginia to this day; also for the origin of old man ALEXANDER RAY, intimate with the CHARLTONS in BERTIE at the beginning of the 18th century (1-029). THOMAS KERBY, of TURKEY CREEK, was a grandson of THOMAS KERBY of the RAY WILL, and a son of THOMAS KERBY and his wife MARY RAY, who had a son ROBERT KERBY, born May 1, 1662, according to the old Charles Parish Register. There is no record of the birth of THOMAS, but he was perhaps a few years older than his brother ROBERT, whose wife was CATHERINE, and who had thirteen children, including a son BENNETT KERBY, who had a son named THOMAS. FRANCIS WHEELER, ancestor of the WHEELERS of TURKEY CREEK, also lived in YORK COUNTY, VIRGINIA.

JONATHAN KITTRELL. JONATHAN KITTRELL, so far as this record shows, appears to have been one of the earliest arrivals of that name. Like WILLIAM and JOHN DANIEL, JOHN ALSTON and the PEELES he settled on BENNETT'S CREEK. This fact alone almost marks him as a comer from ISLE OF WIGHT or NANSEMOND, if his subsequent known transactions with families of that derivation, did not remove any further doubt of it. He and his wife ANN sold lands there as early as 1710 (1-630). The name JONATHAN for many succeeding generations constituted the KITTRELL BRAND. The family married into the SPIVEYS, as a matter of course (2-283, 2-344). JONATHAN KITTRELL, JR. lead the migration westward to GRANVILLE COUNTY, and here the town of KITTRELL was established, which became the seat of this then prominent family. A junction by marriage was effected with the MEMUCAN HUNT family (MAUSEY KITTRELL married WILLIAM HUNT in 1780) and with the HOWARDS (MEMUCAN HUNT of the third generation married a HOWARD) etc. PLEASANT WILLIAM KITTRELL moved down on the PEE DEE after his graduation from the University in 1822 (Wheeler (1) p 120) and there he was elected and represented ANSON COUNTY in the Legislature. There he married a MISS GOREE. He then moved to ALABAMA, and was again sent to the Legislature. Then he "went to Texas" and again was sent to the Legislature in the new State. His sons rose to prominence. JUDGE NORMAN GOREE KITTRELL served with distinction on the bench of TEXAS. His nephew COL. JOHN W. THOMASON, of "FIX BAYONETS" fame, only recently died serving his country.

LACEY, CHRISTOPHER died (1695-6) at the home of MARGARET LAWRENCE 3-402.

LACY, DANIEL, was a school master, and died in BERTIE COUNTY leaving will (1771) 2-345.

LACEY, JOHN died leaving will (1786) and among others mentioned son in law JOSHUA TARLTON and WILLIAM LACEY 3-177.

LACEY, JOSEPH, will (1809) children and daughter ELIZABETH POOL 3-341.

LACEY, NATHAN, will (1798) names children and relatives named EVANS 3-177.

LACEY, WILLIAM, son of WILLIAM LACEY and wife MARY born (1727) 3-387; will 1734 1-60.

LACEY, WILLIAM JR. and wife MARY (1696) 3-369.

LAFITTE, TIMOTHY, died (1744) and SAMUEL STILL - WELL and wife SARAH Executors 1-455.

LAKER, BENJAMIN, of PERQUIMANS, left will (1701) mentions daughter SARAH HARVEY 1-58; account of his family in note 1-58; he married JULIANA TAYLOR in (1696) 3-407; he and THOS KEEPER were JUSTICES (1689) 3-431.

LAKER, JULIANA, was the executor of MRS. MARY SCOTT (about 1700) 1-443; was administra - trix of the will of HUGH DAVIS (1724) 1-41.

LAKER, RUTH, married JAMES MINGE, of MARTIN'S BRANDON in Virginia (1701) 3-409.

LAMANSON, CHARLES, witness to deed by JOHN BALLARD in (1717) CHOWAN 1-618.

LAMB, ARMIGA, died leaving will (1819), witnessed by ABIGAIL LAMB, in which he names wife SARAH and sons HENRY, DANIEL, REUBEN and a JOSEPH LAMB 3-340.

LAMB, DANIEL witnessed will of THOMAS SANDERS in (1828) 3-350.

LAMB, GIDEON, was a Colonel in the NORTH CAROLINA CONTINENTAL LINE 1-420.

LAMB FAMILY. Wills 3-339, 3-340.

LAMB, JOSHUA, his estate mentioned in (1695) 3-259; in (1689) JOSHUA LAMB and a WILLIAM LAWRENCE were neighbors 3-432; WILLIAM COLLINS in (1694) sued MARY LAMB the widow of JOSHUA LAMB, and THOMAS SWANN was her attorney 1-612; he bought ROANOKE ISLAND from GOVERNOR BERKELEY in (1669), who obtained the title through his wife, the widow of SAMUEL STEVENS, and JOHN CULPEPPER witness to the deed 2-101, 2-102, and to 2-108.

LAMB, RESTORE, an executor of GEORGE CARUTHERS in (1821) 3-330; died leaving will himself in (1823), in which he names sons STEPHEN, CALEB and JACOB LAMB 3-346.

LAMB, WILLIAM, an orphan in CHOWAN in (1743) chose THOMAS JONES as guardian 1-447; one WILLIAM left will in PERQUIMANS in (1758) 1-334.

LAMB, ZACHARIAH, died leaving will (1804) wife MIRIAM and RESTORE LAMB, Executors, ELIAB GRIFFIN and REUBEN PERRY witnesses 3-339.

LAMBERT, HERBERT, "late of Maryland" died in (1682) 3-366.

LANCASTER, MARY, died leaving will (1794) and mentions daughter ELIZABETH BRYAN and her children, daughter ELIZABETH SEAY, with sons JOHN ANDREWS and STEPHEN ANDREWS her executors 2-346.

LANCASTER, MICAJAH, in (1768) was appointed guardian of JOHN, MARGARET and STEPHEN ANDREWS in BERTIE 3-444.

LANCASTER, WILLIAM GASTON, was grandson of ELIZABETH RUTLAND who left will in BERTIE in (1836), who named daughters ELIZABETH TYLER, NANCY GRANBERRY and ELIZABETH HELEN LANCASTER and their children, including MARTHA ANDREWS 2-545.

LANDRUM, MARY, mentioned as the daughter of MOORE HOLLEY and wife CATHERINE in will of PENELOPE HOLLEY (1853) in BERTIE 2-522.

LANCEFORD, JOHN, will (1797) wife SARAH WINGATE and son WILLIAM 3-177.

LANCEFORD, WILLIAM, one of the witnesses to the will of JOHN 3-177.

LANE, CHARLES, born HALIFAX COUNTY, N. C. was son of JESSE and grandson of JOSEPH LANE and wife PATIENCE McKINNIE; he married ELIZABETH MALLORY 1-473.

LANE, EPHRIAM, died leaving will in (1773) 1-333.

LANE FAMILY. Wills of WALTER, THOMAS, JOSEPH and CHRISTIAN LANE 1-333.

LANE, EZEKIEL, witnessed the will in (1796) of NATHAN PARK, brother of JOSEPH PARK 3-183.

LANE, GRIZZELL, married GEORGE LILLINGTON RYAN and she was daughter of JOEL LANE and MARY HINTON 1-479.

LANE, JAMES, will in BERTIE (1820), MOSES WARD an executor 3-527.

LANE, JESSE (son of JOSEPH LANE and PATIENCE McKINNIE) married WINNIFRED AYCOCK; childrens' names given 1-473.

LANE, JOHN, called "cousin" in the will of BARNABY McKINNIE, JR. (1735) 1-61.

LANE, JONATHAN, was the son of JESSE LANE and grandson of JOSEPH LANE and PATIENCE Mc - KINNIE, his wife 1-473.

LANE, JOSEPH, and EXUM LANE were witnesses to will of HENRY CHAPPELL in (1829) 3-329; he defended a suit in (1755) with WILLIAM BRYAN and THOMAS DIXON 1-447; he married PATIENCE McKINNIE, daughter of BARNABAS or BARNABY McKINNIE SR. in (1730) 1-469; genealogical account of his family and some of his descendants 1-469 to 1-474.

LANE, THOMAS, bought land in (1728) on CHOWAN river from BENJAMIN PERRY, witnessed by SUSANNAH PERRY 3-445.

LANE, WINNIFRED married PELEG ROGERS and moved to ATHENS, GEORGIA; she was born WAKE COUNTY, N. C. (1780) 1-474.

LANG, RICHARD, sold land to DANIEL CRAWLEY (1720) with JOHN LEONARD a witness 2-618.

LANGDALE, SARAH, will (1843), mentions sons and MARY WEBB 2-527.

LANGSTON, JOHN, and EPHRAIM and WILLIAM HUNTER witnessed deed by MARY BARNES to ALEXANDER CARTER (1733) 2-610; he sold land to WIL- LIAM LANGSTON on ROGERS BRANCH (1739) with JOHN LANGSTON, JR. and ROBERT ROGERS as wit- nesses 3-133; and to RICHARD GREEN JR. in (1739) at a place called SAHUM, the witnes- ses being JOHN, THOMAS and WILLIAM LANGSTON and JOSEPH VANN 3-133.

LANIER, REBECCA, married COL. JOSEPH WILLIAMS- a query from one of his descendants 3-469. (NOTE: From an old Bible record it appears that he also married SARAH LANIER, a sister of REBECCA -WSR.)

LANIER, ROBERT, proved eleven headrights CHOWAN COUNTY in (1711) 3-442; he received the as- signment of a patent from ANTHONY WILLIAMS in (1713) a part of which land had been previously sold to JOHN BEVERLY and GEORGE WINNS; witnesses were JAMES BOON and HENRY BRANSON 1-101; in (1715) he was a witness with THOMAS KIRBY to a deed by WILLIAM DOWN- ING, merchant to WILLIAM SHARP a ship car - penter 1-288; he and EDWARD HOWARD in(1718) witnessed deed of ABRAHAM BLEWETT and .wife JANET to LAWRENCE MARTIN, adjoining land of WILLIAM CRAWFORD 1-625; he died leaving a will in TYRRELL COUNTY in (1744) mentions wife SARAH and children WILLIAM and JOHN & grandsons ROBERT DANIEL and JOHN BRYAN 1-336

LANSTON, LEONARD and WILLIAM LANSTON in about (1737) witnessed deed of JOHN ODOM to EPAP- RODITUS JONES 1-116 in GATES COUNTY; this was land patented in (1718) by RICHARD ODOM 3-130.

LANSTON, WILLIAM, witnessed deed of JOHN ODOM to lands patented to RICHARD ODOM (1737) 1-116 and 3-130.

LA PORT, ARTHUR, placed under care of WILLIAM BADHAM in (1733) 1-450.

LARKER, BENJAMIN. His wife was ELIZABETH 3-366.

LARKER, BENJAMIN, SR. was married to JANE DAY by DANIEL AKEHURST (1685) 3-202.

LARKER, JULIAN, left will in PERQUIMANS in (1735) and in it mentions ABRAHAM SANDERS, MACRORA SCARBOROUGH and BENJ. SCARBOROUGH 1-57.

LARKIN, JAMES, received certain merchandise from CORNELIUS JONES with MAJ. ANTHONY BROCKHOLD in (1691) 3-248.

LASSITER, FREDERICK will in (1787) wife SARAH & children named, RICHARD TAYLOE, DAVID TAY- LOE and TIMOTHY WALTON witnesses 2-345.

LASSITER FAMILY. Wills 2-7, 2-8, 2-345.

LASSITER, GABRIEL, bought land from FRANCIS ROUN- DTREE of NANSEMOND COUNTY, VA. (1735) 3-128.

LASSITER, GEORGE, and FRANCIS ROUNDTREE applied for land warrants through THOMAS LUTEN on line of VIRGINIA and NORTH CAROLINA (1702) 3-269.

LASSITER, JAMES and wife MARY, of NANSEMOND COUNTY, VA. sold lands to JAMES BROWN on BENNETT'S CREEK in N. C. in (1736) wit - nessed by RICHARD MINSHEW and WILLIAM TREVATHAN 3-127.

LASSITER, JOHN received a grant of land in (1721) on the South side of BENNETT'S Cr. 1-10; and also one in (1723) at the head of BENNETT'S CREEK 1-11; bought land also from HUMPHREY WEBB (no date) 1-624; he sold land Near Swamp in (1735) to JOHN WIL- LIAMS, with-JOHN HARRELL and RICHARD TAY- LOR, JR. as witnesses 3-125 (at that time JOHN was (of NANSEMOND COUNTY, VA.); he sold land to WILLIAM DAVIS on BENNETT'S CREEK in (1739) 3-133.

LASSITER, MARY, married JOHN KITTRELL (1794) 2-368.

LASSITER, NATHAN, had a land grant in (1786) adjoining JOB PARKER on CHOWAN RIVER 1-25.

LASSITER, ROBERT, received grant of land in (1720) on BENNETT'S CREEK 1-10; in (1727) ten of NANSEMOND COUNTY, VA. he sold lands on the South side of BENNETT'S CREEK to JAMES BROWN, with THOMAS and FRANCIS ROUND- TREE as witnesses 2-444; in (1757) he pat- ented lands in N. C. adjoining the lands of JOHN MIZELL 1-20.

LASSITER, THOMAS, was placed under the tuition of JOHN SMITH in BERTIE in (1770) 3-448.

LASSLEY, JAMES, mentioned in the will of SARAH DECROW in (1795) 3-169.

LATEN, MARY, married JEREMIAH BARNES in (1705) 3-410.

LATEN, ORPHA, married RICARD MELTON in (1705) 3-410.

LATHAM, PAUL, was Clerk of the Court in CARTER- ET in (1680) 2-301; he died and his widow married DANIEL PHILLIPS in ALBEMARLE by (1697) 1-611.

LATTIMORE, ELIZABETH, died in BERTIE, will proved (1753) JAMES SMITH and RICHARD TOM- LINSON mentioned, or witnesses 1-57.

LATTIMORE, WILLIAM,with JOHN STANCELLE, proved the will of WILLIAM FROST (this was about 1718) 1-153; JOHN LATTIMORE and JOHN SMITHWICK took the inventory 1-153.

LATTIMORE, JOHN, with JOHN SMITHWICK took an inventory about (1718) 1-153.

LATTIMORE, WILLIAM, and LUKE MIZELL with JO- SEPH JORDAN divided the estate of DANIEL HENDRICKS (1744) 2-622; he proved the will of THOMAS ROGERS (1749) 2-632; he witnessed deed of WILLIAM FROST (1717) 1-298; and proved the FROST WILL in (1718) 1-532; wit- nessed deed of THOMAS SPIVEY to his son BENJAMIN SPIVEY (1717) 1-517; with ALEXAN- DER BARRON and JOHN THOMPSON witnessed a deed of WILLIAM FROST to MARTIN CROMENS in (1721) (Must have been a younger Wm. Frost - old one dead) 2-618; he and JOHN ALSTON witnessed deed by ARTHUR DAVIS and wife to BARNABAS McKINNIE in (1720) 1-470.

LAYTE, WILLIAM, died leaving will (1701) son WILLIAM and daughter BARBARA 1-58.

LAUGHTON, JAMES, died leaving will (1813) wife MARY and children all named, including daughter POLLY MIZELL; HENRY RAY a witness 3-526.

LAWLER, DARBY, was a brother in law of JOHN RIVET .(1736) 2-299.

LAWLER, DAVID, sold land and made deed to JAMES HINTON (1732) 3-454; his wife was MARY and he had son in law THOMAS HOLMES 1-58; his widow married JOHN SINGLETON about (1736) 3-299; he had sold land to WALTER PHELPS in (1734) 3-453.

LAWLER, PATRICK, received a land grant in (1722) on Northeast side of BENNETT'S Creek 1-11; before that in (1712) he had patented land on the Southeast side of BENNETT'S CREEK 1-8; he died in (1728) naming wife PATIENCE and sons DARBY and DAVID LAWLER 1-59.

LAWRENCE FAMILY. Wills 3-345, 3-526; births of children shown 3-206. (Name sometimes was spelled LARRENCE without the W).

LAWRENCE, FRANCES, was a niece of JOSEPH PARKER in BERTIE (1770) 3-448; her guardian (1771) was JAMES PERRY 3-450.

LAWRENCE, GEORGE, of BERTIE left will in (1756) children and brother THOMAS LAWRENCE 1-338.

LAWRENCE, JOHN, was the son of WILLIAM LAWRENCE and HANNAH BUNDY and he was married (1692) 3-204; their daughter ELIZABETH was born in (1695) 3-368 (John's wife also was Hannah)

LAWRENCE, MRS. MARGARET, married FRANCIS TOMES, JR. in (1696) 3-407.

LAWRENCE, MICHAEL, lived in GATES COUNTY and his wife was RACHEL in (1792) 2-59.

LAWRENCE, RACHEL, widow of MICHAEL LAWRENCE died in (1792) in GATES COUNTY 2-59.

LAWRENCE, REUBEN, was one of the executors(1841) of MARY HUTSON 3-522

LAWRENCE, WILLIAM, married MARGARET BOGUE ceremony by ALEXANDER LILLINGTON (1689) 3-204; he died in the year (1694) 3-401; left will (1694) in which he mentioned wife MARGARET and brother ISRAEL SNELLING 1-58.

LAWSON, JOHN, letter from to GOV. HENDERSON WALKER relating to BAY RIVER INDIANS 1-598; letter to TOBIAS KNIGHT, Secretary (1705)3-266; died leaving will (1709), mentions HANNAH SMITH, daughter ISABELLA and her brother and sister 1-60.

LAWSON, JOHN, of SCUPERNONG, sold land to JOHN HASSELL in (1717) 1-619; signs petition from BATH COUNTY, with JAMES LEIGH and others before (1711) 3-287.

LAWSON, MARY, witnessed deed (1715) of JOHN TARKINGTON to WILLIAM HARDY 1-286; he was the son of NATHANIEL LAWSON and grandson of MARY PHILLPOT in (1694) 1-67.

LAWSON, NATHANIEL, was son in law of MARY PHILPOT and father of JOHN LAWSON (1694) 1-67.

LAWSON, SAMUEL, will in CRAVEN (1758) wife MARGARET, son DURANCE, dau. MARY LAWSON 1-338.

LAYDEN, FRANCIS, will (1807) wife ELIZABETH, sons THOMAS and JOHN and daughter SALLIE PENDLETON 3-340; an earlier FRANCIS LAYDEN had wife ELIZABETH and children born around (1713) 3-387, 3-388; this last one died about (1729) mentions his sons and a cousin WILLIAM MIDDLETON 1-59.

LAYDEN, GEORGE died leaving will in (1766) gives children, with wife MARY, JAMES GIBSON and JOHN PERRY executors 3-176.

LAYDEN, ISAAC, died leaving will (1786) wife ELIZABETH and "my children". FRANCIS LAYDEN and THOMAS HOSEA witnesses 3-177.

LAYDEN, SAMUEL (spelled LAYTON) will (1791) sisters ESTHER and MARTHA LAYDEN 3-346.

LAYDEN, THOMAS, was witness to the will of WILLIAM HUMPHRIES in (1833) with THOMAS LAYDEN a witness 3-338.

LEAR, JOHN, of NANSEMOND COUNTY, VIRGINIA, sold lands to WILLIAM WILKINSON of ISLE OF WIGHT COUNTY about(1728) which had been patented to JOHN LEAR, the grandfather of the grantor JOHN LEAR. ANDREW MEADE and DAVID MEADE are the witnesses 3-445.

LEAR, COL. JOHN, married the widow of SETH SOUTHEL, ANNA; the wife of SETH SOTHEL was ANNA in (1689-90), and COL. LEAR was her fourth husband 1-74, 3-31; COL. JOHN LEAR was from NANSEMOND COUNTY, VIRGINIA 1-74; the executors of COL. JOHN LEAR brought a suit against THOMAS POLLOCK (no date)3-254, 3-255.

LEARY, CORNELIUS, and wife MARY in (1689) sold 200 acres of land to BENJAMIN LAKER on the SOUND and WILLIAM TETTERTON'S line, which was witnessed by JOHN BENTLEY (son of RICHARD BENTLEY), EDWARD MAYO SR. and SAMUEL PRICKLOVE 3-435; his petition to the PRESIDENT and COUNCIL for a horse seized for Quit Rents in which PAUL LATHAM and FAMILY are mentioned 3-83; births of two of their children 3-213; RICHARD LEARY and wife SARAH had a son CORNELIUS born in (1710) 3-388; births of other LEARY children (mis-spelled LURY)3-210

LEARY, DERBY, will (1789), wife MARY, LAMB HARDY and JOHN CORB, Executors 2-346.

LEARY FAMILY. Wills 1-9, 3-527, 3-346, 1-59.

LEARY, JACOB, died leaving will in (1731) and mentioned son JACOB 1-59.

LEARY, JOHN (Spelled LARY) died in DECEMBER (1682) 3-366; he married the widow of WILLIAM CHARLES 1-58.

LEARY, RICHARD, married SUSAN LONG in (1709) 3-410; one RICHARD'S wife was SARAH(1710) their children's births 3-388; he was the guardian of WILLIAM WILSON, an orphan, in (1734) 1-450; SARAH LEARY was the daughter of THOMAS LONG who died leaving will in (1727) 1-59; Richard Leary died leaving will in (1738) 1-57.

LEARY, SARAH (perhaps the wife of RICHARD LEARY) was the daughter of THOS LONG 1-59.

LEARY, THOMAS, died (1760) 3-469.

LEATHWORTH, JOSEPH, proved his rights when CHAS. SMITH was Clerk (no date) 3-300.

LEDBETTER, WILLIAM in (1721) witnessed deed made to BARNABY McKINNIE 1-470.

LEE, DAVID, bought land from JOHN MARKS and wife MARGARET in (1711), with THOMAS LUTEN, JR. and WILLIAM FALLAUGH witnesses; he then sold 50 acres to WILLIAM FALLAUGH 1-297.

LEE, DIANA (DINA) in (1716) sold land to WILLIAM BONNER 1-299.

LEE FAMILY. Wills 1-333, 1-334, 3-59, 3-60.

LEE, GILBERT (Spelled LEIGH) will (1791) wife ELIZABETH, daughter MARY WHEDBEE, sons FRANCIS, RICHARD, THOMAS, JAMES and BENJAMIN with SAMUEL KNIGHT a witness 3-177;

LEE, JAMES (Spelled LEIGH) signed petition for a road with JOHN LAWSON and others (1711) 3-287.

LEE, MARY of GATES COUNTY left will in GATES CO. in (1836) and gives names of her children and grand-children and other relatives 3-59.

LEE, RICHARD, of EDGECOMBE, died leaving will in (1756) sons TIMOTHY, ARTHUR, RICHARD and SOLOMON LEE and other children 1-333; in(1822) a RICHARD LEE (Spelled LEIGH) was Executor of JOHN MILLER 3-343.

LEE'S MILL was in WASHINGTON, N. C. and JAMES BLOUNT was connected with it 2-312, 2-313; It was in existence in (1706) and was founded by THOMAS BLOUNT 2-133.

LEE, SAMUEL, died in BERTIE COUNTY in (1799) wife MARY, daughter PENELOPE LEE, mentions brother JOSHUA LEE and sister ELIZABETH HARRELL witnessed by ELIJAH HOWARD 2-346.

LEE, STEPHEN, was the son of THOMAS LEE who died in (1716) leaving will 1-59; in a deed to DANIEL GARRETT in (1721) he mentions "my father, THOMAS LEE"; land patented by COL. FREDERICK JONES 2-447; he died leaving will in TYRRELL COUNTY in (1746) Col. ROBERT WEST a witness with CULLEN POLLOCK 1-334; he sold land to EDWARD MOSELEY in (1730) with WILLIAM DOWNING a witness 2-449.

LEE, THOMAS, married the widow of WILLIAM DOWNING, see NOTE 2-133; the THOMAS who died in (1722) leaving will was brother of WILLIAM LEE 1-59; he was probably the father of STEPHEN LEE (1729) 2-447; one THOMAS died in TYRRELL COUNTY in (1751) and left daughter PRISCILLA LEE 1-57; though a note says his father was THOMAS LEE who left will in CHOWAN in (1716) and that his wife was MARY the widow of CAPT. THOMAS BLOUNT 1-59; he, it was, who bought the BLOUNT'S MILL property from THOMAS BLOUNT, eldest son of CAPT. THOMAS BLOUNT in (1716) 1-297.

LEE, WILLIAM, in (1697) appointed COL. WILLIAM WILKINSON his attorney; witnessed by WILLIAM GLOVER and JOSEPH COMMANDER 3-248.

LEEPER, THOMAS, of BATH, left will in (1719) in BATH 1-60; he was a Justice in the year of (1689) 3-429; and he and BENJAMIN LAKER were Justices same year 3-341.

LEGGETT, ABSALOM, was the father of DANIEL LEGGETT of BERTIE COUNTY (1777) 2-215.

LEGGETT, DANIEL, mentioned in affidavit by BENJAMIN HARRISON in TYRRELL COUNTY (1777) 2-208; he makes an affidavit and says he was supplied with vituals by JOSIAH HARRISON 2-297; JOHN STEWART in affidavit tells of conversations with 2-216.

LEGGETT FAMILY. Wills of JAMES LEGGETT (1764) TITUS LEGGETT (1762), ELIZABETH LEGGETT in (1794); JAMES LEGGETT (1796); THOMAS LEGGETT (1799) 2-345. See also 2-526.

LEGGETT, JAMES, married MARTHA TOMLINSON and he left will (1764) referring to her part of the estate of RICHARD TOMLINSON, and also mentions various relatives including the name of WATSON, BATE, JAMES BENTLEY, ELISHA and BENJAMIN WHITFIELD and others 2-345.

LEGGETT, JEREMIAH was a witness to the will of JOHN JOHNSTON in (1790) 2-343.

LEGGETT, SAMUEL, with WILLIAM and ALEXANDER LEGGETT mentioned in the will of CLARISSA LEGGETT in (1842) 2-526.

LEGGETT, THOMAS, with JEREMIAH LEGGETT witness to will of JOHN JOHNSTON in (1790) 2-343.

LEIGH, ANN (See also LEE) of BEAUFORT in a will in BEAUFORT (1733) mentions her sons SAMUEL and JACOB DARDEN 1-58.

LEIGH, DANIEL (See also LEE) mentioned in the will of GEORGE SLADE in (1710) 1-77.

LEIGH, JAMES and JOHN CLAYTON JR. were witnesses to the will of JOSEPH MACKEY in (1801) 3-342.

LEIGH, RICHARD, was the executor of the will of ELIZABETH GOODMAN in (1837); and RICHARD LEE and HUGH GODFREY were executors of the will of JOSEPH GODFREY in (1831) 3-335.

LEIGH, SARAH, left will in (1833) and mentions children and grand-children, including PARTHENIA WILSON 3-341.

LEIGH, THOMAS, of CHOWAN (1711) and members of his family 3-441.

LEONARD, JOHN, witnessed a deed to DANIEL CRAWLEY in (1720) 3-618; in (1718) he bought land from PHILLIP JONES of SURRY COUNTY Va. 1-623.

LETTER, from the GOVERNOR of N. C. to the LORDS PROPRIETORS 3-53, 3-54.

LEWFORD, WILLIAM, of PASQUOTANK in his will in (1732) mentions his mother FEARE 1-58.

LEWELLING, JOHN, mentioned in affidavits relating to revolutionary troubles 2-566, 2-577.

LEWERTON, EPHRAIM, will in CHOWAN COUNTY in (1710) JOHN HARDY Executor 1-60; he left a will in CHOWAN in (1711) 3-441.

LEWERTON, JOHN, BERTIE will (1740 mentions his nephew JOHN GREGORY 1-57.

LEWERTON, WILLIAM, sold land to THOMAS BRAY in CHOWAN (no date) 1-626.

LEWIS, ABRAHAM, mentioned in a true and just account in November (1695) in connection with DANIEL JOHNSTON, JOHN TRUETT, NATHAN BELL, ROSS BELL, JOHN GILBERT, RICHARD BENTLEY, EDWARD ASHLEY and others 1-611; his wife was ELIZABETH, and they made a deed to NATHANIEL CHEVIN in (1699), with RICHARD LEWIS a witness 2-611.

LEWIS, BENJAMIN, of CHOWAN, was the son of RICHARD LEWIS, who died (1719) leaving sons JOHN, BENJAMIN and WILLIAM, and a daughter who married JOSEPH HUDSON and daughter JANE 1-60.

LEWIS, CONNOR, by his attorney THOMAS ROUNDTREE sold lands patented to FRANCIS THORNTON to THOMAS GARRETT (1707) 2-443.

LEWIS, DAVID, of CARTERET, died (1773) leaving wife MARY and mentions children of JACOB SHEPHARD, SOLOMON SHEPHARD, JOHN SIMMONS & witnessed by JAMES and SARAH FRAZIER 1-337; he and WILLIAM and RICHARD SPEIGHT were witnesses to a deed together (1739) 3-135.

LEWIS, EDWARD. His wife was RUTH. Births of JENKINS, EDWARD, VESTY and WILLIAM LEWIS and their ages in (1707) 3-378.

LEWIS FAMILY. Wills 1-60, 1-337, 2-59, 2-7.

LEWIS, ISAAC, with JACOB LEWIS, made bond to one GEORGE SMITH in CHOWAN (1717) 1-625; he had land grant (1717) adjoining RICHARD WILLIAMSON, JACOB LEWIS and others 1-9; bought land from WILLIAM MAULE (1718) witnessed by ABRAHAM BLEWETT and JOHN NAIRNE 1-627.

LEWIS, JACOB, with ISAAC LEWIS, with his wife MARY, made bond to GEORGE SMITH of CHOWAN in (1717) 1-625; in (1714) he bought land on WICACON CREEK adjoining JOHN EARLY 2-455

LEWIS, JOHN, SR. died leaving will in CHOWAN in (1765) leaving children: ISAAC, ELIJAH, JOHN, BENJAMIN, and daughters ELIZABETH, ANN, MARY, MARTHA, ESTHER and SARAH LEWIS and several grandchildren named 2-7; he was son of RICHARD LEWIS and had brother WILLIAM LEWIS in (1729) 2-451; the same (1737) 3-110; his daughter ELIZABETH LEWIS married WILLIAM FALLOW in CHOWAN; the JOHN son of RICHARD LEWIS sold lands to PETER ADAMS in (1737) 1-116; he recorded his mark in BERTIE in (1744) 2-624; he was granted lands on MATTACOMACK SWAMP next to RICHARD LEWIS and JOHN JONES (1720) 1-9.

LEWIS, MICAJAH, was CAPTAIN in the Fourth Regt. of the N. C. Continental Line 1-419.

LEWIS, RICHARD and his wife ELIZABETH sold land in (1712) on what was known as BARROW'S HOLE, witnessed by THOMAS LUTEN and THOMAS LUTEN, JR. 1-98; he and JAMES BLOUNT were witnesses to a deed by ABRAHAM LEWIS (1699) 2-611; in (1715) he patented lands next to SAMUEL PADGETT 1-15; had a land grant(1711) on COWHALL SWAMP 1-7; he had power of attorney with THOMAS HETTERLY, from CHARLES FOSTER in (1719) 1-627; he was the father of WILLIAM LEWIS (1717) 1-618; and of JOHN LEWIS who sold land to PETER ADAMS (1737) 3-130; he and wife ELIZABETH sold lands to HENRY LISLE (1716) with DANIEL HALSEY a witness 1-294.

LEWIS, JOEL, was a Lieutenant in the TENTH REGIMENT, N. C. Continental Line under COL. ABRAHAM SHEPARD 1-425.

LEWIS, JONATHAN, sold lands to ROBERT PATTERSON and EDWARD MOORE (1717) 1-299.

LEWIS, THOMAS, of CARTERET COUNTY in (1740) an account of all his children, etc. He died in (1800) and he had son ISAAC and others 3-317.

LEWIS, WILLIAM of PAMPTICO, signs petition complaining of CAPT. WILLIAM BARROW the collector of Levies. (Must have been in about 1704-5) 3-260; a WILLIAM LEWIS sold land to JOHN LEWIS (1733) with WILLIAM HINTON a witness 2-609; he bought lands from ORLANDO CHAMPION about (1721) 2-614; land grant next to HENRY WARREN in (1706) 1-8; he makes affidavit in (1704) relative to ROBERT BUTT 1-610; was a witness with WILLIAM HOSKINS in (1739) 3-136; had land grant in (1723) adjoining JOHN ALSTON 1-12; one WILLIAM LEWIS in (1742) was ordered to turn over to CHARLES BLOUNT his goods, as he (BLOUNT?) was now of age 1-447; one WILLIAM LEWIS died in BATH in (1732) wife MARY, daughters SARAH SINCLAIR, MARY DUDLEY, MAGDALENE BAGFORD, EDITH HENSON and sons WILLIAM and SOLOMON LEWIS 1-59.

LEWTON, WILLIAM (LUTEN? or LINTON?) died in BATH leaving will (1726) 1-59.

LEWTON, THOMAS JR. (LUTEN?) land grant (1716) adjoining ROBERT WEST and others 1-14.

LIGHTFOOT, FRANCIS, of VIRGINIA. His executors in North Carolina, sued GEORGE RAWLINS of BERTIE COUNTY (1731) 2-298.

LIGHTFOOT, PHILLIP and BENJAMIN HARRISON were executors of FRANCIS LIGHTFOOT of Virginia and sued GEORGE RAWLINS of BERTIE (1731) 2-298.

LIGO, JOHN, died in (1717) THOMAS CARY was mentioned as "nearest of kin" 1-60.

LILES, EPHRAIM, with JOHN COLLINS bought lands from SAMUEL MERRITT in GATES COUNTY in (1719) 1-628.

LILES, GEORGE, died leaving will (1758) CHOWAN COUNTY, sons GEORGE and JOHN, daughters MARY and ANN and "six youngest children" with JOHN CARLTON, JEREMIAH HAUGHTON and JOHN HOSKINS witnesses 1-338; JOHN BEASLEY was guardian of ANN and ELIZABETH LILES daughters after GEORGE died 1-455; GEORGE sold land to JAMES COSTEN (1725) with GEO. ALLEN and JOHN PADGETT witnesses 2-449.

LILES, HENRY, received a land grant in (1714) adjoining MAJOR LUTEN and MATTHEW BRYAN 1-8; and was a witness to a deed by THOMAS BRAY in (1716) 1-298; he appears to have been a brother of WILLIAM LILES who was a neighbor of JOSEPH SMALL in (1738) 3-135.

LILES, WILLIAM, had a brother HENRY LILES & they owned lands next to JOSEPH SMALL in (1738) 3-135

LILES, THOMAS married FANNY COLSTON 1-397.

LILLINGTON, ALEXANDER, was born about 1643 and was thirty-seven years old in (1680) 3-41, 1-477; his first wife was SARAH (maiden name unknown) who died after (1674) by whom he had children JAMES and ALEXANDER 3-205; he married second ELIZABETH COOPER before (1679) by whom he had other children 3-205, 1-477; a daughter ANN LILLINGTON by his 2nd marriage became the wife of GOVERNOR HENDERSON WALKER and then married EDWARD MOSELEY 1-58; he married third ANN STEWARD in(1695) but they had no children 1-477; he died and left will in (1697) and mentions sons JOHN and GEORGE, wife ANN, and daughters ANN WALKER, ELIZABETH FENDALL and MARY and SARAH; the last married first GOV. THOMAS HARVEY and second CHRISTOPHER GALE 1-58 (He had other children not mentioned); he sued WILLIAM CHAPMAN in (1689) 3-431; was executor of RICHARD EVANS in (1692) 1-42; a note states that ALEXANDER LILLINGTON's first wife was SARAH JAMES and that they were married (1668) and that he married ELIZABETH COOKE in (167_) which shows that the genealogy of his family on 1-477 is in error; that his second wife was ELIZABETH COOKE instead of COOPER 3-199; in (1693) MAJ. ALEXANDER LILLINGTON was the High Sheriff of ALBEMARLE COUNTY, as addressed by PHILLIP LUDWELL 2-196; he had a son in law JOHN FENDALL who married ELIZABETH 1-58, 1-335; his executors in (1797) were ROBERT HARMONSON, JOHN BARROW and CALEB CALLOWAY 1-335; in (1693) he performed the marriage of JOHN COOKE to ELIZABETH EIKER (John was perhaps a brother or nephew of his second wife ELIZABETH COOKE) 3-205.

LILLINGTON, ANN, married HENDERSON WALKER (1693) performed by THOMAS HARVEY, ESQ. 3-204, 3-205; ANN (STEWARD) LILLINGTON, widow of ALEXANDER LILLINGTON died leaving will (1725) mentions daughter ELIZABETH LILLINGTON and grandson JOHN SIMONS 1-59.

LILLINGTON, ELIZABETH, died leaving will in BATH in (1741) in which she names sons by name of BARROW - RICHARD, JAMES, JOSEPH, WILLIAM & SAMUEL, daughters SARAH HARRIS and ANNA CAMPBELL 1-57.

LILLINGTON, EDWARD, of NEUSE RIVER in CRAVEN CO. left will in (1736) in which he names all his children 1-479.

LILLINGTON, GEORGE, of CRAVEN COUNTY, died leaving will (1742) wife HANNAH, daughter ANN HUTCHINSON and other children 1-478.

LILLINGTON, JOHN, son of ALEXANDER LILLINGTON & wife ELIZABETH was born (1687) 3-214; in the year (1712) he was the son in law of JOHN PORTER 1-69; he made a deed to his brother in law EDWARD MOSELEY in (1713) 1-231; also in (1719) he sold lands to JEREMIAH VAIL adjoining JOHN PORTER and WILLIAM WILKINSON, with MAURICE MOORE a witness 3-454; in that year he was Treasurer of BEAUFORT PRECINCT 1-444; and in (1708) he was Clerk of the lower House of the ASSEMBLY 1-455.

LILLINGTON, MARY, in (1718) was the grand-daughter of MARY PORTER (and the daughter of JOHN LILLINGTON 1-63; her aunt MARY, daughter of ALEXANDER LILLINGTON, was born in the year (1683) 3-211.

LILLINGTON, SARAH, daughter of ALEXANDER LILLINGTON was born in (1690) 3-216.

LILLY, JOHN and his wife ELIZABETH were married prior to (1671) 3-210; and had children (at least) Ann, William and THOMAS 3-210; he died (1701) at the house of the widow WHEDBEE 3-403; he probably married a second time a wife named HANNAH 3-217; he and his second wife had daughter SARAH born in (1691) 3-217; another JOHN LILLY is mentioned in the will of a WILLIAM KITCHING of PERQUIMANS in (1736) 1-56.

LILLY, THOMAS, sued RICHARD EVANS (1689) 3-430; in his will in (1735) he mentions son in law JOHN RIDDICK 1-58.

LILLY, WILLIAM, SR. died leaving will (1809) names children and grandchildren 3-340, 3-341.

LINDER, MARGARET, died leaving will in (1814) ROBERT PERRY and JOHN OVERMAN witnesses 3-340.

LINDSAY, DANIEL, died in CURRITUCK in (1720-1) leaving will, mentions wife MARY and son DAVID, the witnesses being JOHN NORTON, a WILLIAM JOHNSON and JOHN MARTIN 1-337.

LINDSAY, DAVID, died in CURRITUCK in (1749) & mentions wife ANN, mother SARAH and brother BENJAMIN, with HENRY WOODHOUSE and SOL and M. SMITH witnesses 1-336.

LINDSAY, REV. DAVID. He it was who performed the marriage of GEORGE DURANT and ANN MARWOOD (sic) in NORTHUMBERLAND COUNTY, Va. January 4 (1658-9) 1-203, 3-199.

LINDSAY, JAMES, will in DOBBS COUNTY (1770) mentions brothers WILLIAM, PETER and ROBERT LINDSAY "my mother", with RICHARD CASWELL and JOHN DICKSON Executors 1-336.

LINDSAY, ROBERT, will in CHOWAN, JOHN WILSON & GEORGE FORDYCE Executors, sister MARY HURGIN and children, and ANN MATTHEWS daughter of GEORGE MATTHEWS 1-336.

LINNOT, MICHAEL (Intended for LINTON) in (1747-3) court adjourned to the house where MICHAEL LINNOT lately lived 2-631.

LINTON, JOHN, was a witness to the will in(1751) of JAMES BROWN, of BEAUFORT 1-170.

LINTON, JULIA, left will (1824). Daughter EMILY LINTON and WILLIAM PUGH executors 2-527.

LINTON, LAZARUS, married MARTHA SUTTON (1783) 3-417.

LINTON, MOSES, was a witness to the will (1742) of HENRY ETHERIDGE in CURRITUCK 2-209; & he and WILLIAM PARKER were members of the CURRITUCK COURT (1729-30) 2-467.

LISCOMBE, MARGARET, orphan of JOHN LISCOMBE chose ANNABELLA LISCOMBE as her guardian 3-450.

LITTLE, JOHN, will in ANSON COUNTY in (1755) children THOMAS, WILLIAM, JOHN, ARCHIBALD, JAMES, daughter MARTHA, wife of JOHN REED, MARGARET and ALEXANDER LITTLE 1-57; JOHN of EDENTON, will (1824) related to the BLAIRS, KINGS, SKINNERS and JONES FAMILIES; also mentions THOMAS B. and WILLIAM LITTLEJOHN 2-9.

LITTLE, PENELOPE, was the relict of WILLIAM LITTLE and sold land to JOSEPH ANDERSON (1737) with BENJAMIN HILL, THOMAS JONES and RICHARD WILLIAMS as witnesses 3-130; a daughter PENELOPE had guardian MATTHEW HARDY 1-447.

LITTLE, WILLIAM, was one of the executors of JOHN LOVICK in (1737) 1-57; will of CHIEF JUSTICE WILLIAM LITTLE (1734), mentions wife PENELOPE and sons WILLIAM and GEORGE and daughter PENELOPE; mentions brother ISAAC LITTLE 1-134; JOHN ARBUTHNOT married a sister 1-134; he was witness to a deed by THOMAS POLLOCK in (1720) 2-612; he was Chief Justice of CHOWAN (1733) 1-453.

LITTLE, WILLIAM, of BEAUFORT COUNTY, died leaving will (1756), sons ABRAHAM, WILLIAM, JAMES, JACOB and JOHN, daughter JANE MORING and sons ISAAC and JOSEPH, wife MOURNING 1-339; his brother GEORGE LITTLE left will in HERTFORD (1787) 1-339.

LITTLEJOHN, ANN BLOUNT born (1779) married JOHN LITTLE, a merchant of EDENTON in Chowan County, she being a daughter of WILLIAM LITTLEJOHN and his wife SARAH BLOUNT (daughter of JOSEPH BLOUNT and SARAH DURANT) 1-269.

LITTLEJOHN, ELIZABETH MUTTER, married THOMAS B. LITTLEJOHN, she being nee ELIZABETH MUTTER, a daughter of THOMAS MUTTER and ELIZABETH MOORE who, after the death of THOMAS MUTTER married second GEORGE ALSTON and lived and died in GRANVILLE COUNTY, N. C., where her son in law THOMAS BLOUNT LITTLEJOHN was a merchant and in his old age was "Clerk and Master in Equity", and at one time owned the land on which the town of OXFORD and the County courthouse now stands 1-269, 1-270; for list of their children 1-271.

LITTLEJOHN FAMILY. Genealogy of the descendants of WILLIAM LITTLEJOHN and his wife SARAH BLOUNT, daughter of JOSEPH BLOUNT and SARAH DURANT (who was daughter of GEORGE DURANT & HAGAR CRISP); GEORGE DURANT was the son of JOHN DURANT and SARAH JOORE, and the grandson of GEORGE DURANT and his wife ANN MARWOOD 1-268 to 1-283.

LITTLEJOHN, ELIZABETH, daughter of THOMAS BLOUNT LITTLEJOHN, of GRANVILLE COUNTY, and his wife ELIZABETH MUTTER, married DR. ISAAC N. JONES and they moved to TEXAS and ARKANSAS, and became the parents of HON. DANIEL WEBSTER JONES Governor of Arkansas 1-272.

LITTLEJOHN, MARGARET MUTTER, daughter of THOMAS BLOUNT LITTLEJOHN of GRANVILLE COUNTY, N. C. married ROGER POYTHRESS ATKINSON (son of ROGER ATKINSON and AGNES POYTHRESS, and the grandson of Roger Atkinson and ANN PLEASANTS of Virginia) 1-271.

LITTLEJOHN, WILLIAM, about (1760) settled in EDENTON, N. C. and was ancestor of the LITTLEJOHN FAMILY; and he married SARAH BLOUNT in (1771) 1-268.

LITTLEJOHN, WILLIAM, son of THOMAS B. LITTLEJOHN and MARGARET MUTTER, married JANE McALPIN (widow PATRICK) and moved to GREENWOOD CADDO PARISH, Louisiana, and had among others a son ROBERT McALPIN LITTLEJOHN who married HELEN ENGLAND; they had four daughters but no sons 1-272.

LITTLEWOOD, JACOB, was thirty years old in (1702) 1-610.

LOADMAN, JAMES died leaving will in (1694) and mentions WILLIAM BUTLER, SARAH BEASLEY and TIMOTHY CLEARE 1-58.

LOCKEY, HENRY, died without leaving a will in (1715) and ANN LEWIS, a widow, was his daughter 1-60.

LOCKHART FAMILY. A genealogical account of the family showing connections with the BRYANS, RYANS and others 1-479.

LOCKHART, ELIZABETH left will (1796) and mentions grand-daughters ELIZABETH and MARGARET BRYAN and others; will witnessed by EDWARD BRYAN, JAMES TURNEY and ALEXANDER HOPKINS 2-346.

LOCKHART, GEORGE, left will (1791) and mentions children and son GEORGE RYAN, witnesses are EDWARD WORLEY, EDWARD BRYAN and RICHARD GILL 2-346; he was commissioned as SHERIFF in (1749) 2-632.

LOCKHART, JAMES, in (1767) was ordered paid for repairs to the courthouse at WINDSOR, N. C. 3-443; his father left will in BERTIE in (1754) naming sons LILLINGTON, GEORGE and JAMES LOCKHART and "all my children" 1-57.

LOCKHART, LILLINGTON, was Justice in BERTIE in (1768) 3-445.

LOCKHART'S MILL DAM, was located in BERTIE Co. in (1769) 3-447.

LOCKINGTON, JOHN, of LONDON mentioned 1-626.

LOFTON, EDWARD; his wife was ELIZABETH 3-370.

LOFTON, LEODOVICK, left will in CHOWAN COUNTY in (1720) 1-59.

LOFTON, LEON, proves his rights 3-249.

LOFTON, LEONARD (probably the same as LEON) received a land grant in (1694) 1-4; sold land to COL. THOMAS POLLOCK in (1715) in CHOWAN 1-285.

LOGAN, ALEXANDER died leaving will in (1739) with THOMAS BLOUNT, JOSEPH BLOUNT and TOM CLARK his executors 1-385.

LONG, ALICE, the widow of JAMES LONG married a WILSON in (1682) 3-202.

LONG, ANDREW, was brother of THOMAS, JOHN and JAMES LONG 1-58; was security on marriage bond of SARAH LONG to one HENNESSY (1763) 3-107.

LONG, ARTHUR, of VIRGINIA, died at the home of CALEB CALLOWAY in OCTOBER (1678?) 3-365.

LONG, ELIZABETH, daughter of JAMES LONG and his wife ELIZABETH married JOHN CHASTON in (1684) 3-202; ELIZABETH, a widow, bought land from SARAH SUTTON in (1715) with JOHN WORLEY a witness 1-290.

LONG, REUBEN, witnessed the will of JOSHUA LONG in (1791) 3-177.

LONG FAMILY. Wills 3-340, 3-176, 3-177, 3-52.

LONG FAMILY. Genealogy of the family and descendants of JAMES LONG who died in PERQUIMANS in (1682) bottom note 3-51, 3-52.

LONG, GILES, died leaving will (1691) nuncupative witnessed by EDWARD SMITHWICK and THOMAS HARLOW 1-339; another GILES is said to have left will in TYRRELL (1782) had son named MILES LONG 3-52.

LONG, HANNAH married EBENEZER SPRUILL in (1770) 3-109.

LONG, JAMES SR. died in PERQUIMANS leaving will in (1682) in which he mentions a son JAMES LONG 3-51. also THOMAS and GILES LONG 1-339.

LONG, JAMES, JR. signed ALBEMARLE PRECINCT petition to the KING in (1680) 3-51; witnessed deed from ROBERT HICKS to MOSES FOXWORTH, (1716) but this was the THIRD JAMES LONG, a son of JAMES JR. who died (1711) naming his son JAMES 3-52; will of JAMES JR. who died (1711) had three sons, JAMES, THOMAS & JOHN and daughters MARY and ELIZABETH 1-60.

LONG, JAMES (son of JAMES JR.) had wife ANNE 1-457; and sold land to JOSHUA TURNER (1719) 2-457; a JAMES LONG was mentioned in the division of the estate of JOHN WORLEY 1-446; JAMES JR. (perhaps) sold lands to RICHARD JOHNSON (1702-3) 2-456; left will in CHOWAN in (1734) mentions ANDREW and GILES LONG in the will 1-58.

LONG, JAMES; wife ELIZABETH; grandparents of JOSHUA WORLEY, who had sons THOMAS and JOHN LONG and a daughter who married JACOB BLOUNT and grandsons JAMES LONG, GILES LONG and a JOHN LONG 2-468; a JAMES LONG married MARY BUTCHER in (1775) 3-109.

LONG, JEREMIAH, married PENNY JONES in (1777) 3-109.

LONG, JOHN, contract and agreement between him & BENJAMIN ARCHER in (1697) 3-139; JOHN LONG and ELIZABETH CHARLES were married by ALEXANDER LILLINGTON in (1687) 3-203; JOHN LONG son of JAMES LONG and wife ELIZABETH was married to the widow SUSAN AMES (1697-8) by JOHN BARROW 3-408; JOHN LONG, WILLIAM LONG and THOMAS LONG on list of tithables taken in CHOWAN or EDENTON in (1702) 3-84; JOHN was born in (1673) 3-208; he and his wife SUSAN had daughter ELIZABETH born (1703) 3-375.

LONG, JOILES (JONES?) married his wife ELIZABETH before (1688) 3-215.

LONG, JOSEPH, was Master of the schooner "POLLY" cleared for SPAIN (1775) 2-466.

LONG, JOSHUA, will in PERQUIMANS in (1741) wife is ELIZABETH, sons THOMAS and JOSHUA; brother THOMAS LONG, WILLIAM HOSKINS and JOSEPH SUTTON executors 1-339; JOSHUA was the son of a THOMAS and REBECCA LONG 3-370; mentioned in the will of JOHN WYATT (1739) 1-81; died and left will in TYRRELL COUNTY in (1754) naming wife JEMIMAH, daughters PRISCILLA, KESIAH & ESTHER and nephew STEPHEN LONG 1-57.

LONG, JOSIAH, died leaving will in (1808) mentions brother LEMUEL LONG & ELIZABETH WHITE 3-340.

LONG, KEZIAH married JESSE YOUNG in (1767) 3-108.

LONG, MILES, was the son of GILES LONG who died in TYRRELL COUNTY in (1782) 3-52.

LONG, NATHAN, with DEMPSEY HARRELL, witnessed the will of RICHARD HATFIELD (1805) 3-337; he left will (1816) 3-340.

LONG, NEHEMIAH, was LIEUTENANT in the FIFTH REGIMENT N. C. Continental Line 1-420.

LONG, COL. NICHOLAS, appends a certificate to the application of WILLIS BOONE as a revolutionary soldier 1-426. (This was COL. NICHOLAS LONG, of Halifax, or his son NICHOLAS who had moved to Georgia, the date being 1820.)

LONG, REUBEN. His wife was PENINAH, and he died leaving will (1814) and mentions his daughter REBECCA SHEEY and her children; his wife's will (1817) with ELI BRINKLEY one of executors 3-340.

LONG, RICHARD, sold lands to JOHN KELLY next to land owned by JOHN COTTEN in (1718) 1-628, 1-629.

LONG, ROBERT, sold lands to GEORGE SMITH in (1718) 1-623; and also to JOHN COTTEN in (1718) witnessed by THOMAS SMITH and WILLIAM GREEN 1-623.

LONG, SARAH, was the daughter of THOMAS LONG and his wife REBECCA, and she was born in (1692) 3-219; she left will in PERQUIMANS in (1715), and her sister MARY LONG married THOMAS PIERCE 1-59.

LONG, SIMEON, and JOSHUA LONG are mentioned in abstract of the will of JOHN COLE (1805) 3-339; SIMEON witnessed the will of HENRY SCOTT in (1817) 3-352; he also witnessed the will of JAMES MULLEN in (1796) with a LEAVEN THACH 3-179; SIMEON P. LONG was an executor of JOSEPH BARROW in (1837) who mentioned his daughter MARTHA LONG 3-326.

LONG, SUSAN married RICHARD LEARY (1709) 3-410.

LONG, THOMAS, and wife REBECCA, had son JAMES LONG born in (1689) 3-216; THOMAS received deed from ELIZABETH LONG (1719) with JAMES BLOUNT a witness 2-607; a THOMAS LONG left will in PERQUIMANS (1727) who had daughter SARAH LEARY 1-59; another THOMAS died in (1721) 3-402; a much later one left will (1779) in which MILES SCARBOROUGH is mentioned 3-176; a THOMAS in (1733) witnessed a deed by THOMAS FALCONER 2-611; will of the one who died in (1721) 1-60; THOMAS and REBECCA were the parents of WILLIAM born (1695) 3-368; & the elder THOMAS brought suit in PERQUIMANS in (1688) 3-429; suit also against THOMAS SANFORD (1689) 3-430; witnessed a deed from JOHN to THOMAS SWAIN in (1716) 1-292; the name of his wife was REBECCA WAITE and they were married in (1688) 3-203; one THOMAS LONG left will in PERQUIMANS in (1754) 1-57.

LONG, WALTER, married MARY HUDSON, the executor of THOMAS HOLLIDAY. This appears to have been about (1750-52) 2-305.

LONG, WILLIAM, left will (1701) wife was SARAH, brothers THOMAS and JOHN LONG 1-60; WILLIAM LONG married MRS. SARAH JOHNSON in (1697-8) 3-408; in (1735) WILLIAM LONG was called brother by THOMAS WEST in PERQUIMANS 1-82; a WILLIAM LONG left will in PERQUIMANS in (1758) mentions son REUBEN and others and a son in law JACOB WYATT 1-57; a WILLIAM had wife ANNE and children named in (1742) 3-388; one in (1727) was the executor of HUMPHREY FELTS 1-43; and one who died in (1720) had children and wife MARY 3-388.

LONGLATHER, DANIEL, from KING & QUEEN COUNTY in Virginia left will (1714) 1-60.

LORDS PROPRIETORS: Locke's Fundamental Constitutions reviewed (Document on file in the office of the Clerk at Edenton) 3-27 to 3-29; LORDS PROPRIETORS in AMERICA - their princely Holdings and Regal Rights. An article 1-588 to 1-593.

LOVE, AMOS, will (1770) wife MARY, son AMOS and other children 1-335.

LOVE, DANIEL, will in (1763) wife CATHERINE and children. GEORGE BRUCE and JAMES PAXTON are witnesses 1-335.

LOVE, WILLIAM, bought land from WILLIAM REEVES in (1718) 1-623.

LOVICK, JOHN, sold lands to THOMAS JARRELL on the MORATUCK RIVER (1721), with WILLIAM BADHAM and JOHN PLOWMAN witnesses 2-613; he was given a power of attorney from CHARLES FOSTER in (1718) 1-627; his widow married one GEORGE PHENEY 1-66; with FREDERICK JONES & others he was appointed on commission for adjusting the public accounts after the INDIAN Massacre of (1711) 3-279; he had grant of land in (1719) on the YOPPIM RIVER 1-13; deeded land to THOMAS JARRELL (1721) 2-613; some affidavits made by him in (1725) 3-232, 3-233; he was Secretary of the Colony and married first SARAH BLOUNT, daughter of JOHN BLOUNT and ELIZABETH DAVIS, second, PENELOPE MAULE, widow of WILLIAM MAULE and daughter of GOV. CHARLES EDEN 1-57; he was a JUSTICE with HENRY CLAYTON and CHRISTOPHER GALE in (1725) 3-229; he died leaving will in (1727) mentions wife PENELOPE, JOHN LOVICK, son of his brother THOMAS, and brother JOHN GOLLAND; CHRISTOPHER GALE, EDMUND GALE and WILLIAM LITTLE were his executors 1-57.

LOVICK, THOMAS, was a member of the Court (1727) with CHRISTOPHER GALE, BARNABY MACKINNEY, JOHN ALSTON and HENRY BONNER 3-290; he died leaving will in CARTERET (1759) wife SARAH, son GEORGE PHENY LOVICK, son in law JAMES PARKINSON and grand-daughter SARAH JONES & grandson THOMAS LOVICK 1-338; he was JUSTICE of the General Court East of CAPE FEAR 2-298

LOWDEN, JOHN, left will in PASQUOTANK in the yr. (1719) 1-60.

LOWE, EMANUEL, prays the Court in petition that he be tried for the Treason and Rebellion with which he is charged 1-153; he had brother NEVIL LOWE, daughter ANN LETITIA LOWE and grandson GEORGE LOWE, and a cousin ROBINSON, and left will in (1720) 1-59; he was the attorney of JOHN ARCHDALE and also his son in law. ELIZABETH TWINE & HENRY DAWSON 3-72

LOWE, GEORGE, died leaving will in (1729) naming his children JOHN, GEORGE, EDWARD, WILLIAM, ELIZABETH, MARY and SARAH and wife ELIZABETH 1-58; a later GEORGE LOWE married RACHEL ROBERTS in (1786) 3-419.

LOWE, JOHN, was a brother in law of ROBERT DIXON in (1727) 1-41.

LOWE, JOHN, was Lieutenant in the TENTH REGIMENT of the N. C. Continental Line under COL. ABRAHAM SHEPARD 1-425.

LOWE, NEVIL, was a brother of EMANUEL LOWE and is mentioned in the latter's will in (1720) 1-59.

LOWREY, WILLIAM, will in PASQUOTANK in (1752) names children WILLIAM, JOHN, ROBERT, BETTIE and MARY and wife ELIZABETH 1-335.

LOWREY, JOSEPH, will in PASQUOTANK (1754) sons BENJAMIN, NOAH and other children; SOLOMON POOL and JOHN DAVIS executors 1-335.

LOWTHER, TRISTRAM, will in BERTIE in (1790) wife PENELOPE; SAMUEL JOHNSTON, JAMES IREDELL and brother in law WILLIAM J. DAWSON executors 2-8.

LOWTHER, WILLIAM, will (1782) 2-8; obtained a license for a ferry in BERTIE (1771) 3-449.

LOYD, HENRY, placed under the tuition of one CHARLES POWERS in (1770) 3-448.

LOYD, ROBERT was a Justice of the General Court in (1724) 2-467; he died and left a will in EDENTON in (1726) in which he mentions nephew RODERICK LOYD of ENGLAND 1-59.

LOWE, WILLIAM, sold land to EDMUND ROGERS in (1720) 2-617; WILLIAM LOWE, WILLIAM GRAY and THOMAS WHITMELL lived close neighbors before his death in (1720) 2-617; he died leaving will in (1720) in which he mentions son in law ROBERT DIXON and his daughter ELIZABETH PACE, bequeathing lands in PRINCE GEORGE COUNTY, Virginia 1-59.

LUCAS, HENRY, and WILLIAM MARTIN in (1734) were the uncles of JOHN WOODWARD of BATH who left will that year, and named his brothers JOEL and HENRY WOODWARD and his daughter MARY 1-82.

LUCAS, MARY, died leaving will (1761) in BEAUFORT, mentions her daughter ANN ALDERSON and grandson JAMES ALDERSON, also grandchildren JOEL MARTIN, CHARLES ODEAN MARTIN, SARAH MARTIN, ANN MARTIN, MARY MARTIN and SUSANNAH MARTIN and daughter ANN ELLISON; JOHN SWANN and SARAH HOWARD witnesses 1-338.

LUDFORD, JOHN, died leaving will in TYRRELL COUNTY in (1735) in which he mentions ISAAC FITZPATRICK 1-57.

LUDWELL, COL. PHILLIP, GOVERNOR grants Commissions of the Peace for PERQUIMANS PRECINCT in (1690) 3-436, 3-437; issues an order relating to land grants in (1693) 2-196; in a letter to the General Court of North Carolina he mentions the marriage of SETH SOTHEL to ANNA FOSTER, followed after wards by her marriage to COL. JOHN LEAR of the Colony of Virginia, etc. 3-30 to 3-31.

LUIS, THOMAS (LEWIS?) died leaving will (1720) in PASQUOTANK 1-59.

LUNSFORD, MARY, left will (1806) and in it she names son WILLIAM LUNSFORD and her brother EPHRAIM WINGATE and others; DEMPSEY WINGATE and SIMEON LONG were the witnesses to the will 3-340.

LUNSFORD, WILLIAM, the son of MARY LUNSFORD who left will in (1806) witnessed by a SIMEON LONG 3-340. (NOTE: LUNSFORD LONG was son of COL. NICHOLAS LONG and married a daughter of GEN. ALLEN JONES of HALIFAX COUNTY)

LUNDY, JAMES, married a daughter of MARY COLSON who left will (1732) 1-37.

LUTEN, ADAM, of ONSLOW COUNTY, died leaving will in (1740), making his friend THOMAS JENKINS executor; CHARLES BRYAN a witness 1-333.

LUTEN, CONSTANCE, of BERTIE, with ROBERT BEASLEY and CHRISTIAN BEASLEY sold a plantation to THOMAS LUTEN in (1735) 3-127; CONSTANCE LUTEN and RICHARD WILSON sold land to SAMUEL PADGETT in (1718) 1-624.

LUTEN, ESTHER, the daughter of THOMAS LUTEN was the wife of ROBERT HICKS of SANDY POINT in CHOWAN PRECINCT who died in (1734) leaving will 1-49. See also 1-134.

LUTEN FAMILY. Wills 3-8, 1-134, 2-470.

LUTEN, HENDERSON, obtained a land grant in(1722) 1-11; and a later one had land grant (1793) which joined MILLER on the CHOWAN RIVER 1-34; had an orphan son EPHRAIM LUTEN(1747) who was 14 years old placed under the tuition of WILLIAM BONNER who had married his sister 1-457; the children of HENDERSON LUTEN were JAMES, EPHRAIM, HENDERSON and SARAH LUTEN, who married HENRY BONNER 2-470; the children of the HENDERSON LUTEN who died in CHOWAN in (1791) left will naming wife SARAH, sons EPHRAIM and JAMES and a daughter PENELOPE 3-8; in (1731) HENDERSON LUTEN sold to MARY LUTEN wife of THOMAS LUTEN, deceased, his interest in the will of said THOMAS LUTEN 2-450.

LUTEN, THOMAS. His will was probated in (1731) and in it he names children WILLIAM LUTEN, CONSTANCE LUTEN, CHRISTIAN LUTEN, son CONSTANT and MARTHA HOLLY, daughter RACHEL FARLOW, son THOMAS, daughters ANN BRINN, SARAH STANDING and MARY HAUGHTON, son HENDERSON LUTEN, and his wife MARY, son in law ROBERT HICKS; JOHN LOVICK and JOHN RANDOLPH of WILLIAMSBURG, VA. among the executors named; witnessed by FRANCIS BEASLEY and HENRY BONNER 1-134; this THOMAS had a land grant on TAN YARD BRANCH (1697) 1-5; also a grant in (1721) which adjoined HENRY BONNER 1-10; he and his wife MARY sold land to THOROUGHGOOD PATE in (1704) 2-455

LUTEN, THOMAS, JR. was chosen as her guardian in (1742) by SARAH BAKER, the daughter of HENRY BAKER 1-447; MAJ. THOMAS LUTEN (probably SR.) made bond for the appearance of EDWARD MOSELEY in Court in(1719) 2-83; the same received a land grant in (1703) on MATTACOMACK CREEK 1-6; he sold land to JOHN LILLINGTON about (1718) next to COL. WILLIAM WILKINSON and JOHN PORTER 1-623; in 1720 he bought some lands in PERQUIMANS from JAMES EVANS, bounded by the lands of HENRY BONNER and WILLIAM JONES, the deed to same being witnessed by THOMAS MONTAGUE and ROBERT HICKS 2-613.

LUTEN, CAPT. THOMAS. JOHN HOYTER and other CHOWAN INDIANS declare that the six miles square of land selected by CAPT. THOMAS LUTEN in (1704) is too poor and sandy to raise corn upon 1-614; letter in (1702) to THOMAS SNODEN, Secretary of the COLONY from THOMAS LUTEN, then DEPUTY SURVEYOR of CHOWAN PRECINCT, making request for blank warrants, etc. 3-269, 3-270.

LUTEN, WILLIAM (son of THOMAS LUTEN) sold land in (1739) which he had bought from EDWARD MOSELEY, Treasurer, in (1737), & WILLIAM HOSKINS and WILLIAM LEWIS were the witnesses 3-136; he was Sheriff of CHOWAN PRECINCT in (1741) 1-452

LUTTRELL, JOHN, was a Lieutenant Colonel in the N. C. Continental Line 1-424

LYNCH, GERARD, and his wife KATHERINE (late the widow of HENRY KING) agreement witnessed by THOMAS BOYD and EDWARD MOSELEY (1717) 1-300; he sold lands to EDWARD MOSELEY in CHOWAN (1716) with one JUDITH COX a witness 1-619.

LYNCH, JOHN, married the widow of HUGH ALLEN, whose name was ELIZABETH in (1756) 1-457; he died in GRANVILLE COUNTY, N. C. in the year (1757) leaving will naming his wife ELIZABETH, daughters ELIZABETH and NELLIE and "all my children"; son in law JAMES JENKINS and ROBERT PARKER executors; the witnesses were THOMAS PARKER, JOHN BLAKENEY and WILLIAM FROHOCK 1-337.

LYNCH, MICHAEL, was the step father of JOHN HAWKINS; his mother married (1) HAWKINS, (2) a WADE, (3) MICHAEL LYNCH 3-140.

LYLES, GEORGE with WILLIAM LUTEN, witnessed a deed to THOMAS LUTEN (1735) 3-127.

LYLES, HENRY and wife ELIZABETH sold land to son in law CHARLES RICKETTS(1719) 1-629.

LYLES, JAMES and EPHRAIM LYLES witnessed deed to WILLIAM BENTLEY and JOHN COLLINS 1-628

LYELL, JOHN m. daughter of WILLIAM ROWDEN 2-466.

LUNSFORD FAMILY. Obvious errors are sometimes revealed by the context of some of these notes. In the case of "JOHN LANCEFORD" will 1797 and his witness "WILLIAM LANCEFORD" (3-177) we suspect nothing until a comparison is made with the will of "MARY LUNSFORD" of 1806 and her named son "WILLIAM LUNSFORD" (3-340). Clearly MARY LUNSFORD was a MARY WINGATE, while the wife of JOHN "LANCEFORD" was SARAH WINGATE. The name was either LANCEFORD or LUNSFORD - not both. As a LUNSFORD LONG was son of COL. NICHOLAS LONG, and a SIMEON LONG witnessed the will of MARY LUNSFORD, thus we reasonably conclude that the proper spelling of the name in each instance was LUNSFORD.

JONATHAN LANE. Among the sons of JOSEPH LANE and his wife PATIENCE McKINNIE were JOEL, JONATHAN, JOSEPH and JESSE, and apparently WILLIAM and ROBERT (1-470, 1-471) LANE. The son JESSE LANE had sixteen children, among whom was a CHARLES and a JONATHAN (1-471 LANE. Factual evidence is lacking, but reasonable circumstantial testimony exists in abundance establishing one or the other of the two sons of JESSE LANE as the ancestor of HON. JONATHAN LANE, of Texas, a well-remembered and notable lawyer of Houston, Texas, who died only some twenty years ago. Aside from being a descend- ant of BARNABY McKINNIE and of JOSEPH LANE and his wife PATIENCE McKINNIE, Hon. JONATHAN LANE of Texas had a most interesting genealogical background, which illustrates the remarkable "quirks" that genealogists encounter in tracing the old Southern families. Hon. JONATHAN LANE was the son of REV. CHARLES J. LANE who was born in MORGAN COUNTY, ALABAMA, April 21, 1822, and his wife ELLEN WALLIS, so that his grandparents had migrated to MORGAN COUNTY (North Alabama) and were living there in that year. ELLEN WALLACE (mother of JONATHAN LANE, of TEXAS) was the daughter of one ROBERT WALLIS and his wife ANGERONIA RICHARDSON, who had in all 10 children. ROBERT WALLIS was the son of JOHN McKNITT WALLIS and his wife MARGARET CROCKETT (born 1787). JOHN McKNITT WALLIS was the son of REV. JAMES WALLIS, minister, of old PROVIDENCE CHURCH, in Mecklenburg County, N. C., and his wife MARY ALEXANDER, daughter of JOHN McKNITT ALEXANDER, the Secretary of the Convention which adopted the famous MECKLENBURG DECLARATION. MARGARET CROCKETT, the wife of JOHN McKNITT WALLIS, was the daugh- ter of ELIJAH CROCKETT and his wife MARY DAVIE, of LANCASTER COUNTY, S. C., and MARY DAVIE was a sis- ter of that great patriot and Statesman of NORTH CAROLINA, WILLIAM RICHARDSON DAVIE. ELIJAH CROCK- ETT, brother in law of WILLIAM RICHARDSON DAVIE, revolutionary patriot and statesman, was the son of JOHN CROCKETT, who with his brother, was a member of OLD PROVIDENCE CHURCH in Mecklenburg County, N. C. long before the American Revolution. JOHN CROCKETT'S brother was the grandfather of the famous Tennessee Congressman and Texas hero and martyr, who died in the ALAMO at San Antonio de Bexar back in 1836.   In the old WAXHAW CHURCH cemetery, in Lancaster County, S. C., where repose the remains of HON. WILLIAM RICHARDSON DAVIE, JOHN CROCKETT, great uncle of DAVID CROCKETT, his son ELIJAH and dozens of other CROCKETTS are buried. The first pastor of the Old Providence Church in Mecklenburg was the REV. WILLIAM RICHARDSON, foster father of WILLIAM RICHARDSON DAVIE, the place being later filled by REV. JAMES WALLIS, the son in law of JOHN McKNITT ALEXANDER. Another notable character who is buried with the Crocketts and RICHARDSONS there is ANDREW JACKSON, SR., father of the turbulent ANDREW JACKSON, who became President of the United States. This writer is not writing second -hand. He has visited the old churchyard and has a transcript of all of the old tombstones, while the old records of MECKLENBURG COUNTY at CHARLOTTE have disclosed most of the other information here given. This writer can also boast that as a young lawyer, many decades ago, he has felt the keen blade of the JONATHAN LANE of this sketch as he sat across the table from him in Texas courtrooms.

THE LANIER FAMILY. This writer is convinced that the ROBERT LANIER, who died leaving will in TYRRELL COUNTY in 1744 (1-336) is the same ROBERT LANIER who in 1680 was married and at that time living in the BARBADOES, where his name and mention of his wife is made in the old ST. MICHAEL Par- ish Register; he is further convinced by strong circumstantial evidence that the ANTHONY WILLIAMS from whom he received the assignment of a patent to lands in 1713 (1-101) is the same ANTHONY WIL - LIAMS who appears on the same BARBADOES records; also that the THOMAS DANIEL, who married ELIZABETH LANIER (next to the oldest daughter of ROBERT LANIER) and who died leaving will in TYRRELL in 1749 (1-199) is the same THOMAS DANIEL, son of JOHN DANIEL and wife ANN, who was baptised in the PARISH of ST. JAMES in the BARBADOES September 25, 1675, that his father JOHN DANIEL was the brother of GOVERN- OR or DEPUTY GOVERNOR ROBERT DANIEL, who sailed from the BARBADOES to the CAROLINAS the same year that his nephew THOMAS DANIEL was born (1779).

The most plausible reconciliation of the conflicting accounts of the LANIER family handed down from various sources is that this ROBERT LANIER was one of the sons of JOHN LANIER, who came to VIRGINIA from LONDON after the death of his father JOHN of LONDON, who died in 1650, leaving his wife ELEANOR, who died in 1652. At that time JOHN and a sister ELIZABETH were under 16 years of age. The son JOHN came to Virginia, possibly by way of the BARBADOES, and settled in PRINCE GEORGE COUNTY. He died leaving will in either PRINCE GEORGE of SURRY COUNTY in 1717, in which he named four sons, (1) JOHN (2) NICHOLAS (3) ROBERT and (4) SAMPSON LANIER.

(1) JOHN LANIER. I have found no record of his descendants that can be identified. He is possibly the one who married PRISCILLA WASHINGTON, daughter of RICHARD WASHINGTON, of SURRY COUNTY.

(2) NICHOLAS LANIER was the father of THOMAS LANIER, who married ELIZABETH HICKS and set- tled in GRANVILLE COUNTY, N. C. THOMAS LANIER was born about 1722 and married ELIZABETH HICKS in 1742. He died in 1805, leaving a will in GRANVILLE, from which it has been possible to obtain the names of his children, who were as follows: ROBERT LANIER (b. in 1742), MOLLIE LANIER (b. in 1744), SARAH LANIER (b. in 1748) married first, COL. JOSEPH WILLIAMS, and second, his brother COL. ROBERT WILLIAMS; BETTIE (b. 1750) married COL. JOSEPH WINSTON; CATHERINE (b. 1752); PATSY (b. 1754); REBECCA (b. 1757) see (3-489), the first wife of COL. JOSEPH WILLIAMS; THOMAS (b. 1760); SUSANNA (b. 1763); LEWIS (b. 1765); FANNY (b. 1767), and WILLIAM LANIER (b. 1769).

(3) ROBERT LANIER. The name of his wife was SARAH, as shown by his will (1-336) and in it he mentions his grandson ROBERT DANIEL, while the will is witnessed by ROBERT LANIER DANIEL, which, beyond dought, was the full name of his son in law. According to this record his appearance in CHOWAN PRECINCT was in 1711, when he proved eleven headrights. The chances are that he left the BARBADOES early and came to VIRGINIA where he must have lived for perhaps many years before coming to NORTH CAROLINA. We have searched in vain for a list of the "rights" he proved (3-442) in 1711, but when we count his eight children (named in the will) it is quite obvious that he claimed land rights in 1711 for himself and wife (2) for his next oldest daughter ELIZABETH and her husband, THOMAS DAN- IEL (2) and the balance of his children. By this we conclude that THOMAS DANIEL and ELIZABETH LANIER were married sometime before 1711, as it is evident that his daughter SARAH had married JOHN WILSON sometime before the date of his death in 1749. (See GRIMES p. 90).

(4) SAMPSON LANIER, the fourth son of JOHN LANIER, who died in 1717, married ELIZABETH WASH- INGTON, daughter of RICHARD WASHINGTON, called "of SURRY COUNTY, VA." SAMPSON LANIER lived in BRUNS-

WICK COUNTY, VIRGINIA, at the time of his death, where his will was probated May 5, 1743, same being of record in Will Book 2 pp. 52-53. It is interesting at this point to note that WILLIAM HILL into whose family so many of the LANIERS afterwards married, also died in BRUNSWICK COUNTY in the year 1799 (long afterwards, of course) see (3-511). In his will SAMPSON LANIER names the following children: THOMAS LANIER, SAMPSON LANIER, RICHARD LANIER, ELIZA LANIER (m. BURCH), SAMUEL LANIER and JAMES LANIER.

THOMAS LANIER, of this set of children settled in LUNENBERG COUNTY, VIRGINIA, and was one of the first justices there. He with LEWIS DELONEY or DELANEY, was on the commission to run the dividing line between BRUNSWICK and LUNENBURG COUNTIES. He was a Justice of the County Court of LUNENBURG COUNTY, VA. from 1746 to 1761 (Bell's Cumberland Parish p. 262). In 1751 he owned lands on BUTCHER'S CREEK, not so very far from the line of GRANVILLE COUNTY, N. C. where his 1st cousin THOMAS LANIER had settled, with his wife ELIZABETH HICKS.

SAMPSON LANIER, son of SAMPSON LANIER and ELIZABETH WASHINGTON, and brother of THOMAS of LUNENBURG COUNTY, married ELIZABETH CHAMBERLAIN, daughter of SAMUEL CHAMBERLAINE of BRUNSWICK COUNTY, Virginia, who died in 1752). After the death of SAMPSON LANIER, his widow ELIZABETH, married CUTHBURT SMITH (Vol 45 Va. Mag. pp 86 et seq.). The children of SAMPSON LANIER and his wife ELIZABETH CHAMBERLAINE were: BURWELL LANIER, of BRUNSWICK COUNTY, who later settled in CARTERET COUNTY, then DUPLIN and finally in ANSON COUNTY, N. C.; LEWIS LANIER, BUCHNER LANIER, WINNIFRED LANIER, NANCY LANIER and REBECCA LANIER.

BURWELL LANIER married ELIZABETH HILL, daughter of WILLIAM HILL, of BRUNSWICK COUNTY (See 3-311). He moved to CARTERET COUNTY, N. C. where he bought land in 1763, which he sold in 1767; moved to DUPLIN COUNTY where he bought land, and sold that in 1774; then moved to ANSON COUNTY, where he died in 1812. The children of BURWELL LANIER and ELIZABETH HILL were: WILLIAM LANIER, who was a member of the House of the General Assembly from Anson County from 1802 to 1806; CLEMENT LANIER, who was a member of the House from Anson in 1801; ISAAC LANIER also served in the House from Anson County; THOMAS LANIER, FANNIE LANIER, PATSY LANIER, ELIZABETH LANIER who married MAJ. JOHN JENNINGS, who was Sheriff of ANSON COUNTY in 1798 to 1800; SARAH LANIER married WILLIAM MARSHALL; NANCY LANIER married JOHN McLELLAND, and CATHERINE LANIER who married THOMAS CLINTON. THOMAS HILL, brother of ELIZABETH HILL, the wife of BURWELL LANIER, married FRANCES SMITH, a half-sister of BURWELL LANIER, she being the daughter of CUTHBURT SMITH and ELIZABETH (CHAMBERLAIN) LANIER, widow of SAMPSON LANIER. THOMAS HILL bought land in DUPLIN COUNTY, and he had a son WILLIAM LANIER HILL who married ANNE ELIZABETH DUDLEY, daughter of CHRISTOPHER DUDLEY and wife MARGARET SNEAD, and a sister of GOV. EDWARD DUDLEY (1838-1841) of N. C. JOSEPH HILL, another brother of BURWELL LANIER'S wife, moved to N. C. and became a member of the SENATE (STATE), and he had a son JOSEPH HILL, who married MARGARET WALLACE, daughter of RICHARD WALLACE and ANNE STARKEY (Dau. of PETER STARKEY of ONSLOW). A son WILLIAM STARKEY HILL married FRANCES FOY and (2) ANNE GREEN, daughter of JAMES GREEN, of JONES COUNTY, N. C., and a son THOMAS HOLT HILL married MIRANDA B. GREGORY (Of ONSLOW COUNTY) and moved to GREENE COUNTY, ALABAMA, where he died. To extend this would be too long. See Va. Mag. 45 pp 86-7.

LINDSAY FAMILY. REV. DAVID LINDSAY, of NORTHUMBERLAND COUNTY, Virginia, who on the 4th of JANUARY, 1658, performed the rites that united GEORGE DURANT and ANN MARWOOD in marriage (3-199) was the son of another DAVID LINDSAY, known as the BISHOP OF ROSS, whose second wife and the mother of the Northumberland Rector was ELIZABETH HARRISON, who in all probability was the aunt of that BENJAMIN HARRISON who was Clerk of the Council and the ancestor of two Presidents of the United States (53 V. Mag. of Hist. & Biog. 21). That the DAVID LINDSAY who died leaving will in CURRITUCK COUNTY in 1749 (1-336), and who witnessed the will of MARY JENNINGS twenty years before (GRIMES p. 185), was the son of DANIEL LINDSAY (1-337), was either a descendant or a close relative of REV. DAVID LINDSAY (3-199) is the writer's conviction. This is based upon several propositions that seem plausable. The will of DAVID LINDSAY was witnessed by one HENRY WOODHOUSE. JOHN HARRISON, a brother of ELLEANOR HARRISON, the mother of REV. DAVID LINDSAY was Governor of the BERMUDAS in 1723, and his successor in that office was CAPT. HENRY WOODHOUSE, of Waxham, co. NORFOLK, England, who died in 1637 in ENGLAND (53 Va. Mag. p. 24). This CAPT. HENRY WOODHOUSE and GOV. JOHN HARRISON, while seemingly unfriendly, and perhaps not actually of blood kin, never the less were connected with the BERNARDS and other families by intermarriage. HENRY WOODHOUSE, a son of CAPT. HENRY WOODHOUSE, who succeeded JOHN HARRISON as Governor of the BERMUDAS, like BENJAMIN HARRISON, settled on the South side of JAMES RIVER in Virginia, and was a member of the House of BURGESES from LOWER NORFOLK, it is said, from 1642 to 1652. He was a member of the Vestry of the old Church of LYNHAVEN PARISH in 1640 (40 Va. Mag. p. 134), his wife was MARY, and he died leaving a will in 1655, in which he named his children: HENRY, HORATIO, JOHN, WILLIAM, ELIZABETH, SARAH, MARY and RACHEL WOODHOUSE. ELIZABETH WOODHOUSE, it is claimed by genealogists, married the original emigrant NICHOLAS MERIWETHER, ancestor of a numerous Virginia tribe, connected with many of the old First Families. LOWER NORFOLK COUNTY was the front door to CURRITUCK PRECINCT (later CURRITUCK COUNTY) and a study of the roster of the first settlers in CURRITUCK will disclose even to the casual reader the presence in that territory of the same families that were prominent in LOWER NORFOLK. Notable among these were the WHITES, MOSELEYS, LINDSAYS, CASWELLS (sometimes KASWELLS) LINTONS (particularly old MOSES LINTON), LOWES and a host of others, all of which indicates that HENRY WOODHOUSE'S descendants came down out of LYNHAVEN PARISH to take up lands around DURANT'S NECK and adj. ALBEMARLE SOUND contemporaneous with GEORGE DURANT and his wife ANN. With them, no doubt came the LINDSAYS. The writer has found no LINDSAYS he can identify positively as the sons of REV. DAVID LINDSAY, of NORTHUMBERLAND COUNTY. The grandfather of REV. DAVID LINDSAY on his mother's side was PETER HARRISON, of WARMINGTON, co. LANCASTER, ENGLAND, who had sons RICHARD (?), JOHN, (either of whom may have been father of BENJAMIN HARRISON of the Council) and PETER. DANIEL LINDSAY had a son DAVID (1-337), DAVID LINDSAY (1-336) had a son BENJAMIN, and JAMES LINDSAY had a son PETER. To further strengthen this hypothesis, BENJAMIN HARRISON, of the Council (1633) had a son PETER HARRISON, said to have died young and left no descendants. REV. DAVID LINDSAY, we are told had an older half-brother named JEROME LINDSAY, who probably never came to VIRGINIA, but HUGH LINDSAY, of LANCASTER COUNTY, Virginia, who witnessed a WALTER HEARD deed in 1755, could possibly have been one of his sons. ADAM LINDSAY who left will in YORK COUNTY (1637) was ancestor of a numerous VIRGINIA FAMILY of the name, who were probably related to the same tribe.

MABSON, ARTHUR, was a merchant in BEAUFORT, in CARTERET COUNTY in (1735) 2-302; according to his will in CARTERET in (1748) he had a son ARTHUR, and his wife was SUSANNAH GABLE, a widow, he was an uncle of WILLIAM COLE & his daughter ELIZABETH MABSON married NATHANIEL SMITH, who had a son WALTER SMITH 1-60.

MACKLEY, HENRY, died leaving a will in PASQUOTANK in (1720), and MARTIN MILLER was his son in law 1-63.

MACKEY, JOHN, married FRANCES, the widow of BENJAMIN WEST, who died in (1695) 1-34.

MACKEY, JOSEPH, died in 1802, and his will was witnessed by JAMES LEIGH and JOHN CLAYTON JR. 3-342.

MACKEY, THOMAS, was mentioned in the will of JOSEPH MACKEY in (1802) 3-342.

MACKEY, WILLIAM, of EDENTON, sold land on INDIAN TOWN CREEK in (1734) to ROBERT HALTON, next to JOSEPH ANDERSON 2-454; he had bought land from MARTIN CROMER in (1733) 2-609; and he signed a petition for a ferry in CHOWAN in (1735) 1-447.

MACKUEN, PATRICK (intended for McEWIN) made a bond to CHRISTOPHER GALE in (1711) 3-284.

MADISON, PRESIDENT JAMES, writes letter to GOV. SAMUEL JOHNSTON 3-105, 3-106.

MAFFITT, EMMA MARTIN, an article relating to the COLONIAL DAMES 3-221 to 3-223.

MAGUE, LAWRENCE (May be McGEE) sold land in (1717) on INDIAN TOWN CREEK to THOMAS BRAY, witnessed by JOHN CLARK and JOHN BRYAN 1-616

MAGUIRE, PHILLIP, in (1727) sold land in CHOWAN to JOHN OVERTON, with THOMAS MACKLENDEN as a witness 2-443.

MAINER, JOHN, was witness to a deed executed by FRANCIS DEW in CHOWAN in (1717) 1-618; 3-350

MALBONE, PETER (Probably MELBOURNE) of NORFOLK COUNTY, Virginia, deeded a lot in town of NORFOLK in (1726) to his daughter AFFIA, witnessed by JAMES NIMMO 1-445

MALONE, CHARLES, died in (1744)

MALPES, RICHARD, sold land to JOHN ISMAY (1725) with FRANCIS PUGH and THOMAS SPEIRS witnesses 2-446.

MANDEVILLE, HENRY, had certain headrights including the RICHARD BURTONSHALL family 2-300.

JANE MANERS (Same as JOHN MAINER, above) was married to CALEB BUNDAY in (1690) 3-204.

MANLEY, GABRIEL and RACHEL REDDITT recorded their brands and marks (1744) 2-622; and he recorded his mark in BERTIE (1746) 2-628.

MHOON, JOHN (M'HOON is the correct way) was Executor of the will of WILLIAM WEST in the year (1810), the funeral being preached by REV. JAMES ROSS 2-553, 2-554.

MHOON, JESSE (M'HOON) son of JOSIAH M'HOON who left will in (1772). 1-352.

MHOON, JOSIAH (M'HOON) of HALIFAX County died leaving will in (1772), with NEEDHAM BRYANT and ELIAS BRYANT (BRYAN) Executors, and witnessed by JOHN BRYAN, JAMES BURNETT and WILLIAM BLAND 1-353.(In this item the name is spelled MORHOON, an error).

MANN, BRIDGETT, was the daughter of WILLIAM HOOKER in his will (1718) 1-514 she was the wife of THOMAS MANN 1-103.

MANN, THOMAS and wife BRIDGETT sold lands to HENRY BARNES in HERTFORD COUNTY (no date mentioned, but about (1713) 1-103; he left will in BERTIE in (1735) and names his wife BRIDGETT and his grandson GEORGE WILLIAMS 1-61; THOMAS and BRIDGETT also sold land in HERTFORD (1713) to EDWARD BRYAN 1-103.

MANN, WILLIAM (Spelled MAN on the old register,) had daughter MARGARET MANN born in (1689), her mother was ELIZABETH 3-218.

MANNING FAMILY. An account of this family and its genealogy will be found on (2-461 and 2-462) showing its connection with the BLAIR FAMILY and the JOHNSTONS, and particularly the career of THOMAS COURTLAND MANNING, son of JOSEPH MANNING, whose will, with that of his widow is recorded at (2-13)

MANSELL, WILLIAM, presented his license to practice law in (1748) 2-632; it is perhaps an ancestor WILLIAM MANSELL, who with his wife MARY had a daughter ELIZABETH MANSELL born (1694) 3-367.

MANWARING, HANNAH, was the wife of a STEPHEN MANWARING in (1696) 3-402; they had daughter HANNAH born to them in (1690) 3-217.

MANWARRING, STEPHEN, his wife was HANNAH 3-217, 3-402; he sued EDWARD NORWOOD in (1690) and the same year at the same meeting he was chosen and appointed as guardian of JAMES PERISHO and as the manager of his plantation in PERQUIMANS PRECINCT 3-433; & on the same date STEPHEN was ordered to take into his custody all of the estate of one DAVID BLAKE 3-434.

MARCH, JOHN, died leaving will in GATES COUNTY in (1821) his wife MARY 2-51.

MARCY, THOMAS, and wife SARAH, had daughter ELIZABETH MARCEY born (1684) 3-212.

MARDER (Mis-Spelled MARDRE) JOHN, left will in (1832), ROBERT CREECY a witness 3-343.

MARDER, JOSEPH, left will (1822) and mentioned a son JOHN 3-342.

MARDRUN, BETTIE in (1739) was the daughter of JAMES SPENCE 1-72.

MARE, JOHN (Possibly intended for MARKS) patented lands escheated by THOMAS WRIGHT in (1787) 1-22.

MANIGAULT, JUDITH, (Mis-Spelled MARIGAULT) was of a South Carolina family 2-488.

MARIOT, THOMAS (Mis-spelled MAITT) died in (1693) 3-219.

MARKER, RICHARD, the son of THOMAS MARKER, was born in (1710) 3-388.

MARKHAM, ELIZABETH, was the God-Daughter of EPH-
RAIM COSTE in (1719) 1-39; ANTHONY MARKHAM
was the executor (GRIMES p. 83).

MARKHAM, JOSHUA, will in PASQUOTANK (1747) mentions ANTHONY MARKHAM and his son CHARLES, &
ANTHONY is executor 1-340.

MARKHAM, LEWIS, died in PASQUOTANK in (1744), and
ANTHONY MARKHAM and WILLIAM WALLIS were his
executors; JEREMIAH SWEENEY and ANN BOYD were
witnesses 1-340.

MARKHAM, WILLIAM, was Governor of PENNSYLVANIA in
(1695); and his signature appears on a POWER
of ATTORNEY to DANIEL AKEHURST in (1685)1-513.

MARKS, JOHN, was the son of THOMAS MARKS; THOMAS
sold his son JOHN 200 acres on ROCKYHOCK Crk.
in (1706) with DANIEL HALSEY and JOHN HARRIS
as witnesses 1-95; JOHN made deed to lands to
WILLIAM WOODLEY in CHOWAN PRECINCT in (1715)
with THOMAS LUTEN, SR. a witness 1-290; JOHN
MARKS and THOMAS MARKS in (1715) witnessed a
power of attorney from MARTIN CHARLES and his
wife MOURNING of ISLE OF WIGHT COUNTY, Virginia 2-519; JOHN bought land from EDWARD COCK-
RELL in (1717) 1-617; his wife was MARGARET,
and with her he sold lands to DAVID LEE in
(1711) 1-297; he had a land grant in (1717)
in BEAR SWAMP 1-17; he witnessed a deed By
EDWARD COCKRELL to DANIEL HARRISON in (1716)
2-519.

MARKS, THOMAS obtained a land grant in (1702) on
ROCKYHOCK CREEK 1-6; he and JAMES BUSH wit -
nessed deed by RICHARD BURKE and wife in(1702)
2-456; his wife was ELIZABETH and with her he
deeded lands to WILLIAM EARLY in (1702) which
was witnessed by WILLIAM JONES, DANIEL HALSEY
and DANIEL LEIGH 1-98. (DAVID LEE 1-297 may
also have spelled it LEIGH) THOMAS MARKS and
wife ELIZABETH sold land to THOMAS AVERITT
who was their grandson in (1702) with JAMES
FLEMING and JANE BOON as witnesses 2-612.

MARRIAGES in BERKELEY COUNTY (Perquimans Precinct)
3-199; in BERTIE 2-314, to 2-320; 2-364 to
2-379, 2-589 to 2-593; 3-107 to 3-113; CHOWAN
COUNTY 1-235 to 1-255; 1-392 to 1-414; 2-89
to 2-100; 2-227 to 2-233; PERQUIMANS PRECINCT
3-199 and 3-411 to 3-422; TYRRELL COUNTY 3-107
to 3-113.

MARSH, DANIEL, was a brother of JONATHAN MARSH
who married ANNIE BONNER, daughter of JAMES
BONNER and wife SARAH WILSON 2-171.

MARSTON, ELIZABETH of BATH left will in (1733) &
named a grandson WILLIAM MARSTON HOLLAND and
Daughter MARY HAMILTON and MOURNING and ANN
1-62.

MARSDEN, REV. RICHARD, came from ISLE OF MAN to
North Carolina with ROBERT MOORE 2-299.

MARSTON, WILLIAM, his wife was MARY and they had
son WILLIAM born in (1681) 3-211.

MARSHALL, HUMPHREY, with ROBERT SCOTT and JOHN
PARKER witnessed the deed of WILLIAM WILLIAMS
of the Lower Parish ISLE OF WIGHT COUNTY, VA.
to PETER PARKER, of the Upper Parish of NAN-
SEMOND COUNTY, VA., to a tract of land on the
east side of CHOWAN RIVER in (1706) which had
been part of a patent by LEWIS WILLIAMS in
(1697) 1-93.

MARTIN, ALEXANDER, was a COLONEL in the NORTH
CAROLINA Continental Line 1-416.

MARTIN, ALEXANDER, Governor; received a letter
from GEN. GEORGE WASHINGTON (1783) 2-594,
2-502.

MARTIN, ANN, bought land from JOHN RIVETT in
(1737) 3-131; received a deed to lands
from GEORGE PRIVETTS in (1738) (probably
the same person or family) 1-284

MARTIN, FREDERICK RAZOR and wife FRANCES sold
land to THOMAS POLLOCK on the West side
of CHOWAN RIVER in (1718) 1-827.

MARTIN, GEORGE, bought lands from HENRY BON -
NER in (1732) 2-451; he was " Of Maryland,
late of BERTIE PRECINCT" in (1728) 2-298;
died leaving will in (1732) in which he
mentioned his brother in law EPHRAIM VER-
NON 1-62.

MARTIN, JOEL, of BATH, will (1715) in which
he mentions his daughter MARY WOODWARD &
son in law HENRY WOODWARD of Virginia; al-
son ELIZABETH PENNY (a daughter) wife
of JOHN PENNY 1-83.

MARTIN, JOHN, of PASQUOTANK (about 1735)
left will, mentions son NATHANIEL MARTIN
and daughter ELIZABETH BRYANT (BRYAN) his
son in law JOHN MORGAN and other sons JOHN
and JOSHUA MARTIN 1-62; a later JOHN MAR-
TIN left will in BERTIE in (1819) and had
sons SAMUEL and JOSEPH MARTIN and other
children and relatives, including daughter
NANCY BARNES 2-533; another and different
JOHN MARTIN was Sheriff of GRANVILLE COUN-
TY in (1750) 1-448.

MARTIN, JOSIAH. was Governor of N. C. and issued commissions as Judges to JASPER CHARL-
TON and SAMUEL JOHNSTON in (1774) 1-448;
in (1774) BENEDICT ARNOLD made bond to him
signed by JOHN HORNIBLOW 3-299; copy of
letter from him to SAMUEL JOHNSTON in(1775)
2-430; issued a proclamation copied here-
in in (1776) 2-586, 2-587, 2-588.

MARTIN, LAWRENCE and wife PATIENCE sold lands
to JAMES NORVILLE in (1718) 1-626; in
(1719) he sold land to HENRY MILLER next
to lands of WILLIAM BUSH 2-607.

MARTIN, LODOVICK, proved certain headrights
before (1700) 1-305.

MARTIN, MARY, was the wife of ROBERT TUCKER
in (1719) 1-79.

MARTIN, NATHANIEL, was the son of JOHN MARTIN
of PASQUOTANK who left will 1-62; and he
is also mentioned in the will of JOSEPH
OVERMAN 1-64.

MARTIN, RACHEL married HERBARD HIGH (HERBERT,
tho pronounced HARBERT) of WAKE COUNTY N.
C. 2-310.

MARTIN, THOMAS, left will in (1780). His wife
was ELIZABETH, and he mentions his son
JAMES MARTIN and grandchildren NICHOLAS
BAGGETT, NICHOLAS MARTIN, MARY HAYS and his
grand-daughter ANN MARTIN, with ELIZABETH
MARTIN (wife), ABSOLOM CARNEY and HENRY
LEE, Executors; CADER POWELL, THOMAS HOWELL
and JOHN DOUGLAS, Witnesses 2-346.

MARTIN, WILLIAM, and HENRY LUCAS were both uncles of JOHN WOODWARD, who died leaving a will in BATH in 1734, in which he mentioned a brother JOEL WOODWARD, a son HENRY and daughter MARY WOODWARD 1-82. (NOTE: It is interesting to observe that the wife of the famous COL. JOSEPH MARTIN, Indian Agent, was a LUCAS, which suggests a connection with these MARTINS); This WILLIAM MARTIN died leaving will BERTIE in 1736 naming sons RICHARD, MOSES, THOMAS and JOHN, daughters MARY and ELISE (ELSIE) & wife ELSIE MARTIN 1-61; in 1743 another WILLIAM MARTIN was a brother in law of JOHN SNEAD 1-72.

MARTIN, ZEPHANIAH, was Master of the schooner "DOVE" in 1749 1-434.

MASON, HUGH, bought land from RICHARD TURBEVILLE in 1719 1-628.

MASON, JOHN, SR. of HYDE, left will in 1737 in which he mentioned his oldest son ROGER MASON, his daughter MARGARET and youngest son THOMAS MASON and sons in laws THOMAS TYSON and CLINCH HERRINGTON 1-60.

MASON, JOHN, was named as the "servant" of ANTHONY ALEXANDER, the founder of the ALEXANDER FAMILY in Eastern N. C. about 1700 3-356; but JOHN MASON was deceased in 1700 and JOHN BRUSHBY was administrator 2-302.

MASON, JOSEPH was deceased in 1702 and daughter SKITTLETHORP was administrator 1-62.

MASON, RALPH, with JOHN NAIRN was witness to deed in 1720 2-617; in 1714 he sold lands to JOHN GREEN, witnessed by JOHN DEW and WILLIAM BRYANT (BRYAN) 1-629; he bought lands from NATHAN MERRITT in 1721, with WILLIAM LOWE, JOHN GRAY and THOMAS WHITMELL as witnesses 2-617; he was born in 1700 2-466.

MASON, ROGER, of HYDE, died in 1754 wife MARY and all his sons named; sons BENJAMIN and THOMAS executors 1-340.

MASON FAMILY WILLS at 1-340.

MASSAGNEY, BENJAMIN and wife ANNE (1696) 3-371.

MASSEY, HEZEKIAH, SR. left will in 1727 names wife ELIZABETH and their children 1-62.

MASTERS OF VESSELS, coming into the PORT OF EDENTON and ROANOKE 1-433 to 1-436.

MATTACOMACK CREEK, was in SHAFTSBURY PRECINCT in CHOWAN County 1-3.

MATTHEWS, ANN, married WILLIAM HALL in 1703 3-410.

MATTHEWS, CHARITY, was the wife of JAMES MATTHEWS and left will in TYRRELL County in 1772 in which she names various relatives including the ANDREWS family 1-345.

MATTHEWS, EDWARD, of CRAVEN COUNTY, left will in 1753 mentions daughter ANN, the wife of CORNELIUS GRAY, grandson WILLIAM NEVILLE & son of JACOB NEVILLE; also daughters PRISCILLA, LUCHETIA and LUREMIA MATTHEWS, with LAWRENCE HYLAND, Executor, and THOMAS MITCHELL, MARTIN HAGEN and ELIZABETH RIGBEE as witnesses 1-345, 1-346.

MATTHEWS, GEORGE was on the QUIT RENT ROLLS of ALBEMARLE COUNTY before 1700 1-303; he married ELIZABETH WILLIAMS in 1695 3-407; their daughter JANE was born in 1696 3-369.

MATTHEWS, JOHN, died in GATES COUNTY leaving a will in 1836 2-61; he and WILLIAM MATTHEWS (an older John and William, of course) witnessed deed of AARON BLANCHARD in 1736 3-126; he was also a witness with RALPH MATTHEWS in 1718 to a deed by one of the BAKERS in CHOWAN 1-622.

MATTHEWS, THOMAS of KING WILLIAM COUNTY, Va. sold land in N. C. in 1717 witnessed by WILLIAM COWARD 1-619; and THOMAS left will in CHOWAN in 1732 in which he mentions wife PRISCILLA and a grandson RICHARD HOUCK 1-62; he lived near the land grant of ORLANDO CHAMPION, but was deceased before the land was granted 1-12.

MATHIAS, WILLIAM died leaving will in GATES County in 1799, wife PENELOPE and JOHN and KEDAR BALLARD executors 2-60.

MATTOCKS, JOHN died in 1733 wife MARY and his daughters ANN and ELIZABETH 1-62.

MAUDLIN, EDWARD and wife MARY had a son JOHN MAUDLIN born in 1718 and several other children born in the years immediately before and following 3-388.

MAUDLIN, EZEKIEL and his wife HANNAH had children born around 1720 3-388.

MAUDLIN, GIDEON, and MARY MAUDLIN witnessed a will of WILLIAM BATEMAN in 1773 3-164.

MAUDLIN, JOHN and his wife HANNAH (1745) 3-389.

MAULE FAMILY. Some genealogical notes showing connection with the HARE FAMILY 1-61.

MAULE, JOHN, a brother of PATRICK and WILLIAM MAULE married ELIZABETH HARE 1-61.

MAULE, DR. PATRICK, is mentioned in the will of JOSHUA PORTER in 1733 1-67; he died in 1736 and mentions his "cousins" JOHN & WILLIAM GRAY 1-61.

MAULE, WILLIAM, was Surveyor General of the Colony in 1720 and GOV. CHARLES EDEN files a complaint against him 3-151; he married PENELOPE GOLLAND the daughter of GOV. CHARLES EDEN'S first wife who had been the widow GOLLAND 3-152; he died in 1725 leaving will in which he mentions his wife PENELOPE and brother PATRICK MAULE 1-63; in 1716 he sold land to WILLIAM WORRELL witnessed by PATRICK MAULE and THOMAS MITCHELL 1-624; in 1725 HENRY BAKER petitioned the BERTIE PRECINCT court for relief against the claims of WILLIAM MAULE to his ferry between GATES and HERTFORD Counties 3-451.

MAYFIELD, PETER, his deposition relating to tobacco held in the home of THOMAS HARRISON in 1680 3-43.

MAYO, EDWARD, SR. witnessed deed of JOHN BENTLEY to CORNELIUS LEARY in PERQUIMANS in the year 1689 LEARY'S wife was MARY and BENJAMIN LAKER was also a witness. 3-435.

MAYO, EDWARD, was Clerk of the court held at the house of RICHARD POPE in PASQUOTANK (1694 & 1697) 2-465; in (1715) he was the surviving executor of ANN JENNINGS deceased, widow, formerly ANN SCARBOROUGH 2-467; in (1732) ANN STOAKLEY sister of STEPHEN DELAMARE was the widow of "cousin EDWARD MAYO" 1-41; he was also Clerk of the Court in (1790)3-439; he died leaving will in (1724) and mentions son EDWARD and JOSEPH and daughters ANN, SARAH and ELIZABETH, wife MARY, with THOMAS JESSUP, administrator 1-63; the name of wife of an EDWARD MAYO who died about (1702) was EM. 1-610; in (1695) one ARTHUR WORKMAN acknowledges receipt of twenty shillings on account of EDWARD MAYO 3-248; he met with the Court at the home of GEORGE DURANT (the elder) in (1685) 1-613; EDWARD MAYO a witness to inquisition at the house of RICHARD POPE in PASQUOTANK in (1700) with CALEB BUNDY, HENRY PENDLETON, THOMAS PENDLETON and EDWARD MAYO, JR. 3-88.

MAYO, EDWARD, JR. was of age and a witness (1700) at the home of RICHARD POPE 3-88.

MAYO, JOSEPH, was called "son" in the will of MARY NEWBY in (1739) 1-63.

MAYO, NATHAN, was mentioned in the deposition of THOMAS BEST in (1777) 2-403.

MAYO, SARAH married JOHN CULPEPPER August 23 in (1688) being then a widow 3-203; another and conflicting account says she first married JOHN CULPEPPER, second, JOHN LARKIN and 3rd MATTHEW PRITCHARD (1702) 1-610.

MAYO, WILLIAM, mentioned in an affidavit by one JAMES RAWLINS in (1777) 2-400.

McADAM, JOSEPH, witnessed the will of NATHANIEL WELCH in (1789) 3-198.

McADAMS, JAMES, died in PASQUOTANK in (1742-3) his wife SARAH and JOSHUA WHITE executors 1-353.

McALPIN, WILLIAM, died in CRAVEN COUNTY in (1747) formerly of STERLINGSHIRE, England, daughter HANNAH and wife HANNAH; THOMAS RICKEY of JAMAICA and MRS. JANE CROSS, executors 1-353.

McBRIDE, JAMES, was son in law of BENJAMIN COINS in (1734) 1-37.

McCANE, ALEXANDER, with JOHN and JOSEPH MULLEN a witness to the will of JOHN BARCLIFT, uncle of MARWOOD BARCLIFT (said to have been named for ANN MARWOOD?) in (1788) 3-165.

McCARTY, BAILEY, of HYDE, died in (1751) and left will, wife ELINER and brother DENNIS McCARTY with THOMAS SMITH his executors 1-353.

McCARTY, DENNIS, will in HYDE in (1759), with ABEL HUDSON and wife MARY executrix; witnessed by LUKE TOTEVINE, RACHEL WARREN and MARTHA BASLEY (Bailey ?) 1-353.

McCARTY, TIMOTHY, last will and testament proven at a meeting of the Court at the house of WILLIAM BRANCH in CHOWAN PRECINCT in (1717-1718) 1-154; his will was probated in JULY (1718) wife MARY and god-son WILLIAM GULLIERER 1-63; in (1712) he had witnessed a deed by TREDLE KEEFE to WILLIAM HOOKER to lands South side of MEHERRIN RIVER 1-100.

McCARTY, TIMOTHY in (1712) witnessed the deed of GEORGE SMITH and wife SARAH to JOHN SMITH to lands that joined his own lands on WICACON CREEK 1-98.

McCORKLE, JOHN, will in ROWAN COUNTY, N. C. in (1800) CATHERINE and JOEL McCORKLE mentioned 3-471.

McCORKLE, JOEL, will in ROWAN COUNTY in (1818) names children 3-471.

McCORKLE, SAMUEL, will in ROWAN COUNTY, N. C. in (1817) son SANDY and four daughters are named 3-471. See also 3-317.

McCORRY, FRANCIS, bought lands in (1718) from JOHN HAWTHORNE in CHOWAN 1-623.

McCLANAHAM, MARY in her will (1813) mentions JAMES COLLINS and CALEB NEWBY her sons in laws and some of their children 3-342.

McCLENDEN, DEBORRAH (This name often spelled as MACKLENDEN on the records, but the family finally adopted the uniform spelling of McCLENDEN down in Georgia and other places) left will in (1728) in which she mentions only her god-son JOSEPH SUTTON and her son RICHARD WHEDBEE 1-62. (JOSEPH SUTTON made guardian of RICHARD WHEDBEE 1-610).

McCLENDEN, DENNIS (spelled MACKLENDEN) was a member of a jury in ALBEMARLE PRECINCT in (1702), with RICHARD SKINNER, NATHANIEL ALEXANDER and others 1-610; in (1715) DENNIS sold lands on WICACON CREEK to WILLIAM DOWNING, with WILLIAM SHARP, THOMAS McCLENDEN and DENNIS McCLENDEN as witnesses 1-293; in (1719) he sold lands to JOHN MOSELEY on the North side of WICACON CREEK, with WILLIAM CRAWFORD and THOMAS MANERS witnesses 1-629; he married MRS. DEBORRAH WHEDBEE in (1702) in ALBEMARLE (mother of RICHARD WHEDBEE, a minor) 1-609; he received grant of land in (1704) on the North side of ALBEMARLE river joining MARK ASBURY and EDWARD WILLIAMS 1-6; he bought land from JOHN EARLY in (1717) 1-300; sold land in (1719) to JOHN WESLAND 2-454.EDGECOMBE (1725) 1-350

McCLENDEN, FRANCIS, witnessed a deed from FRANCIS BROWN to EDWARD DAVIS in (1717) 1-300; he and DENNIS McCLENDEN and WILLIAM SHARPE entered into an agreement in (1717) and WILLIAM DOWNING was brother in law of WILLIAM SHARPE and witnesses were WILLIAM DOWNING, ELLENER EARLY and JOHN FOOLER 1-618; the wife of FRANCIS McCLENDEN was ELLINER, and together in (1714) they sold lands to THOMAS ROGERS with ANDREW SALSBURY and DANIEL McGEE of BERTIE as witnesses 1-103; in (1717) FRANCIS McCLENDEN and wife FRANCES deeded lands in CHOWAN to EDWARD HOWCOTT 1-616; in (1718) he and SAMUEL BOZEMAN witnessed a deed from THOMAS BRAY to SAMUEL WOODWARD 1-629.

McCLENDEN, THOMAS, bought lands in (1717) from JAMES WILKINSON and his wife SARAH, 250 acres in CHOWAN PRECINCT; the deed was witnessed by JOHN SMITH and WILLIAM BUSH 1-300; with JOHN ISMAY in (1727) he witnessed a deed to lands from PHILLIP MAGUIRE to JOHN OVERTON 2-143.

McCLURE, RICHARD, qualified as Clerk of CHOWAN COUNTY in (1744) to succeed the term of JAMES CRAVEN 1-448.

McCOY, DANIEL, of NORFOLK COUNTY in (1735) mentions sons JOHN and WILLIAM, daughter LYDIA and wife CHRISTIAN 1-62.

McCOY, JOSHUA left will (1820) son MILES and a daughter LYDIA McCOY; wife ELIZABETH; JOSIAH TOWNSEND and STEPHEN ELLIOTT Executors 3-342.

McCOY, JULIA, will (1802) youngest children, MARY, JOSHUA and JONATHAN McCOY 3-342.

McCOY, WILLIAM left will (1795) giving names of his children; JOHN MIDDLETON and son JOSEPH Executors 3-179.

McCRARY, ROBERT, will in BERTIE in (1740) shows relationship to BROWNS and BARFIELDS 1-51.

McCULLOCH, ALEXANDER was the name of the ancestor of FRANCIS IREDELL'S wife MARGARET (Genealogy given) 2-163; another ALEXANDER (who was related to the same family) married SARAH HILL, daughter of BENJAMIN HILL who left will191758) 1-48 (NOTE. In (1724) he witnessed the will of WILLIAM SMITH of Little River (GRIMES p. 348) and the will of WILLIAM POWERS in CHOWAN PRECINCT (1748) (GRIMES p. 299).

McCULLOCH, HENRY, Secretary of the PROVINCE of N. C. left will in (1755) mentions daughters HENRIETTA MARY, DOROTHY BINSFIELD, ELIZABETH MARGARET and PENELOPE MARGARET; wife MARY and JOHN CAMPBELL, Executors; a witness was WILLIAM POWELL (POWERS?) 1-348; his wife may have been MARY MONCRIEF, daughter of JOHN MONCRIEF who died (1712) as his wife MARY and HENRY McCULLOCH were the executors 1-53.

McDANIEL, DANIEL received a grant of land (1733) 1-62; in (1717) he purchased lands from JOHN MILTON which joined JOHN CROSBY and THOMAS VINCENT 1-299; but sold the land to a THOMAS BROWN 1-300; he left will in (1731) naming sons ARCHIBALD and JAMES and daughters MARY, ANN and SARAH and wife SARAH 1-62.

McDANIEL, OWEN in (1720) deeded lands adjoining ANDREW BARRON to PHILLIP CASTELLO 2-618.

McDONNELL, MICHAEL (Spelled MACDONNELL) JANE his wife and daughter MARY FRANCES (1680) 2-301.

McDOWELL, DANCY was the executor of THOMAS SAWYER in (1720) 1-76.

McDOWELL, CAPT. JAMES, was sheriff of BERTIE in (1745) 2-626; in (1744) he and his wife MARGARET proved their rights in BERTIE COUNTY 2-534; administrator (1744) of HOLBROOK 2-623.

McDOWELL, STEPHEN, left will in (1817) and named wife SARAH; grandsons PERRY and MILES MIZELL sons of TIMOTHY MIZELL, grand-daughter RACHEL MIZELL; GEORGE MIZELL and LAWRENCE MIZELL are witnesses; relationship shown with LAYTONS, HARRELL and JONES families also 2-532.

McDOWELL FAMILY. Wills 2-532, 2-533.

McGEE, DANIEL, with ANDREW SALSBURY, witnessed a deed by FRANCIS McCLENDEN and his wife ELLINER to THOMAS ROGERS in (1714) 1-103.

McGEE, JOHN, left will in GUILFORD COUNTY in(1774) sons SAMUEL and WILLIAM and son in law ROBERT LINDSAY 1-349.

McGEE, LAWRENCE, left will (1740) in BERTIE with son in law JOHN BRYAN and his friend EDWARD BRYAN 1-61; a LAWRENCE McGEE (it is spelled McGUE in this note) obtained a land grant on ROCKYHOCK CREEK in(1720) 1-9.

McGLAUGHON, JEREMIAH had son JAMES 2-532.

McGLAUGHON, JAMES, left will in (1829) his wife JUDITH executrix; witnessed by JOHN THOMAS and JOHN H. COBB 2-532.

McGLAUGHON, WILLIAM, will (1826) his daughter SARAH married an OXLEY; JOHN H. COBB, W. H. SPEIGHT and ELIZABETH THOMAS are also mentioned 2-532.

McGREGORY, AFRICA, was the wife of HUGH McGREGORY, and they were executors of EM MAYO. late wife of EDWARD MAYO, deceased (about 1702) 1-610.

McKENZIE, REV. JOHN, of SUFFOLK COUNTY, Virginia, married JANET GRAY, daughter of JOHN GRAY and ANNE BRYAN; they had son JOHN McKENZIE born in NANSEMOND COUNTY, Virginia, (1743) genealogical account of the family 2-603.

McKEEL, JOHN, (spelled here McKELE) married the widow of WILLIAM SMITH 1-76.

McKEEL, MICHAEL, left will (1802) had JOSIAH, REUBEN, AMY and daughter RACHEL SMALL, and his executors were WILLIAM ROBERTS and WILLIAM BENNETT; witnesses RICHARD HOSKINS and JOSEPH SMALL 3-342.

McKEEL, REBECCA died leaving will in BATH in (1720) in which she mentions a son ANTHONY 1-61.

McKEEL, THOMAS left will (1729) with sons BENJAMIN, THOMAS, JOHN and other children 1-62

McKILDO, JOHN, lived in TYRRELL COUNTY near a ferry run by CHARLES JACOCKS (1770) 3-448.

McKINNIE, BARNABY, with WILLIAM DOWNING, EDMUND GALE, JOHN ALSTON, JOHN WHITE and THOMAS LOVICK were JUSTICES of the GENERAL COURT for the PROVINCE of N. C. which lies EAST of CAPE FEAR (No date, but very early) 2-298; the commission appointing them by RICHARD EVERARD and others is dated (1725) 3-284.

McKINNIE, BARNABY, JR. Abstract of will (1736) mentions daughter PATIENCE, BARNABY LANE, son of JOSEPH LANE, daughter MARY, BARNABY McKINNIE son of WILLIAM, wife MARY, and brother WILLIAM; BARNABY POPE, son of JOHN POPE, brothers ROBERT and JOHN McKINNIE, JAMES HOWELL and cousin JOHN LANE 1-470; BARNABY McKINNIE was living in EDGECOMBE in (1736) 2-467. (NOTE: In these abstracts the name is generally spelled "McKINNE - but in notes we have used the modern way of spelling the name).

McKINNIE, DAVID, with WILLIAM MURPHY witnessed a deed to BARNABAS McKINNIE in (1720) 1-470.

McKINNIE, JOHN, left will in EDGECOMBE (1753) son BARNABY and others named 1-344, 1-345.

McKINNIE, MARY, will (1754) in EDGECOMBE mentions ANGELIANY POPE, sons JOHN and BARNABY McKINNIE and daughters MARY, PATENCE and MARTHA, with BARNABY POPE executor 1-345.

McKINNIE, RICHARD, left will in EDGECOMBE (1755) brothers ROBERT, JOHN and wife MARY, BARNABY the son of JOHN, etc. WILLIAM and LEMUEL KINCHEN Executors 1-350.

McKINNIE FAMILY. See Genealogy of the LANE FAMILY beginning 1-469.

McLEMORE, ABRAHAM, will in BERTIE (1736) (Name is spelled MACLEMORE) names sons ATKINS, YOUNG and WILLIAM McLEMORE, with wife (unnamed) Executrix; witnesses WILLIAM GILLIAM, WILLIAM CLANTON and JOSEPH BRAGG (spelled BRAG)1-349.

McLEMORE, ATKINS, was the son of ABRAHAM McLEMORE of BERTIE in (1736) 1-349. (NOTE: he married one of the daughters of EDWARD JONES and his wife ABIGAIL SUGRE).

McLEMORE, CHARLES, with JOHN McLEMORE, with also WILLIAM CLANTON, witnessed deed of EPAPRODITUS BENTON to JOHN BENTON (1730) 2-448.

McLAIN, ARCHIBALD, married a step daughter of MATTHEW ROWAN who left will (1760) 1-69.

McMILLAN, JOHN, a mate to RICHARD POPE deid(1688) 3-363.

McMULLEN, JAMES died leaving will (1775) naming children, including MARY WINGATE and his wife BRIDGETT 3-178.

McREE, GRIFFITH I, was son in law of HON. JAMES IREDELL, having married the daughter PENELOPE IREDELL 2-164.

McRORY, JAMES was an ensign in the NINTH REGIMENT of the N. C. Continental Line 1-424.

McRORY, THOMAS, was a CAPTAIN in the NINTH REGIMENT of the N. C. Continental Line 1-424.

MEADE, ANDREW with DAVID MEADE and DAVID O'SHEAL witnessed deed by COL. JOHN LEAR to WILLIAM WILKINSON about (1728) 2-445.

MEADE, DAVID with JAMES BARRON was a witness to a deed in (1738) 3-132.

MEADE MARY, with ANDREW and DAVID MEADE witnessed deed in (1738) 3-132.

MEADER, JOB, with MARTHA MEADER witnessed a deed by WILLIAM JONES of CHOWAN in (1728) 2-444.

MEADS, JOHN, of LITTLE RIVER, had daughter MARY mentioned in will of WILLIAM BARRY in (1722) 1-71.

MEADS, MARY, was daughter of JOHN MEADS who lived at LITTLE RIVER (1722) 1-31.

MEADS, TIMOTHY (Spelled here MEAD) proves his rights: 2 wives or husbands, ELLINER BROWN, a young daughter, (1680 -about) 3-457; TIMOTHY MEADS of ALBEMARLE COUNTY, will (1685) wife ANN, son JOHN, children of brother THOMAS MEADS of WARWICKSHIRE, daughter in law MARY, DANIEL AKEHURST, ARNOLD WHITE and HENRY LAST, Executors. WILLIAM BENTLEY a witness 1-341-342

MEADS, TIMOTHY, will (1751) sons JOHN and THOMAS and wife MARY; JOSEPH PENDLETON an executor, witnessed by THOMAS McREEL and MARY ANN SMITH 1-343.

MEADS, THOMAS will (1751) in PASQUOTANK, wife and son TIMOTHY executors, with JOHN SCOTT and JOB WINSLOW witnesses 1-343.

MEBANE, A. W. will (1847), THOMAS COBB and JONATHAN TAYLOE witnesses 3-532.

MEBANE, ROBERT, was a COLONEL in the N. C. Continental Line 1-422.

MEHERRIN FERRY was owned by WILLIAM MAULE in (1725) 3-453.

MEHERRIN INDIANS. Letter in (1706) from THOMAS GARRETT relating to them 2-110, 3-111.

MEHERRIN'S SWAMP issued out of BENNETT'S CREEK 3-133.

MELTON, RICHARD married ORPHA LATEN in the year (1705) 3-410.

MERCER, THOMAS married DIANA WHITE (1703) 3-410; He and his wife DIANA brought a suit in Chancery against Hon. Samuel SWANN in regard to lands that had escheated and been patented by SWANN 3-440.

MERCER, THOMASIN (or THOMAZIN) married THOMAS SNOWDEN in (1705) 3-410.

MERCHANT, CHRISTOPHER owned 908 acres of land in PASQUOTANK in (1704) 1-304.

MERCHANT MARINE of the Province, at PORT OF ROANOKE, EDENTON, N. C. giving the names of Masters of vessels 1-433, to 1-436.

MEREDITH, DAVID was Master of the schooner MARTIN in (1774) 1-406; he left will in (1791) saying he was formerly of EDENTON, wife SARAH and brother LEWIS MEREDITH and a half-brother EDWARD ROE JIGGETTS; ELISHA NORFLEET and wife Executors 3-347.

MEREDITH, JOSEPH (of NANSEMOND COUNTY, VA.) sold land to WILLIAM WALTERS in (1731) 2-452.

MEREDITH, WILLIAM will in (1780) sons WILLIAM, DAVIS, THOMAS, JAMES, BENJAMIN and daughters SARAH and PEGGY 3-347, 2-346.

MERRIDAY, THOMAS was a cousin of JOHN HOSKINS in (1717) 1-51; he left will in PASQUOTANK (1740) and mentioned a son in law SAMUEL DAVIS 1-60.

MERRITT, CHARLES sold land to JOHN WOOD in (1719) with JAMES BLOUNT a witness 3-608.

MERRITT, SAMUEL sold land in (1736) to ISAAC WILLIAMS which he had bought from WILLIAM BENTLEY 3-130; deed witnessed by EDWARD and MARY HARE made by him to WILLIAM BENTLEY in (1736) 3-130; he also sold land in GATES COUNTY in (1712) to WILLIAM BENTLEY, with JOHN COLLINGS a witness 1-628.

MERTON, JOEL, was witness to a bill signed by PATRICK MACKUEN (McEWIN) in (1711) 3-284.

MESSLER, CORSMEAR, left will in (1696) and named his son in law RICHARD LEWIS 1-62.

METCALF, CALEB, left will in (1736), with WILLIAM HENTZER executor, ADAM MOORE a witness 1-340.

METCALF, GEORGE, left daughter MARTHA in his will (1795) and named his mother's children who bore the name SUTTON; SETH WHEDBEE and executor and SAMUEL WHEDBEE a witness 3-179.

MEWBORN, THOMAS, bought land from SAMUEL PAGETT on QUEEN ANNE'S CREEK and CHOWAN RIVER in (1729) with ROBERT HICKS and THOMAS LOVICK witnesses 2-446; he sold land to WILLIAM BADHAM (1729) 2-448; died leaving will (1749), with ELENER MEWBORN, Executrix and proved by the oath of EDWARD RUE (ROE?) 2-633.

MIERS, ANN, will (1816) had daughter ELIZABETH WARD and grand-children JOHN MANSFIELD and WILLIAM STAFFORD; THOMAS WARD executor (and probably son in law); THOMAS and DEBORAH BAGLEY, witnesses 3-342.

MIERS, THOMAS, left will in (1815); children of ELIZABETH MIXON, MARTHA REA and SAMPSON WILDER, my wife, JEREMIAH MIXON Executors, and JOB PETTYJOHN and SAMUEL REA witnesses 3-342.

MICHENER, JEREMIAH, was the third husband of MARTHA HALSEY (daughter of DANIEL HALSEY and a brother of JOHN HALSEY (1731) 2-450.

MIDDLETON, HENRY, bought land (1720) from PETER HERD (HEARD?) next to JEFFREY LIIES and HENRY CLARKE, witnessed by ZIPHA and JOHN EDWARDS 2-614; the same year HENRY owned land next to WILLIAM MITCHELL 2-612; his wife was ELIZA - BETH EDMUNDS (1721) and his wife MARY whose Executor was JOHN EDWARDS 1-43; but a HENRY MIDDLETON died leaving will (1738) with wife MARTHA, with sons JAMES, JOHN and HENRY, a daughter MARY and son in law ELISHA FARLEY - 1-61; THOMAS LEE and BENJAMIN WALKER were the witnesses 1-348.

MIDDLETON, JOHN, died leaving will in TYRRELL in (1718) with daughter MARY and wife ELIZABETH 1-348; another JOHN left will in EDGECOMBE in (1750) and still another JOHN MIDDLETON died in ONSLOW COUNTY in (1744) naming children JOHN, JAMES, SAMUEL, ISAAC, SARAH, ANN, SABRA and SUSANNA; wife SARAH and JOHN STARKEY the executors, with ABRAHAM, ALEX and SARAH MITCHELL as witnesses 1-348.

MIDDLETON, WILLIAM, was a cousin of FRANCIS LEY - DON will in (1728) 1-59; one WILLIAM MIDDLETON of (1754) had son JOSIAH MIDDLETON born that year 3-389; JOSHUA MIDDLETON (son of WILLIAM) recorded his mark in (1747) 2-630.

MIDGETT, MATTHEW, and his wife JUDITH sold lands to JOHN MIXON in (1715) 1-621; he died leaving will (1735) in which JUDITH and all of their children are mentioned 1-62.

MIERS FAMILY. Wills 2-528.

MIERS, NATHANIEL and wife MARY sold lands in (1726) to JOHN WELCH with JOHN PARKER and PAUL PALMER the witnesses 2-447; and a much later NATHANIEL MIERS left will in BERTIE (1839) in which he mentions SALLY COBB, daughter of HENRY COBB and others 2-528; his father, NATHANIEL died (1800) in BERTIE, in which he mentioned MARY JERNIGAN and WINNIE JERNIGAN 2-528.

MILBURN, ALEXANDER left will in BERTIE (1806) naming wife SALLY and GEORGE OUTLAW his executors; WILLIAM HAWKINS and JOHN ROWAN witnesses 2-529.

MILBURN, SAMUEL was appointed the guardian of the orphans of JOHN FORD (1771) in BERTIE 3-450; he died leaving will in BERTIE in (1796) in which the name of his wife and all his children are mentioned 2-348.

MILBURN, SARAH left will in (1820) in which she gives the names of certain grand-children, including SALLY MYERS, with JOSHUA TAYLOE and executor 2-530.

MILES, DANIEL. Genealogical query relating to him and his family 3-469.

MILES, STEPHEN; division of his estate (1808) mentions MIRIAM CARPENTER, BENJAMIN WHEDBEE and wife MARY, THOMAS WHEDBEE and wife JEHOSHEBA 2-267.

MILLER, ABRAHAM, obtained a land grant (1782) on TINDALL SWAMP 1-21.

MILLER, JOHN, will in (1822) wife SUSANNAH son JAMES and daughter PATSY, with RICHARD LEIGH, executor 3-343; another JOHN left a will (1817) in BERTIE, in which he mentions JOS. JORDAN, son of JOSEPH JORDAN, lands from the estate of WILLIAM WEST, and WILLIAM WEST son of JOSIAH WEST, with JOSEPH JORDAN executor 2-528.

MILLER, MALACHI, obtained grant of land (1790) adjoining SAMUEL POPHELSTON 1-23.

MILLER, MARY, will (1851) in which connection with the OUTLAW family is shown 2-528.

MILLER, MASON, obtained a land grant in (1793) on TINDALL SWAMP 1-24.

MILLER, RALPH (Spelled RAISH) tutition of EDWARD HARDY and NTHAN MILLER in BERTIE in (1771) 3-450.

MILLER FAMILY. Wills 2-528, 3-343.

MILLER, MARTIN, was son in law of HENRY MACKLEY who died in (1720) 1-63.

MILLER, THOMAS, was administrator of the estate of SETH SOTHEL (1695) 3-250, 3-251; mentions an account against the estate held by JOHN PORTER 3-250; he renders an account of the estate of SETH SOTHEL 3-66; he was a member of the GENERAL COURT of ALBEMARLE with WILLIAM WILKINSON and others in (1683).

MILLHOUSE, WILLIAM, witnessed a deed to JAMES LONG in (1711) with JAMES HOOPER and JOHN WORLEY 2-135.

MILLS, FRANCIS, married PENELOPE LONG in (1783) with ISAAC AYRES (Spelled AIRS) security on the marriage bond 3-111.

MILNER, JOHN, witnessed a deed from JAMES WILSON (Of WARWICK COUNTY, VA.) to NATHANIEL WRIGHT (Of NANSEMOND CO. VA. in year of (1733) 2-610.

MILNER, JOHN JR. was the witness to a deed of land to RICHARD ROGERS by JOHN ALSTON in (1733) 2-610.

MILNER, JOSEPH, sold lands in (1731) to JOHN SUMNER, which had been patented by COL. THOMAS MILNER in (1703) 2-451.

MILNER, THOMAS (COL?) of NANSEMOND COUNTY, VIRGINIA, sold lands to JANE KNIGHT (of the same place), which had been granted to COL. THOMAS MILNER in (1700); this sale was in (1737) and was witnessed by JOHN SUMNER, WILLIAM HUNTER and JOHN KNIGHT 3-130.

MILTON, JOHN made deed to lands in (1717) to DANIEL McDANIEL, adjoining lands owned by JOHN CROSBY and THOMAS VINCENT, with ROBERT HICKS and WILLIAM BRASWELL witnesses 1-299.

MING, DOROTHY (May be intended for MINGE) was owner of lands before (1696) adjoining lands patented to HENDERSON WALKER that year 1-6.

MINGE, EDWARD, left will (1734) in PASQUOTANK, & mentioned wife MARY, daughter MARY and half-sisters ELIZABETH and SARAH; also his wife's father JOSEPH JESSOP 1-62.

MINGE, JAMES, was a JUSTICE of the GENERAL COURT of N. C. in (1708) 3-142; in (1780) a much later JAMES MING (intended for MINGE)owned land next to JOSEPH CREECY 1-21; JAMES MINGE married RUTH LAKER, daughter of BENJAMIN LAKER and after his death she married RICHARD SANDERSON 1-74; he was mentioned in (1713)in the will of MATHIAS GILES 1-46; he is mentioned in regard to a road in PERQUIMANS in about (1695) 3-141; he died JAN. 23 (1723-4) 3-405.

MINGE, JOSEPH, died leaving will in CHOWAN(1751) in which he mentions sons THOMAS and JOSEPH, daughters and wife RACHEL 1-352.

MINGE, THOMAS, left will in CHOWAN (1798) mention of brother JOSEPH MINGE, deceased, and his own children JOSEPH, JAMES, RACHEL GREGORY, son WILLIE, daughter PENELOPE, and his wife DELILAH, witnessed by JEREMIAH MIXON and SARAH PARISH 2-12; a much earlier THOMAS married MARY, daughter of the widow of JACOB BUTLER in (1738) 2-298; the estate of THOMAS MING or MINGE was divided in (1769) by EBENEZER LEARY between his widow SARAH, and THOMAS and SARAH MINGE 2-267; a THOMAS MINGE SR. died about (1772) leaving widow MARY, children SARAH MINGE, THOMAS MINGE and ELIZABETH LEARY, sister of EBENEZER LEARY 2-267.

MINGE, RICHARD, was one of the heirs of a THOMAS MINGE, with WILLIAM BURKETT and a JOHN MINGE 2-267.

MINSHEW, JOHN, lived on CYPRESS SWAMP in the year (1738) 3-132.

MINSHEW, RICHARD was a witness to a deed by JAMES LASSITER in (1736) 3-127.

MINTON, THOMAS, died leaving will in (1804) naming wife SARAH and children; JOSEPH HORNE, LUKE PARKER and JAMES MINTON witnesses 2-529.

MINTON, MARY, will (1854), names children of MARCELLA MINTON, PENELOPE BAKER a witness 2-529.

MISCELLANEOUS RECORDS, of ALBEMARLE COUNTY taken from EDENTON books 2-296 to 2-305, arranged in alphabetical order.

MISCELLANEOUS RECORDS or ITEMS from such records copied at EDENTON 2-465 to 2-471.

MISCELLANEOUS ITEMS copied from LOOSE PAPERS among the records of ALBEMARLE COUNTY at EDENTON, including the rent rolls prior to (1700) 1-301 to 1-306.

MISCELLANEOUS ITEMS found in BOOK "W" "B" No. 1 and "C" No. 1 at BERTIE COUNTY 1-117 to 1-119.

MITCHELL, ABRAHAM, died leaving will in(1746) in CARTERET, and mentions wife and brothers ANTHONY, JOHN and GEORGE and sister REBECCA; JOHN MITCHELL and EZEKIEL HUNTER executors 1-344; an older ABRAHAM (evidently his father) died in ONSLOW (1747) and named wife ANN and sons ANTHONY, JOHN and GEORGE and daughters REBECCA and KATHERINE; JOHN STARKEY an executor and SARAH MIDDLETON a witness 1-344.

MITCHELL, RANDALL, left will (1758) in EDGECOMBE, with BENJAMIN MITCHELL a witness 1-344; and JAMES MITCHELL died at EDENTON (1745) with JAMES and ELIZABETH WALLACE as witnesses 1-344.

MITCHELL, JACOB, was an orphan of JAMES MITCHELL of BERTIE in (1771) 3-450.

MITCHELL, JAMES, will at EDENTON (1745) and left son JAMES MITCHELL 1-344; and CATHERINE MITCHELL was his widow 1-457; the son JAMES paid the tuition of EDWARD HARDY in BERTIE (1771) 3-450.

MITCHELL, JOHN, his orphan THOMAS MITCHELL placed under care of WILLIAM WESTON in (1746) 2-628.

MITCHELL, NANCY had son WILLIAM MITCHELL under tuition of SAMUEL POWERS 3-450

MITCHELL, RICHARD, of GATES COUNTY; lengthy abstract of his will in (1820) in which he names his wife ESTHER, her heir JOHN MITCHELL, TIMOTHY HUNTER OF BERTIE COUNTY, WILLIAM BARKSDALE of HALIFAX COUNTY, with TIMOTHY WALTON and TIMOTHY WALTON Jr. his executors; witnessed by JOHN WALTON, THOMAS LEAK and JOHN L. BILLUPS 2-60, 2-61.

MITCHELL, THOMAS and PATRICK MAULE witness to a deed in CHOWAN (1716) 1-624.

MITCHELL, WILLIAM, received a deed to lands from RICHARD BATCHELDER (1716) 1-293; he sold land to THOMAS STUBBS and HENRY MIDDLETON (1720) 2-612; witnessed a deed from WILLIAM FRYLEY to BENJAMIN BLOUNT (1716) 1-291.

MITCHENER, JEREMIAH, received a land grant in (1740) 1-18; he had married MRS. MARTHA DUNSTON in (1738) 1-448.

MIXON, JOHN, bought tract of land from MATTHEW MIDGETT in (1715) 1-621; and he and others signed a petition in (1713) 2-111, 2-112.

MIZELL, AARON, married POLLY QUALL in BERTIE COUNTY MARCH 13, 1802, with TIMOTHY MIZELL as surety 2-375; a different AARON MIZELL left will in BERTIE (1808) witnessed by a WILLIAM COPELAND 2-529.

MIZELL, ANN, mentions as a sister in the wills of JUDITH and FRANCES BRITTAN in BERTIE COUNTY in (1810-1811) 2-501.

MIZELL, CLARY, was daughter of WILLIAM MIZELL of BERTIE in (1793) and was a sister of AARON MIZELL 2-348.

MIZELL, ELIZABETH, was the daughter of TIMOTHY MIZELL who left will (1792) in BERTIE, witnessed by REUBEN HARRISON and EZEKIEL WHITE 2-348.

MIZELL, HANNAH, will in BERTIE (1823) mentions her brothers, CADER, HENRY, LAWRENCE and JOSHUA MIZELL 2-529.

MIZELL, HENRY, was named as the brother of HANNAH MIZELL in her will (1823) in BERTIE 2-529.

MIZELL, HEZEKIAH, married ANN HOLLEY (2-501) ; and was executor of the will of JUDITH BRITTAN in (1811) 3-501.

MIZELL, ISAAC, married CHARLOTTE HUGHS Feb. (1799) 2-373.

JERMIAH MIZELL married WIRNIFRED SOWELL in BERTIE in (1807) 2-378.

MIZELL, JOHN, owned lands in (1757) near ROBERT LASSITER 1-20; in (1731) he witnessed a deed by JOHN KEATON, SR. 2-450; a later JOHN MIZELL witnessed the will of GODWIN JORNIGAN (1817) in BERTIE 2-523.

MIZELL, LAWRENCE, brother of CADER, HENRY and a JOSHUA MIZELL 2-529.

MIZELL, LUKE, was apparently the son in law of WILLIAM CHARLTON, having married his daughter SARAH, as sometime between (1706 and 1711) WILLIAM CHARLTON in a deed of gift for "love and affection" called them "my son and daughter" and gave them a tract of land on MORATUCK (ROANOKE) RIVER 1-95 (There was in 1764 a CHARLTON MIZELL who married ELIZABETH EVERIT or AVERIT 3-107);in (1744) LUKE MIZELL WILLIAM LATTIMORE and JOSEPH JORDAN divided the estate of DANIEL HENDRICKS 2-622; in the year (1768) a LUKE MIZELL – perhaps son of the first LUKE –signed the marriage bond of JOHN MIZELL who married HANNAH MIZELL in BERTIE 3-108; at a court held in (1718) it was ordered that LUKE MIZELL, WILLIAM MIZELL, JNO. BENTLEY, WILLIAM LATTIMORE, JOHN SESSIONS & NATHANIEL MOORE do certain duties, including the appraisal of the estate of MARTIN GRIFFIN deceased 1-154; LUKE MIZELL and wife SARAH sold lands to GEORGE CLARK, of PERQUIMANS on ROCKYHOCK CREEK (no date) 1-297; LUKE witnessed a deed from EDWARD SMITHWICK (1714) 1-291; and one from WILLIAM CHARLTON to PHIL WARD in (1714) 1-292; he sold lands to TIMO-THY THURLOVE in (1717) with JOHN FALCONER & WILLIAM STEWART witnesses 1-300; he and SU-SANNA CHARLTON witnessed a deed to EDWARD SMITHWICK in (1702) 2-456; in (1744) he and COL. ROBERT WEST and ROGER SNELL were appointed to divide estate of HENRY GIBBS 2-622; he lived near the VIRGINIA LINE in GATES COUNTY about (1730) 2-450.

MIZELL, MOSES in (1759) had land grant on CYPRESS BRANCH 1-20; he married MARY LAYTON (1799) 2-373; died and left will (1845) 3-529. And of course these are different ones.

MIZELL, TIMOTHY, died leaving will in BERTIE COUNTY (1792) naming sons JONAS and JOHN MIZELL and daughter JUDITH HUGHES and certain grandchildren 2-348.

MIZELL, WEST and ANN MIZELL were children of HEZEKIAH MIZELL who married ANN HOLLEY or BRITTAN 2-501; he and HEZEKIAH MIZELL were witnesses to the will of WILLIAM LEARY in (1822), of which CHARLTON LEARY was an administrator or executor 2-527.

MIZELL, WILLIAM died leaving a will in BERTIE County in (1793) in which he named his children SARAH, AARON, WILLIAM, NANCY, JEB-EMIAH, CLARY, SUSANNAH and MARY; his wife MARY and brother JOHN MIZELL executors 2-348; a WILLIAM MIZELL married WINNIFRED WARD in (1806) in BERTIE COUNTY 2-377.

MODLEN, EZEKIEL and wife HANNAH (1698) 3-370.

MOLBY, KATHERINE sold lands to JOHN COOK in (1717), with JOHN CROMBIE a witness 1-298.

MOLBY, GEORGE (Spelled MOIBEE) left will in CHOWAN in (1719) and named a son in law THOMAS MAGALL 1-63.

MOLTON, ELIZABETH, a widow bought lands from WILLIAM REEVES (1718) joining PHILLIP JONES 1-623.

MOLTON, JOHN and THOMAS SMITH witnessed deed by WILLIAM REEVES in (1718) 1-623; and he sold lands to THOMAS VINCENT adjoining the land of JOHN CROSBY in (1716) witnessed by JOHN DICKINSON 1-295; in (1718) he witnessed a deed to ELIZABETH MOLTON 1-623.

MOLTON, JOHN SR. sold lands to JOHN JOHNAKIN (JARNIGAN) in (1716) witnessed by JOHN CROSBY and ROBERT HICKS 1-295.

MONCRIEF, JOHN, left will in (1712) names his wife MARY, sons GEORGE, THOMAS, WILLIAM and JOHN MONCRIEF and daughter MARY. His wife MARY and HENRY McCULLOCH Executors 1-63.

MONK, GEORGE sold land to JOHN BLACHOW(1719) 1-627.

MONTEIGUE, ROGER and SUSANNAH MONTEIGUE were transported by WILLIAM HANCOCK about (1697) 2-299; ROGER was mentioned (1701) in the will of RICHARD COLLINS 1-37.

MONTAGUE, THOMAS (Mis-Spelled MONTICUE in the book) of PERQUIMANS left will(1750) and named wife ELIZABETH and (evidently) children of ZACHARIAH NIXON (who must have been a son in law) 1-351; THOMAS MONTAGUE (so spelled) witnessed a deed in (1720) by JAMES EVANS of PERQUIMANS to THOMAS LUTEN joining HENRY BONNER and a WILLIAM JONES 2-613.

MONTIEZ, LEWIS, with JOHN CAMPBELL, witness a deed by JOHN WORLEY in (1720) 2-515; JOHN WORLEY , after his death in (1732) was administrator on his estate, and the name was spelled MONTEIR 1-450.

MONTFORT, JONATHAN, and others, including JOSEPH YORK and the widow of JOHN MITCH-ELL were owners of the sloop HANNAH AND MARY in (1718) 2-397.

MONTFORT, JOSEPH, of HALIFAX COUNTY, N. C. was the owner of the BRIGANTINE "BETSY" and the SLOOP "HALIFAX" in (1775). It was sometimes customary for the owners of vessels to take charge of them in person. 1-436.

MONTGOMERY, JOHN was a member of the Court in CHOWAN in (1743) 1-447; in (1733) he was the executor of the estate of FRANCIS PUGH 1-66; and he was appointed ATTORNEY GENERAL of the colony of N. C. in (1723) 1-445.

MOODY, WILLIAM, of BERTIE COUNTY in (1709) with his wife ANN sold lands to JOHN BENTLEY on CHARLTON'S CREEK on MORATUCK (ROANOKE)RIVER with EDWARD BERRY and ROBERT HICKSON as witnesses 1-102; MOODY sold land to EDWARD SMITHWICK, SR. on MORATUCK (no date given) 3-131; in(1710) lands he had sold to JOHN FALCONER was deeded by him (FALCONER) 1-296.

MOON, JACOB, was an officer in the AMERICAN REVOLUTION 2-310.

MOON, WILLIAM S. (Spelled MHOON) died in FRANKLIN COUNTY, ALABAMA 2-532.

MOORE, ANN (Of NANSEMOND COUNTY, VA.) in (1734) bought land from SAMUEL MERRITT adjoining JOHN DUKE and JOHN DRURY 2-453; and an ANNE MOORE with AARON MOORE witnessed the will of NATHANIEL ALBERTSON in PERQUIMANS in (1782) 3-163.

MOORE, AARON with ANNE MOORE witnessed the will of NATHANIEL ALBERTSON in PERQUIMANS in(1782) and he evidently married ANNE ALBERTSON, the daughter of the testator 3-163. See 2-347.

MOORE, ABRAHAM, bought lands about (1771) from a JOHN DREW, whose wife PATIENCE DREW lived in NANSEMOND COUNTY, VA. 3-449.

MOORE, ALFRED, with RICHARD WYATT, witnessed the will of ISAAC HALL in (1828) 3-337.

MOORE, AUGUSTUS, died leaving will in EDENTON in (1851) wife SUSAN 2-13.

MOORE, CHARLES, the son of JOHN MOORE and his wife ANN, was born in (1732) 3-389; he married SARAH and had children ANN and ISAAC MOORE born (1756 and 1757) 3-389.

MOORE, CORNELIUS, was brother and executor of NATHAN MOORE who died leaving will (1831) 3-341, 3-342, with WILLIAM EVANS and ISAAC BUNCH as witnesses; (This will shows relation of the MOORES to the EVANS family). See 3-177.

MOORE, DAVID, wrote will MARCH 25 (1670) proved in December same year; in it he names only son KAINE, with JAMES BLOUNT a witness 1-340; in the GRIMES version, the name of the son is given as DAVID, and the witnesses as ROBERT BONEO and JAMES BLOUNT (GRIMES p. 251).

MOORE, EDWARD, bought land from JONATHAN LEWIS in (1717) 1-299; he and his wife MARGARET MOORE witnessed a deed by JOHN JONES (1718) 1-622; he and MARGARET deeded lands to JAMES CORRE in (1722) adjoining MARTIN GARDNER & PATRICK CANADY and WILLIAM JONES were the witnesses 2-141.

MOORE, ELIJAH, Captain in Revolution 1-425.

MOORE, EPAFRODITUS, and ALEXANDER COTTEN are bondsmen for JOSEPH WIMBERLY who petitions for the establishment of a ferry over the ROANOKE river at CONEAT, which was granted at a meeting of the court at WINDSOR in (1744) 2-621; EPAFRODITUS MOORE died in BERTIE in (1757), and from it we learn that he had a daughter who married JAMES HOWARD, one who married a CAIN (Rebecca), one who married a WALSTONE, RACHEL who married a STANDLEY, and PENELOPE, who married a HARE; he had son JOHN MOORE; grandsons THOMAS & ELISHA MOORE, and other daughters MARY, ANN, GRACE and CHRISTIAN MOORE 1-341; still a later EPAFRODITUS MOORE died in BERTIE in (1789) with wife WINNIE and sons AARON and THOMAS MOORE, ANDREW OLIVER and a JOHN SMITHWICK executors 2-347.

MOORE, GIDEON left will in (1763) named mother MARY MOORE, and brothers JOSEPH and CORNELIUS MOORE, sisters MIRIAM and MARY MOORE and BETTIE BARTLETT; MATHEW JORDAN and MATTHEW WHITE executors 3-177.

MOORE, HANNAH, died in (1802) leaving will in which she named sons JOSEPH and ROBERT MOORE and daughters MARTHA and HANNAH HAMLIN, MARY WHITE and SARAH MOORE 3-341.

MOORE, HEZEKIAH, was the son of WILLIAM MOORE and wife ELIZABETH, and was born (1718) 3-389; another HEZEKIAH MOORE, the son of a WILLIAM and wife MARTHA was born in(1734) 3-389.

MOORE, ISAAC, was the son of CHARLES MOORE who left will in (1806), and ISAAC was then in TENNESSEE; the wife of CHARLES was evidently ELIZABETH CREECY, a sister of LEMUEL CREECY, called the "uncle" of his son LEMUEL MOORE 3-341.

MOORE, JAMES, was a COLONEL and a BRIGADIER GENERAL in the N. C. Continental Line 1-415.

MOORE, JAMES, died leaving will in (1733) and he names wife SUSANNA, son MAURICE MOORE and daughter SARAH; JOHN DAWSON named as executor 1-61; the witnesses to this will were JAMES BARNES, ROBERT TENELL, JOHN BROWN. In a codicil in (1735) the witnesses were ROBERT RUFFIN, JAMES TART and SAMUEL COTTEN (GRIMES p. 251).

MOORE, JAMES, with CHARLES MOORE, witnessed a will of ABRAHAM ELLIOTT in (1813) 3-331; in (1790) a JAMES MOORE left will in BERTIE in which he named his son in law LUKE COLLINS, who married his daughter CELIA MOORE, his son TITUS MOORE, his daughters ELIZABETH JOYNER and SARAH ABINGDON; TITUS MOORE and LITTLEBURY ABINGTON were the executors 2-347; there was a JAMES MOORE & wife FRANCES who had a daughter SARAH born in (1691) 3-369; and a JAMES MOORE was the SHERIFF of BERTIE in (1771) 3-449; MAURICE MOORE in (1717) gave a receipt to EDWARD MOSELEY for money received on claims for services rendered by COL. JAMES MOORE in the INDIAN WARS (about 1711) 3-149; the service of COL. JAMES MOORE are mentioned by JOHN CORRIE or CORY, Constable of PASQUOTANK Precinct in (1713) addressed to NATHANIEL CHEVIN and MAJ. CHRISTOPHER GALE which statement is addressed to them and signed by said JOHN CORY 3-274, 3-275.

MOORE, JESSE, late of PERQUIMANS, N. C. but in (1769) left will in ISLAND OF ANTIQUA, mentions brothers WILLIAM, THOMAS and SAMUEL MOORE, and mother LEAH HOLLOWAY, formerly LEAH MOORE, and "brothers" JOSEPH and THOMAS HOLLOWAY 3-177. (CHARLES MOORE who left will in (1789) had daughter LEAH MOORE 3-177)

MOORE, JOHN married MARY RATLIFFE in (1729)3-410; a JOHN was Master of the sloop SEAFLOWER in (1749) 1-435; a JOHN MOORE, son of WILLIAM and ELIZABETH MOORE was born in (1702-3) 3-373; in (1769) JOHN the son of BENJAMIN MOORE was placed under the tuition of JOSIAH WILLIAMS of BERTIE 3-447; JOHN MOORE and wife ANN had CHARLES MOORE born (1732), PRISCILLA born in (1734) 3-389; JOHN MOORE patented lands in (1700) 3-130; JOHN of NORTHAMPTON County left will in (1753) wife TABITHA, with children JOHN, WILLIAM, NATHANIEL, RICHARD and SARAH 1-340.

MOORE, JOSEPH and HUGH MOORE of Mecklenburg County, query relating to 2-471. See 2-84.

MOORE, JOSHUA, was the son of WILLIAM MOORE and wife ELIZABETH, was born (1705) 3-376; JOSHUA MOORE left will (1791) with sons JOSEPH, JOSHUA and ROBERT, and son in law ROBERT NEWBY, B. ALBERTSON, a witness 3-177, 3-178.

MOORE, LUTEN, was grandson or grand-daughter of RACHEL HALL will (1810) 3-337.

MOORE, MARY, of PERQUIMANS left will in (1756) & mentions son THOMAS NEWBY, daughters JEMIMA and MARY ROBINSON, and grandchildren SARAH and JOHN ROBINSON; son THOMAS and NATHAN NEWBY executors 1-340; MARY MOORE was the daughter of DAMARIS RATLIFFE who died (1734) (see John Moore) 1-70.

MOORE, MATTHEW, married NANCY DALTON, daughter of SAMUEL DALTON, of Virginia 2-479, 2-480; he lived in STOKES COUNTY, N. C., an account of his family 2-306.

MOORE, MAURICE, with JOSEPH MOORE and EDWARD MOSELEY indicted by Grand Jury, indictments signed by DANIEL RICHARDSON (1719) 2-81 to 2-82; inscription on memorial erected to his memory at Parish Church of St. Phillip 3-222; query in regard to MAURICE MOORE by a lady in Texas 2-635; MAURICE MOORE the son of JAMES MOORE and wife SUSANNA, who left will in (1735) 1-61; MAURICE MOORE and RICHARD FARIS were Church Wardens in St. James Parish New Hanover County in (1742) 2-304; in (1719) Maurice Moore witnessed a deed by JOHN LILLINGTON to JEREMIAH VAIL, with JOSHUA PORTER and SARAH SWAIN as witnesses also 2-454; JAMES, son of MAURICE MOORE married ANN IVY who was step-daughter of MARMADUKE JONES 2-490; one MAURICE MOORE from near WILMINGTON, N. C. was b. (1771) and died (1854) married MARGARET TWILLY and moved to Kentucky about (1810) and one of his sisters married McCALEB and had son JAMES McCALEB 3-314; MAURICE in(1720) witness to deed by WILLIAM JONES of BATH to EDWARD MOSELEY 2-613; MAURICE MOORE and MRS. MAURICE MOORE, JAMES MOORE, THOMAS CUNNINGHAM JR, MARY GRAINGER, wife of CALEB GRAINGER and others mentioned in will of ALEXANDER DUNCAN in WILMINGTON (1768); testator also mentions his brother ROBERT, and sisters and JOHN RUTHERFORD and daughter FRANCES 1-201.

MOORE, MOSES, left will in BERTIE in (1818) and mentions wife SARAH, daughter TABITHA and daughter PENELOPE GRANBERRY and NELLY CULPEPPER; Langley Granberry and James Granbarry each married one of his daughters; TURNER HORNE was an executor of the will 2-531, 2-532; he and LANGLEY GRANBERRY, JAMES GRANBERRY and PENELOPE GRANBERRY mentioned in will of WILLIAM TILLMAN (wife POLLY) in (1808) 2-550.

MOORE, NATHANIEL, executed power of attorney to WILLIAM CHARLTON to acknowledge deed dated (1716) 1-297; NATHANIEL MOORE bought lands from EDWARD SMITHWICK adjoining EDWARD BERRY in (1714) with HENRY SPELLER & EDWARD SMITHWICK witnesses 2-455.

MOORE, NORTON, and wife MARY sold lands to MARTIN CROMER in (1719) 1-629.

MOORE, RICHARD obtained a grant of land on the Northeast side of CHOWAN RIVER in (1713) 1-13; he witnessed a deed by THOMAS AVENT and wife ELIZABETH to JACOB COLSON (1716) with JOHN NAIRN also a witness; land on MORATUCK (ROANOKE) River 1-295; in (1748) the will of RICHARD MOORE was proven by the oaths of WILLIAM RUE and THOMAS DAVIS 2-632.

MOORE, ROBERT, came from DOUGLAS, Isle of Man to N. C. with REV. RICHARD MARSDEN 2-299; ROBERT MOORE, son of ROBERT and his wife HANNAH was born in (1729) and they also had JAMES MOORE (b. 1717) and MARTHA born (1726) 3-389; a ROBERT MOORE was witness to deed by JOHN BANKS to JOHN URMSTONE in (1715) 2-455; HANNAH MOORE who left will in (1802) had daughters named HAMLIN, and her executors were JOSEPH and ROBERT MOORE, with MARGARET JONES and HULDA NEWBY witnesses 3-341.

MOORE, ROGER, mentioned in the will of JOHN DALRYMPLE, ESQ. in Scotland, as "my good friend"; executors named being MATHA DALRYMPLE, HON. ROGER MOORE, ESQ. and WILLIAM and JOSEPH WATTERS; witnesses JOHN SWANN, GEORGE LOCKHART, GEORGE MOORE; will proved (1767) but written (1742); Roger Moore deceased at time will was proved; ALEXANDER DUNCAN of Brunswick County, N. C. also mentioned 3-465; a ROGER MOORE was CAPTAIN in the Fourth Regiment of the N. C. continental Line 1-419; will (1748)1-342.

MOORE, SAMUEL, son of WILLIAM MOORE and wife ELIZABETH was born in BERKELEY PRECINCT in (1707) 3-377; MARY MOORE, daughter of SAMUEL MOORE and wife MARY was born in (1739) 3-389.

MOORE, SARAH, married WILLIAM GREGORY, with JOHN WYATT as surety on bond in (1785) PERQUIMANS COUNTY 3-418.

MOORE, TITUS, a legatee with the GRANBERRYS and also executor of the will of GEORGE HOUSE in (1795) with SAMUEL GRANBERRY; FRANCIS PUGH and JAMES HOUSE witnesses 2-340; TITUS MOORE died leaving will in BERTIE (1757) mentions his wife ELIZABETH, son JAMES and daughters MARY ODOM and CHARITY MOORE and "my five children" not named. Witnesses were NEEDHAM BRYAN and PATIENCE TURNER 1-341.

MOORE, THOMAS, "late of New York" died in WIL-
MINGTON leaving will (1753), Dr. COSMOS FAR-
QUHARSON, executor; CALEB MASON, SIMON PAYNE
and RICHARD HARTLEY witnesses 1-341.

MOORE, TRUEMAN, died in PERQUIMANS (1752), sons
WILLIAM, SAMUEL, THOMAS and JESSE MOORE, and
daughters JANE and MARY and wife LEAH MOORE
1-341.

MOORE, WILLIAM, and wife ELIZABETH, had son WIL-
LIAM MOORE, born (1699) 3-371; HEZEKIAH born
(1718) 3-389; JOSHUA born (1705) 3-376; he
died in PERQUIMANS (1732) named wife ELIZA-
BETH and children WILLIAM, JOHN, JOSHUA,
SAMUEL and TRUEMAN MOORE; JANE and ELIZA-
BETH and cousin ROBERT BOGUE 1-62; a much
later WILLIAM MOORE died (1807) mentions
brothers THOMAS and SAMUEL MOORE, and half-
brothers JOSEPH and THOMAS HOLLOWELL; MAR-
GARET and THOMAS WHITE, children of JOSIAH
WHITE and THOMAS WHITE son of WILLIAM, with
SAMUEL WHITE and JOHN PERRY witnesses 3-341
in (1722) WILLIAM MOORE was the god son of
PETER ENGLE 1-42; in (1719) WILLIAM MOORE
deeded land to JOHN KING (Of Nansemond Co.
Va.) on the East side of CHOWAN RIVER 2-612.

MORBY, GEORGE, received land grant (1714) 1-13.

MORGAN, ABRAHAM, with CULLEN MORGAN and THOMAS
MORGAN witnessed will of THOMAS LANK in
GATES COUNTY (1829) 2-59

MORGAN, CHARITY, died in GATES COUNTY in (1825)
with ABRAHAM and SETH BENTON witnesses with
son JAMES MORGAN executor; grandchildren
JOSHUA JONES and EMILY and JAMES SMALL 2-61.

MORGAN, CHARLES, bought lands, next to EDMUND
PORTER and MARGARET SIMONS (1716) with JOHN
BENNETT a witness; and he sold lands to
JOHN BENNETT the same year, with JOSHUA POR-
TER and RICHARD BENNETT witnesses 1-618.

MORGAN, ELIZABETH, daughter of JOHN MORGAN was
born (1700) 3-373; and ELIZABETH, daughter
of JAMES MORGAN and wife ANN, was born in
(1739) 3-389.

MORGAN, HENRY. MARY MORGAN petitions for sale
of personalty of his estate (1759) 1-456;
HENRY and JAMES MORGAN witness deed of JOHN
STENGER to ROBERT POWELL (1740) 3-131.

MORGAN, JAMES; his wife was JEAN in (1698) and
they had son JAMES born (1675) 3-377; son
JOHN born (1678) and son WILLIAM MORGAN
born (1679) 3-208; JAMES and wife HANNAH
had REBECCA MORGAN born (1739) 3-389; and
JAMES and wife ANN had ELIZABETH born(1739)
and SETH MORGAN born (1740) 3-389; JEAN a
daughter of JAMES and wife JEAN married
RALPH FLETCHER in (1698) 3-408.

MORGAN, JEAN, daughter of JAMES MORGAN and wife
JEAN married RALPH FLETCHER in (1698) 3-408.

MORGAN, JOHN, married MARY JONES, the relict of
ROBERT BEASLEY in (1699) 3-409; this JOHN
was born in (1678) the son of JAMES MORGAN
and wife JEAN 3-208; JOHN and MARY had a
son JOHN MORGAN born (1705) 3-376; a JOHN
MORGAN died leaving will in BERTIE in (1827)
wife MARTHA, sons SETH, JOHN, PETER, daughters PATSY MORGAN, POLLY COBB (wife of CHAS
COBB)and PENELOPE CULLIPHER 2-531.

MORGAN, LYDIA died in (1802) and in her will
mentions her son in law BENJAMIN MORGAN
and daughters in law PENINAH and SUSAN-
NAH MORGAN (step-children) and daughters
MARY and ELIZABETH MORGAN; her father
JOSIAH BUNDY and JOHN BELL executors, &
P. ALBERTSON and REBECCA ALBERTSON the wit-
nesses 3-342.

MORGAN, MARY, married JAMES PERISHO JR. in
(1696) 3-406; and a MARY MORGAN died and
left will in (1787) with her friend JOHN
PARKER executor 3-178; MARY the daughter
of EDWARD WILLIAMS married a MORGAN and
is named in the will of her father (1739)
1-81.

MORGAN, MATTHEW died leaving will in (1764)
wife was SARAH and his executrix, JOHN
LACEY and JOSHUA DAVIS witnesses 3-178; a
MATTHEW MORGAN died in GATES COUNTY in
(1832) with daughters MARY HOLLAND, RUTHA
PAGE, NANCY BRITT and SARAH COPELAND; and
son in law THOMAS COPELAND his executor
2-61.

MORGAN, OLIVE, (widow) bought land in (1732)
from JOSEPH SMALL, of PERQUIMANS, on which
JOHN SMALL (her late husband) had lived and
which he had aptented in (1714), JOHN WAL-
TERS and JOHN ODOM witnesses 2-452.

MORGAN, ROBERT was called "son" in the will of
PHILLIP TORKSEY (1727) 1-78.

MORGAN, SETH, left will in GATES COUNTY (1866)
2-61; he was son or grandson of JOHN MORGAN
who died in BERTIE in (1727) with son SETH
MORGAN 3-531.

MORGAN, WILLIAM, married SARAH FLETCHER in
(1699) 3-408, 3-409; he was probably the
brother of JEAN MORGAN who married RALPH
FLETCHER in (1698) 3-408; he and his wife
SARAH had son WILLIAM MORGAN born (1703)
3-375; a WILLIAM MORGAN bought lands from
JOHN STONE in (1730) with ROBERT JEFFREY
and GABRIEL COSAN witnesses 2-450.

MORING, CHRISTIAN, left will in (1816) and in
it named his son WILLIAM and son JOHN E.
WOOD; WILLIAM MEBANE a witness 2-531.

MORLEY, JOHN, his wife was ELIZABETH FITZ
GARRETT in (1706) 3-377.

MORRISS, CHARLES and WILLIAM GATLING (1734)
witnessed deed by SAMUEL MERRITT to ANN
MOORE of Nansemond County, Va. to lands adjoining JOHN DUKE and JOHN DRURY 2-453.

MORRIS, WILLIAM SR. left will in BERTIE in
(1807) naming all his children and his wife
SUSANNAH 2-530; ABRAHAM HARMON was his executor.

MORRIS, ZADOCK, died in BERTIE in (1838) and
had son in law LAWRENCE MIZELL who married
his daughter CHARLOTTE and had daughters
MARTHA and CHRISTIAN; his daughter SALLIE
MORRIS also married a MIZELL 2-530.

MORRIS, JOHN, sold lands to MARY SLADE (1711)
in CHOWAN 3-442; left will (1739) naming his
wife MARY and their children 1-61; a later
JOHN died (1774) was brother of CORNELIUS
MORRIS, and possibly JONATHAN and JOSHUA
MORRIS mentioned same page 3-178.

MORRIS, THOMAS was witness to a deed JOHN HINTON (1734) by JAMES BENNETT and the INDIANS 3-125.

MORTON, EDMUND was Master of the Sloop SUSANNAH in (1749) 1-434.

MOSELEY, EDWARD, appointed (about 1704) a Deputy to represent the heirs of JOHN LORD GRAN - VILLE, and is directed to take charge as COL- ONEL of all the Regiments in the Province of NORTH CAROLINA 3-258, 3-258; EDWARD MOSELEY did not appear in the Province until about the time of GOV. HENDERSON WALKER'S death in (1704), and his Commission must have been is- sued about the time of the CARY REBELLION 3-259; he married the widow of GOV. HENDER- SON WALKER 1-58; in and as early as (1706) he sold land with his wife ANN to ROBERT FENDALL and the deed was witnessed by JOHN LILLINGTON and SARAH LILLINGTON 1-99; about (1711-12) he represented EMANUEL CLEAVES in his suit in answer to CHARLES WORTH GLOVER for illegal arrest, etc. 3-269; in (1714) he sold lands to JAMES BARROW, SR. of PERQUIMANS with JAMES BARROW a witness 1-293; he was witness to a deed in WASHINGTON COUNTY in (1715) by one BROWNELL 1-291; in (1719) he was granted lands adjoining THOMAS GILBERT, JOHN TAYLOR, JOHN BLOUNT and JEREMIAH VAIL 1-13; in (1720) he patented lands adjoining those previously owned by THOMAS GILLIAM 1-18; also lands on ROCKYHOCK 1-18; in (1715) he sold lands with his wife ANN to JOHN LILLINGTON in Washington County 1-291; EDWARD MOSELEY, MAURICE MOORE and others were indicted, with DANIEL RICH - ARDSON foreman of Grand Jury 3-91, to 3-98; one grant to EDWARD MOSELEY lapsed to SAMU- EL SWANN (1716) on INDIAN TOWN CREEK 1-16; it had been granted to him 1-11; he sold land in (1714) to COL. THOMAS CARY 1-294; in(1737) EDWARD MOSELEY was a trustee for WILLIAM ROW- DEN and CHARLES WESBEAR in a deed to DR. ABRA- HAM BLACKALL; JOHN BENBERRY and JEREMIAH VAIL the witnesses 3-129; statment of his public accounts signed by DANIEL RICHARDSON, WILLIAM BARROW and NICHOLAS CRISP (1714)3-155; in (1717) he bought lands from WILLIAM BRANCH of CHOWAN 1-618; as TREASURER he executed a deed to WILLIAM LUTEN in (1737) lands next to JOHN OXLEY and GABRIEL COSAND, which had been mortaged to MOSELEY by THOMAS SPIERS 3-135; he died and his will was proven in NEW HANOVER COUNTY in (1749) names wife ANN and children ANN, JOHN, EDWARD, SAMPSON, JAMES, THOMAS and WILLIAM MOSELEY; wife's father MR. SAMPSON, sisters in law MRS. MARY MOORE, and MRS. SARAH PORTER, MRS. ELIZABETH MOORE rel- ict of COL. MAURICE MOORE, sister of ELIZA- BETH, my sister in law; children of late brother-in-law JOHN LILLINGTON; Col. MAURICE MOORE'S "three youngest children", and my mother in law MRS. SUSANNAH HASSELL and my friend JAMES FASSELL 1-355.

MOSELEY, EMPERER, was Master of the Brigantine JOSEPH in (1775) 1-436; his daughter MARY MOSELEY born about (1783) is said to have mar- ried (1) SAMUEL JARVIS and (2) in (1803)WIL- LIAM COATES BUTLER of Philadelphia; it has been suggested that he was a grandson of ED- WARD MOSELEY, who came from PRINCESS ANNE COUNTY, Va to CHOWAN precinct about (1705-6) SAMUEL JARVIS who married the daughter MARY MOSELEY lived in CURRITUCK COUNTY, North Car- olina, but he probably married MARY MOSELEY in PASQUOTANK 3-316, 3-317.

MOSELEY FAMILY. Genealogical account of the family and some of the descendants of COL. EDWARD MOSELEY who was twice married, and his connections 1-638.

MOSELEY, CAPT. JOHN, vestryman of LYNHAVEN PAR- ISH in Princess Anne County, Va. (NORFOLK) and Captain FRANCIS MOSELEY 1-638; JOHN MOSELEY, who in (1719) bought lands from DENNIS MACLENDEN 1-629.

MOSELEY, MARY, daughter of WILLIAM BASSETT and BURWELL BASSETT MOSELEY mentioned 1-638.

MOSS, JOSEPH, married SARAH SHACKELFORD daugh- ter of JOHN SHACKELFORD 1-73.

MOSS, ROBERT, bought lands from JOHN BROWNING about (1720) 3-614.

MOTT, JOHN and HANNAH MOTT, of New Hanover County related to JOB HOWES Sr. and JR. men- tioned in the will of SAMUEL BRIDGEN (1730) perhaps 1-176.

MOUNTFORT, HENRY and DAVID HENDERSON mentioned in document or message signed by THOMAS POL- LOCK in (1704) 3-244.

MOW, NATHAN name mentioned in deed to WILLIAM LATTIMORE in (1716) 1-616.

MOWBRAY, WILLIAM and his wife HANNAH in (1680) 2-301.

MOYE, JOHN (Spelled MOY) died leaving will in CURRITUCK in (1735) mentions daughter JANE, son JOHN and grandfather PIEDERS and his wife AVIS 1-62.

MOYE, MARY, was the grand-daughter of JOSEPH JESSOP who left will in PERQUIMANS (1736), who was brother of THOMAS and JONATHAN JES- SOP; he also mentions grand-daughter MARY MAYO 1-54.

MOYE, THOMAS left will in CHOWAN in (1723) and named wife ELIZABETH, sons THOMAS and JOHN, WILLIAM PHILLIPS and "my wife's daughters " ELIZABETH and PATIENCE. 1-62.

MULKEY, PHILLIP, died leaving will EDGECOMBE County in (1736) sons DAVID, PETER, daugh- ters JANE, EVE, SCARBURGH and JUDITE, son in law GEORGE LAWS; wife SARAH and JAMES SMITH, executors; witnesses JOHN CALIBAN & JONATHAN MULKEY 1-348.

MULLEN, ABRAHAM, died in BERTIE in (1780) and left will naming sons JOSEPH, GREENBERRY & THOMAS; EDWARD TURNER and AGNES TURNER wit- nesses 2-347.

MULLEN, EDWARD, heads a list of Tithables in CURRITUCK COUNTY, the date of which has not been determined, but VERY EARLY perhaps about (1700) or earlier 3-257.

MULLEN, JAMES left will in (1796) in which he mentions ELIZABETH CALLAWAY and her son THOMAS CALLAWAY; wife and JOHN STANTON ex- ecutors; SIMEON LONG, JOAB THOMPSON and LEAVEN THACH, witnesses 3-179.

MULLEN, JOSEPH, will (1791) sons ISAAC and JO- SEPH, daughter MARY WHEDBEE, and grandchil- dren BETTY and TULLY WILLIAMS, names wife ELIZABETH 3-179.

MULLEN, GREENBERRY, left will in BERTIE (1811) names wife HARIET, daughter SARAH, son WILLIAM MULLEN; witnesses ELIZABETH WALSTON, WILLIAM LEE GRAY and TURNER WALSTON 3-530.

MULLEN, ISAAC. His wife was ELIZABETH in (1736) and he had son ABRAHAM MULLEN 3-389.

MULLEN, JACOB, of PERQUIMANS will in (1758) and he names children ISAAC, ABRAHAM, JACOB and THOMAS MULLEN, daughter HANNAH 1-60.

MULLEN, JOHN, was a witness with MARTHA TURNER to the will of ANN TURNER in (1800) who mentions brother HENRY TURNER, cousin JOSEPH TURNER and son HAWKINS TURNER 3-192.

MULLEN, PATSY, was the daughter of SARAH TURNER who left will (1827) and the wife of JOSEPH TURNER 3-354.

MULLEN, THOMAS, was the son of SARAH TURNER, SR. and brother of PATSY MULLEN who married JOSEPH TURNER 3-354.

MULLEN, ZADOCK left will (1813) names wife NANCY son BENJAMIN MULLEN, daughter MARY GODFREY and son ASHER MULLEN and others 3-342.

MUMFORD, DEBORRAH, married JOHN RUSSELL, the son of GEORGE RUSSELL of COUNTY KENT, England in (1679) by the Rev° GORDON 3-201.

MUMFORD, JOSEPH, of ONSLOW POINT, left will not dated (GRIME p. 260 says 1732) wife ANN and daughter ELIZABETH and sons JOSEPH and EDWARD. Executors EDWARD HOWARD and THOMAS FULLARD; JAMES MURRAY, EDWARD HOWARD and ELIZABETH MURRAY witnesses 1-62 and GRIMES p. 260.

MUNDAY, ALICE, in (1716) with JOHN ODOM witnessed Power of Attorney from WILLIAM DOWNING to WILLIAM SHARPE, relating to a sale made by one MACLENDEN. 1-293.

MUNDEN, WILLIAM left will in (1793) wife HANNAH and children named 3-179.

MUNDEN, ELISHA left will in (1821) wife NANCY & children, including CHRISTOPHER and JOHN MUNDEN 3-343.

MUNDS, JOSEPH, will (1832) wife HANNAH, with JOSEPH WHITE a witness 3-343.

MUNDS, THOMAS (Spelled MUNS) received grant of land in (1714) next to lands owned by JOHN ROBINSON 1-8; he sold lands in CHOWAN to THOMAS KIRK in (1718) with DAVID ATKINS a witness 1-622; a THOMAS MUND (Spelled MAND in Hathaway's print) left will in (1736) mentions "my children and grandchildren" and grandchildren MANDUE and PRISCILLA DORTHY or DORTHRY, son WILLIAM and daughter MARY 1-61; another entry purports to be the will of a THOMAS MUNS in (1693) which only mentions "Wife ANNE MUNS" 1-61.

MURDAUGH, JOHN and wife SARAH, had daughter MIRIAM born (1753) son JOSEPH born (1755) daughter MARY born (1758) son LEMUEL born (1760) and son JOHN MURDAUGH born (1762) 3-389, 3-390.

MURDAUGH, JOSEPH, died and left will (1768) & mentions a sister MIRIAM HUNNICUT (the one born (1753); SAMUEL BOND, JOHN TAYLOR and JESSE MOORE were the witnesses 3-172.

MURPHY, JEREMIAH, died leaving will in CRAVEN COUNTY in (1752) mentions son THOMAS, GEORGE LANE, THOMAS MURPHY and JOHN LANE Executors; witnesses were JOHN MURPHY & JOHN and JANE CARUTHERS 1-351.

MURPHY, THOMAS left will in CRAVEN in (1746) sons THOMAS and JEREMIAH, JOHN and daughter BRIDGETT MURPHY 1-351.

MURFREE, COL. HARDY, Lieutenant Colonel in the N. C. Continental Line 1-416.

MURFREE, WILLIAM, father of COL. HARDY MURFREE, of the N. C. Continental Line is mentioned as having been a delegate to the Convention at HILLSBORO, N. C. in (1775) 3-316.

MURPHY, WILLIAM, will in EDGECOMBE (1737) in which relatives are mentioned 1-351; he witnessed deed BARNABAS McKINNE (1721) 1-470.

MUTTER FAMILY. Genealogical account. Its connections with the BLOUNTS, etc.1-522-3-4

MULBERRY HILL was the name of the home of JAMES BLOUNT on ALBEMARLE SOUND 1-9.

MARKS FAMILY. PETER MARKS of "Ye Little Creeke" (will 1656) in Lower Norfolk County, Virginia, was the ancestor of JOHN MARKS of 1706 (1-95) and THOMAS MARKS of 1702 (1-5, 2-456, 1-88) who acquired lands on ROCKHOCK CREEK, as shown by this record. He was the father of STEPHEN MARKS who died in ANSELMOND COUNTY, Virginia in 1670, who left sons STEPHEN and JOHN, and the latter two were the ancestors of numerous sons, including the JOHN and THOMAS who about 1700 settled in ALBEMARLE PRECINCT; also of JOHN, PETER and HASTINGS MARKS who migrated up the RAPPAHANNOCK to SPOTTSYLVANIA and HANOVER COUNTY, and from there "spread out". In 1734 "JOHN MARKS, Planter, of St. MARKS PARISH, Spottsylvania County, on the South side of the RAPIDAN had wife MARY and a daughter MARY" and in 1733 "PETER MARKS was licensed to keep an ORDINARY at the Courthouse in HANOVER COUNTY, Virginia, with one THOMAS PROSSER his bondsman. (1 Crozier's County Records, and W. & M. Mag 1912 p. 55). This was the same house of entertainment, which many years later, was presided over by one JOHN SHELTON, whose daughter married PATRICK HENRY. "JOHN MARKS, planter" of St. Mark's Parish, had a son JOHN MARKS, who settled at SHEPHERDSTOWN, Virginia, up around HARPER'S FERRY, and married ELLENER MORROW, sister of HON. JOHN MORROW, member of Congress from that District, long years later, and a distinguished Colonel in the American Revolution. JOHN MARKS, of Shepherdstown, was also a revolutionary soldier, and the builder, it is claimed of the first Presbyterian Church in Fredericksburg Virginia, where he removed some years prior to his death, about 1812.

HASTINGS MARKS, brother of JOHN (Of St. Mark's Parish), PETER (Of Hanover County), and WILLIAM MARKS (of Middlesex County, Va.) who sold lands to JAMES BATCHELDER that he had purchased from ROBERT MICKLEBOROUGH in 1740, was the ancestor of an interesting and numerous family of children, one of whom, HASTINGS MARKS, JR., married ANNE SCOTT JEFFERSON, sister of THOMAS JEFFERSON, the President, and another, JOHN MARKS who married LUCY MERIWETHER (then the widow of WILLIAM LEWIS) and the mother of NICHOLAS MERIWETHER LEWIS, of Expedition fame. It is through this alliance and others with the MERIWETHER FAMILY that we are able to trace this MARKS FAMILY back to old PETER MARKS of "ye Little Creeke" in LOWER NORFOLK. Consider these facts:

In 1650 COL. WILLIAM BERNARD was overseer of the will of JUSTINIAN COOPER (whose wife was ANNE HARRISON) of ISLE OF WIGHT COUNTY (pp. 531-532 Boddie) and who owned lands in LOWER NOR-FOLK. Margaret Bernard, his sister married DANIEL GAINES and had BERNARD GAINES, father of another DANIEL GAINES who had MARTHA GAINES who married JOHN HARVEY, of Charlottesville, the parents of ELIZA-ABETH HARVEY who married JAMES MARKS, son of HASTINGS MARKS, and brother of JOHN MARKS who married LUCY MERIWETHER. MARTHA GAINES HARVIE, JOHN MARKS, the TALIAFERROS, THE MOORES, JAMES MARKS and the GAINES FAMILY all settled after the American Revolution on BROAD RIVER in GEORGIA. As for the MERI-WETHERS, they also settled on BROAD RIVER, though originally they came down from old NICHOLAS MERI-WETHER and his wife ELIZABETH WOODHOUSE of LYNHAVEN PARISH in Lower Norfolk County. MARTHA GAINES HARVEY died in the Broad River settlement. The theory has been indulged by the MARKS genealogists that JOHN MARKS, the ancestor of this family of Upper Virginia, married a daughter of a LORD HASTINGS, based on the name of a son "HASTINGS", but no actual proof has been advanced to establish the claim, and the compiler accepts it only as a romantic dream having no basis in fact, since the surrounding historical data makes out too plain a case of mistaken identity, and establishes, beyond doubt that PETER MARKS "of ye Little Creeke" was the ancestor.

THE MOORE FAMILIES. This remarkable record certainly contains an abundance of material for a study of the MOORE FAMILY. The writer thinks he is able to identify among all of those mentioned at least three distinct families, though it is impossible to separate from the mass of names all those assignable to each group. (1) The BARBADOES, or GOOSE CREEK MOORES; (2) THE LOWER NORFOLK, or BERMUDA MOORES, and (3) the BRISTOL PARISH MOORES. This is a grouping that will fur - nish a basis for a study of these records, and I am frank to confess that I find evidence in some instances that suggests a relationship existed between nearly all of them. Following is a brief paragraphic outline of each of the three families:

(1) GOV. JAMES MOORE, who is said to have married a daughter of SIR JOHN YEAMANS was the ancestor of the BARBADOES set. These all came to the CAROLINAS from the BARBADOES with JOHN YEAMANS, ARTHUR MIDDLETON, GOV. ROBERT DANIEL, the BROUGHTONS and others and settled between the Ashley and Cooper Rivers in South Carolina about the same time (about 1678-9). It is probable that GOV. MOORE had brothers. Possibilities: DAVID MOORE (1-340) and NATHANIEL (1-297) also a ROGER MOORE (not mentioned). GOV. JAMES MOORE was certainly the father of a JAMES, a MAURICE and a ROGER MOORE, and probably of a NATHANIEL, JOHN, JOSEPH, RICHARD and EDWARD, all of whom appear on the records, but unidentified as his children. It is known that GOV. JAMES MOORE, who married MISS YEAMANS had a large family (McGRADY) and certainly only the three KNOWN sons would not have complied with that description. The son JAMES was also Governor, but died in 1723-35? (1-61), and he left a son MAURICE, but not the one who established BRUNSWICK and lived and died there in 1777. MAURICE MOORE, brother of the second GOV. JAMES left sons MAURICE and JAMES, mentioned in the will of ALEXANDER DUNCAN (1-201) and ROGER MOORE mentioned in the will of JOHN DALRYMPLE (3-465). What became of MAURICE MOORE, son of GOV. JAMES MOORE, these records do not show. Not all of these MOORES remained in South Carolina, nor did they all live in WILMINGTON, but moved to the ALBEMARLE SOUND region where they multiplied and replenished the earth.

(2) The LOWER NORFOLK or BERMUDA MOORES were all descendants of RICHARD MOORE, the first Governor of the BERMUDAS, whose father was SIR GEORGE MOORE, son of SIR WILLIAM MOORE whose first wife was MARGARET, the daughter of RALPH DANIEL (ALEXANDER BROWN), and who lived in SWAFFHAM, county NORFOLK, ENGLAND, from whence came the WOODHOUSE FAMILY. Richard Moore had a son EDMUND MOORE, who with his son in law HENRY WOODHOUSE (also son of a Governor of the BERMUDAS) settled at LYNHAVEN PARISH in Lower Norfolk County (or PRINCESS ANNE). He was the father of CASON MOORE who married SARAH WOODHOUSE, THOMAS MOORE, WILLIAM MOORE who married MARY WOODHOUSE and ELIZABETH MOORE who became the wife of HENRY WOODHOUSE, who will be found on these records. These Lower Norfolk Moores spelled the name MORE for a time, but later adopted the usual spelling of MOORE. OBEDIAH MOORE of ONSLOW County was a descendant of this set. The WILLIAM MOORE and his wife ELIZABETH of the BERKELEY PRECINCT records (3-371) belonged to this set, and the careful researcher in these records will find it possible to trace the line therefrom. MORGAN MORE or MOORE was of this clan.

(3) THE BRISTOL PARISH MOORES . On the old Register of BRISTOL PARISH in Virginia will be found a list of MOORES, apparently the descendants of a "Great John Moore" there mentioned, in which the names SETH, ROGER, JAMES, JOHN, THOMAS, ALEXANDER, GEORGE, SAMUEL and MARK MOORE are mentioned. SETH MOORE, son of "GREAT JOHN" was born in 1692, and reasonably may have been the father of the others, or most of them. That some of these MOORES went to ALBEMARLE is evident by the presence of the names on the North Carolina records. JOHN MOORE and his wife CATHERINE had a BETTIE RUTHERFORD MOORE born in 1731, and JOHN RUTHERFORD and his daughter FRANCES are mentioned with MAURICE and JAMES MOORE in the will of ALEXANDER DUNCAN of WILMINGTON in 1768 (1-201).

PHILLIP MULKEY. Will in 1736 witnessed by JONATHAN MULKEY (1-348). REV. PHILLIP MULKEY born near HALIFAX, N. C. in 1732, was probably the son of the brother JONATHAN who witnessed the will. In 1757 REV. PHILLIP MULKEY organized the famous SANDY CREEK Baptist Church on DEEP RIVER. In 1760 he carried several members of the Church with him to Little River in South Carolina, where they organized another Church. From there he went to GEORGIA where he died. His son REV. JONATHAN MULKEY was a famous pioneer churchman on the Watauga in East Tennessee in 1787, and he had a son REV. PHILLIP, famous in S. E. Kentucky, who with his family settled in MULKEYTOWN, ILLINOIS, named for him, where he died and is buried. The descendants are legion all over the Southwest.

NABSON, ARTHUR, of CARTERET COUNTY left will in (1748) and had a daughter ELIZABETH married NATHANIEL SMITH 1-60.

NAIRNE, JOHN was neighbor to ABRAHAM BLEWETT in (1718) 1-627; he and wife MARY sold lands to WILLIAM UMFLEET of Nansemond County, Va. in (1728) 2-443; made deed to THOMAS RODES in (1721) 2-617; in (1721) sold lands to CORNELIUS HARNETT joining EDWARD WINGATE and WILLIAM COWARD on the West side of QUEEN ANNE Creek 2-617; sold land to JOHN BRYAN in (1720) on CYPRESS SWAMP, with ROBERT HICKS a witness 2-612.

NANSEMOND COUNTY, Va. was the home of LEWIS WILLIAMS, WILLIAM WILLIAMS and PETER PARKER 1-5.

NAPIER, ROBERT, in (1707) was "late of NEW KENT County, Virginia 1-613.

NASH, FRANCIS was a Colonel and Brigadier General in the N. C. Continental Line 1-415.

NASH, JOHN, for himself claimed a headright about (1701) 2-300.

NASH, THOMAS, with JOSEPH HEWES, EDWARD VAIL and CULLEN POLLOCK signed a bond in (1767) 2-226; he died leaving will in CHOWAN in (1769) and named son CLEMENT, wife, daughter ANN OWEN, MRS. REID of Virginia, sons HENRY and JOHN & "four children by my second wife" and brother ABNER NASH. JOSEPH MONTFORT, ABNER NASH & SAMUEL JOHNSTON executors 2-13.

NASH, ABNER, was brother of THOMAS NASH who died in (1769) 2-13.

NEAL, ABNER of CRAVEN county will in (1772) names grandchildren, wife ELIZABETH, JOHN BRYAN & others 1-355; ABNER NEAL married MILDRED HARVEY 3-480.

NEAL, HENRY, left will in (1735) wife SUSANNA & her son JOHN SIMPSON and the NEAL children are mentioned 1-355.

NEALE, JOHN was sued by JONATHAN JACOCKS and his wife ELIZA 3-283.

NEEDHAM, JAMES and RICHARD SANDERSON witnessed the will of LEMUEL REED in (1816) 3-347.

NEELAND, JONATHAN will (1747) and ELIZABETH NEELAND was executrix 2-631.

NEVILL, FRANCIS, left will in (1725) and in it mentions JAMES COLLINS and his wife MARY 1-64.

NEWBERN, ELIZABETH left will in (1823) names son NICHOLAS and others; HARDY WHITE was a witness 2-534.

NEWBOLD, MIRIAM was the daughter of RALPH FLETCHER in (1785) 3-171.

NEWBORN, MOSES. His estate divided in (1767) & also that of EZEKIEL HARRELL 3-443; THOMAS NEWBORN was one of his orphans and was put under tuition of JOB HUNTER in (1769) 3-447.

NEWBY, BENJAMIN will in (1739) had sons JOSEPH and BENJAMIN and daughter SARAH 1-63.

NEWBY, EDWARD left will in (1717) and mentions his brother WILLIAM NEWBY 1-64.

NEWBY, ELIZABETH, was the sister of WILLIAM TROTTER in (1729) 1-78.

NEWBY, EXUM, was the son of THOMAS NEWBY, who in will (1793) mentions his grandson EXUM WHITE and son in law JOSIAH WHITE 3-180.

NEWBY FAMILY. Wills 3-179, 3-180, 3-344.

NEWBY, FRANCIS married HULDA HONEYCUT and had MARGARET (b. 1728) and ROBERT, MARK and MIRAM NEWBY 3-390.

NEWBY, GABRIEL in his will is called "brother" by MATTHEW JORDAN in (1763) 3-175; his wife was MARY in (1695) 3-372; and she was perhaps MARY TOMS whom he married at some date before (1709) 1-679; a later GABRIEL NEWBY left will in (1824) and mentions his brother in law JOSEPH CANNON 3-344; he was a Deputy of Governor JOHN ARCHDALE in (1708) 2-302; met with the Assembly (1708) 1-454; signed proclamation in (1706-7) with WILLIAM GLOVER, JOHN HAWKINS, JOHN PORTER and FRANCIS FOSTER 3-261; left will (1735) and names wife MARY and sons JOSEPH, FRANCIS, JESSE, WILLIAM and SAMUEL NEWBY 1-64.

NEWBY, JAMES. His wife was SARAH in (1702) and they had son JAMES born that year 3-374.

NEWBY, JOSEPH, left will in PERQUIMANS (1735) and his wife was MARY 1-63.

NEWBY, MARY, was MARY JORDAN sister of MATTHEW and the wife of GABRIEL NEWBY 3-372; and a MARY NEWBY left will in (1822), with a JOSIAH TOWNSEND as executor 3-344; another MARY NEWBY left will (1740) and mentions son JOSEPH MAYO and son in law JOHN WILSON and niece ELIZABETH WINSLOW 1-63.

NEWBY, NATHAN left will in (1735) in PERQUIMANS with ZACHARIAH NIXON his executor 1-63.

NEWBY, SAMUEL, was the grandson of RICHARD TURNER in (1718) 1-79; and the son of MARY NEWBY will (1739) 1-63; his wife was ELIZABETH in (1741) and they had children born then 3-390; one left will in PERQUIMANS in (1737) in which he mentions his cousin THOMAS OVERMAN 1-63.

NEWBY, WILLIAM was the brother of EDWARD NEWBY and left will (1720) wife ANN 1-64.

NEWMAN, JOHN in (1716) sold lands to JOSHUA WAYLES, with ANTHONY and JOSEPH ALEXANDER as witnesses 1-621.

NEWSOME, DANIEL left will in (1811) and names son BENJAMIN NEWSOME 2-534.

NICHOLS FAMILY. Wills 2-348, 2-349; 2-533 -534.

NICHOLS, GEORGE, and his wife MARY had daughter REBECCA, born (1753) 3-368. See also 3-219.

NICHOLS, JOHN left will in (1762) wife SARAH, JOHN HILL and ROBERT WEBB witnesses - 2-348; another JOHN left will (1791) and REUBEN KNIGHT and WINNIFRED WHITE were the witnesses to his will. Name of his wife not mentioned 2-348.

NICHOLS, HUMPHREY was a Justice in BERTIE in (1757) 3-443; was Sheriff of BERTIE (1769) 3-446, 3-448.

NICHOLSON, ABIGAIL married in (1705) to NATHANIEL ALBERTSON 3-410.

NICHOLSON, ANN was the daughter of CHRISTOPHER NICHOLSON 3-215; and ANN NICHOLSON, relict of CHRISTOPHER NICHOLSON married RICHARD DORMAN 3-204, 3-211.

NICHOLSON, BENJAMIN, died leaving will in (1712) and mentioned brother NATHANIEL 1-74.

NICHOLSON, CHRISTOPHER, his wife was MARY (1717) 3-390; he was the son of CHRISTOPHER NICHOLSON 3-213; CHRISTOPHER NICHOLSON died in (1688) 3-365; and he had a daughter married JOSEPH SUTTON 3-200; the father of CHRISTOPHER NICHOLSON was EDMUND NICHOLSON 3-200; he had a daughter ELIZABETH NICHOLSON 3-201; the one in PERQUIMANS died leaving will in (1723) with JAMES NEWBY and SOLOMON and RICHARD POOL witnesses 1-356.

NICHOLSON, EDMUND, was the father of CHRISTOPHER NICHOLSON 3-200.

NICHOLSON FAMILY. Births 3-211; wills 1-356, & births also 3-208.

NICHOLSON, JOSEPH, died in CURRITUCK in (1697) with brothers JOHN, BENJAMIN, SAMUEL, NATHANIEL and CHRISTOPHER 1-356.

NICHOLSON, JOSIAH, died in CURRITUCK in (1750) and named children 1-356.

NICHOLSON, HANNAH, was the daughter of SAMUEL NICHOLSON 3-218; one HANNAH died in (1678) 3-365; and one was a daughter of CHRISTOPHER NICHOLSON 3-201; a HANNAH NICHOLSON married STEPHEN SCOTT in (1721) 3-410; and a HANNAH was the wife of JOSEPH NICHOLSON 3-367.

NICHOLSON, NATHANIEL married SARAH HARRIS the daughter of THOMAS and his wife DIANA 3-274; they had a son NATHANIEL who was born in (1716), SAMUEL born (1722) and JONATHAN born (1730) 3-390, 3-391; an earlier SAMUEL married ELIZABETH CHARLES (1688) 3-203; NATHANIEL died in (1731) leaving will 1-63.

NICHOLSON, SAMUEL, and wife ELIZABETH had daughter IDA born (1694) 3-367; a SAMUEL married ELIZABETH CHARLES (1688) 3-203; he left will in (1727) and named son in law JOHN ANDERSON 1-64.

NICHOLSON, SAMUEL THORNE was the son of a BLAKE BAKER NICHOLSON of HALIFAX COUNTY, N. C. who married LUCY THORNE 2-604.

NICHOLSON, SARAH was relict of THOMAS NICHOLSON and died leaving will (1787) and mentions a son THOMAS NICHOLSON 3-181.

NICHOLSON, SOPHIA, was the daughter of a SARAH SMITH left will (1721) 1-76.

NICHOLSON, THOMAS was a son of CHRISTOPHER 3-215 he had a wife MARY in (1733) 3-391; and another THOMAS had wife SARAH (1774) 3-391; a THOMAS witnessed the will of JOHN TROTTER in (1768) with WILLIAM BOND 3-191.

NICHOLSON, WILLIAM was the brother of a MARY TOMS, widow in (1713) 1-79.

NIMMO, JAMES, of NORFOLK COUNTY, VA. witnessed a deed to PETER MELBOURN in (1726) 1-445.

NIXON, CHRISTIAN, married ABRAHAM WHITE in (1870) in CHOWAN COUNTY 2-422.

NIXON, DELIGHT witnessed the will of JOHN PETTYJOHN in CHOWAN in (1832) whose daughter POLLY PETTYJOHN married a RAY (REA) 2-19; she left will (1801) 3-343

NIXON, DEMARIS, married JOHN PIERCE in the year (1699) 3-408.

NIXON FAMILY. Wills 3-343.

NIXON, JESSE married ABSILIA PRIVOTT (1869) in CHOWAN COUNTY 2-420.

NIXON, MARY FRANCES (POLLY) married CHRISTOPHER C. RAY (REA) in CHOWAN in (1840) 2-90.

NIXON, PHINEAS and wife MARY (1741) 3-390.

NIXON, RICHARD and WILLIAM BRYAN were CHURCH WARDENS in CRAVEN COUNTY in (1744)2-304.

NIXON, SAMUEL had a son in law HENRY COPELAND mentioned in his will (1815); and he had a daughter PENINAH NIXON and a "brother" WILLIAM JONES 3-343.

NIXON, ZACHARIAH married ELIZABETH NICHOLSON in (1739) their children 3-390; he was the executor of the will of NATHAN NEWBY in (1735) 1-63.

NOBILITY - ORDERS OF IN NORTH CAROLINA - By WADDY THOMPSON and JOSEPH McLEAN 1-584, to 1-588.

NORCOM, CORNELIUS, died in (1744) and he was a schoolmate of RICHARD and ALEXANDER HOUGHTON 1-455.

NORCOM FAMILY. Wills 2-14.

NORCOM, JOHN was Master of the Schooner POLLY C. in (1775) 1-436; he received a land grant in (1782) adjoining the lands of JOHN BAPTIST BEASLEY 1-22; also a land grant on YOPPIM RIVER 1-14; he was twice married and left will in (1728) and gives names of children 1-64; received a land grant in (1795) at the head of PARADISE SWAMP 1-24; one died about (1754) and JASPER SPRUILL and his wife ANNA were the executors 1-456.

NORCOM, JOSEPH, witnessed the will of SARAH DECROW in (1795) 3-169.

NORCOM, MARY was the wife of ABRAHAM WARREN of LITTLE RIVER 1-84; she left will in PERQUIMANS in (1718) and mentions her grandson ABRAHAM WARREN 1-64.

NORCOM, THOMAS and wife MARY lived in BERKELEY PRECINCT in (1696) 3-368.

NORCOM, WILLIAM was the son of THOMAS NORCOM and his wife MARY and was born May 31, (1696) in BERKELEY PRECINCT 3-368.

NORFLEET, ABRAHAM, was the son of JOHN NORFLEET who was the son of JAMES, who had brothers MARMADUKE and ELISHA NORFLEET who were in NANSEMOND COUNTY, Virginia, in (1695); JAMES grandfather of ABRAHAM died in CHOWAN COUNTY N. C. in (1732) 2-313; ABRAHAM NORFLEET, son of ABRAHAM, called "SR" died in CHOWAN leaving will (1784) and sons ABRAHAM, ISAAC, BENJAMIN and ELISHA, and daughters MARY & SARAH and wife SARAH, THOMAS HINESLEY and JACOB GORDON witnesses 2-13.

NORFLEET, ELISHA, was the brother of JAMES NORFLEET and ABRAHAM NORFLEET of NANSEMOND CO. VA. in (1695) 2-313; he is said to be the father of JAMES NORFLEET, father of WILLIAM and JAMES ELISHA NORFLEET 2-313; one ELISHA NORFLEET died in CHOWAN in (1811) with sons THOMAS, WILLIAM, ELISHA BENNETT and a JOHN PARKER NORFLEET and several daughters named 2-14.

NORFLEET, ISAAC was the father of ROBERT NOR - FLEET who died in (1872) leaving sons LEON, EDGAR and ROBERT NORFLEET 2-313; a later ISAAC married CHRISTIAN WARD daughter of a JAMES WARD who died in (1843) and had children SALLIE and MARGARET NORFLEET 2-552.

NORFLEET, JACOB, died in GATES COUNTY in (1780) and had son KINCHEN NORFLEET and a brother ABRAHAM NORFLEET 2-62.

NORFLEET, JAMES, was brother of ABRAHAM and MARMADUKE NORFLEET of Nansemond County, Va. in (1695) 2-313; he died in (1732) leaving will and named sons THOMAS and JOHN, wife MARY & daughters MARY, MARGARET, SARAH and PHILLISIA 1-64.

NORFLEET, JOHN, was the son of JAMES who died in (1732) 2-313, 1-64; he bought lands on THICKET SWAMP in (1734) from JOHN POWELL and wife HESTER, of PERQUIMANS 3-126; in (1738) he again bought an acre of land from JOHN POW - ELL, with JAMES SUMNER and SAMUEL POWELL as witnesses (GATES COUNTY) 1-284.

NORFLEET, KINCHEN, the son of JACOB, died GATES COUNTY in (1849) with sons MARMADUKE, SETH, JAMES and JOHN NORFLEET, daughters NANCY JORDAN and SUSAN WALTON (He could have been a son of ISAAC who married CHRISTIAN WARD, and his son SETH named for SETH WARD) 2-52.

NORFLEET, MARMADUKE, brother of JAMES and ELISHA NORFLEET (Of Nansemond County, Va.) (1695) 2-313; one MARMADUKE died prior to (1750) in NORTHAMPTON County, N. C., married first, ELIZA GORDON, and had REUBEN and JAMES NORFLEET, then married, second, JUDITH RHODES and had JUDITH and MARGARET NORFLEET 2-506; his son REUBEN had son MARMADUKE 2-534; the MARMADUKE NORFLEET of HALIFAX died in (1762) but named no children, but sister ELIZABETH NORFLEET, father in law JAMES HOGAN and JOHN YOUNG and JOSHUA BELL'S children 1-63.

NORFLEET, MARMADUKE, son of REUBEN and grandson of MARMADUKE (1766-1815) married HANNAH RUFFIN and had LUCY, MARY, LOUISA, OLIVIA and MARMADUKE; the daughter LUCY married HON. WELDON N. EDWARDS, OLIVIA married THOMAS COX, and LOUISA married DAVID CLARK. See genealogy of the family, including that of REUBEN, his father 2-606.

NORFLEET, REUBEN was the son of MARMADUKE NORFLEET and ELIZA GORDON; he was born (1730) and died (1801) and was the father of MARMADUKE and others 2-606; he married second MARY EXUM (nee FIGURES) and had daughter REBECCA who married THOMAS B. HILL, THOMAS married MARGARET ANDREWS and JOHN who married MARY GRANBERRY; THOMAS B. HILL and REBECCA NORFLEET had a son WHITMELL HILL 2-606.

NORFLEET, STEPHEN married SARAH GORDON, daughter of JOHN GORDON and his wife MISS BAKER and had SARAH WALTON NORFLEET who married WILLIAM RUFFIN SMITH of GATES COUNTY 2-635.

NORFLEET, THOMAS left will (1838) and named a daughter MARY wife of DR. RICHARD URQUHART and other children LOUISA, STEPHEN, MARGARET, FRANCES and THOMAS; WHITMELL J. HILL an executor 2-534; in (1731) an earlier THOMAS NORFLEET, of NANSEMOND COUNTY, Virginia, bought land in CHOWAN from BENJAMIN SMALL adjoining JOHN KING, DANIEL PUGH and his brother JOSEPH SMALL 2-450.

NORMAN, HENRY lived on the West side of SCUPERNONG (no date, but shortly after 1711) 3-268; he was a member of a jury with DENNIS MACLENDON and others in (1702) 1-610; his wife was ANNE and in (1700) they had a daughter MARY born 3-372; 97 years later a HENRY NORMAN left will in TYRRELL COUNTY & named wife SARAH and friend FANNY RAY, and with JAMES BLOUNT a witness 1-132.

NORVILLE, JAMES bought lands from LAWRENCE MARTIN in (1718) 1-626.

NORWOOD, EDWARD, at a court held in PERQUIMANS at the home of MRS. MARY SCOTT, he filed suit against one TAYLOR, which was dismissed with costs 3-429 (1688); in October following (1689) he was sued by ELIAS OSBORNE who obtained judgment; this was followed by another by NORWOOD against Osbourne, which was non-suited for OSBOURNE 3-430.

NORWOOD, GEORGE, died in NORTHAMPTON CO. N. C. in (1749) sons SAMUEL, NATHANIEL, WILLIAM, ELIZABETH, MARY and SARAH; WILLIAM WOOTEN a witness 1-357.

NORWOOD, JOHN, guardian of FREDERICK JAMES, son of ANN, 7 years old (1768) 3-445.

NORWOOD, THOMAS, died in CRAVEN COUNTY in (1758) will son WILLIAM and wife FRANCES; HENRY TRICE and SISELY NORWOOD witnesses 1-357.

NORWOOD, WILLIAM patented 300 acres in GRANVILLE COUNTY in (1746) 1-447; he left will CRAVEN County (1748) sister MARY LANE, brother THOMAS, nephew JOHN NORWOOD, niece MARY RAVEN and THOMAS PEARSON SR. and JR. witnesses 1-357.

NORRIS, WILLIAM, left will in PASQUOTANK (1724) 1-64.

NORTH, RICHARD, will (1805) BELSOM KITTRELL Executor 2-534.

N. C. GLEANINGS in ENGLAND 3-463.

N. C. TROOPS IN REVOLUTION 1-415 to 426.
NOWELL, RICHARD: WEST headrights claimed 3-139.

OAKMAN, SAMUEL and ROBERT PEYTON, JR. moved to NEW ENGLAND 2-305.

OATH OF ALLEGIANCE. Copy of same required, as signed by JAMES BLOUNT (1777) 2-305.

OATH OF OFFICE HOLDERS in early NORTH CAROLINA 1-367.

OATS, JAMES and wife ELIZABETH, had son JOHN born (1697) 3-369; when he made his will in(1703) he named only a son JOSEPH 1-64.

O'BRIEN, KENNEDY and JOHN JENURE were witnesses to a deed in (1729) 2-448.

OCRACOCK. Origin of the name 2-130, 2-131.

O'DANIEL, CHARITY (Dau. of FREDERICK) married DANIEL HERRING, husband of her sister SARAH, and was the mother of BENJAMIN and WHITFIELD HERRING 1-568. See 1-360.

O'DANIEL, FREDERICK, married CHARITY WHITFIELD a daughter of WILLIAM WHITFIELD, and cousin of BETSY WHITFIELD (dau. of MATTHEW) who married AARON DANIEL. For Genealogy of these O'DANIELS and WHITFIELDS see 1-567, 1-568.

O'DEARE, DENNIS, son of DENNIS O'DEARE and wife MARY, was born (1685) 3-213

ODOM, AARON bought 140 acres of land from THOMAS JERNIGAN of BERTIE about (1737) ANN ODOM is a witness 1-115.

ODOM, ABRAHAM, bought land from EDWARD DOWDY of NANSEMOND COUNTY, VA. in (1732) 2-452; also sold lands to EPAPRODITUS BOYCE, patented by ABRAHAM ODOM and EDWARD DOUGHTIE (1735) witnessed by JOSEPH VANN and CHRISTOPHER BOYCE 3-128; in (1735) he sold lands to HENRY DILLDAY which had been given him in the will of RICHARD ODOM in (1728) 1-113; and in (1737) ABRAHAM ODOM with JOHN MONTGOMERY witnessed deed of JOHN ODOM to WILLIAM JONES 1-114; and the same year ABRAHAM ODOM sold lands to WILLIAM JONES joining JOHN WINBORNE and EPHRAIM HUNTER and JACOB ODOM 1-114; his wife appears to have been ANN 2-257; he made deed to BOYCE in (1735) 1-108; and one to WILLIAM WATERS next to EDWARD DOUGHTIE in (1735) 3-129.

ODOM, ANN, in (1737) was witness to a deed made by THOMAS JERNIGAN to AARON ODOM 1-115.

ODOM, CHARLES left will in (1736) and named sons RICHARD and CHARLES and brother JOHN ODOM 1-64.

ODOM, CADER, mentioned as a legatee in the will of DARKIS VANN in GATES COUNTY in year(1793) 2-77.

ODOM, ELIZABETH, mentioned in will of DARKIS VANN in GATES COUNTY (1793) and was related to the LANGSTONS 2-77; witnessed deed JACOB ODOM to JOHN COLLINS in (1717) 1-618; she was a daughter of RICHARD ODOM 1-360.

ODOM, JACOB, received land grant (1738) in fact two of them 1-19; and one in (1749) 1-20; his wife was SUSANNA and they sold lands to JOHN COLLINS (1717) 1-618; sold land to WILLIAM GATLING next to MOSES HARE (1733) 3-128; was son of RICHARD ODOM and had brothers JOHN, AARON and ABRAHAM 1-360.

ODOM, JOHN, sold lands bequeathed to him by his father RICHARD ODOM to ANDREW ROSS (1735) at mouth of ROBERT ROGERS BRANCH 1-109; in (1727) he and his wife SUSANNAH made a deed to JOHN COLLINS, witnessed by RICHARD ODOM, JACOB ODOM, JR. and SUSANNAH ODOM JR. 2-443; he received a land grant in (1692) which he sold to NICHOLAS STALLINGS of NANSEMOND COUNTY, VA. 1-292,1-89; about (1737) he sold lands to EPAPRODITUS JONES in GATES COUNTY, deed witnessed by WILLIAM & LEONARD LANSTON 1-116; about (1720) he sold land to MOSES HARE 2-607; in his will(1741) he names children, JOHN, RICHARD, CHARLES, MARTHA, ANN, LYDIA and EDY ODOM 1-64; he & wife SUSANNAH sold land to MOSES ODOM (of NANSEMOND COUNTY, Virginia), with JOHN COLLINS a witness 1-618; he was on the Quit Rent Roll of ALBEMARLE PRECINCT before the year (1700) 1-304.

ODOM, JOHN, JR. bought a tract of land adjoining JAMES BOON, from PETER GRAY in (1720) 2-608.

ODOM, MATTHEW sold land in (1730) to MARY BARNES adjoining the lands of HENRY KING 2-610.

ODOM, MOSES, of NANSEMOND COUNTY VA., obtained a grant of land on BEAVER DAM SWAMP in (1716), with JOHN COLLINS mentioned 1-618.

ODOM, MOSES, JR. in (1747) lived on a road to where ROBERT ROGERS formerly lived by an old plantation where SIMON DANIEL once lived on CHOWAN RIVER 1-450.

ODOM, RICHARD, owned lands (1725) next to those sold by WILLIAM HUGHES to JOSEPH VANN in GATES COUNTY 2-291; he died leaving will in CHOWAN in (1729) and named sons RICHARD, JOHN, JACOB, AARON and ABRAHAM and daughters ANN, SARAH, ELIZABETH and JANE and granddaughter ANN VANN; EDWARD VANN evidently married one of his daughters 1-360.

ODOM, THOMAS proved his rights in (1744) and mentioned wife SARAH, SUSANNAH and JACOB ODOM 2-624.

OGILBY, PATRICK, of CHOWAN, sued JOHN SALE of NEW ENGLAND in (1720) 1-444; he left will in EDENTON in (1726) and mentions a daughter MARY CHARLTON 1-65.

OLDEST LAND GRANT in North CAROLINA issued to JOHN VARNHAM at SKINNER'S POINT 1-3.

OLDEST DEED to LANDS recorded at HERTFORD in (1661) 3-423.

OLD TOWN CREEK, on the land of COL. THOMAS POLLOCK, and the land of COTTON ROBINSON was also there 1-5.

OLDNER, RICHARD married the widow of TREDLE KEEFE in (1725) 2-470.

OLDS, JAMES, married ELIZABETH EVINS in (1694) 3-406.

OLD, JOHN, probably married the daughter of RICHARD FRENCH before (1712) 1-44; he was a member of an inquisition at the house of GABRIEL NEWBY (1707) 3-278; he and his wife SUSAN had a son JOHN born in (1705) and the record of his birth appears in the Register of BERKELEY PRECINCT 3-376.

OLD, THOMAS mentioned in the will of THOMAS VEN-DERMULLEN in (1720) 1-80.

CLIVER, AARON, with ISAAC PARKER witnessed deed by PETER PARKER and wife ELIZABETH to JOHN WELCH in (1717) 1-616, 1-617.

OLIVER, ANDREW, looked after the tuition of one LEWIS DARBY, then 2 years old (1771) 3-450; in (1747) long before the above ANDREW was deceased, and JAMES CAMPBELL was appointed to sell his property 2-630; he died leaving will in (1793) wife MARY ANNE, and had children including daughter SARAH MOORE 2-349.

OLIVER, DAVID, was brother of THOMAS OLIVER will (1765) with JOHN KITTRELL an executor 2-349; and ANDREW OLIVER had a son DAVID 2-349.

OLIVER, JOHN, died in (1774), will witnessed by JOSEPH JORDAN and THOMAS EDWARDS 2-349; another JOHN died (1793) wife MARY sons MARTIN MALACHI and SHADRACK OLIVER 2-349, 2-350.

OLIVER, THOMAS, left will (1765) 2-349.

OLIVER'S FERRY in BERTIE mentioned (1770) 3-448.

OLIVER, ISAAC will (1732) friend EDWARD SALTER is mentioned 1-64.

OLIVER, MOSES, will (1728) children of CHARLES RICKETTS are named 1-64.

OLIVER, NATHANIEL and wife MARTHA, of BOSTON in NEW ENGLAND execute deed to OLIVER NOYES in (1719) 2-106, 2-107.

O'NEAL, CHARLES left a deed in the place of will in (1711) sister DORCAS, MARY and DANIEL O'NEAL named administrators 1-64.

O'NEAL, JOHN married ELIZABETH TOMS in JULY in (1794) JOSEPH ALBERTSON surety 3-421.

O'NEAL, MICHAEL, SR. and his wife DEBORAH (1697) proved their rights 2-299; he and his wife DEBORAH appeared in court as witnesses(1697) 1-444; he died leaving will in CURRITUCK in (1721-2) and names children CHARLES, MICHAEL, MARY, ELIZABETH, SARAH WALKER, DEBORAH PELL, and REBECCA PARKER 1-64; about (1697) he had a daughter ANN O'NEAL not mentioned in will 2-299.

O'NEAL, PETER, left will in CHOWAN in (1803) his wife KESIA, sons CHARLES and TULLY and daughters KATHERINE and ELLENDER, with JAMES & EDMUND JONES witnesses 2-15.

O'NEAL, WILLIAM called the grandson of MARY Mc-CLANAHAN in (1813) with JAMES COLLINS the husband of his aunt ELIZABETH 3-342.

ONSLOW COUNTY, N. C. Account issued against the home of GOV. GABRIEL JOHNSTON in (1742)2-203

O'QUINN, PATRICK died leaving will in (1746) his wife MARTHA O'QUINN Executrix 2-627.

ORDINARIES. Rates to be charged by those in N. CAROLINA (1743-1746) 2-189, 2-190.

ORENDELL, EDWARD and JOHN STEPNEY were witnesses to deed of WILLIAM CROPLEY to CORNELIUS LEARY to certain lands situated on REEDY BRANCH in the year (1738) 3-131.

ORMES, SAMUEL and NATHANIEL DUKENFIELD were to keep a FERRY in (1747) with THOMAS BARKER and THOMAS WHITMELL as their security and bondsmen 2-629.

ORMOND, WHYNOTT, was granted a license as a lawyer in BERTIE in (1771) 3-449; but back in (1747) a certain WHYRIOTT OR-MOND appears to have been the KING'S AT-TORNEY in BERTIE 2-630.

ORR, HUGH in (1775) was Master of the Brig EX-PERIMENT 2-465.

OSBORNE, ELIAS brought suit against EDWARD NORWOOD in (1689) 3-430; and preceding that NORWOOD had sued OSBORNE, but lost his case 3-429.

OSBORNE, OBEDIAH, died leaving will in ONSLOW COUNTY in (1758) and named wife ELIZABETH and a son JOHN J. OSBORNE, EDWARD and E. WARD witnesses 1-360.

OTWAY, JOHN was a witness with ABRAHAM ODOM to a deed of gift from HENRY HACKLEY to THOM-AS HARRIS in (1728) 3-129.

OUTLAND, JOSEPH left will in (1790) with FOSTER TOMS and SAMUEL ADNDERSON Executors 3-182.

OUTLAW, DAVID, records his mark or brand in BERTIE in (1769) 3-446.

OUTLAW, EDWARD brought suit against WILLIAM DOWERS in BERTIE in (1725) 2-470.

OUTLAW, ELIZABETH and ANN MIZELL were sisters of FRANCES BRITTAIN will (1810) 2-501.

OUTLAW, FRANCES and JOSEPH OUTLAW witnessed the will of JAMES WILLIFORD in (1825) & GEORGE OUTLAW was Executor 2-553.

OUTLAW, GEORGE, left will in (1825) and mentions a daughter MARGARET E. LEGGETT 2-535; Executor of JAMES WILLIFORD 2-553; 2-379.

OUTLAW, JAMES left will in (1808) and mentions brothers AARON, LEWIS, JOSHUA and JOHN A. OUTLAW 3-535.

OUTLAW, JOSEPH BRYAN, with J. W. WARBURTON was witness to the will of MARY BRYAN in (1810) 2-500.

OUTLAW, RALPH, left will in (1790) and named his children DAVID, EDWARD, GEORGE, ELIZABETH MIRES, MARY RAY, PRISCILLA WATFORD, CHARI-TY ALEXANDER, grandson JOHN RAY, and his brother GEORGE OUTLAW 2-349. (ANDREW SOUTH a witness).

OVERMAN, CHARLES died in PASQUOTANK (1756) and in his will names wife ANN and children & grandchildren including ARMOUR family members, with JOSEPH MOORE a witness 1-359, 1-360; a later CHARLES left will in (1774) with wife and son CHARLES Executors 3-131.

OVERMAN, JACOB died leaving will in PASQUOTANK in (1715) wife DOROTHY sons EPHRIAM, JACOB, CHURCH and WILLIAM HAIG, with THOMAS WOOD-LEY a witness 1-359; a later JACOB died & left will (1786) naming wife and children and mentions "three children of my son JACOB, deceased"; wife RACHEL and son JOHN OVERMAN executors 3-131, 3-132.

OVERMAN, JOHN, was the son of THOMAS OVERMAN & was born in (1733); he married HANNAH SCOTT in (1755) and had AARON OVERMAN born (1756) SARAH born (1759) THOMAS born (1761) MIRIAM born (1764) JOHN born (1767) JESSE born in (1769) and MARY OVERMAN born (1772) 3-391; he witnessed the will of WILLIAM ARNOLD in (1774) 2-163.

OVERMAN, JOSEPH, died leaving will in PASQUOTANK in (1739) in which he mentioned NATHANIEL MARTIN and his own brothers EPHRAIM, NATHAN and JESSE OVERMAN 1-64.

OVERTON, CHRISTOPHER died leaving will in (1819) wife RACHEL, son CHRISTOPHER and other legatees; Sparkman Stone and JAMES LEWIS witnesses 2-535.

OVERTON, ELIJAH, married ANN FOREHAND in (1785) with ROBERT DEEL a witness 3-418.

OVERTON, JAMES had a son NATHANIEL in (1747) committed to the care of THOMAS CLIFTON 2-627 & a JAMES S. OVERTON married PATIENCE RAY(1794) 2-368.

OVERTON, JOHN with JOHN PARKER was a witness to a deed by JANE PARKER in (1735) 3-127.

OWENDELL, EDWARD (See ORENDELL) sold lands to JOHN BRAVEBOY before (1732) 2-452.

OWEN, FRANCIS, son of WILLIAM OWEN and his wife DIANA OWEN was born in (1686) 3-214

OWENS, ALSIE, left will in (1814) had daughter DELIE who married a PAGE and her children are mentioned in the will as those of NATHAN PAGE also son in law(?) SIMON PIERCE 2-535.

OWEN, JOHN died leaving will in (1779) wife ELIZABETH and children AGATHA, WILLIAM, JOHN and ELIZABETH OWEN 2-350; an older JOHN died in TYRRELL in (1750) leaving sons ZACHARIAH, THOMAS and JOHN and his wife ANN 1-361.

OWEN, WILLIAM "late of the port of BATH in North Carolina, bachelor, deceased"; administration (1734-5) to his uncle THOMAS WALKER, ELIZABETH OWEN spinster, sister and next of kin 3-467; the wife of one WILLIAM OWEN was DIANA 3-214.

OXLEY, JOHN in (1717) bought land from DAVID ATKINS and his wife ELIZABETH adjoining the land of JOHN JONES and the DEVIL'S WOODYARD 1-617; JOHN OXLEY SR. died in (1767) in BERTIE; sons GEORGE and JOHN OXLEY and wife OLIVE; son in law a JOHN PARROTE and wife ELIZABETH; son in law JOHN RAY and wife ELIZABETH; son in law WILLIAM FLEETWOOD and JAMES BAKER and a grand-daughter SUSANNA FLEETWOOD; WILLIAM GRANT and SARAH LANGSTON witnesses2-350; had charge of orphans of JONATHAN MILLER in (1747) 2-630; owned lands next to GABRIEL COSANDS in (1737) 3-135; a JOHN OXLEY, orphan in BERTIE (1767) was ward of CHRISTOPHER HARRISON 3-443; in (1732) he sold land to STEPHEN ARCHER adjoining the land of JOHN JONES and RICHARD LEWIS, the witnesses were WILLIAM HARDING JONES and FREDERICK JONES and WILLIAM LILES 2-450.

OXLEY, JOHN JR. married FANNY SHOULDERS (1799) with AARON SWAIN security 2-373.

OXLEY, SARAH, married LODOVICK REDDITT in BERTIE COUNTY in (1794) 2-369.

NASH FAMILY. Wheeler (p. 111) says ABNER NASH was born in PRINCE EDWARD County, Va. He was a brother of FRANCIS NASH and of THOMAS NASH (2-13). ABNER's first wife was the widow of ARTHUR DOBBS and his second wife a MISS JONES of the WILLIE JONES family. WILLIE JONES married a daughter of COL. JOSEPH MONTFORT and his wife PRISCILLA HILL, daughter of COL. BENJAMIN HILL, who was a son of HENRY APPLEWHITE HILL, son of THOMAS HILL and MARY MARSHALL (Daughter of HUMPHREY MARSHALL). COL. THOMAS HILL, son in law of HUMPHREY MARSHALL was the father of HENRY APPLEWHITE HILL, ISAAC HILL and THOMAS HILL, the latter the father of HUMPHREY HILL. ISAAC and THOMAS HILL of this family settled in KING & QUEEN COUNTY, VA., the home of HUMPHREY HILL, whose descendants married into the BAYLORS, GWATHNEYS, DABNEYS and other old families, not to neglect the WALKER FAMILY. ISAAC HILL (uncle of COL. BENJAMIN HILL, of North Carolina) had at least three very interesting children: SUSANNA HILL who married BENJAMIN CLEMENT (d. 1780); WILLIAM HILL, married (1) CATHERINE (2) PRISCILLA EMBREE (3) SARAH LANIER (See 3-310, 3-311, 3-312, 3-313 of this record); and MARY HILL married COL. CLEMENT READ, of VIRGINIA. ISAAC HILL died in CAROLINE COUNTY, Virginia in 1734. His wife is said to have been a MARGARET JENNINGS.

COL. CLEMENT READ who married MARY HILL belonged to an old Colonial Family in YORK COUNTY, VIRGINIA, if the genealogical accounts are to be credited, but in his own right he had a very distinguished career as a lawyer in MECKLENBERG and PRINCE EDWARD Counties. It was into his interesting family that no less than THREE of the NASH FAMILY married. His children and the names of their several spouses were as follows:

(1) MARY READ married COL. THOMAS NASH who went to North Carolina and joined his distinguished brother, who became the first Speaker of the Senate and the second Governor elected by the Legislature in 1781. He died in CHOWAN in 1769 (2-13).

(2) MARGARET READ married COL. PAUL CARRINGTON, well known in the Virginia annals.

(3) COL. CLEMENT READ, JR. married MARY NASH, a sister of GOV. ABNER NASH.

(4) COL. ISAAC READ married SARAH EMBREE, relative of the wife of WILLIAM HILL.

(5) COL. THOMAS READ married ELIZABETH NASH, another sister of GOV. ABNER NASH.

(6) EDWARD READ married (1) MISS LEWIS (2) PAULINA CABELL, of an old family.

(7) ANNE READ married (1) WILLIAM JAMESON (2) COL. RICHARD ELLIOTT.

(8) CAPT. JONATHAN READ married JANE LEWIS, of the LEWIS FAMILY of "THE BYRD" over in GOOCHLAND COUNTY, Virginia.

MISS JONES, Governor ABNER NASH'S second wife, through her connection with COL. JOSEPH MONTFORT traced her ancestry back to THOMAS HILL and his wife MARY MARSHALL, while the wife of his brother THOMAS NASH and the husbands of two of his sisters, could trace their ancestry likewise back to the same source. This THOMAS HILL appears to have been a son of JOHN HILL, a son of THOMAS HILL and his wife MARY PERCEY , daughter of ABRAHAM PERCEY, who married second THOMAS BUSHROD.

PACE, JOHN, left will (1726-7) and mentioned a daughter MARY MELTON, and JOHN BRENT was a witness 1-67.

PADERICK, JOHN was Master of the schooner WALKER in (1775) 1-436.

PAGE, THOMAS, will in BERTIE (1786) sons THOMAS, SOLOMON and JOSHUA and SAMUEL PAGE'S plantation, and daughters 3-351.

PAGETT, EDWARD, was granted land in (1716) on YOPPIM RIVER 1-16; also a grant in (1720) 1-9; was an executor of the will of DANIEL HARRISON in (1726) 1-50; two different records of his will (1727) both mention wife MARGARET and brother SAMUEL PAGETT 1-68 & 1-69.

PAGETT, JAMES. His wife was SUSANNAH and they had JOHN PAGETT born (1722), JAMES born in (1724), ELIZABETH born (1726), SUSANNAH born (1729) SAMUEL born (1731), PRUDENCE born (1734), SARAH born (1737), LEAH born (1740) and JOAB PAGETT born (1743) 3-391, 3-392.

PAGETT JOHN, had grant of land near HENRY BONNER and JOHN JONES 1-13; sold land to RICHARD FULLINGTON in (1730) 2-448.

PAGETT, MARGARET (widow) made deed of gift to her children SAMUEL, WILLIAM, ELIZABETH and MARY in (1729) 2-447.

PAGETT, SAMUEL had land grant on OLD TOWN CREEK in (1728) 1-12; SAMUEL died in (1745) in CHOWAN 1-457; he left four children, three of whom were ELIZABETH, PENELOPE and SARAH 2-470; he deeded lands to THOMAS LOVICK in (1729) 2-447; sold land to W. ASHLEY adjoining WILLIAM WOODLEY in (1733) 3-126; & his widow was under 21 when he died, and she then married JAMES QUINN 2-470.

PAGETT, WILLIAM, was granted land in (1713) next to CHARLES GAVIN 1-15; he and his wife SARAH sold lands to LUKE WHITE in (1737) on Rockyhock Creek 3-135.

PAIGE, NICHOLAS, and ANNA PAIGE, his wife of NEW ENGLAND, their will (1703) 1-103, 1-106.

PAINE, JOHN (See PAYNE also) owned lands in (1726) next to THOMAS JONES 1-19.

PAINE, SAMUEL, his land joined that of THOMAS WILLIAMS and JOHN JONES 1-14.

PALIN, ANN, wife of HENRY PALIN, who died (1699) leaving will 1-363.

PALIN, HENRY died in (1699) leaving will in it he mentions wife ANN and sons JOHN and THOMAS PALIN, also RICHART HEATT and wife ELIZABETH and others 1-363; he died Feb.4 (1699) 1-443; he had been sued by WILLIAM GASKINS in ALBEMARLE in (1697) 1-611.

PALIN, JAMES in (1728) was the son in law of one THOMAS PARRIS 1-68.

PALIN, JOHN, ESQ. " Our Chief Justice" in (1732) 2-129; he was Chief Justice in CHOWAN PRECINCT in (1731) 1-456, and was overseer will of HENRY WARREN in (1716) 1-63.

PALIN, THOMAS, of PASQUOTANK will in (1733) sons HENRY and THOMAS and daughters ANN and MARY; one married JOHN ROSS and it appears her name was GLAISTER, also 1-67; his name was mentioned in (1718) in the will of JOSEPH GLAISTER 1-46; and he was a brother of GEORGE ELLIS (1721) 1-42.

PALMER, JAMES and his wife KATHERINE had a daughter ELIZABETH born (1694) 3-367.

PALMER, PAUL and JOHN PARKER were witnesses to deed by NATHAN MIERS (1726) 2-447; he was REV. PAUL PALMER and his license as a minister was issued in (1738) 2-195; in (1734) he was witness to a deed from ROBERT WILSON to WILLIAM COTEREL 3-125; he married JOANNA PETERSON the widow of THOMAS PETERSON who owned the town site of EDENTON; after his marriage he sold this land to JAMES PALIN, of BOSTON, according to the report of a lawsuit 3-284.

PALMER, ROBERT, left will in (1740) named his wife MARY ANN and sons ROBERT, BENJAMIN and JOSEPH, and grandsons ROBERT and THOMAS PENDLETON, grand-daughter NANCY PENDLETON and grandson EVAN JONES; also daughter SARAH wife of THOMAS PENDLETON in PASQUOTANK 1-65.

PALMER, SAMUEL was related to the SCARBOROUGH LARKERS and WORTHENS 1-57; he died in (1739) 3-405.

PALMER, THOMAS, died in (1720) leaving will in which he mentions only son THOMAS and daughter MARY 1-68.

PAMPTICO. Petition relating to a road running to 3-286.

PAQUINIT, MICHAEL, left will in CARTERET (1745) mentions nephews JAMES and MICHAEL 1-364; the son MICHAEL left will CARTERET (1772) named wife MARY, and children including a daughter CHARITY 1-364.

PARCOT, JACOB, will in BERTIE in (1738) with William Fleetwood and EDWARD RAZOR his executors 1-66.

PARGITER, WILLIAM, was an uncle of GREGORY GARFOOT (1702) 1-45.

PARK FAMILY. Wills of 3-346.

PARKS, SAMUEL, left will in CHOWAN in (1769) wife ELIZABETH and sons JOHN, DANIEL and SAMUEL, daughters MARY and ELIZABETH; the witnesses: E. CUMMINGS, NATHAN PARKER & JEREMIAH CANNON 2-18.

PARK, NATHAN left will in (1796) and names his brothers HUMPHREY and JOSEPH PARK, and the witnesses were EZEKIEL LANE and SARAH PARK SR. 3-183.

PARKER, ANN married ISAAC WILLSON in (1701) at a Quaker meeting at the house of FRANCIS TOMES 3-409.

PARKER, AZARIAH, and TIMOTHY JOYS were the owners of lands that joined lands patented by JOHN REYNOLDS in the month of OCTOBER in (1716) 1-16.

PARKER, DANIEL left will in GATES COUNTY (1780) mentions sons DEMPSEY, ISAAC, ROBERT & LUKE PARKER (and LUKE had son DANIEL) daughters SARAH HORTON, RUTH RIDDICK and JUDAH GRIFFIN — wife MARY; witnesses ELISHA and PETER PARKER, THOMAS FRYER and JACOB SUMNER 2-63; in (1734) a DANIEL PARKER bought lands from FRANCIS PUGH next to WILLIAM SPITES and JOHN KING, witnessed by ABRAHAM HILL and ISAAC HUNTER 3-131; a DANIEL married PATSY JOHNSON in BERTIE in (1805) 2-377.

PARKER, DEMPSEY (son of DANIEL) left will in GATES COUNTY in (1808) and had son MILES PARKER and daughters ABIGAIL, BETHANY, SALLY and EDITH PARKER; GOODMAN kin 2-64.

PARKER, ELISHA, left will in GATES COUNTY (1793) had sons PETER, JOHN, JESSE and ELISHA PARKER, daughters PEGGY, CHRISTIAN and NANCY & grandson JOHN GRIFFIN 2-63; the son ELISHA died in CHOWAN (1830) wife Elizabeth and sons JOB, JACOB and PETER and daughters 2-18; ELISHA patented lands in (1790) 1-23; he married ELIZABETH AVERY in (1790) with a ROBERT AVERY on his bond; an earlier ELISHA PARKER was administrator of JOHN PARKER in (1759) 1-451.

PARKER, ELIZABETH was the wife, and another one the daughter of ELISHA PARKER of CHOWAN in (1830) 2-18. See also 2-470, 3-435, 1-616.

PARKER FAMILY. Wills 2-17, 2-18, 2-63, 2-64, 2-65, 2-538, 1-362 (Early ones FRANCIS, 1746, WILLIAM 1751, HENRY 1733, THOMAS 1753, THOMAS 1717, AZRICOM 1738, JOSEPH 1749, RICHARD 1749, MARY 1753, SIMON 1750, WILLIAM 1750, PETER 1750 and 1722 all 1-362 et seq.)

PARKER, FRANCIS and WILLIAM PARKER were sons of THOMAS PARKER of CHOWAN in (1716) 1-617; he left will in EDGECOMBE (1746) and had sons FRANCIS, JOSEPH and SIMON PARKER, daughters ELIZABETH FOREMAN, CHARITY BRETT and CATHERINE HODGES 1-362; a later FRANCIS left will in GATES COUNTY (1791) sons WILDAY and MILES with WILLIAM GOODMAN executor 2-63 (See DEMSEY PARKER).

PARKER, HENRY, died in CRAVEN in (1734) wife CATHERINE and god-son HENRY GREEN; JOHN BRYAN and BENJAMIN GRIFFIN witnesses 1-362.

PARKER, ISAAC, witnessed a deed with AARON OLIVER in (1717) from PETER PARKER and wife ELIZABETH to JOHN WELCH 1-617; ISAAC PARKER SR. left will in GATES (1802) sons JONATHAN, DANIEL and SAMUEL, daughters MARY and SARAH, ANN WILLIAMS, ZACHARIAH PARKER and DEMPSEY WILLIAMS, JR. also ISAAC PIPKIN 2-63.

PARKER, JACOB, married MARY BUNCH in (1828) in CHOWAN COUNTY, with PETER PARKER as security on the bond 1-560; he left will in CHOWAN in (1842), with JOHN BUSH and JAMES T. CANNON as witnesses 2-18.

PARKER, JAMES with WILLIAM PARKER and JAMES HUBBARD in (1734-5) witnessed the deed of MOSES HALL, of NANSEMOND COUNTY, Virginia, to JOHN HUBBARD 3-128; a later JAMES PARKER is mentioned as the son of WILLIAM PARKER, GATES COUNTY will in (1789), with brothers JOHN, WILLIAM, KEDAR and WILLIS PARKER; he had an uncle named AMOS PARKER also named 2-63.

PARKER, JANE (a widow) in (1722) sold lands to PAUL PHILLIPS in CHOWAN 2-443 (JOHN CHAMPION was a witness); in (1735) this widow made a deed to BENJAMIN EVANS lands adjoining JOHN OVERTON and JOHN PARKER 3-127; she appears to have been widow of THOMAS PARKER, and had sons JAMES and FRANCIS who were deceased in (1738) 1-284; she deeded lands to JOHN PARKER in (1739) witnessed by JAMES and PETER PARKER 3-135; in (1719) she bought lands from PETER PARKER, with THOMAS PARKER and ROBERT HICKS witnesses 2-515.

PARKER, JESSE, left will in GATES COUNTY in (1800) wife and two children not named in the will 2-63; one of them may have been the JESSE PARKER mentioned in will of JESSE WIGGINS in GATES in (1826) 2-80; the one who died (1800) may have been son of the ELISHA who left will (1793) 2-63.

PARKER, JOHN with PAUL PALMER was witness to a deed in (1726) 2-447; he was deceased in (1751) and ELISHA PARKER was his administrator 1-451; JOHN S. PARKER in (1800) was witness to will of SIMON STALLINGS in GATES COUNTY 2-75; JOHN SR. left will in (1803) had son SETH PARKER, and grandsons NATHAN and NOAH PARKER and daughter PENINAH NICHOLSON 3-346; in (1719) JOHN PARKER witnessed deed from JOHN JORDAN to PHILLIP MAGUIRE 1-628; JOHN patented lands next to PETER and THOMAS PARKER in (1715) 1-15; & in (1714) adjoining THOS PARKER, JOHN JORDAN and W. COPELAND 1-8; the JOHN who left will in GATES in (1825) had an oldest son ISAAC PARKER 2-64.

PARKER, JONATHAN bought land from FRANCIS PUGH in (1734) 3-127; in (1795) JONATHAN PARKER son of NATHAN, had daughters LEAH and MIRIAM PARKER 2-17 (He had sister RACHEL who married ARTHUR WOOTEN, also).

PARKER, JOB, left will in CHOWAN in (1812) his wife was ISABEL and he names his children and PENINAH MOORE wife of JOSEPH MOORE 2-18; he was the son of ELISHA PARKER who died in GATES in (1793) 2-63.

PARKER, JORDAN, with JOSEPH JONES witnessed the will of BRINKLEY KNIGHT in GATES COUNTY in (1852) 2-58.

PARKER, JOSEPH, married SARAH WELCH, the oldest daughter of JOHN WELCH, who died in (1730) 2-299; he was (or one was) the uncle of FRANCES LAWRENCE of BERTIE in (1770) 3-448; in (1742) he owned lands adjoining SAMUEL JOHNSTON 1-18; he was a brother of JOB PARKER and left will in CHOWAN in (1764), witnessed by NATHAN PARKER & JOSIAH and WILLIAM COPELAND 2-17; in (1798) JOSEPH PARKER left will in BERTIE COUNTY naming sons RICHARD, JOSEPH, THOMAS, REUBEN and JAMES, and daughters ANN, ELIZABETH KING (son in law JOHN HOBSON KING) and SARAH PARKER. His wife was AMELIA 2-537; in (1793) he was Executor will of LYDIA STONE 3-191

PARKER, LUKE, was the son of DANIEL PARKER who died in (1780) 2-63; it was perhaps a later LUKE PARKER who witnessed will of WILLIS THOMPSON in BERTIE in (1834) with SIMON D. RHEA (RAY) 2-550.

PARKER, NATHAN will in CHOWAN (1797) wife SARAH, son in law ARTHUR WOOTEN (Married RACHEL) & land in NORTHAMPTON COUNTY, bought of CHARLEY COUNCIL, son JONATHAN PARKER and grandsons JONATHAN and NATHAN WOOTEN, brother JOB PARKER and cousin JOSEPH PARKER; JOSEPH SCOTT, SR. and JR. witnesses 2-17; NATHAN PARKER received land grant East side Chowan River (1790) 1-23.

PARKER, NOAH, was grandson of JOHN PARKER, SR. who died (1803) leaving will naming his wife JAEL and children and grandchildren 3-346.

PARKER, PETER died in CHOWAN COUNTY in (1785) & named sons ELISHA, PETER, WILLIS, SETH and ISAAC PARKER; JACOB JORDAN and son PETER Executors 2-17; an earlier PETER with JOSEPH and JANE WICKER patented lands on BEAVERDAM and JUNIPER SWAMP in (1716) 1-16; in (1716) in and of NANSEMOND COUNTY, VA. he sold land to LEWIS WILLIAMS on CHOWAN RIVER 1-5; one married GRACE COPELAND in (1714) the daughter of WILLIAM COPELAND and wife CHRISTIAN 2-456; in (1717) a PETER and wife ELIZABETH sold land to JOHN WELCH the deed witnessed by AARON OLIVER and ISAAC PARKER 1-616,1-617; he and WILLIAM CRAWFORD were witnesses to a deed by JOHN EARLY in (1716) 1-615; the one with wife ELIZABETH died in (1720) sons JOHN, THOMAS, JOSEPH and daughters MARY and ANN 1-68; in (1706) PETER PARKER, of the UPPER PARISH of NANSEMOND COUNTY, bought land on the East side of CHOWAN RIVER, from WILLIAM WILLIAMS of the LOWER PARISH ISLE OF WIGHT COUNTY, Virginia, with JOHN PARKER, ROBERT SCOTT and HUMPHREY MARSHALL witnesses 1-93; he also bought land from ROBERT EVANS in (1720) 2-615; he made a deed to JEAN (JANE) PARKER (widow) in (1719) 2-615; in (1714-15) he bought land from RICHARD CHURCH and wife JANE through EDWARD HOWARD, with JOHN WILLIAMS, JOHN JORDAN and WILLIAM CRAWFORD as witnesses 1-293; he and his wife GRACE sold land to WILLIAM COPELAND in (1716) with JOHN and JANE JORDAN as witnesses 2-619; as PETER PARKER SR. in (1716) he sold land on W. Side of CHOWAN RIVER to RICHARD WILLIAMSON 1-294; PETER PARKER on a list of Tithables in CURRITUCK very early 3-257.

PARKER, REBECCA, was the daughter of MICHAEL O'NEAL, who died in (1721) 1-64.

PARKER, RICHARD was appointed a JUSTICE for the CHOWAN PRECINCT in (1731) 1-449; that same year he owned lands adjoining FRANCES HARRELL and RICHARD BAKER of NANSEMOND COUNTY, Virginia 2-450; his children in (1753) were RICHARD, JACOB, STEPHEN, FRANCIS and PATIENCE PARKER 2-268.

PARKER, ROBERT and wife HANNAH were the parents of ANN PARKER who married ISAAC WILLSON at the home of FRANCIS TOMES in (1700) 3-409.

PARKER, SAMUEL died leaving will in CHOWAN in (1811) wife SILVIA, son JOHN and several daughters named 2-17.

PARKER, SETH, died leaving will (1820) CHOWAN COUNTY, wife ELIZABETH, sons JESSE, NATHANIEL and SETH, daughters ELIZABETH and MARY and brother WILLIS PARKER; 2-18; he was the son of JOHN PARKER, SR. who died leaving a will in (1803) 3-346 (NOTE: No. He was son of PETER PARKER who died (1785) 2-17).

PARKER, THOMAS bought land from RICHARD FELTON in (1737) with JAMES GRIFFIN, SR. a witness 3-130; in (1716) he had sons WILLIAM and FRANCIS PARKER, with WILLIAM CRAWFORD and JOHN PARKER witnesses 1-617; he and THOMAS MUNS witnessed a deed by JOHN ARTHUR in (1712) 1-289; he executed a deed to JOSEPH JONES in (1738) in BERTIE 3-134; he had sons WILLIAM and FRANCIS and son in law BENJAMIN EVANS (1716) 1-617; he owned lands joining MOSES FOXWORTH 1-17; he left will in CHOWAN in (1762) names children PRISCILLA, SARAH, ABRAHAM, ABSOLOM, JUDITH, RUTH, ZILPHA, THOMAS and MARGARET; daughter PRISCILLA & JETHRO BENTON Executors, with WILLIAM and JAMES PARKER, JAMES HARRIS and JACOB NORFLEET witnesses 2-17.

PARKER, WILLIAM was a JUSTICE in CURRITUCK in (1729) 3-467; in (1719) he sold lands to a JAMES HUBBARD which had been granted to JOHN SMALL, with JAMES and JOHN BENTON and THOMAS PARKER as witnesses 3-126; he witnessed the will of JOHN BELL in CURRITUCK in (1706) 1-454.

PARKER, WILLIS, left will in CHOWAN in (1843) witnessed by THOMAS SATTERFIELD and JESSE PARKER 2-18; he was a brother of JAMES, JOHN, WILLIAM and KEDAR PARKER 2-63.

PARKER, ZACHARIAH was the son of ISAAC PARKER who died in GATES COUNTY in (1802) and left will 2-63.

PARRIS, GEORGE, an orphan. ELIZABETH CLAYTON to be his guardian 1-448.

PARRIS, JOHN, his wife MARGARET and some of their children 3-392.

PARRIS, SUSANNA. Affidavit and statement made by her 3-231, 3-232, 3-233.

PARRIS, THOMAS left will at EDENTON in (1738) wife SUSANNAH; son in law JAMES PALIN and WILLIAM WILLIAMS and wife SUSANNAH Executors 1-68; he was a brother in law of HENRY SPELLER in BERTIE 1-75; shipment to him from EMANUEL LOWE & CO. 3-271; he and his wife ANN of PERQUIMANS sold lands to THOMAS BETTERLY in (1718) which had been granted to EDWARD SMITHWICK in (1712) 1-628.

PARISH, JOHN, witnessed a deed of gift to SAMUEL HODGSON in (1737) 3-135; his wife was MARGERY, and his daughter ANNE PARISH married BARCLIFT; he had son JOHN mentioned in his will (1739) 1-66.

PARISH, SARAH, had been SARAH GLOVER, daughter of WILLIAM GLOVER of NORTHAMPTON COUNTY, N. C. who left will (1754) and among others had a grand-daughter MOURNING HARRIS 1-216.

PARISH, WILLIAM died leaving will in (1735-6) naming only wife MARY and daughter SARAH 1-66.

PARROTT, MARY. She was an orphan and WILLIAM FLEETWOOD was her guardian (1749) 2-633.

PARSONS, ASA, and JOSHUA SKINNER, witnessed the will of EDMUND HALSEY in (1806) 3-335; he died leaving will in (1826) and mentioned his wife ANNA and JOSEPH and JOHN PARSONS RIDDICK HATFIELD a witness 3-346.

PARSONS, JOHN was the Executor of the will of a
HENRY DAIL in (1828) with WILLIAM SUTTON a
witness 3-331; a JOHN PARSONS, son of SAMU-
EL PARSONS and wife SARAH was born in(1723)
3-392.

PARSONS, SAMUEL and wife SARAH had a son SAMUEL
born in (1726) 3-392.

PASQUOTANK COUNTY in(1713)extended to and took
in ALAGATOR CREEK, which is now in TYRRELL
COUNTY 3-365; Account of certain fees collected in that county 3-255; ROBERT WEST the
father of ROBERT and THOMAS WEST first settled there on FLATTY CREEK 3-265; petition
of the Church Wardens of PASQUOTANK PRECINCT
2-160.

PASSINGHAM, THOMAS and JOHN PORTER were witnesses to a deed by FRANCIS WELLS in (1708)3-136.

PASSONS, LINELLE, and wife MARY, of BEDFORDSHIRE
ENGLAND in (1695) mentioned 3-407.

PASSONS, SAMUEL, son of LINELLE PASSONS and wife
MARY, married ELIZABETH FLETCHER, daughter
of RALPH FLETCHER in (1695); his father lived in BEDFORD, DORSETSHIRE, ENGLAND 3-407.

PASSONS, BARTHOLOMEW, son of SAMUEL PASSONS and
wife ELIZABETH was born (1698) 3-370; they
also had a son WILLIAM born (1707-8) 3-378.

PASSONS, WILLIAM, son of SAMUEL PASSONS and wife
ELIZABETH was born (1707-8) 3-378.

PATCHETT, JOHN (Probably PAGETT, which see) a
land grant on ROCKYHOCK CREEK in (1711) 1-7;
another one in (1719) adjoining JOHN JONES
1-13; he married a duaghter of HENRY BONNER
and was his son in law (1710) 1-69.

PATCHETT, SAMUEL, land grant in (1715) on TIN-
DALL'S SWAMP 1-15; in (1721) he obtained another grant adjoining JOHN HARLOW and others
1-10; grant on COWHALL SWAMP (1717) 1-17; &
he obtained three land grants in (1715) 1-14.

PATE, CHARLES, sold land to NATHAN MOORE (1731)
on KEZIAH RIVER 1-625; he deeded land to
MATTHEW EDWARDS in (1718) 1-622; sold land
to ROBERT HICKS in (1722) 2-449; also sold
lands to PHILLIP WALSTON adjoining THOROUGH-
GOOD PATE in (1718) 1-622.

PATE, THOROUGHGOOD, owned lands adjoining CHAR-
LES PATE and PHILLIP WALSTON in (1718) 1-622
and was a nephew of NATHANIEL CHEVIN 2-455.

PATNALL, JOHN died leaving will in (1711) names
brother WILLIAM and THOMAS BUSTIN 1-69.

PATTER, ROBERT sold land to HENRY KING in (1711)
deed witnessed by THOMAS DOIELE (DOYLEY) and
LEONARD LANGSTON 1-237.

PATTERSON, JACOB (son of JACOB) married RE-
BECCA SUTTON in (1695) 3-407.

PATTERSON, MOSES W. will in BERTIE (1825) mentions brother in law STARKEY SMITH and others 2-540.

PATTERSON, COL. ROBERT, roster of his Company in
(1720) from both sides MEHERRIN RIVER 1-443;
he died leaving will in (1721) and mentioned only one son JOHN PATTERSON 1-68.

PATILLO, REV. HENRY, he and SAMUEL JOHNSTON
appointed guardians of children of ANDREW
KNOX and wife CHRISTIAN in will of (1776)
3-176.

PATTISON, GEORGE and EDWARD BRYAN were JUS-
TICES of BERTIE in (1746-7) 2-629.

PAYNE, EZEKIEL, was the son of PETER PAYNE &
grandson of THOMAS TAYLOR in (1736) 1-78.

PAYNE, JOHN is mentioned in the will of RICH-
ARD HANDRICK in PERQUIMANS (1712) 1-52.

PAYNE, MICHAEL granted lands (1787) escheated
from CLARK & WEIR 1-23; and in the same
year obtained grant at New EDENTON 1-22.

PAYNE, PETER, was the son of THOMAS TAYLOR of
CURRITUCK who left will (1734) (in-law)
1-78; he married HANNAH SLAUGHTER daughter
of MICHAEL SLAUGHTER, and left will in
(1755) 1-65; in (1754) he petitions for a
division of the estate of JAMES BEASLEY
1-457; he was a member of the Court in
CHOWAN in (1743) 1-447; in (1743) he was
chosen guardian in CHOWAN of ELIZABETH
SLAUGHTER 1-447; in (1748) he was appointed to raise JOSHUA JOHNSON, the orphan of
JOHN JOHNSON 1-452.

PAYNE, RICHARD (Spelled PANE) sold lands to
CULLEN POLLOCK in (1720), with JONATHAN
RIDINGS a witness to the deed 2-613.

PAYNE, ROBERT, died sometime in APRIL (1672)
3-365.

PAYNE, SAMUEL served on the jury in ALBEMARLE
PRECINCT in (1702) 1-610.

PEACE FAMILY, of GRANVILLE COUNTY, NORTH CAR-
OLINA, and the KITTRELLS of the same locality were descended from CHRISTIAN REED
and MARGARET JORDAN; see genealogy 3-134.

PEARRE, DEBORRAH, died the year (1678) 3-365.

PEARRE, JOHN and his wife MARY were the parents of DEBORRAH PEARRE 3-365.

PEARCE, ABRAHAM, left will in GATES COUNTY in
(1834) JOSEPH RIDDICK Exr. 2-66.

PEARCE, AARON will GATES (1845) 2-66.

PEARCE, CHRISTOPHER will in GATES (1801) sons
ISAAC and WILLIAM, with FREDERICK JONES a
witness 2-66.

PEARCE, ISAAC, will in GATES (1834), MARY GREEN
and JOSEPH GORDON Executors 2-66, 2-67.

PEARCE, JACOB, will in GATES (1802) 2-66.

PEARCE, JEREMIAH will in BERTIE (1801) mentions
ELLERSON FAMILY 2-536.

PEARCE, LOVICK (PIERCE) ancestor of family of
BISHOP PIERCE of GEORGIA 1-166.

PEARCE, ROBERT, late of EXETER, ENGLAND, his
wife living in DEVONSHIRE in (1729) 1-67.

PEARCE, THOMAS was the administrator in (1749)
of JOHN PEARCE 1-451.

PEARCE, WILLIAM will (1775) BERTIE COUNTY 1-351.

PEARSON, ELIZABETH, married REUBEN PERRY in JAN-
UARY (1780) with JAMES WILSON surety on bond
3-417; another ELIZABETH probably the wife
of PETER PEARSON and the daughter of ARTHUR
CROXTON who died (1765) 3-167.

PEARSON, ELEAZER, died in (1795) laving will his
wife BARSHEBA, with CALEB ELLIOTT and REUBEN
PERRY, Executors 3-183.

PEARSON, JOHN, appointed to take care of tuition
of SARAH and DAVID BENTLEY, orphans of PETER
BENTLEY (1771) 3-450; also the tuition of a
HEZEKIAH ANDREWS of BERTIE (1768) 3-446; he
was attorney for SIR NATHAN DUKENFIELD (1771)
in BERTIE 3-449; JOHN PEARSON of KENT COUNTY,
DELAWARE, left will (1755) 1-361; he was of
DUKENFIELD, N. C. and an attorney at law and
left will (1777), with wife MARGARET and
JASPER CHARLTON, ABIGAIL CHARLTON and MILES
SHEHAN, witnesses 2-351.

PEARSON, MARGARET (widow of the lawyer JOHN
PEARSON) died in (1785) leaving will; her
plantation called DUKENFIELD was left to
CULLEN POLLOCK and SAMUEL JOHNSTON in trust
for her son SIR. NATHANIEL DUKENFIELD, mentions her son ROBERT DUKENFIELD, her watch
to MRS. IREDELL (wife of JAMES; the witnesses were MARY VAIL and CHRISTOPHER CLARK
2-351.

PEARSON, PETER witness to the will of ARTHUR
CROXTON in (1765) and perhaps his son in law
3-167; he died in (1735) leaving will, mentions children JONATHAN, NATHAN, PETER, JOHN,
BAILEY and daughters RACHEL and MARY PEARSON
1-87; there was a PETER son of WILLIAM PEAR-
SON who died (1807) 3-346.

PEARSON, WILLIAM, died leaving will (1807) men-
tions one son PETER and daughters MIRIAM &
LILLIA PEARSON, PENINAH ELLIOTT and ELIZA-
BETH and ESTHER; wife MIRIAM and THOMAS the
son of JOSIAH WHITE, executors; MARY & SAR-
AH HOLLOWELL, witnesses 3-346.

PEED, PATIENCE will (1831) mentions grandchildren named JENNINGS; JAMES and MARY SUTTON
witnesses 3-346.

PEEK, JAMES, bought land from THOMAS STURGIS in
(1719) 2-613.

PEELE, JOSIAH, SR. will in BERTIE (1843) names
sons JOSIAH and JAMES and the heirs of DEMP-
SEY and WILLIAM PEELE; COX FAMILY connection
shown 2-540.

PEELE, JUDITH, died in NORTHAMPTON COUNTY, N. C.
in (1756) names sons JOHN, ROBERT, JOSEPH,
JOSHUA and JOSIAH PEELE, daughters SARAH
PEELE, MARY (wife of WILLIAM GRANBERRY) and
son in law WILLIAM GRANBERRY 1-371.

PEELE, WILLIAM bought 200 acres from WILLIAM DAN-
IEL on the NORTH SIDE of BENNETT'S CREEK in
(1727), with FRANCIS PUGH and WILL ASHLEY the
witnesses 1-112, 3-127. CHARITY PEELE, 1-200.

PELL, URSILLA, petitioned for a road in (1745);
2-526; see will of MICHAEL O'NEAL, SR. in
CURRITUCK (1721) 1-64.

PEMBRACE, DANIEL departed this life (1688) 3-365.

PENN, JOHN (The Signer) letter (1777) written
to Governor CASWELL 2-252, 2-253.

PENNSYLVANIA. JOHN PORTER claims rights for
transporting persons into the Colony of
NORTH CAROLINA from 3-250.

PEDERTON, WILLIAM witness with JOHN STEPNEY
to deed of JOHN SHOIER (1717) 1-617.

PENNEY, JAMES, will (1792) in BERTIE wife was
ELIZABETH, JOHN MIZELL married daughter
LYDIA PENNY; son THOMAS, JOHN CAKE and
JOHN MIZELL Executors 2-351.

PENNEY, JOHN, married ELIZABETH MARTIN, daughter of JOHN MARTIN, who died in BATH in
(1715) 1-63.

PENNEY, THOMAS (Son of JOHN) died leaving
will in (1795) in BERTIE; mentions ANN
MIZELL, daughter of JOHN MIZELL "land bought
by my father from EDWARD ACKEE"; MALACHI
CURRY, JOHN WOLFENDEN and JOHN MIZELL are
executors, and ROBERT HUNTER, JAMES CURRY
and WILLIAM COWARD witnesses 2-351.

PENNEY, WILLIAM, died in CHOWAN in (1766) and
daughter ELIZABETH WESTON named; wife and
ZACHARIAH WEBB, Executors; JOHN BEASLEY &
FREDERICK NORCOM witnesses 2-18.

PENNIBACKER'S MILL. Letter from GENERAL GEORGE
WASHINGTON written from (1777) 2-250, 2-251
and 2-252.

PENDLETON, HENRY, left will in PASQUOTANK in
(1727) mentions daughter ELIZABETH WOODLEY,
wife of THOMAS WOODLEY, daughter ANN, wife
of THOMAS DAVIS and grandson HENRY PENDLE-
TON 1-65. (Also mentions sons THOMAS PEN-
DLETON and JOHN PENDLETON). See 3-88.

PENDLETON, THOMAS in (1740) was married to
SARAH PALMER, daughter of ROBERT PALMER who
left will that year, and had children
ROBERT, THOMAS and NANCY PENDLETON; also
a son HENRY PENDLETON mentioned by his
grandfather in (1727) 1-65; a THOMAS PEN-
DLETON died leaving will (1732) mentions a
daughter ANN KNIGHT and sons THOMAS, JOSEPH,
GEORGE and TIMOTHY, wife SARAH (PALMER)
and daughter ELIZABETH (PASQUOTANK CO.)
1-67; SARAH PENDLETON mentioned in will
of DANIEL ROCKSAKERS of PASQUOTANK (1732)
(probably a witness) 1-70. See 3-88.

PENDLETON, SALLIE, mentioned in the will of
FRANCIS LAYDEN in (1807) 3-340.

PENDER, ELISHA, will in BERTIE (1830) names
of JOSEPH and MICAJAH GRIFFIN are mentioned 2-536; son of SOLOMON 2-535.

PENDER, GABRIEL and WILLIAM BIRD PENDER are
called nephews in the will of HELEN HUB-
BARD nee PENDER in (1842) BERTIE 2-522.

PENDER, JOHN will in BERTIE in (1805) mentions brothers WILLIAM, ELISHA, STEPHEN
and brother in law JOEL HYMAN and his
children 2-535; in (1794) a JOHN PENDER
witnessed the marriage of PATIENCE RAY
to JAMES S. OVERTON 2-368; see 2-531.

PENDER, PAUL in (1748) executed either a will
or a deed to property to JOHN PENDER and
same was proved by ALEXANDER COTTEN 2-631.

PENDER, RIDDICK was the son of STEPHEN PENDER
who died (1813) 2-535, 2-536.

PENDER, SOLOMON, with SAMUEL RAY was Executor of
the will of ALEXANDER RAY in BERTIE in (1769)
2-352; in (1771) he was charged with tuition
of NATHAN COOPER in BERTIE 3-450; he died &
left will in BERTIE in (1800) in which he
named his cousin SOLOMON CORY, sister PRU-
DENCE CORY, brothers JOHN, ELISHA, WILLIAM &
STEPHEN PENDER; NOTTINGHAM MONK an Executor
and BELSON KITTRELL and THOS. E. HARE were
witnesses 2-535.

PENDER, WILLIAM was one of the witnesses to will
of WILLIAM SEALS who died in (1786), whose
wife MARY and LEMUEL HYMAN were Executors
2-357.

PENRICE, EDWARD and wife SARAH had son SAMUEL
born (1751) 3-392.

PENRICE, ELIZABETH died leaving will in CHOWAN in
(1785) which was witnessed by ANDREW DONALD-
SON and ROBERT MOORE 2-15; an ELIZABETH was
wife of FRANCIS PENRICE in (1738) and they
had several children 3-392, 3-408; members
of family mentioned 1-455.

PENRICE, FRANCIS, died leaving will in CHOWAN in
(1760) named wife SARAH and children THOMAS,
WILLIAM, SARAH, EDMUND, FRANCIS, JOSEPH and
MARY; JOSEPH BLOUNT, JOB CHARLTON and a JOHN
HARLOW Executors 2-15.

PENRICE, THOMAS had a son JOHN PENRICE in (1739)
3-132; and THOMAS PENRICE SR. in (1736) sold
lands to THOMAS and FRANCIS PENRICE, with
JAMES CRAVEN a witness 3-125.

PENLAND, GEORGE, of ASHVILLE, N. C. -- query in
regard to his family 3-316.

PERKINS, DAVID left will in (1733) had daughter
ELIZABETH WORSLEY, daughter MARY PUTNELL and
D. AFRICA HARVEY, sons JAMES and JONATHAN &
daughters SARAH and DOROTHY 1-67.

PERKINS, HENRY, of CURRITUCK; his petition in regard to his levies dated (1702) 3-62.

PERKINS, ICHABOD, of EDENTON was a meriner (1780)
and he left will, in which he mentioned his
MOTHER, CHARITY KEARBY, wife of THOMAS KEAR-
BY and sister MERCER KERBY in Dartmouth, R.
Island 2-16, 2-17.

PERKINS, JOHN and wife LEVY, had a daughter DOR-
OTHY born in (1695) 3-368.

PERISHO, ELIZABETH, will (1785) names her husband
JOSEPH PERISHO, cousins named SAUNDERS and a
JOSEPH ANDERSON her executor 3-182.

PERISHO, JAMES, died in the month of MARCH in the
year (1678) 3-366; his wife was HANNAH and
they had son JAMES PERISHO born in (1676) and
daughter ELLENER born (1673) 3-210; JAMES
PERISHO, JR. married MARY MORGAN in (1696)
3-407; another JAMES PERISHO and his wife
SARAH had JAMES PERISHO JR. born in (1700-1)
3-372; JAMES PERISHO and wife SARAH had four
children born 3-392; the orphan JAMES PERISHO
in (1690) selected STEPHEN MANWARRING (Spelled Manneringe) as his guardian, and it was
ordered that he manage the orphan's plantation until he comes of age or cause it to be
managed to the advantage of said orphan and
give bond therefor 3-433.

PERISHO, JANE was the daughter of JAMES and
MARY PERISHO born (1697) 3-371.

PERISHO, JOHN, left will in PERQUIMANS (1759)
and named children JOHN, JAMES, JOSEPH,
VINES and JOSIAH; ELLENDER, BETTY, MARY &
JEAN BUNDY; PETER PEARSON and CORNELIUS
MOORE, witnesses 1-369; JOHN was the son
of JAMES PERISHO and wife MARY and was
born in (1703) 3-375.

PERISHO, JOSEPH, was one of the executors of
the will of THOMAS SANDERS in (1789)3-189.

PERISHO, MIRIAM and JOHN BATEMAN were married
in July (1767) 3-380.

PERQUIMANS PRECINCT: Births, deaths and marriages recorded in 3-363 to 3-410; petition from the inhabitants of the upper part
of same 2-96; other births, deaths and marriages in 3-199 to 3-220; marriages from
1740 to 1799 3-411 to 3-422; ABSTRACT OF
WILLS in 3-163 to 3-198; 3-323 to 3-363.

PERRY, ABRAHAM, with JOHN CAPEHART and HERBERT
PRITCHARD was an executor of the will of
JEREMIAH HALLOM in BERTIE in (1784) 2-341.

PERRY, BENJAMIN married MILLICENT REDDICK were
married (1785) and had MARY, THOMAS, JAMES,
JOSEPH and CHRISTIAN PERRY all born by
(1798) 3-392; BENJAMIN PERRY SR. died in
(1788) and BENJAMIN PERRY JR. son of BENJA-
MIN PERRY and wife SUSAN died (1784) 3-406;
in (1728) BENJAMIN PERRY sold lands to one
THOMAS LANE on the N. E. Shore of CHOWAN
RIVER adjoining the lands of JAMES FARLOW,
the witnesses being ROBERT HICKS and SUSAN-
NA PERRY 2-445; BENJAMIN PERRY witness to
will of ISRAEL PERRY in (1779) 3-183; in
(1790) he also witnessed the will of JACOB
PERRY SR. 3-183, with JACOB and JOSEPH RID-
DICK; HANNAH his wife d (1799) 3-406.

PERRY ISAAC left will in (1834) named wife CHAR-
LOTTE, daughters RACHEL, JUDY and HATTIE
PERRY and BARSHEBA DANIEL, and EDY SMITH; &
sons JOHN, JEREMIAH, WRIGHT and ISAAC PERRY
2-540.

PERRY, ISRAEL, died in (1779) and left will in
which he named sons JOSIAH, ISRAEL, JOHN,
CADER and JACOB, four youngest daughters
MILLICENT, RUTH, RACHEL and ANN and daugh-
ter PRISCILLA TWINE; PHILLIP PERRY and
THOMAS TWINE Executors with wife 3-183.

PERRY, JACOB, died (1777) sons JACOB, ISRAEL &
REUBEN and DEMPSEY and JOHN and son in law
CALEB WINSLOW and ISAAC WILSON 3-183; JACOB
PERRY SR. will (1790) wife MARY, son MILES
PERRY and son LAWRENCE and BENJAMIN PERRY
Executors 3-183.

PERRY, JAMES was the guardian of FRANCES LAW-
RENCE in BERTIE (1771) 3-450.

PERRY, JEREMIAH, died leaving a will in (1694)
in which he mentions his wife JANE and
CHRISTIAN BLOUNT, the daughter of THOMAS
BLOUNT in CHOWAN PRECINCT 1-67 (Grimes p.
285 adds the witnesses were THOMAS POLLOCK,
ALEXANDER McFARLAND, NEAL McKING and JOHN
BUNTIN) ISAAC PERRY had son JEREMIAH in
(1834) brother of BARSHEBA PERRY who married
a DANIEL 2-540; Query, who did CHRISTIAN
BLOUNT MARRY? See note bottom of 1-67.

PERRY, JOHN, and wife ELIZABETH, of NANSEMOND COUNTY, VA. in (1720) sold lands to GEORGE EASON of PERQUIMANS which adjoined THOMAS SPEIGHT 2-612; (THOMAS EASON witness).

PERRY, JOSEPH proved his headrights, including himself and wife ANN, ELIZABETH, his second wife, JOSEPH, SUSANNA, ALICE and SARAH PERRY and OBEDIAH FAIR 2-300; through his attorney MR. BARKER he took an order (1744) for the sale of part of the estate of MARY SPEIGHT 2-622; had son JACOB 1-368.

PERRY, NICHOLAS in (1745) was appointed Constable in BERTIE in the place of JOHN ROBINSON 2-625.

PERRY, PHILLIP died leaving will in PERQUIMANS in (1751) mentions children JESSE, PHILLIP, MARY, ELIZABETH, RACHEL, JUDE, MIRIAM and SARAH FIELD, and brother JOHN PERRY 1-368.

PERRY, REUBEN, married ELIZABETH PEARSON with JAMES WILSON security in PERQUIMANS (1780) 3-417.

PERRY, RUTH married MICAJAH HILL in PERQUIMANS COUNTY in (1763) 3-413.

PERRY, SAMUEL left will in BERTIE in (1774) and named wife PRUDENCE and daughter PEGGY and with HUMPHREY HARDY Executor 2-350.

PERRY, SUSANNAH married MOSES HOWARD in PERQUIMANS in (1790) BENJ. PERRY security 3-419.

PERRY, WILLIAM bought lands from WILL COTTERELL on INDIAN TOWN SWAMP (1735) with JOHN and CHARLES JORDAN witnesses 3-125.

PERSEY, WILLIAM died in BERTIE COUNTY in (1782) with wife ELIZABETH and children WILLIAM, KADER, ZADOCK, NANCY and BLAKE PERSEY, and JAMES WILSON and JOHN PERSEY were witnesses 2-350.

PERVIS, MOSES left will in BERTIE in (1812) son MOSES and others and grandsons named HARRELL 2-539.

PETERSON FAMILY. Wills 2-538, 2-539; Genealogical notes relating to 3-473, 3-474, 3-475.

PETERSON, MRS. ANNA, married MacRORA SCARBOROUGH (By Sir Richard Everard) in NOVEMBER (1729) 3-473; ANN PETERSON, daughter of JACOB and wife MARY was born in (1698) 3-369.

PETERSON, JACOB. His wife was MARY in (1698) 3-369; he was the father of THOMAS PETERSON upon whose land the town of EDENTON was built; the first deeds being signed by THOMAS PETERSON and NATHANIEL CHEVEN, Commissioners to make the deeds in (1714) 3-143; in (1704) JOHN BYRD and his wife REBECCA were the Executors or Administrators of the Estate of JACOB PETERSON 1-612; JACOB PETERSON came to NORTH CAROLINA from MARYLAND about 17 years prior to (1701) or about (1684) 3-143; JOHN BYRD married REBECCA, the widow of JACOB PETERSON in (1697) 3-408.

PETERSON, MARY, was the relict or widow of JACOB PETERSON, SR 3-369; and after his death before (1698) she married JAMES COLES Jr. son of JAMES COLES of NANSEMOND COUNTY, VIRGINIA 3-408.

PETERSON, THOMAS (Son of JACOB PETERSON, SR.) was a JUSTICE of the General Court (1714) at the time of GOV. EDEN 3-267; his wife was JOANNA and after his death she married JONATHAN JACOCKS merchant, of PASQUOTANK Precinct 3-284; he served with NATHANIEL CHEVEN in signing the first deeds to lots in the town of EDENTON, which had belonged originally to his father JACOB 3-143.

PETTYJOHN, ABRAHAM. One ABRAHAM died leaving a will in CHOWAN in (1818) with wife SUSANNA and who had JOHN, JR., ISAAC, ABNER, JACOB, JAMES, WILLIAM and ABRAHAM PETTYJOHN, the witnesses being MICHAEL WILDER and JOHN PETTYJOHN 2-16; he was perhaps the son of THOMAS PETTYJOHN and wife FRANCES who died in (1767) 3-16; another ABRAHAM died at EDENTON in (1717) with wife FRANCES, and JOSEPH B. SKINNER and HENRY KING were his Executors 2-16.

PETTYJOHN, ABNER was one of the sons of ABRAHAM and his wife SUSANNAH (1818) 2-16.

PETTYJOHN, JOB with SAMUEL REA were witnesses to the will of THOMAS MYERS in (1815) who mentioned among others his daughter MARTHA REA 3-342; in (1822) JOB PETTYJOHN left a will in CHOWAN, with wife ELIZABETH, in it names grandsons AUGUSTUS P. and RICHARD T. REA, with MYLES EVERETT and MARTHA REA among the witnesses 3-16.

PETTYJOHN, ELIZABETH was the wife of JOB PETTYJOHN in (1815), 2-16; and either she or another ELIZABETH left will (1844) 2-16.

PETTYJOHN, FRANCES died leaving will in CHOWAN in (1845) naming brothers and sisters with MARTHA SKINNER a witness 2-16.

PETTYJOHN, JAMES left will in (1849) names sisters SARAH and RACHEL and ELIZABETH HAUGHTON (husband of FRANCES who died (1845) 2-16; they married in (1800) 1-255.

PETTYJOHN, JOHN died in CHOWAN in (1832) and left will, his wife being NANCY, and names his daughter POLLY REA 2-16, 2-19 (He had WILDER grandchildren).

PETTYJOHN, SARAH left will in (1855) witnessed by THOMAS and JOSEPH T. WAFF 2-16.

PETTYJOHN, THOMAS died in CHOWAN in (1767) and left children THOMAS, JOHN, ABRAHAM, SARAH and FRANCES and wife FRANCIS; the witnesses were THOMAS BURKETT, NATHANIEL MING and a WILLIAM BENHITE 2-16.

PETTIT, FRANCIS was a witness to a deed by JOHN HARRISON in (1727) 2-444; a FRANCIS PETTIT died and left will in CHOWAN in (1712) and in it mentioned his cousin JOHN CHESTER, a son FRANCIS, daughter SARAH and brother JESSE PETTIT; children of EDWARD NORRINGTON COMFORT; JOHN BARROW guardian of son FRANCIS, and wife MARY; witnesses were JENKINS WILLIAMS, SAMUEL BARROW and FRANCIS SMITH 1-369, 1-370; a FRANCIS PETTIT with THOMAS PIERCE witnessed a deed (1732) 2-452; in (1720) he owned lands next to IRA SMITH & EDWARD HARRINGTON 1-9.

PETTIT, SARAH was called the daughter of MARY SIMONS in her will in (1722); and she also mentioned son THOMAS PIERCE 1-76.

PETTIVER, ANN. She was the mother of ISAAC WILSON, who died in (1724) who had brothers ROBERT and BENJAMIN WILSON, and they had an uncle RALPH BOZEMAN (So she may have been ANN BOZEMAN) 1-83; See 2-152.

PETTIVER, JOHN had an invoice of goods assigned to him in YORK RIVER, in VIRGINIA in (1699) per ROBERT STARKEY, who was his agent; they came from DANIEL ZACHARY of BOSTON, who was represented by his attorney THOMAS PETERSON 2-151; he sold lands to JOHN BURKETT (1720) 2-454; WILLIAM GLOVER, President, HON. THOMAS CARY, JOHN PORTER and FRANCIS FOSTER rendered a bill for having stayed at the home of JOHN PETTIVER during the meeting of the Council in (1708) 3-361; he married ANN the widow of HENRY NORMAN who left son HENRY and a daughter MARY 2-152; JOHN PETTIVER was deceased in (1738) and another JOHN (his son?) sold lands to his brother in law BENJAMIN TALBOT, some in PERQUIMANS and some in CHOWAN 3-131; JOHN PETTIVER was a member of the Court in CHOWAN in (1712) 1-444; the later JOHN was nephew of the first JOHN "late of LONDON, now of PERQUIMANS (1738) and the deed included a tract of land in ONSLOW and was witnessed by MacRORA SCARBOROUGH and ZACHARIAH NIXON 1-284; JOHN PETTIVER and his wife ANN sold lands to JOHN BURKETT in(1720) 2-607; JOHN sold lands in (1713) to ANTHONY HATCH and GEORGE DURANT on South side ALBEMARLE SOUND next to SETH PHELPS and FRANCIS JOHNSON 1-102; in (1725) he sold lands on the head of SCUPERNONG RIVER as deed of gift to JOHN OGILBY 2-291; in (1716) he was granted lands at the head of INDIAN TOWN CREEK 1-15; JOHN proved his rights about (1694) at Court held at home of RICHARD POPE in PASQUOTANK, himself, William DAVIS, EDWARD CLARKE, DANIEL DYER, JUDITH CLARKE and MANDY DOUNE 2-465. (No Will found - GRIMES gives none).

PETTIGREW, REV. CHARLES, first Bishop-Elect of North Carolina married MARY BLOUNT 1-132.

PETTIGREW, EBENEZER, son of CHARLES PETTIGREW & MARY BLOUNT 1-132.

PETTINGER, JAMES proved rights for himself, his wife ELITIA and MARY JOHNSON assigned to ISAAC GUILFORD (1759) 2-299.

PEYTON, BENJAMIN, of BATH COUNTY administrator of the estate of WILLIAM BELL SR. and orphans ANNE, SARAH and KEZIAH BELL also for JOHN WOODHOUSE (no date) 3-282, 3-283.

PEYTON, ROBERT, of BATH left will written(1733) proved (1739-1754) children THOMAS, ROBERT, WILLIAM, AMBROSE, BENJAMIN, SARAH, DOROTHY PORTER and wife MARY 1-65.

PICKETT, REV. JAMES T., of EDENTON, an account of his life and career 1-574.

PICKERING, RICHARD, will in BERTIE COUNTY(1740) mentions ROGER SNELL and his children 1-65.

PIDERS, THOMAS and wife MARY 3-368.

PIERCE, BETSY, had a daughter MARGARET mentioned in the will of BENJAMIN SAUNDERS (Son of JOHN SAUNDERS) which was proved in year (1830), which will was witnessed by ABRAHAM WHITE 3-350.

PIERCE, COPELAND was the son of JOHN PIERCE and his wife SARAH in (1719) 3-393; his father JOHN died leaving will in (1727) in which COPELAND is mentioned together with his GRANDFATHER CHAPMAN 1-68.

PIERCE, EDMUND was commissioned a JUSTICE of CHOWAN PRECINCT in (1701) by HENDERSON WALKER, along with EDWARD SMITHWICK, JOHN BLOUNT, THOMAS GARRETT and others 3-142.

PIERCE, ELIZABETH died in (1739) 3-405; the one who was daughter of JOHN and SARAH was born (1721) 3-393; the wife of RICHARD PIERCE died (1762) was ELIZABETH 3-182.

PIERCE, DEBORAH, daughter of JOHN PIERCE and wife MARY was born (1678) 3-208.

PIERCE, GEORGE. His wife was MAGDALENE and they sold lands to ROBERT HERRICK at DRUMMOND'S POINT in (1711) with THOMAS HORTON and ALEX SMITH witnesses 1-102.

PIERCE, HARTWELL (female) married DEMPSEY TURNER in (1762) with JOSEPH TURNER security on marriage bond 3-413; she was daughter of JAMES PIERCE and wife ELIZABETH and was born (1743) 3-393.

PIERCE, JAMES and his wife ELIZABETH had several children, HARTWELL, MILES, FIORELLA & FANNY PIERCE, all born by (1750) 3-393.

PIERCE, JOHN and wife SARAH were the parents of COPELAND, ELIZABETH, THOMAS and HANNAH all born by (1725) 3-393; he either married second MARY, or another JOHN and MARY were parents of JOSEPH PIERCE who married DAMARIS NIXON (Daughter of ZACHARIAH NIXON) in (1699) on Little River 3-408; JOHN whose wife was SARAH died leaving will in (1727) mentioning children MARY, COPELAND, ELIZABETH, THOMAS, HANNAH and their grandfather CHAPMAN and his brother in law PETER JONES 1-68; a JOHN witnessed the will of JOHN NORCOM in (1745) 1-133.

PIERCE, JOSEPH, was the brother in law of JOHN WILLIAMS who died in (1727) 1-83; JOSEPH of PERQUIMANS died in (1736) leaving will in which he mentioned wife ALICE, son THOMAS, daughters MIRIAM and REBECCA, brother THOMAS and brother in law PETER JONES, Executor 1-56; the daughter REBECCA PIERCE was born in (1729-30) 3-393; JOSEPH PIERCE and DANIEL WRIGHT refused to serve on the highways about (1701) HENRY NORMAN surveyor, JAMES MINGE & ROBERT JONES did NOT refuse 3-141.

PIERCE, MARY was the wife of JAMES SKINNER and the daughter of JOHN PIERCE and she died in (1741) 3-396.

PIERCE, MILES was the son of JAMES PIERCE and his wife ELIZABETH 3-393.

PIERCE, PHILLIP married LYDIA CULPEPPER, and they were the grandparents of BISHOP GEORGE F. PIERCE of the M. E. Church, of GEORGIA 1-637.

PIERCE, REBECCA, was the daughter of JOSEPH PIERCE who died (1736) 1-66; in (1715) a REBECCA PIERCE was witness to a deed of one GEORGE FORDYCE to THOMAS HORTON, and HENRY HORTON was also a witness 1-293.

PIERCE, THOMAS in (1722) was granted 364 acres adjoining the lands of EDWARD PORTER; and in (1727) 119 acres on YAWPIM RIVER and ALBEMARLE SOUND 1-11; he was assessed tithes on 300 acres in PERQUIMANS before 1700 1-301; he and THOMAS BARROW signed a petition by some members of the House of Burgesses to the GOVERNOR and COUNCIL probably before the year (1700) 3-74, 3-75; while WILLIAM WILKINSON was Speaker he signed as a member of the House of Burgesses (before 1704) with EDWARD SMITHWICK, THOMAS and JOHN BLOUNT & ISAAC WILSON, TIMOTHY CLEARE and RICHARD COMINFORT 3-60; THOMAS LONG and THOMAS PIERCE were called "brothers in law" in the will of SARAH LONG of PERQUIMANS in (1715) 1-59; he was a collector of Quit Rents from MITCHELL McDANIELL as early as (1685) 3-270; in (1691) his wife was MARY and they had a son JOHN PIERCE who was born that year 3-217; and they had a son THOMAS PIERCE born in (1693) 3-219; THOMAS PIERCE and FRANCIS PETTIT in (1727) witnessed a deed from WILLIAM HARLON, JR. to JOHN HARRISON 2-444; in (1722) THOMAS PIERCE JR. had acted as a Deputy Collector of the Revenue for JOHN BLOUNT 1-445; THOMAS PIERCE JR. and MARY COPELAND were married in (1719) 3-393; THOMAS PIERCE received a land grant in (1722) adjoining THOMAS PORTER 1-11; THOMAS sold lands to JOHN PIERCE, known as the GOOSE POND in (1740) adjoining JOHN FALCONER, with JOHN JOHNSON and SARAH PIERCE as witnesses 3-134; in (1718) THOMAS PIERCE JR. bought lands from MARY SIMONS the relict of NICHOLAS SIMONS 1-525; and in the year (1732) he bought lands from THOMAS MEWBORN 3-452; THOMAS PIERCE and wife MARY had a son JOSEPH PIERCE born in (1705) 3-376;he and JOHN PIERCE were witnesses about (1735) 3-131; in (1733) a THOMAS PIERCE was the god son of EDWARD ORENDELL 1-64; his will was proven in (1732) in which he named sons THOMAS and JOHN and wife MARY; son JOHN'S three children, daughter MARY JONES, his son JOSEPH, grandson THOMAS PIERCE, grand-daughter MARY, daughter SARAH and son in law PETER JONES 1-69.

PIERCEY, GEORGE received a grant of land (1694) 1-5.

PIEDRAS, "GRANDFATHER" mentioned in will of JOHN MOYE (1735) 1-62.

PIKE, SAMUEL and his wife JANE (1701) 3-300; he left will in (1719) names wife JEAN and his children JOHN, SAMUEL, BENJAMIN, SUSANNAH & ANN 1-68.

PILAND, GEORGE received a grant of land in(1753) on SAHUM SWAMP 1-20.

PILAND, THOMAS in (1736) sold lands, part of his patent of (1728) on the South side of MILLS SWAMP to STEPHEN SHEPARD, deed witnessed by HENRY BAKER and others 1-114, 1-115; he and CHARLES KING in (1723) witnessed a deed by RICHARD BARNES 2-449; in (1729) he bought some land from JAMES HAMBLETON adjoining the lands of RICHARD WOODWARD 2-446; in (1732) he was appointed overseer of the road leading to BENNETT'S CREEK BRIDGE 1-450; about (1734) he again bought lands from JAMES HAMBLETON 2-453; he owned lands near by and was neighbor to the HAMBLETON FAMILY in (1734) as is shown by the various deeds executed by and to him 2-454.

PILKINGTON, SARAH, married SETH PILKINGTON; & she was a sister of EDWARD PORTER of CHOWAN who died in (1737); her sister ELIZABETH married first THOMAS FRY and second DR. PATRICK MAULE 1-133.

PILKINGTON, SETH, and DR. PATRICK MAULE mentioned in the will of JOSHUA PORTER in (1734) who calls DR. MAULE his brother in law, and EDMUND PORTER his brother 1-67.

PINER, PETER, of CURRITUCK left will in(1758) and names wife SOPHIA, sons JOEL, BENJAMIN, NATHAN, daughters SOPHIA HARRIS, MARY MERCER, ESTHER, ABIE and KEZIAH and JOSIAH PARKER; William BRAY, JOSHUA BELL and REUBEN BRAY witnesses 1-365.

PINKETT, ELEANOR, left will in BEAUFORT (1758) with WILLIAM DANIEL PINKETT and THOMAS PINKETT, Executors; they were her sons & she had daughter HANNAH and a son ZACHARIAH PINKETT; son in law WILLIAM MOORE & a granddaughter RACHEL CASON 1-367.

PINKETT, WILLIAM DANIEL, is called "my wife's grandson"in the will of WILLIAM DANIEL in (1741) 1-198.

PIPKIN, ISAAC, left will in GATES COUNTY in (1837) and says that his son JOHN D. PIPKIN is contemplating marriage into MRS. PENELOPE PERKIN'S family in Virginia 2-67.

PIPKIN, JOHN sold lands to MOSES HARE which he had bought from JOSEPH RAWLEY in (1736) & the witnesses were ISAAC WILLIAMS, MOSES ODOM SR. and MOSES ODOM, JR. 3-135; he and his wife SARAH sold lands to CHARLES GAFFIN which adjoined ALEXANDER CARTER in (1730) 2-451; JOHN sold lands to JOHN PIPKIN JR. which had been patented by CHARLES SCOTT of NANSEMOND COUNTY, Va., in (1733) and witnessed by HENRY GOODMAN, WILLIAM BENTLEY & SIMON DANIEL 2-609.

PITTS, DOZIER, was son in law of EDWARD JAMES who left will (1720) 1-55.

POINDEXTER, RICHARD is mentioned in the will of WILLIAM SWAIN in (1810) 2-545.

POISON, EDWARD, married MRS. FOSTER KNIGHT the relict of LEWIS KNIGHT in (1701) with CAPT. JAMES COLES, Justice of the PEACE 3-410.

POINTER, HENRY left will in (1800) names wife SUSAN and his former wife's son WILLIAM JONES, shows relation to the SWEPSONS and ENOS FAMILY of Gloucester County, Virginia 3-344.

POLK, THOMAS, listed as a COLONEL in the NORTH CAROLINA Continental Line 1-419.

POLK, WILLIAM listed as a MAJOR in the NORTH CAROLINA Continental Line 1-424.

POLLOCK, CULLEN and THOMAS POLLOCK were the sons in laws of SAMUEL SCOLLEY 1-72; CULLEN was the guardian of the estate of GEORGE WEST the orphan of ROBERT WEST in BERTIE in (1771) 3-450; he was a JUSTICE in BERTIE in (1767) 3-443; division of the estate and names of heirs in (1754) 2-268; genealogical note relating to the POLLOCK FAMILY at bottom of page 1-65; will of CULLEN POLLOCK proved (1751) names heirs 1-65.

130

POLLOCK, CULLEN. In the division of the estate of CULLEN POLLOCK in (1754) the heirs are listed as the widow FRANCES, STEVENS LEE & FRANCES POLLOCK, GEORGE POLLOCK, MARY POL - LOCK (died before the division), CULLEN POLLOCK (died before the division), MARTHA POLLOCK married STEPHEN LEE, FRANCES married DR. ROBERT LENOX, and ROBERT WEST married the widow of CULLEN POLLOCK 2-268.

POLLOCK, ELIZABETH, was the daughter of RICHARD SANDERSON of PERQUIMANS, who died in(1733) and who was brother in law of HENRY WOODHOUSE 1-74.

POLLOCK, ESTHER, the widow of THOMAS POLLOCK was married three times, first to JOHN HARRIS, second to COL. WILLIAM WILKINSON, and third to THOMAS POLLOCK; she died and her will was proven in (1712) and a very full abstract of same is given 1-134.

POLLOCK, FRANCES, the relict of CULLEN POLLOCK (she married before her death ROBERT WEST 2-268)'died in (1757), though CULLEN POLLOCK had died in (1750) 2-471.

POLLOCK, GEORGE, the son of GOV. THOMAS POLLOCK married in (1734) ELIZABETH WHITMELL; she then married second in (1737) THOMAS BLOUNT, who died that year, whereupon she married third, WILLIAM WILLIAMS 2-471; the will of GEORGE POLLOCK was proved in (1738) and in it he mentions his nephews CULLEN and THOMAS POLLOCK, brother CULLEN POLLOCK and brother in law COL. ROBERT WEST 1-66.

POLLOCK, JAMES died leaving will in (1700) with only BILAH BLOUNT and WILLIAM WARD mentioned 1-87. (GRIMES p. 292 gives the legatees of JAMES POLLOCK of CHOWAN as BULLAH (BULAH) BLOUNT, WILLIAM WARD, THOMAS POLLOCK, EDMUND PEARCE, JOHN WACKER, and the witnesses as THOMAS BLOUNT, SAMUEL SWANN and THOMAS COOPER).

POLLOCK, COL. THOMAS, was born at GLASGOW, SCOTLAND in (1654) and came to N. C. in (1683) and married MARTHA CULLEN; see genealogy of POLLOCK FAMILY 3-156, 3-157, 3-158. (MARTHA CULLEN was born at DOVER, ENGLAND); in (1709) COL. THOMAS POLLOCK made a deed of gift to sons, CULLEN, THOMAS, GEORGE and his daughter MARTHA 1-66; he died in (1722) but before his death was elected President of the Council and Ex-Officio GOVERNOR of the Colony of N. C. 3-156; he and his wife MARTHA CULLEN (who had first married ROBERT WEST, son of ROBERT WEST) had two sets of twins named MARTHA and ELIZABETH, all four of whom died in infancy, and a fifth child named MARTHA (3-156) but called MARY in the GRIMES ABSTRACT (p. 292) who married THOMAS BRAY, of NEW KENT COUNTY 3-156; in (1704) with SAMUEL SWANN he signed a proclamation issued by GOV. THOMAS CARY 2-220; between (1699 and 1704) he signed a petition to the Court of Chancery 3-70, 3-71; an order for merchandise was sent to him by THOMAS EVANS in (1701) 1-557; in (1720) he bought lands from THOMAS WEST and wife MARTHA 3-612; in (1713) he signed order for the adjournment of the Assembly 3-228; in (1697) he was granted land at the mouth of OLD TOWN CREEK 1-5; and in (1720) on CHOWAN SOUND (which included a former grant to COL. WILLIAM WILKINSON) 1-9.

POLLOCK, COL. THOMAS (Continued) Another land grant in (1705) on OLD TOWN CREEK; ESTHER, the widow of COL. WILLIAM WILKINSON was the second wife of COL. THOMAS POLLOCK 1-65 (See genealogical note at bottom of page); after his death in (1722) his widow ESTHER married SAMUEL SCOLLEY; and ESTHER was a daughter of RICHARD SANDERSON who mentions a daughter "ELIZABETH POLLOCK" in his will in (1733), but ESTHER may have been a sister of this RICHARD and a daughter of the RICHARD SANDERSON who died in CURRITUCK in (1718) 1-74 (and note); THOMAS POLLOCK sold land to FULLINGTON SANDIFOOT in (1700) 3-611.

POLLOCK, THOMAS (Son of GOV. POLLOCK) was the Chief Justice in (1724) after his father's death, with WILLIAM DOWNING, ISAAC HILL and JOHN ALSTON 2-302; he left will in (1732) & mentioned sons CULLEN, THOMAS, GEORGE and MRS. ELIZABETH DICKSON 1-67; a THOMAS POLLOCK of NEW JERSEY executed a Power of ATTORNEY at Elizabethtown, N. J. proved by EDWARD RAZOR in conjunction with CULLEN POLLOCK 3-445; THOMAS POLLOCK married EUNICE EDWARDS, in NEW JERSEY, and they had several children 3-157.

POLSON, JOHN and DANIEL STALLINGS witnessed the will of HENRY STALLINGS in (1835) 3-352.

POOL, MARTHA, married JAMES FRUGEEFF in (1694) in HENRICO CO. VA. 3-409.

POOL, SOLOMON, of PASQUOTANK left will (1740) and named wife GRACE 1-66.

POPE, ANN, a widow in (1701) 2-300

POPE, EDWARD died leaving will in PASQUOTANK in (1721-2) his wife SARAH POPE 1-68; also 1-365; he was called "son" in the will of ANN JENNINGS, widow of JOHN JENNINGS of PASQUOTANK in (1720) as were STEPHEN and ANNE DELAMARE also 1-55.

POPE, JACOB, was the son of WILLIAM POPE who died in EDGECOMBE COUNTY in (1749) and had brothers STEPHEN and WEST POPE 1-369.

POPE, JOHN was called the "friend" of JOHN BRYANT (or BRYAN) who died in EDGECOMBE in (1735) 1-30; BARNABY POPE, the son of JOHN POPE is mentioned in the will of BARNABY McKINNIE, JR. in (1736) 1-61; JOHN POPE bought land from BARNABY McKINNIE in (1721) and he lived on MEHERRIN SWAMP in North CAROLINA 1-470.

POPE, RICHARD, left will in PASQUOTANK in the year (1701), wife ANN, and children MARY, ANN and EDWARD POPE 1-67; Court for PASQUOTANK PRECINCT in (1694) was held at the house of RICHARD POPE 2-465; another meeting called an "inquisition" was held at his house in PASQUOTANK PRECINCT in (1700) before WILLIAM GLOVER, escheater, relating to the estate of WILLIAM MOWBRAY, with PENDLETONS, MAYOS and BUNDYS present, a report of which mentions "the heirs of RICHARD POPE 3-88.

POPE, SAMUEL proves his headrights, himself two times and his wife JANE 2-300.

POPE, WILLIAM and WILLIAM LEDBETTER in (1721) witness a deed to lands issued to BARNABY McKINNIE 1-470. See 1-369, also.

POPHELSTON, SAMUEL owned lands adjoining MALACHI MILLER in (1790) 1-23

POPPLEWELL, WILLIAM bought land from JAMES WIMBLE in (1733) with ISAAC ALEXANDER a witness 2-610.

PORDAGE, GEORGE was part owner of ROANOKE ISLAND in (1701) 3-152.

PORK BARRELS. Copy of Act of Assembly regulating their size 3-150.

PORTER, EDMUND bought land from WILLIAM STEWART which had been sold by JOHN LOVICK in (1721) 2-619; owned lands adjoining those granted to GEORGE HAUGHTING in (1716) 1-14; he died leaving will in CHOWAN in (1737) wife ELIZABETH, sisters SARAH PILKINGTON and ELIZA-BETH MAULE, nephew JOHN PORTER of CAPE FEAR nephew JOHN FRY and neice ELIZABETH FRY, and FREDERICK BRICKELL son of THOMAS; witnesses A. BLACKALL, THOMAS ROWAN and MILES GALE 1-133

PORTER, JAMES died leaving will in GATES COUNTY in (1853), JOHN PORTER and MILES PARKER the witnesses 2-67.

PORTER, JOHN met with the ASSEMBLY in (1708) at the home of JOHN HECKLEFIELD 1-454; he was SPEAKER of the House of Burgesses in the days of SAMUEL SWANN (no date) 3-268, 3-269; he proves his rights for the importation of persons into the Colony of N. C. from PENNSYLVANIA 3-250; this last appears to have been in (1699) and he had wife and four children 1-613; his will proved in (1713) named wife MARY, sons EDMUND, JOHN and MATTHEW, & son in law JOHN LILLINGTON, daughters SARAH and ELIZABETH 1-478; his wife's will(1718) mentions also a son JOSHUA and several grandchildren 1-478; his daughter ELIZABETH married CAPT. THOMAS FRY of BATH 1-478; in(1720) he obtained a land grant on YOPPIM RIVER 1-13; he lived on lands called PIPER'S in CHOWAN PRECINCT 1-623; he and THOMAS SIMONS were members of the Court of Admiralty in N. C. in (1705) 1-611, 1-612; he was appointed a Justice of the General Court by HON. THOMAS CARY in (1705) 3-142; he was one of the trustees in a marriage contract (1730) (young JOHN) 1-445; he and WILLIAM WILKINSON signed the bond of ROBERT STARKEY master of a sloop in (1698) 3-204; was administrator of the estate of SIMON KNIGHT (1716) 1-56; JOHN PORTER, JR. patented lands(1696) on ALBEMARLE RIVER 1-5; he owned lands in (1720) next to WILLIAM HAUGHTON 1-10; JOHN PORTER JR. bought land from JAMES BAKER of NANSEMOND COUNTY, VA. in (1728) 2-443; in (1698) he had power of attorney from children and heirs of JOHN WRIGHT, GENT., of NANSEMOND COUNTY, VIRGINIA 2-244, 2-245 (This was in (1702) 1-610) ; RICHARD SMITH complains to the Governor and Council that he was arrested wrongfully by JOHN PORTER (no date) 3-65; JOHN PETTIVER filed a bill for board and keep of JOHN PORTER and others in attendance on the ASSEMBLY in (1708) 3-261; in (1730) JOHN PORTER was executor of will of JOHN KNOX in CHOWAN COUNTY 1-331; JOHN PORTER of BEAUFORT will (1755) with NATHANIEL RICHARDSON Executor 1-366; JOHN PORTER of HYDE died in (1751) will 1-366; JOHN SWAN PORTER of New Hanover left will (1770) 1-366 and JOHN PORTER, SR. of CAPE FEAR died(1728) wife SARAH and JOHN & SARAH children 1-366.

PORTER, JOSHUA was the son of JOHN PORTER & his wife MARY 1-478; he married KATHERINE, the widow of WILLIAM GLOVER by(1723) who had married as her second husband, TOBIAS KNIGHT 2-466; he was a witness for THOMAS CLARK and wife MARY in (1714) 1-293; he sold lands to JOHN LILLINGTON "left me by my father, JOHN PORTER" (no date) 1-624; he died leaving will proven in (1734) named son JOHN PEYTON PORTER, daughter ELIZABETH PORTER, cousins JOHN FRY and ANNE LILLINGTON and ELIZABETH FRY, wife DOROTHY PORTER, brother EDMUND PORTER and brother in law DR. PATRICK MAULE and SETH PILKINGTON 1-67.

PORTER, MARY received a land grant in (1717) on YOPPIM RIVER 1-17; she died leaving a will in (1718) naming sons JOHN, EDMUND & JOSHUA, daughter ELIZABETH, daughter SARAH LILLINGTON and grandchildren JOHN and SARAH PORTER, MARY, ELIZABETH and SARAH LILLINGTON 1-68.

PORTER, NICHOLAS, died in JOHNSTON COUNTY in (1749) naming son SAMUEL and daughters JEANE, ELIZABETH, ANN and AGNES PORTER, with NEEDHAM BRYAN and MARY LEE the witnesses 1-366.

PORTER, SAMUEL died leaving will in BLADEN COUNTY in (1757) children JAMES, JOHN, HUGH and SAMUEL 1-366.

PORTER, WILLIAM, of ROCKBRIDGE COUNTY, VIRGINIA, married FRANCES SHARP and moved to TENNESSEE, and they had a son BOYD PORTER; information of them sought 3-315.

PORTIS, ALEXANDER died in BERKELEY PRECINCT in (1675) at the home of ANDREW ELLWOOD 3-365.

PORTLOCK, POLLY died leaving will in (1815) & mentions brother WILLIAM PORTLOCK 3-346.

PORTLOCK, THOMAS died leaving will in (1789) and mentioned LEMUEL PORTLOCK of Virginia, and children MARY and WILLIAM PORTLOCK & his wife CATRON, with WILLIAM COPPAGE, W. NEWBOLD and WILLIAM STAFFORD witnesses 3-183.

POTTER, JAMES, of EDENTON was of full age in (1725) and was examined by JOHN LOVICK, ESQ., who makes statement in regard to his conduct at the home of JOSEPH YOUNG 3-232, and 3-233; in (1741) he was ordered to teach RICHARD WILLIAM DUNSTON the orphan of JOHN DUNSTON 1-457; he bought lands from EDWARD HOWCOTT in (1738) the deed being witnessed by MATTHEW HARDY, JAMES TROTTER and F. VERNON 3-131; in (1731) he was appointed Constable for the town of EDENTON and in (1729) was a witness with JAMES ANDERSON 2-447.

POWELL, CHARLES received a grant of land near WARWICK SWAMP in (1792) 1-24.

POWELL, DANIEL was the son of MARY POWELL who died in (1833) 2-540, will (1825) 2-67.

POWELL, GEORGE died leaving will in BERTIE in (1736) in which he named his sons KADER, GEORGE, LEWIS and MOSES POWELL 1-66.

POWELL, JACOB died in GATES COUNTY in (1816) leaving will; wife CYNTHIA 2-67.

POWELL, JOHN left will in CHOWAN (1723) & named wife ANN and sons JOHN and BROOK POWELL 1-68; JOHN POWELL of PERQUIMANS sold land in CHOWAN, where he then lived, with JAMES SUMNER & SAMUEL POWELL witnesses in GATES COUNTY - 1-284; in (1734) he and his wife HESTER sold land to JOHN NORFLEET, with ROBERT and JOHN POWELL witnesses 3-121, also 1-111.

POWELL, KEDAR (Or KADER) in (1746) recorded his mark or brand 2-528; he was mentioned as son in the will of GEORGE POWELL of BERTIE (1736) 1-66; still another KEDAR POWELL was son of DANIEL POWELL in (1826) 2-67.

POWELL, MARY was the daughter of DANIEL POWELL of GATES COUNTY in (1826) 2-67.

POWELL, MOSES was the son of GEORGE POWELL and a brother of KADER, GEORGE and LEWIS POWELL in (1736) 1-66.

POWELL, ROBERT left will in CHOWAN in (1773) had daughter RACHEL DUKE and sons JACOB, SHADRACK and DANIEL POWELL and a son in law MOSES SPEIGHT 2-18; he received a land grant (1762) 1-21.

POWELL, WILLIAM bought lands from WILLIAM BOON & wife ELIZABETH in (1721) with THOMAS BOON and ROBERT HICKS witnesses 2-616; in (1734) he & wife MARY sold lands to ROBERT ROBINSON witnessed by GEORGE ALLEN 2-610; the same year he sold lands to JOHN ROBERSON on ROCKYHOCK CREEK, with WILLIAM PERRY and CONSTANCE LUTEN as witnesses 3-125; in (1704) WILLIAM POWELL wrote letter to the GOVERNOR telling about INDIANS who came to his house with KING LOWTHER and all with their guns, etc. 1-437.

POWERS, CHARLES charged with the tuition of HENRY LOYD and orphan in BERTIE in (1770) 3-448.

POWERS, GEORGE, probate of his will in CHOWAN PRECINCT in (1695-6) mention of daughter ABIGAIL and son WILLIAM 1-443; see 1-361.

POWERS, JAMES was the administrator of the estate of THEOPHELUS PUGH in (1747) 1-457.

POWERS, SAMUEL and his wife PRUDENCE charged with tuition of MARY WARBURTON (daughter of MARY) in (1767) 3-444

POWERS, WILLIAM, and CALEB POWERS were Executors of will of ISABEL POWERS in CURRITUCK (1757) 1-351; but another WILLIAM had died before that in (1742) for whom BENJAMIN HILL returns an inventory 2-631.

POYNER, JOSEPH will written (1712) proven (1721) mentions wife ELIZABETH, sons WILLIAM & JOHN and daughter MARGARET (This name may have been adopted from the name PINER or PINNER).

PRATT, DAVID owned lands next to those patented by CHRISTOPHER BUTLER in (1749) on ALBEMARLE SOUND 1-20.

PRATT, GRIZZELL was the daughter of NATHANIEL CALE who left will (1821) 3-389.

PRATT, JEREMIAH left will in (1772) mentions sister MARY PRATT, wife PENINAH and sister DEBORAH HAUGHTON, CHARLES MOORE and brothers RICHARD and JOSEPH PRATT; witnesses JOHN CALE and THOMAS WILLIAMS.

PRATT, JOB, left will in (1737) the legatees being son JOHN, JOHN WILKINS, JOSHUA PRATT and LUKE GREGORY; brother JOSHUA 1-66; a J. PRATT witnessed a bill of sale by JOSEPH BUNCOMBE to GEORGE BURRINGTON (1733) 2-609.

PRATT, JOHN left will in (1740) with wife CHRISTIAN and child unborn 1-65.

PRATT, SUSANNAH registered her mark and brand in (1743) 2-631.

PRATHER, THOMAS, born in (1740) in FREDERICK COUNTY, VA. son of JOHN PRATHER, and married first RACHEL GAITHER, second LENA ROBY by whom he had six sons; descendants to TENNESSEE and KENTUCKY. Query? 2-282.

PRESCOTT, AARON, will written (1709) proved in (1720) names daughter DIANA, MOSES, AARON, JOHN and WILLIAM PRESCOTT 1-68.

PRESCOTT, WILLIAM of CRAVEN COUNTY left will in (1749) names wife MARY, sons AARON, MOSES, JOHN, WILLIAM and RICHARD, also JOB; daughter MARY and grand-daughter ELIZABETH PRESCOTT 1-65; it was probably his son WILLIAM PRESCOTT who died in BEAUFORT in (1755) with son THOMAS and wife AMY 1-65.

PRETLOW, KESIAH left will in (1791) and mentioned son THOMAS NIXON, with JAMES and SAMUEL NIXON witnesses 3-183.

PREDHAM, NOAH, of BERTIE granted license in (1744) to run an Ordinary 2-521.

PRICE, BENJAMIN left will in (1802) wife MIRIAM and son WINSLOW PRICE, brother in law AARON MORRIS, with PENINAH ALBERTSON witness 3-346.

PRICE, JAMES granted land on Green Hall in (1783) 1-21; a JAMES left will in CHOWAN in (1788) children THOMAS, JOHN MYLES & NOAH, ELIZABETH THOMPSON and SARAH BRINKLEY, with RICHARD HOSKINS and JOHN BLOUNT Executors and witnesses 2-15; another & different JAMES left will (1786) daughter TREASY, sons SAMUEL, MILES, JOHN and JAMES daughter ELIZABETH and wife MARY; JAMES & JOHN PRICE and MICHAEL PAYNE Executors & JAMES BUNCH, MILES PRICE and JAMES PRICE witnesses 2-15, 216.

PRICE, MICAJAH, will in BERTIE in (1783) wife SARAH, cousin ELIZABETH URQUHART and ALEX URQUHART 3-350.

PRICE, NOAH died in CHOWAN and left will in (1791) names sister SARAH BRINKLEY and NANCY, SARAH, JEREMIAH, FANNY, ELIZABETH, DOCTON, MILES, JOHN and JAMES PRICE, REBECCA and HENRY THOMPSON, JEREMIAH FLEETWOOD and THOMAS PRICE Executors 2-15

PRICE, THOMAS, died leaving will in (1689) & only mentions wife (ALBEMARLE COUNTY) 1-67. (GRIME p. 301 gives names of godson, ARCHIBALD McDANIEL and other legatees), a THOMAS PRICE died leaving will EDGECOMBE in (1750) naming children WILLIAM, THOMAS, JOHN, daughters ELIZABETH and RACHEL and wife; JOHN HOOKS, WILLIAM RADHAM and JOHN HOOKS, JR. were the witnesses to the will 1-368.

PRICE, RICE died in NEW HANOVER COUNTY in (1756)
and his wife was THOMASIN and his sons EDWARD and RICHARD PRICE 1-368.

PRICE, RICHARD was the son of RICE PRICE whose
will was proved in NEW HANOVER in (1756) 1-368.

PRIDGEON, FRANCIS lived at PRIDGEON'S POINT on
CHOWAN RIVER in (1723) 2-298; he witnessed
the deed of MARY FLEMING in (1717) 1-299.

PRINCE, RICHARD proved his headrights in (1702)
naming DANIEL SULLIVANT and wife ALICE, JERIMIAH SULLIVANT and ELIZABETH LUCAS, JOHN
BERNARD, HENRY SPRING and WILLIAM WRIGHT;
all assigned to THOMAS ARRINGTON 2-300.

PRINCE, THOMAS was Master of the sloop MOLLY in
(1749) 1-435.

PRITCHARD, HERBERT left will in EDGECOMBE (1738)
named sons JOHN, WILLIAM and JAMES PRITCHARD 1-66; another HERBERT died in BERTIE in
(1797) with children ABSOLOM, ELIZABETH,
ZADOCK, HUGH, MARTHA, and other legatees
of other family names 2-350, 2-351.

PRITCHARD, JAMES charged with the tuition of an
orphan NATHAN COBB, son of JOHN COBB (1769)
3-447; and a JAMES died in BERTIE in (1785)
wife DORCAS and children JAMES, REUBEN, RIGON, PENNY, DAVID, LAMB and STEPHEN PRITCHARD
and brother HERBERT PRITCHARD 2-350.

PRITCHARD, MARY who died leaving will in (1765)
had brother BENJAMIN PRITCHARD, sisters
ELIZABETH and MIRIAM PRITCHARD, mother in
law SARAH PRITCHARD, aunt SARAH ALBERTSON,
grandmother RACHEL WHITE, and a lot of other relatives named WHITE; witnesses were
JOHN WHITE, ISRAEL PERRY and RACHEL WHITE
3-182.

PRITCHARD, MATTHEW. He and his wife SARAH were
administrators of the estate of PATRICK HENLEY, deceased; also the executors of JOHN
CULPEPPER in (1702); his wife SARAH had been
the wife of JOHN CULPEPPER 1-610; MATTHEW
PRITCHARD was plaintiff in the suit against
BRYANT FITZPATRICK in (1701) 3-145; petition of PRITCHARD and wife SARAH in their
suit against CAPT. JOHN HUNT 3-88, 3-89.

PRITCHARD, SARAH. She first married JOHN CULPEPPER, second PATRICK HENLEY and third MATTHEW PRITCHARD 3-88, 3-89; one item is erroneous that says she married JOHN LARKINS
of NEW ENGLAND 1-610; she married PRITCHARD
about (1696-7) 3-89.

PRIVETT, GEORGE deeded lands to ANN MARTIN (1738)
with HENRY BONNER and HENRY BAKER as witnesses 1-284.

PRIVETT, JACOB deeded lands to JOHN CHARLTON in
(1723) with JEAN BONNER as witness 2-607; he
and wife ELIZABETH sold lands to WILLIAM
ROWDEN joining the lands of JOHN JONES and
MAJOR BONNER in (1728) 2-446.

PRIVETT, WILLIAM, sold land to JOHN BENNETT SR.
in (1714) which is described as "part of a
patenet to me" 1-293; and WILLIAM PRIVETT
was granted a tract of land adjoining lands
owned by VINES CROPLEY and JOHN VOLWAY on
ALBEMARLE SOUND in (1714) 1-8.

PROCLAMATION making void all offices, signed
by WILLIAM GLOVER and others 3-261.

PROCTOR, JOHN in (1718) he bought 80 acres of
land adjoining RICHARD WASHINGTON on WASHINGTON BRANCH from THOMAS KERBY and his
wife ESTHER; this was in MAY, and in AUGUST he assigned this deed to JOHN COLSON
1-622.

PROCESSIONING LANDS. Acts of the ASSEMBLY of
N. C. relating to the method of 3-71, 372.

PROTESTANT DISSENTERS. Petition from those of
BAY and NEUSE RIVERS 2-198.

PRUDEN, ESTHER left will in GATES COUNTY (1824)
names children and grandchildren 2-67.

PRUDEN, JAMES will in GATES COUNTY in (1823)
names wife ESTHER, and RACHEL RICE granddaughter of ABRAHAM PRUDEN, all my children
and sons DAVID and JOHN 2-67.

PRUDEN, LODOWICK died in (1815) wife ANNA and
RACHEL RICE (Daughter of JOHN, etc) son in
law DAVID TAYLOE, witnessed by CHRISTOPHER
PRITCHARD 2-539.

PRUDEN, MARTHA will (18390 mentions neice SARAH
LeFELLIER and her mother 2-539.

PRUDEN, PATIENCE will in BERTIE in (1797) names
sons ELISHA, JOHN, STEPHEN, SOLOMON and
WILLIAM PRUDEN, daughters MARY PRUDEN and
PRUDENCE CORY, with BENJAMIN CORY a witness
2-351, 2-352.

PUGH, DANIEL lived near the head of BENNETT'S
CREEK in (1715) 2-453; he was "of NANSEMOND COUNTY, VIRGINIA" when he sold lands
to SAMUEL SMITH (1707) on CHOWAN 1-616; he
and JOHN KING and JOSEPH SMALL witnessed a
deed by BENJAMIN SMALL in (1731) 2-450; a
DANIEL PUGH was the son of JOHN PUGH who
died in (1740) 1-65.

PUGH, ELIZABETH left will in BERTIE in (1818)
and named her brother JONATHAN STANDLEY,
daughter PENELOPE IRVIN and other relatives
2-537.

PUGH, FRANCIS died in (1807) named wife ANN &
children, had brother JOSEPH PUGH and a
sister PENELOPE GALE and NANCY HARRELL
2-537; see 1-451.

PUGH, FEREBY, was the daughter of FRANCIS
PUGH and probably married MR. BARKER the
attorney of JOSEPH PERRY by (1744) 2-622.

PUGH, FRANCIS received a land grant in (1737)
on the East side of CHOWAN in GATES COUNTY 1-12; he was a JUSTICE for CHOWAN in
(1731) 1-449; he died by (1737) and his
land was partly bought by DANIEL PUGH
3-127; in (1751) a FRANCIS PUGH chose BENJAMIN WYNNS his guardian 1-451; he sold
land to JONATHAN PARKER in (1734) 3-127;
his two sisters MARGARET and MARY PUGH
married BENJAMIN WYNNS and JAMES LUTEN
1-451; his estate divided in (1744) & Mr.
BARKER (the lawyer) in right of his wife
PHEREBY, JOHN HARRELL, NEEDHAM BRYAN, THOS.
WHITMELL, WILLIAM TAYLOR and RICHARD WILLIAMS were called on to divide the estate
2-622; in (1728) he sold lands to a JOHN
DAWSON that had been THOMAS JONES' 2-608.

PUGH, FRANCIS lived in BERTIE COUNTY, and his wife was PHERIBE SAVAGE, of an old VIRGINIA FAMILY; after his death his widow married THOMAS BARKER, the attorney of BERTIE but afterwards of EDENTON; their daughter ELIZABETH BARKER married COL. WILLIAM TUNSTALL of PITTSYLVANIA COUNTY, Va. 1-66; a daughter MARY PUGH married JAMES LUTEN 2-8; FRANCIS sold lands in (1734) to DANIEL PARKER adjoining lands of WILLIAM SPITES (SPEIGHT) and JOHN KING 3-131; he had son THOMAS PUGH who was 19 years old in (1745) 2-626; a FRANCIS PUGH, then 17, chose JAS. LUTEN (his brother in law) his guardian in (1750); FRANCIS witnessed a deed to land by WILLIAM DANIEL in (1727) 1-112; he died leaving a will in BERTIE in (1736), leaving son JOHN son THOMAS and a child in esse (who was son FRANCIS -see note) and "their sisters" 1-66; his widow married THOMAS BARKER 1-66, 2-470; he sold land to JONATHAN PARKER in (1734) 3-127; and to JOHN DAWSON in(1728) which joined THOMAS JONES 2-608.

PUGH, HENRY died in GATES COUNTY in (1833) with wife ANN and children; DAVID DUKE and NANCY SPEIGHT witnesses 2-65, 2-66.

PUGH, JAMES, of SUFFOLK in NANSEMOND COUNTY, VA. deeded lands to THEOPHILUS PUGH, a merchant, in (1739) which adjoined lands of a DANIEL PUGH 3-131, 3-132.

PUGH, JENNET, MRS. was the widow of THOMAS WHITMELL PUGH and before her marriage JENNET BRYAN, daughter of EDWARD BRYAN and wife MARTHA WEST, the latter being the daughter of THOMAS WEST and wife MARTHA BLOUNT; JENNETT BRYAN'S first husband had been HARDY HILL, who was descended from JOHN HARDY and wife REBECCA. See note 2-536.

PUGH, JOHN, of PASQUOTANK, died in (1741) and DANIEL and THEOPHILUS PUGH were the executors of his will 2-466; Theophilus and DANIEL were his brothers; his wife was HANNAH and in his will he mentions a son named JOHN PUGH 1-65; a JOHN POUS (perhaps intended for PUGH received a land grant to a lot in EDENTON which had escheated from JOHN HENLEY 1-23.

PUGH, PHEREBY and ROBERT WEST the executors of FRANCIS PUGH in (1737) deeded lands to DANIEL PUGH, adjoining SOLOMON ALSTON and others, with THOMAS JENKINS a witness 3-127; she had been PHERIBE SAVAGE 2-8; and married THOMAS BARKER the lawyer 2-470.

PUGH, THEOPHILUS, was the son of JOHN PUGH who died in (1740) and had brothers DANIEL and JOHN PUGH 1-65; he was deceased in (1745) and JOHN HODGSON was administrator 1-452; he came from NANSEMOND COUNTY, VA. 2-627; in (1744) he was granted license to run an Ordinary 2-624.

QUARLES, MARY, was the daughter of ALEXANDER SMITH in (1711) from VIRGINIA 1-77.

QUINCE FAMILY, from LONDON 3-7; PARKER QUINCE of NEW HANOVER COUNTY 3-464.

QUINN, JAMES married MARY PADGET widow of SAMUEL PADGET about 1750 2-469.

QUINN, THOMAS witness MOSES HILL will (1762)2-339

PUGH, THOMAS, of BERTIE COUNTY, in (1767) was guardian of JOHN HARRELL, the orphan of JOSEPH HARRELL; at that time THOMAS PUGH was called MAJOR 3-443; he gave a bond in (1744) to keep a ferry on CHOWAN RIVER opposite to his lands in BERTIE COUNTY, which formerly had belonged to OUTLAW 2-469; another THOMAS PUGH, who must have been younger, but lived in BERTIE, was only 19 years of age in (1745) 2-626; he was a witness to an affidavit or statement made in deposition form by MICHAEL WARD in BERTIE COUNTY in JULY (1777) which had to do with the Tory and Loyalist troubles of that period 2-215; a alter THOMAS PUGH left will in BERTIE COUNTY which was probated in (1806), which was witnessed by JOHN KING, CULLEN COOK and TURNER CARTER and in which he mentioned his son WILLIAM and a deceased son THOMAS PUGH, and grandsons FRANCIS, JOSEPH, WILLIAM, JOHN HILL PUGH; ESTHER PUGH (widow of son THOMAS) and her children WHITMELL, JAMES and AUGUSTIN PUGH; ELIZABETH PUGH daughter of THEOPHILUS PUGH (another son?) children of deceased son FRANCIS PUGH; SAMUEL W. JOHNSTON and JOHN HILL PUGH executors 2-537.

PUGH, THOMAS WHITMELL (probably the son WILLIAM PUGH, son of THOMAS who died in (1806) left will in BERTIE in (1802) and his wife was JENNETT (BRYAN-HILL) PUGH and he mentions daughter POLLY PUGH wife of WILLIAM JORDAN, and makes sons in law RICHARD SANDERSON, WILLIAM JORDAN and JONATHAN JACOCKS his executors 2-536.

PUGH, WHITMELL is called "cousin" in the will of JOHN HILL in BERTIE in (1802), who also mentions JOHN HILL PUGH, son of WILLIAM PUGH, and brother THOMAS B. HILL 2-518.

PUGH, WILLIAM died leaving will in BERTIE in (1809) in which he names sons THOMAS, AUGUSTIN and WHITMELL HILL PUGH and HENRY and JAMES PUGH 2-537. (TUNSTALLS also mentioned).

PULLEN, HENRY was Master of the sloop SWEEP in (1764) 1-436.

PURSER, ROBERT died leaving will in (1733) & names sons RICHARD, JAMES, BENJAMIN and ROBERT 1-67.

PURSELLS, JOHN and SARAH PURSELLS witness deed to THOMAS BRAY (1718) 1-626; and bought land from SAMUEL BOZEMAN (1718) 1-627.

PURSELLS, WILLIAM bought lands(1719) 1-627.

PURYEAR, JOHN, will (1725) 1-66.

PUTNELL, WILLIAM will (1734) son AARON 1-67.

QUIT RENTS. Act of the Assembly relating to payment of and levy, signed by WILLIAM WILKINSON, Speaker in (1703) 2-224.

QUEEN ANNE'S CREEK was called MATTACOMACK CREEK 1-284; courthouse at 2-84.

QUEEN ANNE'S TOWN, later was called EDENTON Account of the cost of the courthouse erected in (1718) 2-100, 2-101.

PARKER FAMILY. In order to convey to the reader of these notes an adequate conception of the VIRGINIA origin of the PARKERS who practically over-ran the old ALBEMARLE PRECINCT in NORTH CAROLINA near the close of the Seventeenth Century, it will be necessary to present some brief sketches of the families with which they were connected. THOMAS PARKER of "MACCLESFIELD" in ISLE of WIGHT COUNTY, Virginia, married the widow of PETER MONTAGUE. (Vol. 6 Va. Mag. of Hist. & Biog. p. 420). This reference does not give the name of the widow of PETER MONTAGUE, so recourse is had to the will of PETER MONTAGUE, proved in May, 1659, in LANCASTER COUNTY, Virginia, as shown on page 57 of the "History and Genealogy of Peter Montague" by GEORGE WILLIAM MONTAGUE (1894) in which her name is given as CICELY. And thereby hangs a most fantastic tale of marital adventure:

THE MYSTERIOUS CICELY JORDAN. At or about the same time, if not on the same vessel, in the year 1611, a ten year old girl named CICELY REYNOLDS, and a comparatively young widower, who had left his small sons behind him in England, arrived at JAMESTOWN in the Colony of Virginia. The young widower was SAMUEL JORDAN, who afterwards established a seat on the JAMES RIVER near its confluence with the APPOMATTOX, which he called "JOURDAN'S JORNEY". Almost contemporaneously with the coming of these two, but perhaps a year earlier, Sir. THOMAS GATES and his companions of the ill fated "SEA VENTURE" had landed, among them being CAPT. WILLIAM PIERCE. This was followed by JOANE PIERCE, the Captain's wife on the "BLESSINGE". CAPT. PIERCE was a relative in some degree of the young girl CICELY REYNOLDS, and doubtless the advance arrival of CICELY was known to both CAPTAIN PIERCE and his wife. Besides, SAMUEL JORDAN was a near-relative of CICELY and her mother's cousin, & still another cousin (of her mother) SILVESTER JORDAIN, came about the same time, so there was no lack of relatives to look after the ten year old child, whose mother, still living in Dorsetshire, for some reason had consented to her coming. Twelve years later, her brother, CHRISTOPHER REYNOLDS, arrived on the "JOHN and FRANCIS" and may have discovered for the first time that his sister was then married to her second husband SAMUEL JORDAN and the mistress of JORDAN'S JORNEY, with a six year old daughter by her first husband, named TEMPERANCE BAILEY.

These sudden and swift transitions in the life of CICELY REYNOLDS were characteristic of one of such adventurous spirit as to undertake a long sea voyage into strange lands, even though accompanied by near relatives. She was ten years of age in 1611, and must have married her first husband BAILEY when but about 14 years old, as in 1623-4 her daughter TEMPERANCE was seven years of age (Vol. 51 Va. Mag. of Hist. & Biog. pp. 384-385). The Christian name of her first husband has not been found, but it is safe to say he was of the same family as the SAMUEL BAILEY who is known to have married a grand-daughter of CAPT. WILLIAM PIERCE, her relative. The grandfather of CICELY REYNOLDS was THOMAS JORDAN, of DORSETSHIRE, England, grand daughter, the mother of CICELY married a REYNOLDS. Her mother's maiden name was CICELY FITZPEN or PHIPPEN, and she was the daughter of ROBERT PHIPPEN and his wife CICELY or CICELLIE JORDAN. ROBERT PHIPPEN was the son of one JOSEPH PHIPPEN, whose mother was ALICE PIERCE, and thus CICELEY REYNOLDS was related to CAPT. WILLIAM PIERCE and his wife JOANE. This last couple were the parents of JANE PIERCE who married as his third wife another celebrated Virginia character - JOHN ROLFE. But to continue the story:

SAMUEL JORDAN, of JORDAN'S JORNEY, became the second husband of this adventurous daughter of his first cousin CICELY PHIPPEN, and at their home on the JAMES he and his wife and their household survived the Indian uprising that occurred in 1622-3. But not long after that SAMUEL JORDAN died. By his first marriage in England he is said to have had three sons THOMAS (b. 1600), SAMUEL and ROBERT JORDAN (W. & M. 7, 121) and in all of the genealogical accounts of these Jordans, each of whom came to Virginia, there continual bobs up the name of a certain RICHARD JORDAN whose parentage is unaccounted for. Incidentally he married before 1654, ELIZABETH REYNOLDS, a daughter of CHRISTOPHER REYNOLDS, of Isle of Wight County. Very shortly after the death of SAMUEL JORDAN, of "Jordan's Journey", one of the legatees in the will of ABRAHAM PERSEY, a certain REV. GREVILLE POOLY, vociferously "woed" the widow CICELY JORDAN, who rejected his early advances on the ground that she was with child; but thereafter she married CAPT. WILLIAM FARRAR, a prominent man of the VIRGINIA COUNCIL. Thereupon the parson brought what has been called by Alexander Brown "the first breach of promise suit in America". The astute third husband, being a lawyer, succeeded in quashing the proceedings, and Parson Pooly went on his way. BUT THE CHILD WAS BORN. His name was RICHARD JORDAN, and he married his first cousin (as they so often did in those days) ELIZABETH, the daughter of CHRISTOPHER REYNOLDS. (See Boddie's 17th Century Isle of Wight). Thus CICELY REYNOLDS had been married twice and was the mother of one child by each of her first two husbands. By CAPTAIN WILLIAM FARRAR, she became the mother of two sons CAPT. WILLIAM FARRAR JR. and LIEUT. COLONEL JOHN FARRAR, of HENRICO COUNTY, who left no children and never married, so that the girl-emigrant thus became the ancestress of the numerous FARRARS of Virginia, through her son WILLIAM FARRAR, JR. Her third husband, CAPT. (or COLONEL) WILLIAM FARRAR died about 1635-6. But CICELY was not near through. In 1621 PETER MONTAGUE, then a very young man, came to JAMESTOWN in the "CHARLES" and was living in JAMES CITY in 1624 aged 21 years. He was two years younger than CICELEY FARRAR, the widow after 1636. He too, had been previously married and had two daughters, then very young, named DOROTHY and SARAH. He married the widow CICELY as her FOURTH HUSBAND. His will in Lancaster County names seven children, all obviously her children, but obviously also, not all of his family, thus reflecting his previous marriage. It was proven in 1659. SARAH MONTAGUE, one of the. daughters of his first marriage married JAMES BAGNALL (6 Va. Mag. of Hist. & Biog. p. 420) and the same authority tells us that the widow of PETER MONTAGUE became the wife of THOMAS PARKER. As Cicely was born in 1601, she was 58 years old at the time of the death of PETER MONTAGUE, therefore it is patent that this latter marriage was one of convenience, and that no children resulted. But this alliance with CICELY MONTAGUE, alias CICELY JORDAN, nee CICELY REYNOLDS readily suggests an explanation of the persistent intimacy which through the long years existed and continued to exist between the JORDANS, PARKERS and REYNOLDS families as reflected by these records (1-16), (1-8), (1-628), (2-619) and other items throughout the list. It is claimed by one writer (Boddie's 17th Century Isle of Wight p. 239) that the PETER MONTAGUE of LANCASTER (will 1659) and the one in ISLE OF WIGHT, whose un-named widow married THOMAS PARKER were different persons. This statement is refuted by our records. The author of the MONTAGUE GENEALOGY did confuse the parentage, but not the identity of his subject. Our records disclose that both THOMAS PARKER, who first patented lands in ISLE OF WIGHT COUNTY in 1650 (Vol 6. Va. Mag. of Hist. & Biog. p. 420) who married the widow of PETER MONTAGUE, and JAMES BAGNALL, who married his daughter SARAH MONTAGUE were living in LANCASTER COUNTY after 1650 (Fleet's Colonial Abstracts 22 pp 8, 9 and 78). All of the records we have examined however, tend to show that perhaps not only JAMES BAGNALL and THOMAS PARKER but also PETER MONTAGUE had been previous residents of ISLE OF WIGHT COUNTY, and further show that THOMAS PARKER and JAMES BAGNALL were living in the latter county towards the latter end of the century. JAMES BAGNALL was the son of ROGER BAGNALL, who died leaving will in Isle of Wight in 1647, at which time his son JAMES BAGNALL was not of age. (Boddie's 17th Century Isle of Wight p. 514). These early emigrants to Virginia moved about a great deal in their furious search for vast tracts of land and for social and economic advantages, just as the people of this day and time and it would perhaps be a misnomer to say that Peter Montague, or James Bagnall or Thomas Parker were either "of Isle of Wight" in a strict sense, until they had finally settled down at an advanced age. In 1624 Peter Montague, then 21 years of age was in Jamestown (Hotten) and in 1631 he was witness to a will in Yorktown, or in York County (Fleet's Colonial Abstracts No. 24 p. 11). He was perhaps "of York County" at the time he married the widow of CAPT. WILLIAM FARRAR, and he was certainly "of Lancaster County" when in 1658, a year before his death, he was a Burgess from that county.

THE PARKER FAMILY, ITSELF. Enthusiastic genealogists of the PARKER FAMILY. ITSELF. have made valient efforts to set down the history of the tribe. In none of these efforts has there been a reference to the NORTH CAROLINA PARKERS, so often mentioned in these records. In one of such articles, evidently written with much care, we are told that two PARKER BROTHERS, a THOMAS and a GEORGE PARKER took up lands in Virginia, the former in ISLE OF WIGHT COUNTY and the latter in ACCOMAC (on the Eastern Shore) in 1650. (We think they came much earlier than that.) THOMAS, of ISLE OF WIGHT, called his home "Macclesfield" as they were descended from the "Macclesfield" Parkers of England. The remainder of this fine article is devoted entirely to the descendants of one ALEXANDER HYDE PARKER, a grandson of GEORGE PARKER, who settled in ACCOMAC COUNTY, and who moved to TAPPAHANNOCK, in ESSEX COUNTY, Virginia, and became the ancestor of a numerous tribe of PARKERS many of whom distinguished themselves in the wars of their country, including the AMERICAN REVOLUTION and on the bench. (Vol. 61 Daughters of the American Revolution Magazine, p. 1) Any genealogical account of a large family that deals exclusively and solely with the descendants of one lone grandson cannot possibly give one any conception of the family with which it deals. This article is valuable as a history of the "Northern Neck Parkers" only, though they are by no means unimportant, and were beyond question distant cousins of our North Carolina tribe. A much better conception of the ACCOMAC COUNTY PARKERS is given in another account of CAPT. GEORGE PARKER, GENT. (the supposed brother of THOMAS PARKER of "Macclesfield", Isle of Wight County) who was HIGH SHERIFF of Accomac County, Virginia, and a member of the County Courts of both ACCOMAC and NORTHAMPTON COUNTIES about 1656 (Vol 6 Va. Mag. of Hist. & Biog. pp 412-414). It was his grandson, ALEXANDER HYDE PARKER who is said to have removed to ESSEX COUNTY where he became the ancestor and progenitor of the "Northern Neck Parkers". But the exasperating thing is that, though he appears to have had many grandchildren and grandsons listed in this account, we search among them in vain for an ALEXANDER HYDE PARKER. But if this last article be credited, CAPT. GEORGE PARKER had not only a brother THOMAS PARKER, but also brothers ROBERT, JOHN and PHILLIP, though PHILLIP is alleged to have returned to ENGLAND to live. As for children CAPT. GEORGE PARKER had GEORGE, JOHN, HENRY, THOMAS, LEVIE, CHARLES, CLEMENT, ANN, SARAH, PRISCILLA and ELIZABETH. With a list of eleven (11) children, including SEVEN sons, CAPT. GEORGE PARKER must have had a small army of grandsons, so it is therefore little wonder we can't find ALEXANDER HYDE PARKER in the scimpy list available.

THOMAS PARKER, of "MACCLESFIELD" in ISLE OF WIGHT COUNTY, was apparently the ancestor of most, if not all of the PARKERS who settled in NORTH CAROLINA (Albemarle Precinct) at about the end of the Seventeenth Century. He is said to have patented land at "Smith's Neck". We think perhaps this was in NEWPORT PARISH. His lands adjoined those of MR. NORSWORTHY. According to the article on which we rely he had FOUR children (all imported), JOANE, ELIZABETH, THOMAS and FRANCIS PARKER. Like the previous article discussed the only light thrown on the entire family pertains solely to the descendants of the son THOMAS PARKER who died leaving a will in 1688, aged 56 years, which is proof that the son THOMAS PARKER was born in 1632. Presumable the other three children have relatively approximate dates. It is the writer's conviction that if this account had included the children of the son FRANCIS we would have much more light on our NORTH CAROLINA PARKERS. As it is, however, we must conjecture and "conjure" with the descendants of THOMAS PARKER JR., who had (from his will) JOHN, THOMAS, FRANCIS, GEORGE, ELIZABETH, MARY and ANN. Of these four sons we do not have descendants of any except FRANCIS PARKER, who had MARTHA, NICHOLAS and NATHANIEL. Nicholas doubtless had sons of whom we know nothing. NATHANIEL married ANN and had NICHOLAS, NATHANIEL, MARTHA & MARY. The last NICHOLAS married ANN COPELAND, and had COL. JOSIAH PARKER (of the revolution) and COPELAND PARKER. (Vol 6 Va. Mag. of Hist. & Biog. p 420). Here we begin to connect, for COL. JOSIAH PARKER married the widow of COL. JOSEPH BRIDGER, who had been MARY PIERCE, daughter of COL. THOMAS PIERCE. THOMAS PIERCE JR. married MARY COPELAND in 1719 (3-393). ANN COPELAND was the sister of THOMAS COPELAND and the daughter of THOMAS COPELAND who married HOLLAND APPLEWHITE, daughter of THOMAS APPLEWHITE (Boddie's 17th Century Isle of Wight pp 214-215). HOLLAND APPLEWHITE was mentioned in the will of HENRY WEST in 1752 (1-80), and this particular HENRY WEST came from NEWPORT PARISH in ISLE OF WIGHT COUNTY, Virginia. Add to this the fact, as shown by these records, that PETER PARKER, of CHOWAN, before 1714 had married GRACE COPELAND, the daughter of WILLIAM COPELAND and his wife CHRISTIAN, and that this same PETER PARKER sold lands to WILLIAM COPELAND in 1716 with JOHN JORDAN and JANE JORDAN as witnesses (2-456) and (2-619) and little room is left for doubt as to the fact that THOMAS PARKER of "MACCLESFIELD" who married as his second wife CICELY MONTAGUE alias CICELY JORDAN, nee CICELY REYNOLDS, was the ancestor of the PARKERS of NORTH CAROLINA.

The remaining space available here will not permit, at this particular point, the account of the COPELAND FAMILY (mostly from YORK COUNTY, VA.) which would further clarify this record.

RABY, ADAM, will in BERTIE in (1765) wife JUDAH and sons ADAM and LUKE 2-352.

RABY, LUKE will in BERTIE in (1789) wife HESTER and her HARRELL children 2-352.

RABEY, JETHRO, proved the will of WILLIAM HILL in CHOWAN (1751) 1-451.

RABEY, WILLIAM, with LUKE RAWLS and JOHN WEBB in (1737) witnessed a deed by THOMAS JERNIGAN to ANN ODOM 3-129.

RADWELL, WILLIAM was the orphan of THOMAS RAD-WELL in BERTIE (1767) under the tuition of WILLIS HARGROVE 3-443.

RAGAN, DANIEL will in (1727). Children DANIEL, SARAH, ANN, MARY and PRISCILLA and wife SARAH and brother THOMAS RAGAN 1-380.

RAINER, MOSES served on a jury of inquisition under CHRISTOPHER GALE in (1716) 3-131.

RAMEKE, DR. FREDERICK patented lands in (1787) which had escheated from JOHN HENLEY 1-22; he committed suicide in (1800) after wounding CAPT. BUTLER of Edenton in a duel 2-306.

RAMSEY, ALLEN, died leaving will in CHOWAN (1799) mentions children of his brothers JOHN, JAMES, WILLIAM and WILLIS RAMSEY. Will witnessed by DR. FREDERICK RAMEKE and JOHN LUTEN 2-21; JOHN RAMSEY who died in BERTIE in (1806) had a son ALLEN RAMSEY 3-542.

RAMSEY, JOHN died in BERTIE in (1806) leaving wife ELIZABETH and children; LEWIS OUTLAW and HARDY FREEMAN executors 3-542.

RAMSEY, SARAH died in BERTIE (1825); the daughter of JOHN RAMSEY and sister of ALLEN; JAMES WILSON, executor 3-452.

RANDOLPH, WILLIAM of HENRY COUNTY, Virginia, employs SAMUEL SWANN his attorney (1701) 1-610.

RANKHORN, AMOS, with JOHN OVERMAN witnessed will of SAMUEL WEEKS in (1815) whose daughter married CORNELIUS RAPER 3-356.

RANDALL FAMILY. Information sought and information wanted about 3-314.

RANDALL, FRANCIS owned a store in EDENTON built on lot owned by NATHANIEL ALLEN; he had a wife and four children who are mentioned in his will, with a history of himself and family in (1795); STEPHEN CABARRUS and Executor 2-21.

RAPER, ENOCH died leaving will (1791) and named children LUKE, ROBINSON and FANNY and brother JOHN RAPER 3-186.

RAPER, JOSEPH left will in (1802) with wife MARY and children JOSEPH, NATHAN, THOMAS, and several daughters named 3-347.

RASBERRY, JOHN in (1719) sold lands to JOHN WOSLAND 2-608; he died leaving will in BERTIE in (1749) and mentions daughter REBECCA who married ARTHUR PINNER, wife BRIDGETT and other children; witnesses were ISAAC HILL & EDWARD WILLIAMS 1-378.

RASCOE, ARTHUR died in BERTIE in (1796) in which mentions son DANIEL and DANIEL'S children; JOHN BENTLEY a witness 2-353.

RASCOE, DAVID married MARY HUNTER in (1807) 2-378.

RASCOE, ISAAC witness to will of JAMES JONES of HERTFORD COUNTY in (1771) 1-133.

RASCOE, ROBERT, was the first husband of ANNA SOTHELL, Governor, whom she married as a third husband; her second was JAMES BLOUNT from Isle of Wight County, Virginia, and after SOTHELL'S death she became the second wife of COL. JOHN LEAR of Nansemond County, Virginia 3-21.

RASCOE FAMILY WILLS 2-542.

RATLIFF, CORNELIUS was the brother of JOSEPH RATLIFF who died leaving will in (1787) & they also had brother THOMAS 3-186.

RATLIFF, DAMARIS was the mother of JOSEPH, JOHN and JAMES THOMAS in (1727) 1-79; in a will she left in (1734) she mentions son JOSEPH, MARY MOORE and SARAH 1-70.

RATLIFF, MARY (daughter of DAMARIS RATLIFF) married JOHN MOORE in (1729) 3-410.

RATLIFF, SAMUEL died leaving a will in (1733) and mentions son ISAAC, PARTHENIA BALL, & daughters ELIZABETH and ISOBEL and WILLIAM BALL and ANNE BALL; Nathaniel HILL and THOMAS ASHLEY executors 1-70; the widow of SAMUEL RATLIFF (Spelled here RATCLIFF) married PATRICK BAILEY about (1703-4)1-305.

RAWLINGS, BENJAMIN died in EDGECOMBE COUNTY in (1738) and mentions EDMUND KEARNEY (son of THOMAS and wife SARAH), ELIZABETH ALSTON wife of JOHN ALSTON, ELIZABETH WILLIAMS the wife of SAMUEL WILLIAMS and DAVID COLTRAIN an executor 1-379.

RAWLINS, GEORGE was sued in (1731) by PHILLIP LIGHTFOOT and BENJAMIN HARRISON the executors of FRANCIS LIGHTFOOT. Rawlins lived in BERTIE where the suit was instituted 2-298.

RAWLINS, JAMES accused of a conspiracy against the State of N. C. makes a statement under oath in (1777) 2-400.

RAWLS, JOHN, of NANSEMOND COUNTY, Virginia receives a deed to lands in (1716) 1-298; in (1739) he sold lands to WILLIAM WOOD, witnessed by JOHN LANGSTON and SAMUEL PARKER 3-132.

RAWLSON, JOSEPH in (1715) witnessed a deed by WILLIAM BRASWELL to HENRY WHEELER 1-299; and in (1719) he and JOHN McCLEESE witnessed a deed executed by THOMAS BROWN 1-623.

RAYFORD, MATTHEW left will in BLADEN in (1758) in which he named his children and which was witnessed by MARGARET ARMSTRONG and by FRANCIS ARMSTRONG 1-379.

RAYMOND, THOMAS left will in (1730) in which he mentions daughter ELIZA RAYMOND 1-70.

RAYNER FAMILY WILLS 2-353, 2-543, 2-544.

RAZOR, EDWARD left will in BERTIE in (1776) & names two youngest children CHARLOTTE and JOSIAH and others, and wife ELIZABETH and WILLIAM, son of LAMB HARDY; will witnessed by EDWARD HARDY, JR., JESSE HARDY and LAMB HARDY 2-353.

RAZOR, EDWARD was a member of the Court for BER-
TIE COUNTY in (1768), and he and CULLEN POL-
LOCK witnessed a power of attorney from
THOMAS POLLOCK that year 3-445; he was
succeeded as Constable by JOHN ROGERS in
BERTIE in (1744) 2-625; in (1770) he and
DAVID STANDLEY were sureties for JAMES CAM-
PBELL 3-448; he and WILLIAM FLEETWOOD were
executors in (1738) of JACOB PAREOT 1-66;
member of the County Court in BERTIE (1757)
3-443.

RAZOR, FRANCES was the daughter of SUSANNAH
JOHNSON who left will (1718) 1-55.

RAZOR, FRANCIS died leaving will in BERTIE in
(1748) mentions daughter ELIZABETH HARDY,
grand-daughter FRANCES HARDY, son EDWARD
and daughter in law ELIZABETH RAZOR, daughter CHRISTIAN BELL and son in law LAMB HAR-
DY 1-376.

RAZOR, MARTIN FREDERICK and wife FRANCIS (1718)
1-627; in (1719) he and JOHN HOWCOTT were
witnesses to a deed of THOS. GARRETT, SR.
1-628; in (1718) he executed a deed to COL.
THOMAS POLLOCK 1-627.

RAY, ALEXANDER in (1718) executed a contract of
indenture to WILLIAM CHARLTON, which was
witnessed by WILLIAM BONNER 1-629; he died
in BERTIE COUNTY leaving will (1769) and in
it mentioned children JAMES, JOHN, SAMUEL,
STEPHEN, WILLIAM and daughters ELIZABETH
RAY, MARY HYMAN and ANN DEW, with son SAMU-
EL and SOLOMON PENDER, executors, and WIL-
LIAM SWAIN and JAMES SWINNOW GROVER as witnesses 2-352; ALEXANDER RAY among the list
of tithables taken by JAMES COLE in BERTIE
in (1702) 3-84, 1-142.

RAY, CHRISTMAS, witnessed the will of DAVID DOUG-
LAS in NORTHAMPTON COUNTY, VA. in (1753) &
DAVE DOUGLASS had a daughter MARTHA who married a CARROLL and one who married a HARWELL
1-198, 1-199.

RAY, CROPLEY married MARY EVANS in (1765) with a
JASPER HARDISON as security; and was himself
security on the marriage bond of JOHN RAY &
MARY GRAY in TYRRELL COUNTY in (1763) 3-107.

RAY, FANNY was mentioned in the will of HENRY
NORMAN of TYRRELL COUNTY in (1797) whose wife
was SARAH, though another HENRY NORMAN in
(1700) had a wife ANNE 3-372, who left a son
HENRY; and JOHN PETTIVER from YORK COUNTY in
VA. (1699) who was connected with ROBERT
STARKEY married the first HENRY NORMAN'S
wife ANNE 2-151, 2-152.

RAY, HENRY died leaving will in BERTIE in (1830)
and named daughters WINNIFRED WARD and SARAH
BIRD, son THOMAS, son JACOB and daughters
DICEY WARD and FRANCES GASKINS; his wife JU-
DITH and THOMAS COWAND were executors, and
witnesses were WILLIAM MIZELL and W. AARON
MIZELL 2-541; his wife was JUDITH WHITE whom
he married in BERTIE March 1, 1794 2-369.

RAY, HESTER ANN, was called "cousin" in the will
of ELIZABETH CHRISTIAN SMALL in (1864) which
was witnessed by ANNIE E. PARKER and THOMAS
SMALL 2-75

RAY, JAMES married POLLY NOWELL on JANUARY 9 in
(1799) in BERTIE COUNTY with SOLOMON PENDER
as surety on marriage bond 2-373.

RAY, JOHN married MARY GRAY in TYRRELL COUN-
TY, N. C. in (1763) with CROPLEY RAY as
security on the bond 3-107; he was the
guardian of STEPHEN RAY in BERTIE COUN-
TY in (1769) 3-447; in (1767) his wife
was ELIZABETH OXLEY, the daughter of JOHN
OXLEY who died leaving will that year
2-350; in (1791) a JOHN RAY is called a
grandson in the will of RALPH OUTLAW in
BERTIE COUNTY, who mentions a daughter
CHARITY ALEXANDER and a daughter MARY RAY
among others; also a grandson RALPH MIERS;
this will was witnessed by DAVID STANDLEY
and ANDREW SOUTH 2-349; one JOHN RAY evidently unmarried left a will in BERTIE
in (1801) in which he left all of his estate to his mother; it was witnessed by
JOHN PENDER and EDWARD WALKER 2-541.

RAY, JUDITH, the wife of HENRY RAY was the
daughter of MEEDY WHITE, who died leaving
will in BERTIE in (1804); she had brothers and sisters CADER, GEORGE, WILLIAM,
EZEKIEL, REUBEN, and WINNIFRED, KERREN-
HAPPUCH SKOLAR and ANNIS MIZELL 2-552.

RAY, LAMB, married PENNY GREGORY in (1831)
with THOMAS RAY as surety on bond 2-592.

RAY, MARY, was MARY OUTLAW, daughter of RALPH
OUTLAW in (1790) 2-349.

RAY, NATHANIEL was surety on the marriage bond
of ALLEN BRYAN and SARAH ARPS (1784) in
PERQUIMANS County 3-418.

RAY, PATIENCE, married JAMES S. OVERTON (1794)
with JOHN PENDER, security 2-368.

RAY, SAMUEL (See REA) in division of estate
CHRISTOPHER, ARTEYES, WILLIAM and WILEY
RAY and LAVINIA JACKSON are mentioned as
the heirs in (1833) 2-268; his widow was
MARTHA, who left will in CHOWAN in (1846)
and mentions ARTEMUS MANSFIELD a daughter
and ELIZABETH JANE RAY, daughter of son
WILLIAM RAY 2-22.

RAY, SARAH, married ROBERT GORDON in TYRRELL
COUNTY in (1769) 3-108.

RAY, STEPHEN was one of the son of ALEXANDER
RAY in (1769) 2-352; and the same year
his guardian was JOHN RAY in BERTIE
3-447.

RAY, WILLIAM in (1719) acknowledged an indenture to WILLIAM CHARLTON to serve seven
years 1-156; he left will in BERTIE CO.
in (1834) mentions wife NANCY, and daughters ELIZABETH PERRY, RACHEL HENRY, NAN-
CY HENRY, PENELOPE MILLER, ANGIE LAYTON
and MARY GASKINS, with NATHANIEL MILLER,
RODERICK PERRY and WILLIAM J. HARDY as
witnesses 2-541.

REA FAMILY (See RAY) Genealogical note on
the BRYAN, HILL, HARDY and PUGH FAMILIES
which shows connection with the REA family, also kin to BRINKLEYS and BUTLERS
2-536 at bottom of page.

REA, CHRISTOPHER C., was a son of SAMUEL REA
and brother of WILEY REA (1833) 2-268;
he married MARY FRANCES NIXON in CHOWAN
in (1840) 2-90.

REA, J. K. married MAGGIE REED BUTLER 2-536.

REA, JAMES (See RAY) left will in CHOWAN in (1829) names wife MARTHA, sons RICHARD T. REA, of Kentucky, AUGUSTUS REA (Ky.) and daughter AGNES P. REA; JOHN H. LEARY executor and THOMAS CHARLTON, and NATHANIEL J. BEASLEY, witnesses 2-22; he (JAMES) a creditor of JOHN COLLINS, of CAPE FEAR in N. C. in (1753) 3-467.

REA, JERMIAH M. (Of Kentucky) was a son of a JAMES REA of CHOWAN in (1829) 2-22.

REA, MILLICENT left will in (1823) and named the following daughters: SARAH WHITE, MARY ALbertson, MARGARET LACEY, NANCY ALBERTSON & HARRIET REA 3-048.

REA, POLLY (MARY) was POLLY PETTYJOHN, daughter of JOHN PETTYJOHN and wife NANCY in (1832) 2-19.

REA, SAMUEL, and JOB PETTYJOHN witnessed the will of THOMAS MIERS in (1815), who named the children of ELIZABETH MIXON, MARTHA REA and SAMPSON WILDER 3-342.

REA, SIMON D. was witness to the will of WILLIS THOMPSON in BERTIE in (1734) with LUKE PARKER 2-550.

REA, THOMAS married RACHEL ARRENTON in (1785) & THOMAS WHEEBEE was surety, 3-418; and MARY ARRENTON married JAMES JACKSON in (1791) 3-420.

READING, CHURCHILL left will in BATH in (1734) and mentioned brother in law JOHN CALDRON 1-70.

READING, JONATHAN left will in (1754) naming a son JOSEPH, and daughters MARGARET, ELIZABETH and DOROTHY 1-69.

READING, LYONELL; letters from relating to INDIANS, mentions SAMUEL SLOCUM and brother JOSEPH READING; letters were written from BATH 2-193, 2-194; left will in year(1708) names wife MARY, sons NATHANIEL and CHURCHILL and THOMAS, daughters SARAH, MARY & ANNE READING; his "widow" called GRACE READING (?) (She may have been a daughter) 1-71.

READY, WILLIAM sold lands to RICHARD RICKSON in (1719) 1-622.

REDDING, JOSEPH, died leaving will in PERQUIMANS in (1753) 1-69; and a JOSEPH "REDDIN" (perhaps the same) was a neighbor of ABRAHAM HILL on HORSE PEN SWAMP (1726) 2-446.

REDDITT, ISAAC, an orphan, was committed to the care of JOHN CRICKETT; one of the orphans of WILLIAM REDDITT and wife SUSANNA (1747) 2-630.

REDDITT, JOHN (Spelled REDDICK) and his wife MARGARET, were the parents of ELIZABETH, RACHEL, THOMAS and SARAH REDDITT born about(1730-35) 3-393.

REDDITT, JOSIAH, SR. died leaving will in BERTIE in (1811) named sons THEOPHILUS, WILLIAM and JOSIAH and a daughter SARAH who married HARDY FLEETWOOD; also sons ASA & AQUILLA & DAVID REDDITT; JONATHAN JACOCKS and Executor, witness HUMP. HARDY 2-543.

REDDITT, WILLIAM left will in BERTIE (1739) mentions THOMAS YATES and wife SUSAN 1-69.

REED, ANDREW and wife DELIVERANCE had daughter ELIZABETH born in (1697) 3-370; he lived on LITTLE RIVER in PERQUIMANS and in his will (1728) he mentions his brother WILLIAM WOODLEY and children, ANDREW, WILLIAM and MARY WOODLEY, who were REED'S nephews and niece; also mentions grandchildren JONATHAN and ELIZABETH KEETON 1-70.

REED, CHRISTIAN, of BERTIE, was Master sloop CHARMING BETSY in (1773) 1-436.

REED, CHRISTIAN, was the wife of GOV. WILLIAM REED, and they had a son CHRISTIAN married MARY DURANT (great grand-daughter of GEORGE DURANT, the elder); the son married MISS MARY DURANT, sister of his brother JOSEPH REED'S wife, ELIZABETH. See genealogy of this branch of the REED FAMILY 3-184, 3-185.

REED, DURANT, left will in (1767) and in it he mentions TULLE WILLIAMS, DUKE WILLIAMS and cousin BENJAMIN WILLIAMS, and brother WILLIAM REED 3-184; see note at bottom of 3-184, 3-185.

REED, JOHN, was the administrator of WILLIAM REED (grandson of GOV. WILLIAM REED of PASQUOTANK) in (1782); WILLIAM REED died after (1776) 2-468; a JOHN REED married MARTHA LITTLE, daughter of JOHN LITTLE of ANSON COUNTY who died in (1755) 1-57; in (1747) in BERTIE, JOHN REED recorded his mark 2-629.

REED, JOHN HATCH, was one of the Executors of WILLIAM REED whose wife was ALICE, who left will in (1800) 3-185.

REED, JOSEPH, left will in CHOWAN in (1774) wife ANN and "mother" ELIZABETH JACOCKS witnessed by THOMAS REED and THOMAS STEVENSON 3-185.

REED, THOMAS. One witnessed the will of JOSEPH REED in (1774) and a leter one the will of SARAH STACEY, the wife of ROBERT STACEY in (1826) 3-353.

REED, TULLY WILLIAMS died leaving will in (1802) names brothers GEORGE DURANT REED, WILLIAM REED and JOHN HATCH REED and a number of nephews, witnessed by ELIZABETH DAVIS 3-347.

REED, GOV. WILLIAM, inventory of his estate in (1729) 1-70, 1-71; appeared first in CURRITUCK in (1692) so it says, and gives a brief account of his acreer in NORTH CAROLINA in footnote 1-70; a WILLIAM REED married ELIZABETH HATCH and she married (2) MacROBA SCARBOROUGH 1-70; a REV. WILLIAM REED of GATES COUNTY died in (1859) and his will gives names of his children and relatives 2-72; the name of WILLIAM REED signed to proclamation by ASSEMBLY in (1717) 2-113; petition by WILLIAM REED in CURRITUCK relating to JOHN GIBBS 3-142; his name signed to a statement signed also by CHARLES EDEN, THOMAS POLLOCK and FRANCIS FOSTER and RICHARD SANDERSON, but without exact date given 3-281.

140

REEVES, WILLIAM, sold land to ROBERT SMITH in
(1718) adjoining the widow MOLTON 1-623;
and in the same year he owned lands next
to land bought by JOHN LEONARD from PHIL-
LIP JONES 1-623; in (1720) he made a deed
to RALPH MASON, with EDMUND ROGERS one of
the witnesses 2-618; in (1725) he bought
land from THOMAS WHITMELL and his wife
ELIZABETH, which deed was witnessed by
WILLIAM GRAY 2-614.

REGNOR, RICHARD, died leaving will in (1763)
in which he mentioned sons LUKE, RICHARD &
THOMAS 3-183, 3-184.

RELFE, CORNELIUS, of PASQUOTANK died leaving a
will in (1750) which shows he had a daughter MARY RELFE, who married DEMPSEY GREG-
ORY 2-297.

RELFE, JOHN in (1711) was indebted to CHRISTOPHER
GALE the consignee of BARON STEPHEN DE GRAF-
FENREID 3-272; in (1732) he was married to
the daughter of JAMES COLLINS 1-38.

RELFE, THOMAS, of PASQUOTANK, was 93 years of age
in (1707) and knew DARBY SEXTON thirty years
before; he was born about (1614) 1-611; in
(1703) THOMAS was appointed Surveyor General
of NORTH CAROLINA 3-61; an earlier or much
younger THOMAS RELFE died in NOVEMBER (1690)
and another THOMAS left will in PASQUOTANK in
(1720) with wife MARY, daughter DOROTHY and a
son THOMAS, and provides that "I give to WIL-
LIAM REED a tract of land if he remains with
his aunt until he becomes of age". 1-71.

RELFE, WILLIAM was present at a Court held at the
house of WILLIAM REED in (1697), with JOHN
HUNT, JOHN JENNINGS, WILLIAM COLLINS and JER-
EMIAH SYMONDS, with EDWARD MAYO, Clerk 3-439.

RELIGIOUS LIBERTY. Copy of document on file at
EDENTON relating to 3-59.

RESTON, THOMAS left will in (1724) in which mention is made of his wife ANN 1-71.

REVOLUTION. Affidavits relating to ROYALISTS and
TORIES activities in NORTH CAROLINA from
(1775 to 1777, inclusive) by various persons,
many of whom are well known in History; 2-556
to 2-577; 2-390 to 2-404; 2-208 to 2-217; &
items and letters and other documents of JOHN
PENN, GENERAL WASHINGTON and others to persons
in NORTH CAROLINA 2-234 to 2-254; 2-430 to 2-
442.

REVOLUTIONARY SOLDIERS OF NORTH CAROLINA. Roster
of the OFFICERS of the N. C. Continental Line
1-415 to 1-425; names of soldiers beginning
with A and B (partial) 2-125 to 2-129; those
beginning with B and C 2-383 to 2-390; those
beginning with B 2-179 to 2-186; those beginning with C and D 2-578 to 2-585; those from
D to F 3-95 to 3-104; those from G to part of
H 3-291 to 3-298; those finishing the letter
H and part of I 3-454 to 3-462. BALANCE OF THE
ALPHABET never completed by MR. HATHAWAY.

REYNOLDS, HEMPSTEAD and attorney from CONNECTICUT
leaves will in BERTIE COUNTY, N. C. and names
his brothers and other relatives, including a
brother ZADOCK; will witnessed by JOHN R. GIL-
LIAM and JOHN HAYWOOD 2-544.

REYNOLDS, JAMES, of BATH, mentioned in will of a
THOMAS CREECY (1730) 1-37.

REYNOLDS, JOHN, was granted lands in (1716)
which joined AZARIAH PARKER and TIMOTHY
JOYS 1-16.

REYNOLDS, NATHANIEL is mentioned as one of the
brothers of HEMPSTEAD REYNOLDS (1837)
2-544.

REYNAUD, BENJAMIN, left will in CURRITUCK in
(1712) mentions sons MOSES REYNAUD and
sons HENRY and LUKE GRACE, daughter SUSAN-
NA ROBINSON and ELIZABETH BOND 1-71.

RHODES, WILLIAM of PASQUOTANK left will (1734)
and mentioned wife ELIZABETH, sons THOMAS
and WILLIAM RHODES and daughters SARAH,
DOROTHY, ELIZABETH and MARY RHODES 1-70;
another WILLIAM RHODES (perhaps the son)
died in TYRRELL COUNTY in (1753) wife was
ELIZABETH, sons WILLIAM and JOHN RHODES &
daughter MARGARET COLLINS and ELIZABETH
GARRETT 1-69.

RIBBITS, GEORGE received a grant of land in
(1740) on BENNETT'S CREEK 1-18.

RICE, BENJAMIN left will in BEAUFORT (1746)
and names sons ZEBULON, BENJAMIN, JAMES,
EVAN, CIANERY, EPHRAIM, GIDEON and HEZE-
KIAH RICE; wife MARY; NATHANIEL DRAPER &
THOMAS WILLS, witnesses 1-375.

RICE, EDWARD, will in (1753) sons JOHN and
daughters MARY and BETTIE; witnesses were
JOHN COKE, SR., JAMES HAIR and WALTER and
ELIZABETH IVANS (EVANS) 1-375, 1-376.

RICE, DANIEL, signed a petition of sundry persons addressed to GOV. ROBERT DANIEL in
(1704-6) 3-259.

RICE, DAVID together with SOLOMON RICE were
witnesses to the will of WILLIAM HOGGARD
in BERTIE in (1823) 2-521; an earlier
DAVID RICE was one of the Executors of the
will of MILLS RIDDICK in (1777) 3-125.

RICE, JAMES and THOMAS PIERCE were witnesses
to a deed by JOHN SIMONS in (1729) 2-446;
and JAMES and JOHN RICE witnessed a deed
by WILLIAM WARD of NANSEMOND COUNTY, VA.
to SAMUEL HARRELL to part of a patent by
JOHN MOORE about (1736) 3-130.

RICE, JEPTHA, was an ensign in the NINTH REGT.
of the N. C. Continental Line 1-424.

RICE, JOHN deeded land to WILLIAM HINTON in
(1718) witnessed by ROBERT HICKS and a
CHARLES WILKINS 1-624; JOHN RICE died and
left will in CHOWAN in (1764) and mentions
wife ELIZABETH, son JOHN RICE and brother
DAVID RICE, and WILLIAM and JAMES RICE the
sons of his brother WILLIAM RICE; the witnesses were JAMES PARKER, SAMUEL HARRELL
and JAMES HODGES 2-191 an earlier JOHN
RICE left will in CHOWAN in (1753) wife
SARAH and brother EDWARD RICE; the witnesses to this will were HARDY HURDELL, BENJA-
MIN BERRYMAN, THOMAS ROUNDTREE, SR. and a
JOSEPH HAIR, JR. 1-376

RICE, JUDITH, died leaving a will in GATES CO.
in (1808) in which she mentions several
children and grand-children named CREECY
with WILLIAM and NATHAN CREECY Exrs. 2-71.

RICE, MARY will (1774) in WILMINGTON 1-376.

RICE, MORGAN died and left will in ALBEMARLE CO. in (1684) and mentions SARAH BURNBY, JR. a daughter of JOHN BURNBY, SR. whom I appoint my Executrix, with WILLIAM BURNBY and ANTHONY HATCH, witnesses 1-375.

RICE, NATHANIEL, was Secretary of the Province of NORTH CAROLINA in (1744) 2-620.

RICE, SOLOMON, with DAVID RICE and ZACHEUS CHAMPION witnessed the will of WILLIAM HOGGARD in BERTIE in (1823) 2-521.

RICE, WILLIAM, left will in BERTIE in (1853)2-544 but a much earlier WILLIAM left will in BERTIE in (1762) with sons WILLIAM and JAMES and daughters MARY and SARAH 2-352.

RICH, OBEDIAH was in the Colony of NORTH CAROLINA as early as (1699) 1-610.

RICHARDS, JANE married RICHARD WOOLARD in (1703) 3-410.

RICHARDS, JOHN. His wife was MARY. In (1744) he was administrator of JOSEPH BOYINTONE 2-469.

RICHARDS, MARY married JAMES FISHER in ISLE OF WIGHT COUNTY, VA. in (1701) 3-409.

RICHARDSON, BENJAMIN married SARAH MIZELL (1767) 3-108.

RICHARDSON, DANIEL was attorney general of NORTH CAROLINA in (1719) 2-84; he qualified as such in (1711) 2-149; he witnessed a deed from CHRISTOPHER GALE to JOHN PALIN(1717) 1-815; in (1719) he signed the indictments against MAURICE MOORE and EDWARD MOSELEY 2-33; he was mentioned by GOV. CHARLES EDEN in his will in (1721) 1-43; he died in PASQUOTANK in (1723) "no kinspeople mentioned in his will" 1-71 (NOTE: but JOHN LOVICK, GEORGE BURRINGTON, MARGARET DERNSBEE - see will of MORGAN RICE - and a MRS. ANN KNIGHT wife of LEWIS McALEXANDER KNIGHT, are Legatees, according to GRIMES' account p. 313).

RICHARDSON, JOHN was a brother in law of WILLIAM TAYLOR who left will in PASQUOTANK (1773) 1-493.

RICKS, BENJAMIN died leaving will in (1721) mentions brother ROBERT RICKS SR., brothers ISAAC RICKS, ABRAHAM RICKS and JAMES RICKS and sister JANE and WILLIAM BROWN son of BEAL BROWN 1-71.

RICKS, ISAAC, was the son in law of BARNABAS McKINNIE, who made a deed in (1722) 1-470; he and RICHARD JACKSON witnessed a deed by BARNABAS McKINNIE in (1720) 1-470.

RICKS, LUCY (Spelled RICS) widow left will in (1721) in which she mentions her cousin EVAN JONES 1-71.

RICKS, SAMUEL, witnessed a deed executed by THOMAS KIRBY, JR. about (1718-19) 1-630.

RICKETTS, CHARLES married ELIZABETH LYSLE (LYALL) daughter of HENRY LYSLE or LYALL and wife ELIZABETH in (1719) 1-529; he deeded lands to JOHN PARKER 3-132, and is mentioned in will of MOSES OLIVER in (1723) 1-54.

RICKSON, RICHARD bought lands from one WILLIAM READY in (1719) 1-622.

RIDDICK, JOB (Or REDDITT) sold lands to JOHN SIMPSON in (1739) that had been patented by CHARLES JORDAN in (1717) 3-134.

RIDDICK, JOHN (See REDDITT) was the son in law of THOMAS LILLY in (1735) 1-58.

RIDDICK, ROBERT (See REDDITT) sold lands to THOMAS HOLLIDAY in (1730) which JOHN JENKINS had bought from LUKE WHITE; the father of ROBERT RIDDICK was also ROBERT RIDDICK 2-448; ROBERT RIDDICK married ELIZABETH MERONEY, daughter of HENRY MERONEY & his wife MARTHA ALSTON, who was the daughter of JOSEPH JOHN ALSTON, of HALIAX CO. N. C., the son of JOHN ALSTON who patented lands on BENNETT'S CREEK near GATESVILLE, N. C. in an early day 2-70.

RIDDICK, WHITMELL, mentioned as a son of MARTHA RIDDICK in (1832) 2-544.

RIDDICK, WILLIAM, married SARAH HUNTER, daughter of WILLIAM HUNTER in (1754) 1-453; he sold lands to WILLIAM SKOYLES in (1716) and DAVID ATKINS and ROBERT HICKS were witnesses (in CHOWAN) 1-617.

RIDINGS, JONATHAN, and THOMAS POLLOCK, JR. witnessed a deed by MARY GODBY to THOMAS POLLOCK in (1720) 2-613; and he and JAMES TIGNON witnessed a deed to COL. POLLOCK in (1718) 1-627; and another deed to COL. POLLOCK in (1716) 1-298.

RIDLEY, DAY, of HERTFORD COUNTY, N. C. left a will in (1777) and mentions sons NATHANIEL and TIMOTHY SHARP RIDLEY; wife and brother in law TIMOTHY SHARP and HENRY TAYLOR Executors 1-132.

RIEUSSETT, PETER died leaving will in (1734) mentions wife ANN GALLADEE, nephew PETER RAWDON (ROWDEN or WROUGHTON); he was a Collector of Customs at ROANOKE 1-70.

RIGGAN, ARTHUR, bought land from JOHN HAWTHORNE in CHOWAN in (1718) 1-623.

RIGGAN, JOSEPH, of ISLE OF WIGHT COUNTY, VA., had brother DANIEL RIGGAN and a son in law JOHN WEBB in (1727) 1-70.

RIGHTON, JOHN was Master of the Sloop FRANCIS in (1774) 1-436.

RIGNEY, JOHN left will in (1725) mentions daughter ELIZABETH and friend BENJAMIN SLADE 1-71.

RIGSBY, WILLIAM married ELIZABETH RIGNEY the daughter of JOHN RIGNEY in (1739)2-466.

RIVER. LITTLE RIVER was in PERQUIMANS COUNTY or PRECINCT 1-70.

RITE, JACOB (Intended for WRIGHT) left will in (1735) and mentioned his son in law WILLIAM POWERS 1-69.

RIVETTS, GEORGE, deeded or assigned a patent to HENRY BONNER in (1738). The Assignment or deed was witnessed by HENRY BONNER JR. and RICHARD MINSHEW 1-135.

RIVETTS, JOHN, deeded lands to ANN MARTIN in the year (1737) which was part of a patent issued to PATRICK LAWLER 3-131; JOHN RIVETTS married ANNE, the daughter of PATRICK LAWLER and she had a brother DARBY LAWLER in (1736) 2-299.

ROACH, PATRICK died about (1744) and ELIZABETH ROACH was his administratrix 2-624.

ROANOKE ISLAND. One GEORGE FORDAGE claimed its ownership in (1701) 3-152; documents relating to the ownership of 2-101, to 2-108; the ownership of same in (1699); deeds from JOSHUA LAMB and others of ROXBURY, MASSA - CHUSETTS 2-101 to 2-108.

ROBERTS FAMILY WILLS 2-20, 2-21, 2-71, 3-135, 3-348.

ROBERTS, JAMES, was granted lands in (1790) on BEAR SWAMP and SANDY RIDGE 1-23.

ROBERTS, JONATHAN, died leaving will in (1785) in GATES COUNTY; sons JOHN and ELISHA and wife CHRISTIAN 2-71.

ROBERTS, PHILLIP, patented lands in GRANVILLE COUNTY in (1746) 1-447.

ROBERTS, RACHEL married GEORGE LOWE in the year (1786) 3-419.

ROBERTS, RICHARD, JR. recorded his mark and his brand in (1746) 2-629.

ROBERTS, WILLIAM, received a grant of land which had escheated from JOHN HENLEY (1787) 1-23; he also received grant in (1783) at GREEN HALL on COWHILL SWAMP 1-21.

ROBESON, THOMAS, left will in PERQUIMANS and was "of LITTLE RIVER" in (1719) naming sons JOSEPH and JOHN and daughter ANN 1-71.

ROBERTSON, HUMPHREY. In (1752) his wife was ELIZABETH BRANCH a daughter of WILLIAM BRANCH 1-69.

ROBERTSON, JOHN was witness to a deed by JAMES BLOUNT in (1716) 1-294; in (1730) with HENRY BOND he witnessed a deed by ROBERT HICKS 2-449; he bought land from ROBERT HICKS in (1719) the deed being witnessed by EDWARD HOWCOTT 2-454; in (1718) he owned lands near lands bought by SAMUEL WOODWARD from THOMAS BRAY 1-639; he deeded lands to RICHARD TAYLOR in (1715) with CALEB STEVENS as a witness 1-290.

ROBINS, JAMES, died leaving a will in (1726) in which he named THOMAS BOYD and wife as his Executors 1-71.

ROBINS, JOHN is mentioned in a deed by a RALPH BOZEMAN in (1732) 2-452; he left will (or one JOHN did.) in (1792) in which he mentioned daughters MARGARET BOOTH and a MARY GORDON 3-186.

ROBINS, WILLIAM, left will in (1817) and named sons JOSEPH, JOHN and GEORGE ROBINS; and the witnesses were JAMES and MARTHA SUMNER 3-348.

ROBINSON FAMILY WILLS. JOSIAH ROBINSON in (1803) another (1807) ORPHA (1819) THOMAS in (1820) 3-347.

ROBINSON, CORNELIUS (Certainly should be ROBERTSON) Genealogical account of his family and some of their descendants 1-632, 1-633.

ROBINSON, COTTON, in (1697) he was granted 300 acres on the FOQUOSON of HATTACOMACK CREEK, and 500 acres on OLD TOWN CREEK 1-5; he is on the list of tithables and land owners in CHOWAN before 1700 1-303.

ROBINSON "COUSIN" mentioned in the will of EMANUEL LOWE in (1720) 1-59.

ROBINSON, HUMPHREY (Probably ROBERTSON - See HUMPHREY ROBERTSON) died leaving will in CHOWAN in (7153) mentions ELIZABETH and SUSANNA CLELAND and JOHN CLELAND and JOHN WILKINS, Executors 1-69.

ROBINSON, JOHN (May be ROBERTSON) in (1715) sold lands next to JOHN SKINNER to one JOHN GORDON; then there is a record on the same page of where "JOHN ROBERTSON" sold lands to RICHARD TAYLOR in (1715) with CALEB STEVENS and ROBERT HICKS as witnesses 1-290; he left will in CHOWAN proved (1720) and mentioned children MARGARET, GEORGE and ELIZABETH 1-71; a JOHN ROBINSON was granted land in (1714) which joined RICHARD SKINNER and a WILLIAM WOODLEY 1-3.

ROBINSON, JOSEPH and wife MARY had a son THOMAS born in (1730) 3-393.

ROBINSON, ROBERT bought land from WILLIAM POWELL in (1734) 2-610; he sold lands to JOSEPH ANDERSON in (1739) which was part of lands patented to MARTIN CHARLES in (1714) known as the "HARRISON PLANTATION"; the deed was witnessed by THOMAS HOSKINS and DAVID BUSH 3-135.

ROBINSON, SUSANNAH was the daughter of HUMPHREY ROBINSON (ROBERTSON) who left will in (1752) and who married JOHN CLELAND 1-69; another item says she was daughter of BENJAMIN REYNAUD in (1712) 1-71.

ROBINSON, THOMAS and his wife SARAH had a son JOSEPH born in (1712) 3-393.

ROCHELL, JOHN was a Captain in the NINTH REGT. of the N. C. Continental Line 1-424.

ROCHELL, LOVICK, was a Lieutenant in the 9TH REGT. of the N. C. Continental Line 1-424.

ROCKSAKERS, DANIEL, left will in PASQUOTANK in (1732) and in it mentions his daughter MARY MICHAEL and his sister SARAH PENDLETON 1-70.

ROE, EDWARD, left will in PASQUOTANK PRECINCT of ALBEMARLE N. C. in (1696) and named his sons EDMUND, EBEN, EZER, and VALENTINE ROE and daughter DEBORAH ROE and wife SARAH 1-347.

ROE, JAMES of CRAVEN COUNTY in (1737), with FRANCIS STRINGER Executrix; the witnesses were DANIEL SHINE and JAMES MOORE 1-374.

ROE, LUKE, died leaving will in CRAVEN COUNTY in (1775) and mentions brother THOMAS ROE and his son BENJAMIN ROE; MATTHEW STEPHENS and brother in law JOSHUA TAYLOR, and JACOB TAYLOR, his son 1-373, 1-374; a PETER PHYSIOC witness and Executor.

ROE, ROBERT (Of PRINCESS ANNE CO. VA.) left a
will in BEAUFORT in (1756) had daughters
KITTY, BETTY and DALEY; son KITLEY (KIRTLEY)
ROE and wife, Executors; JAMES DEGGE, JOHN
PLOWMAN and HENRY TRIPPE witnesses 1-374;
a ROBERT ROE married MARY COLLINS in PERQUI-
MANS COUNTY in (1769) with JAMES DONALDSON
security on the bond 3-414.

ROE, VALENTINE (Mis-Spelled ROW) was a witness
to the will of CORNELIUS TULLEY in (1708) in
CURRITUCK COUNTY or PRECINCT 2-152; he died
leaving will in PASQUOTANK (1740) in which
he named sons GEORGE, BALLENTINE and MINTENE
and daughters DEBORAH, SARAH ROWSON and MARY
witnessed by RICHARD and THOMAS PRITCHARD &
JOHN HARRIS 1-374.

ROGERS, BENJAMIN, recorded his mark in BERTIE
COUNTY in (1769) 3-447; and another (perhaps)
died leaving will in GATES COUNTY in (1824)
with sons JOHN, DANIEL and TIMOTHY ROGERS
2-71, 2-72.

ROGERS, EDMUND witnessed a deed to RALPH MASON in
(1720) 2-618.

ROGERS, EZEKIEL, died leaving will in (1787) with
wife MARY "and my children", BENJAMIN PHELPS
and JOHN ROGERS witnesses 3-186.

ROGERS, JOHN, proved his Headrights in N. C. in
(1701) when the court met at the home of
JAMES NEVILL 1-305; he succeeded EDWARD RA-
ZOR as Constable of BERTIE in (1744) 2-625;
in (1718) he bought land from the widow —
CHRISTIAN BROWN next to WILLIAM BROWN 1-624;
he died leaving will in BERTIE in (1726) &
named only his son JOHN ROGERS 1-71.

ROGERS, JONATHAN, with one RICHARD BARNES was a
witness to the will of JONATHAN WILLIAMS in
GATES COUNTY in (1815) 2-79.

ROGERS, MARGARET recorded her mark when the Court
met in (1688) 3-429.

ROGERS, MARY died leaving will in BERTIE in (1777)
2-353.

ROGERS, PELEG, married WINNIFRED LANE and moved
to ATHENS, GEORGIA 1-473.

ROGERS, RICHARD, bought land from JOHN ALSTON in
(1733) the deed being witnessed by JOHN MIL-
NER, JR. 2-610.

ROGERS, ROBERT, with JOHN LANGSTON, JR. in (1739)
witnessed a deed to land by JOHN LANGSTON
3-133; his plantation was located near the
place called SARAM in CHOWAN COUNTY 1-450;
he was "of NANSEMOND COUNTY, VA." in (1725)
when he bought lands from JOHN WILLIAMS of
the same county and State, with ROBERT ROG-
ERS SR., SIMON DANIEL and HENRY GARDNER as
witnesses 2-291; he and MONTFORD LANGSTON,
JR. were granted lands in (1723) 1-19; one
ROBERT ROGERS died in BERKELEY PRECINCT in
1729 3-405; his daughter ELIZABETH married
SIMON DANIEL, and in his will in (1739) he
mentions his son ROBERT, grandson ROBERT
DANIEL, WILLIAM ROGERS, grandson ROBERT
ROGERS and THOMAS and MARY GALLOWAY 1-69;
he and SIMON DANIEL and THOMAS BARNES lived
near CHOWAN RIVER and SARAM CHAPEL on the
road leading to SARAM 1-450.

ROGERS, THOMAS, was witness to a deed by EDWARD
HOWCOTT to WILLIAM WILLIAMSON in CHOWAN in
(1717) 1-617; he and his wife JEAN sold
land to RICHARD SOWELL in (1716) witnessed
by CHARLES GAVIN 1-294; in the same year
he witnessed a deed by PETER PARKER to
RICHARD WILLIAMSON 1-294; his will in (1749)
was proved by the oath of WILLIAM LATTIMORE
2-632.

ROGERSON, DANIEL and his wife MARY were mentioned in the will of DANIEL SHOOKE (1712)
1-77; in (1731) his wife was HANNAH and
they had children born 3-393, 3-184.

ROMBOUGH FAMILY WILLS: CATHERINE in EDENTON in
(1787); JOHN in CHOWAN in (1773) with wife
CATHERINE; WILLIAM, in EDENTON in (1808)
with wife MARTHA 2-21.

ROOKES, RICHARD and wife MARY had son RICHARD
born (1691) 3-219.

ROOSE, WILLIAM left will in (1722) with GRIF-
FIN JONES administrator 1-71.

ROPER, THOMAS, sold land to RICHARD SKINNER,
JR. of PERQUIMANS, in BATH COUNTY (1720)
2-613, 2-614.

ROPER, WILLIAM, left will in CHOWAN in (1729)
and named friend JACOB BUTLER 1-70.

ROQUIST SWAMP in (1769) was in BERTIE 3-447.

ROSE, RICHARD, witnessed a deed from COLONEL
THOMAS CARY to EDWARD MOSELEY in (1714)
1-294; in (1716) he deeded land to COL.
THOMAS POLLOCK with JONATHAN RIDINGS witness 1-298; he was sold lands by JOHN HAW-
KINS in (1716) 1-298; he sold lands to
JONATHAN STANDLEY in (1716) with THOMAS
WEST and JOHN NAIRNE witnesses 1-298; he
had a daughter SARAH and son in law JOHN
SHORT, and JOHN WORLEY and WILLIAM HARDY
are mentioned 1-618; he witnessed a deed
of THOMAS WEST to JOHN HARDY in (1717)
1-300; he and his wife ELIZABETH had a
daughter SARAH born in (1704) 3-375.

ROSS, ANDREW and GEORGE WILLIAMS were on com-
mittee to lay out a road from BENNETT'S
CREEK to MEHERRIN'S FERRY in (1737) 1-443;
he is mentioned in (1717) as the only son
of ANDREW ROSS of NANSEMOND COUNTY, VA.
mentioned in (1717) in the will of ROBERT
PATTERSON 1-68; he bought land from JOHN
ODOM in (1735) which was willed to ODOM by
his father RICHARD; ANDREW HAMILTON a witness 1-109; ANDREW ROSS and MARY ROSS witnessed a deed of DANIEL PUGH in (1707)
1-616; papers were sent to COL. JOHN LEAR
in the care of ANDREW ROSS 3-254.

ROSS, KALLAM (Spelled CALLUM) received a land
grant in (1738) 1-20; he and ROBERT THOMAS
witnessed the deed of HENRY BAKER to WIL-
LIAM SKINNER in (1739) 3-133.

ROSS, JAMES and NANCY MARSHALL witnessed will
of MILLY BELOTE in (1816) 2-503; a JAMES
ROSS died leaving will in BERTIE in (1853)
witnessed JONATHAN TAYLOE 2-544, 2-545.

ROSS, JOHN was the son in law of THOMAS PALIN
of PASQUOTANK 1-67; he left will in GATES
COUNTY (1781) named children 2-71.

ROSS, MARTIN with STEPHEN SKINNER were witnesses to the will of CHARLES WORTH BLOUNT (1807) 3-325, 3-326; he and MARY WILLIAMS witnessed the will of RHODA WYNNE in (1821) 3-362; REV. MARTIN ROSS left will in (1828) named his son ASHER ROSS; JOHN WOOD and JACOB HARRELL were the witnesses; he organized the N. C. Baptist Convention; his son ASHER never married and another son MARTIN ROSS, JR. married ELIZA TOWNSEND 3-348.

ROULHAC, JOHN G. married JEMIMAH MAULE, see foot note 1-61.

ROUNDTREE FAM. WILLS: THOMAS (1772); HANNAH in (1758); MOSES in (1755); FRANCIS (1745); THOMAS, SR. in (1746) and JESSE ROULHAC in (1777) 1-374; wills in GATES COUNTY 2-67, 2-68.

ROUNDTREE, CHARLES left will in CHOWAN in (1760) mentions , children THOMAS, CHARLES, CHRISTIAN and RACHEL; daughter married FREE MAN & another married a HUNTER; AMOS HOBBS and JAS. SUMER, witnesses 2-19; in (1734) he bought land from MICHAEL WARD on CATHERINE CREEK 2-611; and he received a land grant (1754) 1-20.

ROUNDTREE, FRANCIS in (1727) bought lands on BENNETT'S CREEK in N. C. from ROBERT LASSITER of NANSEMOND COUNTY, VA. 2-444; in (1724) he sold THOMAS ROUNDTREE a water mill on CATHERINE CREEK SWAMP, with WILLIAM HILL & AARON BLANCHARD as witnesses 2-389; as early as (1702) he and ROBERT ROUNDTREE, GEORGE & ROBERT LASSITER, JOHN CAMPBELL, NICHOLAS STALLINGS, THOMAS SPIVEY and BENJAMIN BLANCHARD signed a petition to the Council in N. C. relating to CHOWAN INDIAN LANDS 3-343; in (1702) also, he and GEORGE LASSITER were trying to obtain warrants for lands 3-369, 3-370; he died leaving a will in year 1734 names sons FRANCIS, WILLIAM, JESSE, JETHRO, MOSES and JOHN, and daughters JANE, REBECCA, SUSANNA, SARAH, ELIZABETH and CHRISTIAN 1-70.

ROUNDTREE, JESSE (Too late for the son of FRANCIS) married ELIZABETH WHITE in (1790)3-419.

ROUNDTREE, JETHRO (son of FRANCIS, no doubt) was "continued as constable" in (1747-8) 2-631.

ROUNDTREE, MOSES (son of FRANCIS) sold lands to WILLIAM WALLIS in (1748) 3-131.

ROUNDTREE, REUBEN, served as a Lieutenant in the 10th Regiment of the N. C. Continental Line under Col. ABRAHAM SHEPARD 1-425.

ROUNDTREE, ROBERT (Of Nansemond County, Va.)sold land to GABRIEL LASSITER in (1735) with ELIAS STALLINGS and JOHN ROUNDTREE as the witnesses 3-128.

ROUNDTREE, SARAH, in (1731) married THOMAS WHITE with JESSE ROUNDTREE as surety on the bond 3-420.

ROUNDTREE, THOMAS, SR. died leaving will CHOWAN COUNTY in (1748) and mentions sons CHARLES and THOMAS; son in law ELIAS STALLINGS and his daughter ELIZABETH the wife of ELIAS; he mentions also grandsons WILLIAM WALLIS and THOMAS ROUNDTREE, son of his son THOMAS and his wife MARY; THOMAS WALTON and JOHN FREEMAN were the witnesses 1-374.

ROUNDTREE, THOMAS, the attorney of NICHOLAS HUNTER and wife REBECCA sold lands to WILLIAM HUNTER in (1729) part of lands patented to WILLIAM HUNTER of NANSEMOND COUNTY, VA., the father of said NICHOLAS HUNTER 2-445; about (1720) he and JACOB SPIVEY witnessed a deed of gift from THOMAS SPIVEY and wife MARY to their son-in-law WILLIAM HILL (married MARY SPIVEY) 2-612; he and his wife ELIZABETH sold land to SAMUEL PERRY of PERQUIMANS in (1734) 2-453; he patented lands on CATHERINE'S CREEK in (1716) 1-15; in (1716) he witnessed a deed by THOMAS GARRETT, SR. 1-398; in (1720) he and EDWARD BASS witnessed an ABRAHAM HILL deed 2-615; in (1731) with ELIZABETH BENTON in (1731) he witnessed a deed by JOHN ARLINE and wife MARY to MICHAEL WARD 2-450; in (1713) THOMAS and FRANCIS ROUNDTREE owned lands adjoining MICHAEL BRINKLEY 1-16; in (1707) he was the attorney for CONNER LEWIS 2-443.

ROUNDTREE, THOMAS, of GATES COUNTY, died leaving will in (1781) in which he mentions son SETH and daughters CHRISTIAN, LEAH, RACHEL, LAVINIA, PRISCILLA and FENINAH ROUNDTREE, brother CHARLES ROUNDTREE, THOMAS HUNTER and JAMES FREEMAN, Executors,and SIMON STALLINGS, JOHN BARRETT, JAMES OUTLAW and LUKE SUMNER witnesses 2-67.

ROUNDTREE, WILLIAM and JOHN HINTON owned lands on BENNETT'S CREEK adjoining lands sold by NICHOLAS STALLINGS and wife ANNE of the upper Parish of NANSEMOND COUNTY, VIRGINIA, to JOSEPH WRIGHT, of the same place 1-292; the wife of WILLIAM ROUNDTREE was RACHEL and they lived in PERQUIMANS and sold lands to THOMAS HOBBS about (1734) 2-453.

ROUSE, JOHN, was an orphan of DAVID ROUSE of BERTIE COUNTY, and in (1768) he was placed under the tuition of CHRISTOPHER HARRISON 3-445.

ROWAN COUNTY. Some wills of the McCORKLE FAMILY taken from the records at SALISBURY, N. C. 3-471.

ROWAN, MATTHEW, was Governor in (1753) 2-396; he died in NEW HANOVER in (1760) leaving will in which he mentioned brothers ANDREW, ATCHISON and WILLIAM ROWAN and several other relatives 1-69.

ROWDEN, ELIAS, married SARAH DURANT the daughter of GEORGE DURANT and his wife ANN (the elder); they were married by ALEXANDER LILLINGTON August 14, 1690; he is called ISAAC in the will of ANN DURANT in (1695) 1-41; he is on a list of the tithables from the East side of HARVEY'S CREEK to the West side of FLATTY CREEK (no date) with VINSON WHITE and MAURICE CUNNINGHAM and others 3-253; he is referred to as "ISAAC ROWDEN, and wife SARAH, daughter of GEORGE and ANN DURANT" about 1690 1-139; ISAAC RAWDON of PASQUOTANK patented lands and lived there in (1704) 1-303.

ROWDEN, PETER (Spelled RAWDEN) was referred to as a "nephew" of PETER RIEUSSETT 1-70.

ROUGHTON, RICHARD married MARTHA MANN in TYRRELL COUNTY, N. C. August 1, (1778) with a BENJAMIN MANN as surety on the marriage bond 3-110.

ROWDEN, SARAH is mentioned in the will of SARAH BLACKALL, widow of DR. ABRAHAM BLACKALL, of EDENTON in (1754) together with two sisters PENELOPE and CHARLOTTE BLACKALL 1-28; will of DR. ABRAHAM BLACKALL of EDENTON (1739-40) mentions "infant PENELOPE, born of SARAH ROWDEN, SR., my wife", daughter CHARLOTTE & WILLIAM and SARAH ROUDEN,"children of my wife", witnessed by ROBERT FOSTER, JAMES POTTER and JAMES TROTTER 1-178; in (1754) SARAH ROWDON and FRANCES WILLIAMS witnessed a deed from WILLIAM MACKEY of EDENTON to JOSEPH ANDERSON 2-453; see 1-453 for mention of DR. BLACKALL and JOHN ALSTON about same time; MARY HARRIS alias BLACKALL widow and Executrix of THOMAS BLACKALL brother ABRAHAM BLACKALL (1749) 3-466; MARTHA DUNSTON widow of JOHN mentioned in ABRAHAM BLACKALL deed to JAMES CRAVEN 1-446; the wife of ISAAC (or ELIAS ROWDEN) was SARAH the daughter of GEORGE and ANN DURANT (1690) 3-204; she may have married as a widow DR. ABRAHAM BLACKALL 1-178. 3-129.

ROWDEN, WILLIAM, with THOMAS BETTERLY, witnessed deed of WILLIAM WILLIAMS and wife FRANCES (See 2-453) to THOMAS LOVICK in (1727) 2-294; in (1737) EDWARD MOSELEY was Trustee for WILLIAM ROWDEN and CHARLES WESBEAR and as such sold lands to DR. ABRAHAM BLACKALL adjoining MAJ. HENRY BONNER 3-129; in (1727) COL. THOMAS HARVEY sold 640 acres on the SO. Shore of CHOWAN adjoining WILLIAM FRYERLEY to WILLIAM ROWDEN, which had been patented by EDWARD MOSELEY; THOMAS PARRIS and WILLIAM DOWNING were the witnesses 2-393; in (1728) WILLIAM ROWDEN bought lands adjoining JOHN JONES and MAJ. (HENRY) BONNER, from JACOB PRIVETT; the witnesses were E. PORTER and THOMAS BETTERLY 2-446.

ROYALL, CHARLES died leaving will in ONSLOW in (1755) 1-379, 1-380.

RUFFIN FAMILY WILLS: WILLIAM (1808); THOMAS in (1840); JOHN (1845; and JOHN RUFFIN (1852) 2-542.

RUFFIN, WILLIAM died leaving will in BERTIE in (1781), sons WILLIAM and RICHARD RUFFIN and daughters FAITH FENDER and PURETY DELOACH ; JOHN LAWRENCE and Executor 2-352.

RUSHMORE, CHARLES, of PASQUOTANK died in (1669) 1-443.

RUSSELL FAMILY WILLS: RICHARD (1737); THOMAS in (1744) and JOHN RUSSELL (1751) 1-378.

RUSSELL, GEORGE, died in EDENTON in (1781) and left will; THOMAS CLARKSON witness 2-19.

RUSSELL, JOHN, was the son of GEORGE RUSSELL of KENT, ENGLAND married DEBORAH MUMFORD(1679) 3-201.

RUSSELL, WILLIAM died in (1717) but left no will 1-71.

RUSSIAN, MATTHEW, deeded land to WILLIAM BRIDGERS in (1718) 1-625.

RUTHERFORD, JOHN. JOHN RUTHERFORD, JR., WILLIAM GORDON RUTHERFORD and FRANCIS RUTHERFORD , children "of my friend JOHN RUTHERFORD" are mentioned in the will of MRS. JEAN CORBIN, widow of FRANCIS CORBIN of EDENTON and NEW HANOVER in (1775) 1-187; JOHN and his daughter FRANCES, with THOMAS CUNNINGHAM, JR. and MAURICE MOORE are mentioned in the will of ALEX DUNCAN of WILMINGTON in (1768) 1-201.

RUTLAND, JOHN and wife MARGARET made deed to land around (1700) 2-457; a later JOHN left will in BERTIE in (1804) mentions a son BLAKE BAKER RUTLAND and others 2-542.

RUTLEDGE, JOHN died in BERTIE in (1762) leaving sons BLAKE, JOHN, WATSON and READING RUTLEDGE; JOSEPH and WILLIAM RUTLAND witnesses 2-352.

RUTTER, ELIZABETH married JOHN GRAY in (1703) in BERKELEY PRECINCT 3-410.

RUTTER, JOHN and his wife MARGARET had daughter CONSTANCE born in (1704) 3-375.

RUTTER, MARY with ROBERT CHAPPELL and his son JONATHAN bought lands from EDWARD WOOD in CHOWAN PRECINCT on the North side of WARWICK SWAMP, which WOOD had bought from a JOHN GOODIN; in it he states "my movable estate to be divided between ROBERT CHAPPELL and my daughter MARY RUTTER; this in (1734) 2-453½ MARY was the mother of DANIEL RAYNER in (1737) and they sold land to GEORGE WHITE; the witnesses to the deed being ROBERT CHAPPELL, ELIZABETH ROUNDTREE and THOMAS ROUNDTREE 3-132.

RYAN, ELIZABETH died leaving will in BERTIE in (1805) and mentions sons CORNELIUS, JAMES and GEORGE LOCKHART RYAN, daughters WINNIFRED and ELIZABETH RYAN, the witnesses being CORNELIUS and GEORGE L RYAN 2-541.

RYAN, DAVID left will in BERTIE in (1805) and names his wife MARY BLOUNT RYAN; JONATHAN JACOCKS and THOMAS WORLEY witnesses 2-541

RYAN, GEORGE, built a grist mill in (1771) on the lands of SIR. NATHAN DUKENFIELD 3-449.

RYAN, JAMES died leaving will in BERTIE COUNTY in (1771) in which he mentions his son THOMAS RYAN, his wife and children, and and makes GEORGE RYAN and EDWARD BRYAN his Executor 2-353; THOMAS RYAN was foreman of Grand Jury in Bertie (1749) 2-532.

DANIEL RICHARDSON, who was Attorney General of North Carolina , may have belonged to the MARYLAND family of that name, though there was a YORK FAMILY in Virginia, of which he could have been a member. WILLIAM RICHARDSON, SR., of ANN ARUNDEL COUNTY, Maryland, died leaving will in 1691, in which he named children DANIEL, JOSEPH, WILLIAM, SOPHIA, MARGARET and ELIZABETH. The overseers of his will were RICHARD JONES, RICHARD HARRISON, JOHN TALBOTT and WILLIAM OGLESON. It appears they were Quakers, and it is quite possible they went to MARYLAND from Virginia, and that the eldest son DANIEL, instead, made his way to NORTH CAROLINA, where he played an important role in the affairs of the new Colony. Other RICHARDSONS from Virginia DID settle in ALBEMARLE.

ROBERTSON FAMILY.   From the old BRISTOL PARISH REGISTER in VIRGINIA we learn that one CORNELIUS CARGILL married ELIZABETH DANIEL and that their first child WILLIAM CARGILL was born on June 15, 1727, which gives us an approximate date of the marriage. On OCTOBER 11, 1733, that inimitable character, COL. WILLIAM BYRD wrote in his "Journey to the Land of Eden": "In a distance of about two miles we reached the DAN (river), which we forded with some difficulty into the fork, and then we passed through two good miles across to the STAUNTON (river). COL. COOK had been surveying lands in these parts and particularly that of MR. STITH'S COPPER MINE, and a tract on which CORNELIUS CARGILL has also a mine of fine appearance. We thought best of CARGILL'S MINE." For the years 1751-2 in LUNENBURG COUNTY, VIRGINIA, a complete set of all the tythe lists have been discovered, and they were taken by LYDDALL BACON, WILLIAM CALDWELL and one certain CORNELIUS CARGILL (Sunlight on the South Side p. 178, by LANDON C. BELL). On the list for 1751 appear the names:

                    John Robertson
                    Mark Robertson
                    Edward Robertson   4 tythes
                    John Robertson Junr   1

On page 48 of Bell's Sunlight appears this statement with respect to such lists: "If a person returned his list of tythes of a certain number made up of his own name and certain slaves, there is a reasonable presumption that the tithables bearing his name may be his children, who were that year between the ages of SIXTEEN and TWENTY-ONE years of age", and cites an example from the list of CORNELIUS CARGIE. So we are reasonably certain that JOHN ROBERTSON in 1751 had TWO sons, MARK and EDWARD over SIXTEEN, and one son JOHN ROBERTSON JR. probably married and with several children UNDER SIXTEEN at that time. Any children the elder JOHN had UNDER SIXTEEN are not listed.

JOHN ROBERTSON (above) married a daughter of CORNELIUS CARGILL, who had a copper mine of "fine appearance" when COL. WILLIAM BYRD and his party went to visit him in 1733. The record says he married ELIZABETH DANIEL. She was probably his second wife as she could hardly have been the mother of a daughter with three sons over sixteen in 1751-2. Two more sons, too young to be enumerated in the above list, because under sixteen, were CHARLES and CORNELIUS ROBERTSON. How many other children there may have been we have no way of telling, but of these we are quite sure. It is likely that DAVID ROBERTSON (who appears on the CARGILL list for 1752) may have been another.

JOHN ROBERTSON, JR. married MARY GOWER, of an old VIRGINIA FAMILY, and had JAMES, ELIJAH, MARK, JOHN, CHARLES, ANNE and another daughter who married WILLIAM CASH.

CORNELIUS ROBERTSON (name of wife unknown) most certainly had two sons: CORNELIUS ROBERTSON, who married CLARISSA HILL, and CHARLES ROBERTSON (known as "BLACK CHARLES") of the WATAUGA VALLEY, in TENNESSEE. The U. S. Census of N. C. for 1790 shows CORNELIUS had two other sons & two daughters, but what became of them we do not know, unless perhaps they were the JOHN ROBERTSON & WILLIAM ROBERTSON who appear on the land records of LAURENS COUNTY, S. C. with a CORNELIUS CARGILL in 1834. they might have been.

CORNELIUS ROBERTSON and JOHN ROBERTSON, together with CHARLES ("Black Charles" son of CORNELIUS) appear together on the U. S. CENSUS RECORDS for 1790 in MONTGOMERY COUNTY, NORTH CAROLINA, Charles at that time unmarried. In letters to DR. LYMAN C. DRAPER in 1854, DR. FELIX ROBERTSON, of NASHVILLE, TENNESSEE (Son of JAMES ROBERTSON) says that JOHN ROBERTSON who married MARY GOWER emigrated from Virginia to WAKE COUNTY, N. C. MONTGOMERY COUNTY is directly South of RALEIGH (the State Capital and County Seat of Wake County) while the article in this record (1-632, 1-633) intimates that CORNELIUS married in ANSON COUNTY, which joins MONTGOMERY on the South. The Census record places both JOHN and CORNELIUS in the general vicinity of WAKE, though a little lower down. The same DR. FELIX ROBERTSON wrote DR. DRAPER that "Black Charles Robertson was my father's cousin". He further states that "Black Charles",he is quite sure, was NOT the son of his grandfather's brother CHARLES ROBERTSON, whom he thinks "lived in PHILADELPHIA". He did NOT live in Philadelphia, unless he moved there from Montgomery County, N. C. after 1790. This brother CHARLES ROBERTSON was simply swallowed up in the grand rush of migration that eminated among the members of this family after they began to leave NORTH CAROLINA for different destinations in the South.

The late COLONEL WILLIAM CURRY HARLLEE, in his monmental work on the ROBERTSON FAMILY was extremely loath to depart from his well established traditions and insisted that the statements by DR. FELIX ROBERTSON to LYMAN C. DRAPER regarding the origin of the family were strictly true, and that "My grandfather JOHN was a native of IRELAND, and his father (not named) a native of SCOTLAND." This could have been true and I have no evidence to refute it, but that JOHN and his brother CHARLES came direct to this country from IRELAND by way of PENNSYLVANIA, only two brothers, is I think refuted by the LUNENBURG RECORDS I have quoted, which shows that their FATHER was a tithable in that county in Virginia, in 1751-2. It is also refuted by the MONTGOMERY COUNTY, N. C. Census for 1790. The descendants of JOHN ROBERTSON and his wife MARY GOWER, including GENERAL JAMES ROBERTSON, the oldest son, who founded the Cumberland Settlement (Nashville) in Tennessee, and whose grandsons also established large landed estates in Texas, is thoroughly covered in Col. Harllee's three volume work "KINFOIKS", so the purpose of this sketch, in the main, is to throw some light on the descendants & relatives of CORNELIUS ROBERTSON about whom a "Correspondent in Atlanta, Georgia" wrote MR. HATHAWAY for publication in the last number of his REGISTER (1-632, 1-633).

The four sons of CORNELIUS ROBERTSON, of MONTGOMERY COUNTY, N. C. in 1790, were CHARLES, (then above 21 years of age), CORNELIUS (II), WILLIAM and JOHN ROBERTSON. (The name is spelled as ROBERTSON on the Census, as ROBERTSON on the Laurens County (S. C.) records, and ROBERTSON by the descendants who came to TEXAS, with one exception. TOD ROBERTSON spelled the name ROBINSON, though his KENTUCKY relatives spelled it ROBERTSON. All of the TENNESSEE family spelled the name ROBERTSON, as did GENERAL JEROME B. ROBERTSON and his son GENERAL FELIX ROBERTSON. The name is also spelled ROBERTSON on the LUNENBERG, VIRGINIA records; so we are forced to the conclusion that the "correspondent in Atlanta, Georgia" was in error in spelling the name ROBINSON.

In 1790 when the UNITED STATES CENSUS was taken in MONTGOMERY COUNTY, North Carolina CORNELIUS ROBERTSON (II) brother of "Black Charles" Robertson, of Tennessee, was perhaps a little under 21 years of age, though listed as "over sixteen", which indicates he was born about 1770. He married CLARISSA HILL who was born in 1779, by 1793-4. Notes gathered by this compiler establishes the fact that that CORNELIUS ROBERTSON emigrated from North Carolina to KENTUCKY where he lived for a time, and from there went to ALABAMA, where he was Captain of a Company who went against the Indians sometime during the 1830s in a battalion commanded by R. E. B. BAYLOR, who was also from KENTUCKY. Col. Baylor was both a minister and a lawyer and came to Texas and settled at OLD INDEPENDENCE. He became one of the first members of the TEXAS SUPREME COURT after statehood. The sons of CORNELIUS ROBERTSON also settled at INDEPENDENCE, and CLARISSA (HILL) ROBERTSON died and is buried there in the old cemetery, where this compiler copied her tombstone inscription about 1938, which recites that she died there, the relict of CORNELIUS ROBERTSON on FEBRUARY 5, 1864, aged 84 years and six months. This places her birth in 1779. Who was she?

CLARISSA HILL (who married CORNELIUS ROBERTSON about 1793-4) was a daughter of one ABRAHAM HILL who married CHRISTIAN WALTON. This is a good place to set out what is known of this HILL FAMILY line.

HUMPHREY MARSHALL died in ISLE OF WIGHT COUNTY, Virginia, in 1711, leaving a will in which no sons, but some daughters are mentioned; ANNE, who married CAPT. HENRY APPLEWHITE, and a daughter MARY, who married THOMAS HILL. (BODDIE'S 17th CENTURY ISLE OF WIGHT pp 232-233).

THOMAS HILL and MARY MARSHALL were the parents of HENRY APPLEWHITE HILL, ISAAC HILL, THOMAS HILL and ROBERT HILL. Perhaps others. The son THOMAS HILL was the father of HUMPHREY HILL of KING and QUEEN COUNTY, Virginia, who left many descendants.

ISAAC HILL was the father of WILLIAM HILL who settled in LUNENBERG COUNTY, Virginia, & died in BRUNSWICK COUNTY, who left numerous descendants throughout North Carolina and Virginia. He is said to have married a JENNINGS. He was the father of MARY HILL who married CLEMENT READ and was the ancestor of ABNER and JOSEPH NASH, through their marriages.

ROBERT HILL has been unplaced, as yet, but he may have been the father, among others of SION HILL, whose father was ROBERT.

HENRY APPLEWHITE HILL was the father of COL. BENJAMIN HILL, ABRAHAM HILL (m. JUDITH) WILLIAM HILL (m. JONES) ISAAC HILL (b. 1725) who settled in TENNESSEE, after living for a time in GEORGIA, and GREEN HILL (b. 1714) who married GRACE BENNETT, the daughter of WILLIAM BENNETT of NORTHAMPTON COUNTY, N. C.

ABRAHAM HILL (who married JUDITH) and who died in CHOWAN in 1760, was the father of ABRAHAM, HENRY, ISAAC and THEOPHELUS HILL. ISAAC settled in GEORGIA; HENRY married SARAH COTTON and had eight children; THEOPHELUS HILL married TERESA THOMAS, daughter of JOHN THOMAS SR., and ABRAHAM HILL married CHRISTIAN WALTON. This last couple were the parents of CLARISSA HILL who became the wife of CORNELIUS ROBERTSON. CLARISSA HILL had eleven brothers and sisters, whose names are all listed in the "HILLS OF WILKES COUNTY, GA."

It is possible that CORNELIUS ROBERTSON died in ALABAMA, and that his widow came to Texas to live among her children and numerous other relatives, including the APPLEWHITES and WALLACES. CORNELIUS ROBERTSON and his wife CLARISSA HILL, had among possible others, the following children:

(1) GEN. JEROME B. ROBERTSON, who on the death of GEN. JOHN B. HOOD, was promoted to command the famous "HOOD'S BRIGADE" of Texas Troops. He was the father of GEN. FELIX ROBERTSON who died in WACO, TEXAS, only a few years ago, then the "last living General of the Confederacy". His son FELIX (the Great grandson of CORNELIUS ROBERTSON) was a JUDGE of the District Court in Dallas for many years, but is now deceased. HENRY BELL ROBERTSON the youngest son of GEN. JEROME B. ROBERTSON, died Oct. 23, 1860. The wife of GEN. JEROME B. ROBERTSON was MARY E. CUMMINGS, who died in 1868 at INDEPENDENCE, TEXAS.

(2) HON. TOD ROBERTSON (second son) who married MARY CRITTENTON, of KENTUCKY. He was born in NORTH CAROLINA in 1813, and came to TEXAS and settled in BRAZORIA COUNTY in 1839. He served as a member of Congress of the Republic of Texas several terms before Texas became a State, and he is said to have become a JUDGE in CALIFORNIA. He had a number of children who are listed by the "Correspondent from Atlanta Georgia" (1-633) in this record. One grandson, TOD ROBINSON (so spelled) is a prominent business man in AUSTIN, TEXAS.

(3) MARY ROBERTSON, who became the wife of JOHN ALSTON DUDLEY for whom see (1-633).

(4-5?) GEORGE ROBERTSON and ANDREW ROBERTSON, who were among the very early settlers and members of STEPHEN F. AUSTIN'S "first three hundred" colonists to Texas, may have been sons of CORNELIUS, but there is no proof of this as a fact.

CORNELIUS ROBERTSON, father of GEN. JEROME B. ROBERTSON, and ELIJAH ROBERTSON, father of STERLING CLACK ROBERTSON, the Texas Empresario, were second cousins. In ante-bellam (Civil War) days they lived about 40 miles apart and the two families called each other "cousins" and were socially intimate, according to local tradition in Texas.

ROWDEN (RAWDEN, WRAUGHTON, ROUGHTON, WROUGHTON, RODEN, WROTEN) FAMILY. At (3-204) of this record we are told that ELIAS ROWDEN and SARAH DURANT were married by ALEXANDER LILLINGTON on the 16th of August 1690; an at (1-203) in giving the birth dates of the children of GEORGE and ANN DURANT, we are told that GEORGE and his wife ANN (MARWOOD?) had children: GEORGE (b. 1659), ELIZABETH (b. 1660), JOHN (b. 1662), MARY (b. 1665), THOMAS (b. 1668), SARAH (b. 1670), MARTHA (b. 1673) and PARTHENIA (b. 1675), and that GEORGE DURANT and ANN MARWOOD, the parents, were married JANUARY 4, 1658, in NORTHUMBERLAND COUNTY, Virginia, by REV. DAVID LINDSAY; and further, that these statements are taken FROM THE RECORDS OF PERQUIMANS COUNTY, N. C. In the "record" of their marriage the husband of their daughter SARAH is called "ELIAS" ROWDEN (3-204), but in the will of ANN DURANT he is referred to as "ISAAC" ROWDEN (1-41). On page 11, of GRIMES' ABSTRACTS, the will of one ARNOLD LAWRENCE is witnessed by ISAAC ROWDEN in 1691, so apparently the Christian name of SARAH DURANT'S husband was ISAAC instead of "ELIAS". As to his sur-name GRIMES prints it consistently, all the way through as "ROWDEN" - and "thereby hangs a tale". At (1-70) of this record a PETER RAWDEN is mentioned, and at (3-110) we are told that RICHARD ROUGHTON married MARTHA MANN in TYRRELL COUNTY in 1778, and even our particular ISAAC has his name spelled "RAWDEN" when he obtained a grant of land in PASQUOTANK in 1704 (1-303), so thus it is seen that even these records, voluminous as they are, leave us wholly in the dark as to whether SARAH DURANT married an ISAAC (?) ROWDEN, RAWDEON or ROUGHTON. GRIMES, on page 305, gives us a JOHN ROUTON.

The mis-spelling - sometimes mis-reading and transcribing - of names, in this as well as in hundreds of other instances, has all but relegated to total obscurity, the ancestry of many early American families, making it seemingly impossible for descendants to identify their progenitors. To add to this confusion many of such names, thus mis-spelled, have been perpetuated by erroneous records based on the original errors, as this writer thinks is true in the case of the ANN "MARWOOD", wife of GEORGE DURANT, the "first grantee" of DURANT'S NECK.

ISAAC ROWDEN, who became the son in law of GEORGE DURANT and his wife ANN was a lineal descendant of "EZEKIAH" ROUGHTON, a passenger to Virginia in the "BONA NOVA" in 1619, and MARGARET ROUGHTON, his wife, who came over in the WARWICK. Both were living after the Indian Massacre in the colony. Apparently a son, WILLIAM WRAUGHTON, "beloved brother" of DR. THOMAS ROOTES of LANCASTER COUNTY, Virginia, who, with RICHARD FLINT patented 400 acres of land on the West side of COROTOMAN RIVER in that County in 1652. "EZEKIAH" of course, was probably a contraction of the name "HEZEKIAH" which remained in this family through the centuries, after it had established itself in the "deep South". However, even in those far-flung days of 1652, there appears to have been no uniformity of the spelling of this unusual sur-name, for on the old LANCASTER RECORDS for 1652-1655 by BEVERLY FLEET (Vol. 22 of his Colonial Abstracts, 1945), the name is variously spelled WRAUGHTON, WRATAN, WROUGHTON, WRATTAN, RAUGHTON and ROUGHTON. Among other familiar names appearing on these LANCASTER RECORDS with WILLIAM WRAUGHTON is that of HUGH LINDSAY, believed to have been a son or a brother of the old Rector, REV. DAVID LINDSAY, who performed the marriage ceremony for GEORGE and ANN DURANT in 1658. This suggests strongly that the romance between ISAAC "ROWDEN" and SARAH DURANT had its beginning along the COROTOMAN or RAPPAHANNOCK in LANCASTER or NORTHUMBERLAND COUNTIES where in their childhood days their parents were friends and neighbors.

To carry this interesting story of the name still further, the descendants of this "ROWDEN" FAMILY are even yet "divided" in their method of spelling the name, some writing it ROWDEN, some RHOTEN, some RODEN, some RATTAN, some WROUGHTON, some ROUGHTON, some WROTON and still others WROTEN. The life-companion of this writer, as a girl, was MISS WROTEN, and in the old family "plot" in the cemetery at DENMARK (BARNWELL COUNTY) South Carolina, from whence came her great grandfather HEZEKIAH, moss-covered gravestones, standing side by side, have the name chizeled and spelled in two different ways; while at the little old courthouse on the faded deed records we found the name written "RODEN" in one or two instances, and in each case most certainly intended to apply to this same ancient clan. Also the name PARTHENIA (harking back to one of SARAH (DURANT) ROWDEN'S sisters) continued to persist in this South Carolina family, and followed it through the West into MISSISSIPPI, LOUISIANA, ARKANSAS and TEXAS.

SADLER, ELLENER, was granted land in (1715) adjoining lands of EDWARD and JOHN CHANDLER 1-15.

SADLER, RICHARD left will in CHOWAN in (1753) named wife MARGARET 1-386.

SADLER, WILLIAM left will in CHOWAN in [1727] sons WILLIAM and RICHARD and HENRY BONNER his executors 1-386.

SADLEY, WILLIAM left will in CHOWAN in(1711) in which THOMAS LUTEN is mentioned 1-77.

SAFFORD, ANN in (1719) was the daughter of ELLENER BONNER 1-51.

SAINT, DANIEL died leaving will in (1793) his father in law was JOSEPH JONES 3-191; his father left will in (1772) 3-189, and his mother in (1779) 3-189.

SALLIS, JOHN was Deputy Sheriff of BERTIE in (1747) 2-630.

SALMON CREEK and CASHY RIVER were in BERTIE list of freeholders living there (1719) 1-444.

SALSBURY, ANDREW, owned lands adjoining JOHN WARE in (1717) and witnessed a deed by FRANCIS MACLENDEN and wife ELLENER (1704) 1-103; in (1711) he sold land to one THOMAS BRAY 1-626; his wife was ANN and they sold land to JOHN DOPSON &DAN HALSEY 1-290.

SALSBURY, JAMES, left will in PASQUOTANK (1766) sons JAMES, JOHN, JOSEPH and WILLIAM 1-491

SALISBURY, PETTIGROVE, about 1730 (?) leased lands from or to THOMAS BARKER (the lawyer) for seven years 1-445; he was overseer of a road in (1748) 2-632.

SALTER, EDWARD, who left will in BATH in (1734) mentioned his son in law MILES HARVEY, his daughters and son EDWARD 1-74; his wife was ELIZABETH and in (1732) CHRISTOPHER GALE witnessed their deed 2-609; in (1731) he had married MADAM ELIZABETH HARDY 3-410; & he was a friend of ISAAC OLIVER who left a will in (1732) 1-64.

SANDERS, ABRAHAM and his wife JUDITH, of PERQUIMANS sold land to EDWARD WINGATE (1734) 2-610; he and his wife had ELIZABETH born (1719), ABRAHAM born (1723), JUDITH born (1725) and JOHN SANDERS born in (1729)3-394.

SANDERS, FRANCIS sought permission to erect a mill on CYPRESS SWAMP in (1759) 1-456.

SANDERS, JOHN left will in (1806) naming his children, including JOHN, STEPHEN, THOMAS and ABRAHAM 3-349; and another JOHN left a will in (1818) also naming a lot of children JOSIAH, FREDERICK, BENJAMIN and ABRAHAM SANDERS (This JOHN is spelled SAUNDERS but must be of the same tribe, by the names used) and daughters MILLY TOMS and PARTHENIA BRINKLEY. THOMAS WARD was one of the executors 3-349.

SANDERS FAMILY WILLS: BENJAMIN (1744) ANN (1752) JOHN (1733) (Spilled SANDERS) 1-388.

SANDERS, MARY, will left (1734) mentions son IKE, grandson ISAAC, daughter MARY SNODEN, daughters CHRISTIAN and ELIZABETH SANDERS 1-75.

SANDERS, THOMAS died leaving will (1789) and mentions brothers and sisters RICHARD, ANNE, HANNAH, JOHN and BENJAMIN SANDERS, JOSEPH PERISHO and AARON COSAND 3-189.

SANDERS, RICHARD made Constable in place of JAMES COTTEN in BERTIE in (1744) 2-625; in (1735) his wife was HANNAH 3-394.

SANDERLIN, JOHN, died leaving will in BERTIE in (1838) with REUBEN LAWRENCE Executor 2-548.

SANDERSON, BENJAMIN and THOMAS BONNER witnesses to a deed by JOHN DAVIS and wife MARY in (1720) 2-513.

SANDERSON, BASIL of the ISLE OF ANTIQUA, died at EDENTON, N. C. and buried on the lot of CHRISTOPHER GALE, and in his will mentions WILLIAM HILL of ANTIQUA 1-76.

SANDERSON FAMILY WILLS 1-484.

SANDERSON, HANNAH in (1737) was administrator of RICHARD SANDERSON her late husband, of PERQUIMANS PRECINCT 2-466.

SANDERSON, JAMES married DEBORAH THURSTON, the sister of JOHN THURSTON by (1702) 1-613.

SANDERSON, RICHARD, with CHARLES EDEN and other members signs adjournment proclamation of the Assembly in (1713) 3-228; the Assembly met at his home in LITTLE RIVER in (1716) 2-411; he had daughter ELIZABETH, of PERQUIMANS who in (1725) married JOHN CRISP, son of NICHOLAS CRISP; she married second THOMAS POLLOCK son of Governor POLLOCK, and she married third SAMUEL SCOLLEY 2-355; she died in (1766) and named various relatives 2-355; one RICHARD was executor of the will of THOMAS STEPHENSON in (1802); he signed resolution for investigation of the public accounts when WILLIAM SWANN was Speaker of the Assembly 3-281; he died in CURRITUCK in (1718) and his widow DEMARIS married SAMUEL SWANN 1-74; he deeded lands to EDWARD MOSELEY in (1717) of PERQUIMANS 1-615; this note says his widow married THOMAS SWANN (1718) 1-621.

SANDERSON, RICHARD JR. was the administrator of JOSEPH KING in (1704) 1-56; he was the son of RICHARD SANDERSON of CURRITUCK who died in (1718) 1-74; one RICHARD SANDERSON (later) witnessed will of JOHN CARTER in (1801) 3-328; he died in PERQUIMANS in (1733) and had daughter GRACE who married TULLY WILLIAMS and was brother in law of HENRY WOODHOUSE the nephew of HEZEKIAH WOODHOUSE 1-74.

SANDERSON, RUTH was daughter of BENJAMIN LAKER(& sister of SARAH LAKER)who married first JAMES MINGE, and second RICHARD SANDERSON; SARAH LAKER married GOV. THOMAS HARVEY 1-74.

SANFORD, THOMAS and THOMAS LONG had a lawsuit in (1689) 3-430.

SANDIFOOT, FULLINGTON bought land from THOMAS POLLOCK, on the South side of CONABY CREEK in the year (1700) 2-611.

SANDY POINT, at the time of its seizure, was located 7 miles from the town of EDENTON in CHOWAN COUNTY 2-82; John Porter had a grant of land adjoining it 1-5.

SARAM, a place at the head of SARAM CREEK in CHOWAN COUNTY 1-265; the place was near the plantation of ROBERT ROGERS and the place where SIMON DANIEL formerly lived in (1747) 1-450.

SARSON, LAWRENCE was mentioned in the will of JOHN WEST in (1712) and he sold land to THOMAS WEST in (1720) 2-612; he was from SUFFOLK COUNTY, VIRGINIA, and left a will in BERTIE in (1726) 1-75; he was a witness to a deed by THOMAS POLLOCK (1720) 2-612.

SATTERFIELD, ALFRED left will in CHOWAN in (1834) names sons JAMES and WILLIAM 2-29.

SATTERFIELD, ELIZABETH died in CHOWAN in the year (1838), THOMAS WAFF a witness 2-29.

SATTERFIELD, THOMAS married ELIZABETH HAUGHTON, daughter of CHARLES HAUGHTON (1759) 1-456.

SAUNDERS, ABRAHAM, was the son of JOHN SAUNDERS who died in (1806) 3-349.

SAUNDERS, ALLEN was Executor of the will of THOMAS HARRELL in (1831) 3-337.

SAUNDERS FAMILY WILLS 2-72, 2-73, 3-158, and 3-349. (See SANDERS also) 3-350.

SAUNDERS, JOHN, left will in (1818) and mentions PARTHENIA BRINKLEY 3-349.

SAUNDERS, FATHAN, left will, wife ELIZABETH and JOHN TUCKER a witness 3-350.

SAUNDERS, ROBERT, proved his rights (1702) see list 2-299.

SAUNDERS, THOMAS will in (1828) with DANIEL LAMB a witness 3-350.

SAVAGE FAMILY. Genealogy of the family from THOMAS SAVAGE born (1592) 2-477 to 2-479; wills of in GATES COUNTY 2-76.

SAVAGE, FEREBY (PHEREBY) married (1) FRANCIS PUGH and (2) THOMAS BARKER 2-470.

SAVAGE, HILL was in the Colony as early as (1725) 2-466.

SAVAGE, JOHN in right of his wife SUSANNAH, the executor of the estate of HENRY GIBBS (he had married the widow GIBBS) (1746) 2-627.

SAVAGE, THOMAS, was from CHESTERSHIRE, ENGLAND account of his descendants 2-477 to 2-479; a later THOMAS left will in BERTIE (1762) 2-354.

SAVAGE, WILLIAM left will in CHOWAN (Codicil in BATH) in (1782) of the firm of SAVAGE and WESTMORE; shows connection with DR. WILLIAM FLOOD and son NICHOLAS; with DR. SAMUEL DICKINSON and with families in LOUDON COUNTY and near ALEXANDRIA, VIRGINIA; mentions lands in CULPEPPER COUNTY bought from FAIRFAX, etc. 2-28.

SAWYER FAMILY. This family connected with BLAIR family by marriage 3-461, 3-462, 3-463; some SAWYER family wills 1-386, 1-387.

SAWYER, CATHERINE was the daughter of ALEXANDER SPENCE in (1734) 1-74.

SAWYER, CHARLES, was the son in law of in(1735) JOHN SPENCE 1-73.

SAWYER, DAVID, of PASQUOTANK, is mentioned (1728) in the will of HENRY SAWYER, his father 1-387

SAWYER, DR. MATHIAS, of EDENTON, died in (1835) mentions sons SAMUEL & MATHIAS in his will 2-29.

SAWYER, THOMAS, was Master of the sloop DOVE in (1749) 1-423; there was a THOMAS in PASQUO - TANK, however, prior to (1700) 1-303; and one died leaving will in (1720), and DANCY McDOW-ELL was Executor 1-76; a later THOMAS SAWYER married LETITIA, the widow of JOHN BARBER of CURRITUCK in (1762) 3-297.

SAWYER, WILLIS left will in BERTIE in (1808) and named wife SALLY and children 2-546.

SCARBOROUGH FAMILY. Genealogical account of one branch and some descendants 3-473.

SCARBOROUGH, AUGUSTINE was in ALBEMARLE PRECINCT before (1700) 1-302; he owned lands in(1707) on which DARBY SEXTON had lived in (1677) 1-611; he makes and signs an oath in open court in (1705) 3-349; letter to him by ED-WARD MOSELEY when he was Treasurer of PASQUO-TANK PRECINCT in (1712) 2-189; another of the same 3-228; in (1705) his daughter receives treatment for a peculiar ailment 3-277, 3-278.

SCARBOROUGH, BENJAMIN, was a kinsman or related to JULIAN LARKER, of PERQUIMANS in year (1735) 1-57; was son of CHARLES SCARBOROUGH 1-484.

SCARBOROUGH, CHARLES, left will in PASQUOTANK in (1750) wife JOYCE, son BENJAMIN 1-484.

SCARBOROUGH, JOHN will in PASQUOTANK in (1754) & mentions father in law WILLIAM WILSON 1-484; name on list of tithables in CURRITUCK with-out date 3-257.

SCARBOROUGH, McRORA, married into the PETERSON FAMILY. Some genealogy 3-473; his widow mar-ried JOSEPH BLOUNT 3-459; she had been the widow of WILLIAM REED 1-70.

SCARBOROUGH, MILES and his brother PETERSON were sons of SARAH the daughter of THOMAS LONG who left will in (1781) 3-176.

SCOLLEY, ELIZABETH, was the widow of SAMUEL SCOL-LEY and the mother of CULLEN and THOMAS POL-LOCK (See SANDERSON); she left will in BER-TIE COUNTY in (1766) and mentions names of many relatives and connections 2-355.

SCOLLEY, JOHN, foreman of Grand Jury signs infor-mation about a road against JOHN WALKER the overseer of same 3-282.

SCOLLEY, REBECCA, the wife of THOMAS JACOCKS was from BOSTON 2-296.

SCOLLEY, SAMUEL left will in BERTIE in (1752) mentions his sons-in-law (step-sons they were) CULLEN and THOMAS POLLOCK, and he leaves to TULLEY WILLIAMS his father's sword (His wife was ELIZABETH SANDERSON several times a widow) 1-72.

SCOLLEY, WILLIAM, of BOSTON, wrote his attor-ney in (1724) about a lawsuit 2-466.

SCOTT FAMILY. Wills of MATTHEW, MARY, JOHN (two) STEPHEN (two) and JOSHUA SCOTT 1-382.

SCOTT, BARTHOLOMEW, bought land in (1728) from ROBERT JEFFRIES 2-443.

SCOTT, CHARLES (Of NANSEMOND COUNTY, VIRGINIA) patented lands in ALBEMARLE PRECINCT before (1732) 2-609.

SCOTT, HENRY, died leaving will in (1817) wife RACHEL, sons LEVI and HENRY; the witnesses were SARAH NIXON and SIMEON LONG 3-352.

SCOTT, JOANNA, was the sister of JAMES TOOKE who left will in (1720) and mentions her & JAMES TOOKE SCOTT and cousin MARY RICKS & other relatives 1-79.

SCOTT, JOHN left will in (1738) and mentions his wife SARAH and brother STEPHEN SCOTT 1-73.

SCOTT, JOSEPH, was the husband of MARY SCOTT a widow who married second THOMAS BLOUNT, JR. 1-297; JOSEPH SCOTT died in (1685) 3-366.

SCOTT, JOSHUA and WILLIAM WILKINSON, PATRICK BAILEY and others were members of the Court in ALBEMARLE PRECINCT in (1683-4) 3-283.

SCOTT, MARY (the widow) married THOMAS BLOUNT in (1685) 3-202; MRS. MARY SCOTT died in (1692) 3-218; THOMAS BLOUNT who married MARY SCOTT said to have been brother of JAMES BLOUNT who died that year 3-318; she makes contract in (1690) with ALEXANDER, an INDIAN 3-435.

SCOTT, SARAH, the daughter of JOSHUA SCOTT and his wife MARY was born (1685) 3-212

SCOTT, SEVERN left will in (1799) mentions his son HENRY and HENRY'S wife MARY; REBECCA & SARAH BUNCH witnesses 3-191.

SCOTT, STEPHEN married HANNAH NICHOLSON in the year (1721) 3-410; another STEPHEN died & left will in (1711) wife was ELIZABETH 1-76.

SCRINER, RICHARD and wife MARY had a son JAMES born (1701) 3-373.

SCUPERNONG to the plantation of MRS. ALICE LONG building of road in dispute 3-268, 3-273.

SEALS, WILLIAM died leaving will in BERTIE in (1786) with WILLIAM PENDER a witness 2-357.

SEARS, ANN, died leaving will in (1789) names daughter SARAH SUTTON and brother CORNELIUS MORRIS 3-191.

SEAY, MATTHEW, died leaving an orphan PATIENCE SEAY aged about 6 years (1762) BERTIE 3-444; he also left another daughter named MARY SEAY. Order relating to (1769) 3-447 (Tuition of one CADER CHERRY).

SEAY, JAMES was assigned the tuition of ABRAHAM and SARAH SEAY, orphans of MATTHEW SEAY in (1768) 3-444.

SEAY, PATIENCE was an orphan of MATTHEW SEAY and were placed in the care of EDWARD TOOL and wife MARY 3-444.

SEIRES, SILVESTER, left an orphan named JOHN who is under care of MICHAEL WARD (1748) 2-631.

SESSOMS, SAMUEL (probably SESSIONS) with others of the name were mentioned in the will of WILLIAM FREEMAN (1831) 2-512.

SESSIONS, ELIZABETH asks for letters of administration on the estate of THOMAS SESSIONS in (1711) in CHOWAN 3-442.

SESSIONS, JOHN appointed on a jury to lay out the main road down KESIAH NECK in (1718) with JOHN BENTLEY, WILLIAM LATTIMORE and others 1-154.

SESSIONS, SAMUEL left will in (1837) with son LEWIS OUTLAW SESSIONS 2-548.

SEWELL, RICHARD and one ROBERT HOLBROOK were the witnesses to a deed by EDWARD HOWCOTT in (1718) 1-627.

SEWELL, SAMUEL issued letters of administration by GOVERNOR of MASSACHUSETTS (1721) 2-107.

SEXTON, DARBY mentioned in statement by THOMAS RELFE when WILLIAM GLOVER was Clerk as having thirty years before owned a part of the land now belonging to AUGUSTINE SCARBOROUGH 3-146; the wife of DARBY SEXTON was DOROTHY in (1700) 3-409; he lived in ALBEMARLE later PASQUOTANK in (1677) 1-611.

SEXTON, JEREMIAH, witnessed the will of WILLIAM WINSLOW in (1830) 3-357.

SEXTON, SARAH married ESAU ALBERTSON (1700) 3-409.

SHACKELFORD, CHARLES witnessed a deed from JOSEPH JORDAN to FRANCIS THOMAS (1730) 2-449.

SHACKELFORD, JOHN left will in (1735); his daughter SARAH the wife of JOSEPH MOSS 1-73; he and ENOCH WARD brough suit against the CHADWICKS in (1726) 3-290.

SHADDOCK, SARAH, married JOHN HARE (1698) 3-408.

SHAFTSBURY PRECINCT in CHOWAN contains the oldest land grants in N. C. 1-3.

SHARBO, THOMAS married BARARA LEARY and names of children mentioned 3-394; he and wife ELIZABETH also had children 3-394.

SHARER, ROBERT bought land from HENRY WHEELER in (1715) 1-288.

SHARROCK FAMILY WILLS 2-545.

SHARROD, JAMES. An affidavit by JOHN COLLINS in (1777) refers to his activities 2-575.

SHARPE, ANTHONY was a Lieutenant in the NINTH REGIMENT of the N. C. Continental Line in the revolution 1-424.

SHARP, ARCHIBALD was Master of the Sloop TRISTRAM Feb. 20, (1755) 1-436.

SHARP, JACOB, proved his rights in (1746) & named himself, ELIZABETH SHARP, JOHN GLASS, SARAH BENNETT and STARKEY SHARP 2-627; he died leaving will in BERTIE in (1748) in which he mentioned son STARKEY, nephew SAMUEL TURNER, wife ELIZABETH and PETER EVANS 1-385, 1-386.

SHARP, STARKEY was the son of JACOB SHARP in BERTIE (1746) 2-627; same 1-386.

SHARP, TIMOTHY. He was the brother in law of DAY RIDLEY, of HERTFORD COUNTY, N. C. in (1777), who left son TIMOTHY SHARP RIDLEY 1-132.

SHARP, WILLIAM entered into an agreement with FRANCIS and DENNIS MACLENDEN in (1717) which was witnessed by ELLENER EARLY in 1-618; he made a deed of land to WILLIAM DOWNING in (1722) in which a GEORGE DURANT was a witness 2-143; he had a power of attorney from WILLIAM DOWNING in (1716) 1-293; and witnessed a deed from DENNIS MACLENDEN to WILLIAM DOWNING in (1715) 1-293; in (1712) he received corn from MAJOR GALE for the public service; also from EDWARD MOSELEY 1-439; in (1715) he was referred to as "ship carpenter" 1-288; in (1716) he and RICHARD HAYS witnessed the deed of ROBERT EVANS to THOMAS BRAY 1-616; in (1718) he and THOMAS CRANK witnessed a deed from SAMUEL WOODWARD 1-628; witnessed deed from THOMAS BRAY to ROBERT EVANS 1-300; was in HERTFORD COUNTY in (1715) 1-293; gave power of attorney to TREDLE KEEFE (1716) for sale to McLENDEN 1-293; he bought land from WILLIAM DOWNING in (1715) witnessed by ROBERT LANIER and THOMAS KIRBY 1-288.

SHAW, BENJAMIN was master of the Schooner "ORANGE" (1749) 1-433.

SHEARER, ROBERT, left will in BERTIE (1727) & names sons ROBERT, ARTHUR, JOHN and WILLIAM and daughters 1-485, 1-486.

SHEETES, REBECCA (nee REBECCA EARL) left will in (1730) and mentions mother MARY EARL 1-75.

SHEHAN FAMILY WILLS 2-356.

SHEHAN, MILES had an Ordinary at TOMBSTONE FERRY in BERTIE in (1769) 3-447.

SHEHAN, SARAH in (1770) was placed under the tuition of THOMAS HANDWICK -BERTIE 3-447.

SHELBY, EVAN, had a daughter who married a man named WYLIE 3-315.

SHEPARD, ABRAHAM, was COLONEL of the TENTH REGIMENT of the N. C. Continental line; list of soldiers who served with him beginning with the letter "D" 3-95, 3-98; see 1-425 for the officers; the wife of JOSEPH HARDY (son of HUMPHREY HARDY who left will (1810) in BERTIE) was ELIZABETH SHEPARD, daughter of COL. ABRAHAM SHEPARD 3-519, 3-520; an ABRAHAM SHEPARD was the grandson of DAVID SHEPARD who left will in CARTERET in (1775) 1-387.

SHEPARD, DAVID, died leaving will in CARTERET COUNTY (1775) and gives names of children and grandchildren 1-387; see also 1-49.

SHEPARD, STEPHEN in (1739) bought lands from ROBERT RIDDICK 3-135; and in (1729) he and JOHN MORRIS JR. executed a bond to THOMAS PILAND 3-446.

SHEPARD, THOMAS died leaving a will in CURRITUCK in (1722) names daughters ELIZABETH and GEVINSFORD, son SAMPSON SHEPARD and wife RUTH ; JOHN WICKER and HUMPHREY VINES were the witnesses 1-387.

SHEPARD, THOMAS left will in NORTHAMPTON COUNTY in (1753) named sons JOSEPH, WILLIAM, ROBERT, and THOMAS and daughter CHARITY and other children; JOHN DAWSON and son THOMAS were the Executers 1-435; a THOMAS SHERROD left will in BERTIE in (1731) 1-485; see also 1-74.

SHERRILL, WILLIAM and ALEXANDER LILLINGTON were the "nearest of kin" of THOMAS COOK 1-58.

SHERWINN, THOMAS bought land in (1731) from WILLIAM POPPLEWELL 2-510.

SHERWOOD, DANIEL. In (1693) the name of his wife was JANE and they had children 3-219.

SHERWOOD, DAVID. The name of his wife in (1693) was JANE and they had children 3-369; one DAVID SHERWOOD (Spelled SHERROD) left will in PERQUIMANS (1740) 1-72; one DAVID SHERWOOD married ELIZABETH JONES in (1725) and left children 3-394; a DAVID SHERWOOD recorded his mark (1689) 3-429. See also 1-388

SHERWOOD, DAVID JR. was the son of DAVID and his wife JANE (1700) 3-372.

SHERWOOD, JONATHAN was the son of DANIEL 3-219; he left will in (1765) and mentioned his father JONATHAN; and another JONATHAN SHERWOOD left will in (1769) and mentioned grand-daughter PENINAH ANDERSON 3-187.

SHERWOOD, MARY was the daughter of DAVID and wife JANE born (1702) 3-374.

SHERWOOD, SARAH, was the daughter of DAVID and wife JANE and was born (1706) 3-377.

SHERWOOD, THOMAS, left will in PASQUOTANK (1694) wife ELIZABETH and daughter SARAH 1-388; a THOMAS SHERROD left will in BERTIE 1-485.

SHINE, DANIEL left will in CRAVEN COUNTY in (1757) sons JOHN, THOMAS and WILLIAM and daughter ELIZABETH VAUGHAN, sons JAMES and TAMER SHINE among Executors 1-437.

SHIPP FAMILY. Some genealogy relating to 2-169.

SHIBER, ROBERT and wife DOROTHY deeded lands to PATRICK MAULE in (1706) 2-457.

SHIRLEY, JAMES, of NEW HANOVER, died about (1740) his widow was ANN SHIRLEY 2-166.

SHIVERS, ALEXANDER bought land on MEHERRIN RIVER in (1718) from JOHN COUNCIL (Of VIRGINIA) 1-628.

SHOLAR, JOHN sold land to JAMES SMITH which he had bought from JAMES FALCONER 1-617; and he recorded his mark and brand in BERTIE (1745) 2-627.

SHOOKE, DANIEL left will in PERQUIMANS in (1712) mentions DANIEL ROGERSON and wife MARY 1-77.

SHORT, JOHN is mentioned in the will of JOHN WEST in (1712) 1-83.

SHOWLES, JOHN bought land from JOHN PAGETT in CHOWAN in (1728) 3-445.

SHROCK, PETER CHRISTIAN, bought land from GEORGE CAPEHART and wife MARY in (1746) 2-629.

SLIVERTHORN, GILFORD left will in (1735) and names wife JEAN and ABRAHAM ENLOW 1-73.

SIMONS, ANN obtained a land grant in (1694) adjoining VINES CROPLEY 1-4.

SIMONS, ARGALL sold land on CONEBY CREEK to DANIEL GARRETT in (1712) with THOMAS LUTEN and WILLIAM RAGSDALE witnesses 1-100; he obtained a land grant (1694) 1-4; in (1716) he was the father of JOHN SIMONS 1-293; he was claimed as a headright by ANN STEWART before 1700 3-144.

SIMMONS, EDWARD left will in (1735) an mentions daughters THOMASIN and HANNAH and grandson JOHN JACKSON 1-73.

SIMMONS, GEORGE. In (1716) his wife was HANNAH or SUSANNAH 3-395; the GEORGE who left will in (1720) mentions his mother SUSANNA 1-77.

SIMMONS, JACOB owned lands next to CHARLES and JONATHAN HAUGHTON 1-22; he was granted land in (1784) adjoining PETTYJOHN 1-22.

SIMMONS, JAMES, left will in (1824) and mentions son JOHN CHARLTON SIMMONS 3-353.

SIMMONS JOHN, was dead in BERTIE in (1770) and left MALACHI SIMMONS an orphan, under the tuition of ROBERT HOBDAY 3-448; a JOHN SIMMONS left will (1818) in BERTIE with wife NANCY and the heirs of MALACHI SIMMONS and ZEDEKIAH STONE 2-547; the JOHN who died in (1791) in BERTIE had son MALACHI and brother in law JAMES LANGSTON 2-354; a JOHN was the son of ARGALL SIMMONS in (1716) 1-293; in (1696) the wife of JOHN SIMMONS was BRIDGET 3-370.

SIMMONS, MARY in her will in (1722) mentions a SARAH PIERCE 1-76; also daughter REBECCA TOMS, SARAH PETIT and MARY JONES 1-76.

SIMMONS, NICHOLAS was granted land on ALBEMARLE SOUND in (1694) 1-4; he married MARY BUNDY in (1692) 3-204; MARY SIMMONS the relict of NICHOLAS, deceased, sold lands to THOMAS PIERCE in (1718) 1-625, 1-626 (THOMAS PIERCE JR.)

SIMON, PETER (Of RHODE ISLAND) was Master of the sloop EAGLE (1775) 1-436.

SIMMONS, WILLIAM. In (1739) his wife was MARTHA and they had a son GEORGE who was born that year 3-395.

SIMPSON FAMILY WILLS 1-73, 2-25.

SIMPSON, ALEXANDER left will proved in (1738) & mentioned only JOHN CALDROM 1-73.

SIMPSON, BENJAMIN made a deed to lands to LUKE GREGORY in (1736) -ROBT. KINGHAM 3-126.

SIMPSON, JOHN, was Master of Sloop PROVIDENCE in (1749) 1-434.

SIMPSON, LAZARUS, Master of the Schooner LEMON in (1749) 1-434.

SIMPSON, ROBERT E. in (1806) witnessed the will of JOSIAH ELLIOTT, brother of TOWNSEND ELLIOTT 3-331.

SIMPSON, SOLOMON was grandson of MIRIAM ELLIOTT in (1804) 3-331.

SIMPSON, WILLIAM received a grant to lands (1761) 1-20.

SIMS, HENRY was witness to a sale of land to one JOSEPH SIMS in (1720) 2-619.

SIMS, JOSEPH, bought land in (1720) from a JAMES ANDERSON and wife ELIZABETH 2-519.

SIMS, ROBERT will in BERTIE in (1729) had brother JOHN SIMS and sons ROBERT, THOMAS and JAMES SIMS 1-483; ROBERT and HENRY SIMS lived adjoining WILLIAM BOON and HENRY WHEELER in (1720) 2-617.

SIMS, WILLIAM left will in EDGECOMBE in (1755) & JOHN WHITAKER was his Executer 1-483; in (1755) he owned lands near JOHN SMALL SR. 3-129.

SINCLAIR, SAMUEL, left will in HYDE in (1755) & JOHN STARKEY and STEPHEN LEE were his Executors; he had grandchildren WILLIAM and ANN THOMAS 1-385.

SINCLAIR, SARAH, was the daughter of WILLIAM LEWIS in (1731) 1-59.

SINGLETON, JAMES was granted one acre of land for a CHAPEL in CHOWAN PRECINCT on SCUPERNONG in (1720) 2-614, 2-615; he and his wife ANARITA sold lands to JOSHUA TURNER in (1730) 2-615; he sold land to EDWARD PHELPS deed (1717) 1-622.

SINGLETON, JOHN, married the widow of DAVID LAWLER about (1736) 2-299; he and wife MARY sold land to THOMAS PILAND in (1739-1740) part of a patent to JAMES COLE in (1694) which he had sold to JOHN COLE in (1702) in NANSEMOND COUNTY, VA., who sold same to JOSEPH BIRD in (1716) who in turn sold the land to JOHN SINGLETON; this deed was witnessed by WILLIAM DANIEL, JAMES ALSTON and PHILLIP ALSTON in BERTIE 3-134.

SINGLETON, SAMUEL died leaving will in DOBBS Co. and (1762) mentions daughter MARTHA CASWELL and son in law, RICHARD CASWELL, witnessed by ARTHUR YOUNG and TRAVIS WILLIAMS 1-487, 1-488.

SITTERSON, JAMES and wife PENINA and children (1754) 3-395; JAMES and wife MARY in (1759) 3-395; JAMES SITTERSON SR. and wife HANNAH had son JAMES died in (1768) 3-395; another JAMES SITTERSON and wife HANNAH (1715) 3-395; JAMES and wife KEZIAH in (1718) 3-394; JAMES SITTERSON left will in (1768) son of a JAMES, mentions a cousin WILLIAM PHELPS 3-188.

SITTERSON, SARAH was the daughter of JOHN JOHNSON who died in (1822) 3-339.

SITTERSON, WORTH, mentioned in the will of MARY BARBER in (1807) with HANCE BARBER, WILLIAM BARBER and SAMUEL, ISRAEL, BENJAMIN and JOSEPH LANE 3-326.

SIZEMORE, SAMUEL married the daughter of WILLIAM HOOKER by (1716) 1-51.

SKILES, JOHN died leaving will in BERTIE in (1823) wife CHARITY and children 2-547.

SKILES, WILLIAM, died leaving will in BERTIE in (1820) and mentions sons STARKEY, JOHN, and THOMAS WILLIAM SKILES, grandson STARKEY and other relatives 2-547.

SKILLINGS, WILLIAM left will in (1789) with ROBERT AVERY and JOHN MOORE as witnesses 3-190.

SKINNER FAMILY WILLS 1-486, 2-26, 2-27, 3-351.

SKINNER, CHARLES WORTH was son of JOSHUA SKINNER who died in (1839) who had son in law BAKER HOSKINS, and son JOSEPH BLOUNT SKINNER and other relatives named 3-351; he had daughter EMILY SKINNER who married DR. CHARLES E. JOHNSON. Genealogy of 3-168; a CHARLES SKINNER was Master of the Schooner POLLY in (1775) 1-436.

SKINNER, CHRISTOPHER was MASTER of the Sloop SWALLOW in (1749) 1-434.

SKINNER, ELIZABETH married JOSIAH COTTEN in (1777) and had several children 3-382.

SKINNER, EVAN received a grant of land on BEAR SWAMP in (1761) 1-20; also one same location in (1780) 1-21; he died leaving a will in (1789) 2-26; he was also Master of sloop SUCCESS in (1749) which sprang a leak on the PERQUIMANS river 1-434.

SKINNER, HENRY was named Executor of the will of HALSEY FLOYD in (1828) who mentions the daughter RACHEL SKINNER wife of MILES SKINNER 3-333.

SKINNER, JAMES, wife MARY, dates of birth of their children 3-395, 3-396.

SKINNER, JEREMIAH died (1739) 3-405.

SKINNER, JOHN. One left will in (1781) and had sons JOHN HARRELL SKINNER and WILSON SKINNER and daughters; AMOS HARRELL and LEMUEL HARRELL witnesses 2-353, 2-354; his wife may have been MARY CREECY whom he married in (1780) the daughter of LEVI CREECY 3-396.

SKINNER, JOSEPH BLOUNT had daughter who married DR. T. D. WARREN 1-539; see also 2-168.

SKINNER, JOSHUA died leaving will in (1777) & mentions HARVEY relatives 3-189; one JOSHUA married MARTHA ANN BLOUNT in (1780) and had children 3-396; the elder JOSHUA had married SARAH CREECY in (1745) 3-396; one JOSHUA SKINNER left will in (1831) 2-26, 2-27.

SKINNER, MARY, the wife of JAMES SKINNER and a daughter of JOHN PIERCE died in (1741) 3-396, 3-405.

SKINNER, RICHARD and his wife MARY are mentioned in (1722) 1-456; he was granted lands in CHOWAN in (1718) 1-13; and owned a patent to lands adjoining WILLIAM WOODLEY 1-13; granted lands on BEAR SWAMP (1727) 1-12; & his "wife SARAH" appears with children in (1715) 3-395; sued by JEREMIAH VAIL and wife MARY in (1707) 3-271; RICHARD SR. sold land to ABRAHAM HILL son of HENRY HILL 1-105.

SKINNER, SARAH, died in BERKELEY PRECINCT in the year (1751) 3-405.

SKINNER, GEN. WILLIAM, died and left will (1798) and mentions his wife DOROTHY and daughter ELIZABETH COTTON and son in law LEMUEL CREECY and numerous others; witnessed by STEPHEN SKINNER and CHARLES MOORE 3-190; a WILLIAM SKINNER patented lands in (1740) adjoining ROBERT ROGERS 1-18; his wife received a bequest from THOMAS CORPEW'S estate 1-453; one married about (1752) SARAH VAIL, the widow of THOMAS CORPEW 2-305; see also 3-467; WILLIAM SKINNER and ROBERT THOMAS witnessed deed of JOHN PORTER to CALLUM ROSS in BERTIE in (1739) 3-133.

SKITTLETHORP, "Daughter" was administratrix of JOSEPH MASON in (1702) 1-62.

SKITTLETHORP, ELIZA lived between CASHY RIVER and SALMON CREEK in (1719) in BERTIE 1-445.

SKOYLES, WILLIAM, bought land from WILLIAM RIDDICK in (1716) 1-617.

SLADE, EBENEZER and HENRY SLADE were the grandsons of RICHARD SYLVESTER SR. who died (1728) 1-75.

SLADE, GEORGE bought land from JOHN HAWKINS in (1703) 3-511; in (1710) he left a will in it he mentioned DANIEL LEIGH 1-77.

SLADE, HENRY, brother of EBENEZER SLADE and grandson of RICHARD SYLVESTER SR. 1-75; one lived in CURRITUCK in (1677) 1-73.

SLADE, JOHN, left will in HYDE PRECINCT in (1743) leaving sons BENJAMIN, JOHN, WILLIAM and HEZEKIAH SLADE and daughter MARY and BENJAMIN JEWELL 1-72.

SLADE, JOSEPH left a will in (1710) in which mention is made of EDWARD FRANCIS 1-77.

SLADE, SAMUEL, left will in BEAUFORT in (1746) in which he names sons in law WILLIAM DUNBAR and JAMES BLOUNT 1-72.

SLATTER, ALEXANDER mentioned as the son of OWEN SLATTER of BERTIE in (1767) 2-355.

SLATTER, OWEN died leaving will in BERTIE (1767) in which he mentions EDWARD BIRD and HUMPHREY LAWRENCE 2-355.

SLATTER, THOMAS died in (1741) and THOMAS and MARY SLATTER were the executors 2-468; his wife was MARGARET 3-217.

SLAUGHTER, ABIGAIL was the administrator of estate of EDWARD WOODWARD in (1754) 1-455.

SLAUGHTER, EBENEZER died in BERTIE in (1838) leaving will, with JONATHAN S. TAYLOR Exr. 2-548.

SLAUGHTER, ELIZABETH, the daughter of MICHAEL SLAUGHTER chose PETER PAYNE as her guardian in (1743) 1-447.

SLAUGHTER, HANNAH, daughter of MICHAEL SLAUGHTER, married PETER PAYNE in (1741) 1-65.

SLAUGHTER, MICHAEL, see genealogical note 1-65.

SLEDD, JOSHUA, Master of MARY ANN owned by EMANUEL LOWE & CO., merchants (1716) 3-271.

SLOCUMB, ANTHONY, was 90 years old in (1680) (born 1590) 1-139; he received a land grant in (1684) in CHOWAN PRECINCT 1-3; he left will in (1688) proved in (1689 - 1690) in which he mentions several grandchildren, including THOMAS GILBERT and a THOMAS YELVERTON of ALBEMARLE COUNTY 1-385.

SLOCUMB, JOHN. There were two JOHNS who left wills in CRAVEN COUNTY, one in (1722) and another in (1759) 1-385; another JOHN SLOCUMB left a will in BATH in (1712) and in it mentioned his mother MARGARET DAVIS 1-77.

SLOCUMB, SAMUEL, of BATH, left will in (1712) and mentioned his mother MARGARET DAVIS 1-77.

SLAWSON, EBENEZER, had a daughter ANNA SLAWSON who recorded her mark in (1747) 2-630.

SMALL FAMILY. Genealogical account of SMALL FAMILY and its relationship to the HOSKINS family 3-119; wills of members of the SMALL FAMILY 2-26, 2-75.

SMALL, ABRAHAM was a brother of WILLIAM, MILES, DAVID, DANIEL and ALEXANDER SMALL in (1806) 3-350.

SMALL, ALEXANDER, was brother of ABRAHAM, WILLIAM, MILES, DAVID and DANIEL SMALL 3-350.

SMALL, BENJAMIN received a grant of land in GREEN HALL in (1794) 1-24; his wife was MARY and they sold land to DAVID AMBROSE in (1736) 3-128; in (1734) they deeded lands to ROBERT COLEMAN of NANSEMOND CO. VIRGINIA, which was near the head of BENNETT'S CREEK, adjoining WILLIAM SPEIRS & DANIEL PUGH 3-453.

SMALL, JOHN SR. of NANSEMOND COUNTY, VIRGINIA, granted lands on BENNETT'S CREEK in (1715) 2-453; bought lands from THOMAS HOLLOWAY (HOLLADAY) in (1735) with WILLIAM SIMS a witness 3-129; a JOHN SMALL was Master of the schooner MARY & HANNAH in (1749) 1-433; a certain JOHN HUMPHREY SMALL married SARAH ANN SANDERSON and their son of the same name was CONGRESSMAN from N. C. - the first district 2-533.

SMALL, JOSEPH, administration or division of his estate in (1757) names children 1-466; he was granted land in (1743) which joined that of JOHN LEWIS 1-12.

SMALL, JOSIAH received a grant of land in (1790) on COWHALL SWAMP 1-23.

SMALL, WILLIAM left will in (1802) in which he named his brothers 3-350.

SMALL, REUBEN received a grant of land (1793) in GREEN HALL 1-24.

SMALLWOOD FAMILY. Genealogical notes showing connections with the GRIFFINS and CLARKS in NORTH CAROLINA 2-606.

SMALLWOOD, THOS. J. P. was witness to the will of JOHN ROBBINS in BERTIE in (1846) 2-544; THOMAS P. SMALLWOOD and HUMPHREY H. HARDY willed lands by FRANCIS PUGH in (1845) to build a Parsonage for the Minister 2-537.

SMITH FAMILY. Wills by the SMITH FAMILY are to be found on 1-383, 1-384, 2-73, 2-74, 3-190, 3-351.

SMITH, ABRAHAM and JOHN DUNING witnessed a deed by JOHN JORDAN JR. in (1730) 2-449.

SMITH, ALEXANDER died leaving will (1711) mentions his estate in VIRGINIA, and son FRANCIS SMITH and MARY QUARLES 1-77.

SMITH, DANIEL and MARY JONES were neighbors in (1715) 1-293.

SMITH, EDWARD deeded land to his son JOHN SMITH in CHOWAN in (1715) 1-285; he left will in PASQUOTANK in (1694) with WILLIAM COLLINS & MARY CLARK as Executors 1-443.

SMITH, GEORGE received a grant of land on GILLY CRANKY in (1714) 1-13; he and his wife SARAH sold lands on BROAD CREEK to TIMOTHY McCARTY in (1712) TREDLE KEEFE a witness 1-100; one GEORGE SMITH with wife ELIZABETH died (1736) leaving sons RICHARD, GEORGE, JOHN and LEWIS SMITH and daughter MARY 1-73.

SMITH, CAPT. HENRY proved his "rights" sometime before (1700) 1-305; a later HENRY died and left will in GATES COUNTY in (1787) and had sons JONATHAN and HENRY and daughters 2-73.

SMITH, JAMES. His wife was SUSARNAH in (1721) & they had children 3-396; in (1728) he sold land to THOMAS EVERENDEN at DRUMMOND'S POINT; one before him left will in PERQUIMANS(1719) and he came from VIRGINIA 1-75; the later JAMES sold land to THOMAS HAWKINS in (1728) deed witnessed by JOHN HANSON and JOSEPH CRAIN; the later one died (1735) leaving will with sons SOLOMON and JOHN SMITH 1-73.

SMITH, JOHN, bought land from THOMAS HOOKS and wife ANNA in BERTIE (1771) 3-449; he was to have the tuition of THOMAS LASSITER, orphan in BERTIE in (1770) 3-448; a JOHN SMITH (Of YORK COUNTY, VIRGINIA) had his deposition taken at the home of JAMES BATES in (1713) 2-151; one JOHN SMITH married ANN JASPER, the daughter of RICHARD JASPER before (1742) 2-468; a JOHN SMITH and his wife ANN sold lands to WILLIAM SHARPE in (1717) with DENNIS McLENDEN a witness 1-618; in (1717) JOHN SMITH sold lands to JOHN WARE adjoining ANDREW SALISBURY, with JOHN DIER a witness 1-300; in (1718) a JOHN SMITH and his wife JUDITH sold lands to PHILLIP BROWN, on CHINKAPIN CREEK, witnessed by WILLIAM BRASWELL and wife MARGARET 1-629; in (1703) JOHN SMITH sold land to COL. THOMAS POLLOCK, the deed witnessed by THOMAS DUTEN and WILLIAM EARLY 2-611; JOHN and wife ANN sold land to WILLIAM SHARP in (1715) with WILLIAM DOWNING and JOHN LEVISON witnesses 1-288; JOHN SMITH left a will in (1734) and names only his wife ELIZABETH 1-75.

SMITH, JOSEPH, married HANNAH HILL at the home of FRANCIS TOMES (1695) 3-407; in (1728) JOSEPH of PERQUIMANS was the grandfather of SAMUEL PHELPS 1-68.

SMITH, MARY a widow married JAMES FISHER in (1701) 3-409; and a MARY SMITH left a will in CHOWAN in (1718) in which she mentions her daughter ISABELLA SMITH and sons WILLIAM, FRANCIS and ABRAHAM SMITH 1-76.

SMITH, NATHANIEL married ELIZABETH NABSON of CARTERET COUNTY 1-60.

SMITH, NICHOLAS left will in (1751) named his wife MARY and son SIMON SMITH 1-72; one NICHOLAS SMITH married the widow of THOMAS HAWKINS in (1696) 1-48; genealogical account of the NICHOLAS SMITH family and its connection with the NORFLEETS and others 2-635.

SMITH, RICHARD, an account of his arrest by JOHN PORTER 3-65.

SMITH, ROBERT copy of his letter written to GOV. RICHARD CASWELL from EDENTON in (1777) in which he mentions EGAN 2-244, 2-245; the first ROBERT SMITH left will in (1692) and mentions son JOSEPH and daughter ELIZABETH and a son in law SAMUEL WOODS 1-73; another ROBERT SMITH left will in BERTIE in (1726) wife MARY, son ROBERT and daughters MARY and ELIZABETH 1-73.

SMITH, SARAH left will in (1721) and named her son EDWARD TAYLOR and daughter SOPHIA NICHOLSON 1-75, 1-76.

SMITH, SILAS, left will (1829) and names THOMAS STARKEY, son of EBENEZER STARKEY, and his own son ABRAHAM SMITH and others 2-546.

SMITH, WILLIAM left will in PASQUOTANK in (1719) wife ELIZABETH and father in law JOHN AVERY 1-74; in (1727) another WILLIAM SMITH with THOMAS HARRELL were witnesses to a deed by WILLIAM HARRISON 2-445; in (1716) the first WILLIAM lived on LITTLE RIVER and after his death his widow married JOHN McKEEL 1-76.

SMITHWICK FAMILY. See Petition of EDWARD and JOHN SMITHWICK to GOV. HARVEY and the members of the Council, and of THOMAS GILLIAM and his wife SARAH relating to their land on CHOWAN RIVER for some idea of this family and its connections 3-78, 3-79, 3-80. SMITHWICK FAMILY WILLS 3-354.

SMITHWICK, ANN was the daughter in law (stepdaughter) of FURNIFOLD GREEN, mentioned in his will in (1711) 1-46.

SMITHWICK, EDWARD received a land grant 1-2; he deeded land to WILLIAM LATTIMORE in (1716) witnessed by PETER GRAY, in which NATHAN MOW is mentioned 1-616; in about (1704) he was a member of the HOUSE OF BURGESSES 3-60; he was 33 years of age in (1680) and was born about(1647)1-139; he and his brother JOHN were the sons of HUGH SMITHWICK 1-612; he married SARAH GILLIAM, the widow of THOMAS GILLIAM, who was SARAH WOOLARD before her marriage to THOMAS GILLIAM; they made a deed to WILLIAM WILKINSON in (1703) 1-612; the Court for SHAFTSBURY PRECINCT was held at the house of EDWARD SMITHWICK in (1680)1-613; but his wife was JANE in (1707) when he sold land to JEREMIAH VAIL 1-296; again in (1702) he and wife AFRICA sold lands to JOHN JONES JR. 2-456; the wife of EDWARD SMITHWICK JR. was GRACE (1718)2-285; in (1714) sold land to NATHAN MOORE 2-455; also to WILLIAM MIZELL (1714) HENRY SPELLER & LUKE MIZELL wits 1-291; in(1680) his father HUGH SMITHWICK died 1-613.

SMITHWICK, HANNAH, appears as a witness on bond in (1696) 1-613.

SMITHWICK, HUGH, "late of CHOWAN" came into the country about (1660) and seated on a parcel of land in CHOWAN PRECINCT, and was the father of EDWARD and JOHN SMITHWICK 3-79; on an adjoining tract of land he lived for 21 years or more, THOMAS GILLIAM and his wife SARAH 1-613.

SMITHWICK, JOHN, with his brother EDWARD petition GOV. THOMAS HARVEY in (1696) to (1699) 3-78, 3-79; THOMAS GILLIAM and wife SARAH dispute the rights of JOHN and his brother EDWARD to some of the land, which was located on EDENTON BAY about one and one-half miles from the town of EDENTON 3-80, 3-81; PATIENCE SPELLER had three grandchildren in (1738) named JOHN, SARAH and ELIZABETH SMITHWICK 1-73; a later JOHN SMITHWICK left will in (1803) in BERTIE with wife WINNIFRED and children WILLIAM and CLARRY SMITHWICK 2-546; the elder JOHN owned lands next to ROBERT WARBURTON 1-17; and one was a cousin of JAMES SWAIN in (1738) 1-73; and SUSANNA SWAIN, a daughter of the JAMES SWAIN who died in BERTIE in (1817) married a SMITHWICK 2-546; a JOHN who died leaving will in (1696) mentions only his wife and daughter SARAH 1-74; a JOHN SMITHWICK was foreman of a Grand Jury in BERTIE in (1746) 2-628.

SNEAD, JOHN died leaving will in (1743) naming wife ELIZABETH and HENRY, WILLIAM, JOHN, MARY, ANN, ELIZABETH, SARAH and ANN and his father in law FRY, and brother in law WILLIAM MARTIN 1-72.

SNELL, KATHERINE was the daughter of ROGER SNELL and wife REBECCA and was born (1689)3-216; & her sister MARY was born (1684) 3-212.

SNELL, ROGER and his wife ELIZABETH sold lands in (1702) to JOHN YELVERTON, which had been in possession of RICHARD DARLING 2-456; he was a son of ROGER SNELL and wife REBECCA and was born in (1682) 3-211; a still earlier ROGER SNELL (possibly the husband of REBECCA) married the widow of JOHN HODGSON in (1679) 1-73; one appears to have been the son in law of RICHARD PICKERING in (1740) 1-65.

SNELLING, ISRAEL was the "brother" of a WILLIAM LAWRENCE in (1694) 1-58; his wife was HANNAH and their daughter RACHEL was born in (1690) 3-216, 3-372.

SNOOK, DANIEL, sued DAVID WHITLOCK in (1689)3-431; and JOHN CULPEPPER in (1690) 3-435.

SNOWDEN, CHRISTOPHER, of BERTIE, sold lands to a JAMES WARD on YOPPIM in (1731) 2-451.

SNOWDEN, ISAAC, was a grandson of MARY SANDERS & son of her daughter MARY 1-74.

SNOWDEN, JOSEPH, the son of THOMAS SNOWDEN and his wife CONSTANCE was born in (1703) 3-375; he left will in (1740) in which he names his brothers JOHN, GEORGE and WILLIAM SNOWDEN 1-72.

SNOWDEN, SAMUEL (Spelled SNODEN) left will in PASQUOTANK in (1750) wife SARAH and a ROBERT BAILEY, Executors 1-388; another SAMUEL left will in (1754) same county 1-388.

SNOWDEN, SARAH, married MILES TURNER (1785)3-418.

SNOWDEN, THOMAS married to THOMASIN MERCER in (1705) 3-410; in (1702) he was SECRETARY of the N. C. Colony 3-270; he and his wife THOMASIN had a son JOHN SNOWDEN born in (1707) 3-377; he obtained a grant of land on YOPPIM RIVER in (1704) 1-6; he died & left a will in (1736) and named sons JOHN, JOSEPH, WILLIAM, GEORGE, SAMUEL, SOLOMON and LEMUEL, with SAMUEL SWAIN one of his Executors 1-73; see 3-396, 3-397; fees of Executors accepted by him in PASQUOTANK in an early day 3-255; in (1702) he sued JOHN TARKINGTON in ALBEMARLE 1-610; and was CLERK of the ASSEMBLY 3-301; he was an ATTORNEY in (1715) 3-221.

SOANE, JOHN, left will in BERTIE in year(1732) with LEWIS BRYAN as a witness 1-74.

SOJOURNER, JOSIAH, was the grandson of WILLIAM WEST in (1744) 1-80.

SOJOURNER, MARY was a sister of HENRY WEST who left will in (1752) 1-80.

SOLEAR, MATTHEW, bought land from HENRY FOREMAN SR. in (1717) 1-300.

SORRELL, JAMES left will in BERTIE in (1802) and named wife ANN and sons THOMAS and JOHN and daughters; ABRAHAM PETTYJOHN was a witness 2-546.

SORSBY FAMILY. They were related to the BOZEMAN FAMILY 2-635; and lived in HALIFAX COUNTY, N. C. 3-469.

SOTHEL, ANNA, called DAME ANNA SOTHELL in her bill to GEORGE MUSCHAMP in (1694) 3-247; she is mentioned in interogatory answered by COL. THOMAS POLLOCK (no date) 3-254; she was the wife of GOV. SETH SOTHELL & married second COL. JOHN LEAR of NANSEMOND COUNTY, Virginia 1-74; she was the daughter of EDWARD FORSTER (FOSTER?) 3-31.

SOTHELL, SETH, referred to in Act as "GOV. LORD SOTHELL" in (1689) 2-197; he was issued the first grant of land in BEAUFORT COUNTY in (1682) 3-20; his wife was ANNA, the daughter of EDWARD FORSTER 3-31; his estate was sued for Quit Rents he had collected 3-93, 3-94; and his Executors answer the charges filed against same 3-32, 3-33; THOMAS POLLOCK'S petition in regard to 2-77; he was Governor of the Colony of N. C. in (1689) and left his lands and plantation to FRANCIS HARTLEY, whose widow married WILLIAM DUKENFIELD 2-455; he died in (1689) according to letter signed by ROBERT WINDLEY 2-223; reference to a sale of cattle belonging to him 3-72.

SOUTH CAROLINA. Letter from the Governor (no date) to the Governor of NORTH CAROLINA; GOV. ARCHDALE mentioned on the back 2-222; 2-223.

SOUTH, ANDREW, witnessed the will of RALPH OUTLAW in BERTIE in (1787) 2-349.

SOUTH, ELIZABETH is mentioned in the will of SAMUEL G. HYMAN in BERTIE in (1847) also mentions SAMUEL GILL 2-521.

SOUTH, WILLIAM married ELIZABETH HYMAN 2-521.

SOUTHWICK, WILLIAM was deceased in (1771) and his widow SARAH administrater 3-450.

SOWDEN, GAVIN was a brother in law of EBENEZER TAYLOR, and he also mentions his brother EDWARD WALKER (1711) 1-79.

SOWELL, CHARLES left will in BERTIE in (1739) and named his children, RICHARD, THOMAS, CHARLES JR. and LEWIS SOWELL, wife MARTHA 1-73; in (1770) he was charged with the tuition of the children of BETTIE JAMES 3-448.

SOWELL, FRANCIS left will in BERTIE in (1796) witnessed by MOSES GILLIAM 2-357.

SOWELL, JOHN died leaving will in BERTIE in (1755) naming his sons and daughters and his father RICHARD SOWELL, with ADAM HARRELL a witness 1-489.

SOWELL, OBEDIAH died leaving will in BERTIE (1803) in which he mentioned sons JOHN, ISAAC, OBEDIAH and EZEKIEL, and daughters NANCY, WINNIFRED, SARAH COWAND and MARY DANIEL 3-546.

SOWELL, RICHARD received a grant of land in (1712) adjoining JOHN JORDAN 1-15; he sold lands to his son CHARLES SOWELL adjoining JOHN BALLARD in (1712) 1-629; he and his wife MARGARET sold land to WILLIAM STEMOS in (1703) 2-511; another RICHARD SOWELL died and left will in BERTIE in (1751) witnessed by WILLIAM BENNETT & others 1-489.

SOWELL, WINNIFRED (daughter of OBEDIAH) married JEREMIAH MIZELL in (1807) in BERTIE 3-378.

SPARKMAN, EDWARD left will in BERTIE in (1833) & named wife WINNIFRED and his children 2-547.

SPARKMAN, JOHN was father of MARY SPARKMAN (1734) 1-451; and owned lands next to WILLIAM HARRIS in (1742) 1-18.

SPARKMAN, LUCRETIA left will in GATES COUNTY in (1856) had son DEMPSEY and other children who are mentioned 3-76.

SPARKMAN, MARGARET, widow, sold lands to her son STEPHEN SPARKMAN in (1729) deed witnessed by JOHN SPARKMAN and HENRY BAKER 3-451.

SPARKMAN, MARY was the orphan of JOHN (1734) 1-451

SPARKMAN, WILLIAM died leaving will in BERTIE in (1785) naming his sons WILLIAM, EDWARD and other children, showing his connection with the HYMAN, HUNTER, WARD, WILLIAMS and PRITCHARD FAMILIES; HARDY HUNTER mentioned 2-356.

SPARROW, JOSEPH, of ALBEMARLE petitioned the Court in (1702) 1-609.

SPARROW, THOMAS died leaving will in PASQUOTANK in (1717) in which he mentioned his brother THOMAS HARDING 1-77.

SPEIR, ELIZABETH died leaving will in (1773) and mentions the SMITHWICK (only spelled SMYDICK) and MARY MIZELL daughter of MARK MIZELL and other relatives 1-486.

SPEIR, JAMES, of BERTIE, made deed to WILLIAM EVERETT in (1728), which was witnessed by JOHN THOMAS 2-445.

SPIER, JOHN married MARTHA COTTEN, daughter of JOHN COTTEN 2-298; will (1760) 1-486.

SPELLER, HENRY was given the tuition of THOMAS SPELLER of BERTIE in (1771) 3-450; an earlier HENRY with ROBERT HICKS witnessed a deed by THOMAS PARRIS in (1718) 1-528; he calls THOMAS PARRIS his brother in his will in (1727) in which his wife was PATIENCE SPELLER 1-75; in (1715) he sold lands to JOHN BENNETT; and JOHN BENNETT SR. sold same to WILLIAM WHITE 1-521; in (about 1715) he witnessed a deed by LUKE MIZELL and wife SARAH to GEORGE CLARK of PERQUIMANS 1-297; in (1714) he and LUKE MIZELL and WILLIAM CHARLTON witnessed deed of EDWARD SMITHWICK to WILLIAM MIZELL 1-291; in (1721) he and PATIENCE SPELLER and JAMES SWAIN sold lands on YOPPIM to JAMES WARD 2-288

SPELLER, PATIENCE was the wife of HENRY SPELLER 1-75; she left will in BERTIE in (1738) and mentions her daughter PATIENCE daughter ANN WARD, sons JAMES and RICHARD SWAIN and grandchildren SARAH, JOHN and ELIZABETH SMITHWICK 1-73.

SPELLMAN, JOHN and wife KATHERINE had a son THOMAS born in (1691) 3-217; he brought a suit against WILLIAM STEWART in (1689) 3-431.

SPENCE, ALEXANDER and his wife DOROTHY had a son ALEXANDER born in (1699) 3-371; he died in PASQUOTANK in (1735) and named his sons JAMES, ALEXANDER, JOSEPH, ROBERT and TRUMAN, daughter JANE SPENCE and CATHERINE SAWYER 1-74.

SPENCE, HANNAH and her sister ANN were the daughters of JEREMIAH SYMONS 1-72.

SPENCE, JAMES left will in (1739) and mentioned his daughter BETTY MANCHUM 1-72.

SPENCE, JOHN; his wife was CATHERINE in (1696) 3-369; he left will in (1735) and mentioned daughter DOROTHY DAVIDSON and son in law CHARLES SAWYER 1-72, 1-73.

SPENCE, WILLIAM, left will in (1816) and he was the son of THOMAS SPENCE, of WESTMORELAND COUNTY, Virginia; had sons WILLIAM and JOSEPH SKINNER SPENCE; witnesses were JOHN WOOD and JOSHUA SKINNER 3-352.

SPEIGHT FAMILY. Wills 1-391, 2-74, 2-75; some Genealogical notes 3-471.

SPEIGHT, FRANCIS patented lands in (1743) on West side of GUM SWAMP; two different tracts granted 1-19; but an earlier FRANCIS SPEIGHT was dead in (1732) and his wife was JUDITH 1-450.

SPEIGHT, ISAAC had children MARY, ISAAC and ELIZABETH in (1758) 3-471.

SPEIGHT, JOSEPH died leaving will in GATES COUNTY in (1792) his wife ANN and sons FRANCIS and HENRY and some relatives named FREEMAN 3-74.

SPEIGHT, JOSIAH died in CHOWAN in (1783) and mentioned his cousin JOSIAH FREEMAN (son of WILLIAM FREEMAN) and several brothers in law and relatives 3-25.

SPEIGHT, JUDITH was the widow and executrix of FRANCIS SPEIGHT in the old CHOWAN PRECINCT in N. C. in (1732) 1-450.

158

SPEIGHT, JUDAH (a man) was the husband of a
FRANCES SPEIGHT, and sold land to a WILLIAM
WALTON before (1731) which he in turn sold
to TIMOTHY WALTON 3-131.

SPEIGHT MARY, in (1744) was already deceased and
MR. (THOMAS) BARKER as attorney for JOSEPH
PERRY took an order for the sale of some
part of the personal estate 2-522; then in
(1748) it appears that JOSEPH JORDAN was an
administrator of this same Estate 2-531.

SPEIGHT, MOSES. His widow was MARY and his son
THOMAS SPEIGHT chose his mother as guardian
2-626.

SPEIGHT, NANCY left will in (1834) had sister CE-
LIA WHITE, brothers JOHN and JEREMIAH SPEIGHT,
MARGARET WHITEHEAD was her sister and the
wife of FOSTER WHITEHEAD 3-353.

SPEIGHT, RICHARD was Secretary to GOV. ARTHUR
DOBBS in (1759) 1-457.

SPEIGHT, RUTH was the daughter of THOMAS SPEIGHT
and her sister RACHEL married THOMAS JORDAN;
JOSEPH JORDAN was Executor of the estate of
THOMAS SPEIGHT 1-446.

SPEIGHT, THOMAS in (1733) witnessed deed of ED-
WARD HARE to MOSES HARE 2-611; he and WIL-
LIAM DANIEL on jury to lay out road from BEN-
NETT'S CREEK Bridge in (1737) 1-448; he assigned a patent in (1700) when of NANSEMOND
COUNTY, Virginia, witnessed by ANDREW & MARY
ROSS 1-89; on list of tithables in (1702)
taken by JAMES COLE, with WILLIAM HOWARD 3-85
in (1739) he sold lands to FRANCIS SPEIGHT
with WILLIAM SPEIGHT, DAVID LEWIS and RICHARD
TAYLOR witnesses 3-135; one THOMAS was the
minor son of MOSES SPEIGHT in (1745) 2-526;
he owned lands next to JAMES BATES in (1717)
1-17; THOMAS SPEIGHT (father of ISAAC) had
children, ISAAC, RUTH (m. JOSEPH JORDAN) &
ZILPHA (m. TIMOTHY WALTON), MARY (m. WILLIAM
BENBERRY, _____ (m. SOLOMON SHEPARD) ELIZA
(m. CHRISTOPHER BERN) and PRISCILLA (married THOMAS JORDAN) of Virginia 2-471; he was
son and heir of CAPT. WILLIAM SPEIGHT of PER-
QUIMANS in (1704) 1-303; he owned lands adjoining EDWARD and MOSES HARE in (1733)2-611;
and he owned lands adjoining some owned by
JOHN PERRY and wife ELIZABETH, of NANSEMOND
COUNTY, VA. in (1720) 2-612; a THOMAS SPEIGHT
died leaving a will in BERTIE in (1796) and
named wife ELIZABETH, sons WILLIAM HARDY
SPEIGHT and JAMES SPEIGHT, and daughters WIN-
NIFRED, SARAH, ELIZABETH, LYDIA and FRANCES
SPEIGHT 2-357.

SPEIGHT, WILLIAM (Of NANSEMOND COUNTY, VA.) sold
land to son in law MOSES HARE in (1735) located on HORSE PEN BRANCH, witnessed by EDWARD
HARE, THOMAS and ANN SPEIGHT 3-128; he and
THOMAS GOFFE owned lands that joined JOHN
HAMBLETON of NANSEMOND COUNTY, VA. in (1727)
2-444; he and JAMES WINGFIELD witnessed a
deed to JOHN KING of Va. (1718) 1-627; sold
land to HENRY HOLLAND in (1728) on CHOWAN
RIVER 2-444; CAPT. WILLIAM SPEIGHT owned some
land in PERQUIMANS before (1700) 1-303.

SPIER, JAMES, of BERTIE, left will in (1731) and
mentioned daughters in law SARAH and PATIENCE
STALLINGS 1-75.

SPIER, JOHN was on the Grand Jury (no date) in
the days of GEO. BURRINGTON 3-237.

SPIER, JOHN left will in CRAVEN COUNTY (1767)
wife ELIZABETH and daughters PATIENCE
JEFFREYS and APPLE HOLLAND 1-486.

SPIRES, THOMAS was a witness to a deed by
WILLIAM THOMPSON in (1721) 2-614; and
a THOMAS SPIERS in (1728) sold some land
to EDWARD COCKRILL next to THOMAS and
DAVID JONES, brothers 3-443.

SPIVEY FAMILY. Wills in BERTIE 2-355; also
see 3-24, 3-25 for other wills.

SPIVEY, ABRAHAM, was the son of THOMAS SPIVEY
in (1715) 1-617; in (1734) he had a son
GEORGE SPIVEY who sold land to THOMAS
WALTON, JR. on CATHERINE'S CREEK 1-108;
he and THOMAS ROUNDTREE witnessed deed
of THOMAS SPIVEY in (1717) 1-300.

SPIVEY, REV. AARON left will in BERTIE in
(1822) and named his sons and daughters
including a son MOSES 2-547.

SPIVEY, BENJAMIN was the son of THOMAS SPIVEY
in (1715) 1-617.

SPIVEY, CALEB and one CHRISTOPHER BOYCE witnessed a deed by JONATHAN KITTRELL in
(1739) 3-133.

SPIVEY, GEORGE, was the son of THOMAS SPIVEY
in (1734) 1-108; he sold land to THOMAS
WALTON JR. (1734) 3-128.

SPIVEY, JACOB was a witness to deed by NATHAN-
IEL WRIGHT (Of NANSEMOND CO. VA.) in
(1731) 2-450; he was deeded lands by
ABRAHAM HILL and his wife JUDITH (1732)
2-456; in (1720) he witnessed deed by
THOMAS SPIVEY to CHARLES CAMPBELL (Of
Nansemond County, Va.) 2-614.

SPIVEY, JAMES witness to deed from WILLIAM
WRIGHT to JACOB SPIVEY in (1731) 2-450.

SPIVEY, JOHN was the father of JOHN and LIT-
TLETON SPIVEY 2-610.

SPIVEY, JOSEPH witnessed deed with JAMES
SPIVEY in (1731) 2-450.

SPIVEY, LITTLETON sold lands in (1738) to
JOHN BENTON 2-610; also 1-112.

SPIVEY, SARAH left will in BERTIE in (1848)
and mentioned a great grand-daughter
SARAH MARIA MIZELL and others 2-547.

SPIVEY, THOMAS and wife MARY sold land to
JAMES GRIFFIN (1717) with ABRAHAM SPIVEY
and THOMAS ROUNDTREE witnesses 1-300;
his wife was MARY and they sold land to
JACOB SPIVEY with WILLIAM HILL, RICHARD
BROTHERS and THOMAS ROUNDTREE witnesses
2-612; in (1720) he and MARY sold lands
to MOSES HILL on CATHERINE CREEK 2-608;
in (1720) they sold land to JACOB SPIVEY
with RICHARD HILL and THOMAS ROUNDTREE
witnesses 2-612; he signed a petition
relating to the CHOWAN INDIANS in 1702
3-242; in (1715) he sold lands to his
son BENJAMIN 1-617; in (1717) to his son
ABRAHAM SPIVEY 1-617; he left will in
CHOWAN in (1729) names son in law WIL-
LIAM HILL, daughter MARY HILL, sons BEN-
JAMIN, JACOB, THOMAS and WILLIAM SPIVEY
Grand-daughters MARY & SUSANNAH HILL 1-75.

SPRATT, THOMAS, was a Lieutenant in the 9th Regt. of the N. C. Continental Line 1-424.

SPRING, AARON, left will in BEAUFORT in (1755) & named sons AARON, ROBERT, JAMES and ABRAHAM wife MARTHA and daughters DINA, ELIZABETH; cousin JAMES McGEE and brother in law JOHN BARROW 1-489.

SPRING, ROBERT, signs petition by the Protestant Dissenters of BAY and NEUSE RIVERS, and his house is offered as a place of worship; other signers being JOHN and LAZARUS PEARCE & NATHANIEL DRAPER, JOHN CHURCH and ABRAHAM WARREN 2-198. (no date but JOHN MONTGOMERY was CHIEF JUSTICE).

SPRUILL, JOSEPH and SAMUEL SPRUILL, with JAMES SINGLETON and others resided on the West side of SCUPERNONG after (1711) 3-268, 2-614.

SPRUILL, ELIZA, was called the daughter by STEPHEN SWAIN in his CHOWAN will (1712) 1-76; and ELIZABETH SPRUILL left will in BERTIE (1788) and mentioned her brother ROBERT LAWRENCE & many other relatives 2-357.

SPRUILL, DR. GODFREY left will in (1719) and mentions his son in law CUTHBERT PHELPS 1-77; GODFREY SPRUILL deeded lands to JOSEPH SPRUILL in (1720) 3-615.

SPRUILL, SAMUEL sold lands to JAMES SWAIN (1719) with ROBERT CALF a witness 1-627; and he was a JUSTICE of CHOWAN PRECINCT in (1731) 1-449 and was sued in (1721) by THOMAS GARLAND 1-444.

SAINT PAUL'S CHURCH, of EDENTON, N. C. An account of its erection 1-600, 1-609.

STACEY, CHARLES sold lands to CHARLES MORGAN in (1716) with JOHN VOLWAY, JOHN BENNETT and JOSHUA PORTER as witnesses 1-618.

STACEY, ROBERT was granted lands on MATTACOMACK CREEK in (1719) 1-13; his wife SARAH 3-352.

STACEY, SARAH died leaving will (1826) and named her husband ROBERT STACEY, but this was a later ROBERT than the one on 1-13, 3-353.

STACEY, THOMAS witnessed the will of the widow of ROBERT STACEY in (1826) 3-353; an earlier THOMAS bought land in (1715) from JOHN BENNETT SR. 2-619; he patented lands in (1694) 1-4; in (1714) was granted lands next to ARGALL SIMONS 1-8; his wife was CHRISTIAN and they deeded lands to ALEXANDER SMITH (1715) which he had bought from JOHN BENNETT 2-619; he left will in (1697) and named sons JOHN, THOMAS, CHARLES and FRANCIS STACEY 1-74.

STAFFORD FAMILY WILLS 1-390, 3-190.

STAFFORD, WILLIAM left will in CURRITUCK in (1728) and named sons JOHN, EDWARD, WILLIAM and SAMUEL and daughters ANN, MARY and JANE and wife JANE 1-75; the son WILLIAM died in (1742) and had sons WILLIAM and JAMES and wife FRANCES 1-72; one WILLIAM was the son of WILLIAM and the brother of SAMUEL (1750) 1-446.

STALLINGS FAMILY WILLS 2-75, 2-355, 3-187.

STALLINGS, ELIAS, who died (1785) had daughter SARAH FOREHAND, and sons ELIAS, REUBEN, JOHN, JESSE, CADER and SOLOMON 3-187.

STALLINGS, ELIAS, and NICHOLAS, HENRY and SIMON STALLINGS all lived in PERQUIMANS PRECINCT in (1736) 2-465.

STALLINGS, ELIAS, left will in CHOWAN (1795) wife was RACHEL andhad children who are named; will witnessed by WILLIAM BYRUM 2-25; in (1729) an ELIAS bought land from WILLIAM HORN 2-448.

STALLINGS, GREGORY was appointed Constable of CHOWAN PRECINCT in (1730) 1-448.

STALLINGS, HENRY left will in (1835) witnessed by JOHN POISON and DANIEL STALLINGS 3-353.

STALLINGS, ISAAC was administrator of the estate of his brother JOHN STALLINGS in BERTIE in (1744) 2-622.

STALLINGS, LUKE left will in (1799) and mentions brother RICHARD and JOHN and SOLOMON and other relatives; also brother JESSE and the WHITES and HOLLOWELLS 3-188.

STALLINGS, NICHOLAS signs petition with others relating to the CHOWAN INDIAN lands back in (1702) 3-242, 3-243; his wife was ANN and they sold land to JOSEPH WRIGHT of NANSEMOND COUNTY, VA. in (1716) with WILLIAM ROUNDTREE and JOHN HINTON as witnesses 1-292 and in (1700) he sold lands to ROBERT ROUNDTREE (Of Nansemond Co. Va.) 1-89; in the year (1762) a NICHOLAS STALLINGS with JAMES and JOHN SCOTT witnessed the will of RICHARD HARRELL 3-172.

STALLINGS, PATIENCE and SARAH her sister were daughters in law of JAMES SPIER (1731) 1-75.

STALLINGS, SAMUEL, of PERQUIMANS, in (1735) sold lands on Middle Swamp to CATHERINE BROTHERS, of Nansemond County, Virginia, next to land granted HENRY KING 1-110.

STALLINGS, SIMON, of PERQUIMANS COUNTY sold land to CATHERINE BROTHERS left him by his father JOHN STALLINGS 3-125; in (1781) a SIMON STALLINGS witnessed the will of THOMAS ROUNDTREE in GATES COUNTY 2-67; SIMON died in GATES COUNTY leaving will (1808) and children SIMON, JOSEPH, TIMOTHY, WHITMELL and PRISCILLA, MARY, CHRISTIAN and EMILY RAWLS; witnessed by JOHN S. PARKER 2-75; a SIMON lived in PERQUIMANS PRECINCT in (1735) 2-465.

STALLINGS, WHITMELL left will in GATES COUNTY in (1858) and names among others a son in law W. T. BYNUM 2-75.

STAMP, RICHARD died leaving will in (1722) and names his children 1-76.

STANDIN FAMILY WILLS 2-25, 3-187.

STANDING, EDWARD (Or STANDIN) was the Executor of the will of JOHN SIMONS in (1731) 1-75; he died leaving will in (1738) and had MARY, EDWARD and HENDERSON STANDING, & HENDERSON married a daughter of LUKE GREGORY in (1754); his widow SARAH after his death married JOSEPH CREECY 2-469; he was granted land in (1722) 1-11; ROBERT BEASLEY was guardian of his daughter SARAH (1743) 1-447; his widow called ANEITA in (1756) & another left will (1718) shown on 1-76.

STANDING, HENDERSON chose JOSEPH CREECY as his Guardian in (1742) 1-447; in (1797) a HENDERSON STANDING was granted lands that had been escheated by WILLIAM ARKILL 1-25.

STANDING, SAMUEL (spelled STANDIN) and his wife SARAH had children born from (1736) to (1747) 3-397.

STANDING, WILLIAM died leaving a will in (1815) & mentions sons WILLIAM and JESSE and son in law JEREMIAH SUTTON and his SUTTON grandchildren and also son in law WILLIAM WILLIAMS and the WILLIAMS grandchildren, witnessed by JOHN MOORE and JOSIAH JONES 3-351; the SUTTON FAMILY lived in BERKELEY PRECINCT with the STANDING FAMILY in (1736-1740) 3-397.

STANDLEY, ANN, left will in BERTIE in (1775) and names sister ELIZABETH JERNIGAN and brothers MARTIN, JOHN and JAMES GARDNER 2-356.

STANDLEY, DAVID was a JUSTICE in BERTIE COUNTY in (1770) 3-448; he was SHERIFF in (1768) and was again recommended to the Governor for re-appointment in that year 3-444, 3-443; he died in BERTIE COUNTY leaving a will in (1795) his wife was SARAH and he had sons JONATHAN, JOHN, WILLIAM and THOMAS and son in law FRANCIS PUGH and a nephew JAMES RHODES 2-356.

STANDLEY, JONATHAN was given permission to erect a grist mill in BERTIE in (1744) 2-621; and was a Justice of BERTIE in (1768) 3-445; and DAVID STANDLEY had a son named JONATHAN in (1795) 2-356.

STANDLEY, MARTHA left will in BERTIE in (1800) She died at the house of JAMES BARRADALL WOODS 2-545.

STANFIELD, JOHN died in ORANGE in (1755) with sons JOHN, THOMAS and SAMUEL STANDFIELD; JOHN JONES and JOSEPH MADDOCKS, Executors, and HUGH LAUGHLIN and THOMAS LOWE witnesses 1-380.

STANDFORD, THOMAS and his wife were the parents of SARAH and ELLIN STANDFORD who were born (1684) and (1685) 3-213.

STANTON, JOHN died in (1803) leaving a will and mentions son JAMES and daughter ELIZABETH WINGATE and MARY and SARAH 3-349, 3-190.

STANTON, MARY left will in PASQUOTANK in (1720) and names son in law JOHN ARMOUR 1-76;a later JOHN died in (1799) leaving wife MIRIAM and a son THOMAS and others 3-190; ELIJAH STANTON left will in (1779) 3-190.

STANTON, THOMAS died leaving will in (1720) wife MARY 1-76; another THOMAS left will recorded in (1784) with wife THOMASIN and some nieces and nephews 3-190; and still a later THOMAS left will in (1812) sons IRA and WILLIAM and a son JOHN STANTON, daughters SARAH, NANCY WEDDBEE and ELIZABETH BATEMAN 3-349.

STARBUCK, JOHN was Master of the sleep MARY in (1749) 1-434.

STARKE, ANNIE and FRANCIS STARKE are mentioned away back (no date) in connection with JOHN TARKINGTON 3-140.

STARKE, FRANCIS mentioned in connection with JOHN TARKINGTON and and ANNIE STARKE (no date) 3-140; claiming that he was entitled to their headrights including also the name of WILLIAM TARKINGTON 3-140.

STARKE, JOHN sued WILLIAM LEAKE for certain lands he had leased from OLIVER NOYES of BOSTON in (1729), a part of ROANOKE ISLAND; Leake being the agent of RICHARD SANDERSON 2-304.

STARKE, THOMAS died in (1685) and he was the servant of FRANCIS HARTLEY 3-366.

STARKEY, EDWARD in (1776) was elected to the N. C. Congress that met at HALIFAX 3-17.

STARKEY, JOHN together with JOHN BRYAN was Executor of the will of RALPH EAVES in the year (1741) 2-468.

STARKEY, ROBERT and JOHN PETTIVER handled an assignment of goods in YORK RIVER in VIRGINIA in (1699) 2-151; and CAPT. ROBERT STARKEY was Master of the Sloop DUBARLUS which was seized in (1698) for being loaded with European goods which were picked up at BOSTON; the complaint was signed by WILLIAM WILKINSON and one JOHN PORTER 2-204.

STEEL, WILLIAM, left will in BERTIE in (1816) witnessed by JOHN COBB and MOURNING COBB in which he mentioned sons BEJAMIN, EPHRAIM and WILLIAM, with BENJAMIN HARDY one of his Executors; his widow SARAH died in (1832) naming other children 2-547.

STEELY, EDMUND died leaving will in BERTIE in (1840) wife BETSY 2-548.

STEELY, THOMAS married ELIZABETH LEARY (1783) 3-112; and he died leaving will in CHOWAN in (1719) and mentions his sister JANE ALDERSLY 1-76.

STEELY, WILLIAM and his wife MARY sold land to JOHN WORLEY in (1720) 2-615.

STENGER, JOHN and wife MARTHA sold lands to ROBERT POWELL in (1740) and the witnesses were HENRY and JAMES MORGAN 3-131.

STENMOS, WILLIAM, bought land from one RICHARD SOWELL in (1703); and he and his wife ELIZABETH sold land to JAMES FLEMING the same year, with WILLIAM EARLY a witness to the deed 2-511.

STEPHENS, EDWARD died leaving will in JOHNSTON COUNTY in (1751) wife ANN, brother WILLIAM and sons EPHRAIM, EDWARD and JACOB 1-483.

STEPHENS, JOSHUA was the son of WILLIAM STEPHENS and JOHANNA WILLIAMS and was born in (1685) 3-213.

STEPHENS, WILLIAM, married MRS. SARAH DURANT, the widow of JOHN DURANT in (1703) 3-410; WILLIAM STEPHENS in (1684) was son of ANDREW STEPHENS and wife GRACE of ENGLAND & married JOANNA WILLIAMS in (1684) 3-205; they were married by THOMAS HARVEY 3-220.

STEPNEY, BENNETT was the daughter of a JOHN STEPNEY and wife MARY and was born in FEBRUARY (1686) 3-214.

STEPNEY, ELIZABETH died in (1694) 3-401.

STEPNEY, FRACES was the daughter of SAMUEL BARCLIFT who left will in (1779) who named one of his daughters MARWOOD BARCLIFT for ANNE MARWOOD (?) the wife of GEORGE DURANT the elder, first patentee in N. C. 3-165.

STEPNEY, JANE, daughter of JOHN and his wife MARY was born (1693) 3-219.

STEPNEY, JOHN and his wife MARY were the parents of JANE STEPNEY born (1693) 3-219; he was son of JOHN STEPNEY and his wife BENNETT, London, ENGLAND, and married MARY BAILEY daughter of GRACE BAILEY, of RHODE ISLAND, in (1681)3-201; they had daughter ELIZABETH born in (1684) 3-212; JOHN STEPNEY, JR. died in (1691) 3-364; JOHN died in PERQUIMANS in (1754) wife ELIZABETH and sons WILLIAM and JOHN and daughter MARY; JOSHUA HARMAN a witness 1-487.

STEPNEY, SAMUEL was the son of JOHN and wife MARY and was born (1690-1) 3-217; he died in (1692) 3-220.

STEPNEY, WILLIAM was the son of JOHN and MARY and was born (1688-9) 3-215.

STEVENS, CALEB sold lands called RICH NECK on ROCKYHOCK CREEK in (1720) 3-514; he bought land from RICHARD TAYLOR in (1715) 1-293.

STEVENS, EDWARD was Master of the Schooner DRAKE in (1749) 1-434.

STEVENS, JOHN married MRS. PARTHEIA SUTTON (1726) and they had sons WILLIAM and JOHN STEVENS born (1727 -1729) 3-397.

STEVENS, THOMAS and his wife JANE were the parents of ANN STEVENS born (1695) 3-368.

STEVENS, WILLIAM and his wife SARAH had a son by the name of JOHN born (1724) 3-397; an older WILLIAM STEVENS left will in CHOWAN (1695) and mentions apprentice JOHN HARDY, ROBERT WEST, MARGARET HOULDBROOK and THOMAS GILLIAM 1-74.

STEVENSON, ANDREW, bought land from WILLIAM BUSH in (1717) 1-300; and made a deed of land to JOHN CHERRYHOLM in (1719) 3-516; bought land from EDWARD HOWCOTT in CHOWAN in (1717)1-616

STEVENSON, ELIZABETH died leaving will in (1730) and mentions GRACE, daughter of RICHARD SANDERSON; TULLY WILLIAMS was her Executor 1-74; another ELIZABETH left will in (1800) names ANNE HENDRICKS, and all of her children; and MILES TURNER a witness 3-189.

STEVENSON, GEORGE left will in (1754) and mentions brothers WILLIAM and CHARLES and several sons and wife SARAH 1-72.

STEVENSON, JOHN. In (1749) he was Master of the Sloop SUCCESS; also the TRYALL 1-435.

STEVENSON, PARTHENIA was a sister of THOMAS STEVENSON who died in (1802) 3-349.

STEVENSON, THOMAS, died in (1744) and his widow REBECCA was administratrix 3-620; another one died in (1802) who lived at "STEVENSON'S POINT" who had several sisters, including PARTHENIA 3-348, 3-349.

STEVENSON, WILLIAM left will in (1739) and named grandson WILLIAM STEVENSON and grandchildren named CLARK; son JOHN STEVENSON Executor of the will 1-73.

STEWART FAMILY. Genealogy of the STEWARTS dating back to 1390, and coming on down to the STEWARTS of North Carolina, who married into the LITTLE FAMILY, etc. 3-158, 3-159.

STEWART, ANN, proved her rights, including the name of ARGALL SYMONDS (no date) 1-512; MRS. ANN STEWARD married MAJ. ALEXANDER LILLINGTON in (1695) 3-407.

STEWART, JAMES and brother WILLIAM aged 10 & 14 placed under the tuition of JOHN CAMPBELL in (1747) 1-453.

STEWART, JOANAH was the daughter of WILLIAM STEWART and wife ELIZABETH and was born in (1688-9) 3-215.

STEWART, JOHN, of MARTIN COUNTY makes a long affidavit in (1777) pertaining to revolutionary activities 3-216, 2-217; JOHN STEWART died in CRAVEN COUNTY in (1741) and RICHARD BYRD was one of his Executors and DENNIS O'DYER his father in law; also JOHN STEWART of CHOWAN left will (1702) and one in BERTIE in (1774) 1-385.

STEWART, JOSEPH and wife REBECCA had a son WILLIAM born in (1734) 3-397.

STEWART, WILLIAM left will in CHOWAN in (1709) 1-74; in (1717) he bought land from VINES CROPLEY and wife SARAH, with WILLIAM and JOHN HARRISON witnesses 1-300; the same year he was witness to a deed by LUKE MIZELL to TIMOTHY TRUELOVE 1-300; in (1727) was granted lands adjoining THOMAS STACEY 1-11; in (1735) SARAH WARREN was Guardian of his orphans, and in (1739) his daughter married ISSACHAR BRANCH 3-469; in (1725) was witness to a deed by GEORGE BURRINGTON 3-444; there was a lawsuit between him and JOHN SPELLMAN in (1689) 3-431; and one also one with DAVID BLAKE the same year 3-431; one WILLIAM STEWART'S wife named ELIZABETH 3-214.

STILL, WILLIAM; JOHN DURANT was witness to bill by him in (1696) 3-90.

STILSON, JAMES was Master of the Sloop TRYON in (1749) 1-434.

STILLWELL, SAMUEL and his wife SARAH were the Executors of the will of TIMOTHY LaFITTE in (1744) 1-455.

STOKES, JOHN, died leaving will in (1772) and names son THOMAS and daughter ELIZABETH 3-189.

STOKELEY, ISAAC was a nephew of STEPHEN DELAMARE who also mentions "cousin EDWARD MAYO" in his will (1732)1-41.

STOKELEY, JOSEPH in (1731) is mentioned in the will of WILLIAM CARTWRIGHT 1-38; JOSEPH also left will in (1729) with ISAAC DELAMARE his Executor 1-75.

STOCKLEY, THOMAS died leaving will in NEW HANOVER in (1758) and mentions brothers PETER and CASWELL STOCKLEY and sister ANN and his children 1-390, 1-391.

STOCKLEY, WILLIAM in (1717) sold some land to JOHN CROMBIE 1-523.

STONE, BENJAMIN left will in BERTIE in (1812) with EZEKIEL and JONATHAN COWAND as witnesses 3-546.

STONE, ELISHA left will in (1808) wife LYDIA & brother CORNELIUS STONE 3-349.

STONE, JOHN and his wife MARY had a son JOHN who was born (1725) 3-397.

STONE, MOSES, married MRS. ANN WOODLEY in AUGUST (1764) with WILLIAM STONE, security 3-413.

STONE, WILLIAM, left will in BATH in (1720) wife ANN, son WILLIAM, mother LYDIA DARS and JOHN WINGATE 1-77.

STONE, ZEDEKIAH attended meeting at the house of WILLIAM BLOUNT to investigate the dispute between the INDIANS and WILLIAM KING 3-453; one left will in BERTIE in (1797) and names son DAVID and daughter ELIZABETH CHARLTON & her children 2-357.

STRANGE, LOT, was Master of the sloop KING FISHER in (1775) 1-436.

STREATOR, THOMAS, left will in EDENTON in (1766) wife SARAH and members of the BONNER family 2-26

STRICKLAND, JOSEPH left will in NORTHAMPTON CO. in (1755) names son AXEM and daughters RACHEL, ABIGAIL and OLIVE; wife ELIZABETH 1-489.

STRICKLAND, WILLIAM, left will in (1728) names sons WILLIAM, JOHN, JOSEPH, MATTHEW and SAMUEL STRICKLAND 1-75.

STRAUGHAN, DANIEL and sister RACHEL orphans of GEORGE STRAUGHAN, with ELIZABETH HENDRICKS their guardian 3-446.

STRINGER, FRANCIS, died in CRAVEN in (1749) wife HANNAH; brother in law JOHN SHINE, DANIEL SHINE and others 1-487.

STRINGER, MARY died in CHOWAN leaving will in (1746) and mentions her SANDERS sons and daughters 1-487.

STUART, ROBERT was apprenticed to PETER CARTWRIGHT in PASQUOTANK in (1763) 1-446.

STUART, WILLIAM and JAMES HAMBLETON owned lands adjoining RICHARD WOODWARD in (1734) deed with THOMAS PILAND a witness 2-454.

STUBBS, JAMES was mentioned by MATTHEW ROWAN in his will in (1760) 1-69.

STUBBS, THOMAS left will in (1738) and mentioned sons WILLIAM, THOMAS, BASSETT, JOHN, RICHARD and daughters HANNAH and MARY 1-73; in (1720) he bought land from WILLIAM MITCHELL with JOHN EDWARDS and PETER HERD as witness 2-612; in (1722 he and his wife MARY sold land to NATHANIEL EVERETT next to the lands of WILLIAM BLOUNT 2-144.

STUBBS, WILLIAM married to JEAN CULLEN in (1733) 2-465.

STURDEVANT, MATTHEW and wife SARAH sold lands to JOHN GREEN in (1716), with power of attorney also to SARAH STURDEVANT 1-295.

STURGEON, JOHN married FRANCIS CORWELL in (1676) and they had ANN and MARY STURGEON born in (1767) and (1769) 3-199, 3-207; in (1680) JOHN signed a petition as an inhabitant of ALBEMARLE COUNTY 3-51

STURGIS, THOMAS deeded lands in (1719) 2-613.

SULLIVAN, DANIEL was attorney for FREDERICK JONES and JULIUS DEEDS, London merchants as assignees of ROBERT HARRISON of YORK COUNTY, Virginia, in a lawsuit against WILLIAM DUKENFIELD about (1797) 3-69, 3-70; he and his wife ALICE were claimed as headrights by RICHARD PRINCE.

SULLIVAN, JOHN was deceased in (1746) and left an orphan son MURTER SULLIVAN 2-629.

SUMMERELL, THOMAS brought a suit against WILLIAM WEST of EDGECOMBE COUNTY in (1742) 2-468.

SUMNER, BRIDGET (NANSEMOND COUNTY, VA.) was a widow, and sold lands to JETHRO SUMNER and wife MARGARET, being her half share of certain lands in NANSEMOND COUNTY formerly sold by JOHN KEATON to DANIEL SULLIVAN, his only son and heir, at whose death the same had descended to BRIDGET and MARGARET his sisters. This deed in (1736) witnessed by JOHN and JAMES SUMNER, RICHARD BROTHERS and THOMAS KNIGHT 3-126.

SUMNER, DEMPSEY was a JUSTICE in CHOWAN in (1750) 2-296; in (1759) he petitioned for a mill site 1-456; he died and left will in GATES COUNTY in (1779) and in it named sons DEMPSEY, JETHRO, EDWIN & JAMES BAKER SUMNER, wife MARTHA, and his daughter, late wife of CAPT. JAMES RIDDICK; JESSE and JAMES BENTON were the witnesses 2-72.

SUMNER, JAMES left will in GATES COUNTY in (1787) wife MOURNING, son LUKE and several daughters 2-72; in (1808) a JAMES SUMNER was Executor of the will of SARAH BRAINER 3-327; this latter JAMES died leaving will in (1824) and named a son SETH SUMNER 3-353.

SUMNER, JETHRO was a COLONEL and BRIGADIER GENERAL in the N. C. Continental Line in the revolution 1-418; he may have been the one who died leaving will in GATES COUNTY in (1833) naming sons CHAS. E., JOHN and BENJAMIN and several daughters 2-72; the JETHRO of (1736) was related as brother in law to DANIEL SULLIVAN, having married his sister MARGARET SULLIVAN 1-11, 1-112, 3-126; THOMAS SUMNER was administrator of this one in (1752) 1-451.

SUMNER, JOHN was a JUSTICE in CHOWAN PRECINCT in (1731) 1-449; in (1728) he sold land on HAWKINS CREEK to JAMES BROWN & deed was witnessed by JOHN FANNA and a THOMAS HAWKINS 2-446; also sold land to FRANCIS SANDERS in (1739) 3-132; he and DEMPSEY SUMNER, THOMAS WALTON and RICHARD BOND were Justices of the Peace in CHOWAN in (1750) 2-296.

SUMNER, JOSIAH received shoe and knee buckles left him by his father in (1756) witnessed by MARY SUMNER 2-269, 2-270.

SUMNER, RICHARD and wife SARAH had son RICHARD born in (1717) and son SAMUEL; they were twins 3-397.

SUMNER, SAMUEL was a twin 3-397; he left will in CHOWAN (1765) 2-27.

SUMNER, SETH left will in (1787) and names sons JAMES and THOMAS and other children; NATHAN and ABRAHAM PEARCE witnesses 3-190.

SUMNER, THOMAS, was the administrator of JETHRO SUMNER in (1752) 1-451.

SUTTON FAMILY WILLS 1-487, 2-355, 3-186, 3-187 and 3-352; SUTTON BIRTHS 3-207, 3-208. See also wills 2-23.

SUTTON, BENJAMIN left will in PERQUIMANS (1772) mentions brother JOSEPH and sons GREENBERRY and BENJAMIN 2-23.

SUTTON, BENNETT was the wife of JOSEPH SUTTON & their son JOHN died (1707) 3-404.

SUTTON, CHRISTOPHER was the son in law of JOSHUA TOMS in (1732) 1-78.

SUTTON, DEBORAH. THOMAS FOLTNER died at her house in (1683) 3-366.

SUTTON, GEORGE died in GATES COUNTY leaving will in (1827) naming grandchildren 2-76; and another GEORGE died in (1669) 3-365; GEORGE & wife MARY had daughter MARY born in (1725) & several other children 3-397; he was granted land in (1703) adjoining RICHARD LEWIS on ROANOKE CREEK 1-6; a GEORGE SUTTON died in (1699) and named son RICHARD and daughters ELIZABETH and DEBORAH 1-74; a GEORGE SUTTON and wife REBECCA had daughter ELIZABETH born in (1694) 3-367; SARAH SUTTON in (1724) was the widow of a GEORGE SUTTON and they had a son NATHANIEL SUTTON 1-450.

SUTTON, HENRY married SARAH EARLY, the daughter of WILLIAM EARLY and wife ELLENER; this before (1704) 2-612; he and wife SARAH gave a power of attorney witnessed by WILLIAM CUR-LEE 1-288.

SUTTON, JOHN and wife MARY in (1716) witnessed a deed by JOSEPH WATERS of NANSEMOND COUNTY VIRGINIA 1-616.

SUTTON, JOSEPH, left will in (1724) and mentions brother and son CHRISTOPHER SUTTON 1-75; he and his wife PARTHENIA had son GEORGE born in (1696) 3-369; JOSEPH SUTTON was the son of GEORGE SUTTON and his wife SARAH, and he married DELIVERANCE NICHOLSON, the daughter of CHRISTOPHER NICHOLSON and his wife ANN ATWOOD 3-200, 3-201; they had son CHRISTO-PHER SUTTON born (1685) 3-211; a JOSEPH and wife BENNETT had son JOHN born in (1707) 3-377; JOSEPH bought land from JOHN PLOWMAN in (1715) 2-619; and one JOSEPH married PAR-THENIA DURANT in (1695) 3-407; in (1733) a JOSEPH SUTTON married MRS. RACHEL LEE 3-398.

SUTTON, JUDITH was mentioned in the will of JAS-PER HARDISON in (1733) 1-49.

SUTTON, MARTHA married LAZARUS LINTON in (1783) 3-417.

SUTTON, MARY, married FRANCIS BEASLEY in (1701) 3-409; MRS. MARY SUTTON was alias PAYNE of LONDON 1-65.

SUTTON, NATHANIEL had wife DEBORAH in (1695) 3-407; and wife ELIZABETH with children (1727) 3-398; one NATHANIEL died and left will in (1724) and refers to cousin PARTHENIA SUTTON and other relatives 1-76.

SUTTON, PARTHENIA was the cousin of NATHANIEL SUTTON who left will in (1724) 1-76; she was the daughter of JOSEPH SUTTON and his wife PARTHENIA in (1705) 3-376; she married JOHN STEVENS in (1726) 3-397. (She derived the name from PARTHENIA DURANT)

SUTTON, RICHARD. His wife in (1719) by whom he had children, was MARY 3-397.

SUTTON, SARAH made a deed to land to ELIZABETH LONG, a widow, in (1715) 1-290; one was a daughter of JOSEPH SUTTON born (1711) 3-397.

SUTTON, SAMUEL married MARY BUNCOMBE, daughter of JOSEPH BUNCOMBE and his wife ANN DU-RANT by (1750) 2-469, 1-453; but another SAMUEL had wife SARAH and children born about (1752) 3-398.

SUTTON, THOMAS and JOHN WINNE were CHURCH WAR-DENS in (1735) 2-305; THOMAS left will in (1750) and named his children 1-71.

SUTTON, WILLIAM deeded lands to WILLIAM CHARL-TON in (1717) and his wife was MARY SUT-TON 1-617, 1-618.

SWAIN FAMILY WILLS 3-354, 2-545, 2-546.

SWAIN, JAMES was the son in law of PATIENCE SPELLER 1-73.

SWAIN, JOHN and his wife MARY in (1718) sold to JOHN PORTER "land bought by my father STEPHEN SWAIN from COL. WILLIAM WILKIN-SON" 1-624; one JOHN in (1746) was mar-ried to an ELIZABETH 3-398; in (1716) JOHN SWAIN sold lands to THOMAS SWAIN with JOHN WORLEY and THOMAS LONG witnesses 1-292; in (1720) JOHN SWAIN witnessed deed of GOD-FREY SPRUILL 2-615; he and ROBERT FEWOX, and JAMES SINGLETON were witnesses together in (1720) 2-615; in (1716) he was granted lands on YOPPIM RIVER 1-16.

SWAIN, SARAH and CHRISTOPHER HALL witnessed an agreement in (1717) between CHRISTOPHER GALE and EDWARD MOSELEY 1-615.

SWAIN, STEPHEN left will in CHOWAN in (1712) naming children JAMES, JOHN, RICHARD & daughters ELIZA SPRUILL, MARY and PATIENCE and wife PATIENCE 1-76; he witnessed deed of RICHARD BURKE and wife MARY to WILLIAM DUKINFIELD in (1703) 1-89.

SWANN, MARY, the widow of SAMUEL SWANN was Executrix of his estate in (1704) 1-444; a later MARY SWANN died leaving will in (1771) and mentions daughters MARGARET and SARAH HARRISON and several others 3-188, 3-189; she had daughter MARY also 3-188.

SWANN, SAMUEL held the General Court in PER-QUIMANS in (1700) as Secretary of State 2-302; he was attorney for COL. WILLIAM RANDOLPH of HENRICO CO. VA. in (1701) 1-610; he proved his rights 3-246, 1-612; he was granted lands on INDIAN TOWN CREEK formerly EDWARD MOSELEY'S (1716) 1-16; he imported 13 persons 3-246; married sister of ANN (LILLINGTON) WALKER 3-149; Execu-tor of THOMAS SNOWDEN 1-73; was of NANSE-MOND CO. VA. (1695) 3-407; see also 1-334, 2-149, 3-143, 3-7, 3-398, 3-440, 1-74.

SWANN, SARAH was the daughter of MAJ. SAMUEL SWANN and his wife ELIZABETH 3-371; and MRS SARAH SWANN was his wife, and died in (1696) 3-402.

SWANN, THOMAS was deceased by (1739) and estate was administered by THOMAS HUNTER and wife 2-302; marriage contract of THOMAS SWANN with MRS. DAMARIS SANDERSON, relict of RICHARD SANDERSON in (1713), including deed to WILLIAM LEARY 1-621; THOMAS SWANN and THOMAS DURANT witnessed an agreement between THOMAS WHITE and DAVID BLAKE (1695) 3-247; he and ELIZABETH SWANN witnessed deed to COL EDWARD MOSELEY in (1717) 1-618; COL. THOMAS SWANN left will in PASQUOTANK in (1733) and named sons SAMUEL and WILLIAM SWANN, daughTERS REBECCA and ELIZABETH and wife REBECCA 1-74.

SWANN, WILLIAM renders his account against the QUEEN - itemized 3-150 (1709); a WILLIAM SWANN was named as son of COL. THOMAS SWANN in (1733) 1-74.

SWANSON, SWAN in (1710) witnessed bill of sale to an INDIAN by WILLIAM BRICE 3-270.

SWINSON, RICHARD sold lands to WILLIAM SWINSON by deed in (1719) witnessed by JOHN WORLEY and JOHN EDWARDS 1-629; he and ELIZABETH HAWKINS witnessed a deed from WILLIAM JORDAN to JOHN JAMES in (1729) 3-451.

SWINSON, WILLIAM bought land from RICHARD SWINSON in (1719) witnessed by JOHN WORLEY 1-629; and he sold some stock to his wife MARY in (1716) which he had bought of BENJ. BLOUNT and others 1-299.

SWIFT ADVANCE, a vessel wrecked and plundered on the coast of North Carolina in (1698) 1-33, 1-34, 1-35.

SWEETMAN, HESTER (Or ESTHER) the wife of COL. WILLIAM WILKINSON, first married JOHN HARRIS, and she was from MARYLAND 1-445.

SYGERS, EDWARD and PETER YOUNG witnessed a deed in TYRRELL PRECINCT in (1732) 2-451.

SYKES, LEVI died and left will in PASQUOTANK in (1809) names wife MARTHA and children 3-350.

SYLVESTER, CALEB was MASTER of the Sloop CHARMING in (1749) 1-435.

SYLVESTER, EBENEZER, was Master of the schooner HAWK in (1775) 2-466.

SYLVESTER, RICHARD, SR. was from VIRGINIA and left will in (1728) naming grandsons EBENEZER and HENRY SLADE 1-75.

SYLVESTER, ZACHARIAH died leaving a will in (1810) names wife MIRIAM, sons WILLIAM, JAMES and JOHN, and mother in law MARY WILLIAMS 3-350.

SYMONS, ARGYLE, was one of the "rights" of ANN STEWART 1-512; he left will in (1714) 1-381; he patented lands on TOPPIM RIVER in (1694) 1-4. (See SIMONS - SIMMONS).

SYMONDS, BENJAMIN, died leaving will in (1748) 1-381.

SYMONDS, ANDREW left will in (1752) 1-381.

SYMONDS, JEREMIAH granted lands in (1716) where JEREMIAH SYMONDS SR. lately lived 1-14; he left will (the SR.) in (1713) 1-381; the later one left will in (1740) and mentioned daughters ANN and HANNAH SPENCE 1-72.

SYMONDS, JOHN, left will in (1731) named son ARGYLE SYMONDS, with FRANCIS BEASLEY and EDWARD STANDING, Executors 1-75; and another JOHN left will in PASQUOTANK in (1741) with sons PETER and THOMAS and daughter DAMARIS 1-72.

SYMONS, THOMAS, took an oath as a JUSTICE before (1703)3-60, 3-61, 3-94, 1-611, 1-612.

THE STALLINGS FAMILY came to ALBEMARLE PRECINCT in NORTH CAROLINA from NANSEMOND COUNTY, VIRGINIA, as is evidenced by the fact that NICHOLAS sold lands in that county and State to ROBERT ROUNDTREE in 1700 (1-39), and similar items appearing on this record. The name of NICHOLAS, JESSE, SIMEON, JEREMIAH and other members of this family may be found on the Virginia Quit Rent Rolls as owners of lands there in 1704. How many remained in Virginia and how many came to North Carolina, there is no telling. Some were in North Carolina while some were still living in Virginia and in NANSEMOND COUNTY, according to outside records, as ELIAS BALLARD owned lands on WHITE OAK SWAMP in Nansemond County, Virginia, in (1717) adjoining lands then owned by NICHOLAS STALLINGS in the same neighborhood. Since ELIAS became a family name with the STALLINGS it suggests that there may have been an intermarriage relation between the BALLARDS and STALLINGS sometime back in those very early days. The WILKES COUNTY, GEORGIA records show that a JESSE STALLINGS, probably the son of the ELIAS who died leaving will in 1785 (3-187) in North Carolina, went to BROAD RIVER in Wilkes County following the American Revolution, and took up his quota of lands reserved for soldiers of that conflict and left surviving him a few years later a widow SALLIE and five children, SIMEON, JESSE, JEREMIAH, LOUISA and SALLIE STALLINGS, and that, for a time, at least one JOHN RAY was serving with the widow, as their guardian. Previous thereto in CLEVELAND COUNTY, North Carolina, there had been a marriage between the RAY and STALLINGS family, which had its reverberations in later generations, as the writer once found on a visit on Duck River over in Tennessee, where the RAYS, BALLARDS and STALLINGS families were living side by side in the same prosperous farming community, totally oblivious of the fact that the three families had been probably related for more than two hundred years. As this writer has always been interested in his own family and has studiously followed its migratory perigrinations all over the South, he can say that he is yet to find a family of the same planted anywhere in any Southern State, that like the "gray mule always a red headed girl" tradition did not also turn up a family by the name of STALLINGS not far away. In one instance we were puzzled to discover that a family by the name of LATTIMORE seemed very intimate with both families, but a reversion to the old early VIRGINIA RECORDS showed that these LATTIMORES were of that ELIZABETH CITY COUNTY (Virginia) family, which was allied by intermarriage with CAPT. THOMAS BALLARD'S clan. Which explained the situation.

TABLOCK, JOSHUA (Probably TADLOCK) witnessed the will of ZACHARIAH SYLVESTER, with GEORGE BUNDY in (1809) 3-350, 3-351.

TADLOCK, ABSOLOM, left will in BERTIE in 1816) witnessed by RICHARD POINDEXTER 2-550.

TARKINGTON, CATHERINE, was a minor in 1695, and was living in NORTH CAROLINA COLONY with the family of DAVID BLAKE, and afterwards went to live with THOMAS WHITE 1-613. See 3-247.

TARKINGTON, JOHN, SR. acknowledges an indebted-ness to DANIEL AKEHURST, who lived at the mouth of NEWBEGUN CREEK on PASQUOTANK RIVER same witnessed by JOHN PHILPOTT and SAMUEL MOORE about (1695) 3-246, 3-247; he presents petition to AKEHURST signed by CHARLES THOMAS in (1696) 1-613; he sold lands to WILLIAM HARDY in (1715) with MARY LAWSON a witness 1-286; he proves his rights, claiming himself and MARTHA his wife, WILLIAM TARKINGTON and ANNE and FRANCIS STARKE 3-140.

TARKINGTON, WILLIAM was a headright of JOHN TARK-INGTON 3-140; he lived on the road above JOHN DAVENPORT with RICHARD DAVENPORT, HENRY NOR-MAN, ROBERT FEWOX, SAMUEL and GODFREY SPRUILL CUTHBERT PHELPS, JOSEPH GPRUILL, LAWRENCE AL-EXANDER, MATTHEW CASWELL, SAMUEL HOPKINS, THOMAS WINN, JOHN SWAIN and JOSEPH FISHER, & WILL WEST was moving away 3-153; he died and left will in TYRRELL COUNTY (1748) and named wife ANN, and children JOHN, JOSHUA, BENJAMIN, JOSEPH, WILLIAM, ZEBULON, SARAH, ANN and JOANNA TARKINGTON 1-77.

TARTE, NATHANIEL died in BERTIE in (1826) wife was MARY, witnessed by HENRY and MARY MITCH-ELL 2-550.

TATE, JOHN ran away from MAJOR HECKLEFIELD'S with JANE FENIX alias ANDERSON (1715) 3-285.

TAYLOE, ABRAHAM was brother of DAVID TAYLOE, and left will in BERTIE in (1802) wife ANN and sons RICHARD, BENJAMIN and GEORGE TAYLOE; wit-nessed by MORGAN and WRIGHT OUTLAW 2-549,3-349

TAYLOE, BENJAMIN, left will in BERTIE in (1810) mentions mother ANN TAYLOE and brother GEORGE no children of his own 2-549.

TAYLOE, JOHN S. guardian of the children of MAR-GARET ALLEN (1847) 2-498.

TAYLOE, JONATHAN S. mentioned as friend in will of THEODORE PETERS in (1849) 2-540; in (1836) in BERTIE he was witness to the will of EBEN-EZER SLAUGHTER 2-548.

TAYLOE, JOSHUA, was an executor of the will of SARAH MILBURN in (1820) in BERTIE 2-530.

TAYLOE, RICHARD witnessed the deed of WILLIAM WOOD, to JOHN KITTRELL (1739) 3-133; he died and left will in (1795) in BERTIE and in it mentions son ABRAHAM and other children 2-359.

TAYLOR, EBENEZER left will in (1711) and named wife AGNES and brother in law GAVIN SOWDEN 1-79.

TAYLOR, EDWARD died leaving will in (1710) named wife SARAH and several daughters 1-78; he was foreman of the overseers of the road between CURRITUCK and PASQUOTANK RIVER, or of a jury considering same 3-227

TAYLOR, EDWARD was the son of SARAH SMITH who left a will in (1721) 1-76; he sold lands to JOHN BRYAN in (1717) witnessed by JOHN MANEAR and EDWARD HOWARD 1-620.

TAYLOR FAMILY WILLS: JOHN (1715), SAMUEL in (1746), ANN (1764), ABRAHAM (1751), RALPH (1758), LUKE (1763), JOHN (1772), NATHAN-IEL (1734), ANDREW (1759), JANE (1734) and ROBERT TAYLOR (1758) 1-492, 1-493.

TAYLOR, MRS. JOANNA, married CAPT. JEFFRIES in (1705) 3-410.

TAYLOR, JOHN died in (1688) 3-365; he had land grant in (1681) 1-4; he left a will in CHOWAN in (1763) and mentions sons LUKE & JOHN, daughter PENELOPE and others 3-29; one left will in (1715) with WILLIAM CON-NOR, Executor 1-79.

TAYLOR, JONATHAN and his wife ELIZABETH had a daughter ELIZABETH born (1693) 3-367; and a JONATHAN and wife KATHERINE had chil-dren born (1718) and (1720) 3-398.

TAYLOR, JULIANA married BENJAMIN LAKER in the year (1796) 3-407.

TAYLOR, LEMUEL left will in PERQUIMANS (1720) sons LEMUEL and WILLIAM and wife JEAN 1-79.

TAYLOR, LUKE was the son of JOHN TAYLOR who left will in CHOWAN in (1763) 3-29.

TAYLOR, NATHANIEL, left will in BERTIE (1734) wife was JANE 1-78.

TAYLOR, RICHARD and RICHARD PARKER were close neighbors in (1736) 3-128; he and RICHARD TAYLOR, JR. with JAMES ELLIS witnessed a deed in BERTIE in (1734) 3-125; he deeded lands to CALEB STEVENS witnessed by SAUMEL WOODWARD in (1715) 1-293; in (1727) he was witness to a deed by ROBERT LASSITER of NANSEMOND COUNTY, VA. to JAMES BROWN to land on BENNETT'S CREEK 2-444.

TAYLOR, ROBERT, left will in PASQUOTANK (1700) with wife ANNE 1-78; a ROBERT left will in GATES COUNTY in (1861) showing the descend-ants still there 3-77.

TAYLOR, TIMOTHY granted land in (1714) on WAR-WICK SWAMP 1-9.

TAYLOR, THOMAS, left will in CURRITUCK (1734) sons THOMAS and EDWARD TAYLOR, wife EAST-ER, daughters ELIZABETH wife of CORNELIUS JONES, SOPHIA, wife of PETER PAYNE, SARAH, wife of JEREMIAH STEPHENS, BRIDGETT, wife of SAMUEL JARVIS, BETHIA and grandson EZEKIEL PAYNE 1-78; he signed petition in CURRITUCK at an early date 3-264; which was signed by WILLIAM WILKINSON, Speaker before (1704) 3-271; left will in PASQUO-TANK (1771) mentions son in law LEMUEL SAWYER 3-29.

TAYLOR, WILLIAM was executor of the will of THOMAS BUNTEN, BERTIE (1744) 2-620.

TALBOT, BENJAMIN was brother in law of JOHN PETTIVER (1738), and was witness to JAMES MORGAN deed (1737) 3-131, 3-130.

TAN YARD BRANCH was located on lands belonging to THOMAS LUTEN 1-5.

TANNER, WALTER left will in (1713) and mentioned a step-daughter ELLENER ATTAWAY 1-79.

TANNER, WILLIAM and wife MARY sold land to THOMAS MATTHEWS of KING WILLIAM COUNTY, with WILLIAM COWARD a witness 1-619.

TEA PARTY, AT EDENTON 2-120, 2-124, 2-163, 3-116, 3-163, 3-464, 3-602.

TEMPLE, WILLIAM, deceased, ROBERT TEMPLE and wife ELIZABETH nearest kin (1696) 1-78.

TEMPLEMAN, JAMES, Master of the Brig BOYD (1775) 1-436.

TETTERTON, ELIZABETH in (1698) married JOHN COLES of NANSEMOND COUNTY, VA. 3-408.

TETTERTON, WILLIAM and wife MARGARET had son WILLIAM born (1682) 3-212.

THATCH, ANTHONY died (1762) 3-405.

THACH, EDWARD, formerly a pirate, mentioned 2-82

THACH FAMILY WILLS 3-192, 3-354.

THACH, JOHN, was the guardian of the HUDSON orphans in CHOWAN in (1750) 1-451.

THACKERY, BENJAMIN was Master of the Sloop DESIRE in (1774) 1-436.

THAXTON, JAMES was a Lieut. Col. in the N. Carolina Continental Line, with JAMES ARMSTRONG, Lieutenant Colonel 1-419.

THERRILL, JOHN, died in April (1679) 3-365.

THIGPEN, JAMES, owned lands next to CHARLES McDOWELL and MATTHEW GUMS in (1739) 3-132; he and wife ELIZABETH had daughter ELIZABETH born in (1691) 3-218; he owned lands adjoining WILLIAM JONES in (1727) 1-12; and had a grant of land in (1716) near the lands of THOMAS ELLIOTT 1-14; was on a Jury in ALBEMARLE in (1702) 1-610; JAMES JR. had wife ELIZABETH also in (1710) with children 3-398.

THIGPEN, JOHN, son of JAMES and wife ELIZABETH, died (1692) 3-220.

THOMAS, ABIGAIL died in (1687) 3-364; 3-212

THOMAS, BARNABY, died and left will in (1735) and named son ELISHA THOMAS, brother PHILLIP THOMAS and brother in law JOHN DAWSON 1-77.

THOMAS, CHARLES, filed a petition addressed to the Court (1696) in which JOHN TARKINGTON and DANIEL AKEHURST are mentioned 1-513.

THOMAS, ELISHA, mentioned in will of BARNABY THOMAS in (1735) 1-77; one left will in (1826) in BERTIE COUNTY and named children 2-550.

THOMAS FAMILY WILLS: 1-494.

THOMAS, FRANCIS (Spelled TOMES) was Collector of the Customs 3-277; he married MARY, the sister of JOSEPH JORDAN by (1730) 2-449; his wife ELIZABETH in (1616) 3-398; witnessed a deed between JOSEPH JORDAN and JOHN BYRUM in (1730) 2-449; he (Spelled TOMES) was member of COUNcil with GOV. ROBERT DANIEL (1703) 1-611; the same married ABIGAIL LEARY (1683) 3-202; children born (1684) 3-212; Proprietor's Deputy with DANIEL AKEHURST (1696) 3-263.

THOMAS, GEORGE, died in BERTIE and left will in (1834), ISAAC J. KITTRELL a witness 2-550.

THOMAS, JAMES, 13 years old, orphan, under the tuition of JOSEPH THOMAS (1767) 3-443; he left will in (1780), wife SARAH, and children, ABNER EASON a witness 3-357, 3-358.

THOMAS, JOHN, proved his rights in (1745) and named himself and wife MARTHA, and PHOEBE and ELIZABETH THOMAS, in BERTIE COUNTY COURT 2-626; JOHN THOMAS, of NANSEMOND CO. VA. sold lands on the West side of CHOWAN RIVER to COL. THOMAS POLLOCK "right to said land by MARY my now wife, daughter of JOHN LAWRENCE, deceased (1704) 1-90; he and THOMAS DOUGHERTY, FRANCIS SANDERS and RICHARD TAYLOR witnessed deed of MARTHA JONES in (1738) 3-132; one JOHN was son in law of JOHN COTTEN of BERTIE 1-38; in (1739) he owned lands next to WILLIAM JONES and others 3-133; in (1728) he witnessed deed to WILLIAM EVERITT by JAMES SPEIR 2-445.

THOMAS, JOSEPH, died leaving will in (1735) & names EALES (EARL) THOMAS and sons JOSEPH, MICHAEL, LUKE and JAMES 1-77; a JOSEPH witnessed the will of THOMAS SPELLER in BERTIE in ¦ 1833) 2-548; in(1767) he was guardian of JAMES THOMAS an orphan 3-443; JOSEPH died in (1729) and names brothers JAMES and JOHN and his mother DAMARIS RATLIFF 1-79.

THOMAS, LAZARUS and his wife MARY, sold lands to JAMES PEEK, of BOSTON in (1719) 2-608; in (1715) he sold land to JOHN BARFIELD, with RICHARD WILLIAMSON a witness 1-285; and he and LAWRENCE MARTIN were witnesses to deed in (1719) 2-513; he was appointed CONSTABLE in CHOWAN PRECINCT in (1711) 3-442; was granted lands in (1721) 1-10; he and wife MARY sold lands to THOMAS STURGES in (1715) adjoining LANE MARTIN and the HORSE SWAMP, with RICHARD WILLIAMSON a witness. 2-138

THOMAS, MICHAEL died leaving will in BERTIE in (1766) names sister ELIZABETH and brothers LEWIS and WILLIAM THOMAS; THOMAS PUGH, HARDY HAYES and ANN THOMAS Executors 2-357.

THOMAS MORGAN, died leaving a will in (1709) and mentions only his cousin JAMES MORGAN 1-79.

THOMAS, ROBERT, bought lands from HENRY BAKER in (1733) adjoining the lands of RICHARDS and JOHN THOMAS; THOMAS HOSKINS, WILLIAM REDDICK and WILLIAM DANIEL witnesses 1-115; in (1739) he owned lands adjoining WILLIAM HUNTER and WILLIAM SKINNER 3-133; in (1735) he and RICHARD TAYLOR witnessed a deed by JOHN COLLINS 3-127.

THOMAS, STEPHEN, left will in GATES COUNTY in (1787) and names sister RACHEL WOODWARD and brother JACOB THOMAS 2-76; he is mentioned in the will of JOSEPH JESSUP in PERQUIMANS in (1735) 1-54.

THOMAS, WILLIAM, in (1767) was the orphan of JOSEPH THOMAS and 15 years old 3-443.

THOMPSON FAMILY WILLS: 2-39, 2-30, 2-549, 2-550.

THOMPSON, ANDREW was foreman of the BERTIE COUNTY Grand Jury in (1745) 2-626.

THOMPSON, ANDREW (Mis-spelled)was an executor of the will of DAVID THOMPSON (1773) 1-494.

THOMPSON, DAVID, died leaving will in DUPLIN CO.
N. C. in (1773) and names sons WILLIAM, DAVID,
JAMES and STEPHEN and brother ANDREW; daughters AMELIA and MARTHA THOMPSON and sons in
laws ROGER SNELL and JESSE DARDEN, with JOHN
and THOMAS THOMPSON witnesses 1-494.

THOMPSON, HEZEKIAH, left will in BERTIE in(1771)
naming children HEZEKIAH, LEWIS, NOAH, REUBEN,
ARTHUR and WILLIAM; NOAH HINTON and Executor
and THOMAS WHITMELL, JR. and ANN KITTRELL as
witnesses 2-258.

THOMPSON, JOHN witnessed a deed with ALEXANDER
BARRON and WILLIAM LATTIMORE in (1721) 2-518.

THOMPSON, NOAH was a son of HEZEKIAH THOMPSON who
died in (1771) in BERTIE 2-258; and he witnessed the will of JOHN CHERRY in BERTIE in
(1808) 2-506; will (1799) 2-358.

THOMPSON, ROBERT, was the grandson of ROBERT FUL-
LERTON and obtained lands on BEAVER DAM SWAMP
in N. C. (1749) adjoining JOHN JONES and RICH-
ARD LEWIS 1-19; he helped prove the will of
WILLIAM BRYAN in (1744) 2-520; was granted
land next to THOMAS GARRETT and the ROUND-
TREES 1-16; he bought lands from ORLANDO CHA-
MPION in (1721) with THOMAS SPIERS a witness
2-614

THOMPSON, WILLIAM, left will in BERTIE in (1792)
and named his brotehrs; NOAH HINTON and TITUS
MOORE, witnesses 2-358.

THOMPSON, REUBEN left will in BERTIE in (1780) &
named his brothers 2-358.

THORNTON, FRANCIS sold lands to RICHARD BACON
in (1715); and a few days later he sold same
to EDWARD MASON 1-239; he had patented lands
at EDENTON before (1707) 2-443; he had obtained a patent to lands in (1714) on SANDY
RUN 1-14; he bought land adjoining WILLIAM
COPELAND in (1715) 1-239.

THORNTON, JOHN, married SARAH EATON, a daughter
of WILLIAM EATON of GRANVILLE COUNTY, see
will 1-41; JOHN died in (1754) leaving will
names wife SARAH, son FRANCIS, daughter MARY
and "all my children"; wife and ROBERT JONES
JR. Executors 1-495, 1-496.

THORNTON, MARY died in (1777) leaving will and
names son REUBEN WILSON, some daughters, and
witnessed by JESSE and PENINAH COPELAND 3-192

THREEWITT, JOSEPH (Spelled THEWHITT) left will
in CRAVEN in (1755), wife PRISCILLA and sons
LEVI and JOHN; Luke RUSSELL a witness 1-495.

THORNE, WILLIAM WILLIAMS and his family genealogy
set out 2-604.

THOROUGHGOOD, FRANCIS, left will in BATH in (1714)
names wife ANNE, and children ADAM, SARAH,
ANN, EARLY and daughter ROSE by a former marriage 1-79.

THORPE, RICHARD, died leaving will in CURRITUCK
in (1720) his wife MABEL 1-79.

THURSTON, ABIGAIL was daughter of JOHN THURSTON
and wife MARY & was born (1674) 3-205.

THURSTON, JOHN, son of JOHN and wife MARY born in
(1677) 3-206; his father died in (1692)3-220.

TIGNON, JAMES, witnessed deed (1718) 1-527.

TIGNOR, JAMES, left will in CRAVEN in (1749)
and names children; ABNER NEALE was one
witness 1-496.

TILGHMAN, RICHARD was Clerk of the Court for
Queen Anne County, Md. from (1728) to
(1763) 2-296.

TILLMAN, WILLIAM died leaving will in BERTIE
in (1808), wife POLLY and one child in
esse; MOSES MOORE one of the Executors
2-550.

TINER, NICHOLAS sold land to JOHN NAIRNE in
(1715) with ROBERT FENLEY a witness to the
deed; and the same year he sold lands to
DAVID AMBROSE 1-292.

TINER, WILLIAM, bought lands from JOHN ROBIN-
SON in (1731) 3-131.

TINES, JOSEPH in (1718) witnessed a deed by
ROBERT LONG in CHOWAN 1-623.

TISON, MOSES, lived near Greenville, in PITT
County, NORTH CAROLINA 1-536.

TITHABLES, list of those in EDENTON in (1702)
3-34, 3-35; those from the East side of
HARVEY'S CREEK to the West side of FLATTY
(FLATO'S) CREEK 3-253; list of tithables
in CURRITUCK (no date) 3-257.

TITMAN, EDWARD, a bound boy ordered returned
by WILLIAM BRANCH to his mother JEAN DAWS
and that WILLIAM DAWS pay for the boy's
clothes (1711) 3-442.

TITMARSH, JOHN died at the house of JOHN FOS-
TER in (1692) 3-220.

TITMARSH, RICHARD proved his rights in CHOWAN
in (1672) names wife and sons RICHARD and
JOHN TITMARSH 1-140.

TRUELOVE, TIMOTHY received a grant of land on
YOPPIM RIVER in (1740) 1-18.

TODDE, THOMAS. The name of his wife in (1699)
was ELIZABETH 3-371.

TODD, WILLIAM, died in BERTIE leaving will in
(1769) in which he gives the names of his
sons, including WILLIAM, MOSES and JOHN
2-358; his son WILLIAM TODD, a revolutionary soldier leaves will written (1778)
proved (1795) and mentions his brothers
MOSES and JOHN TODD; will witnessed by
RICHARD DAWSON and JONATHAN JACOCKS 2-359.

TOLL GATES - The first ones established and
set up in North Carolina - Act of the Legislature 1-630.

TOMBSTONE FERRY. Was in BERTIE and MILES SHE-
HAN was the keeper (1769) 3-447.

TOMLIN, JOHN died leaving will in (1719) and
mentions wife, brother WILLIAM and son
WILLIAM 1-79.

TOMLIN, TIMOTHY and his wife ELIZABETH sold
land to A. ALEXANDER in (1718) 1-629.

TOMLINSON FAMILY. The will of JAMES LEGGETT
in (1764) shows connection of this family
with the LEGGETTS and BENTLEYS; witnesses
to the will of JAMES LEGGETT were ELISHA
WHITFIELD, BENJAMIN WHITFIELD and ANNETT
LEGGETT 2-345.

TOMLINSON, JOHN and wife ELIZABETH had daughter ELIZABETH TOMLINSON born (1689) 3-217; JOHN died in (1697) leaving will in which he mentioned wife ELIZABETH, sons JOHN and WILLIAM and daughter MARY and two daughters who married READING 1-78; in (1845), a JOHN S. TOMLINSON with THOS. SMALLWOOD, witnessed will of JOHN RUFFIN 2-543.

TOMLINSON, RICHARD, was related to the wife of JAMES LEGGETT, who died leaving will in BERTIE in (1764) who left a devise to RICHARD'S "two youngest children RICHARD and SUSANNAH TOMLINSON" 2-345; he had died by (1769) and CHARLES BENCH was appointed their guardian 3-447; See 1-57 (1753); Tom COLLINS 3-449.

TOMLINSON, SUSANNAH, was one of the younger children of RICHARD TOMLINSON in (1764) 2-345.

TOMES, FRANCIS (Spelled TOMES, but was possibly identical with THOMAS; the names used and the relationships seemingly the same in many instances) his wife was ABIGAIL (1700) 3-409 (See THOMAS); in (1696) his wife was PRISCILLA 3-365, 3-407; he was Collector of Customs (no date) 3-277 (See THOMAS); and FRANCIS TOMES, JR. married MARGARET LAWRENCE widow of WILLIAM LAWRENCE (1696) 3-407, 3-371.

TOMES, JOSHUA (See THOMAS) in (1727) his wife was REBECCA and they had children 3-399; in (1703-4) his wife was SARAH 3-376.

TOMS, CALEB was the son of FRANCIS TOMS who left will in (1771) 3-192.

TOMS, ELIZABETH, married JOHN O'NEEL in (1794) 3-421.

TOMS, FOSTER was executor of the will of GEORGE HATFIELD in (1775) and probably married MARTHA HATFIELD 3-174; FOSTER TOMS left will in (1779) who mentioned children JOSHUA, JOHN, GOSBY and FOSTER TOMS and daughter MARTHA; another FOSTER (probably the son) left a will in (1794), sons JOSEPH and SAMUEL, his brothers JOHN and GOSBY and wife ELIZABETH 3-192.

TOMS, FRANCIS, SR. died leaving will in (1709) naming wife MARY, daughter MARY wife of GABRIEL NEWBY and PRISCILLA wife of JOHN KINSEY 1-79; a later FRANCIS left will (1729) daughters PRISCILLA JONES and PLEASANT WINSLOW 1-78; still later a FRANCIS TOMS left a will (1771) named sons ZACHARIAH and CALEB daughters REBECCA WHITE and ELIZABETH TOMS; son in law JOSEPH McADAM 3-192; a FRANCIS TOMS was "brother" of HENRY COPELAND (1819) children JESSE and SARAH COPELAND; NATHAN WINSLOW a witness 3-330; in (1689) FRANCIS TOMS made deed to lands to ANTHONY HASKETT witnessed by JOHN FARLOW and MARY TOMS 3-432.

TOMS, JOSHUA, died leaving will in (1732) wife REBECCA, son FOSTER TOMS, daughters SARAH & HANNAH and MIRIAM TOMS married CHRISTOPHER SUTTON 1-78.

TOMS, MARTHA, left will in (1794) and names sons JOHN and FOSTER TOMS, grandson JOHN TOMS a son of JOSHUA; grandson FRANCIS NEWBY a son of FRANCIS NEWBY (her son in law), and a ZACHARIAH TOMS, son of GOSBY TOMS; ZACHARIAH NIXON witness to will 3-192.

TOMS, MARY, widow of FRANCIS TOMS SR. died in (1718) and left will in which she mentions VESTY LEWIS, RACHEL LAWRENCE, ELIZABETH, daughter of my brother WILLIAM NICHOLSON, and JOSEPH GLAISTER and wife MARY, Executors 1-79; a later MARY died in (1816, a hundred years later) naming daughters MIRIAM WHITE, MARTHA NIXON, SARAH ELLIOTT and MARY MORRIS, grandchildren MARY and JOHN WHITE, sons FOSTER, JOHN & BENJAMIN TOMS 3-354; MARY TOMS and JOHN FARLOW were witnesses in (1689) 3-432.

TOMS, PRISCILLA, married JOHN KINSEY by (1709) 1-79.

TOMS, REBECCA was called the "daughter" of MARY SIMONS in her will in (1722) 1-76; one married CALEB WHITE in (1761) and had children 3-400.

TOMS, ZACHARIAH was named as the son of FRANCIS TOMS in will of (1771), he being a brother of CALEB TOMS 3-192; and GOSBY TOMS, son of FOSTER had a son ZACHARIAH 3-192.

TONNAGE DUTIES, payable in powder, shot and Flints; statement of ANTHONY HATCH to the public (N. C.) 2-114.

TOOKE, JAMES, left will in PASQUOTANK (1720) mentions sister JOANNA SCOTT and others 1-79.

TOOKE, JOHN proved his rights about (1701) himself twice, FRANCIS BRITTON, JOHN SWANN, WILLIAM and JAMES TOOKE; MARGARET TOOKE; all assigned to THOMAS ABINGTON, who was Clerk of the Court 2-300; THOMAS of ISLE of WIGHT COUNTY, VA. was called brother of DOROTHY HARVEY, who left will (1720) in PASQUOTANK 1-51.

TOOLE, EDWARD in (1771) administered on the Estate of EDWARD TOOLE 3-450; he and his wife MARY TOOLE had tuition of PATIENCE SEAY an orphan of MATTHEW SEAY in (1768) 3-444; will (1772) 2-357.

TOOLE, JONATHAN died leaving will in BERTIE in (1783), children FREDERICK, ELIZABETH, ANN and FEREBEE 2-357.

TOPPING, SAMUEL died leaving will in CHOWAN in (1814) witnessed by JOSIAH COPELAND, JOB PARKER and SELAH COPELAND 2-29; No, they were witnesses for WILLIAM TOPPING.

TOPPING, WILLIAM, will (1773), with COPELANDS and PARKERS as witnesses; mentions BUSHROD TOPPING, and JAMES IREDELL is mentioned 2-29.

TORRENCE FAMILY. Genealogical account of the family, as sent in, purporting to show descent from JOHN TORRENCE who married a MISS EARL, whose son SAMUEL went to GEORGIA 1-636; a WILLIAM WIRT CLAYTON TORRENCE seeks information of the North Carolina TORRENCE FAMILY 1-480.

TOW, DEBORRAH, was DEBORAH SUTTON, the daughter of JOSEPH SUTTON who left will (1794) who married TAMER TOW 3-187.

TOALER, MATHIAS (TOWLER) binds himself to pay HON. THOMAS POLLOCK three barrels of whale oil (1697) 3-91.

TOWNSEND, JOHN left will in (1737) and mentions brother's youngest daughter ANN TOWNSEND and brother WILLIAM TOWNSEND 1-77; in (1708) in BERKELEY PRECINCT. ANNE TOWNSEND was born to JOHN TOWNSEND and his wife ELIZA 3-378;1-495

TOWNSEND, JOSIAH left will in (1827) naming wife SARAH, daughters MARY SMITH, MARGARET PARKER, ELIZA ROSS, sons JOSEPH W., JOHN P. and CALVIN L. TOWNSEND and daughter SARAH E. TOWNSEND, grandson JOHN F. PARKER, WILLIAM JONES, DAVID WHITE, and brother FREDERICK NEWBY; and WILLIAM JONES and JOHN STANDIN were the witnesses 3-354, 3-355.

TOWNSEND, SARAH, (widow of JOSIAH) left will in (1832) and named the same children, with ELIZABETH SIMPSON a witness 3-355.

TOWNSEND, WILLIAM, left will in (1767) naming his son WILLIAM and daughters RACHEL, BETTY, ANN WRIGHT and SARAH ELLIOTT; wife RACHEL; ROBERT NEWBY and JOHN WHITE (son of JOSEPH) Executors and JACOB WILSON and OBEDIAH WINSLOW the witnesses 3-191; another WILLIAM (the son) left will (1735), sons JOSIAH, WILLIAM and CHARLES TOWNSEND, wife ELIZABETH and father in law WILLIAM WHITE, with brother CALEB WINSLOW and JOSIAH WHITE, Executors; CALEB WINSLOW and ANN WINSLOW witnesses 3-191; in will in (1775) OBEDIAH WINSLOW mentions his brother WILLIAM TOWNSEND, who with his sister MARY and CALEB WINSLOW are made his executors 3-195; WILLIAM TOWNSEND and his wife RACHEL had daughter RACHEL (b. 1754), son WILLIAM (b. 1756), daughter BETTIE b. (1758) and son JOSEPH (b. 1761) 3-399.

TRAVIS, EDWARD, died in BEAUFORT COUNTY in (1740) and named sons JOHN, WILLIAM and THOMAS and daughter MARY TRAVIS 1-495.

TREVETHAN, WILLIAM with RICHARD MINSHEW witness to deed in (1736) by JAMES LASSITER 3-127.

TROTTER, JAMES, his wife MARTHA was the sister of WILLIAM HOSKINS and her first husband was JAMES POTTER 2-305; in (1747) JAMES TROTTER was the grandfather of WILLIAM COLTRANE 2-467; he witnessed a deed by EDWARD HOWCOTT (1738) 3-131.

TROTTER, JOHN left will in (1768) in which he mentions his cousin THOMAS TROTTER of NANSEMOND COUNTY, Virginia; JOHN TAYLOR and WILLIAM BOND, witnesses 3-191.

TROTTER, WILLIAM, died leaving will in (1729) in which he names daughter DOROTHY, sister ELIZABETH TROTTER and wife MARY 1-78.

TROTMAN, EDWARD received a land grant in (1759) close to MEHERRIN SWAMP 1-21.

TROWELL, JOSEPH. The name of his wife was HONOR and they had children 3-214; he married HONOR BRIAN in (1683) 3-202.

TRUEBLOOD, JOHN, left will in (1734) naming wife SARAH and their children 1-78.

TRUELOVE, TIMOTHY left an orphan WILLIAM TRUELOVE tuition to JOSEPH CREECY for seven years 1-457; he bought lands from LUKE MIZELL in (1717) 1-300.

TRURNER, JOSHUA, bought lands (1719) from JAMES LONG and wife ANN 2-457.

TURNEDGE, GEORGE and ROBERT HICKS witnessed an assignment by GEORGE WHITE to THOMAS HOLLIDAY (1725) 3-448.

TURNER, HENRY, of HENRICO CO. VA. will(1712) son ABEL and wife PATIENCE 1-79.

TURNER, JOHN received land grant (1711) 1-7.

TURNER, JOSHUA bought land from JAMES and ANARITA SINGLETON (1720) 2-615.

TURNER, LAZARUS witnessed a deed (1720) from JOHN WORLEY to WILLIAM STEELY 2-615.

TURNER, MILES married MARY SNOWDEN in (1785) 3-418; he left will (1817), sons WILLIAM, EDMUND, JAMES, MYLES, ALEXANDER and GEORGE TURNER; JOHN CLAYTON EXR. 3-353.

TURNER, HARRISON, died (1815) leaving will names mother MARTHA TURNER 3-353; ABRAHAM TURNER will (1801) 3-353.

TURNER, RICHARD was grandfather of SAMUEL NEWBY in (1737) 1-63; will (1719) 1-79.

TURNER, SAMUEL was a nephew of JACOB SHARP of (1748) in BERTIE 1-385.

TURNER, SARAH, left will in (1827) names son THOMAS MULLEN and son in law JOSEPH TURNER 3-354.

TURNER, THOMAS, inspector in BERTIE COUNTY in (1768) 3-444.

TURNER, WILLIAM, of LITTLE RIVER will (1696) wife KATHERINE and children, WILLIAM, JOHN and SARAH 1-78; he married KATHERINE KINSEY in (1693) 3-406.

TURMODGER, GEORGE and JOHN HARRIS witnessed a deed by ANDREW SALSBURY in (1711) 1-626.

TUSCARORA INDIANS in BERTIE (1767) 3-444.

TWIDDY, AARON witnessed will of NATHAN HASKETT in (1832) 3-337

TWIGG, WILLIAM left will in CHOWAN in (1741) PRESTON PERRY a witness 1-496.

TWINE, ELIZABETH, witnessed a power of attorney from JOHN ARCHDALE to EMANUEL LOWE in (1703) 3-72; a much later ELIZABETH TWINE married WILLIAM T. FOREHAND in (1862) in CHOWAN COUNTY 2-415; ELIZABETH the daughter of JOHN TWINE married JOSEPH PERRY 3-192.

TWINE, JAMES, left will in (1829) wife CHRISTIAN sons ALFRED and JOSEPH 3-355.

TWINE, JOEL married SARAH JORDAN in OCTOBER (1847) 2-96.

TWINE, JOHN died leaving will in (1784) names daughter ELIZABETH PERRY, sons JESSE, AARON, JOHN and ELISHA TWINE, wife PLEASANT, son THOMAS JACOB GORDON, with THOMAS, JESSE and ABRAHAM TWINE, Exrs. 3-193.

TWINE, PRISCILLA was the daughter of ISRAEL PERRY, who left will in (1779), with PHILLIP PERRY and THOMAS TWINE Exrs. 3-183.

TULLE, BENJAMIN signed a petition to the GOVERNOR and Council about(1704) 3-264.

TULLY, JANE died leaving will in PASQUOTANK CO. in (1732) names MARY and DANIEL RHODES and grandson DAVID BOIES 1-78.

TYLER, MOSES died leaving will in BLADEN (1762) mentions son NEEDHAM TYLER and others 1-77.

TYLER, NEEDHAM mentioned in will of MOSES TYLER in (1762) BLADEN as son 1-77.

TYLER, NICHOLAS, was the father in law of JAMES BLOUNT in (1712) who married two of his daughters, MARY and KATHERINE TYLER 3-302; NICHOLAS proved his "rights" in (1697) including twice for himself, his wife KATHERINE, KELLAM, MARY, ROSE, ANN, WILLIAM & KATHERINE TYLER; ARCHIBALD McCARRELL, DANIEL BATHELL and FANIFOLD GREEN 2-399.

TYLER, PERRY, left will in BERTIE in (1799) LEWIS THOMPSON and ARTHUR HOLLOWELL the Executors; ISAAC RHODES a witness 3-548

TYLER, RICHARD left will in (1831) sons CALVIN and MOSES 3-548.

TYLER, ROBERT will in (1695) JOSEPH JARMAN an Executor with JOHN HOPKINS 1-491.

TYLER, THOMAS, will in BATH mentions (1722) friend JOHN JORDAN 1-79.

TYNER, WILLIAM sold land to ROBERT HICKS in (1730) witnessed by JOHN ROBERTSON 2-449.

TYSON, THOMAS son in law of JOHN MASON 1-60.
TYRRELL PRECINCT HISTORY 3-308, 3-309, 3-107.

TOWNSEND FAMILY. The TOWNSENDS of this record found their way to the ALBEMARLE SOUND region of NORTH CAROLINA before the year 1700, and certainly prior to 1708 (3-378). Apparently they were headed by JOHN and WILLIAM TOWNSEND (1-77). COL. RICHARD TOWNSEND, member of the COUNCIL of the Colony of VIRGINIA, from YORK COUNTY, as early as 1633, was the ancestor of the family. On the oldest YORK RECORD the name is spelled "TOWNSENE" and later TOWNSHEND. Gradually the name was simplified to "TOWNSEND" as it is now spelled throughout the entire South.

COL. RICHARD TOWNSEND, of the COUNCIL, is credited with being the father of at least two sons, possibly others, (1) CAPT. ROBERT TOWNSEND and (2) WILLIAM TOWNSEND. The first was the ancestor of the NORTHUMBERLAND and STAFFORD COUNTY (Virginia) TOWNSENDS, and the second, of the NORTH CAROLINA TOWNSENDS. Descendants of both branches worked their way Southward into the CAROLINAS and other States.

CAPT. ROBERT TOWNSEND appears in LANCASTER COUNTY as early as 1652, was then of age and engaged in the transfer of property (Fleet's Colonial Abstracts 22, p. 96). He later appears on the records of NORTHUMBERLAND (Fleet 23, p.91, 23 Va. Mag 97). His children were MARY, FRANCES and WILLIAM TOWNSEND. The daughter MARY TOWNSEND, by virtue of her marriage on March 15, 1692 to JOHN WASHINGTON, JR. (Fleet 23 p. 91, Va. Mag. 23 97) in WESTMORELAND COUNTY, became the ancestress of all of the descendants of the emigrant LAWRENCE WASHINGTON, bearing the name of WASHINGTON. The JOHN WASHINGTON, whom she married, was the only son of the emigrant LAWRENCE, though he had two full sisters and one half-sister, the latter born in ENGLAND of a first marriage of his father. JOHN WASHINGTON, JR. and his wife MARY (TOWNSEND) WASHINGTON moved to STAFFORD COUNTY, where he was SHERIFF in 1717-1719. He and his wife MARY had five children, LAWRENCE, JOHN, ROBERT, TOWNSEND and MARY TOWNSEND WASHINGTON. FRANCES TOWNSEND, daughter of CAPT. ROBERT TOWNSEND, married FRANCIS DADE & they were the parents of TOWNSEND DADE. JOHN WASHINGTON (son of JOHN and MARY) died and left a will in 1743 (23 Va. Mag. 98) in which they named children ROBERT, THOMAS, FRANCES TOWNSEND, son TOWNSEND, LUND, JOHN, LAWRENCE and HENRY WASHINGTON. The last named, HENRY WASHINGTON, was the father of LAWRENCE, JOHN and BAILEY WASHINGTON. BAILEY WASHINGTON married, it is said, CATHERINE STARKE, and they were the parents of COL. WILLIAM WASHINGTON, the gallant revolutionary officer, who married JANE ELLIOTT, daughter of CHARLES, and settled in SOUTH CAROLINA and GEORGIA, following the American Revolution. It will be noted that SARAH TOWNSEND, daughter of WILLIAM TOWNSEND, who died leaving a will in (1767) of these records, in NORTH CAROLINA (3-191) married EPHRAIM ELLIOTT, which suggests the almost certain connection between the STAFFORD and NORTHUMBERLAND TOWNSENDS and those in NORTH CAROLINA, descendants of DR. WILLIAM TOWNSEND, of YORK COUNTY, VIRGINIA. HENRY WASHINGTON, another son of BAILEY WASHINGTON, and a brother of COL. WILLIAM WASHINGTON, married MILDRED PRATT & settled in MISSISSIPPI, and his son THOMAS PRATT WASHINGTON moved to TEXAS, where his descendants are still numerous. Descendants of the NORTHUMBERLAND TOWNSENDS appeared in Texas at about the same time in approximately the same locality.

DR. WILLIAM TOWNSEND, of YORK COUNTY, Virginia, (the other son of COL. RICHARD TOWNSEND, of the Council) was living in YORK COUNTY towards the close of the seventeenth century, as is evidenced by the following item which appears on p. 45, of Vol. 8, of the YORK COUNTY RECORDS, for November 24, 1687: "Judgment is this day granted WILLIAM TOWNSEND against MATTHEW HOWARD for the payment of Three Pounds, five shillings, it being for his care and trouble and attendance in surgery on the said Howard's sonne in law, and Physick administered to his wife, which hee, the said HOWARD is ordered to pay with costs of suit, etc."

The other WILLIAM TOWNSEND, son of CAPT. ROBERT, and brother in law of JOHN WASHINGTON, JR., had sons WILLIAM, JOSEPH and JOSHUA TOWNSEND, of Northumberland County. His son WILLIAM married a daughter of WILLIAM HAYNIE, a witness to the will of COL. PETER PRESLEY in 1750, whose wife was WINNIFRED GRIFFIN. PETER PRESLEY'S daughter WINNIFRED married ANTHONY THORNTON and they were the parents of PRESLEY THORNTON. The HAYNIES, PRESLEYS and TOWNSENDS were all intermarried. The children of WILLIAM TOWNSEND and his wife ELIZABETH HAYNIE (as shown by the old St' Stephen's Parish records) were HAYNIE TOWNSEND, SARAH TOWNSEND, ANNE TOWNSEND and GRIFFIN TOWNSEND.

JOSHUA TOWNSEND, (son of WILLIAM, grandson of WILLIAM and great grandson of CAPT. ROBERT TOWNSEND) is believed to have been the father of JOHN and OSWALD TOWNSEND, who settled at BOONESBORO, Ky. about 1778 (Ardery's Ky. Court Records pp. 103, 112, 113), of EWELL LIGHT TOWNSEND (b. Sept. 12, 1757) a revolutionary soldier, THOMAS R. TOWNSEND, who died leaving will in FAYETTE COUNTY, TEXAS, in 1838, and whose wife was ELIZABETH STAPLETON, ASA TOWNSEND (who witnessed said will) and SPENCER TOWNSEND, who also came to Texas. EWELL LIGHT TOWNSEND was a revolutionary soldier, and the grandfather of CAPT. EVERETT E. TOWNSEND, a noted TEXAS RANGER, still living in 1945.

UMFLEET, WILLIAM (Of NANSEMOND COUNTY, VIRGINIA) bought lands in CHOWAN from JOHN NAIRNE in (1728) 2-443.

UNDERHILL, EDWARD was granted license to prac- tice LAW in CHOWAN in (1751) 1-451; he died prior to (1757) and the name of his widow was ELIZABETH; the note says he came from NEW YORK to NORTH CAROLINA 2-469 (This is true, MAYBE, but the UNDERHILLS were an old YORK COUNTY family that married into the RAY and HARRISON and TOMLINSON family).

UNDERHILL, JOSEPH, left will in CHOWAN in (1789) names wife SARAH and "mother ANN UNDERHILL of NEW YORK" and "children of my brothers" SAM- UEL, ANDREW and THOMAS UNDERHILL, children of JAMES MOTT and wife MARY, my sister; and JAMES IREDELL and BENJAMIN WHITE of PASQUO- TANK with wife EXECUTORS 2-30; his wife SAR- AH was the aunt of ANNE JONES 2-271.

UPTON, EDWARD left will in PASQUOTANK in (1755) naming sons EDWARD and JOSHUA and several daughters and wife ELIZABETH; MARY SCOTT & ABRAHAM MILLER witnesses 1-497.

UPTON, ELIZABETH married WILLIAM DANIEL (1799) 3-422.

UPTON, JOHN, left will in PASQUOTANK in (1715) names children JOHN, WILLIAM, JOSEPH, THOMAS and EDWARD, MARY and RUTH 1-79.

UPTON, THOMAS died leaving will in (1799) proved (1804) leaving children and grandchildren & it was witnessed WILLIAM DANIEL 3-355.

URMSTON, JOHN deeded lands to EDWARD MOSELEY by Power of Attorney in (1720) with JO- SEPH WAINWRIGHT a witness 2-613; in year (1717) he and THOMAS URMSTONE were both witnesses for WILLIAM DUKENFIELD 1-618.

URMSTONE, THOMAS was a witness with JOHN URM- STONE to a deed in (1717) 1-618.

URQUHART, ALEXANDER left a will in BERTIE in (1804) in which he mentioned his son JAMES URQUHART, with daughters NANCY, ELIZABETH and MARY; with JAMES URQUHART and ELIZABETH WHITE his Executors; the witnesses were S. R. CLARKSON and BAIDY ASHBURN.

URQUHART, DR. R. A. married MARY NORFLEET the daughter of THOMAS NORFLEET and his wife MARGARET ANDREWS, and among others they had a daughter SARAH URQUHART who married HON JOHN GOODE, of Norfolk, Virginia 2-607.

URQUHART, STEPHEN, son of DR. URQUHART and MARY NORFLEET married SUSAN PLUMMER 2-607.

URQUHART, JAMES B. married ANTOINETTE HILL a daughter of THOMAS D. HILL and REBECCA NORFLEET, and his wife's sister ELIZA HILL married CHARLES URQUHART; REBECCA NORFLEET was the daughter of REUBEN NORFLEET and his wife MARY EXUM 2-606.

URQUHART, WILLIAM died leaving a will in (1738) in which he mentions JAMES MITCHELL and a ROBERT ANDERSON; the witnesses being JAMES WALLACE and JAMES BALLENTINE 1-497.

VAIL, EDWARD was a member of the CHOWAN COURT in (1756) 1-457; he and JOHN VAIL petitioned for setting up a mill in CHOWAN in (1749) 1-451.

VAIL, JEREMIAH, was witness- to a deed by WIL- LIAM ROWDEN and others in (1737) 3-239; in (1719) he owned lands adjoining that of EDWARD MOSELEY 1-13; he was assigned an award by EDWARD SMITHWICK about (1713)1-291; bought land from JOHN LILLINGTON in (1719) 2-454; he and his wife MARY sued RICHARD SKINNER stating they were unmarried before (1707) 3-271; in (1718) he bought lands from EDWARD MOSELEY 1-626; their daughter SARAH E. VAIL married JOHN BLOUNT who left will in CHOWAN in (1754) see genealogical note showing their descendants 1-132, also connection with BEASLEYS 1-522.

VAIL, JOHN, with EDWARD VAIL petitioned for mill in CHOWAN (1749) 1-451; he left will in CHOWAN in (1765) named children, including MOSELEY VAIL 2-30; his son EDWARD VAIL left will in CHOWAN in (1777) 2-30.

VAIL, MOSELEY was son of JOHN 2-30; and was ap- pointed Clerk of CHOWAN COURT in (1733) 1-450.

VALLENTINE, ABIGAIL. There was a person of this name in CHOWAN in (1723) 2-298; see 2-309.

VALLENTINE, ALEXANDER, was appointed with many others to lay out a road in BERTIE (1744) 2-623; see 2-123

VALLENTINE, DAVID proved the will of EDMUND TID- MAN in BERTIE in (1748) 2-631.

VALLENTINE, JOSEPH married ABIGAIL KING. See the genealogical account of the VALENTINE FAMILY descendants and ancestors 2-309, 2-310.

VALLENTINE, RICHARD, left will at CAPE FEAR in (1731) leaving property to JAMES BENNETT, a son of JOHN, and RUTH BENNETT, daughter of JAMES; mentions PENNYSLVANIA 1-498.

VALENTINE, MRS. SARAH, was the wife of ALEXAN- DER VALENTINE, who with JAMES VALENTINE ap- peared in HERTFORD COUNTY, N. C. in (1760) 2-123.

VALENTINE, SOLOMON, was the son in law (having married her daughter MARY LEE) of MARY LEE of GATES COUNTY, who died leaving will in (1836) 2-59.

VANCE, DAVID, was an ENSIGN in the Second Regi- ment of the NORTH CAROLINA CONTINENTAL LINE 1-417.

VANCE, CAPT. JOHN, wrote and addressed a letter to GOV. CASWELL in (1777) 3-344.

VANGALL, ALEXANDER sold lands to TIMOTHY TRUE- LOVE in (1721) with ROGER HAZARD a witness 2-618.

VAN GEILDEN, TUNIS sold land and made deed there- to to WILLIAM RHODES in (1726) 2-449.

VANLUSEN, STEPHEN and JOHN CROMBIE were witness- es to deed by JOHN COOK in (1719) 1-629.

172

VANN, EDWARD bought part of the lands patented by JOHN ALSTON in (1730) 2-450; he died leaving will in CHOWAN in (1752) naming wife MARY and children EDWARD, ANN, SARAH and ELIZABETH; witnesses were JOHN and WILLIAM VANN and JOHN LEWIS 1-497; the son EDWARD left will in BERTIE in (1770) wife MARY and children ELIZABETH, SARAH, MARY and sons KING and KADER; witnesses were MICHAEL, WILLIAM and CHARLES KING 2-359. See also 1-448.

VANN, JOHN and EDWARD VANN, in (1737) were appointed on a jury to lay out a road from BENNETT'S CREEK BRIDGE to the MEHERRIN FERRY, with ANDREW ROSS, JOHN ALSTON, GEO. WILLIAMS, WILLIAM DANIEL and others 1-448.

VANN, JOSEPH was a witness to a deed to land by ABRAHAM ODOM in (1735) 3-128; he and JOHN, TOMAS and WILLIAM LANGSTON witnessed deed in (1739) 3-133; he died leaving will in CHOWAN in (1753) naming sons GEOGE and JACOB and other children; the witnesses being THOMAS and SARAH LANGSTON and JACOB ODOM 1-497.

VANN, WILLIAM, left will in CHOWAN in (1740) & named son EDWARD, grandson WILLIAM, son of EDWARD, daughters SARAH and ANN and his wife SARAH 1-79; it was maybe the grandson WILLIAM who left will in GATES COUNTY in (1789) naming wife RACHEL and JESSE VANN; with his wife RACHEL, JESSE VANN and his son WILLIAM as Executors 2-77.

VANN, DARKIS (DORCAS) died leaving will in GATES COUNTY in (1793) naming her sister ANN and JUDAH LANGSTON, cousin LUKE LANGSTON, CADER ODOM, ISAAC LANGSTON, DEMPSEY LANGSTON, ELIZABETH ODOM and JEMIMAH BRASHEAR 2-77.

VAN PELT FAMILY. Genealogical note and query relating to the family 1-168.

VAN PELT, DANIEL was appointed to sell part of the JOHN VAN PELT estate in (1743) 2-631; he and BENJAMIN WINNS are mentioned together in (1746) 2-627; he was appointed Executor in (1808) of the will of WILLIS SAWYER 2-546.

VAN PELT, HENDRICK, deceased. Will proved by THOMAS HANSFORD and ALEXANDER VALENTINE in (1747) 2-630.

VAN PELT, HERMAN, of BERTIE, was Master of the sloop POLLY in (1749) 1-435.

VAN PELT, CAPT. JOHN settled in BERTIE COUNTY in (1720) account of his family as far as known 1-480; he was (one was) Master of the ship MARY in (1755) 2-296; in (1745) he donated land to WILLIAM BADHAM'S estate for a mill 2-626.

VANTUSEN, CHRISTOPHER accepts a deed to lands from WILLIAM WEST in (1715) 1-298.

VAUGHAN, JOHN patented lands at SKINNER'S POINT in (1679) 1-3; he was from NANSEMOND CO. VIRGINIA and executed a deed to HENRY HOLLAND in (1733) with EDWARD and MOSES HARE and JOHN HOLLAND, witnesses to the deed 2-609; he left will in NORTHAMPTON (1750) naming all his children 1-497.

VAUGHAN, THOMAS, owned lands on the EAST SIDE of CHOWAN RIVER, which he bought from HENRY HOLLAND, of Nansemond County, Virginia; he being of the same place about (1720) 2-444.

VAUGHAN, VINSON (VINCENT) died and left will in NORTHAMPTON COUNTY, N. C. (1749) and in it named his son VINSON and son JOHN and several daughters and sons in laws 1-497.

VAUGHAN, WILLIAM gives his deposition concerning the troubles during the CARY REBELLION 3-226.

VEALE, RICHARD will (1820) 2-556.

VEALE, THOMAS will (1824) 2-551.

VENDERMULLEN, THOMAS left will in CURRITUCK in (1720) mentions Thomas OLD 1-80.

VERLIN, JOHN married the widow of NICHOLAS FAIRLESS 2-626.

VERNON, EPHRAIM, was brother in law of GEORGE MARTIN who died (1732) 1-62.

VERNON, FRANCIS bought land from WILLIAM REEVES in (1720) 2-617.

VINCE, HUMPHREY lived in CURRITUCK early 3-257.

VINCENT FAMILY and its connection with the JESSE BRYAN family 2-565.

VINCENT, THOMAS, owned lands next to JOHN CROSBY and DANIEL McDANIEL in (1717) 1-299; he bought land from JOHN MILTON (1716) 1-295.

VINES, HUMPHREY was a witness to the will of ROBERT IRVING in CURRITUCK (1735) 1-323.

VINES, RICHARD mentioned in bill of sale witnessed by JOHN WHITE & ANTHONY DAWSON 3-429.

VINES, SAMUEL left will in BEAUFORT in (1740) sons JOHN, SAMUEL and WILLIAM 1-497.

VINES, THOMAS, will in CURRITUCK, (1722) sons THOMAS and WILLIAM and brother HUMPHREY & other legatees mentioned 1-497.

VINSON, DAVID a member of PATTERSON'S Company on MEHERRIN (1720) 1-443.

VINSON, PENELOPE was grand-daughter of BENJAMIN WIMBERLY in (1817) will 2-554.

VINSON, STEPHEN left will (1698) 1-497.

VINSON, THOMAS, left will (1720) 1-443.

VINSON FAMILY WILLS 1-443.

VINSON, WILLIAM a member of PATTERSON'S CO. on MEHERRIN in (1720) 1-443.

VIRGIN, JAMES died (1756) son JAMES 1-457.

VOLWAY, JOHN and wife MARY deed land to WILLIAM HAVETT (1720) 3-512; in (1707)his wife was RACHEL 3-377; witness to deed(1716) 1-518.

VOSS FAMILY BIRTHS 3-207, 3-210, 3-203.

VOSS, HANNAH, married CORNELIUS JONES on APRIL 2, (1688) 3-203.

WADDELL, HUGH and JOHN ASHE mentioned on memorial to MAURICE MOORE 3-222.

WADE, ALICE left will in (1701) naming grand-children JOHN, THOMAS, JAMES and ELIZABETH HAWKINS and THOMAS and MARY LONG, and daughter ELIZABETH LONG 1-81, 1-82.

WADE, JOHN, left will in PASQUOTANK in (1750) & named daughters MARY and MAGDALENE, WILLIAM DAVIS and WILLIAM DAVIS SR. and others with JOSIAH CARTWRIGHT a witness 1-510.

WADE, JOSEPH, left will in ORANGE COUNTY (1757) and mentioned wife SARAH and sons JOHN and JAMES WADE, daughters MARY STRAWTHER (STROTHER), SUSANNA HART, ELIZABETH TALLY, LUCY POWELL and son in law JOSEPH POWELL; witnesses WILLIAM BURFORD and SAMUEL BURTON - 1-511.

WADE, MARY, left will in PASQUOTANK in (1736) & mentioned her sister MAGDALENE WADE 1-80.

WAFF, JOSEPH T. married ELIZABETH A. BENBERRY in (1847) in CHOWAN 2-96.

WAFF, SARAH was the daughter of RACHEL HALL who left will in (1810), and the sister of ELIZABETH HARTMUS, and aunt of SALLY ANN, MARY and LUTEN MOORE; JOHN and JOSHUA SKINNER, JR. Executors of the HALL will 3-337.

WAFF, THOMAS left will in EDENTON in (1803) and named wife SARAH, son GEORGE and sons THOMAS, JOHN and EDWARD WAFF, daughter ELIZABETH; ELISHA NORFLEET and executor 2-37; a MARY CARPENTER, daughter of STEPHEN CARPENTER, of EDENTON, married THOMAS WAFF; the witnesses to STEPHEN CARPENTER'S will (1805) were ELIJAH NORFLEET and GEORGE WILKINSON 1-538.

WAINWRIGHT, JAMES (See also WINWRIGHT) with JENNINGS DANIEL witnessed a deed to JOHN WILLIAMS in (1720) 2-613.

WAIR, MARTHA, left will in BERTIE in (1808) and mentioned son GEORGE WAIR 2-555.

WAITE, REBECCA and THOMAS LONG were married by ALEXANDER LILLINGTON in (1688) 3-203.

WAITE, THOMAS was the son of WILLIAM WAITE and wife REBECCA and born in (1684) 3-212.

WAITE, WILLIAM, his wife was REBECCA 3-212.

WALKER, ANN, was the daughter of ALEXANDER LILLINGTON, and married first, GOV. HENDERSON WALKER and second EDWARD MOSELEY 1-58, and 1-291; STEPHEN HANCOCK and one ANN WALKER were married in MAY, (1689) 3-203; in (1704) ANN WALKER, widow of HENDERSON WALKER named her "loving brother" SAMUEL SWANN her attorney 3-149.

WALKER, BENJAMIN bought lands from JOHN ADDERLY in (1733) 2-453; and in (1729) witnessed a deed by JOHN BLOUNT to WILLIAM DOWNING 2-446.

WALKER, ELIZABETH, the daughter of HENDERSON WALKER and wife DEBORAH was born in (1686) 3-214; another ELIZABETH was the wife of GEORGE WALKER and daughter of RICHARD WILLIAMS in (1702) 3-139.

WALKER, GEORGE, married ELIZABETH, daughter of a RICHARD WILLIAMS 3-139.

WALKER, HENDERSON, was Clerk of ALBEMARLE N. C. in (1688) 2-298; he received a land grant in (1697) 1-5; in (1703) he bought land from JONATHAN HAWKINS and wife MARY 2-611; he was Governor of the Province in May (1694) 3-465; address delivered by him to the Court at EDENTON relating to the charges as to the Sloop DUBARTUS by WILLIAM WILKINSON and JOHN PORTER 3-137, 3-138; CAPT. HENDERSON WALKER and ANN LILLINGTON, the daughter of ALEXANDER LILLINGTON and ELIZABETH his wife were married by THOMAS HARVEY, ESQ. in FEBRUARY (1693) 3-304, 3-305; list of head-rights claimed by him (no date) 3-67; his grant was near MOSELEY'S POINT on ALBEMARLE SOUND in (1697) 1-5; he bought land from ROBERT WHITE on CHOWAN RIVER in (1692) 1-297; he had a grant of land adjoining JOHN VARNHAM and DOROTHY MINGE 1-6; he died in (1704) 3-258; and left will dated (1701) in which he mentioned wife ANN and ELIZABETH WALKER, MAJ. SWANN, SAMUEL SWANN, JOHN GEORGE and SARAH LILLINGTON (in CHOWAN) 1-509; genealogical note on his family 1-58.

WALKER, JAMES and his sister MARGARET (who married DR. De ROSSETT) were the children of ROBERT WALKER and his wife ANNE MONTGOMERY who emigrated from IRELAND in (1738) 2-490.

WALKER, JOHN and his "wife and her three husbands" are named in his headrights on paper dated (1695) 3-153; in (1728) he was the overseer of a road from the South shore of CHOWAN to PAMPLICO 3-282; a JOHN WALKER SR. and his two sons and one daughter came to N. C. from the BARBADOES in (1738) and the daughter married JOSEPH ENNIS 2-466; one JOHN WALKER was a Justice in CHOWAN before this time in (1711) 3-442; and he must have been the witness to the deed by JAMES WILKINSON in (1718) 1-621; and perhaps the administrator of REV. EBENEZER, deceased, who appointed MAURICE MOORE and JOHN PORTER attorneys in (1720) 2-612; in (1719) he lived between CASHY RIVER and SALMON CREEK in BERTIE 1-445; a still earlier JOHN WALKER died leaving a will in (1709) and named sons JOHN, BENJAMIN, THOMAS & JAMES, daughters SARAH and ELIZABETH PAULL, with ZACHARIAH GUIRKIN (JERKIN) and WILLIAM MITCHELL witnesses, and THOMAS and ROBERT WEST, the Executors 1-83 (his wife was ELIZABETH); see deed from THOMAS DARLING to CAPT. THOMAS LEE 1-297.

WALKER, MARY makes deposition in which mention is made of THOMAS HARRISON 2-575.

WALKER, ROBERT, married ANN MONTGOMERY and came to North Carolina 2-490.

WALKER, THOMAS was granted a license to run an Ordinary in BERTIE (1744) 2-621; he left a will in (1753) and mentions son JOHN and daughters SARAH and MARY, BENJAMIN CUMMINGS and THOMAS TIGHOR; the witnesses were ABNER NEALE, CHRISTOPHER NEALE and JOHN CUMMINGS 1-509; in (1744) a THOMAS proved his rights, naming SAMUEL, JOHN, WILLIAM and GEORGE WALKER 2-624.

WALL FAMILY. Wills: JOSEPH WALL SR. in BEAUFORT (1756); JOSHUA, CURRITUCK (1749); SARAH, in EDGECOMBE (1754) and RICHARD in NORTHAMPTON in (1755) with son SAMPSON and wife LUCY 1-511.

WALLACE, ELIZABETH, the daughter of JOHN WAL-
LACE (See WALLIS) married PETER PARKER,
and another daughter MARY WALLACE also married a PARKER; JOHN WALLACE died (1756)
2-470.

WALLACE, JAMES was a Lieutenant in the TENTH
REGIMENT of the N. C. Continental Line with
COL. ABRAHAM SHEPARD 1-425.

WALLACE, JOHN (See WALLIS also) was granted
land in (1752) 1-20; a JOHN WALLACE died &
left will in CHOWAN in (1756) mentions a
grandson JOHN PARKER, son of his daughter
ELIZABETH PARKER and her other children &
names his son in law PETER PARKER 2-470; in
(1730) JOHN WALLACE was the administrator
of BARBARY WILLIAMS the relict of ISAAC WIL-
LIAMS 1-448.   See will (1771) 2-37.

WALLACE, MARTHA ANN was the cousin of a SAMUEL
BARBER in (1835) and WILLIAM KIRBY is mentioned also 3-327.

WALLACE, MARY, left will in CHOWAN in (1792) &
the witnesses were SARAH COTTON and ALEXAN-
DER MILLER 2-31

WALLACE, MILES was the eldest son of JOHN WAL-
LACE (See WALLIS) who died (1771) 2-37.

WALLACE, ROBERT (See WALLIS) was foreman of a
jury in a witchcraft case 3-57; his name at
the head of a petition relative to election
of certain officers when ROBERT DANIEL was
Governor (1704-1706) 3-258, 3-359.

WALLACE, SHADRICK was the brother in law of
MARTHA BARBER (1831) and witnessed the will
of SAMUEL BARBER in (1835) 3-327

WALLACE, ANDREW left will in CRAVEN in (1742)
with wife MARY and sons JAMES and ANDREW &
ROBERT JARMAN a witness 1-505.

WALLACE, THOMAS (See WALLIS) left will in
CURRITUCK in (1747) wife SARAH; and another
THOMAS left will in CHOWAN in (1750) with
sons WILLIAM, JONATHAN & JOHN and THOMAS
and TIMOTHY WALTON witnesses 1-505.

WALLACE, WILLIAM (See WALLIS) was one of the
sons of ANN GRAY (her first husband evidently a WALLACE or WALLIS) who died leaving will (1732) 1-46; a WILLIAM WALLACE
left will in BATH (1749) wife MARY, sons
WILLIAM and JOHN, daughter LYDIA BOND 1-30;
one WILLIAM was the guardian of ROBERT WAL-
LACE whose father died in PASQUOTANK (1712)
2-149; a WILLIAM bought land from MOSES
ROUNDTREE in (1748) 3-131. (See WALLIS);
WILLIAM WALLACE of the WAXHAW settlement in
Mecklenburg County, N. C. 2-155.

WALLER, ELIZABETH married JOHN HARRIS 3-203.

WALLER, GEORGE was the son of THOMAS WALLER and
his wife ELIZABETH (1681) 3-211.

WALLER, THOMAS and wife ELIZABETH had son GEORGE
born (1683) 3-213; and THOMAS WALLER died
in (1687) 3-364; he left will, and the witness was JOHN DURANT 1-510.

WALSTON, GEORGE, received a grant of land (1717)
on DEEP RUN, adjoining PHILLIP WALSTON and
WILLIAM NEWLAND 1-9; and another on DEEP RUN
near BEAR SWAMP 1-19.

WALSTON, LONDON, died leaving will in HYDE in
(1729) and named MARY BATTERS, the wife of
THOMAS BATTERS; JAMES BATCHELDER a witness
1-513.

WALSTON, PHILLIP, and wife DOROTHY in (1717)
sold land to CHARLES PATE on KESIAH RIVER
with WILLIAM JONES and MATTHEW EDWARDS
witnesses; in (1718) CHARLES PATE sold
lands formerly located by THOROUGHGOOD
PATE in Bear Swamp 1-522; he was Constable
in CHOWAN in (1719) 1-445; in (1717) he
owned lands next to those patented or
granted to GEORGE WALSTON 1-9; he was constable between Cashy River and SALMON
CREEK (1719) 1-445; he obtained a land
grant in (1717) 1-17; and a PHILLIP WAL-
STON was foreman of the BERTIE grand jury
in (1746) 2-627.

WALSTON, SARAH died and left will in (1821)
and mentioned her brother TURNER WALSTON
and brother in law BENJAMIN MULLEN 3-361.

WALSTON, WILLIAM sold lands in (1718) to
HENRY BONNER with ROBERT HICKS a witness
1-521; in (1719) he owned lands that adjoined HENRY BONNER 1-17; in (1719) he
deeded land to his grandson WILLIAM WAL-
STON 1-529; he had a land grant at the
mouth of TAN YARD BRANCH 1-7; in (1697)
had land grant near GREEN HALL 1-5; and a
grant or patent on BEAR SWAMP CREEK 1-15.

WALTERS, ELIZABETH died in GATES COUNTY in
(1807) leaving will and mentioned son JOHN
SWANN PARKER, and her children ANNE JEN-
KINS, SARAH ODOM, MARY BABB, DOLLY BARR,
ISAAC WALTERS, SUSANNA ODOM and others
with KEDAR PARKER and JESSE SAVAGE as the
witnesses 2-77.

WALTERS, JAMES BRAY left will in GATES COUNTY
in (1784) and names his father WILLIAM
WALTERS, JESSE WILLIAMSON and mother SU-
SANNAH WALTERS; witnesses were PETER PAR-
KER, DANIEL HORTON and ISAAC WALTERS 2-77.

WALTERS, JACOB left will in GATES COUNTY in
(1794) sons BRYAN and HEZEKIAH WALTERS are
mentioned; ROBERT DARDEN a witness 2-77.

WALTERS, ISAAC. One left will in GATES (1801)
with JETHRO SUMNER and ELISHA PARKER as
witnesses; the other left will (1816) his
wife PRISCILLA, with HILLARY WILEY and a
GEORGE KITTRELL as witnesses 2-77.

WALTERS, JOHN in (1732) with JOHN ODOM witnessed a deed by JOSEPH SMALL 2-452.

WALTERS, SARAH left will in NEW HANOVER in
(1756) and mentioned her sister MARY
GRAINGER 1-80.

WALTERS, WILLIAM received a land grant in the
year (1701) 1-6; and a WILLIAM died in
GATES COUNTY leaving will in (1803) with
sons WILLIAM and BRAY WALTERS 2-77.

WALTON, GEORGE was Master of the Brig SALLY
in (1773) 2-468.

WALTON, JOHN was deceased in (1748) and his
widow was ZILPHA who was administratrix of
his estate 1-452; he left orphans, JOHN
and ROBERT WALTON (at least one JOHN did)
mentioned in (1759) 1-456.

WALTON, ROBERT, said to have come from ENGLAND in (1682) with WILLIAM PENN, and was father of ROBERT WALTON of PRINCE EDWARD COUNTY, Va., who married FRANCES and had another ROBERT who married SARAH HUGHES, and were the parents of JESSE WALTON, one of the "signers" of the Declaration of Independence from GEORGIA 3-154; in (1759) a ROBERT WALTON, son of JOHN WALTON, had TIMOTHY WALTON as a guardian 1-456.

WALTON, SARAH was the widow and guardian of JOHN WALTON, orphan of THOMAS WALTON, who had been her husband 1-456.

WALTON, THOMAS, died by (1759) leaving widow by name of SARAH and son JOHN WALTON 1-456; another THOMAS was the administrator of DANIEL COLLY of CHOWAN in (1751), or it may have been the same one 1-451; he bought land from WILLIAM JONES in CHOWAN in (1728) 3-444; a THOMAS WALTON died in KING & QUEEN County, Virginia in (1719) and left three sons and four daughters; his wife was ANNE 1-83; the THOMAS WALTON of CHOWAN died leaving a will in (1751), leaving a son WILLIAM WALTON, and daughters SARAH PERRY, SUSANNA WALTON, ELIZABETH TROTMAN, JUDITH ROUNDTREE and ANN HUNTER, and grandson THOMAS WALTON; the witnesses being WILLIAM WALTON, HARDY HUNTER & TIMOTHY WALTON 1-512.

WALTON, TIMOTHY was the guardian of ROBERT WALTON, the son of JOHN WALTON deceased (1759) 1-456; he was witness in (1751) to the will of THOMAS WALTON, of CHOWAN 1-512; in (1802) a TIMOTHY was one of the Executors of the will of SOLOMON MILLER, with LEWIS OUTLAW 3-527; See also 3-131.

WALTON, JAMES, died leaving will in BERTIE in (1841) and left a son WILLIAM 3-555.

WALTON, WILLIAM obtained a grant of land (1763) on STAFFORD'S BRANCH 1-21; in (1737) he was the guardian of HENRY BOND and orphan 1-448; he sold in (1731) lands he had bought from JUDAH, the husband of FRANCES SPEIGHT, to TIMOTHY WALTON 3-131.

WARBURTON, JAMES died leaving a will in (1780) and named sons JOHN and THOMAS; wife WINNIFRED and LUKE WARBURTON Executors, and WILLIAM PENDER, ZADOCK COWAND and JEMIMAH WARBURTON, witnesses 3-360; another and later JAMES left will in BERTIE in (1818) with one THOMAS TAYLOE and SAMUEL HYMAN Executors 3-555.

WARBURTON, JEMIMAH in (1780) was a witness to the will of JAMES WARBURTON 3-360.

WARBURTON, JOHN, in (1759) received a grant of land adjoining JOHN HARLOW and JOHN BLOUNT 1-21; he died in (1762) and left will in which he mentioned sons JAMES and LUKE and daughters SARAH and PENELOPE, with ROBERT WARBURTON and son JAMES his Executors and JOSEPH JORDAN and GEORGE SAVAGE witnesses 3-360.

WARBURTON, LUKE, was the son of JOHN WARBURTON who died in (1762) and he and the widow WINNIFRED WARBURTON with JONATHAN RHODES were the Executors of the will of JAMES WARBURTON who died in (1780) 3-360.

WARBURTON, MARY, had daughter MARY (1768) 3-444.

WARBURTON, ROBERT, in (1680) was the nearest of kin to JOHN WARBURTON 1-82; a later ROBERT (possibly the same one) died in BERTIE in (1733) and left will naming JOHN and SMITHWICK WARBURTON, wife SARAH and a daughter SARAH WARBURTON 1-82; he had received a land grant adjoining JOHN SMITHWICK in (1719) 1-17.

WARBURTON, SMITHWICK sold land by deed to EDWARD SMITHWICK in (1702) the witnesses being SUSANNAH CHARLETON and LUKE MIZELL 2-456; he was the son of ROBERT WARBURTON who died in (1733) in BERTIE 1-82; apparently he was deceased by (1767) and left an orphan WILLIAM ETENFIELD WARBURTON under the tuition of THOMAS NEWBERN 3-443; in (1694) he received a land grant on MATTACOMACK CREEK adjoining DAVID MORGAN and a MR. SLOCUMB 1-4.

WARBURTON, WILLIAM, died in (1799) leaving will in which he named his wife SUKEY 3-36.

WARD FAMILY WILLS: 3-31, 3-32, 3-33, 3-552, 1-512, and for BERTIE COUNTY 2-361.

WARD, JAMES of CHOWAN COUNTY, left will (1743) naming numerous legatees, which shows the family was connected with the MINGE, BUTLER and JENNINGS family 1-133; he and one GEORGE DEAR witnessed a deed to lands in CHOWAN in (1718) 1-623; in (1731) he bought land from CHRISTOPHER SNOWDEN 3-451; about (1714) he patented lands on the Southwest side of YOPPIM CREEK 1-14; in (1715) he bought land from JAMES WILLIAMSON and his wife CONSTANCE 1-291; one JAMES WARD died and left will in CHOWAN in (1785) his wife MARY mentioned, which was witnessed by SETH WARD and NICHOLAS STALLINGS 3-32.

WARD, JEREMIAH died leaving will in CHOWAN in (1850) wife JEMIAH, and a daughter MARY FOREHAND and her children 3-33.

WARD, JOHN obtained a land grant in (1741) on BEAR SWAMP 1-18; one JOHN left will in TYRRELL COUNTY (1748-9) with sons MICHAEL, JOHN and DAVID and daughters ELIZABETH NOBLE and DORCAS OVERSTREET 1-512; another JOHN left will in CHOWAN in (1750) with sons JAMES, THOMAS, JOSEPH, WILLIAM, JOB, AMOS and BENJAMIN, and daughters ELIZABETH THOMPSON, CATHERINE EVANS, HANNAH, SARAH & JOANNA, and son WILLIAM, Executors 1-512.

WARD, ABSILLA, left will in (1827) and mentions son in law BENJAMIN GREGORY 3-362.

WARD, ELIZABETH made affidavit in (1777) and mentions THOMAS HARRISON 3-576.

WARD, ENOCH, of CARTERET PRECINCT sued (1726) SAMUEL, EPHRAIM and EBENEZER CHADWICK in the Courts 3-290.

WARD, MICHAEL made affidavit in BERTIE COUNTY in (1777) relating to the Tories and their activities 3-215; he was a witness (one was) to deed by THOMAS GARRETT in (1717) 1-299; he sold land to CHARLES ROUNDTREE in (1734) 2-611; in (1748) he was appointed to look after the orphans of a JOHN SEIRES 3-631.

WARD, MARGARET, left will in CHOWAN in (1833) witnessed by ELISHA & THOMAS COPELAND 2-32.

WARD, PHILLIP, died leaving will in (1777) with sons JAMES, DANIEL, GEORGE, MICHAEL and WILLIAM, wife MARY, and daughters ELIZABETH, MILLICENT and SARAH WARD, MARY ANDERSON, with son GEORGE WARD and GEORGE KITTRELL, Executors 2-361.

WARD, SETH, with NICHOLAS STALLINGS, was a witness to the will of JAMES WARD, of CHOWAN in (1785) 2-32.

WARD, THOMAS, obtained a grant of land on YOPPIM RIVER SWAMP in (1784) 1-20; and one adjoining the land of CHARLES WILKINS in (1780) 1-21; one THOMAS WARD left will in CHOWAN in (1793), witnessed by NICHOLAS STALLINGS 2-31; another before him left will CHOWAN in (1772) who had among others a son THOMAS 2-31; another left will in CHOWAN in (1785) with wife MARY and son JAMES and others 2-32; another THOMAS died in CHOWAN (1798) with children WILLIAM, HUMPHREY, EPHRAIM & DEBORAH and ANN WARD 2-32; and HUMPHREY left will in (1821) with wife ABSALA 2-32.

WARD, WILLIAM (Of NANSEMOND COUNTY, VA.) sold land to JAMES SUMNER 1-110, 3-129; a WILLIAM left will in CHOWAN in (1826) wife SARAH, sons NOAH, MICAJAH and HUMPHREY, and grandchildren TIMOTHY and ALFRED WHITE sons of JOHN WHITE 2-32; and another WILLIAM died in CHOWAN in (1829) wife JEMIMAH, with ISAAC and WILLIAM BYRUM witnesses 2-32; WILLIAM WARD of NANSEMOND COUNTY, Virginia, sold land to SAMUEL HARRELL, part of patent to JOHN MOORE in (1700), witnessed by JOHN and JAMES RICE about (1735-C) 3-130.

WARE, JOHN, in (1717) received the assignment of a patent to 250 acres of land adjoining the land of ANDREW SALSBURY 1-300.

WARREN, ABRAHAM served on a jury in ALBEMARLE in (1702) 1-610; his wife was SARAH and they had ANNE and HENRY WARREN born before (1730) in BERKELEY PRECINCT 3-399; in (1701) he married MRS. REBECCA CLAPPER , a widow 3-409; they had a son ABRAHAM born in(1702) 3-374; this young ABRAHAM WARREN was a grandson of MARY NORCOM who left will in (1718) 1-64; the elder ABRAHAM left will on LITTLE RIVER in PERQUIMANS in (1710) and his wife was MARY NORCOM 1-84; (there were three ABRAHAMS in a row, here) the middle one died leaving a will in PERQUIMANS in (1740) named wife SARAH, daughters SARAH & SUSANNA SUTTON, son HENRY, and "my five children" un-named 1-80.

WARREN, BENJAMIN proved his rights, his wife ESTHER and his children JAMES, BENJAMIN, MARGARET, MARY, PATIENCE, WILLIAM and ESTHER in (1744) 2-622.

WARREN, HENRY, of MATETHAPUNGO CREEK, died leaving will in (1716) named wife ELIZABETH and son ABRAHAM and daughters MARY, ELIZABETH and ANNE, with JOHN PALIN overseer 1-83; he received a land grant in (1705) on OLD TOWN CREEK 1-8.

WARREN, EDWARD, died leaving will in GATES COUNTY in (1789) wife MARY and children RUTH, JOHN, WILLIAM, ROBERT, ELIZABETH and MARY WARREN; sons JOHN and WILLIAM Executors & ESTHER LANGSTON, WILLIAM WARREN and a JOHN LEWIS the witnesses 2-78.

WARREN, JOHN, was the orphan of MARY WARREN in (1789) nine years of age and was placed under the tuition of WILLIAM COLE 3-443;1-509

WARREN, ROBERT, of EDGECOMBE left will in (1759) wife MARGARET and five daughters 1-509.

WARREN, SAMUEL, left witnessed deed in (1727) by THOMAS HEATH to WILLIAM HOSKINS 2-443.

WARREN, SARAH, of EDENTON in (1735) given the guardianship of orphans of WILLIAM STEWARD 1-447.

WARREN, WILLIAM died in (1723), with only JOSEPH READING and ALEXANDER CRUIKSHANK mentioned 1-509; one WILLIAM left will in GATES COUNTY in (1797) and mentions his mother MARY WARREN and his brother a JOHN WARREN; JOHN PARKER and PHILLIP LEWIS were the Executors 2-78; another WILLIAM WARREN died in (1788) in BERTIE, his wife ELIZABETH and SHADRICK EARLY the Executors of his will 2-362.

WASHINGTON, JAMES, instituted a suit against a THOMAS WASHINGTON (1742) in BERTIE 2-468.

WASHINGTON, JOHN was sued by RICHARD WASHINGTON of NORTHAMPTON COUNTY, N. C. (1745) 2-468.

WASHINGTON, RICHARD and his wife HANNAH sold land they had bought from WILLIAM HOWCOTT to HENRY WHEELER in (1719), the deed being witnessed by JONATHAN CHRISTMAS and JOHN BAYLIE 2-608; in (1717) RICHARD WASHINGTON witnessed a deed by LAWRENCE HOBBY to THOMAS DRAKE in CHOWAN 1-615; RICHARD lived on WASHINGTON BRANCH on lands adjoining THOMAS KIRBY and JOHN PROCTOR in (1718) 1-622; in (1724) RICHARD WASHINGTON sued THOMAS KERBY 2-297; in (1712) RICHARD was a witness to deed from THOMAS KERBY to HENRY WHEELER 1-295; and in (1717) RICHARD WASHINGTON sold land by deed to JOHN BAILEY 1-299; in (1718) RICHARD WASHINGTON and a JOHN RAINSFORD witnessed a deed to JOHN KERBY 1-629.

WASHINGTON, THOMAS, was sued by JAMES WASHINGTON in (1744) 1-452; probably the same suit referred to on 2-468.

WATERLOE, RICHARD files a complaint against one JOHN KINIZEY, and was given his freedom (as an indentured servant, perhaps); verdict signed by FRANCIS TOMS and witnessed by RALPH FLETCHER and CALEB CALLAWAY 3-429 & 3-430.

WATERS, JOSEPH, of NANSEMOND COUNTY, Virginia, in (1716) made a deed to JOHN MINGE (it is spelled MING all the way through) of the same county which was witnessed by JOHN and MARY SUTTON 1-616; a JOSEPH WATERS died in NEW HANOVER COUNTY in (1739) and his daughter ELIZABETH married JOSEPH HOWES; she had a sister SARAH WATERS and brothers WILLIAM and JOSEPH, and she and her husband had sons WILLIAM, JOSEPH, JOHN and SAMUEL, daughters MARTHA, SARAH and an ELIZABETH who married JOB HOWES, all of NEW HANOVER COUNTY 2-468.

WATERS, WILLIAM and wife ALICE sold lands to WILLIAM BOND in (1699) 2-611; his name was signed to very old document 3-86.

WATFORD, HARDY, died leaving will in (1784) and named his wife WINNIFRED and CAPT. WILLIAM WATKINS WYNNS, his executors 2-362.

WATFORD, JOSEPH, died and left will in BERTIE in (1795) and named his daughter SARAH MARTIN & her children PENINAH, WILLIAM, JOSEPH, WINNI-FRED and SARAH MARTIN, his son JOHN and his sons JOSEPH and GEORGE WATFORD; from the will it seems plain his daughter WINNIFRED married HENRY MIZELL and they had a son MILES MIZELL 2-362.

WATFORD, WILLIAM left will in BERTIE in (1846) and names an interesting lot of children & relatives, including his grandson WILLIAM OUTLAW, son of DAVID OUTLAW of TENNESSEE & JAMES FREEMAN and wife MARTHA 3-556.

WATHEY, HAGAR witnessed a deed (1730) 2-449.

WATKINS, J., of TYRRELL COUNTY was a witness to a deed in (1715) to EDWARD BATCHELDER 1-294.

WATKINS, THOMAS died leaving will in PERQUIMANS in (1754) in which several members of the WHEDBEE family are mentioned 1-510.

WATKINS, WILLIAM, died leaving will in PITT CO. in (1773) naming sons JOHN and WILLIAM WATKINS, son in law FRANCIS BUCK, and daughter SARAH BUCK; other daughters ELIZABETH, ANN and RACHEL WATKINS; wife (not named) and JAMES CASON, Executors 1-510.

WATSON, EDWARD died leaving will in BERTIE in (1810) and made his brother JOHN WATSON his Executor 3-554.

WATSON, JOHN, owned lands adjoining ROBERT HICKS in (1720) 2-454; he left will in (1743-4) & named sons JOSEPH, JOHN, JONATHAN and JOB & wife SARAH and daughter SARAH 1-513; the son JOHN (it perhaps was) who left will in NEW HANOVER in (1774) and named his mother ANN WALSTON, daughter MARY wife of SAMUEL MARSHALL and others; witnesses were JOHN ROBERTSON and WILLIAM NICHOLS 1-513; JOHN WATSON sold land to JOHN HOWCOTT in (1717) 1-617; & in (1716) he and his wife MARY sold lands to HENRY HILL of NANSEMOND COUNTY, VIRGINIA, adjoining the lands of DANIEL HALSEY and JOHN HINTON 1-292; a JOHN left will in BERTIE in (1777) named wife ANN and daughter MARY STANDLEY, sons JOHN, THOMAS, JAMES and WILLIAM & daughters SARAH SMITH, ELIZABETH SMITHWICK, WINNIFRED, ANN and MARTHA WATSON; WILLIAM WHITE a witness 2-360; in (1716) he made deed to HENRY HILL (Of Nansemond Co. Va.) witnessed by CHRISTOPHER DUDLEY and JOHN GORDON 2-447; ZILPHA WATSON was the widow of a JOHN WATSON in (1747) 3-467.

WATSON, DAVID, left will in BERTIE in (1782) and named his wife JEAN, "all my children", ROBERT ADAMS and THOMAS WATSON, Executors; and WILLIAM ADAMS and JOHN VINSON witnesses 2-360.

WATTS, JOHN, formerly of ACCOMAC COUNTY, VIRGINIA died at CALEB CALLAWAY'S house in (1696)3-402

WATTS, THOMAS was MASTER of the Sloop SUCCESS in (1749) 1-435.

WAXDALE, JOHN, died in BATH (1734) 1-82.

WAYMAN, WILLIAM, will PASQUOTANK in (1721) 1-81.

WEAVER, WILLIAM died and left will without date on the record, but about 1730, or earlier; sons WILLIAM, JOHN, HENRY, THOMAS and EDWARD and "all my children" 1-81.

WEBB, ANTHONY was foreman of the GRAND JURY in BERTIE in (1744) 3-624; he left will in BERTIE in (1750) and named wife MARTHA and sons SAMUEL and WILLIAM and daughters PRISCILLA, KEZIAH and ANN; witnesses were WILLIAM and JOHN BARTON and ISAAC PRICE 1-498

WEBB, HENRY, died in CURRITUCK in (1756) wife ELIZABETH and sons WENTWORTH and JOHN WEBB 1-498.

WEBB, DR. JAMES was the father of JOHN WEBB — mentioned in the will of THOMPSON JOHNSTON in (1826) in HILLSBORO, N. C. 3-523.

WEBB, JOHN, was the son in law of JOSEPH RIGGINS, of ISLE OF WIGHT COUNTY, Virginia in (1727) 1-70; JOHN is mentioned in the will of his uncle JOHN LEWIS WEBB in (1848) 3-556; an inventory of the estate of a JOHN WEBB was proved by THOMAS ASHBURN in (1744) 3-634; one had a land grant in (1783) on South side of YOPPIM RIVER 1-22.

WEBB, JESSE, died in CHOWAN in (1803) and in his will named his mother MARY WEBB 2-31.

WEBB, HUMPHREY, sold land to JOHN LASSITER & the deed was witnessed by JOHN SUTTON 1-624.

WEBB, ISHAM signed a bond (1777) 2-214, 2-215.

WEBB, MARY left will in CHOWAN in (1812) and mentioned several grandchildren, and FREDERICK and NATHAN CREECY were the Executors 2-31.

WEBB, MOSES, died leaving will in CHOWAN in (1779) and mentions JAMES WEBB and brothers ZACHARIAH and JOHN WEBB; ZACHARIAH WEBB, JR. a witness 3-31.

WEBB, ZACHARIAH, died and left will in CHOWAN in (1761) naming sons JOHN, MOSES and JAMES WEBB, with SAMUEL WEBB a witness 2-30, 2-31 ZACHARIAH WEBB received a land grant in (1782) on YOPPIM RIVER 1-22.

WEBB, RICHARD left will in (1802) and named wife DELILAH and brothers JOHN and JESSE WEBB 3-355.

WEBSTER, ELIZABETH died leaving will in (1754) and named sons JOHN and BENJAMIN WEBSTER & other children named NOBLES 1-505.

WEBSTER, JOHN left will in CARTERET in (1745) and named sons JOHN, JOSEPH and BENJAMIN and daughters ELIZABETH and MARY; witnesses were MOSES HOUSTON, JAMES NOBLE and RICHARD WILLIAMSON 1-505; he was given a power of attorney in (1714) 1-296.

WEBSTER, WILLIAM died in HYDE COUNTY in (1745) and mentions a grandson THOROUGHGOOD WEBSTER the son of JAMES WEBSTER, his sister ANN, wife ANN, and his son WILLIAM WEBSTER 1-505.

WEEKES, BENJAMIN, with JOHN OVERMAN and THOMAS WEEKES in (1774) witnessed the will of WILLIAM ARNOLD, in PERQUIMANS 3-163.

WEEKES, JAMES left will in (1779) and mentions brother WILSON WEEKES and brother JOSEPH BARCLIFT 3-195.

WEEKES, JOHN died and left will in (1768) named wife SARAH, brother SAMUEL, and sons JOHN, SHADRACK and THOMAS WEEKES, daughters IRENA and SARAH 3-195.

WEEKES, THOMAS died in (1763) and left will naming sons JOHN, THOMAS, BENJAMIN and SAMUEL & JAMES and WILSON, and daughter in law LAVINIA BARCLIFT, wife ELIZABETH 3-195; another THOMAS left will in (1808) 3-356.

WEEKES, SAMUEL died in (1815) and mentions grandson LEMUEL NICHOLSON, son of JOSEPH; JOHN OVERMAN a witness 3-356.

WEEKES, WILLIAM left will in (1816) naming son WILLIAM and several daughters 3-356; another WILLIAM WEEKS left will in (1832) 3-356,3-357.

WEECH, ABNER died in CHOWAN in (1825) and named brother in law ROBERT A. TAYLOR and brothers WILLIS and WILLIAM WELCH; J. W. and WILLIAM LITTLEJOHN witnesses 2-37.

WELCH, EDWARD died leaving will in CHOWAN (1827) names daughter LILLY STALLINGS, SALLY and THAMAR TAYLOR, RACHEL MINGE (MING) and sons EDWARD, MILES and WILLIAM WELCH 2-37; an earlier EDWARD deeded lands to JOHN CHAMPION in (1739) with JAMES WILLIAMS and JOHN PARKER witnesses 3-132; he received a land grant in (1794) adjoining JOSIAH COPELAND 1-24.

WELCH, JAMES died and left will in (1711) daughter MARY and brother in law HENRY BONNER Executor 1-84.

WELCH, JOHN, died in CHOWAN in (1730) leaving his wife, Executrix, who died the same year; they left four children, the oldest GEORGE WELCH; JOSEPH PARKER married SARAH, the oldest one of the daughters 2-299.

WELCH, MILES, died in CHOWAN in (1836) named his wife SARAH, sons BAKER, DREW, GASTON and DORSEY WELCH 2-37.

WELCH, NATHANIEL. The first one died in PASQUOTANK in (1735) and named JEROME SWEENEY, THOMAS GASKILL, JOSEPH and ELIZABETH PENDLETON; THOMAS PENDLETON a witness 1-507; the second NATHANIEL died in (1789) names wife SARAH, son RICHARD, daughter ELIZABETH WINSLOW and son in law WILLIAM JACKSON 3-198.

WELDON, DANIEL, mentioned in the will of WILLIAM EATON in GRANVILLE COUNTY in (1759) 1-41.

WELLS QUARTER SWAMP BRIDGE was in BERTIE COUNTY in (1771) 3-449.

WELLS, DOROTHY died leaving will in (1788) naming ANN ELLIOTT, daughter of JUDITH, and ANN ELLIOTT, daughter of THOMAS and JUDITH; the witnesses were MODECAI and DEPSEY ELLIOTT 3-198.

WELLS, JOSEPH, died in (1816) his wife was CHLOE sons THOMAS, FRANCIS and JOSEPH, with GEORGE SUTTON and EXECUTOR 3-361.

WELLS, THOMAS (son of JOSEPH) died leaving a will (1834) mentions his mother CHLOE HENDRICKS and sister JANE McPHEREN 3-361.

WELLS, FRANCIS obtained a grant of land on CHOWAN RIVER in (1696) 1-4;his wife was ELIZABETH and they had a son FRANCIS who was born in (1706) 3-376; and a daughter SARAH born in (1705) 3-375; he sold land to his son FRANCIS JR. about (1735) with THOMAS PIERCE and JOHN PIERCE as witnesses 3-131; in (1708) he sold the lands he had aptented in (1696) to JAMES BEASLEY 3-136.

WELLS, DR. GEORGE died in CHOWAN in (1767) & his wife was MIRIAM; he had brother RICHARD, brother THOMAS and father in law WILLIAM BOYD 2-33.

WELLWOOD, ANDREW and his wife MARY had a son WILLIAM born in (1673) and twins THOMAS and MARY born in (1669) 3-207.

WENTWORTH, SAMUEL and a JOHN WEBSTER, were mariners of HAMPTON, VIRGINIA, and in (1714) they executed a power of attorney to JOSEPH GLOVER with JOHN ROBERTSON as a witness 1-296.

WEST, ARTHUR, of BERTIE left will in (1730) & mentions ROBERT WEST, son of HENRY, NATHANIEL HICKMAN, wife MARY, brother JOSEPH and sister MARY WEST; WILLIAM WEST and EDWARD POWERS witnesses 1-500.

WEST, ANNE, married CHARLES WORTH JACOCKS of BERTIE COUNTY, and after his death she married SIMON BRYAN, the son of LEWIS BRYAN and ELIZABETH HUNTER; see note 1-28.

WEST, BENJAMIN, of PASQUOTANK, married WINNIFRED BOYD, the widow of THOMAS BOYD in (1720) 2-298; an earlier BENJAMIN WEST died leaving will in (1695) and JOHN MACKEY married his widow and administered on his estate 1-84; MARY WEST was the relict of one BENJAMIN and the administratrix 2-616

WEST, CARY witnessed the will of GEORGE JERNIGAN, SR. in (1778) 2-343.

WEST, CORNELIUS, was the "son" of SUSAN GODFREY who died leaving will (1830) 3-335.

WEST, ELIZABETH, was the widow of THOMAS WEST in BERTIE in (1771) 3-449.

WEST, HENRY, died in (1752) and left will in BATH, naming sisters MARY SOJORNER, SARAH PEYTON, CELIA TYNES and niece HOLLAND APPLEWHITE, nephew JOHN PEYTON; JOHN GILES and WILLIAM PEYTON Executors 1-80.

WEST, CHARLES died in PASQUOTANK in (1748) and named sons LEMUEL and JONATHAN, daughter MIRIAM McKEEL and others; the witnesses were ANN DANIEL and JOHN McKEEL 1-500.

WEST, JOHN, was on jury in ALBEMARLE PRECINCT in (1702) 1-610; in (1690) JOHN WEST was witness to deed by THOMAS POLLOCK 3-281; he took up lands in PASQUOTANK before 1700 1-302; and settled on LITTLE RIVER 1-303; he died in (1712) left will named wife ELIZABETH 1-33; his widow married THOMAS BOYD, though she had several WEST children, with BENJAMIN WEST the oldest of them 1-609, 3-249.

WEST, MARTHA, was the wife of EDWARD BRYAN and had daughter WINNIFRED who married GEORGE D. Reed 2-542.

WEST, MARTHA, the wife of THOMAS WEST, was the daughter of JOHN BLOUNT, and his administratrix in (1722) 1-445.

WEST, MARY, about (1720) was the administratrix of BENJAMIN WEST 2-616.

WEST, PETER, about (1767) left will and in same mentioned sons WILLIAM, THOMAS and PETER & daughters SARAH SMITH, SELAH WEST, MARYAN OLIVER, WINNIE WEST and CHRISTIAN WEST and his wife CHRISTIAN 2-361; PETER WEST was a member of the BERTIE COUNTY COURT in (1741) with NEEDHAM BRYAN, THOMAS WHITMELL and others 2-199; in (1744) he was given charge of BENJAMIN STAPLES then 8 months old 2-520 and in (1722) he sold 150 acres of land to ROBERT MOORE, and 300 acres to MARY WILLIAMS 2-283; he died leaving will in (1749) naming daughters SARAH WEST and ELIZABETH COTTON, son PETER and grandson WILLIAM WEST 1-80.

WEST, PRISCILLA in (1717) witnessed a deed by MARY WILLIAMS, relict of LEWIS WILLIAMS to land on DEEP CREEK to JAMES RUTLAND 1-621.

WEST, ROBERT (COL.) was appointed in (1744) the Surveyor of Roads in BERTIE, over which JOSEPH KNOTT, JOHN JENKINS, JONATHAN KITTRELL and others had been overseers 2-521; he was a brother in law of GEORGE POLLOCK as shown by will in (1736) 1-56; and the son in law of GOV. THOMAS HARVEY in (1747) 2-529; as MAJOR ROBERT WEST he was granted 500 acres near SANDY POINT on the North side of ALBEMARLE SOUND in (1716) 1-395; his wife was MARY and with THOMAS WEST and wife MARTHA they sold lands to THOMAS POLLOCK in (1718) 1-627; he was the Executor of SOLOMON JORDAN in (1722) 1-55; THOMAS POLLOCK, before (1710) deeded lands to "my son in law" ROBERT WEST 1-91; one ROBERT WEST left will in BERTIE in (1771) naming sons GEORGE and ROBERT, daughter ANN WEST, ANN BILLUPS, John, William and Elizabeth (children of ANN BILLUPS) CULLEN POLLOCK and others 2-361; MAJOR ROBERT WEST and MARY HARVEY his wife in (1716) deeded land to JAMES WILLIAMSON 1-295; COL. ROBERT owned lands adjoining ABEL JOHNSON and THOMAS BALL in (1713) 1-620; he had land grant in (1716) joining SANDY POINT 1-16; in (1717) he sold lands to SOLOMON JORDAN adjoining the lands of MARTIN GRIFFIN, with ISAAC HILL one of the witnesses 1-621; see 1-500.

WEST, ROBERT, JR. and ANNE JACOCKS were half brother and sister in (1747) 2-529.

WEST, ROBERT, about (1681) married MARTHA CULLEN, daughter of THOMAS CULLEN, member of the N. C. Provincial Council. See genealogical note at bottom of page 1-500.

WEST, SAMUEL, and MARY and PHOEBE WEST claimed as headrights by RICHARD NOWELL 3-139; SAMUEL S. WEST in (1717) was a brother of WILLIAM WEST 3-148.

WEST, SARAH, a sister of HENRY WEST, who died & left will in (1752) which was proved in BATH, married a PEYTON and had a son JOHN PEYTON, probably son of WILLIAM PEYTON who was an executor of the will; ROLLAND APPLEWHITE was a niece of HENRY WEST and SARAH PEYTON; MARY SOJORNER was another one of the WEST sisters, who is mentioned in the same will 1-80.

WEST, THOMAS, was the son of ROBERT WEST and his wife MARTHA CULLEN, daughter of THOMAS CULLEN; after the death of ROBERT WEST the widow married GOV. THOMAS POLLOCK (1690); she had four sons by her first marriage to ROBERT WEST: COL. ROBERT, THOMAS, RICHARD and JOHN WEST; by her marriage to GOV. POLLOCK she had sons CULLEN, THOMAS and GEORGE POLLOCK (note two sons named THOMAS) and a daughter MARTHA POLLOCK, who married COL. THOMAS BRAY, of New Kent County, VIRGINIA 2-325; THOMAS WEST and wife MARTHA (1720) sold lands to THOMAS POLLOCK 2-612; he was TREASURER of CRAVEN COUNTY in (1719) 1-444; his wife was MARTHA BLOUNT, the daughter of JOHN BLOUNT 1-445; in (1715) he bought land from WILLIAM DUKENFIELD joining the lands of HENRY KING 1-292; sold lands adjoining CHARLES EDEN to THOMAS POLLOCK in (1720) with WILLIAM LITTLE and JOHN LOVICK witnesses 2-612; he left will in PERQUIMANS (one did, at least) in (1735) naming brothers THOMAS, JOSHUA, SAMUEL and JOHN WIATT and WILLIAM LONG 1-32; he was succeeded as TRESURER by JOHN WORLEY in (1721) 1-444; in (1715) he and THOMAS DANIEL witnessed a deed by THOMAS POLLOCK in CHOWAN 1-285; a THOMAS left will in BERTIE in (1795) naming wife SARAH, son JOHN and "all my children" and "each of my daughters", with JAMES LEGGETT and JAMES ROSS, Executors 2-361; THOMAS WEST of BERTIE left will in (1757) with wife ELIZABETH & children WILLIAM and ELIZABETH and brother ROBERT WEST 1-30; in (1721) THOMAS and his wife MARTHA sold lands to ROGER SNELL 2-518; in (1717) he sold lands to a JOHN HARDY on SALMON CREEK, with RICHARD ROSE a witness 1-300; ELIZABETH, daughter of THOMAS WEST and wife MARTHA BLOUNT married THOMAS WHITMELL, and they had a daughter ALICE WHITMELL, who married ELI HARRIS & the last had two sons BLOUNT HARRIS and a WEST HARRIS 2-154.

WEST, WILLIAM left will in (1744) and in it he mentions daughter SARAH PEYTON and grandson JOSIAH SOJOURNER, wife SUSANNA and HENRY WEST, Executors (This the HENRY WEST who died in 1752) 1-80; in (1715) he sold lands to CHRISTOPHER VANTUSEN, with FREDERICK ROGERS a witness 1-298; he patented lands in EDGECOMBE in (1746) 1-447; a WILLIAM WEST left will in BERTIE (1810) naming REV. JAMES ROSS to preach funeral sermon, and friend DAVID KELLY 2-353, 2-554; he married MARY BATE in (1806) in BERTIE COUNTY 2-378; in (1735) a WILLIAM left will naming ROBERT WEST, JR. and THOMAS WEST 1-82; in (1742) WILLIAM of EDGECOMBE COUNTY sued THOMAS SUMMERELL'S estate 2-468.

WEST, MRS. WINNIFRED was administratrix of her late husband JOHN WEST in (1700) 3-302.

WESLAND, JOHN sold lands to JOHN RASBERRY in (1719) which he had bought from DENNIS MACKLENDEN 2-454.

WESSON, EDWARD in (1723) bought lands on WARWICK SWAMP, from WILLIAM KELLY and wife HANNAH 2-295.

WESSON, WILLIAM, bought land from MEDIA WHITE which joined the lands of BENJAMIN SMALL in (1734), the deed being witnessed by JOHN SMALL and BENJAMIN SMALL and the land was on ROCKYHOCK CREEK 2-509.

WESTON, EPHRAIM, died in BERTIE in (1801) naming sons JOHN and EPHRAIM, daughter SARAH and a grandson THOMAS WESTON; SARAH and CATHERINE WESTON, witnesses 2-551; another EPHRAIM (the son, perhaps) left will in (1818) and left several children who are named; WILLIAM R. BOZEMAN and BARNES WESTON as witnesses 2-551.

WESTON, JOHN, was Constable in (1744) in BERTIE COUNTY 2-620; had son SOLOMON 3-444.

WESTON, SOLOMON, was an orphan of JOHN WESTON in (1768) 3-444; a SOLOMON died in BERTIE in (1813) had wife SARAH and four sons, who are not named in his will 2-551.

WESTON, WILLIAM lived not far from ROCKYHOCK FERRY in (1754) 1-452; a WILLIAM left will in BERTIE in (1747) and left children JOHN, WILLIAM, EPHRAIM, THOMAS, MALACHI and daughter RACHEL and wife CATHERINE; MOSES GREEN was a witness 1-511, 1-512, 2-631; in (1746) WILLIAM WESTON was given the care of THOMAS MITCHELL, sixteen years old, the son of JOHN MITCHELL 2-528; in (1749) WILLIAM and JOHN WESTON made a report on the estate of WILLIAM WESTON 2-632; WILLIAM left will in BERTIE in (1696) naming wife SARAH, sons MALACHI, EDMUND and WILLIAM and a daughter WINNIFRED; EDMUND DUNSTON and EPHRAIM WESTON Executors 2-362; in (1755) WILLIAM WESTON was Master of the Schooner UNITY 1-435.

WEYMOUTH, THOMAS was a witness to what is said to be the oldest deed on record in NORTH CAROLINA in (1661) 3-423.

WHALE FISHING in NORTH CAROLINA waters; an article signed by WILLIAM LITTLE 2-187, 2-188.

WHARTON, DAVID, died without a will (1712) 1-84; MARY HOBBS was granted administration on his estate in BATH COUNTY (1712) 2-148.

WHEATON, ROBERT died leaving a will in (1816) & mentions wife ELIZABETH and sister LYDIA; E. BARROW, Executor 3-361.

WHEATON, WILLIAM, was a merchant in HERTFORD, N. C. and died in (1798) naming son ROBERT and daughter LYDIA, and brother JAMES WHEATON as Executor 3-198.

WHEATH, WALTER and wife MARY, bought land from JOHN DANIEL and his wife MARY in (1700) 2-611.

WHEATLEY, JOHN owned lands adjoining that of WILLIAM BRANCH in (1704) 3-455; and he bought land from THOMAS WANE and wife in CHOWAN in (1728) in CHOWAN 2-445.

WHEDBEE, ANN died leaving will in (1834) and in it mentioned her brother RICHARD LEIGH; son GILBERT WHEDBEE and grand-daughters NANCY & SARAH STANTON; JOSIAH JORDAN was a witness 3-361.

WHEDBEE, DEBORAH was the administratrix of the estate of her husband JOHN WHEDBEE (1700) 2-302; their daughter DEBORAH was born in (1689) in BERKELEY PRECINCT 3-216; after JOHN WHEDBEE died his wife DEBORAH married DENNIS MACLENDEN in (1702) in ALBEMARLE PRECINCT 1-609.

WHEDBEE, GEORGE of ALIGATOR, died in (1718) and named sons RICHARD, GEORGE and JOHN, daughter RUTH WHEDBEE and his cousin RICHARD WHEDBEE 1-83; another died (1784) 3-197.

WHEDBEE, JOHN; his name signed to a suit in PERQUIMANS at the house of MARY SCOTT in (1689) with JOHN BARROW and others 3-431; an inventory of his estate was returned into court in (1701) 1-82; his will was probated in CHOWAN in (1803) and mentions wife and child or children 2-37; in (1685) JOHN WHEDBEE, ye son of RICHARD WHEDBEE and ELIZABETH his wife (Late of VIRGINIA) and DEBORAH SUTTON, relict of NATHANIEL SUTTON were married by MR. JOHN WRIGHT, Minister 3-201; they had a son RICHARD WHEDBEE born (1687) 3-215.

WHEDBEE, RICHARD and SARAH DURANT were married in (1709); they had a son JOHN (b. 1715), daughter SARAH (b. 1717), and sons GEORGE, daughter ANN, son JOSEPH and son HEZEKIAH all born by (1728); the wife SARAH died in (1728) 3-399; RICHARD of PERQUIMANS sold land to PAUL BUNCH in (1729) adjoining the land of ORLANDO CHAMPION 2-446; RICHARD of TYRRELL COUNTY died (1739) and mentioned CUTHBERT PHELPS and cousin GEORGE PHELPS 1-80; one RICHARD left will in (1785) and another in (1788) who had a son BENJAMIN WHEDBEE and whose wife was MARY (left will in (1795) 3-197.

WHEDBEE, SETH, died in (1798) naming sons JOSHUA and THOMAS and father THOMAS WHEDBEE; witnesses were MILES TURNER and GEORGE SUTTON 3-197.

WHEDBEE, THOMAS, SR. died and left a will in (1808) with youngest daughters PATSY, MARY, KESIAH and NANCY, wife ELIZABETH, son ROBERT, son GEORGE, sons in law JOSHUA MOORE and MARK NEWBY, son JOHN, and son SAMUEL WHEDBEE; GEORGE SUTTON and LEVI MUNDEN, witnesses 3-361.

WHEELER, HENRY and ELIZABETH WILLIAMS were the witnesses to a deed to JOHN BAILEY (1717) 1-299; in (1718) he had a land grant adjoining the lands of THOMAS KIRBY 1-629; & he sold lands to THOMAS KIRBY in (1716) with JOHN DICKINSON a witness 1-299; and in (1720) he was a close neighbor of one WILLIAM BOON 2-617; he sold lands to ROBERT SHARER (Of ISLE OF WIGHT CO. VA.) in (1715) 1-288; he made a deed to ARTHUR WILLIAMS in (1717) to which RICHARD WASHINGTON was a witness 1-299; in (1715) he sold land to RICHARD WASHINGTON on the So. side of MEHERRIN RIVER, and WILLIAM BRYANT and JOHN NAIRNE were witnesses 1-295; also in (1712) he bought lands on TURKEY CREEK from THOMAS KIRBY 1-295; HENRY WHEELER died leaving a will proved in (1727) and named his wife ANN, sons EMPERER, HENRY and JOHN and daughter SARAH WHEELER 1-83.

WHEELER, JANE was claimed as a headright (1702) by JAMES FEWOX with members of the SMITH, HOUSE and WARD families 2-299.

WHEELER, MARK and also ELIZABETH, DEBORAH and JANE WHEELER were all claimed as headrights by JAMES FEWOX of N. C. in (1702) 2-299.

WHERRY, ANTHONY married SARAH HARMON in (1699) 3-406; they had a son ANTHONY born in (1701-2) 3-373; he was a tithable in BERTIE COUNTY in (1702) 3-85; he was the son of an ANTHONY WHERRY and his wife JOANNA 3-408; his wife SARAH, was the daughter of ROBERT HARMON 3-408; and he is mentioned in will of his brother JOSHUA 1-82.

WHERRY, JOSHUA, left will in (1730) in which he names his brother ANTHONY and sisters RACHEL, ELIZABETH, SARAH and MARY WHERRY 1-82.(They were the children of ANTHONY WHERRY and his wife JOANNA).

WHITE FAMILY. Wills 1-82, 1-83, 1-503, 1-504, 1-505, 3-35, 2-36, 3-79, 2-552, 2-553, 3-193, 3-257, 3-258, 3-359, 3-360, 3-339.

WHITE, ABRAHAM was a witness to the will of BEN-JAMIN SAUNDERS in (1830) 3-350; one in CHOW-AN married CHRISTIAN NIXON in (1870) 2-422

WHITE, ARD, and JAMES and ELIZABETH HOLLOWELL witnessed the will of LUKE STALLINGS (1799) 3-188.

WHITE, ARNOLD, SR., died in (1730) and in will mentioned daughter SARAH and sons JOSHUA & NEHEMIAH WHITE 1-82; see 3-193; 1-504.

WHITE, ANN, the wife of THOMAS WHITE died in (1770) 3-406; ANNA WHITE left will (1796) naming her half sisters and brothers and sister MARTHA SAUNDERS 3-194.

WHITE, CALEB, was the Executor of NATHANIEL CAIN in (1800) 3-169; and he and JOSEPH WHITE wit-nessed the will of SAMUEL SMITH in (1789) 3-190; CALEB WHITE and wife REBECCA had PE-NINA WHITE born (1761) and other children; & CALEB'S wife was REBECCA TOMS whom he mar-ried in (1761) 3-400; CALEB WHITE left will in (1795) and named children FRANCIS, TOMS, CALEB, JAMES, JOSIAH and ELISHA, and daugh-ters PENINAH PRITCHARD, REBECCA ALBERTSON & MARY and BETTY WHITE; WILLIAM SKINNER and CALEB WINSLOW were the witnesses 3-194.

WHITE, DANIEL and NATHANIEL WINSLOW were EXECU-TORS of the will of JOSEPH GRIFFITH (1828) 3-334; he was also an executor of the will of HENRY CHAPPELL in (1829) which was wit-nessed by JOSEPH and EXUM LANE 3-329.

WHITE, DAVID and ROBERT WHITE witnessed the will of EDWARD GARRISH in (1827) 3-335.

WHITE, DIANA, was married to THOMAS MERCER in (1703) 3-410. (She a widow).

WHITE, ELIZABETH married JESSE ROUNDTREE (1790) 3-419.

WHITE, EXUM, was a grandson of THOMAS NEWBY and a son of JOSIAH WHITE in (1793) and was also related to the JORDANS and WATKINS FAMILY 3-180.

WHITE, EZEKIEL, married MARY HARRISON in BERTIE COUNTY in (1780) 2-318.

WHITE, FRANCIS died leaving will in (1813) and in his will mentioned sons CALEB and FRANCIS and other children, and mentions also his brother TOMS WHITE 3-358.

WHITE, GEORGE was the father of JOHN WHITE and was related to JOHN EVANS and JOHN JORDAN in (1717) 1-626; he assigned his interest in a patent to THOMAS HOLLIDAY in (1725) witnessed by GEORGE TURNIDGE and ROBERT HICKS 2-447 & 2-448.

WHITE, GIDEON, was Master of the sloop ELIZABETH in (1749) 1-433.

WHITE, HENRY, under oath about (1700) or ear-lier, declaring he was 57 years old and that he knew SAMUEL DAVIS, of PASQUOTANK in ISLE OF WIGHT COUNTY, VIRGINIA, who was an apprentice to his father HENRY WHITE; that SAMUEL DAVIS married ANN, who was a servant of CAPT. JAMES BLOUNT (also in ISLE OF WIGHT CO. VA.); that the DAVIS family moved to N. C. and SAMUEL DAVIS JR. is heir to the lands in PASQUOTANK COUNTY, being the oldest son of SAMUEL DAVIS, SR. and his wife ANN DAVIS, deceas-ed 3-146; HENRY WHITE was a member of the Court in (1698) that met at the house of JOHN HARRIS 2-298; HENRY WHITE JR. (57) years old) was born about(1642)-1-443

WHITE, ISAAC, witnessed the will of ERI BARROW in (1832) 3-326.

WHITE, JACOB, left will in (1816) and mentioned sons JOSIAH, ROBINSON, THEOPHELUS & JOSHUA and also JOSEPH, daughters JEMIMA GUYER & POLLY WHITE 3-358.

WHITE, JEAN, the relict of ROGER WHITE, married JOHN WILKINSON in (1686) 3-203.

WHITE, JESSE died leaving will in (1814) and in it mentions his daughters and wife and his brother THOMAS WHITE 3-358.

WHITE, JOHN and MARGARET TITERTON were married in BERKELEY PRECINCT in (1685) 3-202; JOHN WHITE left will in PASQUOTANK in (1754) & named children, including JOHN MAN WHITE 1-504 (TIMOTHY MEADS a witness)and anoth-er JOHN left will in PERQUIMANS in (1730) names son JOHN, several daughters and his sister MARY 1-505; JOHN WHITE sold lands in (1717) adjoining JOHN EVANS 1-624; and to MARY BUFKIN in (1729) on CHOWAN river ad-joining ELIZABETH PARKER and THOS HOLLIDAY 2-451; one JOHN WHITE was a grandson of JOHN TOMS in (1808) 3-354; in (1730) JOHN sold land to THOMAS HOLLIDAY 2-449; JOHN WHITE, SR. in (1707) deeded lands to JOHN CHAMPION bought by GEORGE WHITE from EDWARD WILLIAMS 2-448; JOHN SR. also sold land to WILLIAM WILLIAMS in (1700) 3-131; JOHN had a land grant on BEAR SWAMP and SANDY RUN in (1714) 1-6; JOHN WHITE (at an early date)was appointed a Justice of the General Court of that part of the Province of N. C. lying East of CAPE FEAR 2-298; the will of JOHN WHITE was proven in HYDE PRECINCT in (1725) and mentions only his wife SARAH 1-83; in (1716) JOHN WHITE and his wife SARAH sold lands to GEORGE WHITE part of a patent in HOGG NECK, the witnesses being LUKE WHITE and LUKE WHITE, JR. 2-285; & JOHN WHITE SR. and his wife SARAH in (1716) sold lands to JOHN WARD, the witnesses be-ing JOHN WHITE JR., LUKE WHITE and a JOHN GORDON 2-285; he and his wife SARAH also in (1704) sold land to MARY ARLINE which was witnessed by JAMES FLEMING 2-611.

WHITE, JONATHAN, left will in (1823) in which he mentions sons TIMOTHY and JONATHAN & his daughters and wife RACHEL, with JO-SEPH WHITE and NATHAN WINSLOW the witness-es to the will 3-359.

WHITE, JUDAH, died leaving will in CHOWAN in (1770) named wife SARAH, LUKE WHITE SR., with the BYRUMS and STALLINGS as Execu-tors and witnesses 2-35.

WHITE, JOSHUA, died leaving will in (1784) leaving JACOB, ZACHARIAH and JOSHUA, MOURNING, MARY and ELIZABETH WHITE and MARGARET MOORE and son in law SAMUEL MOORE 3-193; in(1806) JOSHUA WHITE was one of the Executors of the will of JOSEPH GILBERT 3-334.

WHITE, LAZARUS, received a land grant in NORTH CAROLINA in (1719) on HOLLY CREEK SWAMP 1-17

WHITE, LUKE, sold lands to JOHN WILLIAMS (1718) on CHOWAN RIVER, which JOHN later sold to SAMUEL WOODWARD 1-625; in (1838) the wife of a LUKE H. WHITE was CATHERINE and she was perhaps CATHERINE JONES 2-265; in (1739) LUKE WHITE kept the ferry from ROCKYHOCK to BERTIE COUNTY, N. C. 2-299; a LUKE WHITE died leaving will in BERTIE in (1796) and mentioned wife MARY, DAVID VALENTINE and NATHAN HARRELL as Executors; the witnesses were NATHAN HARRELL, GEORGE WHITE and POLLY HAGARTHY 2-362; another and later LUKE left will in BERTIE proved in (1837) and named his children as JAMES, ISAAC, MEEDY, JOSIAH, ELIZABETH, MARGARET and SENETH WHITE, with a son AMOS who was deceased; the witnesses were JAMES and TURNER WILSON and THOMAS WARD 2-553. (An earlier LUKE WHITE left will in CURRITUCK proved in (1758) his wife MARGARET and sons VINSON (Vincent) and JOSHUA and daughters CHRISTIAN WHITE, KESIAH ELLES, the wife of MICHAEL ELLES, and MARY, the wife of JOHN TOMSON. GRIMES ABSTRACTS p. 403.) This last will (from GRIMES) appears on (1-503) and spells "ELLES" as ELLIS, which we think correct; and still another LUKE died leaving will in CHOWAN in (1770) named wife SARAH, LUKE WHITE, SR., SOLOMON, STEPHEN, JAMES and JACOB WHITE, son JOHN WHITE, daughters ELIZABETH DISHON and SARAH COPELAND, with AUGUSTINE DISHON and JOHN COPELAND (perhaps his son in law) as EXECUTORS; will was witnessed by DANIEL EARL (the minister, of course), JOHN GREGORY and a WILLIAM BARNES 2-35.

WHITE, MARYAN (the widow of JACOB WHITE) died in (1824) naming sons THEOPHELUS and JOSIAH WHITE, JEMIMAH GUYER, alias WHITE, POLLY WHITE and son JOSHUA WHITE; THEOPHELUS WHITE was married and was the father of a MARYAN WHITE 3-359.

WHITE, MEEDY, died leaving will in (1804) naming sons CADER, GEORGE and WILLIAM WHITE, and EZEKIEL and REUBEN WHITE, and daughters JUDITH RAY, WINNIFRED HALE, KERRENHAPPOCK SHOLAR and ANNIS MIZELL; witnesses were JOHN WHITE, ABSOLOM PRITCHARD and KING WHITE and STEPHEN WHITE 2-552; an earlier MEDIA WHITE died in BERTIE in (1749) naming his wife ELIZABETH, the will being witnessed by ABIGAIL WHITE and JOSEPH BUTTERTON 1-504; this last named MEDIA WHITE sold lands to WILLIAM WESSON in (1734) on ROCKYHOCK NECK, joining the lands of BENJAMIN SMALL 2-609; and in (1729) he sold lands to MARY BUFKIN on CHOWAN RIVER 2-448.

WHITE, MILES (Spelled MYLES) was the son of a FRANCIS WHITE who died leaving will (1813) and MILES was brother of CALEB, FRANCIS, JOHN and TOMS WHITE 3-358.

WHITE, NOAH, married TABITHA COLLINS in BERTIE COUNTY in (1792) with FREDERICK WHITE, who married JUDITH BYRUM, the same year, as security on marriage bond 3-367.

WHITE, NATHANIEL, was the brother of MILES WHITE (will in 1788) and of SETH WHITE; these were the nephews of BENJAMIN WHITE 3-193.

WHITE, NEHEMIAH, died leaving will in PASQUOTANK in (1751) wife MARTHA and children BENJAMIN, JOSHUA, SARAH, MARY and MARTHA and his father ARNOLD WHITE 1-504 (Two ARNOLD WHITE wills on same page). The ARNOLD who died in (1690) was brother of HENRY WHITE, whom see.

WHITE, PENINAH, witnessed the will of a SARAH DAVIS in (1817) 3-330; PENINAH WHITE, as daughter of CALEB WHITE, married a PRITCHARD 3-194.

WHITE, ROBERT, died in ALBEMARLE COUNTY (1698) in which he mentions (in will) his sons VINCENT and ROBERT and a daughter MARY & a THOMAS JONES; 1-504; a later ROBERT left will in (1733) naming sons JONATHAN, ZEPHANIAH, JOSEPH and ROBERT WHITE and his daughters ANN, ELIZABETH and MARY and wife REBECCA 1-82; in (1692) ROBERT WHITE sold lands to HENDERSON WALKER on CHOWAN RIVER with STEVEN MANWARING and PETER GRAY as witnesses 1-397.

WHITE, SETH died leaving will in (1826) naming brothers NATHAN and JONATHAN WHITE sister ELIZABETH GRIFFIN, with DEMPSEY WHITE as a witness 3-359.

WHITE, SAMUEL died in (1779) and left will naming his youngest sons GABRIEL and JOSHUA WHITE, and WILLIAM, BENJAMIN and ARNOLD WHITE other sons; his wife was HEPSIBEE & HENRY WHITE is an Executor 3-193.

WHITE, SILAS, died leaving will in CHOWAN in (1841) and left sons MOSES, JOHN, HENRY, SILAS, JACOB and JORDAN WHITE, wife ELIZABETH and daughters MARY FOREHAND, CHRISTIAN GOODWIN and ELIZABETH WHITE; ELISHA TWINE and ELISHA GRIFFIN a witness 2-35.

WHITE, THEOPELUS was the son of JACOB WHITE & his wife MARYAN (She left will 1820); he had a daughter MARYAN WHITE 3-359.

WHITE, THOMAS and ANN BARNES were married in (1755), and they had MILES, NATHAN, SETH, ORPHA, ELIZABETH, JONATHAN and MIRAIM WHITE all born by (1768); ANN (BARNES) WHITE died in (1770) 3-399, 3-400; another THOMAS WHITE died in (1762) and left children BENJAMIN, JOSHUA, JOSEPH, THOMAS, JOHN, MATTHEW and CALEB, and daughters MARY WINSLOW and SARAH WHITE, and a daughter ELIZABETH who married PRITCHARD and had children; his will was witnessed by THOMAS NEWBY, MARY PRITCHARD and ISRAEL PERRY 3-193; one THOMAS WHITE married to SARAH ROUNDTREE in (1791) 3-420; Court was held at the home of a THOMAS WHITE in CHOWAN in (1694) 1-611, 1-612; he married DIANA FOSTER (who had been DIANA HARRIS) and the widow of WILLIAM FOSTER 1-611, 3-200, 3-146 where he and DIANA sued PATRICK HENLEY; in (1695) THOMAS entered into an agreement with DAVID BLAKE, which they both signed 3-247; THOMAS WHITE, a son of JOSIAH WHITE is mentioned in the will of WILLIAM MOORE in (1808); BENJAMIN and JOHN WHITE were among the heirs of THOMAS WHITE in (1815) 2-260, 2-261.

WHITE, VALENTINE (apparently) the son of LUKE WHITE and wife MARY, will (1796) with brothers NOAH and DAVID WHITE 3-362.

WHITE, VINCENT (Sometimes spelled VINSON, but I am sure it was VINCENT) son of LUKE WHITE (1758) 1-503; and ROBERT WHITE, who died in (1698) also had a son VINCENT 1-504; and ROBERT WHITE and VINCENT WHITE appears on a list of tithables from the East side of HARVEY'S CREEK to the West side of FLATTY CREEK taken by FRANCIS DELAMERE, and ISAAC ROWDEN and MAURICE CUNNINGHAM, JOHN and BENJAMIN WEST and CHARLES JONES appears on the same list 3-253; THOMAS JONES, with VINCENT WHITE is also mentioned in the ROBERT WHITE will in (1698) 1-504.

WHITE, WILLIAM, is called "father in law" by WILLIAM TOWNSEND in his will (1785) and CALEB WINSLOW is called "brother", with JOSIAH WHITE, the Executor 3-191; in (1770) DEMPSEY WHITE was 17 years old and the orphan of WILLIAM WHITE, and was placed under the tuition of MORDECAI WHITE 3-448; WILLIAM WHITE died in CHOWAN in (1724) and left wife MARY and a daughter MARY 1-83; a WILLIAM WHITE died in (1772) naming children, sons JOSEPH, WILLIAM and JOSIAH, daughters ELIZABETH JORDAN, MARGARET TOMS and SARAH WHITE and wife MARGARET 3-193; a much later WILLIAM died leaving will in CHOWAN in (1849) 2-36.

WHITEHALL, JONATHAN, of LONDON died at Lieut. COL. BIGG'S house in (1681) 3-366.

WHITEHALL, ROBERT, was the Collector of the PORT of CURRITUCK in (1755) 1-448.

WHITEHEAD, ALICE died leaving will in CRAVEN COUNTY in (1742) and mentioned brothers EDWARD & WILLIAM WHITEHEAD and their children, and her cousins TABITHA SMITH, ANN HOPKINS and SUSAINA HERRITAGE wife of WILLIAM HERITAGE, & MRS. BRICE, wife of WILLIAM BRICE 1-80, 1-81, (a better abstract) 1-510.

WHITEHEAD, FOSTER, was brother in law of a NANCY SPEIGHT who died in (1834) who also mentions her sister CELIA WHITE, her brother JOHN SPEIGHT, sister RUTH ELLIOTT and MARGARET WHITEHEAD; WILLIAM JONES and JOHN SPEIGHT were witnesses to the will of this NANCY SPEIGHT 3-353.

WHITEHEAD, JOSEPH, with ROBERT WILSON was a witness to the will of ELISHA STONE in (1808) whose wife was LYDIA and who mentions his brother CORNELIUS STONE 3-349.

WHITEHEAD, MARGARET, was perhaps MARGARET SPEIGHT and the wife of FOSTER WHITEHEAD 3-353.

WHITEHEAD, WILLIAM sold lands to MABEL KING who was a daughter of NATHAN KIRBY in (1721) and with HENRY COUNCIL a witness to deed 2-619.

WHITEHORN, JOHN was Master of the Sloop SWALLOW in (1749) 1-435.

WHITEHURST, THOMAS was a Lieutenant in the ROYAL NAVY, and died in NEW HANOVER in (1766) and among the legatees mentioned in his will was a sister ANN WHITEHURST 1-512

WHITLOCK, DAVID and wife SARAH (1688) had daughter ANN 3-216; sued DANIEL SNOOK in (1689) 3-431.

WHITLY, SAMUEL, of TYRRELL COUNTY died and left will in TYRRELL COUNTY in (1739) and mentioned his son in law WILLIAM ARCHDEACON 1-80.

WHITEMAN, JOHN died in (1831) and in his will mentioned his brother FREDERICK WHITEMAN and NANCY WALKER'S heirs 3-362.

WHITEMARSH, JOHN signed a statement by the Justices and Jury in (1716) 3-131; in the same year he sold lands to WILLIAM BONNER with ROBERT HICKS a witness 1-299.

WHITLEDGE, THOMAS CUMMING. In (1771) his widow was RUTH 3-449.

WHITNEY, JOSHUA, died leaving will in (1736) sons DAVID, JEREMIAH, SAMUEL, JOSEPH and FRANCIS WHITNEY, and daughters KETRING & KEITH 1-81.

WHITFIELD FAMILY. Genealogical account of the descendants of WILLIAM WHITFIELD and his wife ELIZABETH GOODMAN of GATES COUNTY, whose son WILLIAM WHITFIELD married RACHEL BRYAN, daughter of NEEDHAM BRYAN, & showing their connection with various other N. C. families 1-567 to 1-576.

WHITFIELD, CHARITY (sister of MATTHEW) married FREDERICK O'DANIEL, and had OWEN, WILLIAM, ALEXANDER and ELIZABETH O'DANIEL who married WINGFIELD; she married second (CHARITY DID) one DANIEL HERRING and had two HERRING CHILDREN 1-568.

WHITFIELD, ELISHA, was one of the executors of DANIEL HENDRICKS, of BERTIE, whose daughter SARAH married a DANIEL by (1769) 2-340; he and BENJAMIN WHITFIELD were witnesses to the will of JAMES LEGGETT in (1764) who in his will claimed that part of RICHARD TOMLINSON'S estate " to which my wife is entitled" 2-345.

WHITFIELD, GEORGE, the noted evangelist, visited BATH in (1765) 3-26.

WHITFIELD, LUKE (son of WILLIAM and ELIZABETH GOODMAN married a MISS WARREN 1-568.

WHITFIELD, LUCY, daughter of NEEDHAM WHITFIELD and LUCY HATCH married ALLEN WOOTEN 1-569.

WHITFIELD, MATTHEW son of WILLIAM WHITFIELD & ELIZABETH GOODMAN married a WARREN and and a daughter BETSY WHITFIELD married AARON DANIEL 1-568.

WHITFIELD, MARY married JOHN GRADY 1-568.

WHITFIELD, NANCY, daughter of BRYAN WHITFIELD married JOHN COBB 1-569.

WHITFIELD, NEEDHAM, married LUCY, the daughter of EDMUND HATCH 1-569; NEEDHAM was the son of RACHEL BRYAN and WILLIAM WHITFIELD 1-471.

WHITFIELD, WILLIAM, of BERTIE, sued WILLIAM BADHAM of EDENTON in (1732), with THOMAS JONES his attorney 2-302; in (1726) he also brought a suit against WILLIAM DANIEL 1-457; he and EDWARD HARE and one ISAAC WILLIAMS were the witnesses to a deed to WILLIAM SCOTT in (1736) 3-130.

WHITMELL, ELIZABETH, was married three times as
follows: (1) in (1734) GEORGE POLLOCK, son of
GOV. THOMAS POLLOCK (no issue) and (2) she
married THOMAS BLOUNT, and had WILLIAM and
WINNIFRED, the last marrying her first cousin HON. WHITMELL HILL; in (1746) she married
(3) WILLIAM WILLIAMS 2-297; an ELIZABETH
WHITMELL, widow of THOMAS WHITMELL, married
ROBERT HUNTER who left will in BERTIE (1753)
1-47; this ELIZABETH WHITMELL was daughter
of LEWIS BRYAN and his wife ELIZABETH HUNTER,
and HENRY, son of ROBERT HUNTER (by a former marriage) married SARAH WHITMELL, daughter of THOMAS WHITMELL 1-47; ROBERT HUNTER
in his will (1753) mentions his daughter in
law ELIZABETH WILLIAMS, wife of WILLIAM WIL-
LIAMS (figure this out yourself) 1-47.

WHITMELL, SARAH, was the daughter of THOMAS WHIT-
MELL and married HENRY HUNTER of BERTIE in
(1771), or by that time 1-47, 3-449.

WHITMELL, COL. THOMAS left will in BERTIE (1735)
and mentions sons THOMAS, LEWIS and WILLIAM,
daughters ELIZABETH POLLOCK, SARAH, MARTHA
and WINNIFRED and MARY; son THOMAS WHITMELL
and brother JOHN GRAY, Executors 1-81; he is
said to have come to BERTIE COUNTY, N. C.
from SURRY COUNTY, Virginia in (1713) and to
have married ELIZABETH HUNTER BRYAN b. (1690)
daughter of LEWIS BRYAN and his wife ELIZA -
BETH HUNTER; a list of his children from the
family Bible are given in the note at bottom
of 1-81; THOMAS WHITMELL, JR., ELIZABETH and
MARTHA WHITMELL are mentioned in the will of
GEORGE EUBANK, of BERTIE in (1732-3) 1-42;
an order was issued to him by the BERTIE CO.
COURT in (1748) 2-531; he and his wife ELIZ-
ABETH deeded lands to JOSEPH COLSON in(1720)
2-613; he was appointed Sheriff in (1745) &
JOHN GRAY and JOHN BLOUNT made his bond
2-626; he was referred to as Ex-Sheriff in
(1768) in BERTIE 3-444; in (1715) ARTHUR KAV-
ANAUGH (Of SURRY County, Va.) sold lands on
the North side of MOHRATUCK in N. C. to THOM-
AS WHITMELL (Of SURRY COUNTY, Virginia)
1-286; he and JOHN HILL and JOHN HURST were
appointed or petitioned to be appointed as a
commission to lay out the town of WIMBERLY
at BLACKMAN'S LANDING in (1752) 3-92; THOMAS
was a member of the County Court of BERTIE
which met on TIMBER BRANCH in (1741-2) with
NEEDHAM BRYAN and others there named 2-199;
MARTHA, the daughter of THOMAS WHITMELL and
ELIZABETH HUNTER BRYAN married HENRY LAWRENCE
BATE, of BERTIE, brother of HUMPHREY BATE and
LAWRENCE left will (1740) in BERTIE 1-28;
THOMAS WHITMELL and THOMAS BARKER in (1747)
were sureties on the bond for a FERRY given
by WILLIAM DUKENFIELD and others 2-629; and
a THOMAS WHITMELL died leaving a nuncupative
will in BERTIE in (1779), proved by WILLIAM
and FRANCIS PUGH 2-360.

WICKER, JOSEPH, with PETER PARKER and JANE WICK-
ER received a land grant in (1716) on BEAVER
DAM SWAMP 1-16.

WICKHAM PRECINCT, in BATH COUNTY, petition of the
inhabitants when THOMAS CARY was GOVERNOR of
North Carolina 1-441.

WICKLIFFE, WILLIAM left will in CRAVEN COUNTY in
(1754) with JEREMIAH VAIL and DANIEL DuPREE
the witnesses 1-514.

WILSON, WILLIAM left will at NEW BERN in (1773)
TIMOTHY CLEARE and WILLIAM RAMSEY named as
the Executors 1-514.

WIGGINS, AMBROSE, of GATES COUNTY died and
left will in (1805) and named his brother
PUGH, THOMAS and JACOB WIGGINS, and a
DEMPSEY KNIGHT was Executor 2-80.

WIGGINS, ELIZABETH was the daughter of JOHN
KEATON in (1734) 1-56.

WIGGINS, JAMES, sold lands to RICHARD BROTHERS
before '(1732) 3-135.

WIGGINS, JESSE, left will in GATES COUNTY before (1826) naming sons JESSE and WILLIS
WIGGINS and others, including grandsons
JOHN W. and JESSE PARKER, the witnesses
being GEORGE KITTRELL and WILLIAM PARKER
and ROBERT PARKER 2-80.

WIGGINS, JOHN, died and left will in GATES CO.
in (1839) and mentioned his brother JESSE
WIGGINS, and property from SIMON and PETER
BRINKLEY estate. COL. JESSE WIGGINS made
the executor, and WILLIAM HUDGINS and JOHN
P. BENTON witnesses 2-80.

WIGGINS, MATTHEW left will in (1820) in BERTIE
COUNTY, and left to ISAAC GARDNER land
of the Testator in TENNESSEE in the hands
of WILLIAM WHITE 2-555.

WIGGINS, RICHARD was claimed as a headright
by JOHN BIRD (no date) 3-139; 3-451.

WIGGINS, SARAH was only five years old (1769)
and was orphan of WILLIAM WIGGINS and was
placed in the care of JOSIAH GODDIN 3-446

WIGGINS, THOMAS sold land to RICHARD WIGGINS
in (1728) with JOHN SUMNER a witness to
the deed 2-451; THOMAS left will in CHOWAN
in (1760) had son WILLIS son JAMES and a
brother JAMES WIGGINS 2-34; in (1769) a
THOMAS WIGGINS was the guardian of CATHER-
INE HUNTER 3-447; in (1736) his wife was
CHRISTIAN 3-400.

WILDER, JOHN died in CHOWAN and named brothers
MICHAEL, NATHANIEL, FRANCIS and STEPHEN
CABARRUS as his executor 2-37.

WILDER, MICHAEL was the brother of JOHN WILDER
2-37; and owned lands next to GEORGE RAINES
JR. in (1794) 1-24.

WILEY, REBECCA married WILLIAM JONES in PER-
QUIMANS in (1790) 3-419.

WILEY, STEPHEN married MARY FLEMING in (1761)
3-412.

WILEY, THOMAS was the witness to a deed of a
THOMAS HAWKINS in (1716) 1-394; and was
born about 1662, being 40 years of age in
(1702) 1-443.

WILKES, JAMES died and left will (1831) 2-555

WILLIE, MATHIAS died in HALIFAX COUNTY, N. C.
in (1802) leaving will in which he named
sisters ELIZABETH GRIFFIN and RACHEL PAR-
KER, with HENRY JOYNER Executor 2-551.

WILLIE, HILLARY, died in GATES COUNTY (1838)
2-80.

WILLIARD, DANIEL witnessed the will of JOHN
GUYER in (1804) 3-334.

WILLARD, JOHN, and wife CHRISTIAN (1734) 2-611.

WILLARD, THOMAS was the son of PENINAH, the daughter of TIMOTHY JESSUP, who left will in(1805) which was witnessed by CALEB ELLIOTT and RESTORE LAMB 3-338.

WILKINS,ANTHONY. MRS. SARAH WILKINS, JAMES, JOSEPH and WILLIAM 2-273; 2-34.

WILKINS, CHARLES, sold land to JAMES BRETON and wife in (1721) 2-283; he and ROBERT HICKS witnessed deed of WILLIAM HINTON in (1718) 1-624; he left will in (1733) named brother in law NICHOLAS CRISP, and LUKE GREGORY married his daughter SARAH WILKINS in CHOWAN 1-82.

WILKINS, JOHN, mentioned in the will of JOB PRATT in (1736) 1-66; GEORGE WILKINS left will in CHOWAN in (1803) 2-34.

WILKINS, MICAJAH (mis-spelled WILKES) left a grandson WILLIAM WILKINS and one named WHITMELL WILKINS, and also had a son JESSE WILKINS 2-556.

WILKINS, WILLIAM, left will in CHOWAN in (1773) naming children JOSEPH, WILLIAM, JAMES, ANTHONY and others 2-34.

WILKINSON, JAMES and his wife SARAH, deeded land to THOMAS MACLENDEN in (1717) with WILLIAM BUSH as witness 1-300; they bought or owned lands adjoining COL. THOMAS POLLOCK and HENRY KING in (1718) with JOHN WALKER a witness 1-621.

WILKINSON, JANE married WILLIAM VOSSE in BERKELEY PARISH in (1688) 3-203.

WILKINSON, WILLIAM, received a land grant (1684) in CHOWAN 1-3; he was Speaker of the HOUSE of BURGESSES about (1703) 2-223; signed a statement relating to ROBERT STARKEY in (1698) with JOHN PORTER 2-204; he was 36 years old in (1680) 1-139, 2-146; mentioned in minutes of first church erected in NORTH CAROLINA in (1701) 1-256; in (1703) he bought lands patented by THOMAS GILLIAM from EDWARD SMITHWICK and wife SARAH 1-612; in (1695) he and HENDERSON WALKER were barred from the General Court 2-301; he was Executor of ROBT FISHER in (1702) 1-43; in (1714) witnessed a deed of WILLIAM HARDY and wife EDITH 2-139; made deposition during the CULPEPPER REBELLION 3-48, 3-49, 3-50; issued receipt (1695) to ARTHUR WORKMAN on account of EDWARD MAYO 3-248; land grant on YOPPIM RIVER in (1696) 1-6; his former land grant was patented to THOMAS POLLOCK in (1720) 1-9; COL. WILLIAM WILKINSON died leaving will in CHOWAN proved in (1706) wife ESTHER, WILLIAM GLOVER, CAPT. THOMAS LUTEN, THOMAS and JOHN BLOUNT and several others mentioned 1-508.

WILLIAMS, ANTHONY, assigned a patent to ROBERT LANIER in (1713) 1-101.

WILLIAMS, ARTHUR in (1717) bought lands from HENRY WHEELER 1-299; and he and P. WILLIAMS were witnesses to a deed by JOHN PROCTOR in(1718) 1-622.

WILLIAMS, BENJAMIN, left will in BERTIE COUNTY in (1817), JOHN WATSON in trust for ELIZABETH, wife of JOHN BLOUNT, and nephew THOMAS CURTIS of SOMERSET COUNTY, Maryland; BENJAMIN B. WILLIAMS is mentioned as son of FRANCIS WILLIAMS in will in (1816) 2-551.

WILLIAMS, DANIEL served as a LIEUTENANT in the Sixth Regiment of the N. C. Continental Line 1-421.

WILLIAMS, EDWARD. One left will in (1714) and names son JOHN and wife MARY 1-83; another EDWARD left will in PASQUOTANK in (1739) naming son LEONARD and son JOSIAH, son JOSEPH and some daughters, and son LODOVICK and brother WILLIAM WILLIAMS, daughter MARY MORGAN and others 1-81.

WILLIAMS, ELIZABETH married GEORGE MATHES in (1695) 3-407.

WILLIAMS FAMILY. Wills 1-501, 1-502, 1-503, 2-34, 2-35, 2-78, 2-79, 2-359, 2-360, 2-551, 2-552, 3-196; BIRTHS 3-208. GENEALOGICAL NOTE relating to 1-68; also 1-509,showing connections with the DURANT FAMILY.

WILLIAMS, GEORGE, died leaving will in EDGECOMBE in (1759) naming sons GEORGE and SAMUEL WILLIAMS, wife CHLOE and daughter CHLOE; brother WILLIAM WILLIAMS his Executor 1-80; an older GEORGE left will in BERTIE in (1735) and mentioned his brother RICHARD and father GEORGE 1-82; 2-396 also; in (1736) a GEORGE sold land to WILLIAM CRAWFORD, part of a tract of land bought of NATHANIEL WRIGHT of NANSEMOND COUNTY, Va. 3-128; JOHN BENTON, RICHARD TAYLOR and RICHARD PARKER witnessed the deed to him from WILLIAM CRAWFORD 3-128.

WILLIAMS, HESTER, married WILLIAM WHITFIELD in (1736) the son of RACHEL BRYAN 1-472, 1-568.

WILLIAMS, ISAAC and his wife MARY, of BERTIE, sold land to EDWARD HARE, with JOHN DAWSON, a witness 2-610; in (1728) he sold land to SAMUEL WOODWARD adjoining JOHN WHITE 2-445; BARBARA WILLIAMS was the relict of ISAAC WILLIAMS around (1735)1-448; with WILLIAM JONES he was appointed as an overseer of a road leading to SARUM which ran by SIMON DANIEL and WILLIAM VINCENT in CHOWAN 1-450.

WILLIAMS, JAMES, married ANN, formerly the wife of JOSEPH HARRELL by (1767) 3-444; JAMES SR. died leaving will in PASQUOTANK (1757) left wife ANN, son WILLIAM and a daughter MILLY 1-329.

WILLIAMS, JANE, daughter of RICHARD WILLIAMS and wife MARGERY was born (1681) 3-211.

WILLIAMS, JENKINS and his wife JOHANNAH, had son ROGER WILLIAMS born (1694) 3-367; & their son JOHN was born (1691) 3-217; this JENKINS was on a jury in ALBEMARLE in (1702) 1-610, 1-612; JOANNA was the wife of JENKINS WILLIAMS 1-612.

WILLIAMS, JOHANNA and WILLIAM STEPHENS, son of ANDREW STEPHENS and his wife GRACE, were married in BERKELEY PRECINCT in (1684) by THOMAS HARVEY, ESQUIRE 3-205.

WILLIAMS, JACOB, was son of GEORGE WILLIAMS, who died leaving a will in NORTHAMPTON CO. N. C. in 1750. This GEORGE WILLIAMS was a brother of SAMUEL WILLIAMS and he named several other children besides the son JACOB, with NICHOLAS and WILLIAM MONGER & JOHN SIMPSON, witnesses to his will 1-502.

WILLIAMS, JOHN left will in (1728) mentions his wife SARAH, brother NATHANIEL, and brother in law JOSEPH PIERCE 1-83; he deeded lands to his neighbor (as a gift) JAMES BLOUNT about (1720) 2-618; sold lands to NICHOLAS CRISP (1727) 2-616; recorded his mark in BERTIE in (1771) 3-449; received a land grant in (1714) on HORSE SPRING BRANCH 1-15; and in (1719) he lived between CASHY RIVER and SALMON CREEK in BERTIE 1-445; JOHN P. WILLIAMS was a COLONEL in the N. C. CONTINENTAL LINE 1-426; one left will in (1722) an mentioned brothers THEOPHILUS, JAMES, ISAAC & ARTHUR WILLIAMS, cousin ANTHONY HERRING and Cousin WILLIAM WILLIAMS, son of brother THEOPHILUS WILLIAMS 1-83; in (1735) JOHN bought land from JOHN LASSITER (Of NANSEMOND WO. in Virginia) deed recorded in BERTIE 3-125; in (1717) he and HENRY WHEELER witnessed a deed by RICHARD WASHINGTON 1-299; in (1720) he bought land from WILLIAM HAVETT and wife MARY with JENNINGS DANIEL a witness 2-613; JOHN, SAMUEL and THEOPHILUS WILLIAMS all married into the LANE FAMILY 1-472; in (1716) JOHN deeded lands to his daughter ANN HERRING and her heirs adjoining THOMAS JONES, with THOMAS BROWN and JOHN EDWARDS as witnesses 1-296; in (1711) he bought lands from JOHN BURKETT in CHOWAN 3-442.

WILLIAMS, COL. JOSEPH, married REBECCA LANIER, of SURRY COUNTY, N. C. Genealogical note relating to the family 3-318.

WILLIAMS, JOSEPH JOHN, was the son of SAMUEL WILLIAMS who left will in EDGECOMBE in (1754) and had brothers WILLIAM, SOLOMON and SAMUEL WILLIAMS; PHILLIP ALSTON was witness to his father's will 1-80.

WILLIAMS, JOSIAH, was the guardian (1769) in BERTIE, of JOHN and BENJAMIN MOORE 3-447.

WILLIAMS, LEWIS received a grant of land on CHOWAN RIVER in (1697) and this land in (1706) was conveyed by WILLIAM WILLIAMS to PETER PARKER, of NANSEMOND COUNTY, Virginia 1-5; in (1717) LEWIS WILLIAMS lived near WILLIAM WILKINSON in CHOWAN 1-616; he sold land to WILLIAM SHARP in (1715) with TREDLE KEEFE a witness to the deed 1-285.

WILLIAMS, LUODOVICK in (1702) claimed the headrights of HANNAH and ELLINER WILLIAMS 2-300; his wife was MARY 1-621.

WILLIAMS, MARY was the relict of LEWIS WILLIAMS in (1717), with PRISCILLA WEST and GEORGE LUMBRY witnesses 1-621.

WILLIAMS, NANCY was the wife of JAMES WILLIAMS of BERTIE in (1767) 3-443.

WILLIAMS, NATHANIEL, and his wife ELIZABETH had son TIMOTHY and sons JOHN and JAMES WILLIAMS all born by (1732) 3-400; NATHAN left will in (1773) and named sons NATHANIEL, WILLIAM and CHARLES, daughter MARY and wife MARY & JOHN and THOMAS HARVEY were Executors; with BENJAMIN and JAMES HARVEY as witnesses 3-195; NATHANIEL was Sheriff of NORTHAMPTON COUNTY, N. C. in (1754) 1-448.

WILLIAMS, RACHEL, left will in (1777), and named sons CALEB WINSLOW, WILLIAM TOWNSEND, daughter BETTY CANNON, grand-daughter MARGARET WHITE, daughter of THEOPHILUS WHITE and numerous others 3-196

WILLIAMS, RICHARD, had three daughters, ELIZABETH who married GEORGE WALKER and JANE and RUTH WILLIAMS 3-139; in (1746) he was Executor of the will of THOMAS ANDREWS 2-627; his wife was MARYDAY and their daughter RUTH WILLIAMS was born in (1686) 3-369; he sold lands by deed to EDWARD HOWCOTT in (1717) with ROBERT CALF and a JOHN SMITH as witnesses 1-617; he was given the care of WILLIAM BRASWELL, fourteen years old in (1744) 2-625.

WILLIAMS, ROGER, was the son of JENKINS WILLIAMS and his wife JOHANNA and was born in (1694) 3-367; he had brother JOHN WILLIAMS and JOHN BENTLEY, who died (1695) was their uncle and brother in law of JENKINS WILLIAMS 1-30.

WILLIAMS, SAMUEL, was granted lands in EDGECOMBE COUNTY in (1749) 1-447; in (1790) one SAMUEL was the brother in law of JOHN JOHNSTON 2-343; in (1739) he sold land to JOHN KITTRELL adjoining JAMES RIDDICK 3-132; he died leaving will in EDGECOMBE in (1753) and named sons WILLIAM and SOLOMON and JOSEPH JOHN WILLIAMS; his wife was ELIZABETH and PHILLIP ALSTON and BENJ. WYNNS were the executors 1-80.

WILLIAMS, THEOPHELUS, was brother of JAMES, JOHN, ISAAC and ARTHUR WILLIAMS and he had a son JOHN WILLIAMS in (1722) 1-83; three brothers, JOHN, SAMUEL and THEOPHELUS WILLIAMS were the sons of ISAAC WILLIAMS and his wife RACHEL SMITH 1-472; THEOPHELUS WILLIAMS lived between CASHY RIVER & SALMON CREEK in BERTIE in (1719) 1-445.

WILLIAMS, THOMAS was Sheriff of CURRITUCK in (1740-1741) 1-456; he had a grant of land in (1719) which joined lands of MATTHEW BRYAN 1-18; and in (1716) on DEEP BRANCH 1-14, 1-9; he died in (1733) and left sons JOSEPH and SAMUEL WILLIAMS, wife MARY and daughter MARY 1-82.

WILLIAMS, TULLE, married ELIZABETH, the widow of ANTHONY HATCH, and she was ELIZABETH DURANT, daughter of JOHN, and grand-daughter of GEORGE DURANT the elder and his wife ANN; HATCH died in (1726) 1-50; he was an Executor of the will of DANIEL BUDGATE in (1770) 3-164; and Executor of the will of ANN SAWYER in (1807) 3-350; he inherited the sword of his father from SAMUEL SCOLLEY in (1752) 1-72; he was the son of WILLIAM WILLIAMS and his wife MARY TULLE, who came to North Carolina from CALVERT COUNTY, Maryland, about (1700) 3-411; he married MRS. ELIZABETH HATCH in (1742) with EDMUND HATCH security on the marriage bond 3-411; he was Executor of the will of ELIZABETH STEVENSON in (1730) 1-74; he married GRACE SANDERSON in (1733)3-400; his father WILLIAM WILLIAMS died in CURRITUCK leaving will in (1726) naming sons THOMAS, STEPHEN and TULLE, wife MARY, and daughters JANE BRENT and ABIGAIL PHILLIPS 1-83.

WILLIAMS, WILLIAM, was the brother in law of JOHN JOHNSTON in (1790) 2-343; a WILLIAM WILLIAMS and wife FRANCES sold lands to THOMAS LOVICK in (1727) the deed witnessed by THOMAS HETTERLY and WILLIAM ROWDEN 2-294; sold land to PETER PARKER of ISLE of WIGHT COUNTY, VA. (1706) 1-93.

WILLIAMS, WILLIAM. One died leaving a will in (1704) in which he named his wife MARY, sons SAMUEL, JOHN and STEPHEN WILLIAMS and "each of my daughters" 1-84; a WILLIAM WILLIAMS was the third husband of ELIZABETH WHITMELL, the widow of GEORGE POLLOCK and THOMAS BLOUNT 3-297; another WILLIAM left will in EDENTON in (1732) named wife FRANCES, sons WILLIAM & THOMAS and daughters SARAH and ELIZABETH WILLIAMS 1-83; in (1728) a WILLIAM of EDENTON was the Executor of THOMAS PARRIS 1-58; one proved his rights in CHOWAN in (1711) 3-442; this last WILLIAM was a JUSTICE in CHOWAN in (1711) 3-441

WILLIAMSON, CHARLES, died leaving will in ONSLOW in (1746), named wife HANNAH and two brothers and a sister 1-510.

WILLIAMSON, CONSTANCE was granted a FERRY at her home at QUITSNEY in BERTIE in (1744) 2-621; she died leaving will that year and WILLIAM PIERCE qualified as the Executor 2-624;1-291.

WILLIAMSON, HANNAH left will in BERTIE in (1781) names legatees and makes WILLIAM WILLIAMSON her Executor 2-359.

WILLIAMSON, HENRY witnessed the will of SARAH SUTTON (widow of JOSEPH) in (1772) with a JOSEPH CLAYTON 3-186.

WILLIAMSON, JAMES and wife CONSTANCE, of PERQUIMANS sold land to JAMES WARD in (1715) 1-291; in (1716) he witnessed a deed by MAJ. ROBERT WEST and wife MARY 1-293; the same year he witnessed a deed of ROBERT DOUGLAS 1-395; in (1718) he and DAVID BUTLER witnessed a deed by CHRISTOPHER BUTLER 1-624; in (1722) he sold land to WILLIAM HAUGHTON 2-283.

WILLIAMSON, JOHN died in (1734) leaving will in which he named sons CHARLES, ZACHARY and CHARLES and wife ROSE 1-82, 1-510; in (1719) he and ROBERT HICKS witnessed deed of JONATHAN KITTRELL to SAMUEL GILLIAM 1-630; in (1716) he witnessed BATEMAN deed to lands on SCUPERNONG ROAD 1-294;

WILLIAMSON, RICHARD, witnessed a deed in (1715) by LAZARUS THOMAS 1-285; in (1716) he bought land from PETER PARKER 1-294; he received a land grant in (1713) on LITTLE TOWN PATH 1-9

WILLIAMSON, THOMAS, lived between CASHY RIVER & SALMON CREEK in BERTIE in (1719) 1-445; will proven in BERTIE in (1744) and MARY WILLIAMSON and WILLIAM WILLIAMSON qualified as the Executors 2-622; he sold lands to EDWARD HOWCOTT next to LEWIS WILLIAMS in CHOWAN in (1717) 1-616; he and ROBERT HOLBROOK witness to deed by EDWARD HOWCOTT in (1719) 1-628; in (1717) EDWARD HOWCOTT sold land to WILLIAM WILLIAMSON adjoining DENNIS MACLENDEN 1-617; in (1790) a WILLIAM WILLIAMSON witnessed a deed by DAVID YEATS 3-363.

WILLIFORD, BENTON was given the care in (1767) in BERTIE of an orphan EDMUND BIRD who was 14 years old 3-443.

WILLIFORD, ABNER left will in BERTIE in (1712) sons JOHN, RICHARD and JAMES 2-553.

WILLIFORD, JAMES will in BERTIE (1825) wife JUDAH; GEORGE OUTLAW, SR. Executor, and JOSEPH and FRANCIS OUTLAW witnesses 2-553.

WILLIFORD, JOHN left will in BERTIE (1833) ZADOCK WRIGHT a witness 2-553.

WILLIFORD, RICHARD witnessed a deed by WILLIAM BUSH to ANDY STEVENSON (1717)1-300.

WILLMOT, DANIEL was Master of the sloop LITTLE HESTER and LITTLE MESTER (1775)2-465. and 2-466.

WILLIS, ANNIE, married second, JAMES BLOUNT, who came to CAROLINA from ISLE OF WIGHT COUNTY, Virginia 3-31.

WILLIS, HUMPHREY. His wife was MARY and she died in (1689) 3-353.

WILLIS, WILLIAM, died leaving will, but date is not shown; wife MARY and son WILLIAM 1-511

WILLOUGHBY, JOHN was sixty years old (1680) and was born (1620) 1-139; his wife was DEBORAH and son JOHN was born (1685) 3-213.

WILLOUGHBY, THOMAS died leaving will in PASQUOTANK in (1753) names brother THOMAS EVANS "half blood by my mother"; SOLOMON and PATRICK POOL witnesses 1-513.

WILLOUGHBY, WILLIAM died in (1701) at the home of JIM FEWOX 3-402.

WILSON FAMILY. Wills 1-506, 1-507, 2-555, 3-197, 3-361.

WILSON, ABRAM died leaving will in (1795) & named grandchildren, including MILES and ABRAHAM ELLIOTT 3-198.

WILSON, EDWARD and wife RACHEL, had son EDWARD born (1687) 3-215; daughter SARAH born in (1795) 3-368; daughter ELIZABETH was born (1692) 3-218.

WILSON, ISAAC, left will (1724) mentions his brothers ROBERT and BENJAMIN WILSON, mother ANN PETTIVER and uncle RALPH BOZMAN 1-33; ISAAC WILSON married ANN PARKER in (1701) 3-409; they (ISAAC and ANN) had ROBERT WILSON born (1790) 3-216; he applied to GOVERNOR ROBERT DANIEL for a position as Chief Ranger for PERQUIMANS COUNTY 3-141; he had a son ISAAC born in (1702) 3-374; he and JOHN ROBBINS witnessed a deed by RALPH BOZMAN in (1717) 2-452; ISAAC, the son of ROBERT and grandson of the first ISAAC recorded his mark 3-429 (This in (1689); he and NICHOLAS CRISP present a petition as members of the HOUSE in (1708) 1-454.

WILSON, JACOB, left will in (1793) naming his sons JONATHAN, and brothers ZACHARIAH and MOSES WILSON and numerous other connections 3-197, 3-198.

WILSON, JAMES, from WARWICK COUNTY, VA. accepted a deed from NATHANIEL WRIGHT in (1738) with JOHN MILNER a witness 2-610; the wife of JAMES WILSON was ALICE and their son JOHN WILSON died in (1691) 3-363; he died by (1759) and SENSABROOK WILSON asked for letters of administration on the estate of JAMES; an inspector on BENNETT'S CREEK in (1748) 1-452.

WILSON, JOHN recorded his mark in (1744) 2-624;

WILSON, JOSEPH administered on the estate of SARAH WILSON in (1769) 3-447.

WILSON, REBECCA died and left will in (1795) & THOMAS and SAMUEL SITTERTON and ANN ELLIOTT were the witnesses 3-198.

WILSON, REUBEN (husband of REBECCA) died(1794) had sons JACOB, ROBERT and SYLVANUS WILSON; HUMPHREY PARKS a witness 3-198.

WILSON, RICHARD sold land to WILLIAM COWARD and THOMAS MATTHEWS was witness (1721) 2-618; he bought land from JOHN YELVERTON in (1718) 1-620.

WILSON, ROBERT granted land on INDIAN TOWN CREEK in (1716) 1-14; his wife was ANNE in (1701) 3-409; his name mentioned in an affidavit in (1689) 3-432; he died and left will in CUR-RITUCK in (1694) and named wife ANN and sons ISAAC and ZACHARIAH WILSON and several daughters 1-82.

WILSON, SAMUEL, will in PASQUOTANK (1720) and mentions uncle in law JOHN SCARBROUGH, brother DANIEL BELL and father and mother 1-83.

WILSON, SOLOMON, late of NORFOLK, VIRGINIA, died leaving will (1775) mentions daughter ANN, COL. SAMUEL BOUSH, JAMES IVEY, TABITHA(wife of WILLIAM FREEMAN), son LEMUEL, daughters MASON, ELIZABETH; JOHN DUKE and JOHN LAW-RENCE, Executors 2-361.

WILSON, THOMAS left will (1785), witnessed by JACOB CANNON and GABRIEL NEWBY 3-197.

WILSON, WILLIAM, left will in CHOWAN in (1771) mentions son in law MICHAEL WILDER, JAMES BAKER, THOMAS HOSKINS and wife SARAH 2-33; he was administrator of HUMPHREY GARRETT in (1752) 1-451; in (1734) he was the orphan of WILLIAM WILSON and was placed under care of RICHARD LEARY 1-450.

WILSON, ZACH (ZACHARIAH or ZACHEUS) was son of ROBERT WILSON in (1694) 1-82.

WILLS, WILLIAM left will in ONSLOW in (1743) and named sons WILLIAM, NATHANIEL and daughters ELIZABETH, SARAH EVANS, and sons JOHN, JO-SEPH and HENRY WILLS 1-80.

WILLS in BERTIE COUNTY 2-323 to 2-363; 2-497 to 2-556; at EDENTON IN CHOWAN COUNTY 2-3 to 2-39; 1-516 to 1-557; 1-132 to 1-134; in GATES COUNTY 2-39 to 2-80; in PERQUIMANS COUNTY 3-163 to 3-198; 3-323 to 3-363; from SECRETARY OF STATE'S OFFICE 1-26 to 1-84; 1-163 to 1-234; 1-325 to 1-390; 1-483 to 1-515.

WIMBLE, JAMES sold land to WILLIAM POPPLEWELL in (1733) witnessed by ISAAC ALEXANDER 2-610

WIMBERLY, BENJAMIN left will in BERTIE in (1811) and had grand-daughter PENELOPE VINCON, and THOMAS CONE was a witness 2-554.

WIMBERLY, ELIZABETH died and left will in (1845) in BERTIE; sister MARY SHARROCK 2-554.

WIMBERLY, EZEKIEL was Guardian of SILVA ELLIS in (1771) in BERTIE 3-450.

WIMBERLY, JOHN died and his will was proven in (1749) in BERTIE 2-633.

WIMBERLY, JOSEPH was foreman of the Grand Jury in BERTIE in (1746) 2-627; asked for license for a ferry over ROANOKE in(1744) and made bond with EPAPRODITUS MOORE & ALEX COTTEN as sureties 2-621; in (1744) he was the executor of the will of JOHN COWARD 2-623.

WIMBERLY, THOMAS, left will in BERTIE (1733) and named sons GEORGE and JOSEPH, daughter SARAH and wife SUSANNAH 1-83.

WINANTS, WINANT, left will in BERTIE (1796) naming sons HENRY and DAVID and "all my children" and wife MARY 2-362.

WINDLEY, ROBERT received a land grant (1680) 1-3; and the same year he proved the will of DANIEL ADAMS 1-613.

WINDLEY, WILLIAM was witness to a deed by a JOHN DANIEL and wife MARY in (1700)2-611.

WING, JOSEPH was Master of the sloop ELIZA - BETH in (1749) 1-433.

WINGATE, JOHN was mentioned in the will of a WILLIAM STONE in (1720) 1-77. (These WIN-GATES mentioned in the will of MARY LUNS-FORD in 1806 -3-340).

WINGATE, EDWARD bought land from JOHN BLOUNT in (1718) 1-626.

WINGATE, WILLIAM, left will in (1774) and in it mentioned sons EDWARD, WILLIAM, JOHN and EPHRAIM, daughters MARY, ELIZABETH CREECY, SARAH STAFFORD and HANNAH 3-196.

WINGFIELD, JAMES and WILLIAM SPEIGHT witnessed deed to JOHN KING (1718) of VIRGINIA 1-627.

WINGFIELD, RICHARD left will in (1733) and in it mentions sons ROBERT and JOHN and his daughters SUSANNA, ELIZABETH, MARY, ANN & PRUDENCE WINGFIELD and wife MARY 1-82.

WINN, GEORGE, sold land to WILLIAM BUSH in (1718) deed witnessed by WILLIAM CRAWFORD and JOHN DAVIS 1-620.

WINN, JOHN left will in PASQUOTANK in (1739) and names nephew DANIEL JESSUP 1-81.

WINN, JOSEPH received a land grant in (1745) 1-20.

WINN, RHODA (WYNNE) left will in (1821) and names JOSHUA WINGATE and others, witnessed by MARTIN ROSS and MARY WILLIAMS 3-362.

WINN, THOMAS appointed overseer of the high - ways on the South shore in (1720) at QUEEN ANNE'S TOWN (Edenton) 3-287

WINSLOW FAMILY. Wills 1-507, 2-36, 3-357.

WINSLOW, BENJAMIN died leaving will in (1794) and named all of his children; will wit- nessed by LAWRENCE and ISRAEL PERRY 3-195.

WINSLOW, CALEB one of the Executors of the will of JACOB PERRY in (1777) 3-183.

WINSLOW, CALEB was called "brother" in the will of WILLIAM TOWNSEND in (1785) who also named his wife ELIZABETH and father in law WILLIAM WHITE 3-191; in (1784) he witnessed the will of JOHN HOLLOWELL with JOHN TWINE 3-172; he died and left will in (1811) naming his wife PEGGY, son NATHAN, daughter RACHEL WHITE & grandson JOHN COPELAND; CALEB ELLIOTT, DAVID WHITE and JOSIAH TOWNSEND witnesses 3-357.

WINSLOW, ELIZABETH, was the niece of MARY NEWBY in (1739) 1-63.

WINSLOW, HESTER was the daughter of HANNAH CLARE in (1726) 1-39

WINSLOW, ISRAEL left will in (1762) witnessed by JOSEPH PERRY and JOHN and RACHEL WHITE 3-194

WINSLOW, JACOB was an executor of JOHN HUDSON in (1772) 3-172; he died and left will in (1807) wife MILLICENT 3-357.

WINSLOW, JOHN left will in PERQUIMANS in (1755) witnessed by NICHOLAS STALLINGS and JOSHUA and THOMAS WHITE 1-408.

WINSLOW, JOSEPH left will in (1766) naming his children and brother BENJAMIN WHITE 3-194; one died about (1782) with children JOB, ISRAEL and JESSE WINSLOW 2-373; another left will in (1750) in which WILLIAM WHITE is mentioned 1-498.

WINSLOW, NATHANIEL was an executor of a HENRY COPELAND in (1819) 3-330; he and DANIEL WHITE were executors of JOSEPH GRIFFIN in (1828) 3-334.

WINSLOW, OBADIAH, with JACOB WILSON was witness to will of WILLIAM TOWNSEND in (1767) 3-191 and with DAVID WHITE he was executor of the will of ISRAEL SMITH in (1825) 3-351

WINSLOW, PLEASANT was the daughter of FRANCIS TOMS in (1729) 1-78.

WINSLOW, WILLIAM, received a grant of land in (1805) on OLD TOWN CREEK 1-25.

WINSTON, ISAAC, of NEW KENT COUNTY, VIRGINIA is mentioned on the records at EDENTON in (1735) 2-465.

WINTHROP, WAIT, of NEW ENGLAND COUNCIL certificate to statement in N. C. (1692) 1-614.

WINWRIGHT, JAMES was a friend of ARTHUR GAFFIS in (1729) 1-46; mentioned as Provost MARSHALL in the deposition of SUSANNA PARRIS in (1725) 3-233.

WITCHCRAFT IN N. C. Petition of THOMAS BOUCHER relating to 3-68, 3-69; SUSANNA EVANS complains and seeks damages on account of in 3-56, 3-57; suit for damages (1702-1712) 2-207.

WOOD FAMILY. Wills 1-499, 1-500, 2-34, 3-355.

WOOD, EDWARD was high sheriff of ALBEMARLE CO. in (1688) 2-298; his daughter MARY was MARY RUTTER in (1734) 2-453; EDWARD WOOD left a will in (1734) and mentions his son JONATHAN CHAPPELL and MARY RUTTER on FOX BRANCH in CHOWAN PRECINCT, and land he had bought of JOHN GOODIN (GODDIN) in (1715; THOMAS ROUNDTREE a witness 2-453.

WOODS, JAMES, sold land to JOHN WOODS, witnessed by FREDERICK JONES, the CHIEF JUSTICE (1720) 2-608; JAMES BARRADOL WOODS gave a home to MARTHA STANDLEY who died at his house (1800) 2-545.

WOODS, JOHN bought land in (1719) from ROBERT EVANS and wife ANN; also bought land from JAMES WOODS in (1720) 2-608.

WOODS, JOSEPH (Spelled WOOD) died and left will in (1802) named wife ELIZABETH and sons RICHARD, CALEB, NATHAN, daughter PENINA, son in law NATHAN WARD, daughter ABIGAIL WOOD; THOMAS HOLLOWELL one of his executors 3-355.

WOODS, SAMUEL was the son in law of ROBERT SMITH in (1692) 1-73.

WOOD, WILLIAM, the father of WILLIAM WOOD died and his widow MARY married BURDNELL (or BURKETT) 2-469; one WILLIAM WOOD married DEBORAH SUTTON in (1718) and had children whose births are shown 3-400, 3-401; in (1739) WILLIAM WOOD sold land to JOHN KITTRELL and SAMUEL PARKER 3-133; about (1739) he sold land to JAMES BRADY 3-136.

WOODHOUSE, HENRY in (1749) was a witness with SOLOMON SMITH to the will of DAVID LINDSAY of CURRITUCK, whose wife was ANN, whose mother was SARAH and who named a brother BENJAMIN LINDSAY 1-336; HENRY was a brother in law of RICHARD SANDERSON who died in (1733) 1-74; he left will in CURRITUCK in (1751) wife KEZIAH, son HEZEKIAH, daughter in law MARY JONES, daughter MARY WEST'S son, ABRAHAM LINCHFIELD and a WILLIAM ABENTON (ABBINGTON); JOHN WOODHOUSE was a witness 1-512.

WOODHOUSE, HORATIO, died in ONSLOW in (1755) & named daughter ALIFF (ALICE) HAINS (wife of ERASMUS HAINS in Virginia) son JOHN & wife CATHERINE; HENRY RHODES and WILLIAM GRAY, Executors; HENRY MOORE, CASON MOORE and WILLIAM WILLIAMS, witnesses 1-512.

WOODHOUSE, HEZEKIAH, the son of HENRY, was the brother in law of RICHARD SANDERSON who died in (1733) 1-74.

WOODHOUSE, JOHN was a beneficiary of the estate of WILLIAM BELL, SR., late of CURRITUCK of which BENJAMIN PEYTON of BATH COUNTY appears to have been administrator 3-282, 3-283; in (1751) JOHN was a witness to the will of HENRY WOODHOUSE 1-512; CAPT. JOHN WOODHOUSE, RICHARD CHURCH, THOMAS TAYLOR and CAPT. JOHN SANDERSON were members of the CURRITUCK COURT in (1728) 2-467.

WOODLEY, ANDREW, then a minor, was one of the distributees of the estate of WILLIAM WOODLEY in (1737) with his sister MARY WILCOX 2-272.

WOODLEY, MRS. ANN, a widow, married MOSES STONE in (1764) 3-413.

WOODLEY, THOMAS, left will in (1753) in PASQUOTANK and named son WILLIAM, daughters MARY SPEIGHT and ELIZABETH TAYLOR, THOMAS TAYLOR and COL. WILLIAM GREGORY; grandsons WILLIAM and THOMAS TAYLOR, and grand-daughters MARY, ELIZABETH and PEGGY TAYLOR; & JONATHAN RIDING was witness 1-511.

WOODLEY, THOMAS, was the son in law of HENRY PENDLETON, having married his daughter ELIZABETH PENDLETON; by this marriage he was the brother in law of JOHN BROTHERS, JOSEPH REDING and THOMAS DAVIS, each of whom married a sister of his wife ELIZABETH 1-65 (HENRY PENDLETON died in 1740). THOMAS WOODLEY had a grant of land on the line of CHOWAN and PERQUIMANS in (1716) 1-14.

WOODLEY, WILLIAM bought land from WILLIAM FALLOW adjoining the lands of WILLIAM BLOUNT and MATTHEW BRYAN in (1718) 1-620; in(1714) his joining neighbors were DANIEL HALSEY, RICHARD SKINNER and HENRY LYLES 1-3, 1-13; in (1703) he had land on HORSE POOL SWAMP 1-6; he sold lands adjoining SAMUEL PAGETT in (1733) 3-126; in the will of ANDREW REED of LITTLE RIVER in PERQUIMANS (1723-4) the testator calls WILLIAM WOODLEY "brother" and ANDREW and MARY WOODLEY his children named as REED'S grandchildren 1-70; in the division of his estate in (1737) his children are ANDREW WOODLEY and MARY WILCOX 2-272, 1-448.

WOODNUT, STEPHEN and ROBERT BOLE bought lands from EDWARD MOSELEY in (1718) with ARCHIBALD CAMPBELL a witness 1-626.

WOODROW, ALEXANDER died in WILMINGTON (1754) and left will 1-513, 1-514.

WOODWARD, EDWARD died in CHOWAN in (1822) with JACOB PARKER and SAMUEL PRIVITT as witnesses 2-38; the estate of another EDWARD WOODWARD was administered by ABIGAIL SLAUGHTER (1754) 1-455.

WOODWARD, HENRY, died in CHOWAN (1824) will 2-38

WOODWARD, HENRY (Of VIRGINIA) married MARY MARTIN daughter of JOHN MARTIN of BATH who died in (1715) 1-63.

WOODWARD, JOHN died leaving a will in BATH in (1734) in which he mentioned two UNCLES, as WILLIAM MARTIN and HENRY LUCAS 1-82; see also 1-513.

WOODWARD, RICHARD owned lands next to THOMAS PILAND and JAMES HAMBLETON (1729) 2-446, 2-454

WOODWARD, SAMUEL, bought land from THOMAS BRAY next to JOHN ROBERTSON (1718) 1-629; made a deed to PAUL BUNCH in (1735) witnessed by ROBERT ROBERTSON 3-128; in (1750) married MRS. SARAH PURCELL with LUKE WHITE security on the bond; 1-237; bought land from JOB MEADER in (1728) next to JOHN JORDAN and ISAAC WILLIAMS 2-445, 2-444; he was receiver of POWDER MONEY (1739) 2-301; made deed to PHILLIP BROWNE about (1715) 1-206; and one to WILLIAM YATES in (1721) 2-616; his wife was ELIZABETH and they sold land to ISAAC ZE.INDEN (1713) 1-99; that same year he witnessed a deed by ARDEN CARLTON 1-296; he bought land from EDWARD HOWCOTT in (1718) 1-620; he bought land from CALEB STEVENS in (1720) 2-614; also from LUKE WHITE in (1718) 1-625; had land grant (1719) 1-18; he sold land to THOMAS BRAY which he had bought from JAMES BLOUNT in (1718) with WILLIAM SHARP as a witness 1-628.

WOODWARD, WILLIAM, left will in (1691) and in it named his wife SARAH his Executor & EDWARD WADE a Trustee; EDWARD BONNER and WILLIAM CHARLTON among witnesses 1-510.

WOODWARD, WILLIAM obtained a grant of land in (1719) next to DAVID AMBROSE 1-18.

WOOLARD, RICHARD married JANE RICHARDS in the year (1703) 3-410; he had lands in N. C. before (1700) 1-303;(his lands were on YOPPIM RIVER).

WOOLARD, MARY, left will in CHOWAN in (1788) and mentioned THOMAS BEASLEY, MILLIE PAYNE and others 2-31.

WOOLARD, WILLIAM, died leaving will in CHOWAN in (1762) wife MARY and children 1-67; he married SARAH, the widow of THOMAS GILLIAM and second, of EDWARD SMITHWICK 3-78, 3-79.

WOOTEN, ALLEN, married into the WHITFIELD FAMILY 1-569.

WOOTEN, ARTHUR, married RACHEL PARKER 2-17.

WORLEY, JOHN in suit with MARY BLOUNT in ALBEMARLE (1707) 1-610; sold land to DENNIS CALLAHAN (1725) 2-446; lived neighbor to JOHN EDWARDS 1-629; was Treasurer of CHOWAN after (1722) 1-444, 3-273, 3-236; bought land from WILLIAM STEEL and wife in (1720) 2-615; he sold land to JOHN BENNETT in (1717) 1-619; he was administrator of LEWIS MONTEIR (1732) 1-450; witnessed deed of WILLIAM SWINSON (1716) 1-299; witness to deed with RICHARD CANADY (1715) 1-290; was connected with WEST and BLOUNT families 1-35; estate divided (¢ no date) but JAMES LONG and wife mentioned 1-446; left will in TYRRELL COUNTY (1740) 1-500; one JOHN was of age in (1726) 2-298; CAPT. JOHN WORLEY mentioned in (1720) 3-287.

WORLEY, JOSHUA, the son of JOHN, was the grandson of JAMES LONG and wife ELIZABETH 2-468;

WORLEY, LOVICK, left will in TYRRELL and mentions his uncle JAMES BLOUNT and brother in law WILLIAM GRAY 1-80.

WORKMAN, ARTHUR left will in (1696) and mention is made of CAPT. JOHN HUNT of LITTLE RIVER and ANTHONY HATCH and others 1-82; see also 3-248.

WORDEN, PETER, made an affidavit relating to evasion of the customs 3-82, 3-83.

WORRELL, JOHN left will in GATES COUNTY 2-30; he bought land from WILLIAM WORRILL in (1718) 1-624.

WORRILL, WILLIAM sold land to JOHN BARDIN adjoining WILLIAM BRIDGER (1718) 1-624.

WORTH, JOHN left will in BLADEN in (1743) 1-31.

WORTH, JOSEPH left will (1775) with JOSEPH HEWES the executor 2-35.

WOSLAND, JONATHAN to THOMAS YEATTS lands next to THOMAS POLLOCK and ISAAC HILL (1720) deed 2-614.

WRIGHT FAMILY. From NANSEMOND COUNTY, VA. 3-244, 3-245, 1-503.

WRIGHT, DANIEL and his wife AGNES, had a daughter ELIZABETH WRIGHT who was born in (1703) 3-375.

WRIGHT, MR. JOHN, Minister (1685) 3-201.

WRIGHT, JOHN, GENT. (Of NANSEMOND COUNTY, VA.) had heirs ANNE, WILLIAM and JOSEPH WRIGHT, who in (1698) gave a power of attorney to JOHN PORTER 3-244, 3-245.

WRIGHT, JOSEPH (Of NANSEMOND COUNTY, VIRGINIA) bought land from NICHOLAS STALLINGS and others in (1716) 1-292.

WRIGHT, NATHANIEL (Of NANSEMOND COUNTY, VA.) sold lands to JAMES WILSON (Of WARWICK CO. VA.) in (1733) with JOHN MILNER a witness 2-610; and in (1731) he sold lands that had been patented by CAPT. JOHN WRIGHT (also of NANSEMOND COUNTY, VA.) to GEORGE WIL - LIAMS, with JACOB SPIVEY a witness 2-450.

WRIGHT, THOMAS died leaving will in (1790) sons JOHN and WILLIAM and JOSEPH and JAMES and daughters SARAH and ANN BRIGGS 3-197; his lands in N. C. escheated to THOMAS BLOUNT 1-22.

WRIGHT, WILLIAM left will in CHOWAN in (1839) & named sons JAMES, WILLIAM, MILES, HUMPHREY, EDMUND and TOWNSEND WRIGHT 2-38; he and JOSEPH WRIGHT (Of NANSEMOND COUNTY, VA.) in (1702) were executors of JOHN WRIGHT and gave power of attorney to JOHN PORTER 1-610.

WYNN, BENJAMIN. His estate was divided in HERT- FORD COUNTY in (1800) 1-449; he was appoin- ted Deputy Clerk of BERTIE in (1744) 2-622; he married MARGARET PUGH, a sister of FRAN- CIS PUGH 1-451; in (1751) he was guardian of FRANCIS PUGH, a minor 1-451.

WYNN, DANIEL (Spelled WYNNS) left will (1813) in BERTIE and named sons and daughters MARY JENKINS, ELIZABETH BARNES and SARAH ROBERT- SON; had son DANIEL VAN PELT WYNNS 2-554.

WYNN, JOHN (Spelled WYNNS) was foreman of a grand jury in BERTIE in (1747) 2-629, 2-630; was surveyor of BERTIE in (1744) 2-620.

WYNN, JOSEPH (Spelled WYNNS) proved rights and named (wife?) JUDITH, GEORGE PALLACIAH WYNNS, JOSEPH PERRY WYNNS and ANNA HUB- BARD, his children (1744) 2-624.

WYNN, LAVINIA left will in BERTIE in (1821) & named PEGGY NORTHCUTT, a daughter, and several other children 2-555.

WYNN, WILLIAM (Spelled WYNNS) was foreman of the grand jury (1744-5) 2-625.

WYATT FAMILY. Wills 1-81, 3-362; BIRTHS 3-208, 3-401.

WYATT, AMBROSE, was executor of the will of JOSEPH MARDRE in (1822) 3-342.

WYATT, JACOB, died leaving will in (1788) and named sons JAMES, WILLIAM and JOSHUA WYATT and other children 3-198; his wife was MARY LONG, daughter of WILLIAM LONG who died in PERQUIMANS leaving will in (1758) 1-57.

WYATT, JOHN, of PERQUIMANS was Master of the sloop SALLY in (1775) 1-436.

WYATT, JOHN, was called "brother" by THOMAS WEST who died leaving a will in (1735) 1-82; he died in (1739) and left will in which he named his daughter SARAH STANDING, daughter ELIZABETH OATES, wife RACHEL his brother JOSHUA LONG and son WILLIAM WYATT 1-81; their children JOHN and MARY WYATT were born (1714 & 1717) 3-401; JOHN WYATT was Executor of ROBERT HARMON in (1717) 1-51.

WYATT, JOSHUA married ELIZABETH SCRYMSHOE in (1768) for children see 3-401.

WYATT, SAMUEL and his wife ELIZABETH had chil- dren JACOB, JOSHUA and ELIZABETH WYATT born by (1725) 3-401.

YANCEY, CHARLES was a LIEUTENANT in the NINTH REGIMENT of the N. C. CONTINENTAL LINE 1-424

YEAMANS, SIR JOHN, mentioned in connection with the DeROSSETT and other notable CAROLINA FAMILIES 2-485.

YEATS FAMILY. Wills 2-362, 2-363.

YEATS, DAVID, left will in BERTIE in (1795) and also probated in BALTIMORE COUNTY, MARLAND in (1794), in which the MANNINGS and BAYLEY families are mentioned; the witnesses were JONAS OSBORN, JAMES LANE and WILLIAM WIL - LIAMSON 2-363; he may have been the DAVID, son of ELIZABETH, who left will (1792) 2-362.

YEATS, JAMES, died in CARTERET, leaving will in (1750) wife MARY and daughter MARY NASH and HARRY and LEMUEL OSTERN (OSBORN?) 1-515.

YEATS, REBECCA & daughter MARY YOUNG 2-470.

YEATS, TIMOTHY, married the widow YOUNG 2-469 in CHOWAN 1-451.

YEATS, THOMAS, land grant 1-16, deed to EDWARD BRYAN 2-631; wife SUSAN 1-69.

YEATS, WILLIAM, will (1826) 2-556; land lapsed 1-11; grant (1717) 1-17; will BERTIE 1-514

YELLET, USLEY land patent (Va) 1689 3-129.

YELVERTON, JOHN. Wife ELIZABETH 1-99; lived in CHOWAN (1711) 3-442; sold land to RICHARD WILSON (1721) 2-618; bought from ROGER SNELL (1711) grant (1711) 1-7; next to Wm. COWARD 2-618; 2-457, 1-620.

YOPPIM (YAWPIM) RIVER boundary between CHOWAN and PERQUIMANS 1-6.

YOUNG, GEORGE, will (1697) son FOSTER 1-515.

YOUNG, JOSEPH, of EDENTON mentioned 3-232; he and WILLIAM BADHAM witness deed 2-607.

YOUNG, JOHN, and DANIEL wills BERTIE 2-556.

YOUNG, JOSHUA married SALLIE BOZEMAN 3-472.

YOUNG, PETER died (1750) widow married TIMO- THY YEATS 1-451; 2-296, 2-451; WILLIAM YOUNG, orphan of HENRY YOUNG 3-447.

ZEHENDEN, ISAAC and wife MARY (1716) 1-296; deed to EDWARD HOWCOTT (1716) 1-293.

WASHINGTONS. The JOHN, JAMES, RICHARD and THOMAS WASHINGTON, of CHOWAN COUNTY in this record must have been descendants of another and different emigration of WASHINGTONS who came early to AMERICA and settled in VIRGINA. Possibly their ancestors, whoever they were even preceded First Mate JOHN WASHINGTON of the "Seahorse of London", who with CAPT. EDWARD PRESCOTT in 1656 got stuck in the mud in the middle of the POTOMAC, opposite the home of ALEXANDER POPE and his wife ANN, who afterwards married the luckless adventurer, who was to become the ancestor of the First President of the United States. (Fleet's Westmoreland Abstracts Vol 23). None of the numerous attempts to straighten out the WASHINGTON FAMILY history appear to agree, and this writer has relied more upon an account written by one WILLIAM WINSTON FONTAINE for a Texas branch of the WASHINGTONS nearly 75 years ago, than any other. Mr. FONTAINE was a contemporary and close friend of ALEXANDER BROWN, and knew his Virginia families. We have several most interesting MSS in his own handwriting, long before the fountain pen was born, and near the close of the "goose quill" era. They are priceless. There is no place in the JOHN and LAWRENCE WASHINGTON family for the CHOWAN COUNTY, N. C. Washingtons; nor is there a niche for RICHARD WASHINGTON of SURRY, the father in law of the two LANIER brothers, mentioned in another note. Richard of Surry and Richard of "Washington's Branch" were not the same. The wife of one was ELIZABETH, and the wife of the other was HANNAH (2-608). ELIZABETH, widow of RICHARD of SURRY left will in 1730 and named children WILLIAM, JAMES, ARTHUR, ELIZABETH LANIER, PRISCILLA LANIER, FAITH BARKER, MARY WARD and ANN WASHINGTON. The photostat of the will in the Archives at RICHMOND, VIRGINIA, which the writer examined, unmistakably identifies the testator as the "Widow of Richard Washington". However, it is not only possible, but probable, that RICHARD of SURRY COUNTY (Va.) and RICHARD, of CHOWAN were kinsmen, and had a common ancestry in early Virginia.

COL. WILLIAM WASHINGTON, of GRANVILLE COUNTY, who for many years was preacher at the little Tar River Church below OXFORD, and whose revolutionary record is known to history, was a son of BAILEY WASHINGTON, who was the son of HENRY, the son of JOHN, the son of LAWRENCE, the first mate's brother. COL. WASHINGTON, after the revolution, moved to SOUTH CAROLINA, and later to GEORGIA where he settled on LOG DAM Creek in HANCOCK COUNTY and died leaving a will dated August 12, 1799. His children were JOHN, EPHRAIM, WILLIAM, MARY and SARAH, and his executors were MILES GREENE, BRITTAIN ROGERS and WILLIAM HART. One of his daughters, MARY, married PLEASANT ROSE, of a well known NORTH CAROLINA FAMILY, which will be found mentioned often in these records.

WOODWARD FAMILY. One of the most colorful characters in CAROLINA HISTORY was HENRY WOODWARD, in all likelihood, a close kinsman, if not an ancestor of the HENRY WOODWARD and others of the name who appear in these pages (1-63). About the time that GEORGE DURANT was dickering with the old Indian Chiefs for his choice tract on the "neck of land" on ALBEMARLE SOUND, HENRY WOODWARD and his companions were exploring the region around the mouth of the Ashley River and learning from the Indians something about the country. Left there by his companions the intrepid explorer remained among these Indians many long months, and was finally captured and acrried to San Augustine; after his escape he became a ship's doctor in the West Indies, was finally wrecked on St. Nevis, and picked up by the Sir John Yeaman's contingent, which was trying unsuccessfully to reach the Carolinas. Later he came to the settlements on Ashley River and, finally became an Indian Trader, of note, whose headquarters were mainly around what is now Augusta, Ga. I would call it a genealogical co-incidence that a hundred years later, one of the striking characters of that new era, who stalked among the Indians of the same general area was COL. JOSEPH MARTIN, whose wife was a LUCAS, and who was almost surely a kinsman of the famous HENRY WOODWARD, since the HENRY of (1715) married MARY MARTIN,(1-63) and WILLIAM MARTIN and HENRY LUCAS were both the uncles of a JOHN WOODWARD, who died leaving a will in (1734) 1-82, 1-513.